The
FIFTY-YEAR
WOUND

The

FIFTY-YEAR

THE TRUE PRICE OF AMERICA'S

WOUND

COLD WAR VICTORY

Derek Leebaert

Little, Brown and Company
Boston   New York   London

First Edition

Library of Congress Cataloging-in-Publication Data

Leebaert, Derek.
    The fifty-year wound : the true price of America's Cold War victory / Derek
Leebaert. — 1st ed.
       p. cm.
    Includes bibliographical references and index.
    ISBN 0-316-51847-6
    1. United States — Foreign relations — 1945– . 2. United States —
Politics and government — 1945– . 3. United States — Social
conditions — 1945– 4. Cold War — Influence. 5. Cold War — Social
aspects — United States. 6. Cold War — Moral and ethical aspects — United
States. I. Title.

E744 .L426 2002
973.92 — dc21

                                         2001034452

10   9 8 7 6 5 4 3 2 1

Q-FF

Book Design by Meryl Sussman Levavi/Digitext

Printed in the United States of America

To the memory of Onno Loobacrt,
my father

Contents

Introduction

Right after the Second World War ended in 1945, a new challenge to democracy arose from the ally that had just been indispensable in crushing Nazi Germany. The resulting conflict was soon known as the Cold War. It was characterized by the procedures, emotions, and perverted legalisms of a military conflict, but the Cold War never involved final combat between the United States and the Soviet Union, an empire (including its Eastern European "allies") half again as large as today's Russia. Instead blood was spilled on fields far from Washington and Moscow. How long could this standoff endure, sensible people asked, until by purpose or miscalculation the superpowers went at each other's throats?

Even for the victor, so great a struggle had to be a disaster, like any other war, no matter the good that was accomplished. Resistance to the Soviet Union was led by the United States not because it was the most virtuous of the nations in opposition, but because it was the most powerful. This is the story of what the Cold War did, is doing, and will do to America. How was that war waged? Why did Americans commit so much in lives and opportunity with such little sustained complaint when, as is apparent only in retrospect, they helped maintain the longest great-power peace since Rome fell? What was sacrificed, how wisely, and at what future cost?

Many of the attitudes and institutions that America is taking into the new century have their roots in an adventure that cost more and shaped more lives than any other in history. Today's world has been molded by the Cold War, as has the world of skill levels, technology, business, and finance. Debates about missile defense, energy, taxes, and terrorism all reflect the experience of these decades just past. So too does the way that America is responding after being attacked in September 2001 — the new fight itself being an outgrowth of the struggle.

For the United States, the Cold War was contemporary with — and closely related to — the passage toward racial justice, the construction of interstate highways, the public backing of science, the first global dedication to free trade, and the serious aspiration that everyone have a chance to pursue higher education. It worked its way into everything from polar visits, to floundering into the paddies of Vietnam, to incubating the Internet, to reddening the national ledger with trillions in debt. These were years when the prosperity of Americans was never the nation's priority, something that seemed strange in the first decade of fulfillment, less so today. Wealth was secondary to a "security" that could never fully be established, one that always seemed easy to lose. The Cold War was so huge that it would take volumes to consider an alternative history. But it is hard to believe that America — and so much of the world — could not have grown further and faster over the second half of the twentieth century without that titanic struggle, or even if it had been fought on different terms.

Although this book focuses on the price of victory to America, the cost must be seen as part of a much larger story. The Cold War began as a contest for a ruined Europe, but soon it was leaping from continent to continent into realms that neither side knew, fueled by issues that neither understood. It was woven into old Latin American intrigues and into the hot, unformed politics of just-minted states in Asia and Africa, and it brought new threats, prizes, resources, and rationalizations — as well as old dishonesties — into the fight. Just as the seventeenth-century implosion of the European political order known as the Thirty Years' War was at least a dozen wars unified by a common breakdown, so each continent, each decade, perhaps each country had its own cold war. For "cold war" was an idea exemplified differently in each place and time that it touched. By showing what that war did to America, this book also addresses how the rest of the world was affected.

There have been longer struggles among nations. However, none has bridged so vast a stretch of human change. The Cold War began within months of the start of the nuclear and missile ages. It embraced half of the electronic and aerospace eras to date. It is intertwined with the evaporation of colonial empires and the eco-

nomic awakening of Asia. Whether we look at the independence of
Mali or flights to the moon, the struggle for the world was a driving
force in these events.

The price of victory is especially harsh because it was levied
during the most creative half century ever, one in which countless
opportunities fostered by the new awareness of scientific power
were waiting to be pursued. The Cold War's duration meant that its
demands could grind at the whole world for a lot longer than any
ordinary war. Nothing that pervasive can be switched off solely by
the passing of what occasioned it, in this case the disappearance of
the Soviet Union. The Cold War remains an unwanted part of millions of lives, and it will so remain well after our generation. The
past dies hard. Tolls exact themselves, even when forgotten.

For the United States, the price of victory goes far beyond the
dollars spent on warheads, foreign aid, soldiers, propaganda, and
intelligence. It includes, for instance, time wasted, talent misdirected, secrecy imposed, and confidence impaired. Particular costs
were imposed on industry, science, and the universities. Trade was
distorted and growth impeded. Today's national skepticism toward
government "peacekeeping" is part of that Cold War price still being
paid. The patriotism that followed devastation in New York and at
the Pentagon is unlikely to revive earlier, more trusting attitudes.

Throughout, the story returns to promises unkept — at the
same time that the United States and its allies escaped the vaster
costs of defeat. America was hurt simply by having to accept its role
as a superpower. This came about as the country was starting to
speed into a future in which it could have used its resources in exciting new ways sooner — not deployed to fund a fleet here or an
embezzled subsidy to some tropical gangster there, but to support
the development of improved food strains, better means of teaching,
a sleek national transport system, or an economic momentum that
might have persisted after the 1960s boom. Perhaps America's poor
could have been lifted up around 1970, just at the time when the
U.S. economy began to stumble for a dozen perilous years.

The Cold War forced America to live in the past. These were
years of exciting technologies, a population unusually young for
that of a developed nation, and a passion for work reinforced by the
Depression. Yet the country was preoccupied with the prospect of
an attack far worse than another Pearl Harbor. Its leaders feared
risking "appeasement" or "losing" this or that distant "bastion."

Wrestling with the Soviet Union — a ghastly hybrid of seventeenth-century quasi-Oriental despotism, nineteenth-century messianic radicalism, and twentieth-century total war — was no stimulus to exploring the possibilities of cybernetics or the genome. Material benefits certainly arose from this struggle, as they had from the First and Second World Wars, but most were short-lived or could have otherwise been achieved.

Catastrophe-impelled decisions were initially undertaken in the Depression and then during the Second World War. Not long after 1945, a pattern of alarm appeared. To be faced with obsessively secretive Soviet regimes in parallel with several concurrent technological revolutions inevitably made crisis a way of life. Soon the cry of emergency came to ring hollow, resulting in a situation all too easy to exploit. Thus the National Candlemakers' Association in the late 1940s insisted on payments to ensure that it would meet the demands of any wartime destruction of electric power, and physicians later drew down billions of dollars for "Star Wars." "For if war and hell have the same dimensions," Stephen Vincent Benét wrote in the 1920s, "Both are as paved with the best intentions / And both are as full of profiteers."

Throughout the Cold War, enormous amounts of talent were used for fundamentally unproductive purposes. The Cold War consumed the energy, genius, and character of people ranging from first-rate mathematicians to military officers who might otherwise have spent their time revitalizing cities or revamping the automobile industry. At one end of American society, the country's most formidable amateurs — bankers, law partners, CEOs — spent countless hours talking about the intricacies of NATO's chronic "disarray" at New York's elegant Council on Foreign Relations. At the other end, military draftees and recruits lost millions of man-years in places such as Kiska, Alaska, belowdecks on some stinking supply ship in the Pacific, or stenciling jeeps at Fort Ord, in California. Most of these men's first impression of public service was that it wasted their time. Later, when others were conscripted after them, they believed that it wasted their money as well.

Institutions were not merely put in place, but Cold War personality types also were rewarded. Careers of particular politicians, experts, and journalists (the ones who thrived on adrenaline) were boosted. The results were excesses and disorder, as well as projects that shuffled forward even after those in charge lost sight of their original purposes. Among influential segments of the press, a condescending impatience emerged toward a public whose fitful passions could be blamed for the incoherence of national purpose.

The blend of emergency and overbearing personalities led to many activities being obscured by the enfolding mysteries of "clearance." Unknown officials pawed through dossiers that were hidden from the people they concerned. "Secure" factories and labs, as well as millions of background investigations, did not come cheap, especially when Washington moved from World War II insouciance toward Soviet espionage, through 1950s alarmism, and into 1970s fatalism. Most knowledge is made to be shared; some is meant to be deeply private. The cult of secrecy all too often reverses the categories. Energetic, if by no means always stringent, secrecy and security diluted the quality of policy decisions, slowed innovation, warped government performance, and, ironically ended up jeopardizing the secrets themselves.

Emergency played into the penchant for bigness that was a child of earlier industrialization, of the radical insecurity that the Depression inflicted on small organizations, and of the cooperative giantism of World War II: big unions, big corporations, and big government, with little concern for the market. High technology, even high culture, came to be government and establishment matters during much of the Cold War. Everything from *Doctor Zhivago* to undersea exploration had a political dimension. More and more spheres of life were intruded on by politics — from which Americans have historically sought their distance as a necessary condition of well-being. The Cold War helped to persuade them that their difficulties and opportunities were such that the state should be waiting around every corner to help. If "war is the health of the state," as the radical Randolph Bourne said acidly in World War I, then cold war is the health of the state's clients in industry, agriculture, universities, media, and many other places.

Along the way, defense spending bore down on U.S. public finance and on the value of the dollar. War affects how a government pays its bills. When a struggle lasts nearly half a century, the problem becomes one of waging war while trying to accomplish other goals that are expensive and intricate, but secondary. The net products are likely to be sloppy. Consider the impact of waging the Cold War and building the 1950s infrastructure of roads and education; implementing the 1960s vision of the Great Society; dealing with the 1970s growth of entitlements and regulations; and, finally, facing down the Soviet Union in the 1980s while cutting taxes. And, after the Cold War was ostensibly over, consider the cost of the 1990s misdirected "war" against terrorists whom the original conflict had helped spawn. All this can vastly inflate the original bill. As Senator Everett Dirksen (R-Ill.) said with complicit geniality, "A billion here and a billion there, and before you know it you're talking about real money."

As the Cold War rapidly became a muffled world war, moving ever outward beyond Europe and Japan, Washington assumed that whatever happened in, say, Angola ("Portuguese, right?") or Penang ("Where?") would likely bear on the military balance in divided Germany or on Moscow's belief in U.S. "resolve." Buying the goodwill of kleptocrats (a fascinating cadre created by Cold War aid) or upholding democracy in lands where it had never arrived was too often claimed to be tied to global strategies — ones that existed only in the minds of their proponents and that make little sense to those looking back on them today. What Winston Churchill called "the Great Republic" found itself propping up a sinister array of third world criminals who insisted on being called heads of governments. The term "free world" was tainted by the all-too-usual emergency rhetoric. National interests in places unknown to most of the nation were compulsively discerned by highly placed, highly energetic officials.

Ultimately, the cost of America's effort was felt as a waste of spirit. The Cold War, after all, was a struggle of hearts and minds — in the end, a struggle for sincere belief and the willingness that flows from it. Yet this war nurtured an increasingly weary awareness of decisions too often rationalized by "national security." From these years has grown public resentment not only toward often hypocritical allies, who have frequently doubled as rapacious yet cosseted trading partners, but also ambivalence toward Washington. The First World War, which set off the whole age of extremity by making possible both the Soviet Union and the rise of National Socialism, was said in Europe to have consumed legitimacy. If that is so, what legitimacy did the decades of the Cold War consume?

The Cold War was the fourth great global tragedy of the twentieth century, after World Wars I and II and the Great Depression. Much effort has been devoted to explaining it: learned debates over its origins; biographies of its great actors; analyses of its char-

acteristic sciences, technologies, armaments, and espionage. Recon-
siderations of Vietnam will continue as long as a single soldier,
demonstrator, or professor still breathes. The Cold War's tunnels into
Afghanistan and international terrorist networks are just beginning
to be clarified. Excellent monographs have assessed particular prices
paid: How many dollars were spent on nuclear weapons? What were
the costs of vicious incursions on personal liberty? What sacrifice
has been made in mortal sickness from fallout? But this book, I
believe, is the first to bring together the Cold War as a state of mind
(the politics, fears, and visions that gripped the world) and the vast
labyrinth of costs and consequences that followed. It shows the
power of the undertow that has dragged for so long on the nation's
energies, while also showing what was won.

It is timely to tell this story now. An entire generation in the
industrial democracies is (happily enough) growing up with the
dimmest memories of the Cold War. Yet at the same time, they hear
that a new struggle — the one begun in fall 2001 — will be much
like the Cold War in its combination of force, politics, secrecy, and its
likely duration.

We all see the immense economic and technological achievements that keep pushing the world forward. But it is important to
understand how the journey to this point of progress was bent by
the pressures of 1946 to 1991 and how the world has not fully
sprung back. Addressing the subject ten years after the Soviet collapse adds perspective. Materials released since then can be called
upon, at the same time that key participants (not necessarily the
wise men of legend or the people who appeared in the news) are still
around to share their thoughts.

The fifty years here invoked may be seen as running from 1939
to 1989 — successively embracing one form or another of extreme
conflict with history's two worst cults of state worship. Or, rather
less exactly, they may be assigned to the explicit struggle with the
Soviet Union from 1946 to 1991 and its immediate aftermath.
Indeed, the years at hand could be the half century since 1950,
when the Korean War propelled the United States into a worldwide
political-military role, and 2001, when another global vulnerability
made itself painfully felt. The number confronts us at each turn,
but, in fact, it is proving to be a grave underestimate.

Like all great tragedies, the Cold War has a beginning, a middle,
and an end. Part I, or the beginning, can be assigned to the years

1946 to 1961 (chapters 2 to 5), as the democracies, having gained one desperate victory for liberty, came to terms with the dangerous truth about their greatest ally. Leaders born in the 1870s and 1890s sought to steer their countries, and the civilization of which they found themselves the dismayed trustees, through a brave new world. Part II, the middle, covers 1961 to 1981 (chapters 6 to 9), when the widening of the terrain excited and then disoriented the new generation of American leaders. The clarion calls of John F. Kennedy and the worldly misconceptions of Richard Nixon permeated this time. Part III covers 1981 to 1989 (chapters 10 to 11), starting with the inauguration of a president who spoke of "transcending communism" and closing as Eastern Europe raced to freedom, democracy steadily replaced dictatorship in much of the world, and the United States pressed ahead to greater vitality as a society. How that occurred has never been examined in detail. Chapter 12 covers the outcome. It explores how the Cold War formally ended, as the hammer and sickle came down from over the Kremlin domes, and then shows how a dramatic political conclusion was not a final resolution.

Over and above the broad questions traced here, other issues keep forcing their way to the surface: the demands imposed by technological change (as shown, for example, in immense recurring efforts to shield the American continent from nuclear missiles); the roles of government, and of elites in general; and the impact of the CIA. The last emphasis derives not from the Agency's being more or less competent than other arms of the government, but from the fact that its own story brings together the many sources of the Cold War's destructiveness: the web of unaccountability, the allegedly expert authority of eccentric talents, and the fact that even those who were apparently best positioned to divine what was going on were hopelessly underinformed. What precedent does this offer for new fights ahead?

Many myths arose during the Cold War decades. They range from the origins of the Korean War; to the dangers of the Cuban missile crisis, which continues to be celebrated as the ultimate crisis "managed" and surmounted; to the benefits of arms control; to the way the whole thing ended. To offer some different interpretations, the following chapters draw on newly available documents, as well as on interviews, recent memoirs, and the valuable research of other scholars.

The State Department and the Defense Department, as well as the White House, are releasing more and more relevant files, although many of the more interesting ones from the CIA remain hidden or are reported to have been destroyed. Official British records contribute important insights, especially for the first decade, when Britain could still present itself as one of the Big Three. Russian archives are problematic and can create confusion. Some from the Politburo, the Central Committee, and the Foreign Ministry have been opened rather selectively. Yet essentially nothing is available from the Ministry of Defense, let alone the KGB, nor is anything at hand that directly concerns weapons development. However, valuable fragments can be pieced together from an array of historical studies by former Soviet military officers and weapons designers. They yield revelations about the Soviet Union's arsenal, remnants of which could still easily destroy the United States or any other target.

Each of the twelve chapters intends to cover as recognizably coherent a period as possible. I write often of "Americans" and "Soviets." This is a practical matter. It assumes that each people was generally unified by a common culture and political system. Similarly, in discussing "Western Europeans," I assume that the peoples of these nations were evolving an increasingly greater sense of what they had in common than of what divided them as they strived toward unity. "Washington," "Moscow," and "Beijing" may present a false illusion of both united governments and united peoples, when this most certainly was not always the case. But in general, such entities embracing millions of individuals, especially in their international dealings, are more crudely unitary than the peoples whom they claim to represent.

Writing in a century free from so many of the old one's worst fears, yet energetically advancing new terrors of its own, I realize that it is too easy to judge how decisions might otherwise have been made. Any author has an enormous advantage over the distant times and people he or she is describing. None of us, even the early participants who are still around, and who have seen so much, can convey that world in all its complexities. Mistakes that now appear obvious, such as the terrible slide into Vietnam, were exceedingly difficult to detect at the time. Even so, many decisions that were widely denounced as wrong when they were being made, such as Washington's shortsighted defense strategies of the 1970s, were as clearly misguided then as they appear today.

The specific efforts that did the most to bring success will likely never be known. A dean of Harvard Medical School used to tell the entering class that half of what it would be taught would eventually be proved wrong; he just didn't know which half. We might also recall Hippocrates' axiom "First, do no harm." So much that was harmful to American life crowded aboard the Cold War bandwagon and rode expensively to the end — even as the world was saved from becoming prey to adventurist tyrannies. But we cannot determine how much of the huge effort it required went to no purpose, or worse. Still, it is worth examining what was lost, what was gained, and how each outcome weighs on us today.

The

FIFTY-YEAR
WOUND

1

1945: At the Top
of the Wave

*The interregnum of the next decades will be a time of distress
and of gnashing of teeth. We shall live in the hollow of the
historical wave.*

Arthur Koestler, 1944

The war that opened with an order to British officers to sharpen
their swords, and that climaxed as proudly modern Germany blitzed
into Russia with more horses than trucks, ended in nuclear ash. The
world was being transformed by factories that could assemble aircraft faster than wheelbarrows had been made forty years before.
Jets, missiles, atomic bombs, and computers were propelled into sustained development by the demands of war. What was not anticipated was how much faster *everything* was going to change.

This chapter is a snapshot of the way Americans saw themselves in the world of 1945. It emphasizes the utter lack of precedent that soon begot ad hoc, sporadic, reactive, expensive, and
open-ended decisions; the reality of Stalinist Russia; and a nation
coming simultaneously to believe in a sunny future and a limitless
danger.

The Cold War did not metastasize overnight sometime during
1946 or 1947. It was brought about by the ghosts of the Great War
of 1914 to 1918, and it took thirty years to attain full, deadly life.
The First World War had made the second one almost inescapable:
it ensured that politics and war technology, rather than trade
and general civilized habits, would frame international relations. It

became ever more difficult to achieve a just and enduring world system. Once the precedent of totalitarianism taking over one great country was set, the next likely step was for it to be countered by its mirror image in a rival tyranny. Lenin became Hitler's alibi. Communism enabled Hitler to fulminate about ultimate danger and to posture as the savior of Germany. The Cold War and all its sacrifices would have been extremely unlikely without World War I's destruction of the old European order. Our children will keep hearing the guns of August even as they embrace the wonders ahead.

✪

Within the lifetimes of many people still living today, the twentieth century appeared destined to be the century of collectivism and, if civilization did not take care, of totalitarianism. The 1930s "waves of the future" — Russian Communism, Italian Fascism, and German National Socialism — seemed only a beginning. Fascist and semifascist regimes arose from Spain to Eastern Europe. In Asia, Japan's ambition was imbued with its own themes of divine preeminence and race mastery. There and in Africa, European elites could still be confident that they controlled most of the world's destinies, and Washington was happy to let them do so, even in the Middle East. On its island continent, America remained remote.

The country had some experience with quarrels over the size and nature of its armed forces. In the 1920s, for instance, General Billy Mitchell had warned about the harm of placing U.S. defense in the hands of the "merchants" — the "people with something to sell" (apparently not weapons). If Americans didn't look out, he insisted, its soldiers and sailors "might as well stop work."[1] In this view, George F. Babbitt would sacrifice sound preparation for country club dues. All sorts of ironies were being set in place.

During the interwar years, Japan, the only exclusively Pacific power of the early twentieth century, was increasingly seen as America's most likely opponent. However, there was puzzlement over the more daunting British Empire. Was it a bosom partner or a fearsome rival? In deadly serious strategic planning right into the 1930s, the sharpest minds on the U.S. general staff could think of no greater danger than that of six million British troops rolling down from Canada to destroy the competitive challenge from the Midwest, as Japan locked the arms of American power in Asia.[2]

Come the end of 1940, Britain was barely holding out against Hitler, while America was still at peace. Franklin Delano Roosevelt, elected president in 1932, made plans to lend or lease supplies to Britain, backed by a petition from 170 Americans that had been drafted by Lewis Douglas, a copper millionaire from Douglas, Arizona, and president of Mutual of New York Life Insurance. Douglas also wrote a characteristically intense letter to his friend James Conant, president of Harvard. "Our endeavor and England's endeavor," he mused, "should be aimed at the resuscitation of a world order in which . . . the United States must become the dominant power." He saw little hope in his lifetime if that remained undone. The lofty reply from Massachusetts Hall read, "I believe the only satisfactory solution for the country is for the majority of the thinking people to become convinced that we must be a world power, and the price of being a world power is willingness and capacity to fight when necessary."[3] This correspondence was one grace note in the grand opera of geopolitics, played in the better drawing rooms on the coast of the Northeast. It presumed both that the British Empire was expected to serve as a butler realm and that influential people of all sorts were anticipating American predominance, whatever that might gain for the United States in a strange new world.

Lewis Douglas's brother-in-law, John J. McCloy, became assistant secretary of war as the United States approached full involvement. *Harper's* magazine would eventually describe him as "the most influential private citizen in America." McCloy unabashedly injected into this discussion his belief that "I would take a chance on this country using its strength tyrannously." He anticipated some sort of "Pax Americana." An unimaginative man with no sense of irony, he added that "in the course of it the world will become more receptive to the Bill of Rights."[4]

There was agreement among men such as Lewis, McCloy, Conant, publisher Henry Luce, and their friends that the United States was destined to replace the British Empire as the world's foremost economic and military force. Since Britain did not remotely have such a role even at the start of World War II, this shows how far behind the times eminent men can be. Such datedness set the tone for half a century.

Only a few months before the United States entered the war, Luce, the unrivaled media titan of his day, declared that this was to be the "American Century." American or not, the rest of the twentieth century would be shaped by the Cold War, one of whose poles was America. However, such ambitions — whether voiced by Wall Streeters, by the president of Harvard, or by other enthusiasts who expected to direct in some way a Pax Americana — were not shared in Minnesota, Oregon, and Pennsylvania. There was no consensus in 1940, at the war's end in 1945, or as the rest of that bloody decade unfolded, that "America would turn outward and assume global responsibilities," as legend now has it.[5]

The world that these and other grandees hoped to lead — once the approaching cataclysm had passed — was expected to be quieter and safer than the one that arrived. They had no inkling of thermonuclear threats, globe-girdling alliances, insular European allies whom they had thought to be world powers, defense budgets in the hundreds of billions, and, above all, the recurring "savage wars of peace," which Rudyard Kipling at the turn of the century had exhorted Americans to take up. Body bags from places like Chosin and Khe Sanh and a national debt in the trillions were inconceivable. That embodiment of Republican faith and statesmanship, Senator Robert Taft, remarked in 1940 that it was about as unlikely that a German army would invade America as it was that an American army would invade Germany, and yet within five years, GIs from Ohio were crossing the Rhine. For the next decades, the best-informed people would be eating their words about whatever political conjunction or technological achievement they had previously deemed unthinkable.

Army Chief of Staff George Marshall and one of his predecessors, General Douglas MacArthur, military adviser in the Philippines until five months before Pearl Harbor, were the two curiously contrasted American geniuses of World War II. They would have been at least equally appalled had it been prophesied to them as eager young cadets during the late 1890s that in their old age, they would have to come to terms with the power to end the human race. This was not soldiering, which they viewed as an exercise of discipline and sacrifice. Nor did it have anything to do with their studies, such as understanding Clausewitz's writings on the capacity to harness violent nonreason with the would-be stylized workings of state policy. From the beginning of history, strategists at their most desperate had never contemplated *mutual* destruction.

On November 29, 1941, a picture of the USS *Arizona* was displayed in the Army-Navy game program, with a caption stating that "no battleship has ever been sunk by air attack."[6] Eight days later, at least 1,177 men went to their deaths on that very ship in one fiery moment. A luncheon meeting of the Cleveland Council on World

Affairs listened raptly on Sunday, December 7, to several renowned visitors, such as Count Sforza, Fascist Italy's most eminent political exile, explaining how Japan was too intelligent to do anything but accommodate the United States in the Pacific. As the meeting adjourned, news arrived that the fleet was burning.[7]

That bright Sunday dawn awoke a fear that would endure throughout the Cold War and after: one moment's inattention, and the unparryable blow might fall. The country's leaders were learning to expect anything. Nothing could be certain, nothing secure. At Harvard, nearly everyone had been intensely isolationist. The most prominent exception was politics professor William Yandell Elliott. His colleagues derided him for his sense of emergency and for advising the Roosevelt administration on military affairs. The following day, the faculty gathered in Memorial Hall, dedicated to the university's Civil War dead. They would hear Roosevelt declare war together. As Elliott entered, he was greeted with rapturous applause. Many beliefs would be changing fast: the ablest people had no idea of what was and was not possible, of what would happen next.[8]

Before America entered the war, the public had few opinions about either how the world worked or what their country might need from it. The America that fought the war was still homespun and often ill informed, its citizens and even leaders not knowing much about the rest of the globe. GIs going to Europe were incredulous that the *Queen Elizabeth* was not American; what other nation could build on such a scale? After two years of fighting, nearly a third of the country did not know that the Philippines had fallen, and twice that many had never heard of the Atlantic Charter. Somewhat more than half thought that the United States had been a member of the League of Nations.[9] Public ignorance might have been the same or worse in France or Italy, but those countries were not about to change history.

Winston Churchill chose the name United Nations from a line by Byron. Other international arrangements also born during the war would become significant to restoring international prosperity. The Bretton Woods monetary conference of July 1944, attended by representatives of forty nations, pegged gold to the dollar at $35 an ounce, with the various national currencies connecting to the dollar like spokes to the hub of a wheel. The American economy was thereby recognized as the centerpiece of international exchange. To pay for postwar recovery and to ensure currency stability, corollary agreements reached by the contracting parties at this New Hampshire resort also created the International Bank for Reconstruction and Development (the World Bank, which McCloy would head) and the International Monetary Fund: "This Fund that you call a Bank," noted the sardonic economist and negotiator John Maynard Keynes, "and this Bank you call a Fund." Imprecision was of little significance in the urgent present.

Breathtaking inventions were coming into being toward war's end, as the gates to progress seemed to fly open for a generation that was encountering "thinking machines," jets, penicillin, and atomic energy. The industrial revolution of rail, steel, telegraph, and turbine was being leapfrogged by that of radio and automobile. Bizarre new materials were undermining the certainties of statesmen — plutonium, for instance, which its discoverer would say "is so unusual as to approach the unbelievable."[10] Nearly $2 billion of that era's money was going into the Manhattan Project for building the atomic bomb — in present-day terms (reckoning not only inflation but a sixfold increase in the size of gross domestic product) about $86 billion.[11] And it was done in secret.

As victory approached, America's economy was booming. It nearly doubled in the war years, with the country having been pulled out of the Depression by war far more than by Franklin Roosevelt's New Deal. Many Americans nonetheless feared that this was a mere digression. Always a people inclined to overvalue recent experience, they recalled that war booms had habitually been followed by peace busts. Whether consumer demand, as well as unrealized new technologies pent up for a decade or more, could now keep the ball rolling was anyone's guess. Technologically, America was optimistic; economically, it was hypochondriac.

Other world leaders, whether in London or Moscow, had little faith in America's financial stability. Men of sixty could remember a long chain of U.S. excesses: the economic crisis of 1893; the alarms of inflation as manically urged by presidential candidate William Jennings Bryan and his "cross of gold"; the roller coaster of the 1920s, when U.S. tariff walls made it impossible to settle European debts. A history of fevered boom and bust in international markets can be charted at least as far back as Charles Dickens's Ebenezer Scrooge, who fears that the riches the Ghost has shown him are mere "United States securities." Perhaps America's moment would be a fleeting one.

✪

In 1945, Lenin's arrival at the Finland Station to take over the Russian Revolution was about as recent as the end of the Vietnam War is today. The organizers of victory during that bewildering autumn easily remembered that a handful of Marxist dogmatists had just hammered a large part of the world into strange new shapes. Now city-evaporating weapons arrived seemingly out of nowhere. Who could tell what was next? Einstein himself had come late to the belief that nuclear fission was possible. Anything in politics or human behavior was beginning to seem likely, whether through the evils of totalitarianism, the wonders of science, or, even more unsettling, the binding of the two.

Stalin's mass tyranny was troublingly familiar, but its secrets and cruelties ensured that virtually no one knew what was actually happening within. Even now that the Soviet Union is on the ash heap of history, we know little about the inner workings of the Politburo, the KGB, or the Ministry of Defense. What was this place that the United States faced on the other side of the globe, the land to which, since 1941, it had provided $11 billion in aid — not only munitions, thousands of bombers, and hundreds of thousands of trucks, but also millions of tons of food and clothing, as well as entire factories — and which in turn had ripped the heart out of the Wehrmacht? To the United States, Russia was not unlike what China seemed to the Russians: vast, ancient, pitiless, unfathomable, and with its own (unlikely to be pleasant) agenda.

The Soviet Union, during its Great Patriotic War, had lost around 27 million combatants and civilians, many of them murdered by Stalin's own secret police under Lavrenti Beria, the other Georgian who smilingly administered mass extermination. ("Our Himmler," Stalin called him during talks with FDR at Yalta, speaking of the Reichsführer SS.) Even at the moment that Hitler shot himself, the Reich had yet to surpass the numbers of murders inflicted on the world by Stalin, who, appropriately, had from August 1939 until Russia was invaded in June 1941 been a more faithful ally of the Nazis than Mussolini.[12] Arthur Koestler's *Darkness at Noon*, published in 1943, was the one serious imaginative treatment of a Soviet system of precisely the sort that had produced this worst of all wars — a Great Terror too immense to neglect (though many tried), too hard to understand. We know about

Stalin's techniques, his foreign policy, and the extreme limitations on his intellectual processes. But there is no insight even today as to what drove the man to destroy somewhere between 17 million and 22 million of his people just during the 1930s. Who would bet on his staying sane, in the most crudely operational sense of not actually starting another world war, by the time it was thought he had atomic weapons?

The Soviet Union came to appear at once terrifyingly inescapable and fundamentally unreal. It was not like confronting the Third Reich, or even the USSR that Lenin left at his death in 1924. At least in Germany, the high command, the diplomatic service, Krupp, I. G. Farben, and generally the universities were in the hands of people who would also have been in place under the Kaiser. At least some aspects of Hitler's Germany had been possible to understand and, had the will been there, to prepare for. Alternatively, so little was known about the Soviet Union and the people who ran it — such as how much of its workforce was slave labor, even if 15 million, or 8 percent of the population, was a good guess.

George Orwell was finally able to publish *Animal Farm* in August 1945, so pointed a tale of revolution betrayed that it had repeatedly been rejected for publication during the war, including by the reactionary T. S. Eliot at Faber & Faber. Orwell, a staunch socialist, was attacking hypocrisy on the democratic left no less than Stalinism. The book's revolutionaries are clever pigs who turn into a master race. In the showdown between men and animals, only the pig supremo, Napoleon — greedy, paranoid, grandiose, and clearly modeled on Stalin — stands up to human explosives, as had Stalin himself to the Germans.

This "fairy story," as Orwell subtitled it, is intended to show how the most exalted ideals are degraded by despotic power. It also underscores the democracies' ambivalence toward Stalin as representative of a people unbelievably long-suffering, decidedly brave, unconquerably determined, so recently allied, and so suddenly threatening. Two months after publication, Orwell coined a phrase to describe the new landscape: "Cold War."

Well into 1945, the White House and most of America's leaders remained optimistic about Russia's intentions. Come V-E Day, the West was watching half of Europe being assimilated into a system whose plans were not just unknown but deeply concealed. The political obscurity was bad enough, but the combination of size, technology, and reach was truly chilling. Stalin added nearly 100 million souls in Eastern Europe to his 200 million Soviet subjects, and he undertook a violent campaign to drag back all displaced persons born in any part of his realm. Key members of liberal non-Communist political parties disappeared in the night and fog of the occupied nations. More than 1 million of his German prisoners of war also simply vanished, all unaccounted for except several thousand who had been classified as war criminals.

Totalitarianism considers that nothing has countervailing rights against it and acts on that assumption. In Stalinism, it became increasingly easier to conclude that civilization faced another "odious apparatus," as Churchill had called Nazism. Extreme violence had become a fact of life.

There was a real possibility that such a deadly ascendancy would cast itself over Western Europe. This is a point now much debated, but nothing had stopped Hitler, ruler of a lesser power, between the Channel and Moscow, and only his bad judgment had halted him there. What made the Soviet Union all the more alarming was that its international reach might not even require such an assault. Anything like a "National Socialist International" was absurd and could be ridiculed by P. G. Wodehouse's portrayal of the blustering Spode and his farcical band of Home Counties "Black Shorts." The Communist International was by no means so preposterous. The Red Army did not have to keep heading west for Stalin to extend his hand.

An hour before the Gestapo shot him, a Communist leader in Paris had scratched on the wall of his cell that he was going out "to prepare the tomorrows that sing."[13] (André Malraux seeks to catch this spirit in *La Condition humaine*.) It was still possible for communism as a Western popular movement to appeal to the noblest hopes and to offer itself as a barrier to the deepest fears. Its epitaph was unconsciously written by Jean-Paul Sartre: "To be unsparing in telling the truth about the USSR was to deprive the automobile workers of hope." In France and Italy at war's end, Communists in the government coalitions and in the big trade unions were candid about where their loyalties lay.

Much of Europe at the end of the war — those parts not occupied by the Red Army — seemed to be tottering into chaos. Inspecting Germany's devastation, McCloy described it as "unparalleled in history unless one goes back to the Roman Empire, and even that may not have been as great in economic upheaval."[14] On the other side of the globe, and two days after Hiroshima, Stalin had finally declared war on Japan. Carleton Swift of the Office of Strategic Services (forerunner of the CIA) accompanied Mao Tse-tung's great Marshal Chu Teh to Manchukuo, where every industrial plant built by the Japanese had been stripped bare by the Russians. Above all, he recalls "desolate silence except for the grinding of Chu Teh's teeth."[15] This sort of vicious world did not look particularly welcoming for an American Century.

After the terrible years just past, that the Soviet Union should be thoroughly armed, thoroughly suspicious, and even rapacious was understandable. But Russia's visceral fear for its safety had nothing to do with packing whole nationalities on to their doom, with the deadly show trials of Eastern European Communist cadres, or with ongoing disappearances, such as that of the heroic thirty-one-year-old Swedish diplomat Raoul Wallenberg, who likely perished in the secret police's Lubyanka Prison two years after he was kidnapped in Budapest toward the war's end. Most sinister because most crazy, Russia's own distinguished genetics profession was destroyed in order to forward the catastrophic doctrines of Trofim Lysenko, charlatan-biologist-cum-secret-policeman, who insisted that Charles Darwin was wrong — his purpose being to prove that "socialist man" could rapidly be developed. Something far stranger was at work in the Soviet Union than the currents of Russian history or the dogmas of Marxism-Leninism. Indeed, the notable Marxist-Leninists, such as Bukharin and Pashukanis, had all been shot. This behavior was not geopolitics: it was despotism run frantic.

Yet from the Soviet Union — a political order based on terror and forced on a much-invaded country — it could have been assumed that such ferociousness was how things worked, world without end. "Neither war nor peace," Lenin had said of Soviet dealings with the capitalist powers right after the First World War. Whereas that situation seemed unlikely to be bearable or, in the longer run, even sustainable by democracies, the Cold War was not a new experience for land-besieged Russia or revolutionary Bolshevism. For Stalin, it even possessed a certain homecoming quality.

✪

Eric Hoffer, in *Working and Thinking on the Waterfront*, tells of celebrating on the docks on V-E Day and of a longshoreman friend who anticipated that the heroic ally Russia would be the next power to confront. Wouldn't the kid most energetic in downing the school-yard bully promptly take his place?

By V-J Day, however, Abraham Lincoln's belief that the United States was "the last best hope of earth" seemed an invocation not just of the republican dream, but of a burdened world at last set materially free. One of the best reflections of 1945 America is *On the Town*, the Jerome Robbins–Leonard Bernstein musical celebrating the strut and swagger of a confident nation beating back tyrants and saving democracy. Its citizens at that time were prepared on the one hand to become more engaged commercially with the world while on the other (having become newly instructed in totalitarian horror), they were intent on keeping its more sordid political and military aspects at arm's length.

The United States by its mere existence exercised an effortless leverage. It had 7 percent of the world's population in 1915, but it possessed nearly half of the world's manufacturing and productive vitality. What horizon need be imposed on its vision? The country was alive with strength and purpose, and there was so much to put this strength and purpose to. Americans had spent more than $230 billion to fight the war — more than the equivalent of the (war-expanded) gross domestic product for 1945 and more than $2 trillion in today's dollars. They had been hoping for a good life since the start of the Depression. Now, with victory, the scientific knowledge developed during the war catalyzed the tremendous pent-up consumer demand and the backlogs of U.S. industry. These two forces hit Main Street together, further driven by an extraordinary reassertion of fertility, the unlocking of wartime savings in bank accounts and liberty bonds, and a crackle of popular electronics.

After nearly fifteen years of postponement, people believed that they could safely be caught up in a whirlwind of change that in less purposeful times would have been demoralizing. By contrast, so much deemed to be provisional during the Depression and the war continued to be so after the outbreak of peace. Among these things were agricultural subsidies, price controls on railroad tickets, public money lavished on science and technology, spy services woven out of exotic material, pension vesting, and industry's military contracts. Unprecedented roles for government were already coming to be accepted as normal. After all, government was clearly the patron of so much that was worthwhile. For instance, a new American middle class was about to be made by the GI Bill of Rights, which allocated $3.7 billion for higher education and (white suburban) home buying at a time when annual per capita disposable income was $1,074. It was a superb investment — so superb as to convince people that all such government outlays could have corresponding benefits.

Scientific American would later distill the surge of all this energy into the telling phrase "acceleration of history."[16] From now on, history would speed forward, bringing about an ever more pervasive technological — and therefore social, economic, political, and military — transformation. Less justifiably, an outsize faith was being placed in some newly applied fields of study, such as economics. An awkward balance was struck between the social and the natural sciences. For example, absurdly too much was expected of analytic psychology, whereas too little attention was given to, say, neurology. For the moment, these were merely details; the world appeared to be made for America. Yet all too soon, this prospect was undercut by a renewed struggle. Acute hope was clouded by a sense that something had gone terribly wrong.

The rest of the world was exhausted, and much of it needed to be propped up. That was an emergency exercise well fitted to the national spirit. However, the country soon found itself far deeper in world events than even exponents of the American Century had dreamed. By the fall of 1945, there was a rough consensus for a more alert, more generally engaged foreign policy. America would stop things from happening — tariff-precipitated depressions and the triumphs of power-mad dictators, for example — but such a strategy would entail doing other things. How many? For how long? At what price? Much of the hoopla about "the leadership of the world" implied that the world would come to learn at America's feet — not that America would plod along the globe's most dangerous roads and jungle trails.[17]

It is strange that a single American generation would so rapidly move into the world to pursue an ideal of national defense that hinged on protecting far-off places about which it knew little and ultimately backing those commitments with immensely destructive devices about which almost everyone knew even less. As remarkable is that a public with opinions still so ill formed would, however grumblingly, drag from its pockets the trillions of dollars to be spent over the next forty-plus years. One need not believe in conspiracies at the Council on Foreign Relations or within a military-industrial complex to detect something incredible about this venture. "The counterintuitive," often remarked Noam Chomsky, as bitter an enemy as the whole enterprise ever had, "is always the most interesting."

To what extent America's "rise to globalism" was reluctant continues to be argued by historians. Yet the very word *globalism,* implying a doctrine and a state of mind, is tricky. America's amazing outreach between Pearl Harbor and Hiroshima had been global, not globalist. Its forces had struck around the world because the country's enemies were there. There was no purpose beyond battle. What happened once these enemies were defeated was a slow, reluctant engagement, nearly always trying to substitute technology and money from afar for an actual presence.

By the end of 1945, five motivating influences bore down on the assumptions most Americans had about the world. One was *speed,* the simplest and most obvious acceleration. No one other than science fiction writers had believed in atomic bombs before 1935, but in August 1945, the bomb was there for the world to see, the simple greatest fact of power. In 1935, no one had realized that a fortress could be taken by air assault. At Eben Emael, on the Belgian border, German commandos showed that it could be done. But by 1950, such a fantastic operation had become old-fashioned and would have been disastrous against any competently prepared enemy. And by then, the Soviet Union had its own bomb, well before almost everyone except Stalin expected. "If it works, it's obsolete," General Dwight D. Eisenhower was fond of saying. It was a time of incredible promise and of incredible threat — in that sense, the best of times and the worst of times.

Another influence was a sense of *luck.* The Allies had won because they had more people, a greater economic base, and the advantage of being the forces of liberation and resistance. At the vulnerable outset, they had had enough nonessential space to lose in the short term, as the Germans had learned in Russia and the Japanese had discovered in the Pacific. Even so, the margin of victory had still been heart-stoppingly slender. A couple of decisions the other way by Hitler and his generals or by a pair of Japanese admirals, and the outcome might have been different. No country — not the richest and remotest — could rely any longer on apparently heaven-sent good fortune. Otto von Bismarck's irritable assessment that God looks after fools, drunkards, and the United States of America could not carry into the atomic age.

There was also the influence of *size,* and here there was a contradiction in American perceptions. The world had become much smaller, whether it be the electronic world of the fascinated consumer or the thermonuclear world of the alarmed citizen. Boys from Butte and Joliet were crashing on the Hump, drowning off the island of Ascension, and bringing brides home from Okinawa. Technology was pulling people together. Yet it also became apparent that the sheer bigness of geography could lift certain countries into another order of magnitude from those historic entities Japan, France, Britain, and Germany — all a great deal smaller than Texas. The United States, Russia, and China are in a class by themselves, as is India. Size can multiply the components of power, and this would be the age of continental might: populations, resources, and, if worst came to worst, capacity to absorb nuclear punishment.

Additionally, there was the realization that security was something that had to be worked at, to be *managed*. Clearly, Americans could not turn their backs on the world and return to their business of doing business. They had done that after the Revolution, the War of 1812, and the Civil War; during the 1870s, when America was a tariff-wrapped autarky; and after 1919, when the country withdrew behind moralist rhetoric and interest-ridden protectionism. Not again.

Finally, it was self-evident that Europe had once more — and perhaps terminally — made a mess of things. Life would only become worse if these exhausted, discredited sovereignties were left to their own tortured histories of unsteady power balances, mercantilism, colonialism, and military adventure. The United States trusted neither its friends not its former enemies to rebuild themselves properly. It had reasons.

Such an anxious understanding of the world was darkened by the loss of the sturdy, if rarely tested, axioms that had guarded American foreign policy from the early days of the Republic: no entangling alliances and the avoidance of Old World quarrels. These axioms were being replaced by new generalities: "Munich," the assumption that any concession brings catastrophe; "free trade," a belief vulnerable to being compromised for the sake of other foreign policy objectives or of not offending rich domestic interests; and, increasingly, "collective security," rather a wet firecracker if taken literally.

Nor was it apparent whom could be relied on for insight into this postwar kaleidoscope: the WASP upper classes, which until the Depression had seemed to gather economic decisions effortlessly into their hands; the scientific elite, so largely a mass of Central European genius, which had spilled into the startled university towns; or the generals and admirals who were beginning to move into high government and corporate positions.

Americans were willing to pay to ensure that there would be two potent mediating bodies between them and everyone else: the United Nations, to be sure, and the British Empire, that globally deployed, high-tech entity that was presented as the archetype of a "super power" when a Columbia University professor coined that term during the last year of the war. To most Americans, the British Empire at the end of World War II appeared to be second among world powers, perhaps third, the more or less consistent American ally in a generation's struggle to save the world from its worst predators. The territory of the Empire and Commonwealth was half again as large as the Soviet Union, and its population at least double. Britain itself perhaps held the lead in jet engines, computers, and atomic research. Maybe it could be America's "outer fortress," as it was soon called by Senator Hubert Humphrey, and would uphold its (quite chimerical) role as maintainer of the Pax Britannica.[18]

No one in America was ready to substitute U.S. strength for whatever worldwide peacekeeping services the British Empire might provide as part of its nature. The story of this "outer fortress" is a strangely Jamesian one of barely uttered commitment, unclear reasons and objectives, and seemingly bold but ultimately empty gestures. Like the British Empire, America was deeply and historically averse to the well-known costs of establishing (and maintaining) balances of power. Island nations, after all, have a peculiar view of such balances: they find their part to be agreeable only after the main equilibrium has been hammered out exhaustingly by others. Unlike Britain, the United States of the next four decades rarely kept its eyes on the stakes of power — losing so much by its discontinuities and distractions, yet finally winning by its unparalleled ability to adapt.

The contest that America was about to enter would become by far the greatest cold war ever. Hot wars have horizons: roughly speaking, the closer the horizon, the more destructive the war. Cold wars — for instance, the war for control of North America between the British and French in the seventeenth and eighteenth centuries, or the nineteenth-century Anglo-Russian "Great Game" in Central Asia — can continue for decades but historically have not drained the societies involved. In the years ahead, however, America would largely end up standing alone against a terrible opponent. The Cold War dragged on — expensive, sleepless, and, at its worst junctures, primed to produce new dangers that threatened to dwarf the World War II cataclysms that had brought it about in the first place. "Hope deferred maketh the heart sick" (Proverbs 13:12).

All the uncertainties that arose in the early winter of 1945–1946 and that presaged the dangers to come for most of the century did not lead to final catastrophe. Some bloodshed was expected, and it came. But it was not a death grapple on the European plain or a nuclear haze over China. Instead, it came in the form of vast sub-wars, weird hybrids of confrontation. There was an endlessness to this struggle, which combined with a global battlefield to make the Cold War so wounding.

At the end of the century, the Pentagon issued a certificate of Cold War meritorious service to Americans who had served in the military between 1945 and 1991. Smithsonian museums also describe the Cold War as covering those years. But the dates are not so tidy. Although there was no shortage of East-West antagonism in 1945, it took a year after World War II ended for tensions to freeze between Britain and the Soviet Union, and more than another year for them to freeze between Washington and Moscow. The world between 1946 and 1950 went back into "some sort of nightmare of aggression we thought we had buried by disposing of Hitler," the hard-boiled British Labour Party minister Herbert Morrison said.[19] History's greatest war had been replaced by history's least plausible peace.

PART I

PART 1

2

Back to the Future

(1946–1950)

For I dipt into the future, far as human eye could see,
Saw the vision of the world, all the wonder that would be.

Alfred, Lord Tennyson, the lines that Winston Churchill called
"the most wonderful of modern prophecies," from "Locksley
Hall," the poem which Harry Truman carried in his wallet
throughout his life

The first year after World War II was, at least for Americans, one of hope and wonder. There were many reasons to be confident about what lay ahead. Anger toward Russia took time. Perhaps the most striking feature of 1946 was not the vigor of Communist pressure, but the weakness of American reaction. Theorists began speaking of "containment," but not until the return to war in 1950 did such thinking take on the material procedures and the global scope of policy.

The Soviet Union stepped up its already absurd mythology of democracy, even renaming its commissars "ministers." Its pretensions as a revolutionary power nonetheless still rested on terrorist industrialization from the top. But outside the areas newly "liberated" by the Red Army, the Soviets could orchestrate mass parties driven by the hope of revolution from below. In February 1946, the new U.S. ambassador to Russia, General Walter Bedell Smith, diffidently asked Stalin how much further he intended to go into Europe. "Not much," was the casual reply.[1] No one knew what that meant to this Moloch who ruled across twelve time zones.

British socialists who arrived in office with Churchill's defeat the previous summer were rarely so uncertain. Many of them had personally confronted communism before the war. In the 1920s, for example, the formidable figure who became the Labour government's foreign secretary, Ernest Bevin, had fought to defend his Transport Workers' Union from subversion. Attentive Americans were startled to see these men face off with Moscow. For instance, Wall Street lawyer and Republican foreign policy adviser John Foster Dulles had been taken aback as Bevin "blustered and stormed," in Dulles's words, during the Council of Foreign Ministers' meeting in London the previous September. Serving as a U.S. delegate, Dulles reported that Soviet Foreign Minister Molotov "told [Bevin] that other conferences had proceeded more smoothly because Churchill and Roosevelt were at them." Three months later, in Moscow, Bevin simply called Molotov's assertions about the tightening Soviet grip on Eastern Europe "Hitler theory."[2]

Bevin was not finished. If the Labour government did not immediately set a firm example for the United States, argued this former wagon driver and son of a washerwoman, "all Europe will fall."[3] Well into 1947, many Americans saw his confrontations with Moscow — whether over Iran, Greece, or Eastern Europe — as reruns of nearly century-old imperial quarrels. He in turn worried that the United States was trying "to take a mediating line or to remain neutral."[4] Right up to the Korean War, he shivered over U.S. delays in moving from broad and desirable principles into action. Didn't Americans see what was at stake?

By the fall of 1947, Stalin was assigning important places in the demonology of imperialism not just to Bevin and Prime Minister Clement Attlee but also to France's Léon Blum, Italy's Giuseppe Saragat, Austria's Karl Renner, and all other leading European democratic socialists. "Western" became a political rather than a geographical term, applying to countries that had not been occupied by the Soviet Union, did not have a Communist government, and intended to remain free of Soviet control.

The world was soon bleeding again. The succession states to the British Empire in India became independent that year and killed a couple of million of their own people along the way. Terrible, confused reports arrived from Eastern Europe and then from China. There was suspicion that the V-2 was likely to become merely the Model T of missiles. To Americans, the globe began to look like "One World," but not in the reassuring sense that the intellectual parents of the United Nations had envisioned. What motivated them to start accepting so many of the sacrifices that before long became commonplace, including the previously unknown concept of foreign aid and the entangling alliances that had been forsworn in 1797? The answers lie in a story that is familiar — but only on first encounter. It includes Churchill's "Iron Curtain" speech in 1946, the Marshall Plan and its origins in 1947, the drama of the Berlin Airlift in 1948, the founding of the North Atlantic Treaty Organization (NATO), and the triumphant arrival of the People's Liberation Army in Beijing in 1949. Beyond these events, we see a half dozen influences whose ties remain little understood.

What occurred was the down payment on a goal that had no final price. First, this chapter shows how, in 1946, Americans tried to use money and technology, among other means, to support the hope that their country might again be able to keep itself apart from the rest of the world. Second, it examines why early alarms were so quickly replaced by anxieties about overreaction — a swing exemplified by one persuasive figure, who is still respected today. Third, it revisits the pivotal year of 1947: unprecedented overseas engagements, reorganization in Washington, and an increasingly hostile view of Russia. Fourth, we bring several new insights to the moral compromises — the politics of dirty hands — that are part of the Cold War story from start to finish.

An official culture of overseas emergencies and accumulating "shocks" had arrived in the United States roughly by 1948. This is the focus of the chapter's fifth part and reminds us that the way "crises" are identified today may be not much different from how they were identified then. Sixth, we look at the seemingly clever, seemingly cheap covert operations that came into being and that were inseparable from the many accumulating secrets. We then arrive at 1949. With mixed feelings, Americans entered an alliance that remains at the core of U.S. foreign policy and the triggering mechanism of which would only be activated in 2001. They also encountered the deep vulnerabilities of their strongest ally around the same time that the Soviet Union suddenly appeared even more daunting. Nineteen forty-nine saw new problems in Asia, as Stalin — much earlier than has previously been understood — began preparing to unify Korea by force. In 1950, America's world role was transformed.

Throughout these years, America's leaders had a good sense of the problems of Western and Central Europe; rather less of an understanding of the nature of revolutionary communism; much less of a grasp of the vast rest of the world; and no idea at all, in the aftermath of Hiroshima and Nagasaki, of the technological future. The peppy, straight-talking Truman, as John Updike wrote soon after the president left office, "gave the impression of being an unnerved riverboat gambler improvising his way through the biggest crap game in Western history."[5] Nearly everyone else in Washington was rolling the cosmic dice, too. General George Marshall, who served as secretary of state between January 1947 and March 1949, was one of the few men who possessed the capacity and the aura to make a difference, as did his deputy, the sober New York banker and former Assistant Secretary of War for Air Robert Lovett. Despite his temper and hauteur, the elegant Dean Acheson, who succeeded Marshall at State, also had this presence. Lewis Douglas, appointed ambassador to London in early 1947 and called by *Time* magazine "the most important diplomat of the most powerful country in the world," was similarly formidable, as were several giants on Capitol Hill, such as Michigan's Arthur Vandenberg and Texas's Tom Connally, who helped redirect the Senate.[6] Like many Americans, these men knew that two decades of shortsightedness since 1919 had been paid for and the United States could not afford a vainglorious rerun in the years ahead. Yet hasty impressions too often passed as wisdom, all based on ever less applicable lessons from the past.

✪

America had been at peace in 1940, but within five years, it had hurled atomic fire out of the heavens, covered the seas with the greatest of all navies, and driven armies numbering in the millions into its enemies' heartlands. Yet in that first year after its hard-won victory, a terrible question already hung in the air. Was this the final peace, or might horrendous new weapons soon make it America's turn to perish? What if the inferno of total war was in fact the face of history?

John Maynard Keynes was beginning to pass into journalistic folklore. He had argued that under certain circumstances, an economic system is not self-sustaining. This was a doctrine that after 1945 often seemed to extend into the notion that *nothing* was self-sustaining. Here perhaps was the dirty big secret of industrial civilization: countries couldn't modernize so rapidly without hitting the sound barrier and losing control. Germany was the home of Beethoven and Goethe, the high point of Jewish culture. If Germany could turn into a savagely messianic Leviathan, what next? The Soviet Union, for its part, was growing more powerful, while inflicting on itself the equivalent of a Holocaust every half dozen years.

That most cultivated pseudoprophet, the prodigious British historian Arnold Toynbee, claimed a mystical sense of great essential movements of humanity, which, when he intuited them, seemed always to climax in violence. He began lecturing in the United States, riveting the bankers and lawyers at the Council on Foreign Relations, while more than two million average Americans bought his *Study of History* and his more concise *Civilization on Trial*. Many of them came to think about the burning cities and stumbling columns of refugees of the present with the newfound perspective of Ibn Khaldun and the Emperor Baber: contemporary problems somehow seemed, if not diminished, at least understandable against the breadth of time. The political culture became soaked in this search for past wisdom. Despite all the new attitudes and technologies, the preoccupation of statesmen and intellectuals (quite as much as of the general public) was with the lessons of history. Henry Kissinger would make his name with a study of the last serious European peace settlement more than a century before, inaccurately titled *A World Restored*. The North Atlantic basin was still "the world" for an amazing number of practical and scholarly people.

At the center of that world was America's closest ally of World War II, now the largest debtor nation after losing a quarter of its imperial wealth in the war. Americans became bound to Britain's desperate finances as the simplest way to maintain democracies in Europe and stability elsewhere in the world touched by British strength. The $3.75 billion loan grudgingly made in early 1946 was the first distinctly postwar commitment of U.S. economic and political power. It was also an attempt to put postwar burdens on someone else's back, as impatient Senate committees (in the words of one Englishman) endured "the spectacle of a wily sponging Socialist Britain attempting to outwit the open-hearted, open-pursed Americans and steal their legitimate markets by indefensible trading practices."[7] Precisely the same proportion of Americans said that they opposed the British loan as claimed they would oppose one to the Soviet Union. Most regarded its terms, with an effective 1.62 percent interest rate stretched out to 2001, as being generous to the point of foolishness. Americans generally began to fear — not without reason, as the next forty years would show — that much of their foreign aid would be pumped down one "Operation Rathole" or another.[8]

National security was a strong but not decisive influence in overcoming Congress's opposition to the loan. "Credits would strengthen Britain as a frontier outpost against communism," its proponents argued, without emphasizing Moscow. Leaving aside the question of will, who in America had the experience to play the Great Game and supposedly undertake the mastery of so much of the world? Lewis Douglas sounded like a British Foreign Office aristocrat when he reminded a Senate committee nodding in agreement that "through lack of training," the United States was unable to assume the British burden of power in distant and unfamiliar lands.[9]

And there just might be much to protect against in the reeling world of 1946. Churchill's speech at what the *New York Times* called "obscure Westminster College in even obscurer Fulton, Missouri," not only denounced the "Iron Curtain" and urged the saving of "Christian civilization" but also, as is less remembered, outlined a breathtakingly ambitious new global alliance with the United States. He dismayed Americans, already impatient with Washington's delays in the rush to peacetime life, with talk of revived military planning, shared bases, and joint weapons production. It was not difficult to read between the lines and anticipate that Britain might also expect its positions in the Near East and even in Asia to be underwritten.

What Americans of course feared was direct commitment. Right after Fulton, both Washington and the Labour government in London quickly let it be known that Churchill had spoken in a private capacity (albeit as the salaried Leader of His Majesty's Opposition). Stalin scoffed. "There are no such private individuals in this country," he coldly reminded the British ambassador.[10] Walter Lippmann, "public philosopher" of his generation at a time when newspaper columnists wielded outsize influence in national politics, had a further reason for condemning Churchill's enthusiasm. The day after the speech, he came across Churchill's son, Randolph, drinking no more heavily than usual at lunch. "We'll show you," Randolph warned. "You don't understand the British Empire. Just let me tell you this. We dragged you into two wars and we'll drag you into the third." Considerably shaken, Lippmann recalled believing that this outburst was "undoubtedly reflecting something of the old man."[11] Had not Americans just fought to free themselves — and the world — from such costs and combinations?

The United States neither looked nor felt ready to contain anybody. It kept fruitlessly conferring with the Soviets, snapping at the British, and fantastically trying to arrange a settlement in China between Mao Tse-tung's Communists and Chiang Kai-shek's Nationalists.[12] By summer — ten months after war's end — not one U.S. Army division or Air Force group could be rated ready for combat. Out of 12.1 million men in service when Japan surrendered, some 9 million had been granted outright discharges, with Congress soon deciding to authorize an army of only 669,000. The Army was 127,000 men short. "The people demobilized themselves," said Marshall, describing this overwhelming homecoming as a "rout" and terming such forces as remained a "hollow shell."[13]

Moreover, Stalin knew how many atomic bombs the United States did *not* have: the American monopoly embraced elements of three or four, none assembled. Anyway, what were three or four Hiroshimas to the man who had plowed under the Russian peasantry? To be sure, Moscow had made its own cuts after the war, dropping the Red Army to around 2.8 million men through 1948. Soviet secrecy ensured that the world did not know this for decades. Thereafter, as Russian archives would show, came resurgence.[14]

At home, the Communist Party was loudly (and falsely) denying that it received either money or instruction from Moscow, although conceding that its members would never fight against the Soviet Union. What some attentive people were learning about Soviet activity in the United States was worrisome. After the Hitler-Stalin pact in 1939, Whittaker Chambers, the disheveled, sullen-looking associate editor of *Time* magazine, had risked his life by breaking with the party's underground espionage apparatus. He began his long ordeal of trying to alert the U.S. government to the extent to which its ranks had been penetrated, finally identifying the State Department's Alger Hiss, a pillar of the establishment if there ever was one, as a Soviet agent. Not that many people paid much attention — for the moment.

Igor Gouzenko, a young Red Army cipher clerk who had defected during 1945, accurately characterized Soviet espionage during and, for a while, after the war as "mass production." Over the years, it included flights to Moscow of dozens, then tons, of diplomatically sealed black suitcases containing secret State Department and military documents, proprietary industrial plans, and information spirited out of Los Alamos, the laboratory in the mountains of New Mexico that gave birth to the atomic bomb. The flow came to be known in Moscow as "Super Lend Lease." Of course, the pipeline worked in reverse, as hundreds of unidentified, uncredentialed Soviet personnel simply walked off planes landing in the United States and vanished. Gouzenko made possible the first atomic counterespionage breakthrough, with no thanks to Western intelligence.[15] The following summer, U.S. Army Signal Intelligence broke a Soviet diplomatic transmission to Moscow. Thereafter, the mounting body of what came to be called the Venona intercepts inescapably outlined the success of Soviet penetration, although the full scope remains unknown even today.

Congress, for its part, was loath to know these nuclear secrets. It had brought the Atomic Energy Commission (AEC) into being that summer, with the authorizing legislation establishing an unprecedented government monopoly over the development and use of an entire form of energy. However, nervous members of the Joint Committee on Atomic Energy, a congressional watchdog, asked not to be told details of "the bomb," as it was trustingly called — certainly not the numbers available. Saying he understood nothing of these arcane scientific matters, the committee's chairman focused Congress's oversight responsibilities on examining the price of garbage containers at the Oak Ridge National Laboratory and on other routine issues of spending and patronage in the multibillion-dollar program.[16]

Nevertheless, the world's attention could not but turn in July to remote Bikini Atoll, thirty minute coral dots twenty-four hundred miles southwest of Hawaii, as "the bomb" was to be used for the first time during peace. "We located the one spot on earth that hadn't been touched by war," joked Bob Hope, "and blew it to hell." It was a portent of how the Cold War would extend everywhere and of how exorbitant its merely mechanical costs could be. Someone had the uneasy wit to name these tests Operation Crossroads, as the Navy anchored ninety-eight ships in Bikini's ten-by-twenty-mile lagoon, including now supposedly surplus battleships, carriers, cruisers, destroyers, and transports — some $400 million worth of hardware, or about $3.6 billion in today's dollars. Congressmen who worried about the expense were told that the Navy was getting a bargain, since the salvage value of these unneeded warships was about 1 percent of the book value. Forty-two thousand military and civilian personnel carried out the operation. Navy publicists organized correspondents' trains, specially fitted boats, and live radio feeds, and they invited a Russian observer. Preparing the test probably cost the life of Louis Slotin, a Los Alamos scientist exposed to a lethal dose of radiation.

Bikini's 162 residents were picked up and moved elsewhere in the Marshall Islands. The Navy then got the Department of the Interior's Fish and Wildlife Service to assert that there was no need to worry about the large numbers of whales and tuna that might be killed. This was the first round in what would be decades of mounting quarrels concerning the environmental damages of testing and storing the bomb — and of the mountingly complex machinery of evasion needed to camouflage the consequences. Also familiar would be exchanges of letters between Washington and its more troubled citizens whenever atomic testing was publicized. For the Bikini detonation, 40 people volunteered to place themselves at ground zero. The Navy declined. The only immediate lives lost were those of the 204 goats and 200 pigs staked out for the blast.

Only the device itself was hidden, but it was known to be at least large enough for a twelve-inch picture of Rita Hayworth to be pasted on the side. Millions listened to broadcasts of the A-bomb's fourth detonation. The result was anticlimactic: five ships and small craft were sunk. "Not so much, after all," the Russian was reported to have muttered.[17] It was the unexpected poison boiled up from the water that brought the eventual scrapping of the whole target fleet, but only after sailors were ordered to scrub the decks.[18] Divers were sent below to examine the damage. The next explosion three weeks later got fewer headlines. The bomb appeared manageable in the hands of experts. A second test site would be built at nearby Eniwetok Atoll within a year, its people also relocated and the island closed. From now on, tests would be cloaked in mystery.

When even the most responsible citizens tried to pierce the atomic future, the result could be chilling. In June, literary popularizer Norman Cousins joined with Wall Street lawyer Thomas Finletter to coauthor a startling article in the *Saturday Review* that has largely been forgotten. They warned that the "atomic armaments race" would inevitably entail the redistribution of America's population, the decentralization of its cities, and the dispersal of its industries.

Its momentum would imminently compel the U.S. military "to carry out the biggest and most complicated physical change-over of a nation in the world's history."[19] What was still known as the War Department then announced that it had completed a preliminary survey of underground building sites in preparation (no matter how far-fetched) for atomic war. Even though nearly all serious people knew that Stalin was a long way from matching U.S. wizardry and building a bomb, some were already arguing that the "redistribution" and "decentralization" of U.S. industry would demand untold billions of dollars to compensate the owners of city property all over the United States.[20] After such visions of a world truly remade, any proposition was moderate, any expense tolerable.

Alternatively, maybe these atomic technologies might obviate the need for military manpower, while still keeping the world at a mailed arm's length. No matter what the role of the bomb, government was stumbling only half aware into an unconsidered peacetime preeminence in research and development (R & D) extending naturally from both triumph in war and the arrival of new weapons. The Navy, for instance, was advancing a partnership of science and government, building on wartime successes by academic operations analysts. In 1946, it negotiated contracts with more than forty-five universities and corporations — including Harvard, MIT, Columbia, General Electric, Firestone, and Sperry Gyroscope — for studies in electronics, physics, metallurgy, chemistry, and ballistics.

Though evolving from World War II, this was a new scale of peacetime preparation. Within half a dozen years, spending would spread far beyond the elite institutions to Louisiana State, Ohio State, and Penn State. Professors flocked to such largesse and, in beginning to propose their own projects, opened the new era of grantsmanship. The Navy was highly receptive to being told what its research needs might be, encouraging scientists to dream freely — with the Navy, of course, having "hopes that their dreams might metamorphose into military reality."[21] It began to fund nerve chemistry, dwarf-star research, econometrics, low-temperature physics, psychological studies of leadership, an electronic machine expected to process 40,000 ten-digit numbers per second, medical technologies, and even an entomologist's study of the army ant. Almost any area of pure research might be relevant.

However, the intricate task of identifying concepts and technologies for funding was being done hurriedly, on a suddenly large scale, and with no market-imposed discipline as to what might be rated a success. Much would be arbitrary, and would keep on being so. For example, a major step in the development of the computer had occurred in the war's last months when Princeton mathematician John von Neumann and RCA scientist Vladimir Zworykin called on Lewis Strauss (later chairman of the AEC) at the Navy Department. They presented their ideas for assembling electronic memory tubes to record, by the standards of the time, an immense body of information. If successful, this device might be elaborated into an apparatus capable of predicting weather patterns (with all the military advantages flowing therefrom). Once the war ended, Navy officials balked at the $200,000 such research required, suggesting that it might be better developed within the Department of Agriculture. The Army, however, was intrigued. An early "electronic brain," as such things came to be called, began to be built near the Institute for Advanced Study at Princeton, which brought the Navy rushing back into competition. The first large problem submitted to this complex machine would concern thermonuclear weapons development.

The newly pronounced peacetime roles for the military and government — and the money that began to flow — helped create a myth. For much of the Cold War, there would remain popular notions on the left about the democratic market economies "needing an enemy" to fuel themselves. In 1946, a story appeared in *Lilliput*, a general-interest British magazine, about how a suddenly unchallenged Britain was menaced by mass nervous breakdown until it got someone to bomb it again. It was an amusing tale, but as far from reality for the United States as for Britain. In the view of Averell Harriman, financier/industrialist and wartime ambassador to Moscow, Americans wanted nothing more than to "settle all our difficulties with Russia and then go to the movies and drink Coke."[22] Truman expected that total federal spending would decline from the $34.5 billion in fiscal year 1947 to a peacetime level of $25 billion, more in line with the 1930s. Price controls would probably have died in any event after the war, but instead they were upended by Republicans amid fears of sliding back into a depression.[23] In part by emphasizing domestic issues, the Republicans went on to take both Houses of Congress in November. The wartime practice of withholding tax dollars stayed in place.

Americans of all persuasions, however, were anxious to find ways to buffer themselves from the almost overnight bridging of their ocean moats. Already strategists were thinking about the possibility of long-range Soviet bombers leaping over the pole. Less than a decade before, after all, Brigadier General George Marshall had been surprised — calling it a "most interesting experience for the U.S. Army" — when Soviet transpolar aviators landed in front of him out of the blue early one Sunday morning at Oregon's Vancouver Barracks in 1937.[24] Now Canada was expected to be responsible for helping shield the far north — a division of labor that implied the first postwar alliance in all but name.

James Blish's science fiction tale of that time, "The Box," captures both this chilly new exposure and the paradox of all the new technology. Although Russia is never named, New York City wakes up one morning to find itself under an impenetrable dome and certain to asphyxiate within days. A European refugee — a survivor of the uniquely depraved concentration camp Dora — realizes that this is not an attack, but rather a test to see whether the United States can extricate its greatest city. If the dome, or "box," is indeed impenetrable, the refugee surmises, then defensive domes will overnight seal off the cities of the unnamed enemy while America is bombed flat. He goes on to destroy the dome. The world is made safe for mutual assured destruction. And the growing New York skyline remained open to the world.

It was only prudent for Americans to search for ways to protect their continent — or, one might say, to create some sort of "box." Increasingly sophisticated efforts toward a nationwide shield have continued into the twenty-first century. At the start, however, in December 1946, Washington sent what the Canadians called "its best men" north to expedite the Joint Defense Review Board over which Ottawa had been stalling for six months. "So far from being in an excitable or panicky frame of mind," reported Canada's surprised Foreign Minister, Lester Pearson, "the Americans have shown themselves very cool, level-headed and realistic. . . . There was no question of their wishing to rush feverishly ahead with preparations of all kinds."[25] Moreover, as he immediately passed on to an immensely relieved London, the American leadership seemed to be secretly but determinedly ready to fight the Soviet Union in Europe and the Mediterranean if worse came to worst.

✪

The embodiment of the postwar danger felt by much of the American elite is George Kennan, one of the most influential voices in U.S.

foreign relations during the twentieth century. He is widely revered as "indisputably an American sage" and "one of the great American statesmen of the twentieth century."[26] Kennan was among the "best men" who had arrived in Canada.

Kennan's long career — from publicly warning of Soviet intentions in 1947 to decrying the way America has stumbled through the world right up to today — has come to personify many of the more taxing habits of America's international behavior: intensely emotional, backward-looking, dismissive of the details of economics and technology, often racist, and occasionally "reckless" and riddled with "impulsiveness." These are characteristics that prominent men of the time discerned in him.[27] The often misguided influence of this extraordinary diplomat and scholar on fifty years of U.S. foreign policy, as well as the authority he brings to our memory of how the Cold War began, has had more than a little to do with making the effort against the Soviet Union so arduous. It is, therefore, useful to meet Kennan and to trace his many appearances over these decades.

In English, we lack a phrase corresponding to *l'émigration intérieure*, meaning a flight from the social and political realities of one's country into enclosing institutions — such as the army, the church, or the diplomatic corps — while despising the regime in whose service one finds oneself. The phrase was coined for the nineteenth-century French aristocracy and sadly applies to George Frost Kennan of Milwaukee, Wisconsin. He was from a solid, small business family, lost his mother early, and graduated from Princeton in 1925. History can impose labels on its subjects — "statesman," "conservative," or "visionary," for example — often failing to stress the most important one, "product of his or her time." Kennan moved through the twentieth century as a highly polished time capsule of the disillusioned 1920s, during which his generation found, as F. Scott Fitzgerald announced, "all Gods dead, all wars fought, all faiths in man shaken." Disgusted with excesses at home and dismayed by miseries abroad, Kennan seems to have viewed the Foreign Service as an escape. Not only did he choose the Foreign Service, but he chose to become one of a handful of diplomats focusing on huge, burgeoning Russia, so recently ruled by the czar.

All sorts of ambiguities and inconsistencies can be found in Kennan, as in his country. He reflected the nation's contradictions: pride in power, perfectionist expectations, readiness to despair, suspicion of leadership, and confident ignorance. Dean Acheson, who for the rest of his life was amazed that a person he thought merely a "footnote of the Truman presidency" would be embraced as a central influence, simply concluded that Kennan never "grasped the realities of power relationships but takes a rather mystical attitude toward them."[28] As for his increasingly benign views of the Soviet Union and his prescriptions as to how the United States should conduct itself abroad, they were described by a leading socialist politician at the height of the struggle as "wishful thinking."[29]

Kennan was not a man at home in postwar America. From both childhood and residence in Berlin during the early 1930s, he was a strong partisan of German culture. His imagination moved, like Toynbee's, along vistas of human suffering. The crude struggle for individual betterment and technological progress passed him by. He became increasingly skeptical of America's abilities and of the buoyant social differences within it, which make this country not only strong but a model to much of the world.

Kennan was pleased that you could "comb [his] family records for three centuries back and you won't find a person who wasn't of straight Anglo-Saxon origin." When he heard that Winston Churchill had once written to his bachelor son that what the Churchill family needed was a draft of Jewish blood, he was astounded. He worried about democratic principles being applied to African-Americans and offered "a tough statement of the Negro situation" when he spoke overseas even in the late 1960s, letting it be known that his black fellow citizens simply "had to have a separate state."[30] For much too long, he was unappalled by apartheid South Africa.

Kennan made it a practice to have the fewest possible contacts with either Congress or the press. Congressmen, he insisted in luxuriant despair, should all be "men of means" and thus "above petty corruption."[31] Other eccentricities spewed out, distancing him not only from the pulse of Washington and his native Wisconsin but also from what sensible officials in other foreign ministries were thinking. Among public men, he more than anyone else reflected the conscientious pessimism of that sort of conservatism that comes within hailing distance of despair. If Kennan had confidence in any society over the long term, it was probably in Germany: hierarchical and dynamic, yet orderly. He believed that in the late 1940s Germany would recover its rightful primacy in Eastern and Central

Europe. The Nazis, he thought, had inflicted little suffering on France, whereas the French after 1945 were being "evil and uninhibited in their treatment of the Germans."[32]

Knowing of these aberrations in so prominent a man is important. It helps put in perspective those demanding Cold War moments that he affected and lets us read his many writings on these years with an overdue skepticism.

At the beginning, Kennan's legendary 1946 "Long Telegram" to the State Department, from his post as chargé d'affaires in Moscow, correctly discerned in Soviet conduct an extension of Russian imperial drive. How the United States responded would pose "the greatest task our diplomacy has ever faced" (not to mention the task faced by industry, public finance, and America's democratic traditions). He warned, with a vividness he has spent many years papering over, that Russia viewed the United States as an implacable opponent of these ambitions, indeed that "the Soviets consider[ed] it necessary that our traditional way of life be destroyed."

"There is no reason," he lectured the War College several months later, "why it should not be possible for us to contain the Russians indefinitely by confronting them firmly and politely with superior strength at every turn."[33] Fair enough. But Kennan wrote as if he were discussing the containment of the czardom rather than Stalin. Within a decade, he was arguing for U.S. withdrawal from Europe, and soon thereafter, he was insisting that the allies defend themselves through some form of passive resistance. He would come to describe Soviet Communism as "just another form of government," rather than as something uniquely dangerous. Just as he never took notice of technological change, he ignored economics. He wrote fine "state papers," but they were just that, curiously European for America, which the English journalist G. K. Chesterton, chiding American moralism, described as "the country with the soul of a church" and with a low tolerance for *raison d'état*. Where are the military concerns in his writings? France had fallen in six weeks only seven years before; it was frailer now. And what would follow the V-2 rocket? A consideration of those facts is hard to squeeze from his pages.

Kennan, fascinating as his evocation of the eternal Russia is, gives little room to Lenin as an intellectually formative force in Soviet policy. He slights the notion of a global contest, which would be vastly more complex than the traditional "struggle for mastery in

Europe." Those Old Bolsheviks who had not been shot by 1947 seemed to be running a sizable part of the world.

Kennan's intellectual leverage became greatest as the Truman Doctrine and the Marshall Plan unfolded in the summer of 1947. He published what would become a landmark article in *Foreign Affairs,* the Council on Foreign Relations' influential quarterly journal. It was reprinted for a much wider audience in Henry Luce's *Life* magazine. Signing it "Mr. X," now that he was director of the State Department's new Policy Planning Staff, Kennan implied that the principle of containment should cover all points of Soviet expansion firmly but courteously. The article wound down with a gloss that could have been signed with equal sincerity by Pollyanna and the elder Field Marshal von Moltke. He hoped that his readers should "experience a certain gratitude to Providence which, by providing the American people with this implacable challenge, has made their entire security as a nation dependent upon their pulling together and accepting the responsibilities of moral and political leadership that history plainly intended them to bear."[34]

War, even cold war, Kennan asserted, may not only build the health of the state but perhaps also be seen as beneficial to the moral health of the people. This is a troubling view. In dispensing such wisdom, the socially ambitious Kennan kept trying to be more Foreign Office than the Foreign Office, to whose bemused principals he insisted that Americans would just have to steel themselves to fighting "frontier wars," given his belief (at the time) that the Soviet Union would push outward. Two, possibly more, fully mechanized U.S. Army divisions would be needed to fight these local wars, he rhapsodized — at least until the Joint Chiefs of Staff curtly stated that his expensive notions were out of the question. Gladwyn Jebb, British ambassador to the UN and the personification of a class Kennan revered, particularly doubted whether this U.S. diplomat's "competence matches his learning."[35]

It was not an idle criticism. While Air Force General Curtis LeMay, for instance, was redesigning cartography to catch the sudden menaces of airpower (by rotating a globe ninety degrees sideways to show the short polar distance between North America and Russia), Kennan's vision of conflict made no concession to this new world. The oceans and the sky held the possibility of ruin, yet he was preoccupied with the grapple of cultures as practiced in Bismarck's mighty day. The fact that cultures now opposed each other across bandwidths and in the stratosphere was merely a vulgar interruption of his arguments. Bolshevism as a contagious idea had alarmed the great men at Versailles thirty years before; now it spoke to millions around the world.

Kennan would spend the rest of his days insisting that his initial alarm over Soviet ambitions had been misunderstood and that the Truman administration — as well as all subsequent ones — had militarized his recommendations for containing Moscow. As a North Atlantic defense alliance was organized in 1949, for instance, he was urging the creation of a disarmed, neutralized, but strong united German state. He argued against signing the North Atlantic treaty, in part because he was certain that a *West* Germany (proclaimed in September 1949) would be economically unviable. Today, he argues that the Soviets "would have paid a higher price than most might think to get the American forces out of the greater part of Germany." Too bad, he claims, that the British and French were "afraid of their own shadows."[36]

By the century's end, he would write as if Stalin had been purely a Russian statesman, someone who might have conceded Russia's traditional inferiority to Germany if given half a chance. "The unification of Germany under a single Communist government," he mused when it was all over, "was the last thing Stalin would have wanted to bring about."[37] Stalin did not intend to reunite Germany, even as a Communist realm, he argued, because such steps would have inevitably returned Germany to dominance. His notion that Stalin, whose life epitomizes the brutal confidence of ignorant power, or that the Red Army, which had just fought its way west with the cry "Blood for our blood," would roll over in the face of a reviving united Germany is a reminder of how far from reality the writing of state papers can become.

At the beginning of a new century, many of Kennan's political opinions sound reasonable. They might even suggest that the United States was mistaken in most of its decisions concerning Russia from 1946 to 1950. Except that the regime that existed under Stalin operated under some very different reality checks than appear in Kennan's more recent writings. Ernest Bevin and similar hard men of Britain's Labour movement knew that. They understood that the Soviet Union was on the verge of making dangerous use of Europe's fears, either with or without direct force. Convinced that Western Europe's confidence would not be restored by anything the

Europeans could do for themselves, they knew that American money and men were needed fast.[38]

Yet Kennan came to see it differently. Stalin was shrewd and fearful enough to realize that any overreaching into Western Europe — even to help install puppets in France and Italy — could undercut "his absolute control over the movement and the country that he headed," since losing "his pre-eminence in the world communist movement would be to endanger his position at home." Russian power in 1947, Kennan argued nearly fifty years later, was already overextended and had begun to retrench. He cited Moscow's refusal to attack Marshal Tito's dissident Yugoslavia as an example, although that was more likely prevented by U.S. intervention in Korea, as is argued in chapter 3. He also cited the eventual Soviet withdrawal from Austria, although that occurred in 1955, half a dozen years after the United States explicitly had tied itself to Western Europe's defense and soon after the GIs had returned to Europe in force.

If, in 1947, the Soviet Union felt sated, indeed overextended, it is easy to conclude, as Kennan came to do, that the suspicions of Soviet ambitions that "flowed in part from the rigidities of the American military mind" and from "our political-military establishment" were "insubstantial." So why yield to a "primitive assumption" of further Soviet aggressiveness?[39]

Marshall, Acheson, Lovett, Navy Secretary James Forrestal (who went on to head the Pentagon), and Truman himself instead saw in Stalin a short-term operator who might have no understanding of Marx and who might have got Hitler wholly wrong, but who had a master's grasp of intrigue and the uses of terror. Churchill tells us of Stalin's witty observation that the problem of Hungary was simply one of cattle trucks, meaning that nationalism was just a logistical question of shipping entire races of people to the gulag. Stalin was no stranger to the idea of redissolving Germany into its preindustrial chaos of numerous petty jurisdictions, perhaps superintended through periodic famines by the Red Army.[40] This was one of the scenarios America was becoming prepared to prevent at any price.

As for his personal power at home being endangered, Stalin had destroyed Old Bolshevism. He broke Marshal Zhukov, who had led the Red Army through fifteen hundred miles of savage combat from Stalingrad to Berlin. A church figurehead, the patriarch of Moscow, hailed Stalin as "Our Father." Stalin had leveled all of Russia to his power, and no one would dare criticize him during his lifetime. This was not a man who had to worry about losing control over his vassals and subjects, had he worked to thrust his domain farther west. Europeanist diplomats today might see an uneasy, over-extended Russia "Under Western Eyes," haunted by a sense of its inferiority before the developed world, including Germany. By 1947, however, the view from the Kremlin was surely vaster and more opportunistic.

The Bolshevik state had grounds for confidence, having grown from persecuted sect to world power in less time than Churchill had taken to rise from junior minister to premier. And now China, the most populous nation in the world, was apparently coming into Moscow's orbit. Wasn't all this the mark of truly scientific destiny? Stalin had kept one crude tenet of Marxist ideology: the conviction, not unjustified by history since 1914, that the old order would founder in its slumps and wars.

The future of Western Europe was much more perilous in 1947 and 1948 than Kennan recalls. Would the United States, citadel of capitalism and former invader of Russia at Archangel and Vladivostok after World War I, not be drawn eventually into a death struggle with its dialectical opposite? If so, wasn't its recoil from Europe in the moment of victory likely to prove a window not long left open? Large-scale Communist parties and mass movements with resistance credentials in France and Italy were significant assets, but not necessarily lasting ones.

Probably no one will ever be able to reconstruct the Soviet leadership's attitudes from the spring of 1946 to the spring of 1947. Surely, these men experienced great weariness, but this was not a system shaped for ease, nor one that can be compared to those of the democracies. Today, the release of Soviet archives is ever more unkind to such interpretations of postwar Soviet behavior as Kennan offers. Other experts argue that the arrival of Stalinism in Eastern Europe was "reactive" and merely "a response to Western initiatives." Stalin, some say, was "provok[ed]," as the United States failed to keep its word regarding wartime and postwar agreements.[41] Even Frank Freidel, eminent Harvard historian and author of the standard biography of Franklin Roosevelt, writes that agreements among the wartime allies over Eastern Europe's political future "were not precise enough, and they received different interpretations in the Soviet Union" — as if the Cold War began because of a legal misunderstanding.[42]

These sympathetic views of Russia's early Cold War ambitions lead to conclusions, such as Kennan's, that Washington exaggerated the danger practically from the start. Therefore, so much of the sacrifice that followed was unnecessary. Yet any state that had lost around twenty million dead just from invasion and was run by survivors who had killed millions more of their own countrymen had a reflex of "toughness" indeed.[43] The only question in 1947 was whether Moscow would be as "tough" with the United States as it was with everyone else — or perhaps, logically, tougher.

Having watched Stalinism rise, Kennan had a civilized doubt that it could be permanent, but the belief today that he long anticipated the collapse of Soviet power is one of the common myths of the Cold War. Kennan expected change more than collapse, likely within ten to fifteen years. Other men — ones who did understand power — started involving that the Soviet Union could implode, if kept under steady pressure.

By 1947, it was apparent in Washington that the Soviet Union was dangerous — unassessably so, because it was so unknown. But a return to war was barely imaginable, and within two years there would be a serious drive again to reduce the military budget. In so unstable a world, a stalemate seemed improbable. A prolonged, shifting armed truce was outside the American experience. A mixture of all three, such as occurred for the next forty years, was not contemplated.

The U.S. leadership came up with a sound first approximation, with which Kennan, for the time being, generally concurred: the Stalinist Soviet bloc was a danger perhaps as ominous as the one just defeated, a continent-size threat, which was intensified by the shared ideological tenets of Marxism-Leninism, largely as defined by Moscow.[44] So here was the problem: there literally was no solution, at least none that was ethically acceptable. The questions were how to maintain and institutionalize vigilance; how to create unity in the West — to put heart into smaller client nations and make them think of themselves as allies; and, not incidentally, how to pay for all this.

✪

It is hard today to recapture the beliefs of men and women conditioned by the arithmetic of public spending between 1775 and

1941, as well as by the Great Depression — let alone by the newly revealed prospect that America, previously so remote, had become so vulnerable. In 1947, the country still felt economically constrained, with a $300 billion debt from the war. This was an alarming 113.9 percent of the gross domestic product (GDP), meaning the total value of goods and services produced within its borders. Each new outlay weighed like lead. That recession followed peace had been a sound generalization since at least the War of 1812. Plenty of people on the left and right were waiting for the appropriately gigantic sequel to the greatest of history's wars. Cyril Connolly, founder of an eclectic literary monthly in London and an old friend of George Orwell, offered an unforgettable dirge: "It is closing time in the gardens of the West."

For the first time, in January 1948, the president's State of the Union address was accompanied by his budget message. The explicit tie between the available resources and what Truman hoped to accomplish was novel and a crucial step toward a "presidential program" of legislation, something equally new. It reflected the increased primacy of the chief executive, ever more exalted by nearly two decades of emergency.

To some degree at some time, the United States would likely have taken many of the steps advanced in 1947 toward systematic international engagement: underwriting Europe's recovery, energizing the General Agreement on Tariffs and Trade (which evolved into today's World Trade Organization), and even dispatching military advisers to friendly states. Appeals for defense necessities before joint sessions of Congress were not essential to a larger peacetime presence in the world, but such appeals made these steps easier. They became less challengeable and more unequivocal. Cries of national security brought persuasive considerations of righteousness and urgency to foreign policy making. The alternative might have been a sequence of disorder into collapse, which could have slid Europe's industrial potential toward the Soviet side.

It is generally forgotten how far Washington went out of its way to appear unprovocative to Moscow. The State Department even tried to block the founding of an Anglo-U.S. Old Comrades veterans' organization. The administration refused to sell Army-surplus Garand rifles to Denmark, of all places. Joint maneuvers were forbidden with the Royal Navy, and British officers had to wear mufti on U.S. warships. The air defense contacts with Canada were kept strictly secret. London described all this diffidence as "a certain girl-ishness on the part of the State Department."[45] When the United States did begin to show signs of resolve later in 1947, it was Labour that congratulated itself for helping America "to realize the responsibilities of her power before it was too late."[46]

To many people in Washington, it looked as if Britain — despite its tough talk — was shirking its own responsibilities. For instance, it ended financial aid to Greece and Turkey. If it also pulled 8,000 troops out of Greece amid a civil war with the far left, as Bevin threatened to do in February 1947, where could London be relied on to help? Having dropped that bombshell, the British sat back to see "how far the U.S. are prepared to go financially to keep the Soviet within bounds, and how far the Republicans will swallow their own election pledges of retrenchment."[47]

With the ruin of war imposed on an economy that was never strong and a tradition of implacable domestic conflict, Greece had become a seedbed of subversion and revolution. Roughly 20,000 guerrillas swimming in a sea of perhaps 250,000 sympathizers were a serious challenge to a corrupt royalist dictatorship and a nation of 7.5 million very tired people. The rebels were supplied from "sanctuaries" (a word just entering the Cold War idiom) in Communist Yugoslavia, Albania, and Bulgaria. Stalin remained aloof. Within a year, however, Communist terror would extend to the *pedomasoma*, the gathering up of village children between the ages of three and fourteen. The kidnappers sent about 28,000 children, few to be seen again, to the "People's Democracies" to deny them to the "monarcho-fascists."[48]

More than Greece seemed to be falling apart. Washington feared that the British were no longer able to block Russian expansion southward, as they were credited with having done for a century. The day before declaring that it was apparently pulling out of Greece, Britain had announced that independence would be accorded to India within months. That suited America's noisy anti-colonialism, but some people were thinking ahead. What about the future of Afghanistan and the passage of tankers through the Strait of Hormuz? That same day, to make matters worse, the Soviet ambassador to the UN, Andrei Gromyko, curtly rejected U.S. proposals for joint inspections as a means of controlling the atom.

Yet contrary to Cold War legend, it was hardly the case that "Great Britain had within the hour handed the job of world leadership with all its burdens and all its glories to the United States," as a State Department official recalled. The British could not really quit Greece as they claimed: for one thing, they lacked the ships to evacuate their battalions even by the end of the year. Although there was not the remotest chance that "what empire was left would be liquidated," the United States was being maneuvered to start paying to shore up this "outer fortress."[49] Even without India, Britain retained most of its possessions.

London's notice of imminent withdrawal had been handed to Undersecretary of State Dean Acheson. He was one of the lawyers whose flexibility and resourcefulness in creating postwar institutions so impressed Lord Keynes, who hitherto had relegated that profession to clerkly obscurity. Son of an English enlisted man who had become Connecticut's Episcopal bishop, and a graduate of Groton, Yale, and Harvard, Acheson had already passed the test of principle over ambition by quitting as acting secretary of the treasury in 1933 — still only forty — when he was unable to win Roosevelt to his notion of sane economic policy. Acheson, of all the cabinet members in the past two-hundred-plus years, came closest to blows with a U.S. senator in committee. Yet he had a sensitive mind, startling hypermodernist art collectors with an intimately informed admiration of their peculiar treasures. It was he who would make an issue of Washington's Cosmos Club's silent exclusion of blacks. And it was he who would dedicate his brilliantly crafted memoirs to the somewhat less reflective Truman as "the captain with the mighty heart." Acheson's temper was epic; he was appalled by Bevin's decision.

Washington entered into a competition of bluff with London, asserting that it could replace any departing British troops only by drawing GIs from Germany, which scared all the Western European governments. Admiral William Leahy, the president's key military adviser, instructed the Pentagon that the British "will not be told that we actually have ready to move upon order 5,000 trained marines."[50] Operation Workdog has remained a publicly unknown contingency, its name showing how a put-upon Washington felt about being forced into a swift response, while still hoping that Western Europe could be pushed into saving itself. In any event, British troops remained in Greece until the Greek Communists began to collapse into the adjacent satellites two years later.

Meanwhile, the United States could at least help with cash and a few military and economic advisers. Truman's speech to Congress in mid-March requesting $400 million for the first year of aid to Greece and Turkey (for its border disputes with Russia) was intended "to make the flesh of the die-hard opposition creep."[51] This meant most of the Republicans. What every member, with one exception, rose and applauded was a hurried improvisation. Few people knew what the president actually intended (other than fighting "terrorism" and "terrorist activities"), much less what he feared: he spoke of making an "investment" of "one tenth of one percent of the investment" just made to win World War II. The chairman of the House Appropriations Committee, John Taber of upstate New York, was a strong opponent of foreign aid of any sort. He also detested the expanding federal bureaucracy, which to him and many other Republicans emphatically included generals and admirals, let alone intelligence officers.

A vital step had been taken to protect Europe, as Bevin understood. But what became known as the Truman Doctrine also enunciated a heavy precedent for un-thought-out aid and commitments to unassessed regimes in ill-defined places. Truman had pledged his country "to support free peoples who are resisting attempted subjugation by armed minorities." The vague assumptions and very real spending that summoned the energy for this portentous step eventually created an assembly line of involvement that would grind on for decades, repeatedly fixed by ever more strained rationalizations. In retrospect, it is not much of an exaggeration to say that the passage of aid to Greece meant that "the road from Athens ultimately led to Saigon."[52]

Massively expensive for the time, the Greek-Turkish Aid Act never received overwhelming public support. Americans were not going to accept such supposed responsibilities easily. The millionaire cotton broker and assistant secretary of state Will Clayton reminded the soon-to-depart Acheson that "the United States will not take world leadership, effectively, unless the people of the United States are shocked into doing so." Although Bevin and his colleagues were still thinking of U.S. "partnership" rather than "leadership," the foreign secretary used the same word. "If the Americans are to be made conscious of anything," he noted, "they have to be shocked into consciousness."[53] Even so, Bevin's sense of the threat did not prevent other parts of the British government from allowing the sale of the world's most sophisticated jet technology to Moscow — an export that horrified those Americans who soon found out about it and that U.S. pilots would soon pay for over Korea.[54]

The famed broadcaster Edward R. Murrow understood this reluctance well. "It seems," he wrote an English friend some time later, "the only way to induce action in this country is through the creation of fear and hysteria."[55] Other than for the one moment in Congress, there was no jubilation. At best, such Americans as cared fell in prudent acceptance of the inevitable. The British had grander hopes. Should this venture prove successful, their diplomats told each other, "the USA will no doubt be encouraged to repeat the experiment of intervention whenever other analogous instances occur."[56]

Bevin nonetheless still dreaded that the United States would be all too eager to escape any peacetime military-related involvements anywhere. Offering few reassurances, Marshall at least told him during a foreign ministers' meeting in Moscow that America was willing to "pay a price" for what he simply styled the unity of Europe.[57] Where exactly Europe began and ended, he did not say. Stalin, who anticipated an imminent depression in the United States, asked Bevin, with a minimum of gloating, when the economic decline would begin.

If Moscow was on the move (or worse, riding movements from which it could plausibly be dissociated), it might not challenge the West only on the relatively defensible ground of Western Europe. Indeed, hours before Truman made his dramatic declaration about Greece to Congress, General Douglas MacArthur, Supreme Commander Allied Powers in Tokyo, summoned the foreign press corps to his headquarters. He urged his government to accept a peace settlement that would help consolidate Japan as an eastern bulwark of democracy. At a time when it looked as if grave trouble might lie ahead for the U.S. economy, however, Americans were reluctant to agree. Starting to work out a balance sheet of U.S. commitments and resources, Robert Lovett (who replaced Acheson as undersecretary in mid-1947), found "even a tentative list to be terrifying in scope. . . . We were spread all over from hell to breakfast."[58]

What the United States wanted, Lovett recalled, was to get "a viable geographic unit big enough and diverse enough to take the monkey off our backs" — the monkey being the alarmingly vulnerable continent of Europe. The Labour government, in the form of Bevin, again stepped forward. This time he worked to keep Stalin out of a recovery effort that would have to be coordinated carefully among all the recipients.[59]

Serving as secretary of commerce during 1947, Averell Harriman tirelessly sold to skeptical Americans the importance of what would become known as the Marshall Plan. The Harriman Committee, consisting of powerful corporate leaders, labor officials, and academics, helped recommend the billions of dollars involved. Harriman himself was an international polo star, the son of a railway king, a film entrepreneur and banker, a New Deal convert, and an unapologetic Gilded Age hardballer who would become known among the U.S. Foreign Service as "the crocodile." He was a classic transition figure for a commercial democracy entering upon world power.

Today, even knowledgeable people still believe that the Marshall Plan's $13 billion in grants and loans over four years — more than $80 billion in today's dollars — paid for Western Europe's revival. In fact, it simply primed the pump. The Marshall Plan operated on a frightened yet advanced society, which had in place virtually all the skills and resources to repair itself. Once the American spigot turned, European investment poured from its hiding places. More than capital, America contributed confidence. Money was authorized by Congress on a quarterly basis and spent largely in the United States for equipment and materials. Yet the Marshall Plan would forever be cited in American politics as the sort of immense cash infusion that should be applied to other enormous problems. It was hardly a phenomenon transferable to the Mekong Delta, Central America, or, much later, the former Soviet Union, the Balkans, or Afghanistan.

"I preferred red ink to red blood," said *New York Times* publisher Arthur Hays Sulzberger about the plan's impact on the U.S. budget.[60] The commitment absorbed 1.2 percent of the nation's total economic output at the time — a percentage that today, over four years, would total around $450 billion. Contrary to still-potent myths that the United States strong-armed its aid recipients into U.S. visions of order, several visionary leaders in western Europe recognized the importance of federation. Frustrated by the Continent's continuing squabbles, at least one top official would lament the lack of preconditions behind Washington's urgings of political as well as economic unity. Perhaps this was the last, indeed the only, moment when American energy could have cast Western Europe into a single mold.

For years to come, European ideologues on the left and right would be united by their belief that the fortress of egalitarian capitalism could never be anything but rapaciously selfish. They actively searched for any slights to their sovereignties and suspected that the Marshall Plan was somehow essential to America's own prosperity. It would have been painful to acknowledge that, economically speaking, European recovery was useful, but certainly not essential, to America, West Germans, as well as citizens of the countries that Germany had occupied, were prepared to reflect on the moral record because that had affected the world. Europeans were not, however, ready to dwell on the fact that their economic primacy was gone for good.

From then on, the United States would hear three enduring refrains from Western European leaders: (1) they could not do more for their own defense because such levels of spending would undercut the very prosperity that the Marshall Plan sought; (2) their first line of defense was social welfare, and their societies could never tolerate the relatively lean level of government support found in the United States; (3) it was economically vital for them to export almost anything short of outright munitions to the East. Thus, for nearly a half century, an ever more prosperous Europe pulled ever less of its weight in the struggle against Russia.

Foreign aid like this had never been seen before in history, with the only similar effort being U.S. famine relief to the new Soviet Union after World War I. Critics feared that the plan would ignite a ruinous inflation at home. Yet more and more Americans increasingly recognized the need to maintain a strong, united Western Europe capable of protecting itself. The governments that began to receive the money concluded that the plan, in its original conception "little more than an economic measure, has come to be the principal weapon in the American armory against Moscow."[61] This was an objective that might — as an ongoing policy, not a frantic fix — just pass Congress. However, as a hardened old Minnesota congressman observed sourly, "If Communism could be halted with money, there wouldn't be any Communism in Hollywood."[62]

Walter Lippmann responded to Kennan's "Mr. X" manifesto of summer 1947 by arguing that the country simply did not have enough men, money, and industry to mobilize "counter-pressure" fast or effectively enough. Lippmann might visit as an equal with any European head of state he pleased, but he seems never to have internalized what was happening in his own country to the south and west of the Potomac. Although he was shrewd about long-term attitudes, his understanding of U.S. capabilities was, as Marx might have said, classically finance capitalist. Like Keynes, he had no real sense of U.S. industrial power. The "House of Morgan" he knew well, but he was not close to grease-under-the-thumbnails tycoons such as Ford, Kaiser, and Martin. Whether in 1941 or 1947, he fell far short in assessing his country's potential.

By contrast, Curtis LeMay, of the new Strategic Air Command (SAC), was shaping much of the thinking. He was a gruff, machine-loving, non-Academy fireplug who stuck to hardware and what it could do, leaving the implications to the civilians. But he made one overall prophecy: the United States, with its vastly stronger free-enterprise economy, could spend the Soviets into the ground. This utterance survives because it was later quoted mockingly by Professor John Kenneth Galbraith.[63]

In debating the European Recovery Act, as the Marshall Plan was formally called, its supporters had to turn back attempts in Congress to attach the quid pro quo of obtaining military bases from the British Empire. Why would the United States want them? It was better to be paying for Britain to man the ramparts, if such they were. By the fall, however, a classic postwar inflation (driven by pent-up demand and forced savings released) had already cut the buying power of the original loan to Britain by $1 billion. Additional help was needed as those 1946 credits evaporated. Loaning Britain further billions to finance its growing deficit with the United States and Canada was vital "not at all because Shakespeare was born here," as Stewart Alsop, the more down-to-earth of the two increasingly influential journalist brothers, wrote from London, but for reasons of U.S. defense.[64] So the United States, having become commercial as well as central banker to the industrial democracies, started on the road to being their insurance company, too, all increasingly justified as a way to resist communism.

Bevin lectured visiting congressmen on how the Soviets united the passions of communism with a czarist Great Russian imperial craving to master the Middle East and the Mediterranean by way of Iran and Greece. The congressmen, like an ever more decisive majority of the American public, felt relieved that so substantial — if perhaps slightly chipped — a power as the British Empire stood between them and Stalin. As the U.S. Navy's commander for Northern Europe, the Mediterranean, and the Persian Gulf recalled in speaking of how America's leaders regarded their country's overseas presence in mid-1947, "We'd gotten as far as Greece and Turkey, and they thought they'd bitten off more than they could chew."[65] The groundwork was already being laid, however, for a large Air Force base in Dahran, Saudi Arabia, the first significant arrival of U.S. military men in that isolated kingdom.

By October, a reorganization of government was under way of the kind that habitually follows a convulsion. Washington created twelve new agencies and departments organized around national security, including the CIA and the National Military Establishment, which within two years evolved into the Department of Defense. The National Security Council (NSC), composed of key department heads and eventually backed by its own staff, would serve as coordinator. Yet nowhere in legislation or executive order was there explicit enunciation of the role of science in U.S. growth and security, a neglect that would make the billions about to be spent on R & D all the more ad hoc. The economic and financial underpinnings of the international system also came to be treated with ever more improvisation in this new structure.

The *New York Times* reported that Americans were facing a test as real as that after Pearl Harbor.[66] At least the country's wealth was unprecedented. America's GDP stood at $235 billion in fiscal year 1947, having had not only been spared war's destruction but having benefited that year from unusually bountiful harvests. America was a strong country in a weak world. Looking back from the beginning of the twenty-first century, however, it is still astounding to see a nation with resources comparable to, say, Brazil today, prepared to accept such unprecedented burdens. The task of underwriting, then manning defense and recovery ought to have been too complicated. Yet it happened too fast for people to realize this. As Hilaire Belloc said of the water spider, "But if he ever stopped to think / How can he do it, *he would sink*."

✪

By the beginning of 1948, America was losing any belief that winning a war brought security and at least several decades of peaceful development. Instead, it brought further troubles. "The feeling of being lost in the universe," New Deal brain truster Rexford Tugwell wrote of the eighteen months after Hiroshima, "engulfed even those people who ordinarily had taken life as it came without question as to where it was going or what it meant while it was going there."[67] Seemingly overnight, considering the impractical had become a deadly practical business. Americans were utterly unprepared for this disruption.

The physicists, cried the Manhattan Project's science chief, J. Robert Oppenheimer, had known sin. So it seemed would many more Americans as they became involved with thugs in the Mediterranean, Nazi war criminals, and macabre secret experiments backed by the U.S. government itself. The explanation for so many of the new efforts was that they were undertaken to "defend civilization." But other than in several Western European nations and in anxious-to-learn Japan, the United States was rarely helping to defend "free peoples" or beleaguered democracies. As W. H. Auden had said before the war, the task was again to "defend the bad against the worse."

Thirty-two years before the Truman Doctrine's arrival, with all the money for Greece and Turkey, the Turks had sent some 1.2 million Armenians on a death march into the Syrian desert. Greece, for its part, was more immediately unpleasant. The discredited king and his graft-ridden oligarchy faced an enemy that was not only more ruthless than they but that seemed to have allies in a position to threaten the whole Eastern Mediterranean.

Stewart Alsop described the inept Athens government as having no higher ambition than to taste the profitable delights of the free economy at American expense.[68] Another correspondent, thirty-four-year-old Murrow protégé George Polk, covered this graft all too well. Immediately after his bound body was found in Salonika Bay, the Overseas Writers Special Committee to Inquire into the Murder of George Polk was set up in New York to augment the work of British, Greek, and U.S. authorities. It comprised the top Washington and New York journalists — men who, in the words of Kati Marton, "perhaps supped too often at the tables of the powerful men they or their staffs purported to cover."[69] For all their assistance, or because of it, the story took forty years to unravel.

It did not help that so many journalists spent their time trying to see the world through the eyes of those in power, or at least in office. This manipulation of knowledge and perspective, continuing into the 1970s, became another cost of the Cold War.

Headed by Walter Lippmann and bankrolled with $43,000 in private funds, the committee selected as counsel and chief investigator General William Donovan, founding father of the OSS. He was the country's most decorated citizen, a superbly connected corporate lawyer at Donovan & Leisure, and a daunting figure of whom even Truman would admit he was afraid. He seemed an inspired choice, but bringing the murder home to the Greek right (and to a foreign minister busy pocketing U.S. aid dollars) would undercut Washington's efforts to uphold the regime. It was more convenient for Donovan, the new CIA, the U.S. Embassy, and a troublingly uncurious Lippmann to finger the Communists.

Athens effortlessly came up with a usual suspect, a confession was gouged out of him, and he was dispatched to long imprisonment. Social chronicler I. F. Stone described Polk as the first casualty of the Cold War. As Polk's family tried futilely into the 1950s to unearth the real story of what became known as "the Polk conspiracy," they came under FBI surveillance for alleged Communist involvement.

Aid to other parts of Europe could have equally sordid destinations. Harriman, who was now serving as the Marshall Plan's representative, would warn the State Department that "French spending in Vietnam was about as much as we were giving them in Paris" to repair themselves at home. He was referring to the vast sums that France was already devoting to crush the Democratic Republic of Vietnam, which the fervent nationalist Ho Chi Minh had declared in 1946. Acheson would snap that Europe, and not the Far East, was Harriman's concern.[70] Similarly, aid to the Netherlands in 1948 almost exactly matched what the Dutch were spending on trying to kill the newly proclaimed Republic of Indonesia. With few vested interests yet to protect, the CIA was already warning that U.S. objectives in Europe and the Far East appeared mutually and dangerously exclusive.

Worse expediencies were being made. During the war, Albert Einstein and several colleagues — upright Jews justly sickened by the surrender to evil of the country that had been their intellectual homeland — had sat around at Princeton discussing the far-reaching penalties that would be exacted once Hitler was overthrown. Then the penetrating voice of a visitor broke in. "The victors would lend money to the German government," predicted Bertrand Russell, the great Welsh mathematician and philosopher, "and would forget the German crimes."[71] Einstein and his friends were appalled.

As predicted, the notion quickly arose that it was not the German people whom the United States had been fighting. "The Cold War and the need to rehabilitate Germany made it essential to have this view of terrible Nazis oppressing Germany," notes one historian.[72] There was nothing wrong with rehabilitating Germany, but several programs were created to employ German nationals whose pasts Washington was all too willing to whitewash. The most important program, Operation Paperclip, began in 1947. Specialists in each of the military services submitted to the State Department the names of experts they wanted to recruit. The Commerce Department compiled its own list, known as Operation 63. The U.S. occupation authorities ostensibly performed background checks. About 260 scientists were singled out as "critical personnel."[73]

From mid-1945 into the early 1950s, these and other men were courted by U.S. officials and given contracts and money. The muffled transactions were initially rationalized as the extraction of "intellectual war booty,"[74] and the price was cheap: importing 140 German scientists in 1948 cost around $900,000. Their salaries ranged from $3,000 to a rare $10,000 maximum. Thereafter, the Germans would accept lower wages than their increasingly annoyed U.S. counterparts. Further, because they were already supposed to have been subjected to background investigations, security clearances were granted much faster than to U.S. employees. Stalin, for his part, had a more efficient approach: around 16,000 German scientists and engineers were simply rounded up and forced to work on Soviet missile programs — which did not prevent a number of the best from being well paid and well treated. They induced other scientists to join them in living arrangements much better than the lean conditions prevailing in the U.S. occupation zone. Right through the summer of 1948, most senior U.S. personnel in Germany, including intelligence officials, saw no reason to be worried by field reports of this competition.[75] The results would be apparent in about ten years.

Several of the German rocketeers who arrived in America after the war had been deeply complicit in the concentration camp labor procedure of "annihilation through work." Arthur Rudolph, for instance, had been production manager at Dora, the gigantic Nazi tunnel in Thuringia that sheltered the factory where Hitler's V-1 and V-2 "vengeance weapons" had been made by slaves. Rudolph was accompanied to America by his close friend Wernher von

Braun, an SS officer to be sure, though one primarily focused on space flight. As the Cold War continued, the Pentagon would have ever stronger motives to edit the résumés of such soon-to-be senior NASA executives.

In any event, security investigations were usually falsified to skirt immigration laws. Initially, the State Department refused entry to former Nazi Party members, but 80 percent of the talents desired had been Nazis, and so these restrictions were relaxed. U.S. officials in Germany then had to certify that a would-be immigrant had been coerced into joining the party. This was not too difficult once the Joint Intelligence Objectives Agency (JIOA), coordinating the program for the Pentagon, urged other authorities to "tone down" the background checks.[76] Soon Congress passed the CIA Act of 1949, which allowed the immigration of one hundred useful future citizens a year, who would otherwise be likely to be arrested for war crimes.

The case of Walter Schrieber is telling. Here was a man who had authorized funds for many of the so-called experiments conducted in the camps, ranging from injecting salt water into the veins of living people to scouring their lungs in high-altitude chambers. Captured by the Russians, he had been used as a witness at Nuremberg. Learning about his work, U.S. officials in 1948 discussed picking him up should he become available. The following year, he resurfaced in the West, claiming to have escaped, and was promptly brought to the United States. This was tricky to conceal. Once New York Congressman Jacob Javits threatened an investigation, the JIOA advised the State Department that "allegations by minority groups" of Schrieber's human experiments could not be proved. Foggy Bottom conveniently defused the controversy by helping him move to South America.[77] Similarly, in a scene that could have been taken from the movie *Marathon Man*, a Jewish immigrant living in New York was horrified in 1949 to encounter Theodore Dussik, a Nazi neurologist, in the Alamac Hotel, which housed the new recruits while their contracts were being written. He immediately contacted New York Senator Herbert Lehman, who was falsely told by unspecified officials in Washington that Dussik had never entered the country. In Europe, Klaus Barbie, the Gestapo's "Butcher of Lyon," was protected by Army counterintelligence, apparently in exchange for access to anti-Communist agents. U.S. officials then connived in his escape to Bolivia.

These were not rare incidents. Otto Ambrose, high in the war effort of the I. G. Farben industrial empire, was enjoying American hospitality along with colleagues whom he identified as having been vital to his wartime research, which included producing poison gas for Auschwitz. Settling in at Maryland's Edgewood Arsenal, headquarters of the U.S. Army Chemical Corps, they extended their studies to nerve gas and to aerosols for delivering anthrax.

Former Nazis were not alone. The CIA's Special Operations Division at nearby Fort Detrick became the center for developing psychotropic drugs such as LSD, considered useful for interrogations. Human beings were thought necessary to the research, and its own employees were not off-limits. One member of this outfit, science officer Sidney Gottlieb, found it necessary to slip LSD into a colleague's glass of Cointreau. Thereafter taken to New York, ostensibly for psychiatric help, the man plunged (or was thrown) ten stories to his death. The CIA's general counsel recommended disciplinary action against Gottlieb, who instead received only a mild reprimand and whose career flourished. A lawsuit against his estate was under way in 2001 as the story was brought before the nation.[78] He who fights dragons, as perhaps the cultivated Dr. Ambrose had read in Nietzsche, becomes a dragon himself.

Within a few years, the Defense Department would chronicle what it saw as the immense benefits of employing its own galaxy of dark stars, proudly calculating the returns: $750 million and ten years of research saved on guided-missile R & D; five years of research avoided by a German-constructed supersonic wind tunnel; "unmeasurable amounts of time and money" obviated by a German developer of submarine snorkeling devices; rich innovations in cold-state steel processing and magnetic generation. The department climaxed its summary with the triumphant intelligence that "Dr. von Braun's rocket research has saved an unknown amount of time and vast amounts of money (estimated to be in the billions)."[79] By that time, John McCloy, serving as High Commissioner in Germany, would extend odious but convenient clemency to two dozen unambiguous Nazi criminals, including high-ranking judges and other concentration camp "doctors."

Social-critic-as-cartoonist Jules Feiffer evoked in one of his drawings the sentimental amnesty exemplified by Irwin Shaw's *The Young Lions,* a novel that appeared in 1948: "Next time I want to be the Nazi," shrieks a little boy who is playing a GI, contemplating the

lush martyr's role assigned to the victim. In Hollywood, Paramount
Studios demanded of Billy Wilder, when he was directing *Stalag 17*
four years later, that the villain be a Pole rather than a German.
Germany's image became refurbished as whole categories of its
population were, according to literary aesthetc Dwight Macdonald,
"transmuted from cowardly accomplices of one kind of totalitarianism into heroic resisters of another kind."[80]

Washington also was not about to help repatriate the Nazi loot
that its various friends hoarded. For instance, Swiss assets in America were not frozen when the gnomes of Zurich coughed up just
$58 million of some $400 million in Nazi gold or when the Swiss
refused to liquidate other Third Reich assets valued at between
$2.1 billion and $6.1 billion today. The State Department feared
that Switzerland would react badly to "being bullied by the greatest
power in the world."[81] Nor did Washington strong-arm Portugal,
which surrendered only about one-tenth of the loot it held. Spain
eventually forked over just $114,000 from a stash of around
$30 million. Turkey, which held some $44 million in Nazi assets
and $5 million in looted gold, saw fit to make no restitution at all.
Argentina's Central Bank served as a laundry for such ill-gotten
treasure. "In the cold war," recalls diplomat Richard Holbrooke,
"the rule was that you didn't rattle the cage."[82]

Some of the worst Japanese war criminals also received immediate benefits. Major General Shiro Ishii, for instance, had overseen
biological experiments on Chinese captives. His Unit 731 killed
about 850 "patients" by exposing them to infected fleas in order to
study the mortality rate of anthrax. Some were subjected to a hem-
orrhagic fever similar to the Ebola virus, which might make an even
better weapon. The U.S. Army gave Ishii and his colleagues immu-
nity from prosecution in exchange for fifteen thousand slides of
specimens from more than five hundred human cases of deliberately applied disease.[83] Also unaccountable was Emperor Hirohito,
who had been a determined, hands-on strategist of Japan's aggression — right down to helping plan the attack on Pearl Harbor. He
was directly responsible for blocking reform-minded visions of a
truly open Japanese society and for the deaths of millions of people.
Following V-J Day, General MacArthur found it convenient to keep
him in place. Thereafter this culprit is best seen as "a cold war tem-
plate," among the first of many unsavory figures Washington
befriended in the name of democracy.[84]

Unlike Germany, and with the smallest of exceptions, Japan would never pay individual reparations to its wartime victims. In the case of Unit 731, for instance, Tokyo still claims ignorance, despite piles of evidence of grotesque experiments and of cruelties no different from the worst Nazi crimes. The deaths of American, Australian, and other slave laborers in Japanese mines would also be skirted. No compensation, let alone apologies, from companies such as Mitsui. Only in 2001 would Chinese plaintiffs seek legal redress from Tokyo, as would surviving American prisoners of war who pressed their case in the widest read U.S. weekly magazine.[85] Being the greatest power might not always be pleasant for the United States, but it was already a poor thing for the country if its strength could not serve basic justice on either side of the globe.

Totalitarianism naturally sees everything as tactical. In the free countries, too, the dark notion arose that so much could be expedient. For instance, the Atomic Energy Commission (AEC) characterized its own experiments on human beings at the time as possessing "a little of the Buchenwald touch."[86] The AEC began to violate the Nuremberg Codes, promulgated in 1947 and requiring that human subjects consent to being experimented on. Radioactive materials, for example, were tested on patients being treated for illnesses on which radioactives had no bearing. Hundreds of different experiments were making their way into the long, demanding inquiry into what atomic weapons might wreak on military formations and civilian populations. They ranged from marching soldiers, unwarned of the attendant risks, through nuclear explosion sites to irradiating individuals' entire bodies.

The AEC would later explain that it had been necessary to determine at what level radioactivity became "dangerous" in order to avoid "an ultimate harvest of defective individuals" in the aftermath of atomic war.[87] Truman agreed at the time with what he understood of that twisted reasoning, and he directed the National Research Council, drawing on government agencies as needed, to undertake specific studies. When thirteen-year-old Gary Hearne of New Mexico wrote to the White House to offer himself as a "guinea pig to an Atomic Bomb blast," his inquiry was matter-of-factly forwarded to the AEC's Division of Biology and Medicine. It replied with a form letter: "Needless to say, we are interested in exploring all possible means of evaluating the biomedical effects of atomic blasts . . . [but] the Commission does not deliberately expose any human being to nuclear radiation."[88] Not quite.

The AEC understood how the nation would react should the mutated cat be able to claw its way out of the bag. One 1947 document, titled simply "Medical Experiments on Humans," insisted unequivocally that "it is desired that no document be released which refers to experiments with humans and might have adverse effect on public opinion or result in legal suits. Documents covering such field work should be classified."[89] Only a quarter century after Nuremberg did the Oak Ridge National Laboratory get around to signing a General Institutional Agreement that required subjects' informed consent before experiments proceeded and ensured that the risks were outweighed by the potential benefits.[90] Only after the Cold War was the Advisory Committee on Human Radiation Experiments appointed to uncover the full story.

Against this backdrop of what appears criminal may be found men like Thomas Finletter, who went on to high official responsibilities. During his mellow old age, back at his partnership in Coudert Brothers, he observed that it was curious how some of the brightest Americans in forward positions of the Cold War had shown signs of "going native" — in the special sense of coming to admire, and perhaps with American energy going on to outdo, the British political officers with whom they were assigned to work.

Ernie Cuneo, an OSS veteran who would establish the CIA-connected North American Newspaper Alliance, was an example of someone who never ceased to admire the *arcana imperii* of the Great Game. At lunch with Finletter, a mutual friend quoted Cuneo's repetition of a British colonial aphorism: "Always have 'em rubbed out by a plausible enemy, best if it's religious, but you can always find somebody, the trick lies in concealment." All geniality departed from Finletter. He leaned forward and said, "Ah yes. We heard about that. Thought he was *so damn clever, didn't he? Thought he was so DAMN CLEVER!*" Heads turned throughout the Downtown Association.[91] Well after Dresden and Hiroshima, a former secretary of the (nuclear-delivery) Air Force knew with merciless clarity that "he that toucheth pitch shall be defiled therewith."

Sow an act and reap a habit, goes an old saying; sow a habit and reap a character; sow a character and reap a destiny. Toward the end of the 1940s, there were already enough terrible secrets that dealing with them was passing from habit to character and rapidly onward into destiny. But whose destiny was being reaped? The statesmen who knew about these events? The people who surrounded them in the shadows? Or the sedulously uninformed nation itself?

✪

To be sure, no one in high position during 1948 was losing sleep over the morality of using atomic bombs in the event of war. By that year, there were about fifty bombs — none assembled, all plutonium implosion devices weighing more than ten thousand pounds, and each of which would take thirty-nine men two days to put together. No one even knew whether "the bomb" would be enough to thwart an outright thrust into Western Europe, the scenario then imagined by many intelligent people. More than vague pledges of U.S. retaliation might be needed to deter Moscow and buoy Europe. Although still practicing law at Sullivan & Cromwell, John Foster Dulles was widely expected to become secretary of state once New York governor Thomas Dewey beat Truman, as surely he would, in that year's election. So Dulles was taken seriously when he testified in early January before the Senate Foreign Relations Committee. There was no reason for the United States to bear the expense and risks of an actual defense treaty with Western Europe, he declared. Why should 140 million Americans protect 200 million Europeans?

The fall of Czechoslovakia's democracy in February, the last Eastern European state Stalin swallowed, promptly offered a convincing answer. The threat was personalized in the West by the midnight death of Jan Masaryk, the internationally respected foreign minister, son of the country's first president and an American mother, and a former diplomat in Washington and London. Even the politically illiterate could read this portrait in blood. "The Communist coup in Czechoslovakia could not have been better timed," noted the British Embassy in Washington.[92]

Two days after Masaryk had been dragged through his bedroom high in the Czech Foreign Ministry and thrown from a window by unidentified killers, Marshall warned the Senate Armed Services Committee that the United States could "no longer count upon others to carry the initial burden of safeguarding our civilization."[93] The crucial word is *initial:* America was now a frontline nation. Emergency would lead to emergency, begetting an atmosphere of crisis. There was the awe of Soviet power, a belief that Moscow would choose world war rather than tolerate the slightest insubordination within its sphere of influence. The "madman theory" of statesmanship, later deliberately fostered by Richard Nixon, was already in bloom.

A critical reason that Moscow tightened its grip on Eastern Europe was that East Germany and Czechoslovakia were Stalin's only ready sources of uranium. Significant deposits within the Soviet Union had yet to be located.[94] In addition, Eastern Europe was wide open to more familiar forms of plunder, as around $14 billion worth of loot was hauled from those countries between 1948 and Stalin's death in 1953. It was the Marshall Plan in reverse.

Most Americans had become convinced that sparks were again drifting down on the powder keg. "Time is a critical factor," Marshall told the Senate Armed Services Committee. The same day, Truman reiterated this thought in his emergency appearance before a joint session of Congress: "Time is now of critical importance." America had a "clearer appreciation than ever before of the value of the time factor in the security problem," added Army Chief of Staff Dwight D. Eisenhower.[95] During these months, it was common to talk of a "rapid" or "heightened" tempo, as the beat of events seemed to be building to a crescendo.

Lippmann, who polished his image as the cerebral master columnist, called for immediate mobilization. He frantically wrote to the commander of the Sixth Fleet in the Mediterranean that "even war is preferable to being paralyzed all over the world with no prospect of a decision and only the prospect of indefinite and unlimited entanglement."[96] Henry Luce's *Fortune* magazine was equally frantic, intoning that a strong and unified Europe had become vital since "the American people placed their frontier in the Caucasus."[97] How would Luce's editors have liked *Pravda* to opine that the frontier of socialism lay in the Adirondacks? It was the certainty of the experts during these decades — all the more absolute because of a lack of background in geography, engineering, and languages — that would make such gung ho geopolitics so peculiar.

Undersecretary of State Lovett appeared on *Time*'s cover for March 25 as it stressed the need for "stepping up" government organization. The task was right up Lovett's alley. He was the preeminent figure to emerge from Wall Street to play a first-class role on a rougher stage as Marshall's loyal deputy. Lovett's father had been chairman of the Harrimans' Union Pacific Railroad, and he and Averell Harriman had been friends since their teens. After attending Yale, he had won the Navy Cross for antisubmarine air patrols along the French coast during World War I. He was a friend of William Faulkner, whose short story "Turnabout" was gleaned from discussing these adventures. But Lovett lived into the 1980s with little hint of this bold character trait. Instead, his hypochondria, the one neurosis that Freud said might be forever incurable, effectively masked the inner man except in true emergencies.

Emergency was what Lovett faced. His cover issue of *Time* concluded that security "would be considerably more reassuring when U.S. policy has matured beyond the state of crisis statesmanship." Lovett added calm. But "crisis statesmanship" would never disappear, as would be seen through the rest of the century. Crisis was then heightened by a submarine scare. Just as the swallows come back to Capistrano in the spring, alarms about Soviet subs began resurfacing during budget time.

With a truly diplomatic synthesis of detached analysis and civilly concealed glee, the British Embassy reported to London that "as in the recent case of 'flying disks' [UFOs], it is likely that 'submarines' will be sighted around the coasts of the United States in large numbers for some weeks to come."[98] In an almost electroconvulsive spasm, Americans were being scared into a grudging recognition of their stake in the world. Marshall began to worry that each squall of citizen passion might upset the steady policy required of the nation. Come the next season, the next cry, would the public not be just as precipitate in retreat as it was becoming headlong in advance?

European ministries, meanwhile, portrayed Washington as either foolishly optimistic or as formulating a Soviet policy so negative "that even the dullest Congressman can understand it."[99] This generation of Europeans had concluded that the United States was ambivalent and oscillatory, intense at any given moment but in sum unreliable until the hour of decision. They also knew that the alarm bells were still likely to ring first in Europe, and whether London liked it or not, "Europe" now included Britain.

The appropriations to fulfill the plan that Truman wanted named after his secretary of state came in April, once an amendment tying aid to the actual formation of a united Europe was defeated. Congress insisted that the recipients finally stop militarily significant exports to what was coming to be called the Eastern bloc. It was the least they could do, although decades of quarreling would follow over what was and was not significant.

As for Europe's defense in the event of outright attack, Washington simply assumed that the Continent's single undermanned

U.S. division would be pulled straight home. Europeans would be left to depend on their own best efforts until America could step in to "cut the enemy's jugular vein" — implying immediate use of the atom bomb against, it was hoped, lines of communication well in the rear.[100] One of the Cold War's single greatest burdens would be the time and money spent to assure Western Europe that it would not be abandoned if worse came to worst.

America's recurring efforts to protect itself at home did nothing to help ease Europeans' minds. When Truman's Air Policy Committee, chaired by Finletter, proposed a 7,000-plane Air Force to defend American skies against sneak attack, the British were uneasy. This unfulfilled ambition was denounced "as equivalent to a sort of Celestial Maginot Line" — a term the French unconsciously would parrot in condemning President Ronald Reagan's Strategic Defense Initiative, as such quarrels and spending carried on for decades.[101]

More than half the American electorate in 1948 was willing to increase taxes to meet defense budgets of a size they had never seen except in war. Reimposing the draft also appeared acceptable, although there were several strong sources of opposition. Senator Robert Taft, among others, warned that peacetime conscription would transform the United States into a "militaristic" country.[102] Another opponent was labor and civil rights leader A. Philip Randolph, who set up the Committee Against Jim Crow in Military Service. Truman's response was Executive Order 9981, calling for "equality of treatment and opportunity for all persons in the armed services." It emphasized the danger of communism. Just as the Confederacy started recruiting blacks a month before the end of the Civil War, so the prospect of mass warfare began the movement toward a crude mass justice.

Other opposition came from scientists and academics who argued that conscription diverted many of the brightest young men from further study that would make them more valuable to the nation. A limited draft was nonetheless revived in 1948 and extracted valuable time from the relatively few unfortunates who were compelled into uniform during their most vital years.[103] It was supposed to be temporary, but it would endure for a quarter century, with an increasingly unfair range of exemptions for millions of draft-age men.

There were reasons most Americans tolerated the draft's return. That spring, the Western powers had introduced a new currency in their zones of occupation, presaging a new government for West Germany. The currency's arrival inspired the Soviets by June (on grounds of "technical difficulties") to cut off road access to Berlin, a city one hundred miles inside their own sector of Germany and to which right of entry had been guaranteed after Hitler's defeat. Berlin and its two million inhabitants quickly took on a symbolic role as capital of the Cold War. The Soviet blockade would not be lifted for eleven months. "Although Greece and the Soviet coup in Czechoslovakia opened the eyes of Congress quite a lot," British prime minister Clement Attlee recalled, "it wasn't until the Berlin airlift that American public opinion really wakened up to the facts of life."[104] Kennan roundly criticized the Joint Chiefs of Staff for considering withdrawal from the city.[105]

Bevin compared this original Berlin crisis with the repulse of the Turks from the gates of Vienna in 1683. Given U.S. support, he roared that he would "drop the submergence of Europe by the Slavs."[106] But this sort of talk within the dusty chanceries of Europe was contrasted with what could be glimpsed behind the scenes. For instance, market forces trumped Communist ideology as East Berliners smuggled additional supplies to West Berlin, and the airlift's provisioning of 2.3 million tons of food and fuel spawned the concept of electronic data interchange, an innovation that would be propelled over the next decades right into Kmart and Wal-Mart.[107]

Following through on a visit that was already planned before Soviet troops closed the roads, two groups of B-29 "atomic bombers" rolled onto British airstrips in June, with eighty-two jet fighters being shipped over for escort. The fact that a dock strike jeopardized the fighters' unpacking caused heads to shake in Washington. Despite excellent morale and nostalgic articles on both sides of the ocean about the revival of a common cause that many were still unashamed to call Anglo-Saxon, it soon proved hard to agree on which country would come up with the roughly $32 million needed to build the requisite airfields near Oxford.

Even though the NSC had ruled that these bases were indispensable to American defense (there was nowhere else from which bombers could prudently operate within range of Moscow), Washington insisted that the cost be borne by the British "since the bases were in the U.K." There followed eighteen months of increasingly futile confrontations, of which the outcome was a munificent concession from the Pentagon to defray one-sixth of the cost. Ambassador Douglas — about to be sidelined as America's "most important diplomat" by a devastating eye injury — finally warned Washington to back off. The bill would be passed back and forth acrimoniously until America agreed to pay the lion's share of the cost — right after the Korean War broke out.[108] From then on, the allies always assumed that the Americans would pay the most for a common defense.

The dramatic Berlin Airlift entailed 278,000 flights, around the clock and in any weather. The Royal Air Force (RAF) contributed one-third the effort. Pentagon planners believed that this was unfair and saw the RAF as shirking. Heroic as it was, the airlift was neither a glorious extension of World War II's "crusade in Europe" nor a preview of enterprise and the Internet. Mario Puzo's novel *The Dark Arena* described the black market underside of an army of occupation, while Hammond Innes's *Air Bridge* explicitly depicts the corruption of blockaded Berlin. Less memorable diversions would occur in the years ahead. As so many Cold War dollars began to flow, many would inevitably go astray — a result of misplaced goodwill, misjudgment, or just plain theft.

✪

By 1948, and more so the following year, anxieties about these foreign dangers came to be reflected in suspicions at home. There was a strong case to be made for greater vigilance when the American Communist Party was essentially running the presidential campaign of Henry Wallace, that brilliant agronomist and self-deceived visionary who had preceded Truman as FDR's vice president. In *Scoundrel Time*, her poisonous memoir of the McCarthy era, Lillian Hellman (a recent party member) recalls having to explain this fact to the dumbfounded candidate. A much deeper, though not necessarily clandestine, Communist penetration of the United States existed in the 1940s than is generally recalled.

True to Cold War form, however, vigilance was indiscriminate and shaped by partisan battles. In 1947, Truman had ordered loyalty boards created within federal departments. This was done for the characteristically local reason that it "should take the Communist smear off the Democratic party" — meaning that the Republicans might otherwise exploit the public's growing disenchantment with Stalin.[109] The attorney general was authorized to identify "subversive organizations," and membership in one of them could be reason for exclusion from federal employment. This list, including the Spanish Civil War's Abraham Lincoln Brigade, of which around 70 percent of the Hemingway-romanticized volunteers were Communist Party members, would remain unchanged for thirty years.[110]

Much of the country still believed that any great technological advance overseas must have been stolen from America. An increasingly wide range of invention was covered in secrecy. Function-lusting civilian security "experts" were drawn into government. Careers could be built. Within ten years, *Business Week* would write about "the cost of doing business" with the government because of elaborate industrial-security procedures imposed on about twenty-five thousand companies. When suspicion and "clearance" pass into a way of life, the cost mounts from that of diligent insurance to those of a war fought against oneself.

Other procedures were coming into place. In May, George Kennan proposed creating a permanent covert action group. Within a month, a new institution within an institution arrived. In the blandest spirit of bureaucratic camouflage, it would be named the Office of Policy Coordination (OPC). It sat within the CIA, its director appointed by the secretary of state. The OPC — its activities regarded as a convergence of the military and the political-subversive — was kept distinct from the Agency's Office of Special Operations, which handled espionage and counterintelligence.

This was a turning point in U.S. clandestine policy. Details would be buried until after the Cold War. Still a ferocious cold warrior, Kennan drafted a mandate to inflict "political warfare" on the Soviet Union. Stalin being well practiced in political assassinations abroad, America would counter the "vicious covert activities of the USSR, its satellite countries and Communist groups." For a country that had ample recent experience in incinerating civilians in Dresden and Tokyo, "fighting fire with fire" was not really new. The result was a peacetime resort to "propaganda, economic warfare, preventive direct action, including sabotage, anti-sabotage, demolition and evacuation measures; subversion against hostile states."[111] There is considerable willed ignorance within all governments. By creating this clandestine outfit, the country's leadership was also enabling itself largely to ignore a range of unsavory activities.

The stakes of these subtle enterprises were the more fascinating for their secrecy. The men who came to practice them were able to think of themselves as a band of brothers and could cast a siren spell on the congressmen who disbursed the money for such adventures. The country was drawn into deeper swamps of compromises invisible from the office windows of greater Washington or from the air-conditioned suites of newly built embassies. The CIA's success in financing anti-Communist electoral activities in France and Italy (as well as in subsidizing friendly European labor leaders, journalists, and intellectuals) seemed easy enough. However, these frequently useful operations coexisted with the OPC's ill-starred undertakings outside the constitutional world.

Political warfare, which Kennan later admitted "did not work out at all the way I conceived it," meant backing the heroic, doomed, national resistances behind the Iron Curtain. Guerrilla tactics and propaganda would be used not only in Eastern Europe but also in the Soviet Union. Once authorized by the NSC, Kennan and friends cobbled together a variety of catastrophic paramilitary operations. Scores of courageous parachutists were dropped to link up with resistance groups. For instance, in the Ukraine, all who were so naively sent to join guerrilla groups in the Carpathian Mountains instead went straight into the hands of the efficient Soviet security forces and disappeared forever. But the authorization had been crafted so that "the originating role of the United States government will always be kept concealed."[112] So, too, of course, was the role of the individuals responsible. This portent for the years ahead entailed the codification of "plausible denial," which meant that the U.S. government could, and most likely would, disclaim responsibility for future operations gone awry. The old rule that no war is just that does not have some prospect for victory was little heeded, and the Joint Chiefs of Staff wanted to distance themselves from Kennan's paramilitary recklessness.

Adventurous men at the newly established CIA were becoming accustomed to working in a sealed universe removed from healthy oversight. For the first time, a President had institutionalized a process of covert action. Frank Wisner, the first head of these operations, was — in his wealth, good looks, and knowledge of the larger world — truly representative of what historian David Fromkin calls such "daring amateurs."[113] By the end of its first year, the OPC had around three hundred employees, a $4.7 million budget, and seven overseas stations. Like so much else, the manpower and money would swell. So did the amateurism — a remarkable mixture of initiative, unconscious "St. Paul's School Chapel arrogance," and the tendency to assume that an excellent liberal education could substitute for the kind of specific understanding of nations that takes a lifetime to acquire.[114]

A federal government office that would become part of the National Security Agency also began intercepting private messages by "borrowing" transatlantic telegrams from the New York–based offices of Western Union and other telegraph companies. Until this blew open in the mid-1970s, these obliging corporations would hand over printed messages, microfilm, and eventually computer tapes for overnight copying by agents masquerading as technicians in a television tape-reprocessing lab.[115]

Most Americans had by now more enthusiasm for opposing communism than they had mustered before Pearl Harbor for a showdown with Germany or Japan. There was surprisingly little difference between Republicans and Democrats — much less between parties than between regions. But Washington did not feel confident that it understood Soviet capabilities, let alone intentions. For intelligence, it still depended on the dated debriefings of Nazis, such as General Alfred Jodl before he was hanged in 1946, and on German aerial photos of the western Soviet Union, as well as on Wehrmacht maps for more distant regions. The Air Force assembled SAC's target lists from publicly available descriptions of Russian cities and industry at the Library of Congress. The Red Army's size was canonically said to be 175 divisions, as during the war, but Washington's ability to track the number of Soviet divisions did not mean it could count how many men were on duty with them. Contrary to myth, U.S. intelligence was not remotely "confident that the Kremlin would never sanction direct military conflict with the West."[116]

The vast federal spending that would be necessary to support the country's new Army, Air Force, and Navy had not yet become part of American life. "All too frequently there is ample justification to the sarcastic insinuations that our strategic planners have been smoking marijuana," future chief of naval operations George W. Anderson noted as a captain, "simply because they have been unmindful of the logistic implications of their plans."[117]

Although U.S. productivity was unprecedented, Americans were not yet immersed in their wealth. They feared that current well-being was an unwholesome side effect of weapons buying and foreign aid. In 1948, for instance, the Republican Congress voted down the single million dollars the administration requested for cancer research. With the addition of a smear from the American Medical Association linking national health insurance to communism, the ensuing Democratic Congress in 1949 killed that possibility, too. However, such thriftiness was disappearing fast. Big problems would be solved with big money and big organization. Many solutions — starting promisingly enough with federal subsidies to school lunch programs in 1946 — were easily justified by claims of "national security."

Military budgets hit the Cold War low in fiscal year 1948 at $9.5 billion, or 3.5 percent of GDP. Right after Czechoslovakia's fall in March 1948, Congress quickly granted a $3 billion supplement. Then it controversially approved defense spending for the next year that was about 20 percent higher. Perhaps because of global tensions, early 1949 was one of only two times during the Cold War when a majority of Americans believed that the amount of federal taxes they were paying was "about right."[118] The country was already spending the then-staggering amount of $6 billion annually on its international needs, not counting defense. Meanwhile, half its adult citizens figured they needed $50 a week to support a family of four comfortably. Americans understood that their new role in world affairs was big, but how big was only gradually becoming apparent, even to the best informed.

The notion of defense officials and industry "entwined like a pair of mating serpents," to use Churchill's metaphor of two big entities coming together, had yet to enter many minds — let alone the term "military-industrial complex," although the more constricted "military-industrial clique" was already being used on the left to describe the pressures exerted on Truman to take a harder line with Moscow.[119] The R & D relationships between universities and the military were meanwhile expanding through a web of advisory panels and other committees that were to become inseparable from much of academic life.

Amid all of these new foreign involvements and domestic repercussions, many Americans were plagued by a question posed by advertising executive Bruce Barton. This former obstructionist congressman of FDR's mocked triumvirate "Martin, Barton, and Fish" asked in November's *Reader's Digest*, the world's most widely circulated magazine and one of immense cultural and ideological weight, "Are We Biting Off More Than We Can Chew?" By the end of 1948, many people suspected that the answer was yes.

★

Nineteen forty-nine was the last year the United States eschewed most of the ongoing involvements that would become second nature for the century's duration. Familiar assumptions still prevailed despite alarms about Moscow: U.S. military spending might be cut further, new peacetime allies more or less in the North Atlantic could mostly provide for themselves, U.S. manpower in Asia might be reduced, and the recovering British Empire should still be able to contribute its stabilizing influence to obscure places in between. Yet decisions were being made in both Moscow and Washington that would upend each of these hopes and connect the globe in ways to be felt by every city and town in America.

Sixty percent of U.S. troops overseas, nearly half the Navy, and most of the Air Force were in the Western Pacific. However, the keen concern that the Pentagon had shown for the Pacific Rim immediately after the war was starting to dwindle amid the growing faith in airpower. A national strategy of nuclear deterrence was adopted by default, in part because higher taxes were politically impossible without actual war and because Truman was a "hard-money" man who refused to spend more than government took in.[120]

Washington had finally written off South Korea, and everyone concerned knew it. Part of the Japanese empire for forty years, Korea had been partitioned in 1945. Three years later, in August 1948, the Republic of Korea was established south of the 38th Parallel under seventy-three-year-old President Syngman Rhee, with its capital at Seoul. The following month, the Democratic People's Republic of Korea was proclaimed in the north by thirty-six-year-old Kim Il Sung. Soviet officials drafted its constitution, which also named Seoul the capital.[121] In March 1949, Kim met Stalin in Moscow, expecting modest industrial help, coastal defense capabilities, and some "supplementary military aid" for his new regime. He apparently did not expect the armory that quickly followed.

The conventional wisdom is that North Korea maneuvered hesitant Soviet patrons into underwriting its 1950 invasion of the South and that Moscow had reservations about the attack until the last months of Kim's plotting. More likely, it was Stalin who initiated the offensive and then opened the door to provide North Korea the "overwhelming military superiority" he insisted was necessary for a quick conquest.[122] Wish lists thereafter came in from the provisional capital Pyongyang, written in tandem with Soviet officers. Particularly given the immense amounts of medicines and lubricants shipped to North Korea in 1949, as well as the buildup of armored divisions, it is hard to believe that Stalin was just thinking about helping a new ally defend itself. The eight divisions that would lead the invasion were formed and equipped by year's end.[123]

The cost of retaining U.S. troops in South Korea was thought to exceed that land's limited strategic value, just as MacArthur had suggested to the world in March 1949, and they were out by June. The $10 million Washington allotted in military aid to South Korea that year was intended to maintain the outmoded artillery pieces, small arms, and strictly rationed ammunition that U.S. forces left behind when they departed. One gets an uneasy feeling that all Washington was seeking was a "decent interval."[124]

Across the Korea Strait, it appeared to Europeans, as well as to Australia and New Zealand, that the United States intended to build up Japan to a recklessly high industrial level. They suspected that Washington would impede cheap exports to America, while letting Japan compete ruthlessly in other world trade. When the Foreign Office's foremost expert on Japan sarcastically asked the State Department why America did not just say it was going to make Japan a colony and grant it dominion status in twenty-five years, he was startled at the ingenuous reply. The idea was appealing but would never pass Congress.[125]

As long as the United States bore the entire cost of the occupation — including $1 billion in outright aid for 1947, 1948, and 1949 — it had a strong incentive to make Japan as self-sufficient as possible.[126] America itself had little fear of commercial competition at a time when the world needed more of everything. Increasingly, however, the desire to rebuild Japan rested more on defense than on economics. Probably that desire went too far. Former investment banker and navy secretary James Forrestal, who served as secretary of defense from October 1947 to March 1949, Kennan, and several other high officials denounced MacArthur's original attempt in 1947 to dissolve Japan's *zaibatsu* (money cliques). They insisted that the loss of these great, centralized industrial and trading combines would cause "near anarchy." Kennan particularly warned that, through ignorance or duplicity, the Supreme Commander was pushing a "vicious" scheme to open Japan to Communist influence by his forced "socialization" of big business.[127] As MacArthur thereafter diluted his efforts to democratize Japan in favor of a "reversed course" favoring central authority, long-term political reform was sacrificed in order to build up Japan as a Cold War bastion — a step that helped perpetuate an arrogant bureaucracy at the price of more autonomy for the ordinary Japanese, and one for which Japan is still paying.[128]

It is now forgotten how much the U.S. commitment to Japan was haunted by issues of geopolitical perspective, open ethnic suspicion, and fear of overcommitment. Army Secretary Kenneth Royall stated at a Tokyo press conference in early 1949 that America was under no obligation to defend Japan in the first place. After all, danger threatened the U.S. East Coast rather than the West, he explained, just as he had done in Europe two months before.

MacArthur let loose. Unlike Kennan, he deplored the idea of simplistically tying Japan to some sort of worldwide containment program, but that hardly meant that he could implicitly endorse the notion of not defending Japan at all. So the Supreme Commander told traumatized allied diplomats in Tokyo and the rest of the world that he "considered it beneath his dignity to make any public pronouncement" about Royall's "stupidity."[129] Not the least cost of this moment was MacArthur's viceregal tones, which would soon work its way back into American public life.

For mercurial America to abandon Japan did not seem to Western Europeans, let alone to Australians and New Zealanders, inconsistent with Washington's emerging doctrine of nuclear retaliation across continental distances. It seemed to harmonize all too readily with rising U.S. despair at the task of bolstering up both extremities of Eurasia. "The suggestion that the United States is losing interest in the Far East," Bevin complained to his ambassador in Washington, "is likely to have most serious repercussions in South East Asia."[130] Would not communism plunge from a bolshevized Vietnam right down through the Thai peninsula and on to Singapore (the British Empire's greatest naval base) like a run in a silk stocking? Not only the British but also the French and the Dutch saw a unified communism pressing on the borderlands of newly independent Burma (today's Myanmar) and what the French called Indochina, an area comprising Cambodia, Laos, and Vietnam. As Soviet ambitions in Europe were construed in the light of Munich, so Russia must be attempting to create another, greater, and much redder East-Asian Co-Prosperity Sphere, as imperial Japan had titled the fruits of its predations.

In early March 1949, the French finally reached a modest agreement with Bao Dai, the genial ex-emperor who fronted for the Vietnamese loyalist coalition. They slightly loosened their grip on Vietnam, then asked Washington for weapons — ostensibly for the new Vietnamese army (that is, an army of Vietnamese in French service). They argued that the British endorsed such a force as a "real contribution to the prevention of communist expansion in Southeast Asia." Washington, however, already had the sense to speak about "the legitimate aspirations of the Vietnamese." State Department officials suspected that Britain and France were colluding to get America to pay the first installment on what looked like potentially unlimited neocolonial presences masquerading as containment.[131]

Such skepticism was apparent that April when Bevin's brainchild, the North Atlantic Treaty, was signed by the United States, Canada, and ten European countries. Fittingly conducted in the American capital, the entire ceremony was broadcast live to the nation. Acheson, who had succeeded Marshall as secretary of state at the beginning of Truman's second term, shepherded this "creation" of his country's first truly entangling alliance, in which an armed attack on one member would be considered an attack on all. Right after the event, Bevin told Acheson that there was an urgent need to establish a "special relationship" with the United States in Southeast Asia, one that included the Dutch and French. A categorical public reply from Acheson followed: the United States was unlikely to participate in "any further special collective defense arrangements."[132]

Yet even previously cautious U.S. opinion leaders were becoming impatient with such hesitancy. "Why at the zenith of American power was American influence in China paralyzed?" asked Lippmann on the eve of Mao Tse-tung's final victory.[133] To reverse the question, why should so first world a phenomenon as industrial-democratic America even try to exercise leverage on an environment so far — militarily, culturally, and politically — from Main Street? Why assume that the outcome in China between Mao's Soviet-backed forces and Chiang Kai-shek's U.S.-supported government could even be determined by what the United States did or did not do?

Nineteen forty-nine was the last full year in which American alarm about communism in Asia stopped at the doors of Fort Knox — although that was also the year in which foreign assistance reached an all-time high percentage of GDP (3.21 percent, which would be $327 billion from today's economy). The State Department recognized that Congress was at the limit of voting fresh funds for aid anywhere, but the "limits" discovered by those who consider themselves practical can be just as myopic as anyone else's. Britain was demanding money for its colony of Malaya, where it had begun what would be a ten-year campaign against some fifteen thousand ethnic Chinese guerrillas. London insouciantly suggested that dollars could be diverted from the funds that Congress had originally appropriated for Chiang's now-disintegrating Nationalist cause, or perhaps from what could be found at the new World Bank.

Yet Mao's rolling triumphs raised a clamor that a line had to be drawn somewhere. The difficulty with drawing lines (which usually meant underwriting withering imperial holdings or purely administrative postwar demarcations) was that often some part of the enemy (or his present friends) was already behind them. America's politicians would be haunted for twenty years by the "lesson" that another "loss" of position only remotely of the magnitude of "losing" China would undercut all their achievements.

The pell-mell flight of Chiang's armies across the 115-mile-wide Formosa Strait that midsummer seemed to have taught Americans never to extend open-ended commitments of materiel and pledges of political solidarity to thieving clients with thin popular support. Although Chiang's incompetent government had never controlled more than half of China, it had received about $3 billion in grants and credits since V-J Day, not counting the amounts of civilian and military supplies sold to the Nationalists at a fraction of the procurement cost. Less forgettably, Chiang's regime had received one of the five Security Council seats when the United Nations was founded.

Disgust with Chiang, however, could not overshadow the apparent dangers of Mao. The "Great Helmsman" parroted Stalin in policy and rhetoric, as in declaring that socialized agriculture was the ultimate goal and that "neutrality is a camouflage and a third way a mirage."[134] This did not sound much like a Chinese Tito, as some hoped Mao might become. Instead, he kept following the "Russian path" of Marxist-Leninist principles wrapped in Stalin-scale carnage.[135]

No matter whether or not the United States decided formally to recognize the men now controlling Beijing, the new China sounded like a threat to Southeast Asia — access to whose markets, it had so recently been asserted by imperial Japan, was a matter of life and death for those islands. Kennan, always a much better cultural morphologist than an economist, was among the first after World War II to strategize about the commercial interdependence of Japan and Southeast Asia. Japan should have "some sort of empire toward the South," he insisted, fearing Communist control of "the rice bowl of Asia" in Indochina, which was the source of Japan's food imports. He also thought that Korea would be better off under Japanese control.[136] Everyone else, including Japan itself, had had enough of empire.

In Western Europe, and increasingly in Asia, military guarantees had come to be accepted as necessary to economic assistance, and vice versa. Development aid was a new idea, military protection an old one. Four days after the Senate ratified the North Atlantic Treaty in July, Truman asked Congress for an unprecedented program of peacetime military assistance, the most difficult foreign policy legislation to enact since Lend-Lease.[137] He was not obtuse in urging these ties, nor was he morally culpable in sending dollars that the colonial powers would use to uphold their fraying empires. As in announcing what other people called his "doctrine" two years earlier, Truman was motivated by the hopes that it would lessen the need for direct U.S. involvement, that it would buy time for other nations to strengthen themselves, and that it would save American lives.

Congress did not overly object to the $314 million in aid eventually allotted to non-Atlantic nations, but it sharply debated the amount of money going to Europe under the Marshall Plan. Truman defended this outlay as "an investment in security that will be worth many times its cost."[138] The focus had to stay on NATO. "Europe is more important from an industrial standpoint than Asia," testified Omar Bradley, who had replaced Eisenhower as Army Chief of Staff in early 1948, adding that there was "no immediately effective way that you can render assistance to Asia."[139]

As for Washington's own hemisphere, Bradley told Latin American military leaders (often the same people who served as political ones) that Europe had priority because there was "no immediate threat of aggression from communism" against their countries. To that end, Belgium and tiny Luxembourg would receive more U.S. aid from 1945 to 1950 than all of Latin America. The United States simply wanted Argentina to stop threatening Britain over the

Falkland Islands, one inducement being that Argentina soon received, for a nominal $4 million, the decommissioned American cruiser *Phoenix*. (Promptly renamed the *General Belgrano*, it would be sunk with 368 men in a war for the Falklands thirty-three years later.) Kennan, on the other hand, was frantic about what he called the "virus of Communism" infecting that largely impoverished continent of around 146 million people.

He admitted to knowing nothing about Latin America. After a brief first visit, however, he sent Acheson a 10,000-word essay containing the sort of meretricious opinions that legitimized U.S. permissiveness toward right-wing thuggery. For reasons of history, geography, and "human blood," he regarded Latin America as the most hopeless region on earth. (Africa was still largely under European domination.) After all, any chances of progress had been lowered by the "unfortunate results . . . of extensive intermarriage . . . [with] Negro slave elements." He was convinced that, in those countries without established traditions of popular government, "harsh governmental measures of repression" might be the "only answer" to Communist inroads.[140] There is nothing so consistently unkind in the writings of Acheson, Marshall, Dulles, LeMay, McCloy, or other men shaping America's role in the world.

As for Europe, the United States in 1949 still had its one division in Germany. It could deploy only a single tank battalion, which — led by Colonel Creighton Abrams, who had spearheaded George Patton's rescue of Bastogne — operated just twelve tanks capable of fighting.[141] Moscow's cutbacks had not been anywhere near this severe. U.S. armored forces were probably inferior in quality and number to those of Britain. The services were squaring off against each other for shares of a defense pie that they expected to be pretty small for the foreseeable future. Such rivalry and redundancy, said a government commission grimly, brought its own "extravagance in military budgets and waste in military expenditure."[142] Spending quarrels and parochial claims of technological primacy became embarrassingly public. Throughout Truman's presidency, U.S. civilian and military officials never "believed that they had enough power to support their diplomatic risk taking," as is now widely assumed. The leadership, in Marshall's words, instead saw itself "playing with fire."[143]

The relatively insular, painless (because conscription-proof), high-tech solution of concentrating on the roles of aviation and the atomic bomb for the Navy and Air Force was also being questioned. Americans were by no means confident even in their airpower. The U.S. Aircraft Industries Association, for example, petitioned the State Department to pressure the British, who had no interest in pooling knowledge with U.S. competitors, into sharing details about superior Rolls-Royce jet engines. The British insisted that their lead in aviation technology was insurmountable.[144] At least they were devoting roughly an equal proportion of their wealth to defense, as were the Dutch (mainly to fight a hopeless war in the East Indies). But Washington was largely disappointed that the British were not living up to its expectations of burden sharing. It kept accusing them of insufficient effort.

Ten years to the day after the invasion of Poland, which had ignited World War II, and just one month before Mao entered Beijing, the Pentagon finally set out to examine why Britain's economic fate was of such significance to America's future. On September 1, 1949, the challenge was to determine what it would cost the United States if it tried to "replace" the British Empire by beginning to take on most of Britain's globe-girdling commitments. The result was NSC 75, a policy document from the National Security Council declassified only after the Cold War. It justly concluded that the costs for America would be so high as to be literally "uncountable."

The question came down to whether London's latest financial crisis in 1949 would "mean a new Greece somewhere in the world where vital U.S. interests have heretofore been protected by the U.K."[145] Washington more than ever assumed that a worldwide British network was vital to its own extended sense of national interest. Although the specifics were unclear, anxiety that Americans might be compelled to replace a dissolving British presence was growing fast. To succeed a strong empire may give the new power a chance to play liberator; to arrive as an empire is crumbling is far less palatable. Replacing the British would involve not only more U.S. troops (ongoing conscription was emphatically *not* to be taken for granted) and more money (about which both elite and public opinion was still jittery) but also more unpronounceable names, more humiliating obligations to odious tyrants, and more frustrated outbursts from Chicago or Richmond.

To that end, Britain had to be saved from going bust, as seemed all too likely a possibility that autumn. If Britain could not be helped, insisted Hubert Humphrey, the new senator from Minnesota, "totalitarianism will have won an important victory." Americans were told by CBS foreign correspondent Charles Collingwood, one of the most incisive American journalists ever to perform such work, that "if Britain goes bankrupt," the whole military position of the Western powers would change.[146] The word *bankruptcy* was bandied about but never clarified, with Senator Taft, fine flower of Harvard Law School, observing that he had no idea how a country could go bankrupt. Yet anyone who had lived through 1919 on knew that financial catastrophes, whatever they might be called, could eviscerate a nation.

The administration and much of Congress believed that Britain's financial failings might result in "military vacua in other parts of the world" besides Europe. The Pentagon particularly understood that even "the idea of undertaking additionally the support of U.K. military commitments on a global basis will be hard to support before Congress."[147] Among the obstacles to helping Britain were men on the Hill such as Pat McCarran of Nevada. He had no qualms about airing "anti-British, anti-socialist, anti-Russian, anti-Communist, anti-Jewish" opinions.[148] A Democrat so right wing as never to have been endorsed for reelection by a Democratic administration, he had become chairman of the Joint Committee on Economic Cooperation when his party had retaken the Senate earlier in 1949.

The British once more asked for a greater share of U.S. aid, stating that without aid, their country might implode — with mere financial disruption just the beginning — and carry with it all European nations in the Atlantic orbit. In fact, more was at stake in Washington during what were called the Financial Talks that September than perhaps in any postwar conference: not simply Britain's economic fate but the international financial role of America, the hope of Western European unity, and the development of Southeast Asia, for starters. The fundamental question for Americans was whether a far longer U.S. military reach into the world could be avoided, or at least postponed.

In his last frustrating weeks as director of Policy Planning at the State Department, Kennan seriously confused these pivotal negotiations. He acknowledged to British officials that he had fomented articles in the American press to push forward his idiosyncratic idea of some form of high-toned Anglo-American union. Denying to his friend, Foreign Service Officer Charles "Chip" Bohlen, that he had done so, he told the British in confidence that they could safely discount State Department and White House insistence that Britain move to integrate itself with a Western Europe becoming increasingly unified under U.S. prodding.

Kennan could be shrewd about Russia, but he had joined the Foreign Service to be distanced from the vulgarities of his own country. He was ill equipped to speak of America. He despaired of all the Continental countries (except, of course, Germany), claiming that there were other men in Washington who wanted to go even further in bilateral relations with comfortably Anglo-Saxon England but who were, like him, blocked by Congress and the Pentagon.[149] This was like saying that America, except for its political representatives and military leaders, was united behind dreams from a mythical past. In fact, such vaporizing about a special relationship would probably have been voted down at the venerable New York Yacht Club.

The United States ended up nudging Britain toward another devaluation and helping with more credits, but the patched-together postwar order was being undermined by events of colossal implication over which America had far less control. September 1949's financial storm was joined by fallout drifting east in the jet stream from Kazakhstan.

Remarkably, a U.S. military intelligence report in early 1945 — unaware of the Manhattan Project and months before the first detonation — had predicted that the Soviet Union would have an atomic bomb in about five years. Once the atomic age arrived in July of that year, the services deemed the prospect of Moscow imitating this accomplishment to be far in the future. When the AEC was created in 1946, its founding commissioners were startled to learn that no monitoring system was in place to discover atmospheric radioactivity from the tests of other nations. Soon thereafter, the Air Force told the AEC that such monitoring would require $1 million and that it "found itself short of funds." The AEC had to fork over the initial money for what was called the Long Range Detection Program. As late as June 1949, the Defense Department Research and Development Board questioned whether such scarce dollars "might be spent more wisely in other fields."[150]

About a year earlier, Vermont Senator Ralph Flanders had urged that the country pledge itself never to be the first to use atomic weapons. His proposal sounded silly when the alternative might be sending thousands or millions of GIs back to Europe. It still looked silly in August 1949 when the State Department saw fit to commission secretly a Gallup poll to discover how many Americans agreed with forgoing "first use." Only 30 percent.

Within two months, Moscow conducted its own atomic explosion. The National Opinion Research Center then discovered that twice as many Americans concluded that they should never be the first to use the bomb. "To the responsible men in government," recalled one sharp commentator about reaction to the detonation, "the shock was extreme."[151] Letting emotion once more overcome reason, Kennan amazed Acheson with the assertion that the U.S. atomic deterrent had become "superfluous." Paul Nitze, a former Wall Streeter who was to be Kennan's successor, recalls thinking that getting rid of U.S. nuclear weapons — unilaterally, if necessary — "was the best way to go."[152] Also distancing itself from reality, the Air Force tried to cancel what it regarded as unnecessary contracts for detecting further tests.

The State Department at least attained the insight that "the idea of a mutual renunciation of the bomb is more attractive when we no longer have a monopoly." The fact of being the world's only nuclear-capable nation had for four years been a pillar of American exceptionalism. "Our civilians," opined Foggy Bottom, "have not been conditioned to taking punishment such as was the lot of Europeans during the last two wars."[153] Truman overrode the attempts of several of his aides to promote the dispersal of U.S. industries, and the factories (not yet manicured corporate headquarters) that began going up beyond the cities were built for unrelated reasons.[154] It would take ten years for all the theorizing and budget drafting of moving underground to take their (really big) bite.

As would only be understood once the Cold War ended, the device that the Soviets detonated was about the only one they had until after Stalin's death. Even limited production of usable weapons would begin slowly, and not until 1954 did Moscow put them into battle standing. Building air-portable bombs was still painstaking, even under Lavrenti Beria's fearsome direction.[155] Perhaps some power/political edge could have been gained had this disparity been known. In any event, Washington began massively overcorrecting, assuming that the Soviets would be producing bombs as quickly as America's weapons plants.[156] Here came another bite of the Cold War, as Americans started perceiving every possible Soviet technical advance as a towering menace.

The country, meanwhile, wrapped its sixth and seventh detonations, at Bikini and Eniwetok, in extreme secrecy. Imaginations ran wild. Connecticut senator Brien McMahon, cochairman of the Joint Committee on Atomic Energy, asked why the size of the atomic stockpile, then around two hundred bombs, should not be made public. Everyone else in government thought the question uncharacteristically naive: the dangerous details of foreign policy should not concern the man in the street. This was a time when there were more and more government activities that the uninitiated did not need to know about, and therefore should not. Among America's leaders, moreover, there was little concern that some malcontent might run to, say, the *New York Times* with troubling revelations. If he did, such material would likely not be deemed fit to print.

People knew it was a new world, but that was about all they knew. They sensed being surrounded by paradoxes — situations that seem to be contradictory or false but are not. Was the atomic bomb, for instance, keeping the Red hordes at bay, or was it making the United States more vulnerable in the long run? Both, of course. And what of China — was it now the greatest long-term asset of Communist tyranny, or might it someday complement American power against Russia? The awful fact was that both possibilities were real.

Ironically, in 1949, President Conant of Harvard and the newly appointed President Eisenhower of Columbia University served on a National Education Association panel that decreed that all Communists "should be excluded from employment as teachers." From here on, leftists in the academy would realize that their greatest direct enemy was not some transient Washington blowhard, "but the opportunism and cowardice" of trustees and administrators, as well as "the high road to professional prosperity" pursued by their own colleagues. Universities themselves were becoming increasingly prone to the scabrous careerism ever more tied to the getting of defense and CIA dollars.[157]

These issues of secrecy and suspicion, of America being spread too thin around the world, of the possible ceaselessness of struggle, came together toward year's end. Congress was cool toward bailing out Britain, toward Truman's proposal of using U.S. technologies to aid developing countries, and even toward additional funding for the Marshall Plan. A brief and mild downturn had caused unemployment to rise, ensuring that most people worried more about recession than about war. Truman might denounce Congress's hesitancy as "the worst kind of false economy," but it showed the temper of the times.[158]

That cranky isolationist, Senator Edwin C. Johnson of Colorado, known for his commitment to a cheap (because ruthlessly nuclear) defense, raged against U.S. atomic scientists, whom he accused of telling anyone who would listen about their secret research. In a plea for even more secrecy, he let it drop that the AEC was hard at work devising a bomb one thousand times more powerful than that used at Hiroshima. This was hardly the first or last time that Washington itself, rather than some goateed subversive, unconsciously alerted the world to America's most cloistered efforts. His harangue could actually be seen on the new medium of television.

If thermonuclear fire was casting shadows even before it was ignited, scientists also were talking about using radioactive substances as an invisible film on the battlefield or, perhaps more effective, circulating them in the air as a "death-sand."[159] How could people go about their lives with this horror overhanging them? Tellingly, one gentle soul could not.

F. O. Matthiessen, professor of English and American literature at Harvard, was one of the country's finest scholars and most morally sensitive people. When he hurled himself from the roof of a Boston hotel, he left a note saying that he could not live helplessly within the atomic nightmare, believing that there was nothing he could do to affect the inevitable progress of events leading to destruction. His never-hidden homosexuality and his humane, trust fund–backed democratic socialism (combined with a desire to be deceived about the nature of the Soviet Union) made him a classic high-wire walker of his age. The country had to think many things through before a decent man like him could be happy in it.

★

What were Americans facing at the start of 1950, less than five years after U.S. and Soviet soldiers had embraced in the middle of Germany? China fell in the autumn of 1949, as Mao exulted in Tienanmen Square that colonized people everywhere were ready to "stand up." It began to seem possible that the still-prodigious residue of British imperial presence — a million men in nearly a thousand garrisons around the world — might dissolve with similar apparent suddenness. Moscow appeared likely to exploit collapses in authority almost anywhere. The strength and the will of the people who had fought under Zhukov were unmistakable, even if the genius of Leninism had perished in execution cellars and death camps years before.

Essentially nothing "that emerged by 1950 had been planned, desired, or foreseen by 1945" — contrary to today's common belief that so much of what followed after V-E Day had already been set in place by the grasping proponents of the American Century.[160] Absolutely no one was thinking of forty more years of struggle in every corner of the globe and through so many facets of human behavior. Each side believed that the other would fall by its own hand: Moscow saw the inevitability of a capitalist crash; the West, less certain that inexorable social forces guaranteed victory, nonetheless hoped that the Soviet system was too irrational to endure, although the isolation and ruthlessness of its leaders might make this end violent.

Perceptive Western leaders of contrary political leanings, such as Marshall and Bevin, insisted that there was not much difference between Nazism and communism. So, too, did some European intellectuals, such as French left-wing activist David Rousset, a Buchenwald survivor who appealed (to the scorn of his confreres) for an investigation into the Soviet labor camps. Faced with Stalinist Russia, these men did not set Hitler's state apart as a singularly terrible regime with which nothing could compare.

In fighting the Axis, Americans — perhaps more so than others — had believed that the predators in Nazi Germany and Dai Nippon could be "taught a lesson" and that, once defeated, they could quickly be separated from their peoples. The taxing frustration of the Cold War was slowly becoming apparent: recent allies-turned-enemies in the Soviet Union and China could not be taught any final lesson without a terminally disastrous war.

To a Depression-stinted U.S. leadership, money was the magic ingredient in building up new allies and in confronting the East. Money had done so much so fast in the war just finished, and it was now doing so much in peace, from creating Levittown to reviving Europe and Japan. However, recent memories of the Depression still constrained America's political and military reach. As late as January 1, 1950, the Dow Jones average stood at only two hundred, less than twice what it had been in 1940, although the GDP had nearly tripled. What engagement there was — the

Truman Doctrine, the Marshall Plan, NATO — would surely be implemented as cheaply as possible through proxies, technology, and secret operations.

The Cold War's first four years were filled with starts and stops rather than any considered policy or long-range goals (other than not having the world fall apart again). But trends and patterns were emerging and would be reflected in the sacrifices ahead. Crises real and imagined intruded. Big government of the emergency years of the Depression and World War II was getting bigger. The secrecy that accompanied it grew darker. Unaccountability followed, and moral compromises became even easier. America appeared a veritable aircraft carrier against the current, borne back ceaselessly into the past, as its officials preoccupied themselves with Europe and as the nation dropped what had so recently been its fervent anticolonialism. It also found itself upholding more than a few brutal regimes, though none as bad as the Soviet one that it had sustained during the war.

The weary, case-hardened men in the White House, on Capitol Hill, in the executive departments, and in the corporations, who framed the issues in these early Cold War years, had been leaders in prenuclear conflict. Mostly born in the nineteenth century, they remembered their country when the very notion of human flight had been humorous. With the sudden rescue in mid-1950 of a distant place whose existence was unknown to virtually anyone outside Washington, the relatively modest East-West contest that had been endured since 1946 was utterly buried by new threats and passions.

Now at the height of his influence, Dean Acheson wanted to know where America was heading. Throughout the preceding thirty-five years, he believed, Washington had been guided by the view that if something "abnormal" happened, it was temporary, and the situation would shortly return back to "normality."[161] In fact, during that entire period, the global realities that America confronted forced it to do nothing but "abnormal" things. He worried that unless America faced up to what it wanted and decided how to get it, the whole Western structure could collapse.

Acheson had come of age just two months before Sarajevo, precisely the date of his "thirty-five years ago." He was now calling, in terms distinctly prophetic of John F. Kennedy's inaugural address a dozen years later, for America to commit itself to meeting the world's seemingly perpetual crisis. His thoughts represent an understanding at the highest level that the clock of world order could not be rewound; it was broken. America's immediate task was to push the hands around as if it were actually working and perhaps, over the long run, to make a new clock.

3

Getting the Habit

(1950–1953)

It was the Korean War and not World War II that made us a world political-military power.

Charles Bohlen, *Witness to History*

The Korean War was the detonator that blew U.S. power around the world. The decision in late June 1950 to shoot it out on that bleak peninsula was made quickly. When Congress learned that Truman had ordered Americans into the fight, nearly every member leaped to his feet and cheered. The generation of 1929–1933 and 1940–1941 felt that anything was better than waiting. U.S. retaliation in this truly obscure theater — never before an American interest, never a European possession, always a byword for savagery — threw together the initiatives of the previous four years.[1] The invasion compelled the United States to make hard decisions, while Europe was still weak and unpredictable. The rich and remote country that would rather have been a younger but predominant partner of the troubled Old World thereby took on an undisguised global role. The Cold War as a planetary struggle began taking shape.

Clausewitz tells us to establish the price of violent action before undertaking it, because once such action is started, rarely is there a chance to change one's mind, except to up the ante. It is also one of the great rules of bureaucratic life that it is easier to start than to stop, especially when a country's security is evoked. What occurred between 1950 and 1953 would institutionalize the means of open-ended conflict. Whether or not they wore uniforms, people could start committing their careers to national security. It became a business like any other, promising to cover a lifetime. From 1950 on, it was easy for a substantial para-bureaucracy to drive its roots outward from Washington into the plains, cities, and mountain power stations, through great corporations, distinguished universities, and discreet law firms. This was a curious growth, spreading branches at extraordinary speed but often flourishing best in the shade.

So much had been temporary and unwanted between 1946 and 1950: the constricted military budgets stand witness, as does the improvised R & D; the on-again, off-again draft (with inductions suspended from early 1949 until June 1950); and the absence of specific transatlantic defense collaboration. Now America had to confront what it had been trying to evade, or at least to ameliorate.

No longer was U.S. spending in Southeast Asia a by-product of Marshall Plan investment in Britain, France, and the Netherlands. Now money was targeted for French Indochina and British Malaya. Paris and London both waited for more dollars to safeguard their colonies. British officials buttonholed Americans: didn't they know that half the world's rubber and a third of its tin came from the Malay Peninsula and that the road to Kuala Lumpur went through Vietnam? They became the first to press upon Washington the notion that if Indochina fell, Malaya would follow, as would the independent nations of Thailand, Burma, India, and who knew what else. Everything seemed so infernally interconnected.

The years 1950 to 1953 were ones of profound transition, as Americans shouldered all sorts of burdens deriving from "world political-military power." The Korean War introduced many of the domestic and international demands that would become familiar for the rest of the century. It was a time of headlong expedience, as General MacArthur pleaded for the "free world" to send him simply "men with rifles." This chapter starts by offering some new thoughts on how the war occurred and how the United States reacted. Second, it discusses why this first "peacekeeping war" began, on the one hand, to distance America from allies who had recently been expected to offer so much more and, on the other, how meeting the apparent needs of those allies combined with the shock of being at war to push America along a path that led to deeper involvements in Asia.

Third, we show how the war nurtured a sense of limitless danger abroad that led to the worst impulses of government arrogance at home. Eisenhower, for instance, attributed the rise of McCarthyism to frustrations Americans felt over Korea. Fourth, we explore how Washington maneuvered to find ways that might make the U.S. role less onerous, whether through new weapons and other technological feats, more allies, or secret manipulations. What policies should the country follow to avoid being pinned down, as in Korea, while Russia watched? Two contrasting architects of the Cold War offered their answers.

Finally, we address the one profound price that Americans did not pay. Amid their desperate responses to Korea, they refused to allow their society to become militarized. Pentagon spending nearly quadrupled, GIs were shipped overseas, and the atomic bomb was hugely surpassed. But the greater peacetime role of the armed services became offset by a remarkably ironic *civilian-ization*.

Americans made promises to themselves during the Korean War's three years. Never again would they buy time with blood because of too few guns, too little training, and not enough warning. They were putting structures into place. They were not, however, embarking on a "crusade," as their efforts are commonly described and as the word was used in 2001 when the country prepared for war.[2] Every crusading quality quickly disappeared from the Cold War struggle — any sense of mission, national unity, unlimited sacrifice, or clear objective. A crusade by definition must be aggressive, and even in World War II, Senator Robert Taft had objected to Americans using this word for the grim work they were undertaking. Eisenhower might reminisce about a "crusade in Europe" (as he titled his memoir in 1948), because the purpose in fighting Nazism was to trample down the iniquity in blood. But it would have been a different Cold War — and it would likely be a different world today — had Korea actually pushed rich, ever more heavily armed America into anything so visceral.

✪

The overriding questions in the first half year of the new decade were whether and on what terms the United States would pay to buttress and even directly defend what Dean Acheson called "situations of weakness." Did the weaknesses thus singled out mean such apparently untenable lands as Taiwan and South Korea — if those were even considered "positions" at all? Or might that description include the new alliance partners in Europe, who could, as it was asserted facilely in Washington, be doing so much more for themselves? What were the positions of strength? Acheson, for once representative of his countrymen, was angry and unspecific.

He worried not only that the imminent fall of Nationalist China's remnant on Taiwan would "boost communism all over Southeast Asia," but also that the "bad boys" of Chiang's failed regime would escape to emerge dangerously in overseas Chinese communities. Nonetheless, he spoke for most of America in saying that the United States "would not agree for one moment to anything bordering on military interference" to save Chiang.[3] Nor, it might have been presumed in Moscow, would force be used to save South Korea.

In the first three months of 1950, the British recognized Mao's regime without the slightest notice to Washington; U.S. aid to South Korea was cut off, then restored, by the House of Representatives; at least $65 million in other assistance began to flow to Southeast Asia; Truman told the world that the United States was going for a "so-called hydrogen or superbomb"; and Stalin and Mao signed a Treaty of Friendship on Valentine's Day. Such friendship included a $300 million Soviet loan, the promise of tens of thousands of Soviet technical advisers, the transfer of entire industries to China, and the joint recognition of Ho Chi Minh's nationalist movement as the government of Vietnam. There was little interest in Washington for examining the underlying hatreds within that threesome. At least some key people from the Foreign Office understood that any Sino-Soviet friendliness would be short-lived, but during early 1950, London and the rest of the allies were more concerned that the "situations of weakness" from which America might retire "will become so numerous that the West will either lose the Third World War before it starts, or arrange for it to begin on a very bad wicket."[4]

The United States, after all, was still a super island state rather than a superpower, feeling little obligation to lead. It seemed everywhere on the defensive. So Policy Planning director Paul Nitze urged upon Acheson the need for a dramatic success, an unambiguous "situation of strength," or perhaps a specific defeat of communism. Anything appeared likely in a conflict whose length, he warned, should now be thought of as indefinite. "The cold war is in fact a real war," Nitze noted, so the United States should devote a fifth of all its output to defense, or somewhere between $40 billion and $50 billion annually, if foreign aid were added.

Nitze was the son of a University of Chicago professor. He graduated from Harvard in 1928, then joined the Wall Street firm Dillon, Read in the 1930s. After a while, he returned to Harvard to earn a master's degree in sociology. He went back to Wall Street for a year, made and married a lot of money, flirted with isolationism, nonetheless hastening to Washington in 1940 to work with James Forrestal and George Marshall. Nitze's wartime focus on economic mobilization and strategic bombing was superb preparation for the decades ahead. Yet he lacked what his admirers too readily took for granted as they acclaimed his charm, ability, and public spirit. He never quite commanded unreflecting trust. He appeared to regard himself as not only a little more privileged but also a great deal quicker than the men around him. That impression almost certainly denied him the cabinet posts he was so qualified to hold.

During April 1950, Nitze distilled his advice in a speculative paper, NSC 68, which has since received enormous attention as a founding document of the Cold War. His arguments for an immense buildup were essentially a polemic, even a fantasy, since there was no chance that Congress would adopt them. Military planners were vastly more conservative, hoping for a budget increase to $18 billion. Truman expected to spend only $13 billion on the armed forces that year and around $1 billion more on military assistance. The Bureau of the Budget warned that higher taxes and military spending would dampen the economy. More in line with the beliefs of the time was Nitze's point that Britain had to retain its potent role — this time in Southeast Asia, where the United States must find additional proxies of some sort.[5]

Actual "allies" in such places, as opposed to proxies and clients, would be too risky. That might mean more treaty commitments, which could drag America into who knew what. MacArthur's Far East Command was hardly as formidable as it sounded. The Eighth Army mustered at most 108,000 poorly trained men dispersed throughout Japan, their divisions each being more than a thousand rifles short of what the U.S. Army required. The understrength Fifth Air Force, with 34,000 men, also was in Japan, but it had no jet fighters — although this did not prevent it from undertaking the first covert overflights of Soviet territory. The Marine Corps was down to two incomplete divisions. The Navy had only 647 active ships of every class (down from its 1945 high of 5,718). The Air Force was somewhat more robust, with a total of 4,700 planes, if one counted all types and ages.[6] There were only 500 U.S. soldiers left in South Korea. Averell Harriman, now serving as Truman's foreign policy assistant, spoke despairingly of the Pentagon's "military isolationism." However, America's nuclear stockpile did contain 298 atomic bombs.

Seoul had reason to be edgy during the first months of 1950. The Soviet-trained "Great Leader" (Kim Il Sung) who ruled the North had been supplied with 258 T-34 tanks, 178 planes, and 1,600 artillery pieces to back up at least eight full-strength, disciplined, modern divisions led by young officers who had served with the Red Army. Some 70,000 soldiers of Korean nationality had been transferred fully equipped from Mao's victorious People's Liberation Army. South Korea fielded its own eight divisions, but they were so ill prepared and supplied that the remaining U.S. military advisers were not permitted to call them an army; the diplomatically correct term was *constabulary*. The South Koreans had neither tanks nor antitank guns.

John Foster Dulles, who had been taken into the State Department that spring in the name of bipartisanship, made a personal appearance before South Korea's National Assembly to offer reassurance. The whole point of remaining firm, he explained in Seoul a week before the invasion, was to buy time for building a prospering, peaceful society that, by its example, would eventually dissolve Soviet-backed communism in the North; unity would follow. Stalin had a more immediate plan for unity. Less than a week later, at four o'clock in the drizzly morning of June 25, some 150 tanks and 90,000 men began pouring into the South. North Korea's battle plans had been drawn up by the Soviet General Staff.

Amazingly, some people today still insist that "the war represented a suckering of North Korea by South Korean provocation," meaning that the Communists were provoked or that a harried Joseph Stalin reluctantly had to "satisfy the demands of an overambitious ally." The fact that a serious historian would argue that the matter of who lit the bonfire in Korea "is the wrong question" shows how some Americans have come to view the Cold War as a sort of disease, at best lacking consciousness and volition.[7] At least Nikita Khrushchev, as Communist Party secretary, would be more categorical: "We started it," he told Molotov.[8] It is vital to be clear on this issue of blame. Washington's assumptions about its origins, after all, became the catalyst for U.S. commitment to a large peacetime military establishment, to deeper involvements in Europe and Southeast Asia, to the belief in a Sino-Soviet monolith, and to much of the effort that eventually defeated the Soviet Union itself.

Conventional wisdom is that Moscow knew of the pending North Korean attack and approved it, but that encouragement was late and halfhearted. Most historians of every stripe emphasize that "Stalin had to be persuaded" by Kim Il Sung's petitioning visits in 1949 and 1950. One leading authority writes of "Soviet acquiescence to the North Korean attack."[9] Another concludes that "the documentary evidence indicates very strongly that from February 1945 to April 1950, Stalin did not aim to gain control over the entire peninsula." Therefore, the view of premeditated, outright Soviet assault that provoked the U.S. response is "false."[10]

These opinions are contradicted by Soviet sources. Moscow's role was even greater than suspected at the time, although Stalin was cautious enough not to commit any forces directly or to make public his air support for Chinese forces once they intervened. Stalin had actually been preparing for nearly three years, not three or four months, to ensure a Communist unification of Korea. He had reconstituted the command for his Far Eastern "theater of military operations" (TVD) in 1947. He had extended his political control into North Korea (and tried to destabilize the South) primarily through Colonel General T. F. Shtykov (known in the Red Army as the "boss" of the North), his first ambassador in 1948.[11] From March 1949, he took the lead in equipping and preparing the North Korean divisions, including the armored one that would ultimately lead the invasion.

The trade and aid agreement reached that March in Moscow was well beyond what Kim had anticipated. It was also much more preparation than would be needed for a quick-and-dirty cross-border incursion.[12] Tens of thousands of tons of equipment, from tanks and field artillery to ammunition and lubricants, began to go east over the Trans-Siberian Railway, to be transshipped at the Manchurian border because of the change in rail gauge.[13] An offensive buildup of this scope could never have been accomplished between April and June 1950, nor, given the sacrifice of the Soviet Union's own petroleum, oil, and lubricant supplies for this purpose, could it have begun the previous December.

In 1949, the Soviet General Staff wrote the Preemptive Strike Plan given to the North Koreans in the spring of 1950. Stalin pulled the trigger on the invasion only after an inspection mission from his Far East Command scrutinized Kim's forces down to battalion level and reported back on June 24 that all was ready.[14] The invasion, in brief, was "preplanned, blessed, and directly assisted by Stalin and his generals, and reluctantly backed by Mao at Stalin's insistence."[15] But it was even more deliberate than has been understood. Truman, Acheson, and Marshall (who would be appointed defense secretary in September) intuitively understood who and what were behind the attack. They then worked intimately with Capitol Hill in committing the country to fight, contrary to another Cold War myth of the president's "failure adequately to consult Congress."[16] After initially backing prompt unilateral military action, George Kennan reconsidered: Washington should agree to neutralize Japan if the Russians would only stop the war. Walter Lippmann, swinging back to caution, thought the commitment of U.S. ground troops a mistake.[17]

Again, Britain's ruling Labour Party may have said it best: what the world faced in Korea was "evil aggression," and if it came to an atomic showdown with Russia, the toughest, most radical elements of British labor unionism would be backing the United States.[18]

With Truman's decision to intervene and to put the U.S. Navy between China's mainland and Taiwan, the one great power to front directly on both oceans was beginning to act decisively in each part of the globe. Its critics were soon to scent imperial designs, but actually it was the opposite: the worldwide backing of a liberal world order, one drawn increasingly to the Pacific Rim, had begun. Washington was showing its new North Atlantic allies — and Moscow — that Europe would not be treated one way and the Far East another. Perhaps the most enduring cost of the U.S. response, however, was that America's outrage at China's involvement would combine with Mao's inwardness to exclude his People's Republic from the community of nations for twenty years.

"The Korean conflict marked the end . . . of the Fortress America era," wrote Matthew Ridgway, one of the few hero-generals of World War II whose fame was polished in Korea. Before then, he recalled, the concept of "limited war" had never been discussed. Eisenhower thought the term to be meaningless.[19] From here, however, it would no longer be a question of whether to fight a limited war, but of how to avoid fighting any other kind. Yet a limited war needs a national objective short of all-out conflict when the fighting bogs down. From the start, it was unclear whether America's purpose was to restore South Korea along the 38th Parallel or to crush North Korea and go to the Yalu River (its border with China), not just as policeman but as unifier.

Although MacArthur had refused to let the CIA operate in his theater, it was beset for not predicting the date of the invasion. Its director, Admiral Roscoe Hillenkoetter, whom British Secret Intelligence Service (SIS) station commander Harold (Kim) Philby described as "an amiable sailor," was promptly replaced by the intimidating Walter Bedell Smith. His "cold fishy eye and . . . precision-tooled brain" alarmed Philby, the charming Cantabrigian who, on his rapid rise toward nearly becoming chief of the SIS, was responsible for all Anglo-American intelligence relations, including code breaking.[20] Within a week, Smith began bringing the eccentric Office of Policy Coordination to heel. It would be folded into the CIA in 1952. He assigned another hardened Army general, Lucian Truscott (like Smith, not a West Pointer and no respecter of elites), to examine the activities of Frank Wisner and friends on the front lines of the Cold War. Truscott wanted to "find out what those weirdos are up to," but the daring amateurs would not be restrained for long.[21] Korea was to become the awful counterexample to what they kept arguing could be cheap and minimal secret operations.

In Japan, Douglas MacArthur reigned. Born in 1880, he had first visited Japan during 1905, when his father, a three-star general for whom the Washington, D.C., boulevard is named, was military attaché. He said that the eight months he spent there were the most formative of his life. He was first in his class and first captain of cadets at West Point and was the second-youngest general in 1917's American Expeditionary Force. He married and divorced a Philadelphia heiress, and became Army chief of staff in 1930 before setting himself up as "Field Marshal" in the Philippines five years later. Franklin Roosevelt said that MacArthur and Huey Long, the "Kingfish" demagogue of Louisiana, were the two most dangerous men in the country. MacArthur was a brave and brilliant man, but one pretty far removed from Main Street America. The European allies were as leery of him as FDR had been.

Repulsing North Korea's invasion ought to have been a snap, given that the United Nations (free to act, owing to the absence of the Soviet delegate and his veto in the Security Council) immediately called on all its members to join the U.S.-led intervention under the light blue flag. Turkey, ancient enemy of Russia, was the first to rally round the United States. Colombian Indians would die on Old Baldy, as would Brazilians and Ethiopians near the Yalu River. Fifteen UN members eventually sent forces. Beyond the heat of the war itself was its significance for the future of Europe, Japan, and Southeast Asia. Yet the war became a protracted agony. At the outset, South Korean forces performed poorly. The North Koreans stormed into Seoul on June 28, rounding up and executing hundreds of Syngman Rhee's supporters.

GIs scuttled from Japan were immediately thrown in front of the highly mechanized and disciplined North Korean troops. They were cut down with ease. Green units rushed over from America, including ones from the National Guard, went through the same meat grinder. Their 2.36-inch bazooka rockets bounced off the heavy armor of the T 34s, perhaps the best tank of the time. American newspapers pictured them fighting with barely reconditioned equipment and inferior training. Likely from panic, as well as from having encountered the North Korean tactic of infiltrating U.S. positions with refugees, GIs shot hundreds of unarmed civilians near the village of No Gun Ri, a tragedy to be revisited a half century later.

Nor was the United States clad in the full armor of righteousness. America was hardly "restoring democracy" to South Korea, controlled by Rhee's corrupt and exploitive government. As would also be revealed fifty years later, for example, his soldiers and police summarily executed more than two thousand political prisoners in the early weeks of the war.[22] The United States was aligning itself not only with Rhee, and with the equally corrupt regime in Taiwan, but also with the likes of Bao Dai in Vietnam and General Phao in Thailand. "Korea is the Greece of the Far East," Truman told an aide, as everything looked more and more the same, often in ways unconsidered.[23]

As in Greece, Washington expected Britain, its strongest and most globally deployed partner, to be on the front lines. Acheson's "tough guy" temper could be fearsome when focused on the shaken and reluctant European allies, but not until the end of July, after a month of slaughter and only after he offered what the British felt was "obscurely worded menace," did they indicate that their men would be sent into action alongside the GIs.[24] Not for the last time in East Asia, London would urge its U.S. ally forward, then hold back. Acheson's outrage was correctly understood to reflect "the mood when the Americans feel they have shouldered the burden of the world and are being criticized by others whose burdens they are carrying."[25] Yet anger could only go so far at a time when Kim Il Sung's invasion was feared to be a feint covering an imminent Soviet thrust into Western Europe.

Although those 175 Red Army divisions rumbled through speeches and committee hearings, U.S. leaders still knew strikingly little about Soviet capabilities. For instance, neither Acheson, Nitze, nor anyone else at the State Department knew whether Moscow would have to mobilize before an invasion, and they doubted whether the Joint Chiefs had the answer either.[26] Moreover, they mistakenly assumed that Moscow possessed usable nuclear weapons. So if world war should erupt, America would again have to work closely with the British, who possessed the only air bases within reach of Moscow that could "be relied on at all," according to the Air Force secretary. Two additional air groups then arrived in England, laden with what the Strategic Air Command (SAC) called its "hardware."[27] In any event, no one in Washington was about to wait while British leaders debated whether a U.S. atomic assault could be launched from their all-too-vulnerable island.

Outnumbered and burdened with a demoralized South Korean ally, MacArthur reversed disaster in September with a breathtaking amphibious counterinvasion, placing a Marine division 150 miles behind enemy lines at Inchon. British forces had by then been dragged in. Losses suffered by the Argyll and Sutherland Highlanders when mistakenly bombed by U.S. planes (a phenomenon labeled "friendly fire" when British troops were again bombed forty years later in the Gulf War) momentarily overshadowed questions about the size of the contribution. France could spare only a battalion, though one that would fight gallantly for its life alongside an American Regimental Combat Team against several Chinese divisions. It was then withdrawn for Indochina.

The Soviets had at least not pounced on Western Europe, and great new weapons were gestating. It was, therefore, in character for MacArthur to demand on October 1, with ill-omened precedent, "unconditional surrender." Then, confident of further vindicating the deifying chatter of his staff, he extended U.S. forces toward the Chinese border. He was certain that China would not intervene and, if it tried, its forces would be crushed. In late November, thousands of Chinese soldiers stormed out of the North Korean mountains where they had been massing secretly. Others swept across the Yalu River in a thrust south, a move that should not have been surprising given Beijing's fear that a U.S.-dominated Korea would threaten its revolution. The mostly American forces were tumbled back over the 38th Parallel and began the longest retreat in U.S. military history. In light of the possibility that they would be annihilated and all of Korea overrun by Chinese troops, more than half of all adult Americans said that they were ready to use the bomb against China should full scale war ensue.

On the peninsula, at least, the debacle already looked "full-scale." Military cameramen, rather than those working for U.S. television networks, filmed the lurid slaughter. Details of the rout were put before a horrified public by several brave journalists, including twenty-nine year old Marguerite Higgins, who showed Americans that a woman could be an ace combat correspondent, an incisive political analyst, and a mother. She would win a Pulitzer Prize for her work in Korea. CIA analysts were reporting to a far more select readership that Mikhail Suslov — boss of the Cominform (the enforcement bureau of Communist Party orthodoxy), editor of *Pravda*, secretary of the Central Committee, and reigning ideologue — believed that Soviet success depended largely on pitting the United States against China. Such a conflict could shake apart all the power structures except Russia's. "Will not the war in Korea now lead to complete disintegration of the Atlantic alliance and to international isolation of the United States?" he asked with statesmanlike concern.[28]

During late October, China had found it convenient to invade Tibet, prompting Truman and Acheson to approve efforts akin to extending the Truman Doctrine there as well, although with much fewer dollars. In Korea, however, the meat grinder started again. As this time it was turned by Chinese "volunteers," the allies were chilled to hear MacArthur talk of perhaps using the bomb against the "privileged sanctuary" of Manchuria. One young congressman, Lloyd Bentsen of Texas, simply urged Truman to drop an atom bomb on North Korea. To the allies, the entire U.S. leadership — not only the Supreme Commander but also Acheson, Harriman, and Dulles as well as hotheads on the Hill — looked like "avenging angels." The wearying pattern was being set for the strangely unsynchronized alliance of the next forty years, with the two sides of the Atlantic never feeling intense or flexible at the same time on the same issues. America never got it straight, complained Europe's dispossessed right and its fervent far left.[29]

In the midterm elections of 1950, both the Democratic Senate Majority Leader and Majority Whip went down in defeat but the party did not lose either House. The losses were said to be signs of outrage over Truman's efforts in Korea, as well as a result of Republican charges of Communist penetration. Democrat Lyndon Baines Johnson, who had served only two years in the Senate, became his party's whip. Two years after that, at age forty-four, he took the Democratic Leader's seat at the front of the chamber when his party narrowly lost both Houses. In short order, he also became a pivotal member of the Armed Services Committee, and the most powerful man in the Senate once the Democrats regained both Houses in 1954.

To underline the Communist threat without actually declaring war, Truman proclaimed a state of emergency in mid-December. It gave him extraordinary powers over industry and the economy, such as being able to take over any radio station in the United States. His State of the Union address the following month called for doubling the size of the Air Force, and the Defense Production Act soon arrived. Charles E. ("Electric Charlie") Wilson, president of General Electric, resigned his $275,000 job to head the new Office of Defense Mobilization at a salary of $22,500 a year.

Seoul fell to the Communists for the second time on January 4, 1951. "This was one of those times of panic when Congress loses all its native caution," reflected Rexford Tugwell sourly. "Matters about which it had been niggardly for years were suddenly financed with ridiculous lavishness."[30] A program more sweeping than anything Nitze had envisioned sprang forth. Military spending multiplied between 1950 and 1953, with Congress appropriating billions of dollars more to supply and stockpile war-making materials such as aluminum and copper. Taxes expanded and revenues jumped, with industry receiving $37 billion in deductions to help boost production.[31] The draft would no longer be temporary, and eligibility was lowered from 19 to 18, while the term of service was extended from 21 to 24 months. The armed forces doubled to three million men within the year. Certain export controls were reimposed. The Voice of America, which Congress had barely allowed to survive over the previous four years, was denounced on Capitol Hill as too faint and immediately transfused with $79 million. As always, it was hoped that other countries would do more in standing alongside the United States. The biggest boost in spending went for military assistance, not just to the NATO allies but also to Greece, Turkey, Iran, Southeast Asia (which largely meant France and Britain), and the Philippines.[32]

Every GI and Marine in Korea was backed by five tons of equipment and sustained by sixty pounds of supplies a day. With almost everything arriving by sea, ships had to be drawn from the two thousand vessels mothballed between 1946 and 1951. Thirteen carriers and two battleships also were activated — "the cheapest insurance policy in history," bragged the Navy.[33] Congress created the Federal Civil Defense Administration to establish community bomb shelters and to instruct people how to protect themselves in case of nuclear war. Dozens of how-to films were made and distributed. Their titles alone tell the story: *Pattern for Survival* (1950), *You Can Beat the A-Bomb* (1950), *Survival Under Atomic Attack* (1951), and the famous *Duck and Cover* (1951) with its cheery sound track.

The nation's economy took all this in stride. America had skirted the prospect of a recession earlier in 1950 to enter what Carl Sandburg called the years of "fat, dripping prosperity."[34] Productivity was humming; Detroit was setting weekly records; airlines were crowding the skies. National income was up to $267 billion in a boom akin to that of the 1920s, but on much wider margins. Federal spending, just 3 percent of GDP in 1940, was now 20 percent, with no apparent harm. War brought long-lasting innovation. Just as bargaining for pensions had come about as a way around World War II's wage controls, for example, management resorted to granting stock options to offset the war-driven top tax brackets of 90 percent. War also brought distortion. Although more than 100 million tons of steel a year were being cast at more than 100 percent of capacity, for instance, Washington demanded that the steel companies produce more. Overproduction became a step to be paid for down the road, as it added to the industry's problems of retarded specialization and long-term rigidity.[35]

No matter how robust the economy might appear, Americans were fervently looking for help. The NATO alliance had to be strengthened. The message was underscored by Eisenhower's appointment in late December as European Supreme Commander Allied Powers. He bridled at that initial title from the Joint Chiefs of Staff. Its acronym, ESCAP, was only one letter shy of what Europeans feared

America would do if Stalin turned on them. Instead, Eisenhower requested the title Supreme Allied Commander Europe, or SACEUR. He joked with Marshall, who had ordered him to Europe in World War II, that perhaps he should be called "Colossal Supreme Commander."[36] Truman announced that the understrength U.S. division "over there" would be reinforced by four full new ones, despite MacArthur's pleas to rush them to Asia. Implicit was the chilling issue of arming West Germany.

The State Department darkly warned the allies that only their own greater efforts could help to counterbalance any tendency in U.S. opinion to shift emphasis to the Far East.[37] Although America's buildup was creating worldwide shortages in raw materials, its industrial boom was feeding Europe's growth. Washington wanted to see some of the result turned into weapons, backed by what had expanded to some $5 billion in military aid to NATO members just for 1951. Some 80 percent of U.S. assistance to Western Europe would go to military uses. Yet cooperation often was lame. While Washington prohibited U.S. firms from selling items such as turbines and machine tools to Russia and oil and rubber to China (against whose forces UN troops were bitterly locked), the allies were filling the gaps. More amazing still, Britain and France were asking for spare parts of various types of machinery, copper, and other items under the Military Assistance Program to make up for exporting exactly the same materials to the East.

Recriminations flew, and Eisenhower (still looking at the short term) thought it "crazy to waste so much talent on this problem."[38] Not quite. The deadly costs of earlier indulgent exports were now being felt, as Soviet-made jets using British technology kept shooting American planes out of the Korean sky.[39]

The Korean War helped spotlight the great geopolitical question of the century: the rival claims of Western Europe and oceanic Asia on America's future. Senator Robert Taft offered a tempting alternative, agreeing with former president Herbert Hoover that the country must maintain an Air Force and Navy "armed to the teeth," while having "little need for standing armies." This was an alchemy of tradition, technology, and wistful geographic determinism, which would haunt Republican politics throughout the 1950s. The high-tech rationale for "cutting the continent's cables and drifting into some more friendly ocean," as Horace Walpole had long ago said about England, fell upon many receptive American ears. Wouldn't the otherwise healthy, self-sufficient U.S. economy eventually face ruin should it have to build forces against the sprawling Red Army, not to mention China?

Couldn't air-age weaponry be the Republic's shield? "America cannot create their spiritual forces," Eisenhower insisted, referring to the will and unity of Western Europeans — something he might have observed had never existed. "We cannot buy them with money." Material support and muscle, however, could instill a sense of confidence that might prevent such tests of the spirit. While Truman spoke of "new and fantastic weapons," it was left to the capable Robert Lovett, Marshall's deputy at the Pentagon and soon-to-be successor, to advise that there was no new inexpensive or magic way to win wars.[40] Just look at Korea.

At the start of 1951, about 270,000 U.S. and allied troops and around 235,000 South Koreans were fighting under UN command.[41] They were outnumbered three or five to one at the front (the enemy virtually did without support formations). Washington spoke somberly of a "planned fighting retreat." But the tide turned again, as the U.S. Eighth Army recaptured Seoul and returned once more to the 38th Parallel in March. Yet only with MacArthur's dismissal the following month, for defying Truman once too often in talk of bringing the war to China, would General Ridgway begin repairing the disaster without fanfare or blame. "Thanks to Mac's handling of the Eighth Army," he wrote thirty years after replacing MacArthur, "it was starved for ammunition, food, clothing, engineering supplies, etc."[42]

MacArthur's firing, and the fiery recriminations that followed, showed that war, cold war, uncertainty, genuine heroism, and leadership had not negated the civil authority hammered out with iron clarity by the Founding Fathers in Philadelphia in 1787. That was not going to change, even though everything else seemed to be. MacArthur rejected the view often ascribed to him that Asia was paramount. He said he could imagine "no greater expression of defeatism" than to doubt America's ability to confront its enemies on both sides of Eurasia.[43] The cautious and collective policies of Truman the failed haberdasher appealed to Americans more than the bold and belligerent ones of MacArthur. They cheered MacArthur from the heart, but weighed the dismal choices that governed their sons' lives, their treasure, and their homes, so fragile before atomic fire. They would not abandon Asia, but they certainly would not raise the stakes by risking a wider war. "We cannot scatter our shots equally all over the world," Acheson told the Senate in trying to limit U.S. commitments. "We just haven't got enough shots to do that."[44] Absent more extensive U.S. involvements in Asia, which would take years to develop, the vote went to Europe by default.

By the spring of 1951, the first of what would be around 400,000 American soldiers began disembarking at Bordeaux and La Pallice, moving to the advance base at Verdun, where farmers still plowed up hundreds of bones daily from the inferno of thirty-five years before. Surely this great deployment of so many Americans in the heart of Europe was necessary only until the allies built up their own strength and resolve. "We cannot be a modern Rome guarding the far frontiers with our legions," Eisenhower remarked with soldierly directness and dated geography. *Far* frontiers? France? "The ultimate cost [would] be excessive," he said, while asserting that no one in Washington "ever believed for an instant" that the U.S. presence could be other than for a few years. To that end, Washington even entertained, and quickly abandoned, the idea of a "Volunteer Freedom Corps" using Germans and other peoples in some form of Foreign Legion. Anything other than U.S. conscripts.[45]

In the summer, Marshall finally decided to leave Washington for the last time. Lovett, the man in government he most considered a friend, succeeded him. They were of vastly different backgrounds, but each had instinctively been drawn close amid the capital's crass manipulations. It was one of the two significant personal relationships for the country during the early Cold War, the other being between Truman and Acheson.

A certain sense of balance was lost with Marshall's departure. He had just completed fifty years of service to his country. Starting the journey as first in his class at the Virginia Military Institute, he ended up restoring order and confidence to the armed forces, as well as to the nation at large. He had been the calming figure of an earlier age, a pared-down citizen-soldier who was almost a statue pointing back to Revolutionary days. Many hated him, but it took a Douglas MacArthur to belittle him, and that very quietly. Marshall had maintained his authority amid the menagerie of egos that had directed the Allied drive to victory in World War II and those that had shaped America's postwar response to Stalin. Yet he could still exact from Dean Acheson as powerfully brief a summary of singular eminence as was ever given: "His goodness put all ambition out of countenance."

Marshall refused a likely $1 million offer for his memoirs, at least the equivalent of a $7 million book deal today. "The people of the United States have paid me for my services" was the gist of his reply.[46] His strengths and limitations lay rooted in the old Republic, which was necessarily passing away. As the *New York Times* reflected after the Cold War, "It is impossible to imagine George Marshall taking a job as a lobbyist for an arms maker or as a consultant to a foreign government or signing on to the talk show circuit."[47] He joined no corporate board and gave no paid speeches.

Also leaving the fight was a man of similar rectitude and purpose, though Marshall's opposite in manner and politics. Ernest Bevin had been the most dramatic, and probably greatest, foreign secretary in Britain's centuries of greatness. He was a harsh, sometimes brutal, overbearing, squat, bulge-faced man. Not generous in feeling, he nevertheless had the hostesses of London at his feet and many of the most aloof Foreign Office dignitaries wrapped around his finger. Churchill called him the workingman's John Bull. There was no fiercer opponent of totalitarianism. He died in the spring of 1951, a month after being eased out as secretary.

The challenge they had responded to in Korea had turned into a midcentury Passchendaele. In 1951, American dead and wounded numbered 100,000, most of them conscripts. During the bloody, seesawing first year and a half, the United States suffered casualties as high as during its first twenty months of combat in World War II — without the consolation of Midway or Sicily. By the end of the year, the *Times* looked over its shoulder and described the previous twelve months as "The Year of World War 2.5." The *Chicago Tribune* called it "The Franklin D. Roosevelt Memorial War." Polls showed that most Americans expected war directly with Russia "sooner or later."

Fighting to the death at the edges of the earth was something Americans had hardly bargained for during 1946 to 1950. Yet Kennan came to regard Korea as the sort of border conflict that they would have to get used to. To the surprise of the Foreign Office officials whom he cultivated, Kennan compared his country's agony to the tribal skirmishes that the British had endured on the North-West Frontier nearly a century before.[48] He was coolly reminded that those had been fought by professional soldiers. In any event,

U.S. resentment of its predicament swelled as the country's two most powerful allies justified their modest presence by saying that they were holding up the front in Indochina and Malaya.

✪

Throughout the Korean War, U.S. decisions were made with an eye to Tokyo. For instance, it was feared that lifting the self-imposed ban on bombing north of the Yalu River would lay Japan open to Chinese or Soviet retaliation. The *Nippon Times,* at least, was not too worried as U.S. forces streamed in and built new bases. It reported without irony that Japan was now "Pearl Harbor proof" against a surprise attack.[49]

The Korean War helped transform Japan's economy, shape trade relations, and corrupt its politics. Korea also brought a peace treaty that allowed a range of war crimes to be excused. Americans came to regard Japan less as an isolated place in need of redemption and more as a democratized ex-great power. MacArthur had valued Japan's loyalty as the most powerful evidence possible of the complete success of "his" occupation, going so far as to describe the average Japanese as a child — "a boy of 12 as compared with our development of 45 years."[50] Even Japan's Communists behaved impeccably, as eighty million people set out to play their part in the war. Japan's shipping was mobilized, with most of the landing crews at Inchon having been Japanese nationals from the skippers on down. The UN Command in Korea secretly used Japanese transport and railroad experts who had served on the peninsula during Tokyo's decades of brutal rule. Washington urged the recent enemy to rearm itself. A 75,000-man National Police Reserve was set in place, with Ridgway insisting that for "each dollar expended," Americans could "purchase more security through the creation of Japanese forces than can be purchased by similar expenditures in any other nation in the world, including the United States."[51] Japan, however, preferred reindustrialization, and its 1951 output returned to the pre–World War II level.

American military spending for the Korean War ignited what would be called the Japanese miracle. Not everything could be sent straight to the war zone from San Francisco and Seattle. Hundreds of millions of dollars in U.S. purchases far surpassed direct aid, as items ranging from electronic components to whole ships were commissioned and millions of more dollars bought munitions. Three thousand Japanese firms held U.S. military contracts.

For example, one struggling truck manufacturer, Toyota, received contracts to assemble jeeps. Japan's high-technology and export sectors in particular were energized. A nation painfully conscious of its special identity began taking advantage of the international division of labor, but without having to submit itself to anything like the acceptance of free trade, which is part of the logic of that division.

Japan's increasingly curious international role was taking shape. The previous half century of conquest meant that no nation was comfortable with a seriously armed Japan — except America, which, for a while in the early 1950s, hoped in vain that a carefully expanded Japanese armed force could set itself up as a barrier against Asian communism. Japan instead started enjoying the luxury of being able to concentrate virtually all its energy on business. The story of U.S. relations with Japan from here on is one of overly generous interpretations that likely would never have been made without the Cold War.

Such condescending attitudes as those displayed by MacArthur, reinforced by Japan's avowed dependence on U.S. protection, persisted through most of the Cold War, blindfolding America to critical realities of industrial competition. Even more than in dealing with Europe, U.S. preoccupation with defense issues blunted trade and other commercial disputes. Washington seldom used the fact that it was protecting Japan in order to pry open its markets.[52] The result, within fifteen years of the peace treaty, would be to help put Toyota and Honda on Main Street, with Sony and Panasonic packed in their trunks. Americans were right to be optimistic about Japan and the "Asian tigers" that would emulate Tokyo's trade practices, but their perpetually shifting attention in world affairs would soon make them unable to recognize what was afoot. South Korea itself would become masterly at milking the U.S. Treasury, as it too began developing a corrosive brand of crony capitalism involving high tariffs and huge conglomerates with intimate ties to politicians and the cheap credit they could provide.

America remained Japan's largest source of cash, and Washington was ready to offset Japan's loss of trade with Mao's China by welcoming whatever exports could be sent.[53] It also insisted that the highly reluctant Europeans open their markets as well, and forced them to accept Japan's entry into both the Organization for Economic Cooperation and Development and the General Agreement on Tariffs and Trade (GATT). Western Europe's memories of fierce competition from the 1930s were overridden by Washington's insistence on making Japan politically strong and economically dynamic. It was to be a major ally, not a dragooned client.

The Stainless Steel Kimono, an allegedly hilarious best-seller published in the early 1950s, reflects American impressions. The U.S. paratroopers whose experiences in Japan the book recounts compare this crowded, "smelly and strange country" to a brimming bedpan that they are designated to defend. Both they and the rest of America seem quickly to have forgotten its underlying strengths. In fact, there were good reasons for mercantilism. Economically, militarily, and culturally vulnerable Japan held itself to a basic self-sufficiency and kept its distance from a world it did not trust. To the classic foreign policies of island powers (understatement, lack of commitment, avoidance of enthusiasm, and separateness), the Japanese added a samurai emphasis on the subtlety that can turn an adversary's strengths against himself. In the early 1950s, they were known for high arts and pathetically cheap goods. They set out to startle a world that, experience taught, was easy for the bold and skillful to surprise.

Japan's vulnerabilities were nonetheless painfully apparent once direct U.S. financial aid ended following the formal peace treaty signed in San Francisco in September 1951 — a treaty that for fifty years would protect Japanese companies from suits by former prisoners of war. The dollar gap was bridged, seemingly only for the moment, by Japan's selling supplies for Korea and by payments from U.S. occupation forces. Inflation raged and trade showed no hope of even an unsteady equilibrium, as U.S. imports accounted for two-thirds of a yawning gap. The treaty also postponed the question of reparations until Japan's economy strengthened. Apparently, it would never be strong enough, since payments were never made. By contrast, Germany would be required to convey more than $80 billion between the end of World War II and 2005.

The security pact that accompanied the peace treaty stated that Japan would take steps "increasingly [to] assume responsibility for its own defense against direct or indirect aggression."[54] But such self-defense would require a level of armament that would contradict Japan's new (and American-inspired) constitutional pledge "forever [to] renounce war as a sovereign right." Once more, illusion reigned.

The Occupation of Japan ended in 1952. It had, of course, been tainted by corruption. Each month, GIs sent home a sum that exceeded their total payroll, and 800,000 carats of diamonds that the Bank of Japan had entrusted to the U.S. Army simply vanished. However, by 1952, every important component of the Japanese economic machine was in place.

It became easier to forget that Japan had visited a world-class holocaust on China, and although its processes were less methodical than those of the Reich, its hands were just as bloody. Not incidentally, 1 in 3 American prisoners of war in Japanese captivity died, as opposed to 1 in 25 held by the Nazis. But accountability might undermine Japan's determination and loyalty. So before departing, Occupation authorities restored political rights to nearly 200,000 Japanese who had been penalized at the outset and absolved Japan of claims for redress that might be made by individual victims. Even the truly guilty, such as Nobusuke Kishi, cosigner of the declaration of war against the United States were forgiven.[55] After the Japanese election in late 1952, 42 percent of the new members of the Diet's lower house were ex-militarists. In addition, Washington secretly involved itself in Japan's party politics to undercut leftist contenders. The CIA pumped more than $2 million into conservative campaigns during the April 1953 election, thereby beginning a habit that helped underwrite the rigidity of Japan's dominant party.[56]

With Japan looking stable in the aftermath of the Occupation, Britain and France could at least turn their full diplomatic energies to bending Washington's attention toward Southeast Asia. Surely, they urged while rattling their cups, America had an equal responsibility to help them defend Indochina and Malaya, with which Japan's future was intertwined. Acheson angrily saw the United States being suckered into financing France's war, with Paris behaving as if it were receiving only "an odd revolver or two."[57] To complicate matters, the deal surrounding NATO's creation had included U.S. guarantees to help build up French forces as solace for Germany's revival. There were unintended consequences. "While France relied upon mercenaries to restore her colonial estates," writes one historian of the early U.S. involvement, "in a broader sense the French Expeditionary Corps was a mercenary army, for America paid the bill for nearly all of them."[58]

That "the future stability and safety of Vietnam will depend on the Vietnamese" was understood by everyone in Washington — if not in Paris, which had chosen to tie down ten French divisions in an apparently endless war.[59] The Pentagon was fully aware of French incompetence and the waste of dollars. That was why, if further help was to be given, each of the service secretaries asked the State Department to demand that a U.S. military assistance group begin training the Vietnamese army directly. France opposed this step as intrusive, jealously guarding its colonies from American interference.

As if France's recalcitrance were not enough, the British were tireless in linking the fate of Indochina to Malaya and the world beyond. "With the loss of Indo-China," they warned, "the rot [will] set in and the whole of South East Asia must go." Once that happened, the argument continued, Soviet and Chinese influence would inevitably extend not just toward Pakistan and India but also into Iran and Afghanistan. Then the Americans would be sorry. Washington had to pay serious attention. In 1951, it went through another drama with London over the value of sterling, as Malaya remained Britain's single largest source of dollar earnings.

Churchill, who had returned as Prime Minister in October 1951, rehearsed all these points before leaving for America that Christmas. Indochina was the "keystone" to halting communism in Asia, and a U.S. role was essential to cementing it.[60] The State Department anticipated his petitions, reminding Truman that London had been trying for several years "to maximize American commitments to Southeast Asia." The Pentagon not only shared such skepticism but was even more "firmly opposed to any statement to Mr. Churchill" that might even imply a direct U.S. role, let alone sending soldiers. Not "a man, a ship or an airplane" would go to Indochina or Malaya.[61] Nitze, among other shrewd officials, had long been warning anyone in government who would listen not to "forget that the majority of Asians are infinitely alien to us," although he needed reminding, as in the Budget Bureau's critique of NSC 68, that it was ludicrous to classify as "free all those peoples whose governments oppose Russia." "Are the Indo-Chinese free?" asked the bean counters.[62] It was not only the difficulty of facing different races, cultures, and definitions of *freedom* that bedeviled Washington as it tried to figure out connections between war in Korea, Japan's prosperity, and upheaval in Southeast Asia. It was also the original haphazardness about what the country wanted to achieve in Asia, how it could do so, and what it would risk.

✪

In 1953, the short story "Top Secret" appeared in the magazine *Authentic Science Fiction*. In the story, a hush-hush factory is

urgently built outside a typical American small town. All the contractors are paid in cash. (Only one Washington institution does
that.) The townsfolk take it for granted that this is a government
plant enshrouded in "national security." It recruits brilliant engineers blacklisted for long-past left-front affiliations. No one asks any
questions. The public-spirited local paper runs an editorial titled
"Don't Stop, Don't Look, Don't Listen!" In fact, readers soon see, the
Russians have infiltrated respectable-looking businessmen who can
faultlessly pass for U.S. defense executives. The story ends with them
purposefully assembling atomic weapons on American soil — ones
that would be delivered, in an early portrayal of nuclear terrorism,
by mail. Might not the enemy find its most effective ally in America's
new, overdriven psychology of secrecy?

The investigations of 1950 to 1953 saw a shift in attention
away from the serious question of espionage and subversion to the
more subjective one of dissent. The United States had only briefly
before thought of itself as the object of systematic alien espionage,
let alone sabotage. Today, we regard the response in terms of
McCarthyism and blacklisting, but such distractions were performed against a backdrop of something more serious than many
people realized at the time. Even Joseph McCarthy, the forty-one-
year-old senator from Wisconsin, whose name has rightly become
synonymous with unsubstantiated smears, was onto something. He
had some sort of list from the House Appropriations Committee in
his possession when he gave his infamous February 1950 speech in
Wheeling, West Virginia, declaring that he had the names of known
Communists in the State Department. In typical McCarthy fashion,
however, he had no idea whether suspects from the personnel files
were still on the payroll. One person being paid turns out to have
been a Soviet courier, and it took another year for her employment
to be terminated.[63] Only days before the speech, Alger Hiss had been
convicted of perjury, the statute of limitations for treason having
expired.

Also among those traitors who were or recently had been at
work during this era were Coplon, Fuchs, Gold, Greenglass, Abel,
the Rosenbergs, Burgess, Mclean, and Joel Barr (who would become
a leading force in the Soviet computer industry). "For the unin-
structed public," novelist John Le Carré recalled after the Cold War,
"the spies popped up like gray ghosts scurrying across the world
stage."[64] The immensely publicized case of Hiss (code-named ALES

by his Soviet handlers) in particular became, in the words of Whittaker Chambers, a "permanent war."[65] As Hiss, the imperially slim State Department and Carnegie Endowment mandarin from Harvard Law School, defended himself with naked elitism and homophobia, Chambers — his heavy, shuffling accuser — had no idea of this war's duration.

Any spy with an ordinary sense of tradecraft could have operated indefinitely in the American system. Perhaps quite a few did. Although much of Moscow's World War II espionage network had been closed down by 1950, the 2,900 Soviet diplomatic telegrams that came to be known as the Venona intercepts contain the cryptonyms of some 140 Soviet agents who have never been identified. Men like Hiss might have been expendable because they were so unsubtle. Those who stayed in the dark as good Republicans and Episcopalian vestrymen will never be known. Had there been real militarists within the Pentagon or wilder Red-hunters in the FBI, they could have whipped up quite a frenzy by telling the country of the undetectable treason that lay behind those names.

In a classic early instance of dangerously ignorant compartmentalization, neither Truman, Acheson, nor Attorney General J. Howard McGrath apparently knew that U.S. counterintelligence was reading Soviet spy traffic. The CIA would not be alerted to Venona's astounding revelations until 1952. FBI Director J. Edgar Hoover kept the information in his personal vault. Organizing and studying the paperwork would continue until 1980, but Truman belatedly understood that Soviet espionage had riddled government activities at least into the later 1940s and likely remained active thereafter. Exposing some of the long-term methodical penetration would be done in the slapdash fashion of a republic that had never confronted anything like it.

Pervasive government secrecy — meaning the compulsory withholding of information not only from the public but from senior officials — was becoming commonplace, as fuel for theories among the paranoid and the merely startled. More materially felt costs of secrecy would for decades include grossly inaccurate estimates of foreign threats and the anger and waste that followed. Such secrecy also prevented Americans from learning about the extent of Communist subversion in the 1930s and 1940s and abetted the fever of charges, countercharges, and inconclusiveness that boiled up from 1950 to 1953 and several years beyond.[66] Among secrecy's other costs, ironically, was a reticence that prevented disclosing, and in several instances prosecuting, treason.

It was said of one of the principal traitors of the time that he had done what a country least forgives — he had made it put aside trust in its own people. Somehow, the State Department's entire Division of Eastern European Affairs had been abolished in 1937 and its library dismantled, likely after pressure from the White House. "Here, if ever," said Kennan, correctly, "was a point at which there was indeed the smell of Soviet influence, or strongly pro-Soviet influence, somewhere in the higher reaches of government." Later in the 1930s, Moscow had saboteurs on the West Coast docks waiting for orders.[67] As recently as 1940, $200,000 (about the income of 180 median American households) had been found in a former Republican chairman of the Senate Foreign Relations Committee's safe-deposit box when he died. Nobody knows how he got it, although the Soviets were far more adept at manipulating American isolationists than their Nazi allies.

This was prelude, as Truman knew. "Our chief concern," Arthur Krock of the *New York Times* recalls him saying just after the outbreak of the Korean War, "is the 'Trojan Horse Commies' in the United States." The president feared that vital parts of the country's defenses were vulnerable, particularly air bases. "Many of the 'fifty thousand Communists in the U.S.A.' in contact with the Russians," Krock reports the president fuming, "are bent on sabotage." Saboteurs and subversives, Truman said, might actually prevent bombers from leaving the ground. Supremely well-connected in Washington, Krock would later note privately that he "knew" that Hiss, as well as the Rosenbergs, were spies, perhaps from Venona. If America at midcentury endured an "unreasonable and unreasoning terror of Communist subversion," as Krock's successors at the *New York Times* casually assert today, such unreason not only started at the top but was found convincing by their savvy Washington bureau chief.[68]

Leaving aside a potential Communist fifth column, Truman was correct in judging that the American Communist Party was never an independent political organization and that its true believers were in thrall to Moscow. In 1951, the Supreme Court ruled that membership in the party was a crime, basing its decision on the premise that it advocated violent overthrow of the government and citing "the inflammable nature of world conditions." Thousands of people went underground, but spies kept surfacing.[69]

A grave and immediate scandal erupted during that year into antidiplomat, antihomosexual, and anti-British tremors when Guy Burgess and Donald Maclean, two British officials in Washington who had been trusted with the gravest allied secrets, defected to Moscow, prompted by at least one even better-placed friend. The Foreign Office at first explained away their absence to U.S. inquirers by claiming that "they merely went off on a prolonged toot to Paris." Suspecting that there was a "third man" among the moles, Walter Bedell Smith forced Kim Philby to return to London under suspicion. Philby insisted to his SIS colleagues that he was the innocent victim of a McCarthyite witch-hunt. He was not fired, as Smith had demanded, but placed on the sidelines, to be publicly cleared three years later. He then went on to become a field agent in the Middle East.

All politics is local, and U.S. counterintelligence would forever be bedeviled by rivalries. The FBI was at daggers drawn with the CIA from start to way past finish. To the seven thousand hardened G-men in the Justice Department, the Agency was just an academy to instruct Ivy Leaguers "how to marry rich wives."[70] At least the CIA had the sense to tell the White House that 90 percent of all top-secret information was already in the press, and implicitly that the Republic was still alive.

Even when treason was detected, retribution often could not be taken. Scientist Theodore Alvin Hall, for instance, had worried while working on the Manhattan Project about the dangers of an American atomic monopoly should there be worldwide depression after the war. So in early 1945, he and his recent Harvard College roommate had given Soviet agents the "implosion principle," a radically efficient way to ignite a nuclear explosion that the Soviets may have found vital.[71] Since the highly secret Venona decryptions could not be used in court, prosecutors were unable to build a case against Hall, who currently enjoys a leisurely retirement in England. Nor could a treasonous cipher clerk who told the Soviets of Venona's interceptions be tried for espionage, even at this time of supposed anti-Communist ferocity. He was sentenced to a year's imprisonment for failing to answer a summons to appear before a grand jury. Nor could Justice Department analyst Judith Coplon, incriminated in 1949 by material from Venona, be jailed. She was arrested while handing FBI files over to a Russian engineer at the United Nations, but her convictions were overturned because she had been illegally wiretapped. There was additional concern as to whether the FBI actually possessed an arrest warrant. She also enjoys a tranquil retirement. The early 1950s saw anything but "a machinery of repression that operated with devastating efficiency."[72]

To be sure, much was being spent in money and morality, particularly to protect U.S. atomic secrets. In 1946, for instance, during the first months of the AEC, decisions on personnel security were taking up so much of the commissioners' time as to impede their main tasks, not to mention that of the actual bomb builders.[73] In its first seven years, more than half a million people were investigated. Slightly over 1 percent were found to be of questionable eligibility, and less than a tenth of 1 percent were actually denied clearance.[74] In a 1953 review of classified papers, the AEC discovered that nearly a third of its "Top Secret" documents and another third of those rated "Confidential" or "Secret" could be declassified completely. The nation was getting wise to all this, and a cartoonist depicted AEC officials presiding over file cabinets stuffed with phone books and newspapers and marked "Top Secret."

Such a wilderness of scrutiny did not come cheap. "If the FBI does not have enough trained manpower to do this job," urged Senator Hubert Humphrey in speaking of the special agents who were required to be either lawyers or accountants, "then for goodness sake let us give the FBI the necessary funds for recruiting the manpower it needs."[75] Of course, the bureaucracy grew. One historian sympathetic to American communism accurately describes the Bureau as "a New Deal agency in that it shared the Roosevelt administration's commitment to big government."[76] By 1953, it had made some 26,000 field investigations under Truman's original sweeping executive order on "loyalty." That was in addition to 2 million "name checks" of federal employees overall, resulting in about 2,700 dismissals within three years. It had 109,119 informants at more than 10,745 "vital facilities," such as defense plants, research centers, dams, and telephone exchanges.[77]

Meanwhile, the real and active Soviet apparat did harm on at least three fronts: (1) through the pivotal information passed to Moscow by the likes of Philby and Hall; (2) through the capacity to obstruct decisions from inside the government, as Hiss had shown; (3) through poisoning the climate of opinion by the discovery of the faithlessness of those who were trusted. Philby repeatedly made sure that brave men parachuted into the East by the Office of Policy

Coordination ended up in the hands of Soviet bloc executioners. Nothing he transmitted to the secret police headquarters at the Lubyanka, however, would match the harm done by the consequent obsessions of the friend he betrayed, James Jesus Angleton, soon the CIA's avenging head of counterintelligence.

It is far-fetched to recall the anxieties and countermeasures of these days as a time of "terror of a widespread level" or of a "great fear" that can be spoken of in "comparison with the Soviet inquisition," or to equate, as did the CNN series *Cold War,* the epoch of Stalinism and the gulag with McCarthyism. Even a former SAC commander laments in one breath the "bloody purges and political inquisitions" that the Soviet Union and the United States endured, respectively, during these years.[78] Still, to describe early 1950s America as a time when wholesale purges of leftists and dissidents were occurring at every level of society is to echo Soviet propagandists, who until the end kept comparing the crimes of Stalin and McCarthy. For such a comparison to have any reality, one would have to imagine the Dulles brothers and Acheson as broken men confessing in open court to conspiracy with Beria right in Washington, D.C., or Joint Chiefs of Staff Chairmen Bradley and Radford shot in the FBI cellar, their liquidation not to become public until the first Bush administration.

It is equally far-fetched to describe Americans as hysterical, despite reckless charges raised in Washington about subversion (which were then parroted locally). Citing a Roper poll, Acheson believed that less than 1 percent of the public considered communism at home their chief source of concern. As if to underscore the issue's volatility, a Gallup poll indicated a high of 17 percent.[79] In any event, the subject of Communist penetration was newsworthy enough to be taken up for topical allusion among the sophisticated: a character in a *New Yorker* short story remarks about having no trouble obtaining a passport post haste, "I know a Red in the State Department who can get it for me." The supposed evils of anticommunism also began to insinuate themselves into intellectual life to such an extent that a recent supplement of the *Dictionary of American Biography* casually describes the great jurist Roscoe Pound as cultivating "anti-Communist and anti-Semitic friends."[80] The equipoise of iniquity between these two categories is interesting, particularly for those who remember the malevolent Stalinist insinuation "rootless cosmopolite."

There would probably have been a major struggle with domestic Communists no matter what had happened internationally. This was payback time: for what the Communists had compromised in the 1930s; for backing Joe McCarthy against Robert La Follette, Jr., in Wisconsin's U.S. Senate race in 1946; for infiltrating labor unions in communications and aviation; for the lists of anti-Communists, in Hollywood and elsewhere, who were denied work when Stalinist influence was at its height. What finally made McCarthy "McCarthyism," as Chambers himself knew in detesting the demagogue as a "raven of disaster," was the contempt for common law and common decency. McCarthy married opposition to widely known Communist tactics with a Midwestern detestation of foreign policy, particularly of the snobs and homosexuals who, everyone (at least in Milwaukee) knew, dominated the State Department. It was an attack initiated by outsiders against government; less so, as Acheson understood, a case of government itself on a rampage.[81] Once the attackers got some official traction, however, the internal security bureaucracies performed with enthusiasm.

Serious people, such as Diana Trilling, of the liberal weekly *The Nation*, would simply conclude that the investigations "weren't that bad."[82] Undoubtedly, there were individual tragedies on both sides. People lost their jobs, as did ex-Communist Sigmund Diamond of Harvard University, who could not clear himself with the FBI when ordered to do so by McGeorge Bundy, the new dean of Arts and Sciences, and David Fox, fired from teaching at Berkeley for taking the Fifth Amendment. But contrary to the legend that now makes a reprehensible situation sound much worse, many people also bounced back as injustices were corrected. Fox, for instance, arrived at the State University of New York later in the 1950s and eventually became graduate school dean. Ring Lardner, Jr., one of the Hollywood Ten, would win an Oscar for the movie *M*A*S*H*. Writer/director Abraham Polonsky, among others, bragged of having a higher income while on the blacklist than he had had before.[83] Alger Hiss had a chair in the humanities named in his honor at Bard College. By contrast, Chambers, whose action against Hiss cost him obscene defamation and his job at *Time*, writes in *Witness*, his 1952 classic of American confessional literature, "It [was] not the communists, but the ex-communists who have cooperated with the government who . . . chiefly suffered."[84] The studio police at Warner Brothers issued Democratic activist and Screen Actors union leader Ronald Reagan with a .32 Smith & Wesson because of death threats.

There "was a kind of droll aspect to McCarthyism initially," admits far-left historian Walter Schneir. Irony and drollness evaporated in 1953, however, when the unprecedented double execution of Julius and Ethel Rosenberg for espionage meant that "everything got serious."[85]

Throughout, the FBI painstakingly kept accumulating archives on seemingly everyone except the officers of the Daughters of the American Revolution: Arthur Godfrey, America's most popular broadcaster; Norman Rockwell; Groucho Marx; Helen Keller, whose 118-page file is only partially declassified forty years after her death; Albert Einstein; and Ronald Reagan. A years-long investigative vendetta was waged over the "hostility" of Senator Albert Gore Sr. for daring to criticize Hoover. More than six hundred heavily censored pages were gathered on Leonard Bernstein from the 1940s to the 1970s, replete with insights from his household garbage. "Between the CIA and the FBI," Bernstein would tell acquaintances after President Richard Nixon's enemies list surfaced, "I'm keeping at least a few people busy."[86]

No bureaucracy can thrive by dealing just with celebrities. Thousands of pages built up around one short, feisty, immigrant Hungarian Jew who, in the words of an FBI report, had "a facial resemblance to Lenin." This blacklisted screenwriter, Gordon Kahn, had refused in 1947 to tell the House Committee on Un-American Activities (HUAC) whether he was a Communist Party member. It was likely he was, but he was also more than likely a patriot, as shown in a line from a novel he wrote in the mid-1950s: "America makes no mistakes from which it doesn't recover" — a point proved within half a dozen years when the courts reversed their overheated rulings against the Communist Party and its adherents.[87]

Hollywood, capital of myth and hyperbole, put itself pretty close to the center of the white terror. As literary critic Leslie Fiedler observed, however, few really persecuted people bring further trouble on themselves by retailing the fact. Hollywood's solicitude tends to be even more selective than that of the rest of us. In 1997, the movie industry would put on a lavish celebration to commemorate the fiftieth anniversary of the refusal of ten aggressively pro-Soviet writers and actors to tell the Committee in 1947 whether they were or ever had been Communists and who else was or ever had been.

Performers such as Billy Crystal and Kevin Spacey reenacted bits of testimony. At this show, there was no clue of the Stalinist blood-baths of the era, and the "Ten" had apparently not been troubled by them at the time. "Witch hunt," scoffed Molly Thacher, a brilliant muse who knew of what she spoke in 1952. "No one who was in the Party and left uses that phrase. They know better." Only one of the ten, Edward Dmytryk, who went on to direct *The Caine Mutiny*, recanted and eventually cooperated with the Committee. He was among those Americans, he now explains, who "prized their country more than the party of Stalin and Brezhnev."[88]

Today, the *Washington Post* writes incorrectly of the Hollywood Ten's "possible Communist associations." A well-received TV documentary recalls the "many actors, directors, and writers [who] swallowed their pride, put aside their sense of honor, and named names."[89] Such naïveté adds to the popular belief that the superpowers were each evil in their own ways, that it was anticommunism that most threatened Americans, that fears of Soviet subversion were uniformly overwrought, and that so much of what Americans did to resist tyranny was wrongheaded.

Misrepresentations continue. Elia Kazan, long one of America's most accomplished film directors, could receive a career achievement award only in 2000 because industry guilds had remained vengeful for fifty years. He had felt duty-bound to disclose the names of eight of his Communist confederates from the 1930s, believing that breaking the secrecy would help destroy the party. What if Kazan, Dmytryk, choreographer Jerome Robbins, and others had been identifying hidden members of the American Nazi Party from those years? Who would write of losses of honor in attempting to break *that* "dangerous and alien conspiracy"?[90] There was no compelling reason, after all, for Chambers to testify against a former comrade, and many people would have lionized him if he had chosen not to do so.

At least the country never had to pay the price of letting anticommunism disrupt the Hollywood studios, which so valuably showcased American life to the world. Although the industry made pallid attempts to avoid producing "un-American" movies and the CIA played at producing a silly animated cartoon film of *Animal Farm* and a reworked version of *1984*, Hollywood, of course, ended up doing whatever was most profitable. Message movies were simply bad business.[91]

Some works of art, if not necessarily good, capture key aspects of their time. In *Big Jim McLain,* a heroic HUAC investigator (John Wayne) is distraught that one "Dr. Carter, professor of economics at the University," has been able to escape prosecution by taking the Fifth and return to campus "to contaminate more kids." McLain then turns to unearthing a Communist cell in Hawaii — against the poignant backdrop of Pearl Harbor — remarking to his soon-to-be-dead partner, "For once, our investigation is adequately financed." The Committee assisted the movie. It also spawned imitators. Always at the forefront of the nation's trends, California formed its own Senate Fact-Finding Subcommittee on Un-American Activities, which targeted Hollywood producers, screenwriters, and actors, as well as union leaders and other citizens thought to be Communist sympathizers. Twenty thousand people were spied on before the records were sealed in 1971. HUAC itself was not disbanded until 1975, its increasingly petty harassments backed by an annual re-authorization vote in Congress.

J. Edgar Hoover — the corrupt, nightclubbing tough guy who defended America from communism, bank robbers, and any sense of irony, along with his best friend, Clyde Tolson — could scare up whatever funds he wanted, privately admitting that he played on fears of espionage. But Hoover was angered by the Committee's sensationalism, not to mention its encroachment. It was the Committee, after all, not the FBI, that had exposed Hiss. Although he gladly made the FBI available for flattering anticrime movies, the director put the studio heads on notice that the entire subject of Communist subversion was a more serious business.[92]

Given today's impression of Hoover's domestic dispositions, it is particularly striking that, by 1953, the belief was widespread that "sexual perversion" was an inevitable peril to national security. The conviction that homosexuals were always blackmailable went unquestioned in government until the 1980s, not only inflicting injustice but also denying the government access to talent at a time when the nation needed it most. Canada, which had first exposed the Soviet spy rings, possessed its own prejudice in this regard. The Mounties formed a special unit, accumulated around nine thousand files, and deployed a device, developed with government money at Carleton University, that measured eye movements to "detect" deviants. They pursued homosexuals with a vigor that, when brought to light after the Cold War, was denounced by Conservative Prime Minister Brian Mulroney as "one of the greatest outrages and violations of human rights," which even "the passage of time . . . [has not made] any less odious."[93]

Bizarrely, homosexuals were also being expelled from the American Communist Party for fear that a vulnerability to FBI blackmail would endanger their comrades. For sheer self-destructiveness, however, the U.S. security bureaucracy was unsurpassed. It was not a question of communism or anticommunism. For example, mathematician and economist John Forbes Nash, Jr., whose previous work would eventually win him the Nobel Prize, was fired from his summer consulting job at the Air Force's Rand Corporation think tank after he was arrested in a men's room sting by the Santa Monica police.[94] Top game theorist and forthright homosexual J. C. C. McKinsey did not survive his 1951 expulsion from Rand; two years later, he killed himself.

All sorts of other expensive mischief began to take place in the name of resisting subversion. The State Department, for instance, enforced a fifty-thousand-name "lookout book" under the McCarran Internal Security Act, essentially a political speech test at the country's borders, which Truman had tried to veto. Vigilantly excluded were such threats to the Republic as actor Yves Montand (who had welcomed American Communist Party members in Paris, but soon called them "Red Nazis") and Arthur Koestler (who had been a Communist before writing *Darkness at Noon*), though not, as the legend of McCarthyism has it, Charlie Chaplin, whom the authorities wanted to question over his heterosexual amusements rather than his Stalinoid delusions.

More foolishly still, the act was a blanket exclusion of vaguely leftist scientists, such as French physicist Alfred Kastler, whose lack of a visa prevented his fundamental work in quantum electronics from being introduced directly to the United States.[95] Additional self-inflicted damage ensued with the forced repatriation of American-trained scientists to China. The politically suspect but uncharged Caltech professor and Pentagon consultant Qian Xuesen, among others, soon began working on his native country's bombs and missiles. As president, Eisenhower would use an executive order to extend Truman's 1947 initiative. Rather than assessing federal employees just for loyalty, after 1953, they could be dismissed for general reasons of "security."

A lot of time and talent also were being lost through harassment of government scientists. For example, thirty-eight air defense specialists at the Army Signal Corps Engineering Laboratories were suspended in 1953 for no reason but to please McCarthy's committee. A year later, other top scientists would quit, and outsiders investigating the situation warned that the labs risked being "incapable of carrying out their assigned missions."[96] At MIT, meanwhile, the chairman and deputy chairman of the Math Department were being investigated by the FBI; both were thought to have once been involved in Cambridge's own Communist Party.

Ever more arbitrary power was being given to the dimmest cadre of bureaucrats — those people handling security clearances. Soon one out of five Americans in a labor force of sixty-two million had to complete a loyalty statement or achieve some sort of clearance as a condition of employment, including one William Shonick, who needed to renew a state license as a dealer in secondhand pianos. Appointed Consultant in Poetry to the Library of Congress in 1952, William Carlos Williams failed to get clearance, and the post remained vacant for four years. Acheson summed up this insidiousness: "The authoritarian mind is not interested in a calculation of the cost of repression, or an appraisal of its effectiveness."[97]

Anti-Communist fears ultimately blunted some overdue concerns about civil liberties. Groups such as Americans for Democratic Action and the American Civil Liberties Union (ACLU) made compromises that they came to regret, spurring the disintegration of the Old Left of socialist aspiration and democratic radicalism and, for better or worse, hastening the emergence of a new liberalism, which adopted the political and philosophical assumptions of the center.

Reaction against Communist penetration probably contributed to the decline of American labor unions. A dozen were expelled from what became the AFL-CIO, as that brotherhood, otherwise dedicated to "aiding workers in securing improved wages," claimed to have "broken the back of the Communist Party in the United States."[98] With wages pegged to productivity amid a growing economy, few members cared about such internal political brawls or regretted the ouster of a large Communist-controlled union such as the Electrical Radio and Machine Workers, especially while the country was at war in Korea. One loss, however, was further delay in addressing racial discrimination, since the leftist unions had been leading the integration of American labor.

Particularly pernicious was the intertwining of anti-Communist insinuations with the civil rights movement, at a time when 75 percent of African-Americans earned less than $1,000 a year (less than one-third of what was deemed adequate to support a family of four). How many other citizens were reluctant to do more on behalf of equality because of the widespread allegation that these efforts were Communist inspired? After all, George Kennan was among those saying that it was the Soviets who were busy fomenting tension between "blacks and whites in America."[99] The charge was difficult to refute when nobody knew who was and was not a Communist and when the National Association for the Advancement of Colored People (NAACP) itself had to make delicate accommodations with the FBI. Truman's loyalty program had been so hastily conceived (as was everything dealing with the Cold War) that it was rife with abuse. Federal agencies, argued the NAACP's Denton Watson, used it to fire blacks who filed discrimination complaints.[100]

Even Thurgood Marshall, the future Supreme Court Justice and a towering figure in the civil rights movement, had to walk a fine line in defending the NAACP. As director-counsel for its Legal and Education Defense Fund, he described Communist penetration of the NAACP as the greatest threat within its ranks, insisting that the Communist master plan was to set aside black people in a forty-ninth state.[101] He cautiously shared confidential information with J. Edgar Hoover, as did the ACLU to demonstrate its patriotism. Yet Marshall was as much a target of Hoover's surveillance as were Martin Luther King, Jr., Roy Wilkins, Clarence Mitchell, and other giants of the movement. In 1949, the FBI zeroed in on Marshall's membership on the Executive Council of the National Lawyers Guild, an organization that the Committee on Un-American Activities had denounced as a Communist front. Forty years later, the Bureau had to pay up in a civil suit after being forced to acknowledge that it had tried for decades to disrupt the guild, which was never shown to have had Communist ties.

Not just racial antagonisms were being exacerbated by threats of communism, but also class, ethnic, religious, and cultural ones. Civil libertarian Nicholas von Hoffman writes of "the ongoing Kulturkampf dividing the society [since] the elites of Hollywood, Cambridge and liberal think-tankery had little sympathy for bow-legged men with their American Legion caps and their fat wives, their yapping about Yalta and the Katyn Forest. It was just too Catholic and kitsch."[102] These were the people who held huge annual Captive

Nations Day rallies across the country, which politicians of taste and sensibility avoided. They were fine examples, no doubt, of "the primitives" whom Acheson grandly disdained. Yet they were among the "responsible anti-Communists" — all those people dismissed as irrational and reactionary in Lillian Hellman's *Scoundrel Time*.

During these years, Hoover transformed himself from crime fighter to scourge of communism. As one former FBI assistant director concludes, with only slight Bureau chauvinism, the FBI "made the McCarthy hearings possible."[103] The amount of money and manpower that the Bureau devoted to tracking "subversives" remains classified — most likely out of embarrassment. Even the files on individuals are largely out of reach for them or their families. Nearly fifty years after Bartley Crum, the idealistic attorney for the Hollywood Ten, reluctantly began his own cooperation with Hoover, 5,000 pages of his 7,000-page FBI file cabinet are still withheld from his daughter because the Bureau considers them "top security."[104]

Give some people secret discretion, and they will abuse it. Perhaps such types are unusually drawn to bureaucracy and its intrigues. For example, the FBI knew the impotence of the American Communist Party because it had informants at the party's highest levels. Indeed, it was recording the serial number on every dollar bill brought in from Moscow. Gus Hall, the party's national secretary, had been convicted in 1949 for advocating the violent overthrow of the U.S. government. After jumping bail and being abducted back from Mexico, he was taken in chains from Leavenworth penitentiary to criminal hearings in New York. He would serve eight years. When he was transferred within the federal prison system, his lawyer frequently would not be told of his whereabouts.[105]

Just as vindictive was stripping J. Robert Oppenheimer of his security clearances in 1954, a personal vendetta by AEC chairman Lewis Strauss against America's most famous scientist and director of Princeton's Institute for Advanced Study. (Oppenheimer had consorted with Communists, but there is no shred of evidence that he ever showed disloyalty.) "The real shame," says Ann Marks, secretary to the head of the Manhattan Project and wife of Oppenheimer's personal lawyer, "was that Strauss knew full well Bobby would also be cut off from so much of what he loved in the universities."[106] Testifying for the prosecution was theoretical physicist Edward Teller, Hungarian émigré wizard and a key figure in inventing the atomic and hydrogen bombs.

Meanwhile, the FBI was embarked on racking up at least 23,800 mostly warrantless "black-bag jobs" (breaking and entering) that would continue into the mid-1970s.[107] While the Bureau was so preoccupied with uncovering Reds, its director denied that organized crime had a presence in America. "It wasn't that the F.B.I. had missed its shots at the top guys," writes a former special agent who finally infiltrated the Mob, "it had never *taken* them. . . . Against the truly organized criminals, the syndicates that controlled the construction gangs, the restaurants, the docks — the guys who added a fat percentage to the cost of living for most, if not all, Americans — we had screwed up big time." By 1959, the FBI had only four agents in New York City investigating the Mafia; around four hundred were dealing with Communist matters.[108]

During World War II, the United States had become involved in a flimsy entente with the Mafia against a common enemy, Mussolini. Then it made a deal with mobster Lucky Luciano to help bring order to occupied Italy. Now fantasy politics was giving the Mafia an even bigger break. As FBI director Louis Freeh would acknowledge before the World Economic Forum in the mid-1990s, the FBI has needed "untold resources" to compensate for the delay in prosecuting the Mob. For Hoover, organized crime was simply "a distraction from the enemy within, which was the Communist conspiracy."[109] Like McCarthy, who was so largely a creation of the press, Hoover took advantage of the career opportunities afforded him by the Cold War.

★

At the start of his last year in office, Truman estimated that the United States had provided around $60 billion since 1945 for the world's rehabilitation (the equivalent of about $400 billion today in a much larger economy). No matter how he calculated the sum, he called this commitment "the most important task of the Twentieth Century."[110] To him, the future was as full of possibility as were those years a half century earlier when the Wright brothers flew at Kitty Hawk. Who could have foreseen the future of aviation, he wondered, or have imagined that this farm boy from Missouri would command the U.S. Army Air Forces that flattened Germany and Japan?[111] But he was dismayed that more than three-quarters of the U.S. budget was being drained by national defense, and particularly by an inconclusive war in Korea.

Immense promise juxtaposed with fear of immense destruction. Hope lay in handling the dangers as cheaply and indirectly as possible, so that the country would be able to explore the wonders ahead. There seemed to be three ways of doing this: (1) trying all the harder to get friends and allies to do more; (2) ensuring that technology could substitute as much as possible for GIs; (3) using the CIA as a means of accomplishing goals quietly and cheaply. These anticipated efficiencies would be emphasized for the rest of the Cold War, although the purposes they served often remained unclear. This was especially so in 1950 to 1953, when the country heard the distinctly different views of Kennan and, once Eisenhower won the presidency in November 1952, of John Foster Dulles.

One way simultaneously to wage war in Korea, defend Western Europe, and "contain" communism elsewhere was to seek help from just about anywhere on almost any terms. Greece and Turkey, which had seemed to Washington far removed from the North Atlantic only three years earlier, were added to NATO in 1952, provoking arguments at home about cost and Russian reaction, which would be repeated nearly verbatim when NATO again expanded in 1999. The heavy-handed regimes of these two new allies made the entry of the dictator Francisco Franco into the common cause unremarkable. Spain could no more be excluded from U.S. assistance than could democratized West Germany. So a separate ten-year treaty of economic aid and military cooperation was concluded with Franco, helped by a $75,000-a-year lobbyist who was said to be getting him money faster than he could spend it.[112] In Spain, SAC set about building three major air bases, and the Navy began preparing a great port at Rota. Meanwhile, the U.S. Treasury paid out $1.8 billion in aid over the next dozen years, bearing much of the expense for modernizing Spain's military forces along the way.[113] SAC also secured access to air bases in the Azores, a group of islands in the Eastern Atlantic owned by Portugal, a NATO member controlled by strongman Antonio Salazar.

In addition to recruiting all sorts of friends to help share the burden, U.S. leaders naturally played to the nation's technological strengths. Military backing of high tech, after all, was bringing nationwide benefits. For instance, in the early 1950s, the Navy developed the world's most powerful transmitter, more than one million watts. The Navy's early work at Harvard led to large, high-speed digital computing machines. IBM soon added its own expertise to Navy research, and together they pioneered breakthroughs such as thin-film electronic circuitry in order to save space aboard ship. Nothing seemed to work like public capital when joined with universities and industries to explore the chasms of basic research. In 1950, the State Department established the post of science adviser to the secretary, which was later enlarged to the Office of Scientific and Technological Affairs.

Herbert A. Simon, the wayward political scientist and economist who conceptualized the emerging field of artificial intelligence in the 1950s, was one of the penetrating minds that Cold War money helped challenge. "I learned many things," he admits in his autobiography, "few more important than how to position the decimal point in a research proposal."[114] Nearly all the worthwhile grants were coming from government, with more than a hundred educational institutions receiving money from the AEC and nearly two hundred from the Defense Department.

As military-related R & D kept pushing ever deeper into academia, however, the sagacious Columbia University physicist and Nobel laureate I. I. Rabi paused to wonder what obliging oneself so thoroughly to public patronage might entail in the long run.[115] Few men were so reflective. Like everyone else, scientists were largely reacting — in this case, to government funding. Whereas it had once taken years to raise some picayune sum for a minor experiment, now they found that the sky was full of free cyclotrons. Everyone could win. And technical problems thankfully had to be tackled in a half dozen different ways to maximize results. That method, after all, had just been brilliantly exemplified by the Manhattan Project. So the United States undertook R & D that led to its buying a missile program *and* a new strategic bomber program, a missile submarine force *and* a surface Navy. No one knew what approach, if any, would be the decisive one.

Money could be found for seemingly any institution, even the most implausible. For instance, the Navy saw fit to contract with Catholic University to form the Mine Advisory Committee of the National Academy of Sciences and to deal with the highly unspiritual matters of helicopter sweeps and pressure munitions. Each part of government naturally wanted its own university relationships. The State Department, for example, lined up to support MIT-managed studies involving any of the sciences that could be harnessed for psychological warfare and propaganda — thereby furthering academic ties to the military and extending them to diplomacy and foreign relations.[116]

The most capable scientists, however, were rarely in positions to drive policy. Oppenheimer, after all, was not shaping the overall U.S. approach to science and defense; the ambitious H-bomb developer, Ernest Lawrence, was. Since Herbert Hoover had left office, there had not been any top U.S. political official with an up-to-date technological background — including AEC chairmen such as David Lilienthal, with a career in utilities, and Gordon Dean, a capable criminal lawyer. The egotistical, self-taught Lewis Strauss knew little of physics.

The great leaps in technology became the deathblow of reflection, postponement, and waiting to see how things worked out. Wartime fears, the intense secrecy surrounding nuclear matters, and the well-placed suspicion of Stalin's own progress guaranteed that there would be no tacit moratorium on the testing of a weapon that was thermonuclear (i.e., one that was based on the fusion, rather than the fission, of atomic nuclei). So Halloween, 1952, was followed immediately by the vaporizing of Elugulab, a Pacific island one mile in diameter. The power of the prototype bomb was about seven hundred times that of the atomic bomb dropped on Hiroshima, nearly as devastating as the incautious Senator Edwin C. Johnson had predicted. The physicists had constructed a working model of the stars and turned it on. Edward Teller, key conceptualizer of what insiders called "the super," apologized to colleagues for its destructiveness. So many people in Washington had been threatening to cut off money for the eighty-two-ton device if the test did not work, he explained, that its builders kept adding to the design anything that would make it more powerful.[117]

Teller's concern about return on investment is significant. There was reason to think that justifying the expense of the atomic bomb had been one of the pressures compelling its use at Hiroshima. Might the same consideration help precipitate use of a hydrogen bomb should worse come to worst? With the H-bomb, moreover, there was no theoretical limit to its destructive force, as it could be made as large as desired. It was no longer entirely science fiction to talk of blowing the earth's atmosphere into space or raising ocean waves that crushed entire nations.

Civilization-ending weapons shared the headlines with a seemingly unwinnable war of dugouts and hand-to-hand combat in Korea. A tempting alternative was at hand. Well supplied by professors and deans such as Bundy, the CIA's daring amateurs were believed to offer economy, exact targeting, smoothness, secrecy, and distance. Perhaps the country could exercise its power more or less remotely. America was institutionalizing a special kind of intelligence service. Pride of place was given to covert action rather than to espionage, let alone to crafting intelligence estimates. Between 1949 and 1952, the covert political action "office" created by Kennan had dilated from 302 staffers to more than 6,000, its budget swelling from $4.7 million to $82 million. In 1949, it had seven stations overseas; in 1952, it had forty-seven. All in all, by 1953 it accounted for 74 percent of the Agency's budget and three-fifths of its personnel. Almost $100 million was being spent annually on operations in Eastern Europe, about half of that on hopeless paramilitary activities.[118] That year, Allen Dulles — brother of John Foster, also a lawyer, and a stalwart of the Council on Foreign Relations, who had been in the Agency since early 1951 — succeeded Walter Bedell Smith as the first civilian director. Bundy had meanwhile helped to recruit a graduate student, World War II veteran Larry Devlin, whose Zelig-like career would become a fascinating reflection of nearly thirty years of CIA intrigue.

Allen Dulles's OSS adventures as station chief in Switzerland made him comfortable with activities that generals such as Smith and Truscott found "weird." Covert action would be applied almost immediately to diverting Chinese attention from Korea, while simultaneously taking the initiative in Southeast Asia. Given the right tactics and sufficient cash, Thailand might prove useful for both purposes. Between 1950 and 1953, $72 million in military assistance was shipped in, as well as around one hundred military advisers, quickly outnumbering the American missionaries there. It was the CIA, however, that furnished the police with even more modern weapons than those supplied to the soldiers.[119]

Truman had overridden Smith's soldierly objections to this adventure, which even included the recommendation to withdraw from Korea to preserve limited U.S. resources for Europe and Japan. The president then approved a CIA project to employ fragments of Chiang's armies that, after losing to Mao, had fled to Burma rather than Taiwan. Thai acquiescence was needed for supplying and concealing their CIA-backed invasion of Yunnan province. The Agency expected a million of Mao's new subjects to leap to arms, but only a few thousand unfortunates raised their heads. The "invasions" of 1951 and 1952 proved miserable failures. Moreover, as Washington discovered when trying to terminate the venture, it could not: it had bought enough time and given enough momentum for a criminal state to establish itself in parts of northern Thailand. As the stranded Chinese Nationalists turned to drug dealing, the corrupt and well-armed police ran interference for them and easily checked any other civil authority. What profited was the opium trade in the Golden Triangle.

Part of that triangle included the northern territory of contiguous Burma. The left-leaning government in Rangoon urged Washington to pressure Taiwan to remove the roughly twelve thousand Nationalist troops encamped there. It suspected that the CIA was backing them, which was true, despite the mistaken denials of the U.S. ambassador. Inanely, the Agency believed that Chiang's troops would be useful in preventing Burma from becoming too familiar with Communist China. Once Burma took the issue to the UN in 1953, the U.S. ambassador, a seasoned career diplomat, resigned in disgust over having been deceived. Left behind in the CIA's busy Rangoon station was an alcoholic operative and his family. That operative, Carleton Cecil Ames, formerly a professor at River Falls State Teachers College in Wisconsin, had been recruited into the Agency because he was one of the few Americans who knew anything about Burma's culture and history.

CIA subtleties and would-be statecraft fared no better in Korea. The station in Seoul had nearly two hundred Americans running covert action and intelligence operations behind the lines. None spoke Korean, its new thirty-two-year-old chief was dismayed to discover, and the "intelligence" being collected was bogus.[120] One hundred one of the Nationalist Chinese agents that the CIA parachuted into Manchuria between 1951 and 1953 were killed, usually on the spot. One hundred eleven were captured, as were two CIA officers, whose unmarked transport plane was lured over the Yalu River into a trap. The American judged the most senior, twenty-two-year-old Jack Downey, just eighteen months out of Yale, was imprisoned in China for the next twenty years, his colleague for nineteen.

With stalemate in Korea, hundreds of millions of dollars going to military assistance, and GIs returning to Europe, it was not surprising that many Americans were ready to reconsider their country's direction. After spending much of 1950 and 1951 on leave from the Foreign Service at Princeton, Kennan published a small, wide-ranging volume titled *American Diplomacy, 1900–1950*, which received considerable attention at the time and has since come to be regarded as a classic. He then accepted in late 1951 Truman's appointment as ambassador to the Soviet Union. Perhaps recalling his "Mr. X" mode, or knowing that Kennan had been instrumental in persuading Truman to establish the secret Psychological Strategy Board that year, Stalin believed that the appointment came at the bidding of anti-Soviet cliques, notably the Catholic Church, which Stalin, once an Orthodox seminarian, perceived as Russia's most dangerous enemy.[121]

Kennan's thoughts at this juncture are again noteworthy. His lucid prose addresses what America was trying to accomplish and whether it was capable of doing so. Finally arriving in Moscow in May 1952, he let other diplomats know that favorable letters from all sorts of prominent people showed that his book "macht schule," and that even Douglas MacArthur had modified his views to jibe with those the book expressed.[122] Significantly, American Diplomacy deals hardly at all with economic policy (so technical and so much the sphere of Congress) and instead primarily with the limitations of democracy. Instead of U.S. foreign policy being seen as an averaging of pressures, initiatives, and influence (as that of, say, the Quai d'Orsay or Whitehall usually was), Kennan portrayed the United States, in Lord Macaulay's terms, as "all sail and no rudder."

In American Diplomacy, in conversations with other Western diplomats in Moscow, and in all sorts of forums for decades to come, he condemned the legalistic, moralizing mentality to which he thought Americans fatally prone, with their weakness for such high-sounding themes as "a world made safe for democracy." To him, this was the critical cause of U.S. misconduct, as well as of the national hangovers of delusion and letdown in world affairs, whether in Europe or Korea. He wrote as that characteristically American type, the moralizing antimoralist. Yet in discussing "the American mind," he dismissed the fact that so much of America's energy, as well as its influence abroad, has lain precisely in offering the world slogans and even such morally charged objectives as "self-determination." The opening paragraphs of the Declaration of Independence are full of what nineteenth-century worldly philosopher Jeremy Bentham scorned as "glittering and sounding generalities." But a country whose title deeds they are finds it difficult to the point of inauthenticity to cut them out of its discourse.

In any event, nothing in Stalin's Russia was going to be affected by the soul-searching and second-guessing of a U.S. ambassador — particularly by a high-strung one who, the CIA's chief of the Soviet division recalled, asked for cyanide capsules in case he was arrested. Stalin lucidly foresaw that capitalist West Germany and Communist East Germany could live indefinitely side by side if each had twelve divisions, but he then lapsed into bizarre vaticinations that there could be no peace in the world until the Papacy abandoned its obsolete dogmas.[123] Had not New York's Cardinal Spellman, Stalin asserted to Italy's flabbergasted foreign minister, attended the Yalta conference in disguise, the better to harden Roosevelt against him? In Washington, it was difficult to imagine what common ground could possibly be established with this potent brew of diplomatic realism and demented projection. Failing such accommodation, what should the United States prepare for?

John Foster Dulles, named secretary of state soon after Eisenhower won the presidency in November 1952, had some answers. He offered a farewell message to the National Council of Churches of Christ on his resignation from its Department of International Justice and Goodwill. The message outlined a U.S. foreign policy that would "still follow the American tradition of openness, simplicity, and morality," but that could offer a new "dynamism" to counterbalance Soviet claims of social betterment. A deeply, at times sonorously, moral man, Dulles — the son of a minister and the grandson and nephew of secretaries of state — gave the impression of otherworldly absoluteness toward the ills of man. Only many years later would his son, a convert to Catholicism and indeed a cardinal, disclose that Dulles was indifferent to religion except as an instrument of the purely secular peace for which he fought. He was impressed by Arnold Toynbee's arguments about the withering of civilizations.

It was in this solemn light that the policy of "liberation" for Eastern Europe — highly controversial in the presidential campaign — was viewed. The "captive nations" were somehow to make their occupation too onerous to continue. They would be warmly encouraged by an America whose posture would remain solely defensive. In a swipe at Kennan, Dulles repudiated the "new realism propounded by some who deplore our legalistic-moralistic approach to international problems." As Edward R. Murrow dryly remarked on CBS, "It rather looks as though those who wanted a change are going to get it."

Dulles was in deep earnest. When Americans are in earnest, they lay out money, rightly preferring this to bloodshed and feeling that high utterances without material backing give no impression of substantial commitment. "I remember," he once let slip with unconscious revelation, "when I was a student at the Sorbonne, I used to go and riot occasionally."[124] He had indeed. This reflected his own lifelong romantic bent, which embarrassed his friends and put his enemies' teeth on edge. He had joined the "riot" against Anatole France's scurrilous *Life of Joan of Arc.* Covington & Burling's Acheson had not rioted. Brown Brothers Harriman & Co.'s Lovett certainly had not rioted, Dean Rusk, deputy undersecretary of state and soon heading the Rockefeller Foundation, would have been on the side of the *flics.* On the one hand, there was the unsettling fact that Dulles sounded like a machine. On the other, he would suddenly display almost manically ingenuous convictions. This apparent contradiction in a man at the heights of power kept many of his American associates off balance and did nothing to put the minds of war-sobered Europeans at ease.

Upon his appointment, Dulles was primed at last to squeeze Kennan out of the Foreign Service. He had the opportunity, since one of Kennan's emotional outbursts (comparing, while in Berlin, life in Russia to that under the Nazis) had given Stalin the excuse to declare him persona non grata. Kennan's wounds still stung a generation later. Yet near the Cold War's end, he had to acknowledge that Dulles had been "clearly well ahead of anyone else on the political scene of the day" in his "critical assessment of the developing problems for American foreign policy." Those qualities did not mean that Nitze, known as a Democrat and probably doing little to hide his opinion of Dulles as a "shyster lawyer," was any more welcome to stay.[125] Despite trying to hang on, he also was pushed out, although both men would be called upon as consultants.

Dulles was not Eisenhower's first appointment. That was Joseph Dodge, an able Detroit banker, to be director of the Bureau of the Budget. The economy was flourishing as Eisenhower and the "eight millionaires and a plumber" of his cabinet prepared to take office in January 1953, along with Republican majorities in both houses of Congress — for the second and last time during the Cold War. Western Europeans worried how deeply Eisenhower would cut defense spending and whether cuts might lower demand for their exports. (After the greatest depression in history, it was not well understood how consumer and business expansion in a dynamic economy could take up the slack.) America had to be a "good creditor," they insisted, and find ways to finance its trade surplus with the world. With Japan and West Germany now taking larger roles in the international economy, the Soviets chimed in: the inevitable disintegration of capitalism must accelerate as the battle for global markets became fiercer.

Churchill was in the United States just before the inauguration and met with Truman in Washington, as well as in New York with President-Elect Eisenhower. In friendly conversation at the White House, Churchill characteristically focused on soldierly details and worried that the United States was lagging behind Russia in building jet fighters.[126] He also probed for information about the H-bomb. Truman simply replied that its power was as much in advance of the Hiroshima weapon as that detonation had been to dynamite.[127] He also reflected on his years in office. The most difficult decision of all, he told Churchill, had been to intervene in Korea. The prime minister rightly responded that rescuing South Korea was far less important than its ultimate consequence — the overnight mobilization of America into a worldwide military power.

✪

As the elements that would make the Cold War so enduring were being set in place, there was one large price that Americans did not pay: they did not let the Cold War weave a net of consuming anxieties and preoccupations around great stretches of the nation's life. According to the Gallup poll's periodic question "What do you think is the most important problem facing the country today?," war or the threat of superpower war was never the biggest concern during the Cold War, even during Korea, when the fear was highest, at some 40 percent.[128] People tended to be more anxious about the economy and politics in general. The Cold War could be fought without even coming close to the "militarization" of America.

Rather than deforming the country, the American military was itself bent during the conflict's initial stage, and not merely into a civilian shape. Politicians (rarely soldiers) who tried to concentrate the nation's resources on military power were repeatedly confronted by Americans' inherent hostility to an overbearing state.[129] Yet today a large proportion of writings about the early Cold War insist that "militarization ha[d] reshaped every facet of American life," that at least "the military-industrial complex dominated postwar American life," and even that Washington, D.C., appeared to turn into a "military headquarters." Kennan writes about "the extreme militarization of American discussion and policy" of the time. To the extent that most Americans then alive think about this era, this is not how they remember it. Chroniclers of a "warfare state" or a "national security state" nonetheless fight hard to control this view of the past.[130]

With fighting in Korea ensuring that the Cold War affected more aspects of day-to-day affairs in the early 1950s, many people worried that the military might be playing too big a role in the country. Truman spoke about the possibility of America becoming a "garrison state" should it end up facing communism without allies. Eisenhower used the term often to resist demands for more defense spending. During the upheavals of the Vietnam years, the notion that America had actually become (or was fast becoming) militarized joined the hyperbole of the times. Today, the argument that militarism leached through America during the Cold War — and that it was responsible for grievous burdens until the end — is a familiar one.[131] It is, therefore, important to put such views into perspective.

Militarism and *militarization* mean a reverence for the cult objects of war, a belief that there are spiritual rewards in sacrificial violence for its own sake. They involve a political, as well as a cultural, preoccupation with military power, a process in which a society organizes itself for violence. And they are the idealization of a determinedly backward stage of life. There has never been a high-tech, basically decent militarized society.[132] By the time a people has adopted advanced ways to communicate and to move around, leadership has to either accommodate itself to expanded expectations or discourage and repress. The United States, as a cheerfully technocratic country, has always taken a different view of military matters than even the most civilian-spirited European states. If anything as rebarbative as militarism had operated in the land during any part of the Cold War, the reaction would have been fearsome. The dislike of being ordered about goes deep.

The Cold War was instead characterized by gigantic, safe, predictable institutions, as well as by unprioritized, expensive efforts. Paid activity could be its own justification for children of the Depression. This was anything but "internal imperial discipline" among the American people.[133] Nor is assigning military purpose to numbers in the budget enough to make it believable that Americans were militarized, though very likely it bureaucratized some of them. The country did not sacrifice its civilian, moneymaking, individualistic character, but it did neglect a lot of the more interesting and worthwhile ways to make money.

Prussian Field Marshal Helmuth von Moltke had declared that a world without war would be lost to materialism. No one of any stature in the United States dared utter anything like that, and, happily, few believed it. Theodore Roosevelt and Secretary of State John Hay, with their dismaying chatter of "splendid little wars," sounded truly archaic by the 1950s. Such doctrines exercised no leverage in Cold War America. The wealth, not the ferocity, of the United States became the classic subject for national assertion.

Militarism also means the cult of authority, the idealization of violence and military power, and the romanticization of uniforms and weapons. Instead, during the Cold War, respect for authority steadily diminished in every part of American life. The exception was the very American eagerness to defer in the short term to alleged experts. In this case, they were the professors and think tank denizens (many also serving as consultants to government when not actually in it) who began to consider the untested theories of ultimate destruction. A nuclear-age military simply could not be an end in itself, as shown by constant budget undulations and political pork barrels. The wider society effectively kept the military, its jargon-spewing civilian functionaries, and the overall pursuit of national defense at arm's length. In fact, the military and its civilian managers were employed to distance the rest of America from the world's turmoil. The moment the butcher's bills came in from Korea (then from Vietnam), there awoke a deep conviction that the system had failed.

"Snow wasn't snow in 1927," F. Scott Fitzgerald wrote in *Babylon Revisited*, "you gave it some money and it went away." A quarter century later, in another economic boom, Americans with varying success would try using money to distance themselves from totalitarianism, dubious allies, and so much else. They delegated responsibility for maintaining a congenial world. The wars of the first half of the century had been true contests between societies. The Cold War, partly because the civilian populations of developed nations were most of the time called upon to do so little except pay taxes, returned war to what it had been centuries before — a conflict of specialists, though very different specialists than of old.

This was mandarinism, not militarism. Between George S. Patton and Norman Schwarzkopf, no fighting commander's name acquired the resonance that accrued to alleged administrative geniuses such as Defense Secretary Robert S. McNamara. Throughout, the most jingoistic language, the most appalling recklessness, and the greatest of the many unnecessary costs by far came not from the military but from politicians and civilian advisers. Yet even these enthusiastic civilians could not reshape "every realm of American life," let alone be while les for imposing "the inescapability of war in American culture," as is now alleged.[134] Even the renown of provocative defense thinkers such as Oskar Morgenstern and Herman Kahn was likely limited to 10 percent or so of the upper middle class.

What occurred during the Cold War was very American and very modern. The country's relationship with its defense — spending lots of money, employing many highly credentialed people, and believing that one didn't personally have to think about the details of total war or even limited war — bought a decade or so of apparent comfort as the Korean War ceased. The dozen years between that war's end in 1953 and the escalation of the Vietnam War in 1965 were a respite, like that of a millionaire who can buy a period of contentment until some ghastly event shatters his happy life.

Certainly, the military and its suppliers became a huge interest. Although this combination was much bigger than, say, the highway interest, which was also growing, it was similar to it. The armed forces were deemed to be providing a necessary service. America's suddenly globalized military position was seen as an unavoidable cost — the greatest and grimmest, but not necessarily the most alien. It was put in the hands of businesslike people: eminent executives drafted to represent the civil power from above, polished young fighting men (slide rules in hand) rising from below. The military not only increased its historic trend toward specialization, but it generally followed that logic into a remarkable secularization of the profession of arms overall.

The technocratic military leadership aspired to by Thomas Jefferson (founder of West Point as an American polytechnical school) and George Bancroft (founder of the Naval Academy and preeminent nineteenth-century U.S. historian) eclipsed the warrior tradition. This was not always to the nation's advantage. West Point became the college that would produce the most major corporate

CEOs, definitely an insight into how far military culture has converged with civilian culture. Jefferson would have been proud. Would Washington have been? Very likely. But would Jackson have been, either as Tennessee rifleman or as vetoer of federal funding for the Maysville Road?

As usual, advertising offers a valuable index of prestige and glamour. When Madison Avenue wanted a he-man to sell cigarettes, they did not have the models portray SAC officers and NSC staffers; they had them portray cowboys. People in uniform were never used to impart an enviable tone in advertisements. On the contrary, advertising executive David Ogilvy used himself, in an earlier incarnation, as the anonymous diplomat in a car advertisement.

SAC's motto "Peace is our profession" was not exactly like, say, the *"Abajo la inteligencia! Viva la muerte!"* of the Spanish Foreign Legion. America was now buying big, corporate, bourgeois defense, almost interchangeable with the rest of the executive world. Even weapons production was outsourced to business, unlike during the country's first 160 years, when the federal government dominated such manufacturing. Already in *Guard of Honor*, a novel that James Gould Cozzens set in 1943, Colonel Mowbray is a visibly old-fashioned character in American life. The military no longer bred its own unmistakable types. Dwight Eisenhower looked as if he could have been a St. Louis utilities executive and indeed had been a football coach and university president. Officers' messes soon moved from the atmosphere of an Elks or Rotary Club — which had already disconcerted European officers and gentlemen in 1917 — to that of a land-grant faculty lounge as each service placed a priority on graduate degrees for its officers. The financial cost was great to the general society, but the cost to the military was greater still in terms of an increasingly bureaucratized attitude toward war.

The prime players in national security matters, including the civilian managers of strategy and intelligence, were making life-and-death decisions for their country, but they were doing so with much less fuss and flair than Teddy Roosevelt displayed when showing off the peacetime fleet. There was far more excitement, for instance, about battleships in 1907 than there ever was about nuclear aircraft carriers. By the 1950s, these immense cities-at-sea were miracles taken for granted. It took the conga dancing of fruitless superpower summits to excite public opinion about the greatest weapons of the age.

The feeling of emergency during these years was not continuous; it rose and fell like an angry sea. There was more than one moment of near panic, but no sustained preoccupation with war as follows naturally in a militarized society. The new forces of nature were indeed as impressive (it was hoped) to enemies as they were to philosophers and to those who believed they were buying peace. Preventive war was a doctrine for cranks, or at least for the most far-fetched Air Force contingency planning. As for any enthusiasm over "frontier wars" or "police actions," the very terms become repellent, with the advent of Korea.

The disgraceful actions taken early in the Cold War — the prompt reemployment of Nazi scientists, secret experiments on hospital patients, McCarthy's slanders, and official backing of assorted overseas thugs — were examples of specialism malign and out of control. But the country was not on a lynching spree. People wanted to hand responsibility over to the experts of war and science, hoping to "see nothing."

There are other telling indices of the perhaps surprising absence of militarism in American life. The books and journalism of these years that concerned war were ones of soldierly ordeal, and indeed of war as comedy or madness, overwhelmingly conditioned by World War II and not some imminent contest. *The Naked and the Dead*, *Once an Eagle*, *Day of Infamy*, *Mister Roberts*, and *Catch-22* are hardly the literature of destiny and triumph.

Writings on defense themes by various intellectuals were no doubt read — more certainly bought — by other intellectuals, but such insights did not form the thinking of educated Americans, let alone preoccupy them. Instead, the works of Vance Packard, David Riesman, and even John Kenneth Galbraith were sold at train stations and in the Book-of-the-Month Club. Writers such as these were earnest discussers of 1950s conformity, the new executive life, and the problems of (a very modest) affluence. Alexander De Seversky's *America: Too Young to Die* and even General Maxwell Taylor's *The Uncertain Trumpet* also sold well, but their concerns did not reach the ever-growing suburbs.

To be sure, metaphors of war were commonplace during the early 1950s, as they would be throughout the Cold War — and as they had been for centuries before the Cold War and still are today. Comparing various events to war is a standard form of human expression, whether in Christian hymns, in talking of wars on poverty or drugs, or in those old alliterations "war on waste" or "war on want." In the decades after World War II, the great theme of war made no conquering entry into general discourse. Indeed, a strong case can be made that talk of war and power made altogether too weak an impression on America as the country jumped from one short-lived yet expensive undertaking to another. Discussion was sanitized, as experts began to speak of a nuclear "exchange" or of "termination with extreme prejudice." This was hardly martial imagery. The billions of dollars being spent on the Pentagon were described as being spent for "defense," and even the historic title War Department was quickly changed to Department of the Army within the Department of Defense.

There were no stars, no charismatic enticers of America into militarism, and thereby into an accompanying repression — certainly not the professors who elbowed themselves onto the NSC staff, then returned to the classroom or sold their connections to foreign governments; not the lawyers and bankers who exercised their cycles of power, then emptied their club smoking rooms for years afterward with reminiscences. Millionists paid heavily for being so, as with MacArthur. Unequaled ambition and a sense of entitlement did not prevent him from being fired, ignored as a potential politician, and finally left to preside over the implosion of Remington Rand. Nor did veterans groups during the Cold War remotely maintain the moral, political, or social standing that they had attained during the 1920s and 1930s. No fully national politician of either party had a power base in veterans politics, with the exception of Louis Johnson, Truman's defense secretary, who had been pushed out after cutting too deep. Americans had been far more military-minded in the nineteenth century, when the U.S. armed forces (above all, the militias) set a tone for society, a note that faded away as America became both patriotic and grown-up.

Defense budgets might be huge, but their impact on the hearts and minds of ordinary citizens was surprisingly small. The United States began to confront the Cold War in its usual mode of facing immense obstacles, such as continental distances and unassimilated citizens, by spending heavily. The new world of transcendent defense outlays of the 1950s met its analogue in the massive social spending of the 1960s and was surpassed in the early 1970s.[135] After the initial military surge caused by Korea, the welfare state would expand much more robustly than the warfare state. No one,

however, speaks of the "socialworkification" of America as entitlements and transfer payments permeated society.

A lot of money was about to be spent on everything, not just the
military. Defense rationalizations hastened or streamlined some of
this spending, such as the Defense Highway Act, the Defense Education Act, and the emerging race into space. But the nation would
have reached for its checkbook to pay for most of this anyway. What
helped make budgets both bloated and arbitrary was the sense of
urgency, of what must be done now. The solution to every urgent
problem seemed to be money.

☆

Despite combat in Korea, the Cold War itself was not seen as a
struggle to be "won." The ultimate horror would be to fight the
Soviet Union, knock it out, and then try to meet the price of holding
it down (if enough of America was left to do so). By the time of
Eisenhower's election, most Americans thought they needed only to
hang on.

The Korean War was the defining event of the early 1950s and
the origin of so much of the outpouring of life and money that followed. What might have been the price had America decided not to
fight, as Lippmann and Kennan advised, and instead allowed South
Korea to be conquered outright? That choice would likely have
undermined much of what had been accomplished in Western
Europe. If Korea didn't count, Americans could reasonably have
asked, why should Berlin? It wasn't the South Koreans who had
been mortal enemies only five years before. Stalin had expected
South Korea to be quickly, if noisily, consumed. He had not anticipated U.S. intervention, let alone in such force. Had the Americans
remained aloof, he most likely would have been emboldened to
crack down on Yugoslavia, the only independent Communist state
in Europe throughout the Cold War. There, too, Soviet preparations
had been under way since 1948, soon after Tito had asserted himself ideologically.

The buildup of Eastern European forces backed by the Red Army
was to be completed in late 1950, according to the general in
charge of Hungary's preparations. As it was, an ominous war game
was undertaken in January 1951 that could otherwise have been a
prelude to yet another invasion.[136] Stalin's military manpower more
than doubled, and production of civilian machinery was frozen

while the Red Army benefited from the bulk of Soviet production. However, it was probably clear to Stalin that war in Korea had braced Americans for an attack in Europe, where the prospects of atomic bombs being used against Russia were greater. His eventual forbearance in Yugoslavia probably had at least as much to do with fear of another U.S. riposte as it did with Tito's renown as a mountain fighter.

For Japan, the consequences of South Korea's fall would have been equally stark. If America had permitted an armed and united Communist Korea to come into being, or if it had initiated a wider war, it is unlikely that Japan would have seen a fruitful destiny in remaining so lightly armed and quietly prosperous, even if the latter were possible.

The agony of the Korean War was multiplied by the UN allies having to fight a formidable but virtually unknown warrior people, as well as the Chinese. As North Korea's armorer, planner, and ideological parent, the Soviet Union was orchestrating the intensity of combat. A total of 70,000 Soviet pilots, gunners, and technicians were in the North by 1953, their commanders reporting back to Moscow's highest officials that they had downed 569 American planes.[137] This was likely an exaggeration, but Russians were killing Americans nonetheless. Soviet jets were said to be faster, Soviet tanks and artillery superior. Next time — a fatalistic prospect — Americans would at least not be outgunned as they bought time with blood.[138] Korea started off being called with mordant wit the "come-as-you-are war." It would soon be called the "forgotten war." And so it became for everyone but the bereaved. Not until 1995 would a monument to the dead be erected in Washington. Sitting on the Mall, directly across the Reflecting Pool from the powerfully dark sunken wall honoring those lost in Vietnam, the Korean War Veterans Memorial forms half of the stone diptych that is unconsciously America's sole public commemoration of the Cold War. The inscription on its apex reads, "Our nation honors her sons and daughters who answered the call to defend a country they never knew and a people they never met."

A lifetime before this war, Bismarck had said wearily that Russia was a force of nature, something one endured like bad weather. Yet every so often in the sweep of history, bad weather turns into an ice age, and here the deepening chill froze a pattern of negations and avoidances, of trying to dodge the expensive mistakes of the well-meaning, inflexible generation that had brought civilization to the edge between 1919 and 1939. By the 1960s, men would talk of "managing" conflict, but the early 1950s were still pure improvisation. The driving force of those years was not high policy, but the determination not to repeat past sins in doctrine and preparedness.

Never again would Americans allow themselves to be overrun on the battlefield, nor to be as unprepared in weapons and attitude as they had been for every world challenge since 1914. Never again would U.S. defense spending fall below $273 billion a year (in today's dollars). The nation was accepting the inevitability of "neither war nor peace" and inexorably preparing itself for the long haul.

4

Nothing So Simple

(1953–1956)

*It is easy to say that man is immortal simply because he will
endure: that when the last ding-dong of doom has clanged and
faded from the last worthless rock hanging tideless in the last
red and dying evening, that even then there will still be one
more soul.*

William Faulkner, accepting the Nobel Prize, 1950

The Cold War was not preoccupying most Americans, as had the
two world wars or the first desperate year in Korea. People went
about their business. The inconclusive armistice that Eisenhower
reached in Korea during June 1953, however, reflects how complicated the world of "neither war nor peace" was becoming. Neither
new leaders in Washington and Moscow, nor additional allies, nor
an expanding economy, nor terrifying new means of intimidation
made America's role any easier. It was never as simple as people
hoped to substitute technology, money, and secret manipulation for
more direct engagement. Puzzling new places and strange new
people captured the headlines, such as Dien Bien Phu and the Viet
Minh, an umbrella group of anti-French nationalists with the
handle held firmly by Communists. At the other extreme of modernity — and even easier to imagine than what would begin to unfold
in Southeast Asia — was the literature of apocalypse that arrived
along with the hydrogen bomb.

Nowhere else in history has the dance of death shadowed a society so growing in wealth and in every possible mode of safety but

one — the prospect of sudden obliteration. American prosperity was joined by the sense that all this success could be blown away, more literally and more finally than had so many hopes in 1914 and 1917, 1929, 1933, 1941. . . .

The little Florida town of Pat Frank's *Alas, Babylon* pulls itself together after nuclear war and, having found the ability to survive, faces "the thousand-year night." The faithful in *A Canticle for Leibowitz* sing in determination as they leave earth to reseed humanity while the second nuclear holocaust completes what the first began. In another story, Ted Sturgeon's simple soldier discovers all those he loves dead or dying of grief and nuclear fire. Having disarmed the doomsday machine, he says wearily to the future, "This time you'd better get it right." Nevil Shute's best-seller *On the Beach,* about the last remnants of mankind in Australia preparing to succumb to radiation, was followed by the Gregory Peck and Ava Gardner movie. But perhaps most chillingly, in "Later Than You Think," two octopuses discuss the wasted land civilization they can now explore. Ironic, muses one, that they had had visions of the gods who named them and created them, and of those gods' terrible apocalypses. But this final tragedy, they had brought on themselves. Oh, their name? Rat. Humanity had already been wiped out eons before.

While such writings began to enter the popular culture, Washington did not know that Moscow, at the time of Stalin's death in March 1953, had a much smaller arsenal than assumed. It contained fewer than 10 atomic bombs, none deployed, rather than the estimated 150 or more. In August, however, everyone was transfixed by the sudden arrival of the Soviet Union as a thermonuclear power. Moscow's H-bomb detonation was far more efficient than the first U.S. one, and it therefore could be crafted as an actual "bomb" about a half year ahead of the Americans'. Whether to the man in the street or the new administration in Washington, the implications of the explosion were terrifying.

Over the Pacific, whole islands were seared out of existence as the United States conducted its biggest blasts ever from a growing stockpile of bombs, with deadly poisons falling on the innocent from thousands of miles away. Britain had finally staged an atomic test off Australia in 1952. Churchill publicly wondered whether God might have wearied of mankind. Bertrand Russell, the World War I war-resister who in 1958 would be a founder of the Campaign for Nuclear Disarmament, cared deeply for peace and knew more than most people about Leninism and logic. He now drew the hard conclusion and seemed to call for the United States to use the nuclear weapon to enforce world order.[1] Science fiction was not looking all that fictional.

Civilization, writes Eric Hoffer, rests on "hope and maintenance." The Cold War began to drink deeply of both. For the United States, the domestically sunny, prosperous years of 1953 to 1956 were accompanied by storm clouds covering the rest of the world. The dread of surprise attack and apocalypse, as shown in the literature of the day, became worse as technologies advanced. With the H-bomb, a sense of precariousness arrived, as reflected in such desperate rituals as training children how to respond in the event of Armageddon.

Yet perhaps the worst hatreds would diminish before they fossilized into the type of historic enmities that Americans believed haunted the Old World. Maybe there was a chance, with Stalin dead only forty-four days after Dwight D. Eisenhower was sworn in as president. Conceivably, the madness would wane, and the Soviet grip might loosen on Eastern Europe. Moscow settled inflammatory territorial claims against Turkey and Iran. The State Department detected an attempt to return "to the conditions that existed under Lenin as distinct from the Fuhrer character of the U.S.S.R. under Stalin."[2] Phrases such as "Malenkov's molasses" (after Premier Georgi Malenkov, who a dozen years previously had purged the captive Baltic nations for Stalin) and, a couple of years later, the "Spirit of Geneva" (after the first summit since Potsdam) began to percolate in the West. By contrast, people could sensibly assume that much blood would be spilled before the Kremlin's wolves determined who would lead the pack.

Not every cause of disruption originated in Moscow. Eisenhower's inaugural address included a fateful phrase that conflicted with much of what he and John Foster Dulles actually believed about the force of the "rising peoples." In the pitting of "lightness against the dark," he spoke of freedom conferring "a common dignity upon the French soldier who dies in Indo-China, the British soldier killed in Malaya, the American life given in Korea." After years of patiently explaining what was to them obvious, the British, French, and even the Dutch finally detected the triumph of what they viewed as common sense in Washington. Eisenhower, taking unspoken office as alliance leader, was subordinating his role as

American statesman by buying into two allied arguments — why they could not do more on behalf of the UN forces, and why the United States had to back their colonial duties, as if those were synonymous with what Americans were still dying for in Korea.

Otherwise, people literally went about their business. Around 40 percent of Americans could not name a single country the Soviets occupied, nor did they bother to keep tabs on who Stalin's successor might be. A national debt of $256 billion (with total federal spending of $78.6 billion) was alarming to them, and due significantly to America again being at war. Some theorists might explain military spending as a form of social policy, not only stimulating the economy as a whole but also benefiting industry and innovation. The Republican bankers and businessmen whom Eisenhower appointed to his cabinet, however, knew it was a sinkhole. Regardless of the effect, what is remarkable about these years is how this huge reallocation of the nation's product and public purse occasioned so little controversy.

First, this chapter shows how the new president attempted to change the dynamics of the preceding six years by making overtures to Moscow while trying to impose economies at home. Second, it discusses how fleeting "successes," as in Iran and Guatemala, ended up being tragic, and how "spending millions to save billions" (as Eisenhower put it) in Indochina laid the groundwork for America's greatest Cold War disaster. Third, we explore how nuclear weapons, which some people thought to be a solution to such draining entanglements as the Korean War, began imposing their own open-ended costs. Fourth, we trace how all this momentum introduced emergency-laden public projects of unprecedented enormity in the name of national defense. Finally, the argument is made that the weight of being a "world political-military power" kept getting heavier precisely because no one was thinking about building an empire. Americans were showing not the manner of Clive of India, but of Mr. Toad, that eager collector of fitful enthusiasms.

On the Somme during World War I, British soldiers forlornly sang, "We're here because we're here because we're here because we're here." Despite strong allies, cutting-edge technologies, and supposedly deft secret operatives from the best schools, American soldiers, sailors, and airmen were nonetheless "over there" — not just in France and Germany but also in the mountains of "frozen

Chosin," on the Greenland ice cap, in the Persian Gulf, and eventually in the South Vietnamese jungle.

✪

The embodying figures of the Cold War begin to appear by 1953. Eisenhower, who looked back longingly to the days when only the Army Chief of Staff had a government car and when other senior officers were simply allotted tokens for the trolley, had a deep sense of the wastefulness of war. The young lions were meanwhile pacing, as Vice President Richard Nixon and Senator John Kennedy awaited their times of greatness. For the power-minded of the next generation, public expenditure was inextricably entwined with personal fulfillment.

Eisenhower's reputation was that of a conciliator, one of the few national leaders in the electronic age who seems to have taken close to a malicious delight in his capacity for incoherence; a figure out of the small-town, small-church past, acclaimed for his "Tom Sawyer grin." Tom Sawyer, it would have been worth remembering, is the supreme American trickster, and small communities (just like the upper echelons of the old officer corps) can be more viciously competitive than larger, impersonal ones. Eisenhower presented a personality to the world that it took another generation to disentangle: the extremely able, indeed shrewd master of deadly practicalities and the apparently bumbling civil politician; the reader of westerns who, when pressed, showed himself to be surprisingly well instructed in history. He clearly found this confusion useful, as clever people celebrated their intellectual superiority to him, while thrusting people stressed their greater decisiveness. What counted to Eisenhower was that he was in command. He was a cold man, but he lacked the chilly self-respect of a George Marshall. Unlike Marshall, he was always impressed by money.

Foreigners were startled to hear the president referred to as *Mister* Eisenhower on the radio, in contrast to General de Gaulle or Marshal Stalin or Tito. Unlike after World War I, when some people clung sedulously to their military rank, the end of World War II brought a determination not to carry things military any further. "Colonel" Dean Rusk or "Captain" McGeorge Bundy were not to be found among the rising young leaders. It would have been pretentious for someone to present himself under such trumpery. What America was undergoing was not "militarization"; it was unprecedented *politicization*. The new president symbolized anything but "a military gaining in stature," as the explainers of American militarism argue today.[3]

Eisenhower was the apostle of managerial calmness. The movement toward management — teachable, rational, reassuring, consolidating, and fundamentally predictable — was the gift of American supercorporations to the Cold War. To the Department of Defense, he sent the impressive Charles E. ("Engine Charlie") Wilson — electrical engineer, labor union member, and president of General Motors. GM was the business equivalent of the Defense Department, the biggest entity in its world, and the largest defense contractor. Now Wilson opened the bitterly fought campaign to get a "bigger bang for the buck" out of the Pentagon. "We believe Uncle Sam's big old pocketbook has been open just too wide," he insisted, as the administration dismantled the industrial planning apparatus imposed at the Korean War's outset and began facing Democratic criticisms of its defense cuts.[4] He immediately axed forty thousand employees from the payroll, drawing on the management theories that business consultant Peter Drucker had introduced to GM during the war. From 1954 to 1960, defense spending would fall 25 percent to consume "only" 59 percent of the federal budget. A million soldiers, sailors, and airmen would be let go, only half attributable to the truce in Korea.[5]

At the same time, Eisenhower brought new talents to Washington, though from predictable places. Undoubtedly, there were many other people of different backgrounds around the country who possessed equal ability and public spirit. Yet there was no time for meticulous national recruiting. Senior appointees had to be identified quickly irrespective of fairness or finding the best. Planes, ships, tanks, missiles, assistant secretaries, and dependable cabinet members were needed *now*. Respectable and familiar men at the Council on Foreign Relations could again contribute. A significant part of foreign policy making continued to be limited to a small elite, as it would be for about fifteen more years. Such invidiousness may have nurtured an unfortunate attitude in an ever-better-educated democracy: other highly qualified citizens could influence little of what was going on at the top.

Eisenhower's was also the first Republican administration in twenty years. Despite the commercial and government-reducing priorities with which the Republican Party has long been associated, the national spotlight remained on political events. The *New York Times* front page, for instance, continued to be the domain of public men — politicians, diplomats, and brass hats. There was no daily business section, no weekly science section. These matters kept being subsumed by politics, a cost in creativity that carried over from the Depression and World War II. The Cold War gave pride of place in national affairs to politicians and generals rather than to the scientists and entrepreneurs who were truly transforming America.

From the start, the tone of the Eisenhower administration was one of sobriety. This was no time to experiment with political and social change. It was a joke during these years that the United States was indeed run by a junta — General Motors, General Electric, and General Eisenhower. George Humphrey, CEO of the Mark A. Hanna Company, a far-flung conglomerate with a supremely Republican name had been appointed treasury secretary. He could persuasively recite every argument for budget balancing and sound finance at the drop of a hat. It seemed as if vaunted American mass production had created a process for stamping out CEOs and high government officials: solid, aging, stress-proven men who were experienced, Protestant, humane, and distinctly children of an older America.

Eisenhower added both the secretary of the treasury and the director of the Bureau of the Budget (forerunner of today's Office of Management and Budget) to the National Security Council. "You can't provide security just with a checkbook," he instructed Congress. Such phrasing is usually a preface to further demands, but here he was a literalist, as he sliced nearly $5 billion from Truman's final Pentagon budget.[6] Combined with "Engine Charlie" Wilson's promises of further cuts, defense-related stocks plunged on Wall Street that spring.

The demand for tax reductions was vigorous, since the bite on profits and other investment income had become far bigger than the New Deal ever dreamed of. Some taxes had diminished at the end of World War II, only to be restored during the Korean War. Eisenhower immediately abolished Truman's wage and price controls. Still-high defense and foreign assistance spending prevented even deeper tax cuts. Hopes that the conflict would moderate were encouraged by saccharine initiatives from Moscow, as anti-American propaganda rapidly toned down. Until then, Russian attacks had been so virulent — unceasing fabrications of U.S. germ warfare, "Gestapo" outrages, and concentration camps in Korea — as to have likely precipitated a break in diplomatic relations during the prenuclear era. A man truly ahead of his time, Soviet Ambassador to the United Nations Jacob Malik had already told U.S. delegates without apparent sarcasm that he hoped Washington would invite the Soviet Union to participate in NATO, especially since, he regretted to say, it was proving to be a bone of contention between the two countries.[1]

Weeks after Stalin's funeral, Eisenhower made his own move for peace. Speechwriters Charles Douglas (C. D.) Jackson, Walt Whitman Rostow, and Emmet Hughes focused on the convictions of that older America embodied by the man in the White House — a country where prosperity was the reward of work and initiative, not state management and emergency-driven spending. George Kennan also was consulted as the speech went through two dozen drafts. "The land where hatreds die," as Stanford University's first president had called the Republic, was a refuge in the new world from the crimes of the old. America would be shown as seeking peace, as well as being able to protect it. Eisenhower noted:

> Every gun that is made, every warship launched, every rocket fired signifies . . . a theft from those who hunger and are not fed, those who are cold and not clothed. The world in arms is not spending money alone. It is spending the sweat of its laborers, the genius of its scientists, the hopes of its children. The cost of one modern bomber is this: a modern brick school in more than 30 cities . . . two electric power plants, each serving a town of 60,000 . . . two fine, fully equipped hospitals. This is not a way of life at all. . . . It is humanity hanging from a cross of iron.[8]

Three million pamphlets of Eisenhower's speech were distributed throughout Western Europe and Latin America. One hundred thousand handbills in eight languages were given away in New Delhi. The text was sent to 921 West German newspapers and magazines. It was broadcast hourly over every channel used by Radio Free Europe.[9] A new institution was established, the U.S. Information Agency, in order, the president said, quoting the Declaration of Independence, to "submit facts to a candid world." The Soviet Union and China were unimpressed. "Red Empire Crumbles" West Berlin's mayor cabled an American friend, as strikes erupted in Czechoslovakia and riots spread across East Germany in June. "Do the men of the Kremlin think they can long rule by means of the bayonet and the tank?" he demanded incredulously. Well, yes. The protests were crushed.

A cease-fire was reached in Korea, almost exactly along the lines where the fighting had begun three years earlier. The president believed that the atomic bomb could be adapted tactically and that it would be "cheaper, dollar-wise," to use it in Korea than to continue the bloodletting. The NSC also endorsed Pentagon plans to use nuclear weapons against China, "from Shanghai all the way north," including "Peiping" (as China's capital was called with deliberately insulting archaism).[10] Eisenhower quietly let "Peiping" know just that — unless the fighting in Korea stopped. At the same time, he ordered the bombing of a series of North Korean dams, releasing catastrophic floods.[11] The fighting did stop. Other than those of South Korea, the casualties of America's allies who had rallied to the UN cause ended up being relatively modest: around 3,000 dead and 15,000 wounded. Approximately 400,000 South Koreans had been killed, and as many more were wounded or missing. North Korean and Chinese casualties were put at 1.5 million.

As for the number of American dead, the vague body count shows how oddly this war came to be remembered. A bogus figure of 54,246 service member deaths was used until the end of the century. On the war's fiftieth anniversary, the *New York Times* breezily noted "an estimated . . . 30,000 Americans" dead. By then, the Pentagon had corrected the record to 36,516, no longer lumping together all the noncombat fatalities that the military had suffered outside the Korean theater during the war's three years, including those in car wrecks from Germany to California.[12] For decades, many accounts also overlooked the missing. Of 8,177 prisoners thought to be held in North Korea, only 4,482 returned. How these unaccounted-for prisoners became nonpersons is one of the era's most unsettling mysteries. There were also the mained, including Allen Dulles's only son, Allen Macy Dulles, who never recovered fully from having a mortar fragment penetrate his brain.

Atomic threat seemed to have worked in Korea. Such weapons appeared to offer a way of substituting technological primacy — in the classic American way — not only for expensive manpower but also for the protracted, draining agonies of these types of wars. To

Treasury Secretary Humphrey, military spending was a necessary evil but otherwise an utter waste that added nothing to the country's wealth.[13] If it was, in fact, U.S. nuclear striking power that "kept peace in the world," he concluded, "all the rest of these soldiers and sailors and submarines and everything else . . . could drop in the ocean, and it wouldn't make too much difference."[14] The price of relying on nuclear weapons, however, was seriously underestimated. This was a consequence of both the fog of institutionalism and the failure from the first to account for what economists term "externalities" — such as hundreds of billions of dollars in radioactive cleanup costs not calculated until the Cold War's end.[15] The financial equation, as with so much else in the Cold War, was very different from what it appeared.

Despite the supposedly cheaper New Look" emphasis on nuclear retaliation, Eisenhower warned that the country must be prepared to "continue, for as long as necessary, a state of limited defense mobilization." John Foster Dulles spoke of being committed for "the long haul." For many critics, this dedication was insufficient. Today, it is easy to forget that throughout the 1950s, it was primarily Democratic liberals who advocated spending more on Army divisions, carrier fleets, and fighter wings, as well as on strategic bombers and missiles — a "strategic" weapon, in the U.S. definition, being a long-range one that could strike Russia from afar. Many Republicans insisted that U.S. forces in Europe should return home, a point Eisenhower disdained, since that would destroy "European morale."[16]

The New Look, one critic noted, could be compared to the local police deciding to use "blockbuster" bombs against citizens who failed to shovel snow from their sidewalks.[17] Illinois Governor Adlai Stevenson, Democratic candidate for President in 1952 and again in 1956, bitingly described the New Look as national security in the large economy size. The obvious question, asked by Democrats and U.S. allies alike, was how the administration thought it might deal with what were called "little wars" if its preferred response was nuclear. Eisenhower, contemptuous of that horrible term, offered an all-too-glib answer: If the country could win a big one, it could certainly win a little one.[18] His prestige overrode any suspicion of illogic. In effect, the New Look was not all that new. Eisenhower had essentially returned to the nuclear-centric pre–Korean War defense strategy of the Truman administration, although one more reliant on allies.

Eisenhower aspired to maintain high employment without the deficits and inflation America had endured under Truman. Never having lived in a big industrial city before becoming president of Columbia University, he was unconvinced that the country could sustain the versatile, globally deployed, conventional as well as nuclear armaments of a superpower at the same time that Americans expected their unrestricted civilian economy to keep growing. Nor was he disposed by experience or temperament to grasp the compounding effects of technology and individual consumption on productivity. Almost everyone else also underestimated the vitality of a consumer democracy with huge resources for innovation. Unfortunately, Eisenhower was more strongly positioned to give important form to his misunderstanding.

He enjoyed economics: he read reports, studied the financial pages, and had a sound understanding of statistics. Yet he reflected his times. Without that pervasive sense of limitation, he could probably have presided over much greater economic growth than 3 percent a year — whether or not more money was devoted to the military, as critics on his left increasingly demanded. What if another 1.5 percent of inflation had been steadily allowed? We now know that around 4 percent inflation can be adjusted to indefinitely, but at the time, an inbred fear of easy money combined with anxiety about immense Cold War outlays to impose a ceiling on expansion. With Eisenhower firmly believing that managing prosperity was a component of national security, this was no time to consider economic policy alternatives.[19] At least defense spending would be held at 10 percent of a growing GDP. How was that target arrived at? "Oh, it was a nice round number," recalled Secretary of Defense Wilson. It could have been 9 percent; it could have been 11.[20]

Among the widespread beliefs of these years was the conviction that government spending provided the dependable countervailing "demand" that stood in the way of renewed depression. John Maynard Keynes had tried, with mixed success, to convince Franklin Roosevelt that this was the way out of the wretched 1930s. Ultimately, the spending came with World War II. Keynesian policies presupposed poorly functioning markets and people who would just not spend enough. In "mature economies," whatever these might be, there was a tendency to save much more than to invest, precipitating stagnation at best. A civilized man with a fine mathematical education, Keynes had thought of neither war nor consumption as forces that would push countries into the sort of dynamic economic future on which America was embarking.

By the 1950s, the possibility of a country actually saving itself into ruin was entering popular wisdom, as in Mark Clifton's 1952 story "Crucifixus Etiam," which logically carries the argument beyond the planet. In brief, the fear that "goods will pile up . . . big depression on Earth follows" justifies expensive settlement on Mars. A neo-Keynesian rationalization then began to surface. It explained defense dollars as the only practically available, politically accept able, and, above all, consistent stimulus to social development. National security requirements, and the industrial production that met them, could be an automatic and more or less welcome pump primer. Thus, the United States was expected to soar on the wings of a truly "military Keynesianism." Past wisdom was again being drawn on, in a strikingly different context.

Amazingly, many well-informed people still believe that "a half-century [of] defense procurement" has somehow been "an engine of American industrial growth," or that "the expenditure on armaments . . . fuelled the American economy" through the postwar boom.[21] They conclude that devoting all those trillions of dollars to building weapons plants, establishing bases, and stationing hundreds of thousands of troops abroad "made the affluent America of the Cold War possible" — or, more foolishly, that "the Cold War helped make America rich."[22] The ideologically inclined write of a "war-sustained U.S. economy," or even a "permanent war economy," in which defense spending elevated aggregate economic activity.

"Military Keynesianism" has been discredited, as has so much of Keynesianism itself. It offered a compelling perspective on 1953 to 1956 only because a few years previously, between the Depression and World War II, government spending had indeed been a crucial stimulus. Sadly, the notion would linger. But even in the early 1950s, it did not make sense. "Military Keynesianism" is a hypothesis that assumes the fallacy *post hoc, ergo propter hoc* (after this, therefore on account of it): unprecedented economic growth supposedly followed unprecedented military spending in magical consequence. In that case, however, Japan and West Germany should have gone bust, while overarmed Latin America should have been a showcase for the twenty-first century.

Today's commonplace notion that Americans had to be willed by government into spending during these years shows how distanced many scholars have become from the ways their own country operates. In fact, it was consumption-driven expansion that made U.S. defense outlays at this level possible, rather than the reverse. Amid the 1953–1956 great leap forward into a consumer society, people were clearly going to be buying more and more in any event.

To be sure, the military was funding important innovation. By 1953, for example, half of Bell Labs' R & D for transistors came from the Pentagon, with transistors quickly going into televisions, stereos, cameras, and computers — in addition to radar systems. But military backing was never "vital for the transistor's success."[23] At a time when the new technologies of affluence combined with wider education and relatively open trade, it is impossible to imagine 160 million Americans sitting on their wallets or otherwise turning their backs on the miracles of technology. The magazine *Popular Mechanics*, for instance, had a huge circulation in the 1950s.

There may have been other, more peculiar reasons for people to spend freely. People hope, build, and save less when they believe that their children will inherit less of a future than offered their parents. Consciously or otherwise, fears of Armageddon may have made Americans less willing to husband their earnings.[24]

Better-invested talent and capital would have been required for the country to have grown faster during these years. Those were precisely the resources being lost, since military spending is a notably inefficient form of investment. If public money has to be spent, it is better directed to building roads and airports, worker training, or anything that reduces the costs of production, as opposed to bombs and bullets, which are virtually useless in terms of productivity. Before people could devote their time and money to other ends, however, Washington was deflecting much of their effort to the struggle for the world. A lot of this sacrifice was necessary, but it was not otherwise beneficial.

In describing the America of these years, it has become popular to exaggerate the clout of the largest U.S. defense contractors, such as GM and GE. More so than today, these companies and their kin produced for both military and civilian consumers. Yet to describe them as "militarized giants of weapons production" that "no one dared cross" makes the burden sound even costlier than it was.[25] In fact, the biggest defense contractors were "crossed" all the time by anyone who wanted defense cuts, including Herbert Hoover and his two beady-eyed commissions on government reorganization, Senator Robert Taft, Treasury Secretary Humphrey, and his successor, Texas lawyer Robert Anderson, fresh from tightening up the Navy Department. In periodic examinations of contracting procedures, congressional committees were compelling some of the country's most powerful corporations (GM, Westinghouse, and the Martin Company, for example) to disgorge millions in overcharges. Industrialist Howard Hughes was excoriated before the Senate for allegedly fleecing the government. It takes more than selling to the military to be militarized. The only militarized aspect of these bureaucratized behemoths were the security requirements for their defense plants. For instance, the fact that Navy shipbuilding "spelled pork barrel politics in capital letters" during the Cold War represents the standard unlovable mixture of civic boosterism, personal ambition, and floods of public money that characterize any large federal program, but not militarization.[26]

Although defense spending has been grossly exaggerated as a factor of economic stability after World War II, it did afford a certain underpinning of expectations and confidence to a Depression-damaged generation. We now know that modern economies can generally work efficiently without tax money being pumped into them. Once we distance ourselves from the 1930s-conditioned attitude that government spending was essential to 1950s prosperity, it is clear that the United States was wasting whatever percentage of GDP it was spending on defense above the minimum needed to confront the Soviet Union. Of course, that minimum can never be known, but it was probably a lot less than was spent. So much more could have been accomplished with the difference.

The cost of defense should be seen as imposing limitations on the lives of ordinary people rather than hastening modernization. This is true no matter how conspicuous the achievements — the technological triumphs of aviation, the computer research, the billions spent in the South to help lift that region out of poverty. America's efforts to maintain order abroad and consensus at home began to acquire much of the character of what Jeremy Bentham called a "sinister interest" — sinister because it appeared good and useful, honestly believed itself to be so, and robotically pursued so many objectives ever less rewarding, even for itself.

Despite pressures to spend, the Republicans were looking with colder eyes not only on Defense Department extravagance, but also on the seriousness of Western European efforts at self-protection.

The allies had reason to worry that, with the Republicans, they were facing the America of Taft, Hoover, and the *Chicago Tribune*. To them, this was "the United States of industry and commerce," ready "to reduce and consolidate her commitments to a burden which could be carried as capitalist insurance," determined to decide alone how "to use her massive retaliatory power."[27] The country more or less wielded its power with a light hand, never insisting on subservience from its allies, but purely private feelings of how America was being taken advantage of could erupt.

Dean Acheson's impatience with America's NATO allies had become notorious. His frustration was shared, though less fiercely displayed, by Charles (Chip) Bohlen, a self-possessed and down-to-earth aristocrat who embodied the best qualities of the U.S. Foreign Service. Most of his classmates at Harvard, when he graduated in 1927, had wanted to go into business and make a fortune. Not Bohlen, although later he could not remember why he had settled on a career in diplomacy. His father was moderately well off, and the family had traveled widely through Europe. His grandfather had been ambassador to France. Like his contemporary George Kennan, a very different man from a very different background, Bohlen selected the Soviet Union as his specialty, although he was never sure why. Two dozen years after joining the Foreign Service, and right after brushing off absurd insinuations by Joseph McCarthy, he became Eisenhower's ambassador to Moscow. Like Acheson, his detachment from ambition made him highly skeptical about the great men in public life. Also like Acheson, he could become pretty nasty when drunk.

A previously untold story about Bohlen is significant in showing how the most informed Americans, not to mention those on the hustings, were getting fed up with the allies for not doing more for themselves. Their colonial wars and garrisons might appear useful to some people in Washington, but they did not compensate for disappointing contributions on the front lines — whether that was the 38th Parallel or the border between East and West Germany. Moreover, allied leaders — in particular, Churchill, given his love of summitry and his suspicion that sooner or later thermonuclear weapons would be used — seemed all too eager to strike a deal with Stalin's successors.

During August 1953, Bohlen stopped in Frankfurt en route to Moscow, where he had arrived early that spring as Kennan's replacement. While dining with the British deputy high commissioner, he began drinking heavily and, as the evening progressed, unburdened himself of extreme bitterness at the unseemly desire of the allies, particularly Churchill, to compromise with Moscow. "If I got the instructions, I could go down any day to the Kremlin and fix things up between the USA and the Russians," he told his disconcerted hosts. "There is nothing the Russians would like better." Since the allies criticized almost everything Washington did concerning Moscow, Bohlen continued, they shouldn't be surprised if the Americans simply cut a deal with the Kremlin and shook themselves loose of their expensive hangers-on. Apparently, Bohlen also claimed that he might soon receive orders to negotiate precisely along such lines. He added that he would certainly be warmly received. Weren't the Soviets far more interested in an arrangement with the Americans at the expense of any other countries than in doing a deal with another country against America?

The next morning, Bohlen apologized profusely and implored his hosts to forget the incident. Fat chance. The whole episode was promptly relayed to London, reinforcing the dread — one of the few sentiments uniting Western Europe — that America would somehow work a disimperial masterstroke and go back to fish in the Mississippi.[28] Constantly reassuring these NATO allies meant putting more soldiers, more families, more bases, and more nuclear weapons into Western Europe. Several hundred thousand GIs plus dependents, as well as thousands of pilots and Air Force personnel, would sit there into the 1990s, marginally calming such fears as Bohlen had stoked. Perhaps most damaging to U.S. interests, the Army would have to pivot its training, doctrine, and equipment around the ominous prospect of fighting about one hundred (when mobilized) Soviet bloc divisions composing the Eastern European coalition that Moscow put in place by early 1955. NATO had twenty-five.

Yet what became known in the West as the Warsaw Pact could not compare to the alliance America had created, however rancorous. The Pact was by no means a "mirror image" of NATO, as some scholars have stated, nor was NATO "basically a mirror image of the Warsaw Pact," as President Bill Clinton strangely claimed. Russians now acknowledge that this military order, directed from Moscow, was a ruthless instrument of Soviet oppression.[29]

Meanwhile, Eisenhower kept reminiscing about the austerities of Coolidge's administration, when paying for European goodwill and effort was inconceivable. At least he could stop the wilder spending on items he knew about. He reduced the Army's budget by $2.2 billion and released sixty-eight thousand men from the Navy in fiscal year 1954, then dispensed with sixty-five thousand more sailors in fiscal year 1955. He knew how to joust with the military chiefs, how to head off their end runs to Congress, and how to counter "secrets" leaked to reporters "proving" that more money was needed for yet another indispensable career-enhancing program. He knew how to cut, he could persuasively claim, without slashing. But he worried that one day, another man would sit in his chair unschooled in a game he had spent half a lifetime preparing for.

✪

J. D. Salinger's 1954 story "Just Before the War with the Eskimos" depicts two intelligent upper-middle-class women contemplating a messy (but not conspicuously nuclear) future: "Who knows whom we'll be fighting next, or when?" To these women, their country's worldwide involvements appear nearly irrational as America becomes entangled in ever-stranger places: Iran, Vietnam, and (closer, if no more familiar) Guatemala. Despite such citizen skepticism, powerful men saw good reasons for all this. To them, the world at large appeared full of dark hatching places for communism, as the increasing disorder of Europe's empires kept jarring their nerves. For example, Indochina's fate really might be inseparable from Malaya's. Malaya, along with Iran, was central to Britain's economy, which was intertwined with Western Europe's defense, which was inseparable from France's military contribution, which was thought to hinge on Indochina. The world looked as if it had come full circle, and arguments could be made for U.S. commitment almost everywhere.

Some of the reasons for involvement, as perhaps in Iran, look persuasive. The trouble arises from the indiscriminate, short-sighted ways in which U.S. efforts were applied. Only rarely did someone cut through the clichés: "What do you mean by the '*survival*' of democracy in South Korea?" snapped Robert Cutler, a Boston investment banker and as close to a professional mean Yankee as the upper executive branch has ever seen.[30] He was the first to hold the new post of special assistant to the president for national security affairs, part of Eisenhower's quest to improve bureaucratic procedures. Few realized that Cutler's was a truly exemplary question, necessary but insufficiently asked, let alone answered.

Despite recent blunders in Korea and Southeast Asia, the CIA increasingly appeared a clever supplement to depending on wayward allies and spendthrift generals. So additional secret cash came forth from both government and U.S. corporations: in the Philippines from Coca-Cola; elsewhere from United Fruit or oil or mineral interests, conveyed via the secretary of state's younger brother Allen Dulles. For instance, Dulles offered Colonel Edward Lansdale, an advertising man before World War II, $5 million to jigger the Philippine presidential election. That legendary operative cabled back that he could sway it for $1 million.[31] Only in the 1960s would such activities come to be rationalized as part of "nation building." In the 1950s, they were believed to be counterpunching. But the blend of corporate money and secret government operations was on its way to becoming septic.

While France's plight in Southeast Asia worsened, the most dramatic counterpunch of Eisenhower's first year was in Southwest Asia, where Britain's future appeared to depend on Iran. Even more so then than today, Iran was a land little known to Westerners. For half a century, Britain (preferably in league with czarist or Bolshevik Russia) had determined Iran's rulers while it relied on the country as its largest source of oil. If Iranian oil was lost, there might come another collapse of the pound, with Western Europe choking for want of energy, or perhaps becoming more dependent on radicalized miners unions.

The Shah's rule was jeopardized by the rise of a popular and fiery prime minister, Mohammad Mosaddeq, exactly the kind of well-meaning nationalist demagogue behind whose eccentric facade hard revolutionaries might move into place. By 1953, powerful men in Washington, as well as in London, were insisting that Iran was about to deliquesce into chaos followed by communism. They could imagine no alternative, and they may even have been right, since that was the only movement in Iran with self-confidence and a coherent agenda. Two years earlier, Mosaddeq had confiscated Britain's refineries — the empire's largest single overseas investment. Washington restrained the British from gunboat diplomacy, since violence would have made it all the easier for Moscow's influence to take hold. While Mosaddeq rode high as the national hero, the British simply shut down their facilities. All oil exports ceased. If

Western Europe was to resist the real pull of communism, London argued, something had to be done to make the oil flow.

The Soviet Union was standing by to help as Iran's throttled finances resulted in chaos. Taking their cue, the British smoothly let Washington know that if they were pushed to compromise in Iran, they just might withdraw from the entire Middle East, as they had threatened to do from Greece. Helpfully, their Secret Intelligence Service (SIS) began sowing bribes and building arms caches in Tehran. The chief of the SIS and some convincing colleagues got themselves to Washington right after Eisenhower's election, equipped with a blueprint for counterrevolution. George Kennedy Young, son of a poor Scottish grocer, recipient of an MA in politics from Yale before the war brought him into intelligence, was the SIS man responsible for the Middle East. He persuaded the CIA to help implement the plan.

For the Americans, Kermit Roosevelt, grandson of TR, ran the Near East and Africa Division of the CIA. He was "a courteous, soft-spoken Easterner with impeccable social connections," Kim Philby recalled, "the last person you would expect to be up to the neck in dirty tricks."[32] Also called "Kim," Roosevelt entered Iran in July 1953 on a passport describing him as "Special Counselor to the President." His suitcase held $1 million in rials. "Failure to act," he told the vacillating Shah, "could only lead to a Communist Iran or to a second Korea." Years later, the SIS let it be known that Roosevelt merely showed up in Iran with CIA money to encourage agents the British had already organized. Perhaps this is true, but in any event, the cash was timely. Mosaddeq was deposed by the mob that had backed him, around three hundred people were killed in the process, and the Shah promptly returned from a brief exile in Rome's Excelsior Hotel, to receive a $45 million emergency grant from Washington (with $5 million secretly added from the CIA) to help him get reestablished. Roosevelt flew to London to convey the details to Churchill, then regaled Eisenhower in Washington with his adventures.

Upending opposition to the Shah during 1953 appeared to be another Agency triumph, and, in the short term, so it was. It also broke the British oil monopoly, and American giants, such as Standard Oil of New Jersey, jumped in. This was the Agency's initial attempt at third world kingmaking, and it was heady. A still heavily redacted CIA history of the events surrounding the August 19 coup would be written the following year. "It was a day that never should have ended," says this account, "for it carried with it such a sense of excitement, of satisfaction and of jubilation that it is doubtful whether any other can come up to it." Nonetheless, there were indicators of the coming years' disasters. The principal operatives at the U.S. Embassy did not speak Farsi, disabling them during the confusion when they could not reach their familiar English- and French-speaking Iranian sources. In addition, toppling the secularist Mossadegh ultimately had little to do with either CIA or SIS participation, contrary to the myths they cultivated. Clerics and other uncompromised Iranians who were eager to see the last of him seized the faltering initiative in the streets at nearly the last moment.

Meanwhile, the ever more autocratic Shah was encouraged to move into the role of exemplary U.S. client until, like several others of the genre, he triggered a reaction nearly a quarter century later that would spiral his country into the past, cripple a U.S. presidency, and cast America for decades in the role of Satan. "For an operation to last 25 years is not so bad," reflected one of Roosevelt's old CIA colleagues right after Roosevelt died in 2000. "It fell apart. Every operation cannot go on forever."[33]

On the other side of Eurasia, Moscow looked to be taking more blatant steps against another strategically positioned American friend. Soviet MiGs, for example, were screaming over Hokkaido, and John Foster Dulles warned the nation on radio and television that "the Soviet Russians are making a drive to Japan."[34] Japan's recovery during these years proceeded in the teeth of Washington's enduringly naive conviction that it would be "extremely difficult" for that exposed archipelago to achieve what the NSC deemed "economic viability." No one seemed to pay attention to Treasury Secretary Humphrey's seemingly petty observation at a 1954 cabinet meeting that Japan's reviving economy was already challenging electrical equipment manufacturers in Pennsylvania. Rather than bothering to worry about nascent competition, the Psychological Strategy Plan for Japan was put in place. Anti-Communist groups would be assisted, and Tokyo would be encouraged "to develop defense forces consistent with [its] economic capability" — a step, had it been followed over the coming decades, that would have redrawn world politics.[35] Japan instead capped what it called its Self-Defense Force at 110,000 men, a third of the level Washington expected. If only out of "self-respect," complained Dulles, Tokyo should "bear some responsibility and a fair share of the common burden of defense of the free world."[36] So much for the original U.S. hope that Japan would renounce war forever, as made in the form of Article 9 of the U.S.-written constitution, one that prohibits Japan from fielding a full-fledged army.

Japan's excuses for not doing more for western defense emphasized economic fragility. They were readily accepted by U.S. leaders of that generation, who tended to overvalue the significance of Europe and to underestimate the modernizing capacity of the East. For example, Japan's ruling party — the inaptly named Liberal Democrats, which the CIA would help finance for twenty years — bemoaned the pressures of a population growing at a million a year over a resourceless archipelago. Prosperity could come only through more exports, the Liberal Democrats complained, and Japan's delicate recovering industries were lacking orders after having been compelled to expand at America's behest during the Korean War. So there was no alternative but to ignore defense and, they threatened, perhaps to trade with China.

Well after the Occupation, therefore, Japan continued to receive the full range of American help: security, technical aid, agricultural surpluses, credits, and running interference with the Europeans over trade. Tens of million of dollars' worth of grain shipments were funded annually. A $15 million grant was provided for school lunches and children's clothing in 1954. Several million dollars' worth of cotton credits were tossed into the pot by the U.S. Export-Import Bank. Yen accruing to the United States under government-subsidized agricultural sales were largely recycled as development loans. About half a billion dollars in U.S. defense materiel was handed over between 1950 and 1956.[37]

One way the Soviets were trying "to get Japan," said Dulles, was "through what they [were] doing in Indochina." He even saw fit to compare France's colonial empire to the British Commonwealth, as a stout barrier protecting small nations from communism. For the secretary of state and the president to keep speaking of Indochina and Malaya in the same breath as Korea was tragic.[38] Such rhetoric was making it increasingly harder to keep America aloof from Southeast Asia's bloodshed. Dulles's fondness for phrases and formulas, however, also led him to pepper his private utterances with references to "disengagement in Asia." In practice, this meant building up South Korean and selected Vietnamese forces so that they could take care of themselves.

"To earn the alliance of the international underclass without jeopardizing relations with its allies was frequently tantamount to squaring the circle," writes one student of Dulles's life and times.[39] No one recognized this dilemma more than Dulles himself. The corporate lawyer and the world visionary coexisted easily in his own mind. He could sympathize with nationalists in the colonies, but he was not ready to distance his country from its most powerful anti-Communist allies in Western Europe. He had to take seriously the mediating institutions of almost-postcolonial government that provided generally unsatisfactory fig leaves for British or French authority. The colonial powers, meanwhile, claimed that these institutions were transitional ones along the path to genuine independence for their protégés. The steps to independence would have to be defended against all comers — if, of course, America could find the odd two or three or more billion dollars to help.

Word in the fall of 1953 that unidentified U.S. civilians (actually CIA contractors) were shuttling C-119 "Flying Boxcars" into Indochina from Japan aroused little interest at home. Had there been less confidence in Eisenhower as a general, more people might have asked where this was heading. The commander of the French Union forces, a technically capable but uninspiring leader, was lauded by *Time* magazine. It quoted an anonymous U.S. official: "Now we can see victory clearly — like light at the end of the tunnel."[40] One of Dulles's successors, Dean Rusk, would find the phrase both useful and regrettable.

The prospective "loss" of Indochina was somehow reckoned (by a logic so arrogantly paradoxical as could only be convincingly advanced by the French) to eviscerate France's ability to defend itself. "France is the keystone of Europe," the Joint Chiefs of Staff intoned, "and the Indochina thing has to be settled before NATO will work." Moreover, according to Eisenhower, who would certainly know, a Communist Indochina surely meant that "the gateway to India, Burma and Thailand would be open."[41] Adlai Stevenson was just as categorical in advancing this theory. "All Asia would slide behind the Iron Curtain," he warned in 1953, should Vietnam be "absorbed into the Moscow-Peking empire."[42]

France's self-interest could not be concealed by its clamor that there would be "no barrier to Communism before Suez" if

Indochina fell. Paris was essentially echoing what Britain's leaders, including Churchill, had been saying about the threat of communism in Southeast Asia at least since 1950.[43] With Washington increasingly attuned to the pleas of the colonial powers after the outbreak of the Korean War, it was difficult to see America as being on the side of "political liberty." Once Congress voted an additional $400 million for Indochina in 1953, the French immediately asked for $385 million more. By 1954, America was paying for around 75 percent of France's war. This amounted to a third of all U.S. foreign military assistance.

France would accept U.S. aid, but still without yielding to any preconditions about granting full independence or permitting U.S. officials any direct contact with its Vietnamese loyalists. French officials also worked hard to prevent Americans from developing their own sources of intelligence. They were absurdly alarmed about U.S. "inroads," even opposing U.S. General Claire Chennault's attempt to establish a volunteer air service into the region, as his "Flying Tigers" had done for Nationalist China before Pearl Harbor.[44] France felt that American taxpayers were obliged to finance the struggle down to the last centime without presuming to require political quid pro quos or even informed access.

"I am afraid we will move to the point from which there is no return," cautioned Mississippi's unequivocally hawkish Senator John Stennis from his seat on the Armed Services Committee.[45] When two hundred Air Force mechanics were assigned to Vietnam that year, he styled this "going to war inch by inch."[46] The notion of American draftees and tanks in Vietnam remained as conceivable as declaring war on the Eskimos. "I'm not going to Indochina," Colonel Creighton Abrams wrote his wife from Korea. "There is in that thoroughly confused situation nothing towards which American combat troops could be directed."[47]

By early 1954, the French command, still fearful that obvious reliance on U.S. personnel would humiliate them before their colonial subjects, graciously agreed to accept two U.S. special warfare officers to instruct anti-Communist tribesmen in the hill country. Henry Cabot Lodge, defeated as senator from Massachusetts by the promising John F. Kennedy and new U.S. representative to the UN, hoped that Indochina could be turned into "another Greece where we trained and helped." This was yet further naive use of the original emergency behind the Truman Doctrine. Comparisons with

Greece were also drawn by the otherwise astute Bohlen in Moscow and by the *New York Times*.[48] Even Secretary of Defense Wilson entertained this parallel to Greece, although he finally suggested that Indochina should simply be written off. Clearly, no one in Washington knew anything about the place.

By then, those U.S. cargo planes, though not crewed by Americans, were being used to drop napalm. U.S. Air Force transports also were flying in French reinforcements, though avoiding combat zones. The American press was angry. At issue was not this creeping commitment, but the fact that India's first prime minister, Jawaharlal Nehru — a sanctimonious Brahmin who believed Americans to be "more hysterical as a people than almost any others, except perhaps Bengalis" — was not allowing overflights.

No one in Washington had any idea what the consequences might be of a French defeat. Nor did anyone know what would and would not work in Vietnam, what was and was not possible. Until the last moment, Eisenhower gave "a soldier's appreciation" that the "odds are all in favor" of the Foreign Legionnaires and French regulars, as they were smothered in the collapsing dugouts of Dien Bien Phu, the defining defeat of that first post–1945 Vietnam war.[49] After all, this most famous of fighting men said that the fate of these hardened professionals would be as historic as the siege of Carthage (which fell). Never having fought guerrillas, Eisenhower kept underestimating the preponderance that a conventional force would need. And if Indochina were "lost," he further insisted, Japan's trade would "have only one place in the world to go, that is, toward the Communist areas in order to live."[50]

At the precise time that France was pleading for U.S. carriers and carrier-based aircraft, and as it accepted a gift of two squadrons of B-29s, it was using the *Belleau Wood*, an aircraft carrier already supplied by America, to transfer from Toulon to Bombay the parcel of navy fighter planes it had just sold to India — a sale that the White House found as "incomprehensible" as was the "maximum degree of trade" with the Soviet Union that Britain was meanwhile pursuing. Each ally had a ready retort: they had to trade almost anything with anyone because America was importing so little from Europe and because West Germany and Japan were now competing — at U.S. insistence — in world markets. England had to sell to the East to keep fifty million people alive on the small island, Churchill melodramatically argued to Eisenhower.[51] The prime minister also found it politic to take a much lower profile on the question of Southeast Asia, as America began getting further involved. After all, he told his cronies, he had lived all his life without ever having heard about places such as Laos.[52]

Should France fail in northern Vietnam, what about creating another buffer state between China and Malaya besides feeble, disordered Thailand? Might not the Americans be counted on to hold southern Vietnam through some sort of Southeast Asian defense pact, which Britain had initially been urging? Of course, London concluded, this could all be sorted out after the forthcoming conference in Geneva concerning Korea and Indochina. For the first time, the foreign ministers of all the major World War II allies — the United States, Britain, France, Russia, and China — would meet. Cosponsored by Britain and the Soviet Union, the conference took place from April 26 to July 21, 1954, in the Palais des Nations, the former headquarters of the ill-fated League of Nations.

With the armistice in Korea holding up, the French turned the conference into one on Indochina. Before it convened, Churchill essentially vetoed any joint military response with America, even though it was what he had long been urging. Still believing that French defeat meant a catastrophic turning point in history, he nonetheless had a greater fear of U.S. and British action provoking war with China. Should that happen, he elaborated, Beijing might invoke its defense pact with Russia, which might then use hydrogen bombs against U.S. bases in Britain.[53]

Eisenhower was livid, knowing that Congress would not permit direct U.S. engagement without Britain. "We failed to halt Hirohito, Mussolini, and Hitler," Eisenhower wrote Churchill, "may it not be that our nations have learned something from that lesson?" He knew that trying to intervene further without Britain would mean that the White House would have to face Congress and "fight for [intervention] like dogs, with very little hope of success." After all, Senate Minority Leader Lyndon Johnson led Capitol Hill's insistence that there would be "no more Koreas with the United States furnishing 90 per cent of the manpower."[54] Here is one of the Cold War's cruel ironies: Eisenhower, popularly remembered as being so cautious in not getting America involved, was urging intervention, while Johnson, doomed in history for reckless, tragic U.S. engagement, opposed it.

As the conference was about to begin, the French conceded that they just might welcome "participation by U.S. forces with possibly token assistance from [the] UK." At Dien Bien Phu, in a mist-shrouded valley near the border of Laos, about thirteen thousand desperate professional soldiers were cornered by a Viet Minh division supplemented with tens of thousands of porters, and many Chinese engineers. French officials fantasized that their men might still be saved by bombing runs from two hundred to three hundred U.S. carrier aircraft, perhaps, for discretion's sake, repainted with French insignia to pass as Foreign Legion (that is, ex-Luftwaffe).[55] Chinese-supplied Viet Minh artillery on the surrounding hills turned Dien Bien Phu into a death trap. U.S. diplomats in Geneva still sought to harness Britain to some form of joint action, perhaps at least to a defense pact, if not to explicit threats of intervention. Without a common front that might buck up France while deterring further Viet Minh offensives, the Communists would keep chipping away

Eisenhower lectured anyone who would listen that he was "gambling thousands to save billions" of future defense dollars in Indochina. He exploded when Colorado senator William Milliken talked about America washing its hands of the colonial powers should they continue waffling — France in continuing to scorn independence for Vietnam, Cambodia, and Laos; Britain in back-pedaling from any involvement beyond squashing insurrection in Malaya. To go in unilaterally," Eisenhower said, "amounted to an attempt to police the entire world," and he would have none of that. For Eisenhower, leadership meant having partners; otherwise, "the leader is just an adventurer like Genghis Khan." However, followers, let alone partners, were proving hard to find. This was particularly so at the conference, where America, with its newfound enthusiasm for taking some sort of anti-Communist stand in Indochina, found itself deserted.[56] In the weeks that followed, even Foreign Secretary Anthony Eden's closest aide feared that London was "getting very near having cheated the Americans" by abandoning its plan for joint protection of the Southeast Asian peninsula.[57]

It was American pilots of the Taiwan-based Civil Air Transport, bought through a cover holding company by the CIA's Frank Wisner for $950,000 from the entrepreneurial General Chennault, who maintained Dien Bien Phu's tenuous aerial lifeline until almost the bitter end. The downing of a "Flying Boxcar" resulted in the first U.S. combat fatalities in Vietnam. Even after the fortress was stormed in May, Eisenhower debated sending Marines, should that be possible politically — meaning if America could align itself with forces from Australia, New Zealand, the Philippines, and ever-helpful Thailand. And if Congress concurred. He fumed that Churchill's inertia was "promoting a second Munich."[58]

In an extraordinary Star Chamber meeting at the White House after Dulles returned in ashen anger from Geneva, the secretary laid out all the duplicity and perceived abandonment by America's putative partners. He delivered his case to the barons of Capitol Hill — Senator William Knowland, a member of the strongest pro–Chiang Kai-shek lobby; Senator Lyndon Johnson and his mentor, the daunting Richard B. Russell of Georgia; Senator Leverett Saltonstall, the model of an Atlantic-first Republican; and a dozen representatives, including Speaker of the House Joe Martin, Democratic Minority Leader Sam Rayburn, and Representative Carl Vinson, the once and future chairman of the House Armed Services Committee. As the undisputed leader of the Senate's inner club, Russell was clearly the most powerful, and he was known to be "weary of seeing American soldiers being sent as gladiators to be thrown into every arena around the world,"[59] He and the others heard Dulles explain how the United States was "obviously subject to U.K. veto, which in turn was in Asian matters largely subject to Indian veto, which in turn was largely subject to Chinese Communist veto" concerning possible ways to keep Indochina out of communism's grasp. Congress was now seeing firsthand how the allies — in this case, Britain as the "outer fortress" — were trying to reassert their past dignity without being able to summon up their past power.

Washington had tried to bluff China and the Viet Minh with the prospect of a united Western-led riposte. The bluff was called simultaneously by Britain and by the tenacious Viet Minh guerrillas. Dulles mused on the seemingly incredible fact of America having become entangled in Southeast Asia in the first place. He believed that the fundamental blunder had been made in 1945 when Washington acquiesced to the demands of the imperial powers that they reassert themselves in their colonies. He was sufficiently fed up with France, he told Eisenhower, and "from time to time he thought it best to let the French get out of Indochina entirely and then try to rebuild from the foundations."[60]

"If we were asked our opinion," Churchill coyly replied to Eisenhower, "we should advise against United States local intervention except for rescue." He explained that Britain would fight in Indochina only if Malaya were invaded, emphasizing that he was ready personally to show the war plans to the Pentagon. To itself, London concluded that in Washington "there is a natural reluctance to see American forces committed to jungle warfare."[61] Of course this was true, especially since Americans could feel not just a lack of alliance loyalty, which they would soon learn to be customary, but an absence of allied dynamism. State Department officials knew that Dulles's threat of an "agonizing reappraisal" of the European commitment in the light of insufficient allied defense spending had not been taken seriously, but currently unstable U.S. public opinion could quickly crystallize to make this impatience a very real threat indeed.

During the night of July 20–21, 1954, a year since the Korean armistice, separate agreements were concluded to stop the fighting in Cambodia, Laos, and in Vietnam. The Viet Minh were also to withdraw themselves from Laos and Cambodia. Like Germany and Korea, there would be a temporary partition, with free elections to follow throughout Vietnam in 1956. Rather than sign the peace accord, the United States merely said that it generally accepted its terms. The partition arrangement along the 17th Parallel between North and South Vietnam was deemed by U.S. critics to be "so economically absurd as to be patently temporary," given that the South produced most of the country's rice.[62] Moreover, it seemed immoral to bless an agreement that surrendered territory and populations not actually conquered on the battlefield.

The recurrent twentieth-century nightmare of hundreds of thousands of exhausted, destitute, terrified people fleeing a collectivist takeover made this much more than an abstract sensitivity. In a huge operation, the U.S. Navy ferried south about 311,000 of the roughly 1 million people who escaped Ho Chi Minh's new regime in the North, then rescued thousands more of the first "boat people." Almost no one went north. Faced with a public relations disaster and the loss of nearly 10 percent of its population within a few months, the Communist regime closed its borders. In the name of either "Western unity" in Europe or "political liberty" in Asia, Vietnam had cost the United States $2.6 billion, a quarter of the annual U.S. defense budget before the Korean War.

Even more troubling than his readiness to involve U.S. fighting men in Vietnam is the fact that Eisenhower still entertained the notion that Chiang Kai-shek might be able to return to the mainland and "conquer all of China," although this might have been a

tactic toward splitting the Sino-Soviet alliance. Characteristically de-
vious, he would insist the next year that, as Dien Bien Phu crumbled,
only he had resisted pressure from "the boys" to back up with U.S.
forces the staggering sum sunk in Vietnam. He had been "the only
one around . . . willing to put the American prestige on one
goldurned thing in there," he confided to one newspaper publisher,
later writing that the "strongest reason of all" for not going in had
been his unwillingness to tarnish America's "tradition of anti-
colonialism."[63] In fact, it had been Congress, and above all Lyndon
Johnson reacting to the prospect of the United States going it alone,
that had barred the way. And the reason for America not further
backing the French was hardly "anti-colonialism" (billions having
already been given to France); it was Britain's reluctance.

More than forty years after the Geneva conference, under a cold
December drizzle in 1996, France would unveil the Memorial to
Indochinese Wars, nestled modestly amid the pines and olives of
Fréjus, outside Toulon. France sent about fifty-five thousand men
to their deaths in Vietnam from 1946 to 1954, nearly as many as
America would send in the years ahead. The names on the wall
show the toll exacted on colonial troops and include thirteen hundred young French lieutenants whom their country needed to
rebuild an army so recently broken in World War II and about to be
undone again by primitive war in North Africa.

As for Japan, in the name of whose needs for rice and markets so
much U.S. effort had been expended in Vietnam, its world trade
deficit was falling fast. By September 1954, Dulles had quickly and
resentfully consolidated the Southeast Asia Treaty Organization.
This ensured that a reluctant United States joined France and
Britain — as well as Australia, New Zealand, Thailand, the Philippines, and Pakistan — to guarantee the defense of Cambodia, Laos,
and the newly created South Vietnam against unspecified "aggression."[64] The Joint Chiefs stubbornly opposed his desire to send a military assistance advisory group to Vietnam. Right after the treaty
was signed in Manila, Dulles flew to Japan to explain the new
arrangement, adding the frank and not unkind advice that Americans, regrettably, really didn't want Japanese products, which made
Japan's trade deficit with America a fact of life. Japan was, of
course, welcome to try to offer its goods, but it would be more fruitful to look elsewhere. Since "the Japanese only produce cheap substitutes of things which we produce in quality," he confided to

others, the ideal solution would be for them to retrace their steps to Southeast Asian markets. Americans believed it harmless enough — even soothing — for Japan to envision its industrial rebirth. The rest of the world was beginning to think otherwise.[65]

Frustrated by Communist advances in Asia, Washington heard the Soviets kicking on its doorstep — or at least it heard possible destabilizing enemies who might be considered similar. Weapons caches were said to be sprouting in Nicaragua. Labor troubles in Honduras and expropriation in Guatemala plagued the United Fruit Company, which immediately charged Communist instigation. U.S. manipulations in Guatemala, as in Iran, appeared to be a success, but they turned out to be tragic over the long term, about which no one was thinking. Nor was much thought being given to obtaining the allegiance of oppressed peoples.

By the late spring of 1954, the stage was set for the overthrow of Guatemala's popularly elected president, Jacobo Arbenz, a thuggish leftist who was nonetheless accomplishing some salutary reforms for his backward people. The CIA-managed coup highlights the arrival of a particular type of American player in "the game of nations" — the phrase being coined by one of them. This was the type that had given rise to Thomas Finletter's loathing for self-important internationalist manipulators, for whom these decades offered a ticket to the greatest game of all. John Le Carré looked back on them after the Cold War:

> They are the global architects, the world-order men, the political charm-sellers and geopolitical alchemists who in the cold war years managed, collectively and individually, to persuade themselves — and us, too, now and then — that with a secret tuck here, and a secret pull there, and an assassination somewhere else, and a destabilized economy or two, or three, they could not only save democracy from its defects but create a secret stability amid the chaos.[66]

"Secret stability" was an equipoise to be discerned with the same eye that saw light at the end of the tunnel or Chiang Kai-shek as a soldier of democracy. Vietnam would be these men's legacy, but for the moment, Central America was more familiar territory. Again, it was the British who first clamored that a particular nationalist movement was a Communist front, thus tarring Arbenz because of Guatemala's territorial claims on British Honduras (today's Belize), although he proved bitterly anti-Communist once in exile.[67] The United States was paying an increasingly expensive price for a relationship ever less "special."

Nicaragua's dictator, Anastasio Somoza, had originally added his two pesetas' worth by proposing to Truman that they cooperate in ousting Guatemala's government, and Truman had told the CIA to proceed. The initial operation failed. Washington needed no encouragement to return to the charge, particularly after a Polish ship with two thousand tons of small arms and ammunition from Czechoslovakia steamed into Puerto Barrios, exacerbating U.S. policy grandees' reaction to Arbenz's agrarian radicalism.

Allen Dulles's new special assistant, the forcefully urbane Richard Bissell, coordinated the dirty work. He was a graduate of Groton and Yale, where he also had earned his doctorate in economics in 1939, going on to teach at MIT, where he became a very young full professor in 1948. Bissell had worked for Lewis Douglas during World War II, and later in the 1940s for the Marshall Plan, from which counterpart funds under his signature had been conveyed to Frank Wisner, deputy director of plans and the CIA's third-highest official, for various tasks. By 1952, he was at the Ford Foundation at a time when more than 170 foundations were coming into place as conduits or fronts for CIA money, with Ford assuming a helpful role in political warfare under its new chairman, John McCloy.[68] Bissell's résumé encapsulates the brilliance, earnestness, and ties to particular elite organizations that for too many years would conceal the crippling unawareness of many of the men who were racking up the Cold War's costs.

The CIA helped draw up a "disposal list" of fifty-eight of Arbenz's supporters, courtesy of the exiled rebel leader Carlos Castillo Armas, who was to be installed after Arbenz's demise. The list made clear the Agency's criteria for death: officials who were "irrevocably implicated in Communist doctrine or policy," or perhaps other people "whose removal for psychological or organizational or other reasons is mandatory for the success of military action." Fifty-eight assassinations might be a bit much, chided one CIA official, while proposing that, "say, 20 would be sufficient." The rebel killers in Honduras received twenty silencers for .22-caliber rifles, and the Agency conducted a self-described "nerve war" of death threats. Apparently with a straight face, it also concocted a nineteen-page how-to manual on murder that says, "No assassination instructions should ever be written or recorded."[69]

Only two dozen or so CIA officers were involved with the force of a mere 480 men (although they let it be known that there were five times that many). They moved on Guatemala City from Honduras and Nicaragua, to which the CIA that spring had airlifted fifty tons of its own small arms. Operation Success, as the Agency hubristically called this enterprise, cost only five or six times the small amount of the previous year's victory in Iran. Choreographing the chaos, the new U.S. ambassador — rushed in from Greece and speaking no Spanish — appeared to other diplomats in the capital as "looking more like a gangster than ever."[70] Lies, overly clever manipulations, and even killings at one remove were becoming policy.

As in other parts of the world, Washington concluded that the Guatemalan military was "the only organized element" with which to work. What followed sent a message to the rest of Latin America for forty years. Foggy Bottom meanwhile declaimed that any suggestion of U.S. involvement was "ridiculous and untrue." At the UN, Ambassador Henry Cabot Lodge categorically denied that Washington had played any role, although it was apparent to Europe's officials that "the rebellion was an outside job."[71] Reaching into the *New York Times,* Allen Dulles found Arthur Sulzberger ready to cooperate in keeping one overly curious reporter, whom the CIA had been tracking, out of Guatemala. The publisher volunteered to monitor the work of this troublemaker.[72] Dulles also had a word with James Reston, who had succeeded Arthur Krock as the *New York Times*'s Washington bureau chief and lead national columnist: there should be no more unwholesome curiosity about where the attacking forces had acquired so many weapons.[73] And there wasn't.

"I'd never heard of this bloody place called Guatemala until I was in my seventy-ninth year," fumed Churchill about this latest poisonous backwater.[74] Then matters got worse. While he and Eden were in Washington during mid-June, getting lectured on appeasement in Indochina by Eisenhower and John Foster Dulles, a CIA officer with the rebel Guatemalan air force incredibly authorized the sinking of a British merchant ship, the *Springfjord,* mistakenly believing it to be carrying gasoline. The Agency had to reimburse the shipping firm to the tune of $1.5 million and send Wisner to deliver a personal apology to the British Embassy. The civilian dead in the bombings of Chiquimula and Zacapa by U.S.-supplied planes were beside the point.

Arbenz's removal seemed so easy; just $20 million had been spent. However, it proved the precedent not for mounting successes, but for confident overreach in the barracks of the Congo, in the Sumatran jungles, and in the alleys of Saigon. Short-term tactical U.S. objectives were attained at the price of undying identification with SAVAK (the Shah's secret police) and United Fruit. Iran-Guatemala (the first time Iran and Central America were linked, a sour precedent for a generation later) left the Agency basking in "success" all right. It was poised to involve the United States far too deeply in a world poorly understood. In Guatemala alone, the CIA's squalid connections began to share responsibility for a horrendous pattern of licensed murder. "We started something and didn't know how to get off the train," admitted an inspector general some years after the Soviet Union fell. The civil war that began at the end of the decade would last until 1996 and take around 200,000, mostly civilian, lives, with an estimated 80 percent of those deaths caused by the U.S.-trained military.[75]

Ernesto (Che) Guevara was a striking everyman for the haunted privileged of a Latin American generation who knew things had to be done better, and who found the United States (for all its ladling out of well-meant aid) on the wrong side. In 1954, he was a twenty-six-year-old, upper-class Argentine physician living among the eclectic community of political exiles in Guatemala City. As the foreign-backed reactionaries grabbed power, the increasingly radicalized Guevara took refuge with other leftists in the Argentine embassy. "I won't rest until I see these capitalist octopuses annihilated," he vowed before fleeing to Mexico City for his fateful encounter with Fidel Castro.[76] The Sierra Maestra, the Belgian Congo, and the Bolivian mountains were in the dim future, as were more of Kennan's desiderated "harsh governmental means of repression."

The myths of success take their own toll, and several of these stemmed from Guatemala. The Agency lied to Eisenhower (as became known decades later) that only one rather than forty-eight of the Agency-backed rebels had been killed and informed no one of the poor security and amateurish planning that had characterized the plot. Within two years, moreover, the British had talked themselves into the profoundly mistaken conviction that Washington would back them in their own conspiracy to topple a supposedly Communist-tainted government in Egypt, given that they had faithfully helped the Americans block Arbenz's final emergency pleas to the United Nations to condemn the U.S. role.[77] And almost the entire cast of the U.S. operation would move on to planning for the Bay of Pigs seven years later. Operation Success consolidated the ascendancy of covert action over espionage and analysis at the CIA.

Allen Dulles remarked with disturbingly matter-of-fact satisfaction that the role of the intelligence authorities had more influence in the United States than in any other country in the world.[78] No matter what the exaggeration, he was saying this about a service unable to discern the number of Soviet nuclear weapons or fully manned divisions. The costs started to add up, as in 1954 Eisenhower gave the Agency an expanded mandate to face down communism throughout the world.[79] The public might have assumed this existed already, but Congress certainly was not offered any serious account of such developments in America's foreign relations. Everything in the tool kit could be used. There was no NSC body charged with reviewing covert action. CIA officials were the only ones positioned to make judgments about whether a covert venture was covered by previous authorization or was significant enough to merit special consideration outside the CIA.[80] This was another dangerous step toward an attitude best described as "if the President says so, it's legal."

Here was a worldwide hunting license indeed. For all its wealth and world power, this heedlessly general policy put the United States at a grave disadvantage wherever there was a determined and potentially majority movement opposed to it. Client regimes look tawdry against real passion. Along the way, U.S. covert operators found themselves free to begin implementing an NSC recommendation "to make more difficult the control by the Viet Minh of North Vietnam."[81] For all his people's poverty in other respects, Ho Chi Minh was holding the trump cards.

These CIA operations were accompanied by other intrigues. Charles Douglas (C. D.) Jackson, former publisher of *Fortune* magazine, became Eisenhower's special adviser for psychological warfare in 1953, after briefly heading the CIA-funded National Committee for a Free Europe (the ostensibly private foundation that launched Radio Free Europe as "a surrogate free press for the captive peoples"). Particularly during the 1950s, psychological warfare was treated like a science, although it merely referred to covert operations that boosted the morale of friends or undermined that of enemies. Like his Agency counterparts, this high-energy Princetonian created all sorts of dangerous mischief, such as launching thousands of balloons to drop propaganda over Eastern Europe and the western Soviet Union. Some 300 million leaflets were sent over the years, as were CIA reconnaissance balloons launched from bases in Scotland, West Germany, and Turkey. Gaining in influence, Jackson noted that Eisenhower considered psywar "just about the only way to win WWIII without having to fight it" because (in an analogy he might not have used to his chief's face) Eisenhower understood "that practically every other golf club in his bag is broken."[82] What he meant was that there were still too many domestic obstacles preventing the direct use of American men and money.

Jackson, the Psychological Strategy Board, and the CIA spent hugely on more refined activities. Moscow's effort to control the world of ideas would be met. For example, secret funds enabled the Boston Symphony Orchestra to tour Western Europe, the hope being to convince condescending allies that the United States also possessed some forms of sophistication. Starting in 1953, the the Agency in London covertly underwrote the influential monthly journal *Encounter* to shape European intellectual opinion. It was bankrolled for years. There was a family of similarly serious publications in other languages: *Preuves, Tempo Presente, Cuadernos, Der Monat, Hiwar*. Private U.S. foundations kept laundering CIA money to sponsor conferences that might quietly introduce Europe's writers, painters, and professors to arguments unfavorable to Moscow.[83] Yet the Agency was hardly strutting the world as "an organization which was as near to being all-powerful as any of modern times," as some of its less-informed critics conclude today.[84] Upon inspection, the invisible empire of the CIA dwindles to an overstaffed bureaucracy, its effectiveness not remotely reflecting its undoubted worldwide presence.

"Like the voyages of Columbus and Magellan," one CIA veteran of the 1950s recalls of Agency bungling, "we were improvising all the way."[85] Such confusion was already leading to deep doubts among some responsible, well-placed Americans. Within two years of Guatemala, Robert Lovett, back on Wall Street, and diplomat David K. E. Bruce would apparently conduct an inquiry for Eisenhower on what the Agency was actually doing. "The C.I.A., busy, monied and privileged, likes its 'kingmaking' responsibility," they are said to have concluded. "The intrigue is fascinating — considerable self-satisfaction, sometimes with applause, derives from 'successes' — no charge is made for 'failures.'" They ended by asking a question that would never be answered: "Should not someone, somewhere in an authoritative position in our government . . . be keeping in mind the long-range wisdom of activities which . . . are responsible in a great measure for stirring up the turmoil and raising the doubts about us that exist in many countries of the world today?"[86] Frank Wisner's story, culminating in his suicide in 1965, poignantly shows how so many of these men of the CIA's founding generation could slide from the soaring life of a Fitzgerald "rich boy" to the agonized self-destruction of Fitzgerald himself.

George Smiley, who perennially combines the ideal and the reality of Britain's SIS in John Le Carré's novels, looks back at the end of the Cold War on the fantasies that underlie the conflicts of nations:

> The sad answer is, I'm afraid, that the Cold War produced in us a kind of *vicarious colonialism*. On the one hand, we abandoned practically every article of our national identity to American foreign policy. On the other, we bought ourselves a stay of execution for our vision of our colonial selves. Worse still, we encouraged the Americans to behave in the same way. Not that they needed our encouragement, but they were pleased to have it, naturally.[87]

Vast resources were being consumed in a struggle that was in great part tangential to the world conflict. The distracting self-deception that everything was understood now looks just as vast. Much of this effort eventually brought as its equal and opposite reaction violent condemnation. It served to energize, even occasionally to justify, many of the West's opponents. And the long haul was just getting started.

✪

At the other extreme of violence and technical sophistication, Washington was pouring more than $2 billion a year into military-related research, out of a total federal budget averaging $70 billion a year. Most of the money was funneled through the Defense Department and the Atomic Energy Commission (AEC), which were busily refining the hydrogen bomb and scaling down warheads to an extent that atomic cannons could roll down Pennsylvania Avenue in Army Day parades. Like the services, the AEC was also funding such worthwhile projects as linear accelerators. People could still assume that their taxes would be put to good use, and the amounts being shepherded to the universities and national laboratories seemed admirable examples. Even atomic testing (at about $100 million per year) held the promise of future prosperity. The all-knowing visitor from outer space in *The Day the Earth Stood Still* surely had it right: the unfolding mysteries of the atom must be used not for war, but for farms, factories, and homes. Might not atomic power, in the words of legislators, "make the maximum contribution to the general welfare" by providing unlimited fuel as well as unlimited defense? Yet pricing, permits, sales, and construction would all be controlled by government, "a far cry from the world of Adam Smith," remarked one observer. Power industry lobbyists had actually been hoping for more generous development subsidies than Congress had allowed.[88]

The AEC studied, as well as funded research into, how the atom's Promethean gifts applied to medicine, agriculture, and industry. It ensured that patent rules were changed to benefit individual inventors. Uranium mining became a major segment of the U.S. non-ferrous metal industry, nourished by an AEC bonus program to encourage prospecting. Groundbreaking ceremonies for the country's first atomic power plant took place in Pennsylvania on Labor Day, 1954. America was embarked on what the *New York Times* called "five thousand years of atomic energy" — such confidently delivered, empirically contentless numbers being part of the era.[89]

Surely, government knew best about these mysteries. "Never did so many trust so few so blindly as the people of the United States and the rest of the free world trust the members of the Atomic Energy Commission," remarked *Time* in January 1952.[90] The "rest of the free world," in fact, was more often scared to death. And the "people of the United States" were paying out unknowingly, as post–Cold War claims for radiation exposure would show. Budget balancing nonetheless had to be considered. Even the emptiness of the Pacific (by the standards of those environmentally unconscious days) could not offset the costs of testing in such distant seas. Detonations were much cheaper in the American West, and bombs were by now being set off at the Nevada Test Site, which was as big as Rhode Island. Camp Desert Rock was built to house soldiers who were ordered to participate in fallout-contaminated maneuvers.

For a single blast in 1953, what was described as a typical American community was created near ground zero to determine what might happen to Anytown, USA. Houses were fully furnished and larders stocked, new cars were parked in garages, and mannequins representing all ages were dressed in the latest fashions. Not surprisingly, all this wealth evaporated with a direct hit. "Things are probably going to look different when you get outside," noted *How to Survive an Atomic Bomb*, a widely distributed AEC pamphlet of the mid-1950s, with Welcome Wagon chattiness. "If the bomb hit within a mile and a half of where you are, things are going to look very different." One wonders what constituency these wisdoms aimed to enlighten.

Adjacent Nevada towns received another pamphlet, *27 Questions and Answers About Radiation and Radiation Protection*, which assured readers that the survivors of Hiroshima and Nagasaki had been examined carefully and much had been learned about public safety. "Studies have shown," said the AEC to Congress and downwind residents alike, that nuclear testing posed only "minimum" (if undefined) risks to human health.[91] The AEC assumed correctly that the uninformed public and an uncurious press were not about to calculate nuances of minor versus major risk. This combination of secrecy and public relations, a powerful synthesis in an age when government was rarely questioned, was captured in a Jules Feiffer cartoon: "Are you sure that the President doesn't have access to classified publicity not available to you?"

Unaccountable officials in a secrecy-shrouded program could find it all too easy to deny, dissemble, or mislead as a matter of course.[92] Still, they could go only so far. Although the public was uninformed, the AEC did confidentially alert executives of Eastman Kodak Company and other film manufacturers about the pervasiveness of fallout. At least these companies would be forewarned about future detonations. After all, Kodak had threatened to sue once it attributed to atmospheric nuclear tests some fog on the film (packed in a material made from corn husks contaminated with iodine 131) that its customers were buying.[93]

Rarely did such concern apply to worker safety. Hundreds of businesses secretly accepted AEC contracts in the late 1940s and into the 1950s, then shifted plants, mills, and mechanical shops to nuclear weapons work. Employees could be assured, as they were at Cleveland's Harshaw Chemical Company, that radioactive dust posed no health risk despite vast overexposure. No one in government considered providing detailed information to people laboring at commercial facilities. Like most weapons program documents, ones on operational hazards were classified. If informed, workers might demand hazard pay or safer conditions, or they also might sue. Thousands of people who cut and pressed uranium and thorium metal into nuclear fuel rods were affected at places such as Joslyn Manufacturing in Fort Wayne, Indiana; Bridgeport Brass plants in Connecticut and Michigan; and William E. Pratt Manufacturing in Joliet, Illinois.[94] AEC medical officials were aware of the problems.

Much safer federal plants built in the 1950s eventually took over the work, although, after the Cold War, the government would still have to pay millions of dollars in compensation for its own unsafe practices, as at the Fernald processing complex in Cincinnati. That was the issue that caught public attention, as did discovery in the 1990s of AEC experiments on humans. The extent of increased cancer, as well as of kidney, lung, and other diseases, among the private workforces remains unknown. No study of them (except a report on each of the two most litigious companies, Mallinckrodt Chemical and Linde Air Products) has ever been undertaken, let alone any settlement reached.

It was easier to make a fuss over livestock. For example, sheep died mysteriously in Utah, and the Los Alamos National Laboratory detected lesions "remarkably similar to severe beta ray burns as demonstrated experimentally." The incisive scientific minds of the U.S. district court determined that the sheep must have perished from "cold weather . . . and infectious diseases."[95] Cattle herds suffered strange diseases, and children complained of swollen tongues. "Blue snow" fell over areas surrounding the Nevada proving grounds. This was trickier to blame on the weather, and claims for damages would reach the Supreme Court.

Having altogether established 447 closed "danger areas" for weapons testing, including the seas around Bikini and Eniwetok, the United States finally performed its largest test ever in the Pacific. On March 1, 1954, the fifteen-megaton thermonuclear detonation Bravo entered history not for its size or for being the first actual airborne "bomb," but because it showered twenty-three Japanese fishermen aboard a tuna trawler, The Lucky Dragon, with gritty ash out of a thick white cloud. They had been about eighty-five miles downwind from Bikini.

When the fishermen were back in their home port of Yaizu, one crew member died of liver failure within seven months. Others were in hospitals recovering from burns or blood and intestinal disorders.

The rest would report stomach and skin cancers. AEC chairman Lewis Strauss first accused the fishermen of espionage, then insisted that they were exaggerating their injuries. John Foster Dulles finally issued a bland apology once Eisenhower weighed in to cut through AEC obfuscation. Washington never acknowledged that radiation killed the first man, although it paid his widow about $2,500 and in 1955, without admitting liability, gave the Japanese government $2 million (paid from military aid funds) against any injuries or damage caused by the blast. Each crew member received roughly $5,500. Total compensation over the following years would total about $16.5 million in today's dollars.[96] Thirty years later, *The Lucky Dragon* would be heard from again.

Every detail of H-bomb testing had to remain secret, the experts said, because sharing fallout data could reveal aspects of weapon design, such as how much of the energy released came from fusion and how much from fission. After Bravo, the world knew that fallout from a single bomb could cover at least ten thousand square miles. No one had any idea how long a political half-life these tests would have. Bravo's poison also sifted down over several islands. "The medical staff," reported Chairman Strauss a few weeks later, "advised us they anticipate no illness, barring of course disease which might be hereafter contracted."[97] "Hereafter" arrived with a vengeance, as nineteen of the twenty-one children under age twelve on the island of Rongelap developed thyroid tumors. A decade after the test, Congress appropriated $950,000 under the Bikini Compensation Act, amended a dozen years later to embrace the inhabitants of nearby Uterik. This was just the start of the payouts.

Forty years after Bravo, Washington would have paid a total of $205 million to Marshall Islanders to redress damage from nuclear testing — by which time, under the usual alchemy of the age, the islands had become inordinately valuable tourist property, offering some of the world's best scuba diving. Bikini's enforced desertion and the eventual dispersal of radioactivity by sea and wind left a white sand island of coconut palms swaying over a perfect turquoise sea, open to all. The head of the Bikini diving school remarks philosophically that "anything bad can be turned into something good" — a fine articulation of the deepest Cold War hope.[98]

Nevada at least remained eager. Testing, after all, brought a permanent and popular payroll to the desert, especially for struggling, small-town Las Vegas. Employment soared, construction boomed, and even the budding tourist industry increased. Some three thousand jobs stemmed from the test site between 1951 and 1958.[99] By 1955, there had been thirty-one detonations and countless reassuring pamphlets. Citizens were glad to help. When a state senator dared to propose that Nevada ask Congress to take its mushroom clouds elsewhere, Las Vegas's two rival newspapers agreed on something for the first time, denouncing him as an "ass" and a "crackpot." He was among those whiners who "spread witches' tales regarding atomic data they know nothing about," succeeding only in frightening old ladies. After all, if "the friendly people of the AEC" did not care so much about public safety, reported these watchdogs of liberty, the "experiments could be conducted at greatly reduced cost and much less bother."[100]

Nevada was also reaping fine publicity and repeated patriotic tributes. If those of little faith elsewhere in the country were worrying about atmospheric radiation, let them think of all the roentgens amok should deterrence fail. A handful of malcontents couldn't be allowed to stand in the way of those "friendly people's" need to keep testing above the desert. The AEC flatly asserted that fallout "does not constitute a serious hazard to any living thing outside the test zone" — a statement it knew to be false. A curiosity of the Cold War is that more nuclear weapons were exploded in the United States than anywhere else. The appalling record of human injury and ecological scarring is still being tabulated. The Rockefeller Foundation nonetheless offered its own authoritative assurances at the time, as did the National Academy of Sciences, which explained that the biological damage from peacetime activities (including the testing of atomic weapons) had been essentially negligible.[101] In the face of such authority, who could dissent?

Behind the scenes, more dubious scrutinies were under way. "If anybody knows how to do a good job of body snatching," declared chemist Willard Libby, a member of the AEC's General Advisory Committee, "they will really be serving their country." The abuses of the late 1940s expanded. The AEC's Project Sunshine, for example, gave top priority to a secret worldwide search for cadavers, on which bone and tissue tests might show the planetary effects of atomic testing. A network of contacts in hospitals and among doctors in the United States, Canada, Europe, Australia, Latin America, and Africa brought the commission as many as fifteen hundred bodies, primarily from cities and from among the poor. The cremated bones of Australian babies were shipped to the United States into the 1970s. There was no need for families or physicians to know. This program, begun in 1953, had to be accelerated in light of the following year's glitches in the South Pacific. Libby was ready to help, and took time away from his pioneering work in radiocarbon dating. He was anxious for tissue and bones from all age groups all over the world and was annoyed at the difficulties, especially of obtaining juvenile samples, complaining that "the supply [of stillborn infants] has now been cut off." A twenty-nine-year old woman who died in childbirth and her dead baby were a fortunate find indeed. New York and Texas were especially good hunting grounds. "Down in Houston, they don't have all these rules," explained one Columbia University scientist. "We can get virtually everybody that dies."[102]

Though not having quite the fog draped drama of Victorian grave robbing for anatomists, this approach to research was prosaically unpleasant. It was the arrogance of men pleased to regard themselves as the vanguard of the dispassionate scientific administration of the future, happily unaware of how steam-driven and gaslit their behavior would look in fifty years.

Today, however, all sorts of silly tales are used to show the extent to which the nuclear prospect was utterly different from all past time and uniquely traumatizing. One of the most tiresome refrains of the atomic era is to hear social scientists describe how 1950s images of atomic testing traumatized an otherwise coddled generation. To be sure, children were generally receiving the most exposure to fallout, three to seven times that of adults, because they drank more milk, which contained a radioactive form of iodine from bomb fallout on grass. Yet it is a stretch to conclude, for example, that "triumphal weapons of a suicidal nature" were "deeply upsetting" for children. The evidence for this conclusion included one young man who told a sympathetic sociologist that he "became hysterical" as a child when in 1950 he saw a picture of an atomic bomb under "A" in an illustrated encyclopedia.[103]

There would have been terror aplenty for schoolchildren, had they only known what the experts were up to. Tattooing them for easier identification after nuclear attack was examined but dismissed as impractical, given that skin would likely be burned off. Issuing metal dog tags made more sense, since they would not melt quite as thoroughly as the child. The New York City school system decided to allocate $87,000 for such a plan.[104] Yet to wallow in all this as a source of adult neuroses today takes attention away from the ever-worsening picture of how the nation really was harming itself.

✪

The fears that compelled nuclear testing and its accompanying deceptions were by no means just a "terrifying abstraction," as some people have recently asserted.[105] There was nothing abstract about the dread of massive air raids. The likelihood that deterrence might fail was a fact. In actual war and in newsreels, too many people had seen what critic Desmond McCarthy evoked: "a little white arm lying in the street" the morning after. Throughout his presidency, Eisenhower, like most Americans, was haunted by the possibility of yet another surprise attack.[106] He was hardly alone, hence all those duck-and-cover drills. They may have seemed like an absurd game to children but were carved inescapably into their parents' experience.

Soviet forces in early 1954 had only a handful of atomic weapons. Moreover, there was no "bomber gap," at least for long-range, heavy bombers. Yet pictures taken at that year's May Day air show in Moscow had an enormous impact on U.S. intelligence and on the public. A fleet of new bombers — for the first time, not derived from U.S. and British designs — seemed poised to threaten the continental United States. Actually, U.S. observers had been deceived by the same squadron flying around in circles, reappearing every few minutes over Red Square.[107] Not until the summer of 1956, after the first five U-2 spy plane flights over the Soviet Union, would the CIA be able to disprove Air Force assertions of such a gap. Allen Dulles would call his results "million dollar photography," providing Eisenhower with the evidence to deny requests for additional B-52 bombers to "catch up" to the Soviets. Money was instead provided for SAC to build new bases in the northern United States. The existing ones had come into being more or less by accident, according to Curtis LeMay, who pointed out that they were merely converted World War II training facilities.[108]

Several polls showed significant numbers of Americans in 1954 anticipated war of some sort. "Threat of war" led "unemployment" and "high cost of living" as the greatest problem facing the country.[109] Many suspected that war might mean another Pearl Harbor, although this time it would be New York and Los Angeles that would be sunk, not a row of obsolescent battleships. The extent of the danger, according to journalists Stewart and Joe Alsop, was deliberately not being shared by the White House for fear of provoking panic. "Unless drastic measures are taken to improve our air defenses," the experts were supposedly telling each other behind closed doors, "the Kremlin will be able to make a totally devastating air-atomic attack on the United States within eighteen to twenty-four months."[110] Such worst-case thinking sounds hollow enough today, partly because the Soviet state was even then undercutting itself through its preposterous economic system, and partly because Moscow chose to start emphasizing missile development programs rather than rapidly building long-range bombers. The genuinely competent, genuinely frightened people who nonetheless envisioned these threats had an answer that still cannot be blunted: they had to be wrong only once to ruin their country and much of the world.

By the fall, however, the administration was expecting to enter an economic heaven. The old deficit-laden, inflation-distended days of Truman seemed a bad dream, although federal spending nonetheless had to rise as the population and production grew. The Dow Industrials had peaked at 381.17 in September 1929 after hitting 300 on the last day of 1928. Only in 1954, a quarter century later, would they again surmount the 300 barrier. This was the year that a Luce magazine came up with the Fortune 500. It did not take long for people to describe the Pentagon as a "Fortune 1" company, an easy analogy since some of the most senior officials spoke in these terms. Thomas Finletter described the Air Force as "the world's biggest business." The Department of Defense was said to "own" property valued at $140 billion.[111] That included such a vast expanse as the White Sands Missile Range, greater in area than Delaware and Rhode Island combined. Of nearly two and a half million civilians working directly for the federal government, half were employed by the Pentagon.

Surely, all this prosperity could be directed toward making the country impervious to a surprise attack — a notion that had been percolating since Kennan had raced to Ottawa in late 1946, and since Finletter had tried to build his air armada. Now the most ambitious construction task ever accomplished in so short a time was tackled, backed by research from the heights of American science: a radar picket line across the northernmost parts of Alaska and Canada.

The "awful urgency" of such a need was publicly championed by MIT's president and by the director of its Lincoln Laboratory, created by the Air Force in 1950 precisely to work on air defense. Lincoln would be responsible for the initial R & D, involving tens of millions of contract dollars; MIT as a whole would get much more. A "distant early warning system" wouldn't cost more than $20 billion, as the Pentagon had feared, said Professors James Killian and A. G. Hill, but even if it did, they were "not convinced that the costs need be backbreaking to the country." How, for instance, did the human and capital value of Manhattan weigh against a defense that "would cost as much as, or more than, all present military expenditures put together"? Once the Air Force was assured that money would not be taken from its bomber wings, it happily agreed to proceed.[112] America's "best minds are working on air defense," boasted the Air Force Chief of Staff.[113] No matter how necessary, this was a sorry admission about the use of talent.

Contractors, inevitably including MIT, were given less than twelve months to make the system operational. By mid-1954, a primitive thirty-station radar fence had been completed fifteen hundred miles south of where the more ambitious distant early warning (DEW) line would run. The Canadians, whose GDP was about a tenth that of the United States, paid a third. At a cost of about $200 million dollars, they then built their own unmanned microwave "fence" about five hundred miles farther north, believing that this contribution would absolve them from having to support the much more expensive DEW line itself. No such luck.[114]

Never before had there been such a mammoth intrusion into the far reaches of the Arctic. In early 1955, Ottawa formally gave the United States permission to begin construction, forgoing any payments of its own, ensuring a role for Canadian companies, and having Washington pledge that no Eskimos would be affected. Americans would be accused of violating all these provisions. AT&T's Western Electric division became the main Air Force contractor, developing radar systems that precluded the need for twenty-four-hour visual monitoring and introducing "scatter communications" to overcome magnetic interference at the pole.[115]

The full strength of American scope and effort was let loose on the Arctic. An immense airlift — three thousand flights for one-third of the first year's supplies — was undertaken. The rest of the supplies were sealifted in, the ships being among the first that had sailed into that ocean. Several thousand stevedores, specially trained for extreme weather, unloaded a quarter of a million tons of cargo and fifty thousand barrels of petroleum during the brief Arctic summer. Five thousand Western Electric engineers were expected to finish by early 1957, at a cost of around $1 billion. "Nobody makes any claims to pinching pennies on the Distant Early Warning Line," the Air Force admitted. " 'Get it done and damn the cost.' "[116]

Innovative radar would enable the warning systems to perform for only $160 million a year, it was said, requiring just twelve hundred men on five-month stints above the Arctic Circle at any one time. Yet truck engines lasted for only two thousand miles. Coal cost $120 a ton to ship in. As much gravel was needed to maintain the new airstrips as would have been used to underlie a two-lane highway, twelve inches deep, from New York to San Francisco. Twenty-six lives were lost in 1956. Nothing that big or dangerous comes without tragedy; the deaths and injuries just tended to be more poignant and often more dramatic.

The Pentagon preferred to emphasize marvelously beneficial spin-offs, as in electronics, textiles, and "opening the Arctic," as well as in the likelihood that "the DEW Line will result in more dollars being made in private profits than were put into it from taxpayers' pockets" (a rationalization for government spending forever to be repeated).[117] In Wilmette, Illinois, the Snow, Permafrost, Ice Research Establishment (SPIRE) was established for Arctic R & D work directly related to construction.

Should enemy bombers be detected, the DEW line was backed by plans to ensure a navigation-blotting blackout throughout the United States. Hundreds of businesses, trade associations, and local governments joined in the Pentagon planning. For instance, the Outdoor Advertising Association pledged to turn off in an emergency any billboard lamps that emitted upward light. Streetlights would be shielded, sky glow from cities reduced, and house and office windows covered.[118] More than 2,500 interceptor jets and 7,000 warheads for continental air defense followed. Advertising and lobbying dollars were added to the defense effort. The Army, for example, encouraged Western Electric to launch a nationwide campaign for the Nike-Hercules surface-to-air missile. The Air Force, working through Boeing, countered with a publicity blitz of its own for the competing Bomarc. A Nike, misfired at Fort Meade, Maryland, swooped three miles to explode over the newly built Baltimore-Washington Parkway. The missile was otherwise part of an efficient approach to air defense and ended up being the one chosen.

These were mighty and large-minded projects, but the decision makers were fighting the last war all over again. Even as workmen started to pour cement for the first Canadian stations, events were being overtaken by technology. Low-flying bombers and intercontinental ballistic missiles (ICBMs) were about to render the system obsolete.

This atmosphere of thinking fearfully, of immense construction, and of assimilating big spending to defense combined with astute public relations to energize the building of what became the interstate highway system. That undertaking became the single largest public works and construction project in history. The United States was going to tie together its continent no matter what happened in the outside world, pouring highways along lines that had been sketched in the early 1940s. Unfortunately, they would be blasted and laid amid the 1950s atmosphere of emergency. Perhaps a road pattern might have emerged that would have been more responsively to the needs of America 2005 or that would not have helped destroy city neighborhoods. Or perhaps other forms of mass transportation would have received more scrutiny. Necessity may be the tyrant's plea, but it is assuredly also the bureaucrat's, union chief's, CEO's, and county road contractor's.

In 1954, Eisenhower asked General Lucius Clay, who had been military governor of Germany during the Berlin Airlift, to recommend a highway system to fit "America's military and civilian defense to the economy." Each had seen how quickly troops could move around Germany on the autobahns. Eisenhower did not start the system, as is commonly believed; he made what had been a state issue into a national one. The Federal Civil Defense Administrator had already determined that at least 70 million people would have to be evacuated from likely target areas in case of nuclear threat, let alone actual attack.

A commission chaired by Clay soon concluded that an interstate network would be "vital as a civil defense measure," with the Pentagon then urging a forty-one-thousand-mile system as "essential to national defense."[119] Military and civilian objectives would be intertwined. After all, Clay testified, "one out of every seven of our workers, directly or indirectly, is supported by an automobile economy."[120] When congressmen initially worried in 1953 about Secretary of Defense Wilson's own conflicts of interest, he had offered the eminently sensible retort that he had often thought, "What is good for the country is good for General Motors, and what's good for General Motors is good for the country." They had not seen anything yet.

It was a more casual, if not a more trusting, time in government, industry, and academia. The President's Advisory Committee on a National Highway System (the Clay Committee) included specially interested participants such as Stephen Bechtel of the giant engineering company, William Roberts, president of Allis Chalmers, the earth-moving equipment corporation, and David Beck, leader of the Teamsters. At the Bureau of Public Roads, Delaware's Francis DuPont, whose family empire was still the largest shareholder in GM, offered his thoughts. No one was about to question the fairness of these experienced and practical citizens.

What began as a marginally popular civil program became wrapped in Pentagon exaggerations. The fevered hearings gave the impression that the United States had never possessed any means for transporting goods and people, although in World War II, as the railroad industry argued, more than 90 percent of the country's military passenger traffic and freight had moved by rail.[121] Searching for signposts, the Army's chief of transportation tried to "look back 30 years" in hopes of learning how to anticipate national needs in time for the next war. That task was futile, as entire cities and industries might now have to be dispersed, hardly something anticipated in planning against an invasion from Britain or Japan.[122]

The legislative history is full of references to crisis. Clay demanded immediate funding, since the interstates would address a defense priority that was "the greatest problem the Government has ever faced" (overlooking, say, the recent world war).[123] SAC's bombers, after all, might soon need to use the interstates of the high western plains as emergency landing strips. The Federal Aid Highway Act swept through Congress in 1956, and its name was changed immediately to the National System of Interstate and Defense Highways to underscore both national security and Washington's new role. Congress's promise to supply 90 cents of every dollar spent was irresistible to local politicians. Lingering opposition was pointless.

Amid such urgency, the Army even promised to tailor its equipment designs to fit highway specifications. However, the Bureau of Public Roads and the Pentagon never communicated on such basic steps as standardizing the tunnels or even the scaffolding on the two thousand bridges built during the next four years. The old-fashioned fourteen-foot clearances dictated by the first headlong rush proved too low for modern military trucks and trailers. Tanks, for instance, could not be hauled through on their transporters. In 1960, ceilings had to be expensively raised, but by then Americans were too preoccupied with other crises to notice.[124] Also by then, the Army was urging that ring roads circling the nation's cities were essential for evacuation. "A plunge route [going] through the center of the city" might be unnecessary, officials concluded, since it had become obvious to them that evacuees would more likely come from the flourishing suburbs than from the aging inner districts. After all, those were the people with cars.[125]

✪

By 1956, the United States was expending great and generally benign energy, although often without adequate information or focus. It was neither acting like an empire nor content to leave other nations to their dangerous ways. For centuries, America had been a place for Europeans and even Asians to escape to. Barely a decade after World War II, the country went into reverse, becoming fully engaged with the rest of the world. Sincerity was often measured by how much was being spent. America was pursuing not only anti-Communist objectives but also less dramatic ones, such as open markets and commercial advantage. It was hardly seeking supremacy. Even where Washington created an alliance (as in Southeast Asia) or installed a regime (as in Iran and Guatemala), its clients were able to defy it from the start. Americans really thought their political involvements were temporary.

Thoughtful officials understood that one of the century's most striking changes was America's transformation from relative economic self-sufficiency to increasing reliance on overseas resources. The last world war had been the turning point. It was easy to exaggerate the danger of such "dependence": this was a generation unprepared to see the extent to which technology can create substitutes for scarcity. Europe's empires still covered many of the distant lands possessing "sources of supply," principally raw materials. There was a general assumption in Washington that primary producers (not, of course, Iowa) were troublingly unstable.

However, the terminology of empire does not apply to U.S. political and military involvements in these places. *Imperial* has the overarching quality of "we're here, we're the boss, you can't get rid of us." Perhaps that would have been a cheaper, more efficient approach to deal with much of the world — as in, say, turning Japan into a colony, about which the British snickered. Among the deterrents to such an approach were at least two big unpleasant facts: it would have been necessary to produce an administrative class or elite cadre to oversee such relationships, and Americans would have had to become even more involved with the complicated politics of foreigners. Although America sometimes exhibited signs of being an empire, the country ultimately did not have the commitment to behave imperially.

Only in America could the plumber drive up to a customer's house *in his own car,* said awed Europeans during the 1950s. This was power indeed — and, in one sense, more than the ordinary imperial power, since it was exercised on the imaginations of developed societies. America's ascendancy was over fellow industrial democracies, which were about to disembarrass themselves from centuries of imperial conquest as they recognized how unprofitable nonindustrial landholdings could be in the modern age. It was the children of Henry Ford, not of Andrew Jackson, who were at work during the Cold War, seeking to build a system, not an empire. Their world role entailed such incredible expense largely because they dealt with the world through fits and starts. Programs would roar upward and fall short — a generalization true of foreign aid, collaborating with allies, language studies, and Pentagon spending. By and large, defense-related programs were not stop and go, but go, slow down, and wander.

This was not world dominion; it was domestic ambivalence. Overseas, it was confusion plus amateurism, as the CIA kept proving. Ignorance of languages, for instance, is highly uncharacteristic of those who intend to run empires. So, too, is having about twelve happy-go-lucky members of the staff at the American Embassy in Moscow sent home during Bohlen's four years after having been photographed secretly by the KGB enjoying sex with Russian "swallows;" or having unsupervised Russian construction crews riddle the embassy building with microphones.[126]

"Our national purpose," Acheson was fond of saying, "is to survive and perchance to prosper."[127] Civilization had so far survived, and prosperity by the mid-1950s seemed to be survival's logical sequel. The real problem, he told a former aide, was that the

Eisenhower administration "is following us too slavishly" and that "containment is being over-sold and over-followed." Right or wrong, this was one observation that he and Kennan could agree on.

Acheson hoped for much more of a power "system" in which the United States could rally or even buy allies to build a greater level of common defense. Ironically, that would require even more military spending. As the most prominent spokesman of the Democratic Party during the 1950s, Acheson, chairing a foreign affairs advisory committee with Nitze acting as his deputy, argued that Eisenhower and John Foster Dulles were being witlessly economical, dangerously trying to give "paramountcy" to America's fiscal and tax questions. Instead, the military had to be equipped "in an all-around manner" to ensure that "those in charge in Washington [are] not thinking of blasting away with nuclear weapons at some place of their own exclusive choosing" no matter what the threat.[128] The approach he envisioned would be more expensive in terms of bombs and bullets, but perhaps ultimately less so if America's client nations could be put to better use.

From his scholarly perch back in Princeton, Kennan offered his own commentary. He published another articulate, much discussed, seriously flawed book, *Realities of American Foreign Policy*. A traditional, highly Anglo-Saxon America, he reiterated, should "leave the cause of freedom to the power of example" (no need to examine how this might be conveyed). So many of Kennan's recommendations, Acheson would recall, were useless or stale.[129]

Kennan was increasingly critical not just of Eisenhower and Dulles but also of what Truman and Acheson had tried to achieve. He argued that Truman had militarized his original recommendation of containment, perhaps forgetting the additional Army divisions he, as State Department counselor, had advocated at the time. In a lecture series broadcast around the world by the BBC and published as *Russia, the Atom and the West*, Kennan offered his "personal assurance" that the Red Army was no threat. He then proposed that Germany reunify and become neutral and that U.S., British, and Soviet troops "disengage."[130] He lambasted Acheson for envisioning an end of the Cold War caused by an eventual collapse of Soviet power — a highly unlikely event, in his opinion.

Acheson dismissed almost anything from Kennan as reflecting "poor George's marshmallow mind."[131] Kennan was hurt and complained that his proposals for withdrawing from Europe were being misunderstood and distorted, as had been his original articulation of "containment." The price to the country of these well-publicized brawls was that U.S. intentions looked even more improvised and emotional than usual, thereby letting the allies rationalize doing even less.

While learned men debated in their law offices and faculty clubs and in the Council on Foreign Relations' mansion at 68th and Park, deadlier and long-denied matters were under way. These were the real costs of wielding power, especially with such uncertainty. The Korean War, for instance, did not close with the 1953 armistice.

Thousands of Americans were still unaccounted for. In 2001, the Pentagon hoped that the remains of half of them could be recovered. Before the POWs were repatriated in 1953, 600 soldiers and 310 airmen known to have been alive in enemy hands had simply "disappeared."[132] Within two years of the armistice, the Air Force had indications that dozens of missing airmen might be alive in Chinese or North Korean prisons, China having taken control of POW camps in North Korea in 1951. For example, a thirty-year-old B-29 pilot and four crewmen had been shot down near Pyongyang in January 1953. Radio contact was made with them during a failed rescue attempt, and a month after the armistice, the crew was reported to have been captured alive. Then there was nothing.[133]

Also in 2001, the Pentagon began looking for the remains of about twelve hundred Americans in former POW camps near the Yalu River. The extent of the number missing and disappeared — more men lost than at, say, First Bull Run — was not addressed until the 1990s. Tales accumulated of tortures and executions and, perhaps worse, of men sent to nameless destinations forever. Chilling new stories of what POWs endured at the hands of North Koreans are still widely published.[134] Not until the turn of the century would North Korea so much as discuss the possibility of helping to unearth the fate of these Americans, and even then, Pyongyang's officials truculently referred U.S. investigators to the Russians. Soon after the Soviet collapse, a joint U.S.-Russian task force would be established to track all unaccounted-for Americans, whether lost in Korea, in Indochina, or over the Soviet Union itself. Although the senior Russian involved denies that Soviet authorities had any direct contact with U.S. POWs, the Soviet documents that can be seen are equivocal. They use the same terms and phrases as are applied to dissidents who "disappeared" under Stalin. The last trace of scores of missing POWs may be otherwise inexplicable bureaucratic indents from various Soviet functionaries requesting more English-language translators.

Americans kept falling into that chasm from which no voices are ever heard again. In 1956, for instance, the State Department told Moscow that it was "informed and compelled to believe" that Americans were imprisoned somewhere in that necklace of labor camps that Aleksandr Solzhenitsyn would chart as the Gulag Archipelago. A U.S. officer, perhaps from a plane shot down four years earlier, had been reported seen in a Siberian hospital. Officially, the Soviets knew of no one. That was the last whisper of one of many Air Force "ferret flights" that probed Soviet borders using electronics to pinpoint radar defenses.

Such flights were child's play compared to reconnaissance intrusions over the Soviet Union, as had been under way since 1951 — a practice that Americans would have found unendurable had MiGs been darting across California and Virginia. The U.S. Air Force also supplied planes and training to the British for their own recurring penetrations. Fierce (though secret) Soviet protests accompanied efforts to shoot down or ram the intruders. There was an air battle over the Kola Peninsula in June 1953.[135] U.S. spy planes also regularly overflew China, and the Air Force abetted reconnaissance flights by the Nationalists on Taiwan. None of this was disclosed until the Cold War's end. When planes were downed, the aircrews' families were told that they had simply vanished or had drifted off course to destruction. The Soviets would fatefully remember these activities into the 1980s, and the Chinese cite them still.

Thirty-one U.S. aircraft (not including those lost in Korea and Vietnam) were shot down between 1950 and 1970, starting in the spring of 1950, when a U.S. Navy bomber with a crew of ten disappeared over the Baltic after encountering Soviet aircraft. Another crew of ten was lost in the fall of 1951. In the spring of 1953, the entire crew of a Lincoln bomber (a British plane with Americans on board) perished when it was attacked by Soviet fighters along the border between East and West Germany. Fourteen more U.S. airmen went down that summer. A B-29 reconnaissance plane was destroyed off the coast of Japan in November 1954. The following year, a Navy patrol plane was blown apart over the Bering Straits, an incident notable because the Soviets, amid that year's "Spirit of Geneva" summitry, paid half the damages and issued an apology.

The Air Force was undeterred. During one seven-week period in early 1956, it flew almost daily missions over the Soviet Union's northern reaches from a base in Greenland. As those flights continued, an unarmed C-130A (not on a spy mission) was shot down in 1958 over Soviet Armenia, the fate of its seventeen crewmen unknown until the 1990s. All had perished. Today, a refurbished C-130 is part of the centerpiece of the Aerial Reconnaissance Memorial and National Vigilance Park near the National Security Agency in suburban Washington. The park, dedicated in 1997, contains eighteen trees, each of which symbolizes a type of reconnaissance aircraft lost during the Cold War — reflecting the scope of the spy effort and the several hundred people who died participating in it.

Eisenhower remained extremely wary (and characteristically ambiguous) about these probes. He tolerated radar-seeking ferret flights along Soviet borders but warned that actually penetrating Soviet airspace was risking war. He personally authorized individual flight plans. Results were mixed; there was still no reliable intelligence on Soviet military capabilities. By the spring of 1954, however, the breathtaking possibilities of U-2 high-altitude reconnaissance came to hand. The U-2 was a hybrid glider and jet that the CIA had developed with the Lockheed Corporation in only two years. Flying at around seventy-two thousand feet, it produced photographs of astounding detail. The president was assured that at such heights, the U-2 would be undetectable. He nonetheless wanted pilots to be non–U.S. citizens so that America might escape the blame in case one was downed. Language and flying ability proved troublesome, so the pilots ended up coming from SAC, although they had civilian (that is, CIA) status. (The transition meant that all the former SAC pilots had to be polygraphed for loyalty and sexual preference.) Should Moscow somehow detect a flight, Washington could then truthfully reply that no U.S. military planes were involved.[136]

The first detachment was based in England, reflecting a still special, though diminishing, relationship. Deployment began in late April; photos would be shared with British intelligence. The planes, however, attracted attention from casual observers near the Lakenheath air base. In June, Foreign Secretary Eden gave the CIA twenty-four hours to get them out of the country. They were moved to West Germany, and this time the hosts were not informed, let alone consulted. The first penetration occurred on July 4, another the following morning. Both Moscow and Leningrad (today's St. Petersburg) were overflown.

Soviet radar was able to track each flight. This angered the president, who declared that he had "lost enthusiasm." He believed that his fellow citizens, should they learn of these missions, would be appalled that their country had violated international law. "Soviet protests were one thing," Allen Dulles was told, "any loss of confidence by our own people would be quite another." Eisenhower was torn between his desire to take a correct and even legal position and his need to know what the Russians were doing. Moscow, after all, had passed up his Open Skies proposal for mutual confidence-building aerial inspections of each other's territory. He ordered the flights to cease. They stopped for four months, briefly resumed, and stopped again.[137] The fact that the president was fretting about proper intelligence collection procedures and about the public's delicate sense of outrage, comes from another epoch. And another epoch it was.

Walter Lippmann meanwhile denounced Eisenhower's budgets as making no practical distinction between being at peace and being at cold war, complaining, with Acheson, that fiscal restraint was jeopardizing the country's defense. Such high critics of the age railed at Eisenhower's America as fat and pleasure seeking, showing it to be anything but militarist and imperial. Writing about this exactly six years to the day before Kennedy's inauguration, Lippmann sounded an early note in the coming chorus for "vigor."[138]

By contrast, John Foster Dulles suspected that the Soviet Union might be on the point of collapse, an opinion he shared with Congress. If so, why shouldn't the United States start splurging and bring the enemy to its knees? Even the wilder-spending liberal Democrats would not go that far in an era when balancing the budget was an enduring bipartisan goal. By 1956, there was no triumphant talk of the American Century. The country faced the possibility of nuclear conflagration, heard Churchill urging the United States to build more bases around the world, and saw communism dominating most of Eurasia. Searing disaster, as envisioned in so much of the popular fiction of those years, was averted. Cold, opportunity-devouring misfortune instead dragged on American life.

5

Settling In for the Long Haul

(1956–1961)

What makes the Soviet threat unique in history is its all inclusiveness. Every human activity is pressed into service as a weapon of expansion. Trade, economic development, military power, arts, science, education, the whole world of ideas — all are harnessed to this same chariot of expansion. The Soviets are, in short, waging total cold war.

Dwight Eisenhower, State of the Union, 1958

Of all the Cold War years, 1956 to 1961 are characterized most by that ancient wisdom *omne ignotum pro magnifico*, "everything unknown is taken as formidable." To complicate matters further, Eisenhower's second term saw the United States become increasingly involved in the developing world, mostly by using various kinds of assistance, but also by CIA plotting and an adventure in Lebanon. Few people knew where the money was going, or what was at stake. These were also the years in which the Soviet Union started arming and aiding a host of nonaligned countries — Afghanistan, Syria, and Yemen during 1956; Iraq and Indonesia in 1958; Guinea in 1959 — with the highest members of the Presidium, as the Politburo was then known, popping up in such improbable places as Burma. No one could know the extent of the payoff for Moscow, but surely there would be one.

During this time, once seemingly potent allies began to shrink before American eyes. Although Britain was able to detonate a hydrogen bomb in 1957 and France an atomic one in 1959, these dubious achievements occurred alongside a startling political and

military retrenchment. Americans began to settle in for the long
and heavy haul, while realizing that they would be traveling virtually alone. They came to respond regularly and directly when communism appeared to leach into nations once overseen from Europe.
Unlike the ten years just past, by 1956 every superpower showdown
seemed to have a chance of going nuclear.

This chapter first discusses how bloodshed in Hungary and
Egypt, during the weeks surrounding 1956's presidential election,
ensured more U.S. burdens for decades to come. Soviet rule became
unassailable in Eastern Europe, while Western Europe jumped into
decolonization, with the pace being a distinct yet rarely considered
cost of the Cold War. Second, the burst of newly independent states
in Africa finally forced questions of U.S. racism to the top of John
Foster Dulles's agenda. Third, the age of the Republic as an invulnerable "city on a hill" died once Americans looked up at the first
artificial satellite sailing among the constellations. With large,
expensive public initiatives followed. Fourth, we examine the price
in dynamism. Big organizations — whether in business, government, or labor — wanted other big organizations with which to
interact, a process that raised decisions to ever higher, less specifically informed, overstaffed levels. Finally, during 1956 to 1961,
America mounted the jet-propelled treadmill of modern arms competition. The weapons so familiar today — ICBMs, submarine-
launched ballistic missiles (SLBMs), B-52s — began to arrive. There
was no way of telling whether the casual overlaps of destructive
power in this arsenal were foolish waste or wise strategy.

All this energy was directed against an opponent that lots of
people thought steadily less malevolent and not preoccupied with
expansion. Hungary's fate in late 1956 dimmed the optimism arising from the previous year's U.S.-Soviet summit meeting. But many
Americans were hopeful about Nikita Khrushchev, the Russian
Communist Party's first secretary. Insiders knew that he had condemned Stalin's crimes before the Central Committee and, sometime
later, that he had denounced the "metal eaters" of the Red Army for
distorting his country's postwar planning. The Cominform was dissolved as a means of holding down Soviet satellites. Molotov was
dismissed as foreign minister. Deportees stumbled back from the
camps and penal colonies. Khrushchev came to be portrayed in
America as a good-hearted, gruff peasant, as in the 1962 best-seller
Fail-Safe. How disappointed he was, it would become known, not to

have seen Disneyland during his 1959 visit to the United States with his wife and son, yet how delighted to have met John Wayne.

To be sure, there was a departure from Stalinism. Khrushchev was a populist and may have felt genuine remorse for some of his own crimes. He outlined a new strategy of "peaceful coexistence," modifying Marxist-Leninist orthodoxy to say that war was not, in his own words, "a fatalistic inevitability." Travel to the Soviet Union became possible. Yet too many prominent Americans were unable to comprehend the radical differences of one of Stalin's prime executioners. There were risks in regarding the Kremlin as ever more "like us" and in yearning for compromise. Even more inconsistent behavior was one. These were the years when it became routine for many pundits to conclude that perhaps the latest Communist Party boss might have his "eccentricities," but surely he was "a figure with whom you could do business."[1]

Philosopher George Lichtheim, writing in *Commentary*, put such humanist moderation in perspective. Had the Third Reich won World War II, he explained, there undoubtedly would also have been a period of de-Hitlerization, probably by the early 1960s, perhaps conducted by Eichmann. In the Soviet case, once Stalin was gone, "moderation" came a little earlier, and it was Lavrenti Beria, maneuvering right after Stalin's death and before his own execution, who first positioned himself as the leading liberal.

Actually, the atrocities Khrushchev revealed amid de-Stalinization were largely those against other party members. The millions of dead or displaced peasants, workers, Chechens, or Jews received little mention. Khrushchev himself had been deeply complicit, running the party in Moscow during the Great Terror and a Politburo member since 1939. "I offer you 50,000 enemies of the people," he had told Stalin as the cattle cars rolled away in the late 1930s.[2] Although the death camps of Kolyma and Magadan had been closed in 1953, thousands of other prisons and labor camps for political prisoners thrived well into Mikhail Gorbachev's period of perestroika. Post-Stalin moderation went only so far. Denouncing Stalin was also a shrewd tactical move. It helped Khrushchev consolidate his supremacy by labeling his opponents as Stalinists. It also enabled him to present the Soviet Union as fully modern, worthy in every respect to challenge the United States across the board. During 1956 to 1961, Americans were discovering just enough about that new regime to be seriously and legitimately scared.

✪

In 1956, the United States had defense pacts with forty-two countries, embracing most of Latin America, Australia and New Zealand, Southeast Asia, Turkey, Iraq, Iran, Pakistan, and Western Europe. With the possible exception of always-contentious NATO, these were anything but strong alliances with real partners. The arrangements involved minimal mutuality and were instead demarcation lines against Soviet interference. The tone of that time was one of relentless legalism, of rationales for endorsing the original European alarms in Southeast Asia and in the Near and Middle East. John Foster Dulles was reluctantly pursuing the treaties that America had passed up in the 1920s. Generals fight the last war; diplomats revisit the last peace.

Just as America decided to act collectively, the country found itself like Gulliver in Lilliput, entangled among the little people's cords. The melancholy, disorganized de-commitment that would characterize U.S. policy during the 1970s largely began during these years. America simultaneously discovered that it would not be a knight-errant in Hungary and that its European allies would inevitably maneuver (while they rode off on their own erratic colonial missions) to leave the bills for the common defense in American hands. This showed in the conjunction of Hungary's rebellion, which began on October 23, and the altogether unrelated Anglo-French-Israeli invasion of Egypt, which got under way seven days later.

When Dwight Eisenhower was a shavetail, Britain and France were towering imperial powers. Now they were at best clients, as dramatized in the falsehood, private threat, and resentment that was Suez. In the 1930s, American opinion had considered these powers decadent, in slow decline. Now America, both more and less confident in its world role than two decades before, was startled when this judgment was proved true. Almost overnight, the Europeans moved from being the great advocates of world engagement to undignified avoiders of obligation, even to their own interests. Outside Europe, Eisenhower's recent inhibitions about "going in unilaterally" and trying not "to police the world" were falling fast.

The extent to which Hungary's tragic uprising resulted from U.S. encouragement remains controversial. The propaganda balloons that dropped leaflets emblazoned "Free Europe" had sailed over the people's republics for three years before the uprising. Mean-while, C. D. Jackson, now a delegate to the United Nations, ever more embodied the energetic assumptions of the John Gunther gen-eration, convinced that one could easily understand the inside workings of any country. He kept insisting to Eisenhower, to his patron Luce, and to anyone else who would listen that the times called for "little bits of cold, hard action." Something was needed that would be inspiring and "visible to the eyes of the millions of little men around the world."[3] Washington's energetic denials that it had any tie to the balloons or to other Free Europe Committee adventures were so unconvincing as to irritate friend and foe alike. Since no U.S. authorities translated, let alone understood, what Radio Free Europe's Hungarian émigrés were broadcasting, even the CIA did not know what it might have been provoking.[4]

The price in duplicity among allies, a bad enough precedent, is insignificant compared to playing at liberation in Eastern Europe. Thousands of those "little men" ended up rioting in Budapest for Imre Nagy, a reforming prime minister from 1953 to 1955 who had been expelled from the party. He was returned to office. Once the rebellion began, the United States may actually have had "a rare opportunity to change the face of Eastern Europe by pressing for a peaceful, negotiated solution," in the judgment of one commenta-tor.[5] Soviet troops and tanks withdrew from the city, and Moscow's divided leadership wavered for eleven days. Why should Washington have assumed that Moscow was *not* equivocating? Meanwhile, Nagy's new, legal government — determined to remove Hungary from the eighteen-month-old Warsaw Pact — proclaimed its neu-trality on November 1, 1956. Nagy announced that his country would no longer be a one-party state. He brought non-Communists into the government.

Dulles hailed these events to Vice President Richard Nixon as "the beginning of the collapse of the Soviet Empire." Kennan thought so too. Radio Free Europe broadcasts likely encouraged resistance, although Eisenhower rejected Agency requests to air-drop arms and supplies.[6] "We've just got to fight on 'til the UN gets here," a bunch of youngsters throwing up a barricade reassured the dumbfounded scholar Tibor Szamuely.[7] After so much Republican talk of rolling back the Soviet occupation, however, Dulles simply let Moscow know that the United States would not try to bring Hun-gary into NATO. There was no attempt to press for permanent Soviet troop withdrawals, no effort to deal directly with Nagy, and no understanding, given Washington's prevailing beliefs in monolithic communism, that Moscow might be enduring pressures from prickly Yugoslavia and even China not to use force. The West shrank from any recognition of Hungary's brief freedom. America's own limp response was essentially a way of telling the Kremlin that it could do as it pleased.

"What will NATO do?" frantic officials in Moscow kept asking their Eastern European loyalists, such as German spymaster Markus Wolf. Nothing, it turned out. The result of unpreparedness, of assuming that a demarche could not be made to the single-minded Soviet behemoth, turned out to be lethal for the rebels.[8] As the Red Army gathered, moreover, the bizarre Middle East war began. Its timing perfectly suited Moscow, which was also fearful that any compromise with Hungary would embolden the "imperialists" to go on the offensive in Central Europe as they were so clearly doing in Egypt.[9] Against the backdrop of Suez, the Red Army smashed into Budapest with 4,000 tanks, slaughtering men and boys in desperate house-to-house fighting. Using overwhelming force, Moscow asserted that its 200,000 troops were there legally under the terms of the Warsaw Pact.

Between 3,000 and 4,000 "freedom fighters" (the first use of the term) were killed, although the number may have been substantially higher, given purges and "disappearances" in the countryside. They took around 700 Soviet officers and soldiers with them. Some 300 rebel leaders were promptly executed. The Brezhnev Doctrine, as it later came to be known, was already in operation. In fact, it had been Stalin who had originally promised to use force against attempts to stray from the Soviet model of socialism. The United States ended up merely aiding the thousands of refugees, with Congressman Gerald Ford being just one of the many Americans standing on the Hungary-Austria border doing what little they could. Conceivably, the United States might have taken quietly firm steps to dissuade the Russians from cracking down in the first place, perhaps even using its nuclear superiority to give force to its principles.

Had Moscow shrugged off Western efforts to help negotiate a settlement, SAC, for instance, might have been placed on alert while Eisenhower cautioned the Kremlin against moving a single division within Hungary. One drawback to such a hypothesis, of course, is that Washington still had no idea of its nuclear preponderance, or whether Moscow would have been intimidated. Judging from what is now known of the Soviet leadership's dithering internal debates, however, a U.S. demand (backed by a range of unspecified threat) for Hungary's neutrality, as had just been established in neighboring Austria, might have begun prying Soviet hands from Eastern Europe several decades earlier.[10] Yet Eisenhower determined that Hungary — "as inaccessible as Tibet" — was beyond the limits of U.S. power. In any event, it was Western "fascism" and "counterrevolution" that were checkmated in the occupied nations. Washington's talk of a rollback evaporated for a quarter century, as the United States acquiesced to the Soviet bloc's western borders.

"The West deserted us once; will it welcome us now?" wondered Hungarian novelist Peter Nadas many years later as his country finally prepared to join NATO. Such memories would help shape the twenty-first-century landscape. Even in 2001, a democratic Hungary found itself putting on trial former border guards, accusing them of crimes against humanity in 1956. Stories were told to a new generation about Russian collaborators' machine-gunning demonstrators. They included the one of how Nagy was kidnapped from his refuge in the Yugoslavian embassy by the tall, gaunt Soviet ambassador, Yuri Andropov, then warehoused for two years until Khrushchev permitted him to be hanged.

Almost any tremor in the world from now on could be expected to court direct U.S.-Soviet confrontation. That became explicit in the Middle East. The violence had fermented at least since 1952, when young Egyptian nationalists had ousted the playboy King Farouk and begun to get truly assertive with London. The eighty-year-old Churchill, his vigor failing, was pushed from office three years later. "He is gaga," said Eden, his longtime understudy. But the old lion was strong enough to disdain any yielding of authority over the Suez Canal, as he bellowed about Eden's "appeasement," sneered that he had never known before that Munich was situated on the Nile, roared that "if we have any more of their cheek we will set the Jews on them and drive them into the gutter from which they never should have emerged," and then collapsed into his armchair.[11]

Washington was by then bidding for influence in Egypt, the apparently pivotal state in the Middle East, now run by obdurately patriotic colonels. In both Washington and London, men assumed that the thirty-eight-year-old colonel who rose to the top, Gamal Abdel Nasser, could be paid for at least some of his favor. They were wrong.[12]

With nearly all the British Empire's troops withdrawn from what had been its most prized bastion at Suez — gateway to Africa, path to India — Nasser was finally able to seize the Suez Canal Company in July. What Eisenhower called "the world's foremost public utility," through which passed most of Europe's oil, lay in his hands. Would Egyptians be able to run it? "An abominable snowman" could navigate the Suez Canal, said the Greek shipping magnate Aristotle Onassis phlegmatically.[13] The British felt otherwise, and they initially planned to poison Nasser. George Kennedy Young, on his way up the ladder to vice chief of the SIS, encountered qualms at the CIA when he broached the possibility of Nasser being "terminated."[14] To reoccupy the canal, the British instead conspired with France (enraged at Nasser's fanning of revolt in Algeria) to back an invasion by Israel (provoked by guerrilla attacks), after which they would flatten Egypt's air force and parachute into Suez to "separate" the combatants. Each of the three swore to Washington that nothing of the sort was afoot.

U-2 flights out of West Germany discovered British preparations, as equipment originally earmarked for NATO was moved into the Eastern Mediterranean. French and Israeli measures were detected as well. Eisenhower released the photos to London in a fruitless effort to dissuade. By October 28, John Foster Dulles predicted what was going to happen. The ten-day war began the following night when Israeli paratroopers dropped into the Sinai and a powerful armored column lashed out to the west. Forty-eight hours later, British and French bombers struck Egyptian airfields. The full Anglo-French assault finally surged ashore on Tuesday, November 6, voting day in America. Standing up for Egypt, Moscow threatened to send "volunteers" and even intimated that "rockets will fly" against London and Paris. Preserving the amenities, Washington let it be known publicly that in the event of such attacks "the Soviet Union will be destroyed."[15]

Within hours of his reelection, Eisenhower augmented the DEW line, prepared to dispatch a carrier task force to the war zone, and placed troop transport wings on alert. Recalling Hitler's last days, he concluded that the Soviets were "scared and furious, and there is nothing more dangerous than a dictatorship in that frame of mind."[16] As for the attack on Egypt, he compared it to behavior from Queen Victoria's day. The bold U.S. response all depended on which nation was being invaded by whom.

The British expected Eisenhower to impede any action in the UN that would undercut their plot to oust Nasser, somewhat as they had done two years earlier for him in Guatemala. He was not unsympathetic, given that Nasser had recognized Beijing and bought weapons from Czechoslovakia. But "nothing justified double-crossing us." Knowing that British gold reserves had fallen drastically, that there was a run on the pound, and that London desperately needed U.S. credit, he used that moment for an ultimatum. The pound sterling would be left naked to speculative pressure if the fighting did not stop. After all, said his treasury secretary in speaking of Egypt's self-determination, the British had "violated the basic principles in which we believe."[17] The same went for Israel, and Eisenhower was ready to cut off aid. Washington spoke forcibly, and when it did so, it spoke in dollars. Britain and France caused the maximum grief for themselves and everyone else, especially America, by mounting a great reassertion of empire, then losing their nerve as they faced threats from both the United States and the Soviet Union. Troops began to be evacuated by month's end. Obloquy without victory, weakness conceded before a weaker enemy, could only entail further disaster. It soon did.

These weeks also marked a turning point for the CIA's seminal U-2 program. Although the spy plane offered valuable coverage of what Britain and France were doing in the Middle East war, Eisenhower's stand-down order against flights over the Soviet Union was still in force. He would not allow U-2 penetration of the Eastern bloc during the Hungarian crisis. Only on November 20 did he permit the first flight since July: a U-2 flown from a secret base in Turkey by Francis Gary Powers, the son of a Kentucky coal miner, and an Air Force captain who had resigned his commission for a contract with the CIA. Three missions over Bulgaria followed during December, as did Soviet protests. "Effective immediately," the exasperated president finally instructed the Pentagon and the CIA, "there are to be no flights by U.S. reconnaissance aircraft over *Iron Curtain* countries."[18]

In comparison with the glimmering early flights of the U-2, the sorting out of colonial and European issues with Britain and France reads as if from the nineteenth century. Even while derailing the invasion, he could still call the British Empire "my right arm."[19] Ten years earlier, it would have been inconceivable to speak of the original "super power" in such modest terms; ten years later, it would be overblown to think of Britain as anything so significant. Suez definitively uncovered how much the postwar greatness of Britain and France had been resting on habit and bluff. At this rate, they would be more trouble than they were worth as proxies. America was being forced to develop a far more complicated perspective on Europe's "end of empire" than it had ever thought necessary in 1946.

The world is still paying for the rapid decolonization that followed. The "stay of execution" that John le Carré's George Smiley recalled was running out. Without the Cold War and its upheavals, decolonization might have proceeded at a pace better governed by reflection than by the threat of convulsion. The Cold War context, however, ensured that late-imperial disorder would end up striking the most sensitive nerves at the State and Defense Departments, in Congress, and among the CIA's world-order men.

Suez was the deathwatch of Britain's sense of itself as the third of the Big Three. Within a matter of weeks, observed political commentator Alan Watkins, bright young people were no longer dressing for dinner. John Osborne had just brought out *The Entertainer*. The sophisticated audiences who attended would laugh bitterly as Archie Rice said, with a terrible lightness, "It's hollow. . . . Don't clap too loud . . . it's a very old building." The will at the center was gone, muttered Harold Macmillan, Eden's swift successor.

Forty new countries, or at least foreign ministries, quickly arose out of what had been European colonies in Africa and Asia, with nineteen scrambling, or being pushed, onstage in 1960 alone. Only two years before Suez, Eisenhower fruitlessly urged Churchill to turn his back on an imperial lifetime by invoking "*a right to self-government* for colonial peoples (presuming they should achieve the necessary political, cultural, and economic maturity) callable in, say, twenty-five years." The emphasis was his. Churchill dismissed the idea, believing that Europe's civilizing mission of "opening up the jungles" had to extend well beyond 1980. The Belgians thought a thirty-year process was ridiculous: it would require at least one hundred.[20]

It was idle to believe that imperial power, established by shattering what indigenous legitimacy had existed, could, just by the fact of European departure, be transformed into deeply rooted constitutional authority. The sudden abandonments propelled by the Cold War ensured a freezing of colonial boundaries, which were often inauthentic ethnically or economically but were nervously consecrated thereafter because of the trouble that would be let loose if any border came under challenge.

The Cold War did not so much accelerate change in the not-particularly-developing world as create it a generation ahead of schedule, short-circuiting what might have been a more considered process. By diminishing the European powers and by fomenting lawless possibilities in the national sovereignties of Africa, it meant that there was no time for second thoughts. The British, for their part, had the site of a huge new Colonial Office already cleared. It stood empty for years, then was quietly built over.

Decolonization in these cases was not like restoring the independence of ancient Vietnam. It was largely preemptive. The Sudanese, in fact, feared that the British would give them to the Egyptians, nominally their co-sovereigns. In non-Muslim Africa, there were few colonial rebellions. White colonials ruled Africa badly in many ways, but the sudden scuttle helped ensure that it would be ruled even worse, starting with what an incisive student of Africa describes as a band of "crocodile liberators, Swiss bank socialists, quack revolutionaries and grasping kleptocrats."[21] The world's largest cathedral rose in the home village of one of the continent's more efficient Big Men. Roads disintegrated with a totality reminiscent of the fall of Rome.

No matter how sharp, the tiny elites of university graduates and soldiers who took over had no choice but to exaggerate their ability. Had Uganda been given twenty years to evolve, for instance, it is unlikely that Idi Amin would have been able to add thousands of dead to his name. Nor would have Sergeant, soon Emperor, Bokassa in the Central African Republic or the worst vampire of all, Equatorial Guinea's Francisco Macias Nguema. By the Cold War's end, the continent's 47 countries and 500 million people south of the Sahara would have, all in all, the same gross domestic product as Belgium, a country of 11 million.

The United States stood clear of these looming catastrophes until it felt it had to compete with the Soviets, and even with the Chinese, in such incoherent third world realms. Moscow, for example, was pouring about 40 percent of its aid money into Egypt. Nasser had little gratitude for his savior at Suez. "The genius of Americans," he is supposed to have said, "is that [they] never make clear-cut stupid moves, only complicated stupid moves; which make us wonder at the possibility that there may be something to them which we are missing."[22]

Unfortunately, there were no secret subtleties. Beginning in 1957, the United States stumbled into the process of third world development aid amid unresolved confusion over aims and likely effectiveness. Urged on by C. D. Jackson, and by his tirelessly ambitious successor, Nelson Rockefeller, Eisenhower and Dulles gingerly backed the creation of the Development Loan Fund. The president spoke of fighting poverty as a means of "defense against Communist conspiracy and encirclement," a concept that Democrats endorsed. From the mid-1950s to 1991, some two trillion nominal dollars in commercial and concessional assistance flowed to aid-receiving countries.[23]

Another cost of the Suez imbroglio for the United States was precisely this focus on "Communist conspiracy" in the Middle East. As in Vietnam, Washington frequently confused anticolonialism with communism (something that Moscow did, too). Beyond its various bilateral arrangements, the United States already had a range of official ties, particularly as an "observer" since 1955 of the Baghdad Pact (organized by the British to associate the defenses of Turkey, Pakistan, Iran, and Iraq), which then becoming CENTO, the Central Treaty Organization, once Iraq was violently broken loose. Eisenhower requested from Congress in January 1957 his own Ali Baba's hoard to funnel into these "northern tier" nations and their neighbors — $200 million in military and economic assistance to be spread around as needed. The proposal included the authorization to use U.S. troops to protect the beneficiaries from "any nation controlled by International Communism." When the bill was passed in March, it became known as the Eisenhower Doctrine. But by early 1958, the Middle East cauldron was boiling from intra-Arab rivalries far more than from Soviet subversion. Soon *The Economist* would define the term "friend of the West" as an elderly Arab statesman about to be assassinated.

Eisenhower was shrewd enough to suspect that America was often aligning itself with "the classes that have been exploiting their own people since time immemorial," a point he made to Harriman.[24] The CIA nonetheless became so thoroughly involved in Middle Eastern scheming that one officer in Beirut wondered if "we'd soon be out of key politicians for CIA personnel to recruit."[25] Several of them were so-called million-dollar agents who steadily received six-figure subsidies.

Lebanon, for instance, had gained its independence from French rule after World War II, and the Agency was dishing out taxpayer money and oil company donations to it, hoping to ensure a government that would be more or less friendly to business. "Throughout the elections I traveled regularly to the presidential palace with a briefcase full of Lebanese pounds," the same officer wrote, "then returned late at night to the embassy with an empty twin case."[26] In July 1958, once Lebanon's president nonetheless cried "Communist" amid incendiary radical politics fanned by Nasser and the overthrow of the monarchy in Iraq, two thousand Marines hit the beaches south of Beirut. They were supported by aircraft from the carrier *Essex* and backed by the Sixth Fleet's fifty or so ships. Five thousand more Marines and nearly eight thousand GIs followed, with the Air Force also playing a role. Eisenhower was inclined to move in sticky third world circumstances only when uncontestable force could preclude resistance, which had not been possible in Vietnam.

At Eisenhower's urging, a British parachute brigade landed in Jordan. Kim Philby was living in Beirut, staying intermittently with his father, the great Arabian explorer and convert St. John Philby. Ostensibly working as a journalist, he was supplying intelligence to both the SIS and the CIA, as well as to Moscow. Paid by the SIS, and perhaps by the CIA, he reserved loyalty for the KGB. Philby would not feel compelled to flee until early 1963, when he appeared in Moscow and thereafter received the Order of Lenin, the Soviet Union's highest honor, for his extraordinary successes at the heart of Western intelligence.

U.S. intervention in Lebanon was in the tradition of Iran and Guatemala, but with its own heavy-handedness. In explaining the operation, Eisenhower preferred comparisons with Greece in 1947 and even the U.S. repulse of North Korea in 1950. Time was supposedly being bought to stabilize Lebanon.[27] What Americans were in fact buying was inflamed Arab nationalism and an imperial caricature. As the NSC recognized, it was easy to blame the United States for upholding the ugly status quo in too many places.[28] However, the $205 million visit to Lebanon (about $1.2 billion today) appeared to be another cheap and easy victory. Within two months, the troops were gone, leaving behind, in the words of Chief of Naval Operations Arleigh Burke, only "a few legal beagles to pay for damage to the olive groves."[29] The fleet's operation order, however, had contained a contingency plan for a nuclear strike on the Soviet Union should matters get out of hand.

But it was not Moscow that responded. Half a world away, Mao decided to shell the small Nationalist-controlled islands of Quemoy and Matsu, in part, he said, to support the "Arab people's anti-imperialist struggle."[30] Had he decided to invade the islands, Joint Chiefs of Staff plans were in place to strike deep into China with "low-yield" atomic bombs — ones comparable to those used on Hiroshima and Nagasaki. Millions of civilian casualties around Shanghai, Nanking, and Canton were expected.

The following year again focused on the Soviet threat to the "northern tier" and to the Middle East as a whole. Eisenhower cemented a virtual bilateral alliance with the Shah when he pledged the use of American forces should Iran be attacked — subject to the approval of Congress, which would then, and only then, have to be told of the deal. The Soviets, however, usually had no need to be so secretive in their international maneuverings. Whether in Bandung or Cairo, they presented themselves as staunch anticolonialists who held the key to rapid industrialization. They pressed the tentative new states toward forced nationalization of foreign or locally owned properties, promising about $5 billion in aid from 1954 to 1960, of which about a fifth was actually delivered. The Soviet money that arrived was a fraction of what the United States was paying out. Helpfully, the newly dynamized Western European industrial democracies were now offering their own development assistance, if only in return for postimperial influence.

The price of playing in the third world kept increasing. Vietnam was adding up, as Washington buttressed Ngo Dinh Diem, the country's most prominent non-Communist nationalist and a former prisoner of Ho Chi Minh's, who had fled in 1950 after the Communists sentenced him to death. Six years later, Diem canceled the elections stipulated in the 1954 Geneva treaty. Nor was North Vietnam about to permit free and secret elections. About $10 million in CIA money had also been instrumental in maintaining Diem during the year after Geneva. Between 1955 and 1961, millions more in aid would make South Vietnam the fifth-largest recipient of U.S. assistance. Cash, of course, was not all that went to Vietnam, or to almost anywhere else that received U.S. aid. As John Kennedy would have said that final afternoon in Dallas, it was "not General Marshall's speech at Harvard which kept Communism out of Europe."[31] Military protection and a CIA presence inevitably accompanied the dollars.

✪

At a time when independent African states were emerging, America was compelled to face its own forms of oppression at home.

Eisenhower believed that every serious domestic problem had to "be examined critically against the background of our international situation." The "international situation" in turn affected which problems to tackle, if not solve.[32] He understood, as did his secretary of state, that America's role in the world was being harmed by the "Negro question."

In 1951, the January graduating class at Cardozo High School, a black school in the District of Columbia's segregated system, had managed to land Nobel laureate Pearl Buck as commencement speaker. The House Committee on Un-American Activities, however, found her Americanism wanting, apparently because of her doubts about Chiang Kai-shek. She was regarded as a poor role model for Negro youth and was disinvited by the school board, with the principal being reprimanded.[33] Half a dozen years later, racial problems had not conspicuously improved but had nevertheless become markedly altered. Race was the most painful contradiction of the country's evangelistic message of liberty.

National security had been a catalyst for civil rights at least since Truman had reimposed the draft. During the Korean War most of the "For Whites Only" signs on public accommodations were removed in California, and the ironic discrimination against Koreans and other Asians eased.[34] Discrimination of any sort was "criminally stupid," Eisenhower had remarked during his first presidential campaign, if simply because America vitally needed the brains and skills of all its people to face communism.[35] Otherwise, he remained personally detached from goals of racial equality.

Cries of "national security" worked both to uphold and to deny liberty for 10 percent of America's population. State and local governments had found it opportune to lump together civil rights and communism at least since World War II. Mississippi even institutionalized the tie in 1956 with its State Sovereignty Commission, which flourished for twenty-one years and accumulated 124,000 pages of investigators' documents with salient observations on skin tone, bloodlines, and suspect affiliations. Only in 1998 would these records be unsealed.[36] The connection made sense to J. Edgar Hoover. Although the Supreme Court by the mid-1950s was reversing many of the laws and penalties of just a few years before, the charge of communism could still be a convenient slander.

At the start of the Cold War, the most admired African-American was also someone whom the State Department labeled "one of the most dangerous men in the world." Paul Robeson —

distinguished artist, all-American football player, and graduate of Columbia University's law school — was never a Communist Party member, although he was reckless enough to assert that he could "walk in full human dignity" in the Soviet Union. FBI scrutiny of Robeson had begun in 1942, soon after he became chairman of the anticolonialist Council on African Affairs. It escalated to harassment in 1947 once Army intelligence concluded that he "managed to further the Communist Party line by his songs." It then grew worse. Not until 1974, two years before his death at age seventy-six, did the Bureau decide that "no further investigation is warranted."[37]

Other heroic African-Americans were singled out. *Exiled in Paris*, the best biography of the renowned author Richard Wright, shows how Cold War reflexes essentially hounded him to death by 1960. At the vanguard of the civil rights movement, W. E. B. DuBois, cofounder of the NAACP and a well-known scholar with (initially) integrationist ideals, was denied a passport to attend Ghana's independence celebration in 1957. (As if that were not enough to antagonize Ghana, its finance minister had been refused restaurant service in Delaware.)[38] His books had already been withdrawn from U.S. Information Agency libraries overseas. Only eighty-odd years of hope deferred could turn the increasingly radicalized DuBois from a Republican into a Communist, and he joined the Communist Party in 1960, long after other American socialists had left it. Still without a passport and having felt compelled to renounce his U.S. citizenship, DuBois died in Ghana in 1963 while in voluntary exile. Any emerging nation looking to America for inspiration during the 1950s could not help but notice something terribly wrong.

Washington feared that African peoples heading toward independence — described accurately, if insufficiently, as living in one-fifth of the world's land area — would be open to Soviet blandishments if the alternative was the land of the Ku Klux Klan. John Foster Dulles and anyone else who followed the issue knew that the rising generation of African leaders visiting as students "obtain[ed] their knowledge of American racial practices the hard way." In Nigeria, new elites could easily conclude that "Negroes in the United States are not included in the 'free world.'"[39] More annoyingly, Western Europeans lectured with visible satisfaction about the regrettable gap between America's high-principled rhetoric and the reality of Little Rock and Birmingham.

So the State Department undertook an ambitious study for Secretary Dulles, although it was not exactly needed to see that race relations were defiling America's role as "champion of freedom and democracy," particularly in "the non-white world."[40] Earlier in the 1950s, those U.S. embassies and consulates that had reason to touch on racial matters reported such comforting scenes as A. Philip Randolph's participating in an event in Japan, which demonstrated the "importance of the Negro in American Free Labor" and had been sponsored by the CIA-funded Congress for Cultural Freedom. Or they might report on the extended tour of *Porgy and Bess* through Western Europe, South America, and the Soviet bloc — a tour secretly subsidized by C. D. Jackson as a "living demonstration of the American Negro as part of America's cultural life."[41] Now something explosive was coming through the cables, as Europeans and Africans alike reacted to particular disgraces, such as the case of Jimmy Wilson, sentenced to death in Alabama for stealing $1.95 from a white woman.

Diplomatic instructions and USIA press kits had to address one indefensible incident after another. Efforts were well-intentioned and usually ineffective: translating and sending throughout France and francophone Africa Robert Penn Warren's monograph *Segregation: The Inner Conflict in the South*; shipping the Harlem Globetrotters to Africa; distributing an embarrassingly superficial tract called "The Louisville Story," which tried to showcase how blacks and whites were happily living together in that troubled Kentucky city.

Some American diplomats were perplexed by the commotion. "Why do you Swedes make so much fuss about the occasional Negro being manhandled in the U.S.," demanded the irritated ambassador in Stockholm, "when 20 million people have been murdered in China?" The ambassador went on, more effectively, to needle his hosts about the way they treated Gypsies.[42] Justice, however, is never a matter of numbers, and the United States could not hide behind Mao when it would not even recognize him. Even more uncomfortably, the condemnatory UN debates on the Soviet invasion of Hungary that finally began in September 1957 sadly coincided with the riots in Little Rock against integrating Central High. Moscow and its Budapest puppets struck back with straight faces: not only was America abusing defenseless black children, but it was hypocritically raising its dirty hands to reproach others. Soviet delegates solicitously warned their Asian and African counterparts to take care where they traveled in the United States.

Little Rock was a milestone. This city's name became a household word in France. Holland's centrist *De Telegraaf* concluded, as did many newspapers in Western Europe, that "the race ideologists . . . are doing more harm to America's moral voice, especially among colored peoples, than is befitting for the leader of the free world." Even West Germans noted how shameful it was for a strong nation to persecute a racial minority, and Nasser's editorialists got specific enough to depict the "terror" brought by "ten thousand 'pure white Americans'" on children in Arkansas.[43] Sukarno, Indonesia's increasingly left-leaning founding dictator, set his mouthpieces to work asking how Asians in general and his people in particular could believe in the United States. He invited Americans from the South to come to his country to learn about racial tolerance.[44] Many Americans, however, still preferred to identify bigotry as something foreign and distinct from their own experience — a "made-in-Europe poison," as Frank Sinatra called it during a television spot for the National Conference of Christians and Jews.[45]

The inevitable press kits were couriered around the world at the end of 1958 when two nine-year-old black boys were locked in a North Carolina reform school for kissing two white girls their age. "Facts on Racism Charge of U.S. Kissing Incident" argued that the Raleigh authorities were institutionalizing the offenders because of neglect at home. America's friends had heard enough. The U.S. ambassador in The Hague warned that just this one drama was "snowballing out of all proportion."[46] No one feared the consequences more than Dulles, who worried about the world's hundreds of millions of "brown" and "yellow" people whose sympathies were not yet held by Moscow or Beijing. By 1958, he telegraphed summaries of his embassies' reports directly to Alabama governor James Folsom, who was already being bombarded by upwards of a thousand letters a day from almost every point on the globe about the Jimmy Wilson case. As U.S. diplomats asked for more men and money to stem worldwide damage, Dulles ordered that all overseas missions report to him regularly on local reactions to U.S. racial turmoil.

In December, he shared a damage assessment with Brigadier General Andrew Goodpaster, a fast-rising officer with a Princeton Ph.D. who served as staff secretary to Eisenhower. "Treatment of

Minorities in the United States: Impact on Our Foreign Relations" was a country-by-country analysis of how white America was soiling itself, particularly in Asia and Africa. The report reviewed the obvious: the televised results of a criminal justice system in the South aimed at controlling rather than protecting black citizens were so harmful in themselves that Soviet propaganda barely had to comment. In fact, Moscow was clever enough to spend only one-sixth of its overseas broadcasting time mentioning American racism. The USIA might try offering a positive spin at the 1958 World's Fair in Brussels, the first such gathering since one in New York during 1939–1940, but its exhibit, "Unfinished Business," was a bit too frank in discussing America's shortcomings. It was closed under Southern pressure.

One of the reasons Eisenhower intensely admired Secretary of the Navy Robert Anderson, and thought he would make a splendid successor, was the quietly effective way he had desegregated installations at Charleston and Norfolk. Secretary of Defense Wilson had tried to desegregate all Defense Department schools. Progress was painfully slow in this wider effort, as it was in the South's other segregated shipyards and shore stations. Only African-Americans actually in uniform and on government property were benefiting from Truman's original desegregation directive. Southerners such as powerful Georgia congressman Carl Vinson felt no rush: he had introduced a bill in 1953 to outlaw any integration activity by military officers. Well into the 1960s, Secretary of Defense Robert McNamara would be compelled to say of his own orders that "not a goddamn thing happened."[47]

✪

At the same time that Americans were coming to grips with their basest emotions, the highest technologies were starting to change their lives. Never before had technology, like fundamental issues of justice, been so tied to national prestige. Twenty years earlier, in 1938, to invent an example, Hitler would not have been technically able to send a thousand bombers on an overflight of London (making a peaceful courtesy visit, of course). Now intimidating spectacles were routine. Immense recurring demonstrations of power, including giant, gloriously filmed bomb tests, were being magnified by seemingly more modest technologies such as television. The U.S. nuclear submarines that broke through the ice at the North Pole were another way to put the world on notice of such strength — ever newer and farther ranging.

ICBMs were already anticipated in late 1956 as the "ultimate weapon," and everyone knew that U.S. and Soviet earth-satellite programs were dress rehearsals for a missile race. Should Moscow be first into space, critics warned, the least of America's worries would be small wars such as those in Korea and Indochina, let alone troublemaking radicals in the Middle East. Thank goodness "a dynamic young German-born scientist . . . and many of his countrymen were recruited by the U.S. Army after the war," gushed the *New York Times* military correspondent.[48] Surely American technology remained unrivaled, especially when catalyzed by Wernher von Braun and friends.

The 1957 movie *Jet Pilot* reassuringly showed that nothing could sneak by that technology. Two formations of four jet fighters flying in perfect unison compose the opening image as the credits roll. The United States is seen to marry unparalleled technology with traditional courage to confound any enemy. Among the recruits is the U.S. Air Force, a star in its own right equal to John Wayne, who, as Colonel Jim Shannon, is the watchman guarding the skies.[49] *Jet Pilot* displayed to Americans the men and machines, far more competent than they, who were defending the country. Shannon's ground-control station is crowded with radar screens, communications devices, and complex maps, with a language all its own. An unidentified plane must be Soviet "because it does not show IFF," and from the moment it swoops into Shannon's radar net from across the Bering Sea, it is clear that he is in control.

The assumed omniscience of this technology formed the cultural background for Americans being crestfallen, as well as scared, after a shattering Soviet success in 1957. Indeed, one *New Yorker* cartoon of the time presents a Russian researcher crying, "Sergei! Sergei! I've just invented something! No, I mean *really* invented something!" But that was before *Sputnik*. Moscow enjoyed a multiple triumph: the launch of the first ICBM in August 1957, carrying only a test payload, was followed by *Sputnik* in October, and then by another satellite, containing a dog, in November.

In scoffing at what had become Curtis LeMay's highly publicized Strategic Air Command, Khrushchev bragged that aircraft could henceforth be treated as museum pieces. Soon thereafter, he crowed that Russia possessed ICBMs with an eight-thousand-mile range and hydrogen bomb warheads — all of which would be put into "mass production." "When will they hit us?" Virginia senator Harry Byrd asked after CIA Director Allen Dulles's briefing on the Hill just weeks after *Sputnik*.[50] The illuminating neologism "Sputnikeria" was coined to describe a fear different from those aroused by the Soviet detonation of 1949 or the bomber gap tales of 1955. Maybe *Sputnik* showed that communism really did possess inherent advantages in concentrating energy, money, science, engineering man power, and basic education into new kinds of world mastery. This was the apogee of central planning, with Russia "ushering in the Space Age," as the saying went. "I had no idea that the American people were so psychologically vulnerable," said Eisenhower.[51] They need not have been.

It was also the year in which investor Sherman Mills Fairchild backed a handful of twenty-something entrepreneurs to form a semiconductor company in the northern end of the Santa Clara Valley. The beginning of the space race coupled the transistor and the computer, leading to the integrated circuit that miniaturized the functions of the mighty military-backed "thinking machines" of a decade before.

The Soviets were never particularly secretive about their satellite work. Descriptions of an imminent launch had appeared in everything from the popular magazine *Radio* to documents circulated at scientific conferences. But the founding generation of the CIA rarely matched general savoir faire with language skills. In fact, great archives of Russian technical literature had been piling up in the Library of Congress. Although frustrated U.S. scientists suspected that these papers contained important information, the $1.5 million required to translate and catalog them could not be found: the task was "too expensive."[52] (Rarely during the Cold War was unclassified Russian material ever taken seriously by what came to be known as the intelligence community.) *Sputnik* once lofted, the Air Force finally gave several universities and publishers, notably McGraw-Hill, the wherewithall to interpret this treasure. More feverishly, it weighed a plan to explode an atomic bomb on the moon's surface. Surely, the world needed to be reminded immediately of America's prowess.[53]

Allen Dulles said that *Sputnik* "came as no great surprise" to him and thanked the Soviets for having dramatized their ability. Americans, he believed, needed such periodic "shock treatment."[54]

Eisenhower let it be known that he had never considered his country to be in a race and that a responsible U.S. satellite effort had to abide by a strict budget. He had offered a hostage to political fortune by not investing heavily in early ICBM development, asserting that a crash program was too expensive. He was correct in having looked at the bigger picture, and in his 1958 State of the Union address, he reminded everyone three months after *Sputnik* that the Cold War was not just a military matter.

He was too good a soldier to be hypnotized by hardware or by the intelligence offered in the CIA's "Estimate of the World Situation," which he concluded "could have been written by a high-school student." It was the strong dollar, he believed, that was ultimately inseparable not only from America's place as sheet anchor of the free world economy but especially from its military alliances.[55] Capitol Hill was hardly so subtle, as the House of Representatives tore apart a switchboard room and reassigned it to the new Select Committee on Astronautics and Space Exploration. The public's fears were echoed by Missouri's Clarence Cannon, one of those titans, often invisible to the public, who wield vast quiet power and are quickly forgotten. America, he said, lagged behind not only in space but in ICBMs, rocket fuel, submarines, radar, tanks, even rifles. Eisenhower, meanwhile, studied photographs from the U-2s.

Also in January 1958, the United States finally, and only after a string of colossally publicized mishaps, got its own satellite off the ground. For this achievement, von Braun received the President's Award for Distinguished Civil Service, to go along with the Knight's Cross granted him by Hitler. Days after von Braun's success on behalf of the U.S. Army, the president authorized work on *Corona*, the first "eye in space" — an orbiting imaging system able to photograph the planet and release pods of exposed film, which would be plucked from the sky by airplanes. It would be developed at crisis speed by a state-of-the-art aerospace industrial coalition. Lockheed Missiles & Space built the satellite. Itek, a new company whose entrepreneurial founders acquired Boston University's Air Force–funded Physical Research Laboratories, made the cameras, with the help of Sherman Fairchild's eponymous Camera and Instrument Corporation. General Electric handled the film-return pods, Douglas Aircraft the rockets. Eastman Kodak had to come up with a new type of film, Estar, which would eventually find many commercial

uses. All would succeed beyond anyone's wildest expectations —
but not for more than two years.

Nothing was more important than immediately remedying the
lack of intelligence about the Soviet Union, which "was just
appalling," according to Lawrence Houston, the CIA's general counsel: "We just didn't know what was going on."[56] The pressure
increased on Eisenhower to use the U-2 for seeing through the fog.
Perhaps slipping in from the south, using bases in Iran and Pakistan
rather than in Western Europe, would skirt Soviet radar networks.
Reluctantly he had allowed overflights of the Soviet Union to
resume in August 1957 because the Agency assured him that technical improvements had really made the planes undetectable.
Although he initialed his approval of the flight map, after examining it with Goodpaster and his son John (an Army officer serving as
a White House aide), the president was unconvinced. Following
another deep penetration in September, there would be only one
more, in March 1958. It was met by a vigorous Soviet protest and
resulted in another angry order from the Oval Office that the flights
be "discontinued, at once."[57]

The Air Force began launching high-altitude photographic balloons that spring to fly across the Soviet Union. Because the balloons were taking advantage of a newly discovered change in the jet
stream, there was (so the president was assured) a "practically nil"
risk of detection. Within weeks, Moscow had shot down one of
these contraptions and put it on display for the world press. "Every
cent that has been made available as part of any project involving
crossing the Iron Curtain," the furious Eisenhower ordered, "is to be
impounded." Had he screwed up like this, said the president, he
would have shot himself. Embarrassment was only part of the problem. He told the Joint Chiefs that if the Soviets were sending balloons and planes over the United States, the country would be
discussing mobilization.[58]

Other alarms were being raised about America's deficiencies.
Critics suddenly insisted, for example, that the United States ranked
seventh behind various European nations in the per capita ratio of
serious scientific achievements. Everything had to be done to catch
up. Lee Auspitz, later head of the Sabre Foundation, tells of a post-
Sputnik White House convocation of corporate chieftains to press
them to drop quotas against Jews.[59] Much talent and unknown
millions (soon billions) of dollars were flowing into the National

Security Agency (NSA), quietly created by executive order on election day, 1952. About nine thousand people already worked at the "Puzzle Palace," as insiders came to call this center of cryptology and signals interception. Its ultrasecret $35 million headquarters outside Washington housed the world's most sophisticated computer complex, and its officials directed the world's largest computer research program, which involved Sperry Rand, IBM, RCA, Philco, and General Electric, as well as MIT, the University of Kansas, and Ohio State. Although the NSA would remain Maryland's largest employer, and the biggest U.S. intelligence organization by far, its very existence was concealed from the public for twenty years.

In 1958, the Pentagon created the Advanced Research Projects Agency (ARPA) to streamline cutting-edge R & D. ARPA was intended to eliminate interservice feuding over the suddenly glamorous mission of military activity in space. It achieved much more. From the start it was a fast-paced, "freewheeling, adventurous" institution — "a 'revolving door' in the very best sense," with identifiably innovative talent drawn from all over the country to circulate among government, industry, and the universities.[60] Deliberately kept lean and distinct from the defense bureaucracies, ARPA opened its doors with a $520 million appropriation and a $2 billion long-term budget. "Come up with a good idea for a research program and it will take you thirty minutes to get funding," one scientist remembers being told. Cost was largely irrelevant; what mattered was encouraging compelling projects beyond the purview of industry.[61] At the same time, other parts of the Pentagon were inadvertently creating actual industries. Air Force R & D money at MIT, for example, brought into existence the computer-controlled machine-tool sector of the world economy.[62]

An AEC commissioner claimed that he did not know of any competent U.S. scientist who suffered from lack of research funding. Yet the National Science Foundation simultaneously concluded that U.S. scientists could achieve a lot more if they only had more money. No one really knew how much was being spent or on what. University deans alleged that the Defense Department's pre-*Sputnik* penny-pinching had already "cut severely into the graduate schools . . . throwing out the planned research programs." Congress's own niggardliness, it was charged, had forced university-administered national laboratories, such as enormous ones at Johns Hopkins and the University of California, to cancel contracts.[63] These complaints

vanished as Congress hurriedly reopened its wallet for those uniden-
tical twins, R & D, with the usually parsimonious president adding
the blessing that "our future security" had to be linked to science
education.

Defense dollars, for instance, fueled much of Harvard's growth
after *Sputnik*. Three-quarters of the university's research budget
came from Washington, at the same time that the CIA was helping
to fund an annual summer seminar for selected foreign leaders
and scholars. Other universities also welcomed the cash and were
equally uncritical of its source. Contracts to the engineering school
or secret subsidies to the government department could be assimilated into general overhead, benefiting fine arts majors or a sociology professor with, perhaps, far-left affiliations.

Responsibility for the country's intellectual strength had to go
beyond such universities as existed. *Life* magazine ran a cover photo
of a determined, scowling Russian student beside that of a what-
me-worry American teenager. The Soviet Union, allegedly deploying
its much smaller but apparently winged economy, was supposed to
be investing the same absolute capital resources in basic education
as the United States, so kindergarten through twelfth grade became
part of the race. Admiral Hyman Rickover, besides developing the
nuclear submarine, presided over a commission to offer rigorous
standards. Grade-schoolers who scoffed at classroom air raid drills
became truly rattled as they heard rumors that the nation would
demand additional homework. Worry over *Sputnik* and the condition of U.S. education also brought demands for efficiency. Small
schools were consolidated into centralized behemoths so as to
add sophisticated labs and advanced courses. Eventually, the sprawling factory-style high schools would be recognized as mediocre, and
the policy vogue would swing back to the obvious: smaller schools
for better learning.[64]

The National Defense Education Act of 1958 arrived to address
the "educational emergency." The four-year, billion-dollar program
doubled the federal education budget. The national security arguments behind universally available higher education were made
explicit. One way of attaining progress, much practiced in business,
is supposedly to improve product quality by renaming it and making
the package larger. Just so, second- and third-rank American colleges began mutating into "universities." Around a thousand new
colleges and universities would be opened or redesignated between

1960 and 1975. The short-term, status-raising advance to so-called higher levels of education began to overshadow the vital signifi-cance of the grammar and high school years — the time of greatest learning capacity, when students can overcome fears of languages and math and are most likely to become lifetime learners.

In the great tradition of American response to educational fail-ure, deficiencies were not reformed; instead, new institutional layers were piled on. More and bigger did not have to mean worse. Fore-shortened perspective and frantic action, however, meant that aca-demic quality would suffer.[65] People began to believe that higher degrees and time served for its own sake meant greater knowledge. "Education is a critical national security issue for our future," a president would assert forty years after *Sputnik*.[66] The link between scholastic and national economic performance was by then discred-ited. Yet using "security" to create a sense of crisis was still useful in trying to introduce new entitlements.

Indiscriminate university building and research center creating also contributed to a Malthusian nightmare: as ever larger hosts of academics received government largesse, each scholar would spawn one to two dozen new Ph.D.'s over a typical career, most of whom would in turn clamor for federal grants and tax-deductible money to start their own labs or policy centers. The great American Ph.D. machine got under way, fueled with taxpayer dollars and graduat-ing all too many of its products into unemployment. Soon the Uni-versity of California would set up the first permanent academic office in Washington, to be followed by dozens of others seeking yet more money. By 2000, around 180 academic institutions would be hiring outside lobbyists to help navigate through Capitol Hill's appropriations bills.

The chasing of contracts often overshadowed teaching. Rapid expansion also meant that university staffs could become loaded with mediocrities. There was little criticism. "Like certain other industries," writes essayist Louis Menard, focusing on growth, "the university was a great beneficiary of the Cold War."[67] Who, before the Cold War, had categorized universities as industries? Enroll-ments would at least double in the 1960s, and more faculty posi-tions were created than had come into being over the previous 310-year history of American higher education. By the late 1950s, the physical sciences were receiving more than 70 percent of all basic research money in the United States. To be sure, government support could often provide a genuine stimulus to study. Yet arguments flared and still smolder today: was all this money the Trojan Horse of university life, bending the world of the mind toward military ends, or could universities remain independent and rigorous while also profiting?

Some people were able to do it all. MIT's Jerrold Zacharias personifies this era's union of defense, scholarship, business-government ties, and startling creativity. A veteran of the Manhattan Project, he was a lifelong friend of Columbia University's I. I. Rabi. He was also a key figure among the physicists who came to prominence during World War II and who dominated American science for thirty years. It was he who had helped create automatic radar detection of an aircraft on the DEW line. Zacharias served on the President's Science Advisory Committee and directed the Laboratory for Nuclear Sciences at MIT, as well as Project Hartwell (on undersea warfare), Project Lexington (on nuclear-powered flight), and Projects Charles and Lincoln (on air defense) for the Navy and Air Force. Backed by the Office of Naval Research, he turned one of his own laboratory prototypes into the Atomichron atomic clock, had it produced by a suburban Boston electronics firm with his colleague Jerome Weisner (later to be President Kennedy's science adviser) on the board, and sold the device to the Pentagon. Along the way, he taught Physics of Atoms, Molecules, and Nuclei and headed a committee to revamp the teaching of high school physics. It is tormenting to think what else along these lines Zacharias might have contributed had the country's needs not made him feel compelled to do so much for national defense.

The structure of the federal research system in place by the late 1950s has remained essentially static through today. Undoubted benefits stumbled forth as the country more than doubled its R & D spending from 1955 to 1960, although nearly all of the money was related to defense and mostly administered by universities or corporations. For example, the Naval Weather Service, whose outposts were scattered across land and sea worldwide, was providing iceberg forecasts and optimal ship-track routing for navigators. When sixty-six nations launched the eighteen-month International Geophysical Year in 1957, this scientific study of the earth, sun, and outer space seemed merely to parallel the Navy's own research in astronomy, astrophysics, nuclear and molecular physics, math, and chemistry. The Army's TIROS series of satellites, begun in 1960, transformed weather prediction. The plate-tectonic revolution's million-year perspectives also benefited from the month-to-month urgencies of the Cold War: a largely Defense Department–supported global network of standardized seismic stations installed during the 1960s would harvest the previously inconceivable body of data necessary to ratify this vision of continents bobbing like rafts across geological time.

By 1960, the Naval Research Laboratory alone was up to 1,200 scientists, backed by support staff and working in 84 buildings on several hundred different projects. This was only one of a chain of coast-to-coast Navy labs, many geared to special missions, such as the 1,000-person Naval Electronics Laboratory in San Diego and the Naval Air Engineering Center in Philadelphia, plus the supersecret Special Devices Center for computer research. Radio signals were bounced off the moon. The dollars pumped continuous life throughout this technosystem. The Navy's deep underwater Sound Surveillance System (SOSUS) spread through the world's oceans and shipping choke points, with corrosion and the crushing depths enforcing "a mini-industry" of repair.[68] Hydrophonic monitors listened twenty-four hours a day for any movement of Soviet submarines but also, in learning of the necessity to distinguish between subs and whale songs, opened to the life sciences a storeroom of sparkling treasures. Oceanographic data from the Navy would advance environmental studies, geology, climatology, weather forecasting, pollution studies, marine engineering, commercial fisheries management, and deep oil and mineral exploration. "The value of that data is measured in tens of billions of dollars," one geophysicist reckons.[69]

Not that any of this was available for public use until after the Cold War — an expensive postponement. Raymond Siever, professor emeritus of geology at Harvard, recalls that he would have been forced to leave oceanography had he insisted on having nothing to do with the Pentagon. The New England seamounts, for example, were discovered and mapped by the Woods Hole Oceanographic Institute with Office of Naval Research money, although their whereabouts were promptly concealed by the Navy, which allowed unclassified maps of the area to be produced only if the seamounts were inaccurately plotted. Soviet oceanographers, it was hoped, would be fooled and thereby mislead their submariners. So were American and other Western scientists without clearances.[70]

The Soviet leap into space nonetheless remained alarming

because it was far more visible than anything else in science and technology. The White House had no doubt that America's prestige and security were being damaged, the two in those days being habitually coupled. Thus NASA, the National Aeronautics and Space Administration, was born under a cloud of confusion in 1958 as the White House debated to race or not to race — whether to request an annual budget of around $100 million a year for practical experimentation or to marshal twenty times as much for an all-out space competition, with clear military implications. Race America would, but in a haphazard drunkard's zigzag of spending. Within a decade, NASA's director would rail about a "crisis in space planning."[71]

Thousands of Americans had more intimate connections with outer space. UFOs were sighted throughout the country. Washington tossed lies to an unconvinced public about people instead having seen ice formations, temperature inversions, and other tricks of nature. A government intelligence panel wondered whether civic groups and even the Disney corporation could be used to debunk UFO reports and whether clubs of too-curious UFO buffs should be investigated for questionable patriotism. Only forty years later did the CIA note that more than half of all UFOs reported from the late 1950s through the 1960s were test flights of advanced espionage aircraft (a typically dubious calculation). All the misinformation "added fuel to the later conspiracy theories," an Agency study finally concluded, at a time of deep suspicion toward the federal government.[72]

✪

In an early John O'Hara novel, a rich man is startled upon reflecting that poverty must be like serving in the army — regimentation, shared sanitary facilities, no privacy, one's fate in the hands of others. By the late 1950s, amid suburbanization and steps toward civil rights, America was becoming freer. Yet from today's perspective, it was still mired in the past. This was no golden age. Despite the promises of technology and education, it was a poorer and more repressive time. Although the economy kept growing spunkily at about 3 percent a year, such growth was only relieving what today would be considered mass poverty.

For better or worse, Washington took a central role in America's transformation. Only a domestic situation as great as the Depression of the 1930s could have brought about this period's faith in the power and wisdom of government — its moral authority and commanding presence, its role as a repository of justice, moderation, and resource. Not just post-Depression but also pre–World War III insecurity was making people commit their lives and hopes to other big institutions in a way that today we might find bewildering. This occurred at a time of sustained unpredictability, which also reinforced the attractiveness of solid and apparently immutable corporations. The growth of business bureaucracy, the delay of pro-market pressures, and the eventual dash into a slew of counterproductive social policies were among the results.

Government, as the administrator of national defense, liked to deal with a reciprocatingly predictable industrial sector, diverse as its components might be. That this "countervailing power" of public and private abrasion was remotely efficient is the belief underlying Harvard professor John Kenneth Galbraith's *American Capitalism*, a much-discussed book of that era. Galbraith articulated the assumptions that, given some twists, business culture itself tended to endorse. Absent significant foreign competition, all companies in an industry could labor under the same regime of government-imposed burdens and benefits. They found the visible hand of federal involvement surprisingly congenial. However, this vision of extolling the big and the centralized came expensively in terms of creativity and speed. The bigger an undertaking, the more likely it is to be wasteful: economies of scale are brought about only by conscious effort and competition.

James Madison said that war is "the mother of executive aggrandizement."[73] During the Cold War, this came to apply not just to the executive branch of government but to every arena where anything "executive" had an impact. The era might be called one of "big engineering" — meaning the deployment of "engineering" in a broad sense on huge, highly material objectives, with an ever-larger directing role for expansive, well-connected organizations. The term "big engineering" is also more useful than is "military-industrial complex" in explaining what was coming about during these years. By now, the peacetime national defense establishment comprised much more than "the military" and "the industrials." Such a "complex" became inseparable from Congress, academia, the large foundations, and often the press.

A "big engineering" phenomenon would have characterized much of 1950s America even if less money had been spent on the military. The country had been moving toward agglomerated institutions for seventy years before 1945. U.S. Steel, GM, GE, and the like were not creatures of the Cold War. However, a belief in dependable, well-policed size was a keystone of Cold War liberal orthodoxy — the orthodoxy of a New Deal great power. The merits of mass and hierarchy had not yet begun to lose their allure. Big government and big business, ideally working together, appeared to be the driving forces of innovation. This seemed to be confirmed by technology. Computers were still housed in glass rooms and attended to by white-coated experts. The machines could even be depicted making government decisions, as in Robert Jungk's *Tomorrow Is Already Here*, a misguided account of the United States during these years. "It was the Cold War that helped IBM make itself the king of the computer business," recalled Thomas J. Watson Jr., about the fact that half his profits as head of U.S. sales at IBM during the 1950s came from contracts for the SAGE air defense system.[74]

The imperious Lionel Trilling writes in *The Liberal Imagination* about his literature students at Columbia being determined to join the largest corporations, such as IBM. A professor schooled in the Old Left who had gone on to master the literary, psychoanalytically sophisticated high culture of the 1950s, Trilling came to regard himself as an aging Machiavelli in a gathering of risk-averse choirboys. It was not just that the people at the top were believed supremely to understand crises and uncertainty but that any rung in the big organization was deemed a wiser, safer place to be than the chilly outside world. Eisenhower himself had been the organization man of the Army — delegating, calculatingly democratic, no more loyal than necessary. It is telling that the idiosyncratic MacArthur went nowhere politically in 1952, although he was the greatest American field commander since Ulysses S. Grant.

The country was in the hands of a leadership generation oddly short on the actual founders of enterprises. With the exception of Fairchild Semiconductor and a handful of other start-ups, few firms begun in the 1950s correspond to the countless high-tech and other enterprises created after, say, 1968, when Fairchild's original engineers, Robert Noyce and Gordon Moore, rounded up $2.5 million to start Intel. Certainly, Fairchild had a plethora of spin-offs in the 1960s, but it was not yet the time for Larry Ellison, Bill Gates, Steve Jobs, and the rest of the last quarter century's startling roster of entrepreneurs. Galbraith, for instance, could easily mock the

business executive for identifying himself with the dashing entrepreneur of economic legend, comparing him to the commander of
an armored division worrying about gasoline while imagining himself at the head of an old-time cavalry charge.[75] Entrepreneurs and
warriors, he reminds people in the know like himself, had both been
euthanized. The future would belong to rigid, pyramidal organizations, whether of business or government. The Cold War did not
create this belief, but it reinforced it by canonizing predictability,
solidity, and size. "The man in the gray flannel suit" of Sloan
Wilson's 1956 novel was a stepchild of these decades. Taxes remained high.

One consequence of extolling size and centralization was that it
became all the easier to assume that the state had a primary role in
American life. "Politicians today hold the key roles crucial to our
country's survival," concluded William Benton, advertising man
briefly turned U.S. senator, when discussing the disruptive new technologies. "The pace of change will make the politician's role ever
more important."[76] After all, what had the "private sector" — as
the world of commerce and industry came to be called — done
recently to match the Manhattan Project; the overthrow of the
Axis; the highways, satellites, and race to the heavens?

Presidential power expanded further. For example, the right of
"executive privilege," at first used sensibly by Eisenhower in 1954 to
shield executive branch witnesses from McCarthy's investigators,
was quickly extended to withhold from Congress any information
that a President might deem secret. Although Eisenhower's predecessors had been more circumspect, the doctrine thereafter came to
be regarded as traditional. It became easy to deify political power,
one aspect of what historian Arthur Schlesinger Jr. would call the
"imperial presidency." An early example is the 1956 election, in
which a TV commercial ended with a cabdriver looking at Eisenhower's White House and sighing, "I need you." This silly bleat
would be echoed twenty-one years later when journalist Barbara
Walters ended her interview with Jimmy Carter by saying, "Be kind
to us, Mr. President. Be good to us." By the late 1950s, a belief was
forming that the people at the center possessed extraordinary abilities, which in turn required that such abilities be exaggerated. The
distance between powerful institutions and the public naturally
increased. What did some "little nobody in a sack suit" (E. B. White's
horrifying description of himself in The White Flag) know anyway?

One of the most popular American novels of the century, Allen Drury's *Advise and Consent*, published in 1959, is about politicians — specifically, the battle over an erudite and wellborn nominee for secretary of state, resembling Alger Hiss before his fall. In the public mind, as well as in both business and government, the Cold War brought a last-chance confirmation of already-fading elites. Its 1950s pantheon was drawn from within the circle of men who administer things as they are, rather than those who bring new forces into being. An immense, institutionally paced quasi-war needed stable administrators rather than bold creators. The secretary of defense was just another good but interchangeable CEO, and so secretaries of defense proved to be. Charles Wilson was followed in 1957 by Neil McElroy, president of Procter & Gamble, and in 1959 by Philadelphia banker Thomas Gates. Government needed men who knew how to run immense organizations, "who [could] move in fast and be helpful right away" — solid, predictable citizens from an exceedingly small circle, even within the world of big business.[77]

The Cold War rested heavily on the shoulders of not only such established executives but also their lawyers: John McCloy, Policy Planning director Gerard Smith at the State Department, John Foster Dulles — all men of an inner circle, entering government at a level beyond the vulgar necessities of election. While serving as a rapporteur for such men at New York's Council on Foreign Relations, Zbigniew Brzezinski, an exiled Polish diplomat's son who rode political science into the position of national security assistant twenty years later, recalled that he felt he was sitting among the very few people who were deciding the fate of the world.[78] All the while, beneath such certified grandees, publicly obscure people were *really* changing it — identifying the coils of heredity and beginning to elicit the powers of the information revolution.

Even with Eisenhower's cutbacks, the Pentagon spent around $330 billion (more than $2 trillion today from a much smaller economy) during his eight years in office. Much of what it bought was aging fast. Nothing becomes obsolete as rapidly as weaponry during an arms race. Proponents of new projects — ICBMs, SLBMs, bombers, and military satellites — clamored for funding. Before the First World War, the great powers' peacetime military budgets (driven by spending on new battleships, the knockout weapons of the day) were repeatedly described as ruinous. That was small change in comparison. The late 1950s were the first years in which a society seemingly at peace became accustomed to continuous spending on a scale that had previously been seen only during war. Because so many constituencies were involved, many Americans came to enjoy it.

It is significant that one of the greatest of America's floating fortresses bears the name not of Benjamin Franklin or John Adams, but of Carl Vinson. This was the first time in the nation's history that one of its warships was to be named after a living person. It was the biggest and newest aircraft carrier. Although everyone understood that Dixie's delegation was seeing to it that the South would rise again, few people in these expansive years criticized how much was being pumped into that ascent by military spending.

Vinson's presence in his country's saga was the product of unspectacular public service and the kind of loyal district that even Georgia's legislature finds hard to create these days. His influence will long be felt. This quiet man, who had become chairman of the House Naval Committee half a dozen years before aircraft sank the smallest warship in combat, went on to preside over the Armed Services Committee less than four years after Hiroshima. He was one of the silent pivots on which turned not just America's defense but much of the nation's economic and political geography as well. It was said that if "one more military base or defense plant were built in Georgia, the state would sink under its own weight."[79] The strategy that justified this had as much to do with the voting booth as with the fleet.

Vinson embodied the defense-driven reconstruction of the South. When elected to Congress in 1914, he represented a region that had lost not just a war but a peace — in tariff policy, bank policy, and internal improvement policy. H. L. Mencken could speak of "the hookworm and pellagra belt." Of course, neither Carl Vinson nor the decisions he shaped for a gallery of presidents were solely responsible for the prospering South that rose between the plunge into the Second World War and the Apollo program. But the Houston Space Center, as well as the growth of Forts Bragg and Benning, are woven into the history of the time. New towns, great highways, and a modern way of life sprang in part from all the dragons' teeth sown.

The little-told Vinson story helps underline the fact that an effort so vast in scope and so long-lasting will metamorphize into much more than intended and that it will work itself into all fields that prove significant to it. The crucial factor is duration, and that, to be sure, is something the Cold War had to offer.

Alongside Vinson were Sam Rayburn, for whom a ballistic submarine would be named; L. Mendel Rivers of South Carolina, who rebuilt Charleston as a Navy town; F. Edward Hebert, who brought so much Pentagon money to Louisiana (while developing the most expensive medical school in the world for the armed forces); and the mighty Senator Richard B. Russell of Georgia, chairman of the Armed Services Committee and indispensable not only to the military but also to the secret agencies whose budgets he blended into regular Pentagon appropriations.

Cold War procurement became a form of crude regional development. It not only helped the South clamber from relative poverty but fueled intense specialization elsewhere, whether it was shipbuilding in New London or military aircraft assembly in Seattle, while adding to the visible per capita incomes of those states stretching from New England down the Atlantic seaboard, across Michigan and Ilinois, and into the lower Mountain and Pacific regions. No one can tell what other forms of enterprise were forgone to pay for this.

More than raising nineteen large military installations in Georgia, as well as others in South Carolina and Louisiana, defense spending came to account for between 20 and 30 percent of manufacturing employment in Kansas, Washington, New Mexico, California, and Connecticut. The Pacific expansion got under way during World War II. Civic leaders in San Diego, Los Angeles, San Francisco, and other already-prospering cities naturally tried to attract the valuable high-tech industries producing military goods and services, especially courting the Air Force, which commanded the highest proportion of service contracts. It followed that when 40 percent cutbacks in Air Force orders fell on, say, the Santa Monica or El Segundo–Torrance plants of Douglas Aircraft, the potent, many-thousand-member locals of the International Association of Machinists would bombard their congressional delegation to block such shortsightedness. The Cold War was becoming a business proposition, a career for both law partners and their friends at the Council on Foreign Relations, and a calling for members of the Union of Electrical, Radio, and Machine Workers in Long Beach.

In budgets for fiscal years 1958 to 1960, totaling $33.8 billion just for procurement, the bulk of the money was divided among a hundred or so large corporations. Ten of those received a total of around $7.5 billion, and the big three — General Dynamics, Lockheed, and Boeing — took down more than $1 billion each, with at least 85 percent of all contracts awarded without competitive bidding. Nobody wanted to take any chances. Hadn't such companies delivered when Franklin Roosevelt, picking a figure out of the air, had called for fifty thousand planes a year? Who knew what the next demands might be?

Naturally, the services laid claim to much more. With the usual spectrum of motivations that come into play with such big, portentous issues, many influential people outside the Pentagon openly insisted that Eisenhower was not doing enough. The Democrats particularly denounced his tightfistedness and, starting with Adlai Stevenson in 1955, hammered the issue home as their main line of attack. Couldn't $44 billion more in deficit-financed dollars be appropriated over the $40 billion defense budget for fiscal year 1958? And what about a crash program for building fallout shelters? All this was needed immediately, the elder statesmen from the Truman administration insisted, because there would be no end to the moves and counter-moves with the Soviet Union.[80]

Yale economist James Tobin, a former destroyer officer (and a minor character in *The Caine Mutiny*), a future member of Kennedy's Council of Economic Advisers, and a Nobel laureate, bemoaned what became known as the "missile gap," as did other learned men. Blaming America's lethargy on alleged laissez-faire capitalism, he derided Eisenhower in the *Yale Law Review* for his "vigorous effort to reduce the rate of spending of the Defense Department."[81] Henry Luce, who would eventually back Kennedy, was not to be left out. Surely, America's economy could "stand the load of any defense effort required" so long as "creeping socialism and the ceaseless extension of government activities" was avoided.[82] The irony was that so much of this creep and extension was being justified on defense grounds.

The attacks on Eisenhower were fueled by an NSC advisory report that had been submitted to the President a month after *Sputnik*. It would be classified for fourteen years, which of course made citizens fear the worst once the general conclusions were promptly leaked. The press portrayed the report as a warning that the United States was "in the gravest danger in its history."[83] By 1959–1960, it was thought, the Soviet Union would possess enough ICBMs to destroy SAC and the many fewer missiles America planned to have by that time. H. Rowan Gaither Jr., a San Francisco lawyer who chaired the Ford Foundation (the world's largest philanthropy) and had been president of the Rand Corporation, knew what should be done, as did other wise men. So did Paul Nitze, who drafted the report. Given Moscow's thrusts, powerful economy, and "spectacular progress" in nuclear programs, America had to develop both a huge, invulnerable ICBM retaliatory force (at the cost of what would be some $149 billion to $300 billion today) and fallout shelters throughout the nation. This report was followed a month later by one from the Rockefeller Brothers Fund: $15 billion more had to go to the Pentagon over the next five years, it said, or "the world balance of power will shift in favor of the Soviet Union."[84]

The president was dismissive as he referred to his country in the old-fashioned way: "I can't understand the United States being quite as panicky as they are." Although spending on missiles, submarines, bombers, and other large projects had jumped after *Sputnik*, he had no intention of bucking the $275 billion debt limit imposed by law, especially when his budget for fiscal year 1958 was nearly balanced. And he knew that the majority of his party still opposed "globaloney," Ohio senator John Bricker's memorable term for underwriting worldwide involvements. He would not devote more to defense even if the country could afford it, Eisenhower snapped; such a path would lead to a "garrison state."

Anything but an ideologue himself, Eisenhower was again using hyperbole to hold the line against the coalition of ideologues and alarmists, which included corporations, unions, universities, foundations, and so many other organizations both patriotic and self-serving. "Security with solvency" was his lodestar. It was also that of the elderly corporate chairman Douglas MacArthur, who was amazed at the "exorbitant funds" Eisenhower was shelling out even before *Sputnik*. (In the 2000 presidential campaign, Ralph Nader would acclaim his critique.) MacArthur suspected that Eisenhower was already going too far in defense spending. So did John Foster Dulles. The man who spoke of "brinksmanship" had doubts that America needed to be the world's greatest military power in the first place.[85]

Ever thereafter, Eisenhower's choice of phrase would be used by critics of just about any amount of military spending. He had made his career before World War II in the small army of a profoundly civilian nation. He was comfortable with the defense structure of a country that was no more than adequately armed in the years immediately after the war. His exaggerated descriptions — whether he was speaking of a "garrison state" or a "military-industrial complex" — reveal the mind-set and fears of the son of a Mennonite. These were hardly depictions of 1950s America or of what it might become.

Eisenhower's leading opponents of the time were united in describing American society as lost — but not to militarism. America was said to be wallowing in the swinish private pursuit of happiness. The puppet masters of Madison Avenue, portrayed in Vance Packard's *The Hidden Persuaders* (1957), were not getting people to sign up for the Army or to cry for more aircraft carriers. The gluttonous consumers presented in *The Status Seekers* (1959) were not swanking around in reserve uniforms like Wilhelmine bankers. If the United States had not been a "garrison state" when spending nearly 40 percent of its wealth per year on the "good war" of 1941 to 1945, it was an unlikely candidate for that title when it was spending 9 percent in 1958. A garrison state is not the creature of a civil society; a civil society is auxiliary to a garrison state.

Doubt about America's continuing prosperity and prevailing attitudes against taxation were among the reasons Eisenhower restrained spending. Responsible but unknowing people shuddered over inflation, which was climbing inexorably at over 2 percent a year. The boom that America enjoyed after 1953 was more a catch-up with reality (given how long stocks had been undervalued) than it was a bull market, which thrives on predictions of a rosy future.[86] A puzzling shift in the U.S. economy brought another reason to worry. For the first time in any country's experience, the number of people employed in producing things — farmers, factory workers, jewelers, builders — had dropped below the number of people providing services. No one knew what this meant in the short term — the long term being clearly revolutionary for life in America. By contrast, the Soviet Union increasingly appeared to be a triumphal industrial giant.

It was becoming conventional wisdom in the West that Russia, purportedly growing annually at 9 percent, would inevitably leave the United States in the dust — although for the moment, its economy was only around two-fifths the size of America's. The textbook written by MIT economist Paul Samuelson, who would be one of

Kennedy's key advisers, put faith in the power of Soviet central planning. The *New York Times* warned that "before the end of this century Soviet industrial output will exceed our own." If anything, that fateful crossover point was expected to be earlier — by 1980, Khrushchev insisted.[87] One set of government projections, based on CIA estimates, indicated that the size of the Soviet economy would be triple that of the United States by 2000.

The Soviets were indeed pumping out a lot of steel, coal, tractors, and tanks, as well as the world's second-largest oil flow, after the United States — not to mention their strength in producing that sternest of war's commodities, the Russian soldier. But all talk about the rising Soviet superstate rested on dubious extrapolation. Most devastatingly for the Communist future, 1959 became the year in which Khrushchev decided to subordinate household consumption and capital investment in Russian society to buying weapons.[88] Moscow, in effect, did not listen to Eisenhower.

A few keen observers were skeptical of Soviet industrial triumphs. Historian Eric Hobsbawm was a Stalinist, but he scoffed at the purported speed of Russian transformation.[89] Oxford economist Colin Clark produced powerful statistical evidence that these impressions of an inevitably booming Soviet Union made no sense. Robert Heinlein, science fiction ace and a Naval Academy graduate, observed the lack of barge traffic on the Moskva River and asked himself where all that productive power might actually be. He found his intelligence contacts equally perplexed. These opinions received little play.

One reason that less incisive people than these believed such projections of the Soviet economy was that, during this era, state direction seemed to equate with economic success. Even Western Europe was growing faster than the United States. Here was the "European miracle" that Kennedy would send his officials to study. Everyone seemed to have it right except America, which, even with respectable growth, felt that under the grandfatherly Eisenhower, the country was not keeping up with more centrally directed economies. Of course, the United States was spending more than twice the percentage of GDP on defense than were the six members of Europe's new Common Market (NATO members all).

Japan, meanwhile, was quietly but quickly outpacing even booming Europe. It enjoyed a growth decade never matched before or since, with annual production surpassing 10 percent and, by the end of the 1950s, reaching twice the prewar total. Yet Washington still saw Japan as uniquely fragile, unlike Russia and Europe. It felt compelled to keep extending aid and private charity, including $37.4 million more for school lunch programs. In the late 1950s, the United States sent hundreds of technicians to Japan to improve its industrial efficiency, and credits were extended to businesses in electric power and steel. U.S. government papers surrounding these various dealings, sums up Chalmers Johnson, a leading scholar of Japan, "sound like those of Roman proconsuls off in the boondocks."[90]

This indulgence can largely be explained by Cold War anxiety. Throughout, Japan's scrounging was courteously mingled with discreet threat. In 1957, Washington bowed to pressure to revise the 1951 security agreement: Tokyo would have to be consulted before U.S. bases in Japan could be used in a conflict. U.S. officials also kept fearing that Japan would disengage from its alignment with the West unless given open access to U.S. markets. Too much was at stake to dicker over reciprocity of any sort. Moreover, secret subsidies to leaders of the ruling Liberal Democratic Party (LDP) — the "party of private enterprise," as it was calling itself — had to continue, since they claimed to be too weak to oppose their socialist rivals. Tokyo's finance minister and other LDP officials sought specific contributions for the 1958 parliamentary election, claiming that otherwise they would "lose out." The finance minister "put a bite" on Washington, according to the U.S. ambassador, for "financial help in fighting communism."

Initially, Washington refused to come up with the requested funds, advising the LDP to look to its own business community, as was done in the United States when politicians needed cash. But the powerful *keiretsu* of Mitsui, Mitsubishi, and C. Itoh, among others, had no need to pay for more congenial politics themselves when money could be extracted from American taxpayers. U.S. reluctance did not last long. "We financed the LDP," recalls the CIA officer who ran many of these operations.[91] Secret payments became routine and perpetuated that party's crony capitalism. Moreover, such political subsidies are tricky to stop, as there is always the danger that an aggrieved former recipient will expose what has been going on.

Despite U.S. underwriting of treaties around the world, including a new one with Japan in 1960 that helped secure U.S. bases, the overarching question of the time was whether an apparently soft, even hedonistic, American consumer society had the stamina for a long, inconclusive contest with communism. Of course it did. But the emphasis on the big, the central, and the indispensability of the state was not helpful.

U.S. and Western European intellectuals kept insisting that America was at best stagnant, merely producing fripperies to satisfy artificial needs created by all those "hidden persuaders." Galbraith's *Affluent Society*, published in 1957, was one of the most influential books nominally on economics in the first thirty years after World War II. The author disdained the splurging on large, powerful cars and other objects deemed trivial. The masses, gerbils on a treadmill, would learn to be happier as their money was better spent with rigorous efficiency by government on worthy causes such as education, atomic research, urban renewal, and especially national defense, which Galbraith saw as being starved for resources. It was less apparent to him, and to other enthusiasts, how inefficiently the Pentagon, as Washington's biggest spending bureaucracy, was handling the earnings of sixty-eight million American workers. Waste on the unique scale that accompanies big government was soon replicated in the new civilian departments and agencies that assumptions such as Galbraith's would spawn in the 1960s.

★

On November 27, 1958, as cancer was closing in on John Foster Dulles, Khrushchev issued a six-month ultimatum. He threatened to sign a peace treaty with East Germany, which would include a provision terminating the Allied presence in West Berlin. "Rockets will fly" if he were opposed. "We are not afraid of May 27, 1959," responded Dulles. On May 27, 1959, with U.S. and Allied soldiers firmly in Berlin, he was buried at Arlington. For a man so often criticized as inarticulate, his words had been clear enough.

By the end of the 1950s, a daunting arsenal enabled the United States to back its men in Berlin and elsewhere in Europe, as well as those in Korea and Japan. Hundreds of B-52s had recently been commissioned. ICBMs arrived, and the first nuclear missile submarines were deployed — the latter being described by the General Accounting Office as "the largest single military program ever undertaken by the United States."[92] What next? Satellites as rocket-launching platforms? Missile bases on the moon? Weather warfare? Edward Teller, who was famous for creating the H-bomb, admitted that even he could not imagine what would be the undoubtedly immense military advantages of space.[93] "Anything's realer than war" goes the refrain in Stephen Vincent Benét's "John Brown's Body."

There was no way to determine what was and was not immediately essential. Almost every technology, like almost every bit of contested territory, as seen by the light of Munich, appeared vital. Technology was disrupting any attempt at anticipation: nuclear, thermonuclear, intercontinental, mobile, and miniaturized weapons kept arriving to demolish all certainties except those of less time and greater expense. Was the notion of a nuclear-powered plane any more preposterous than that of a nuclear submarine shooting off city-destroying missiles from beneath the ocean's surface? Nothing seemed ridiculous anymore. It was just hard to sort the absolutely ridiculous from the slightly eccentric.

The Air Force was swallowing half the defense budget by decade's end. The Navy hardly foundered. Fifteen carrier battle groups, the most expensive of all military instruments, became the national standard. By 1958, some $2 billion had already been spent or programmed for constructing the "Atomic Fleet." The first nuclear carrier commissioned, the USS *Enterprise*, with its twelve reactors (in contrast to the two on modern carriers), still sails. Within ten years, the AEC and the Navy went through $13 billion more, buying 223 reactor cores along the way. Approximately 16,500 officers and men, including recent Annapolis graduate James Earl Carter, had passed through Navy schools to work on "nukes." Surely, the long-term civilian benefit was obvious: men and know-how for the nation's expanding nuclear power industry.[94]

Polaris became the first true fang for this "dragon in the sea," an SLBM with a range of twelve hundred miles. Sixteen of these missiles could be carried on the new class of nuclear submarines, also named Polaris. (Amid the haste and complexity of development, a design flaw in the missile's warhead meant that more than half would not have detonated if fired.) Just building a fleet of submarines cost nearly $10 billion between 1959 and 1964 (at least that was "the amount publicly admitted") and required two thousand major contractors and six thousand affiliates. The Navy let every officer know that "they would not get medals for saving money."[95] Princeton's Oskar Morgenstern, one of the century's great economic thinkers, would meanwhile denounce the president for letting Polaris languish for want of sufficient financial support.[96]

With four emerging ballistic missile programs already belonging to the Air Force (the Atlas ICBM; its backup, Titan; the Thor IRBM; and the new solid-fueled Minuteman), Polaris was the Navy's chance for its own great-power standing. "The incipient waste in such a system was colossal," writes one of the leading historians of the postwar Navy, "but the waste was rarely that of fraud or peculation." Polaris's construction meant that vast amounts of material, of a mass and sophistication dwarfing any national fighting machine of the First World War, had to be produced, assembled, stored, and transported. Computers were used extensively to develop everything simultaneously. Nonetheless, at one point in the early 1960s, critical spare parts worth $600 million were lost in the Navy's own logistics pipeline.[97]

The Navy also designed a new class of nuclear-powered submarine capable of hunting and destroying enemy subs. The *Thresher* was the first, its keel laid in May 1958. Five years later, Navy listeners on the SOSUS system could hear its hull being crushed as it sank a hundred miles off Cape Cod with 129 men. "That accident or one like it was going to happen one day," says its first commanding officer.[98] Political pressures demanded new weapons, and construction standards, it would be charged, were relaxed in the rush to launch.

Procurement of this scope and speed also made inevitable the failed weapons fathered by each of the armed services. Among those that were canceled before being deployed were the Navaho cruise missile, which preceded the ICBMs ($5 billion today); the nuclear-powered aircraft, which consumed even more billions between 1946 and 1961, despite the fact that none were ever built; the nuclear-powered rocket engine, which ate up $4.2 billion in current dollars; and the XB-70 Valkyrie bomber, which taxied through more than twice that amount on its way to Valhalla. There were many others. They all seemed worth pursuing in their time, since military planners had no idea what number and configuration might be needed.

When there are no real answers, anyone can be an expert. Heinlein, who was a competent weapons engineer, used to say that the weirder the vision, the more likely it was to be right. Not only engineers and physicists pressed forward as experts. Wall Street lawyers, political science professors, economists, and psychologists also surfaced. Speculation, presented as categorical assertion, was almost a civic duty among the powerful and ambitious. Given the quality of businesslike apocalypse in so many respected writings of the time, such as those by Morgenstern and the Rand Corporation's Herman Kahn (to name two with a touch of genius), the public could believe that anything short of the tens and hundreds of billions being recommended must be almost timorously moderate.

Excellent reasons could have been given for spending two or three times the amount budgeted for defense during the late 1950s. This was a time, after all, when Khrushchev shouted, "We will bury you" — a pledge rightly taken as more than an economic threat.

If — after Stalin's massacres, Hungary's executions, *Sputnik*'s implications, Khrushchev's bluster about being the leading military power, and repeated intimidation over Berlin — Americans had been as scared as they were entitled to be, heaven knows where the effort might have stopped. A complete intellectual structure was in place for such radical steps as dispersing population and going underground. Given the mobility of Americans, the new highways crashing into midtowns (strategy combined with urban renewal), and the alarm bells from the Ford Foundation, such dispersal and burrowing would not have been fanciful. Even with the U-2 flights, the White House still knew little of what the Soviets did or did not possess. Many Americans were ready to ratchet up the costs. They also were ready to "pay the price" of nuclear war, according to Dulles, if Moscow moved against Western Europe even with non-nuclear forces.[99]

Morgenstern, for instance, berated the Eisenhower administration for not digging blast-proof caverns for millions of Americans. Entire cities should be able to be evacuated fast, he insisted, and the White House was failing "to do its most primitive duty" of protecting its citizens.[100] He urged that a substantial part of U.S. production be put underground so that America could recover after nuclear war: machine-tool factories, refineries, pharmaceutical plants, nuclear power plants, whatever might flourish in the dark. "The cost of the sub-economy would be great — but only the initial investment." There could be tax advantages, and private investors might see such steps as a way to insure themselves against losses from war damage.[101]

To be sure, perhaps a hundred million people would be killed once the Soviet ICBMs started falling. To Morgenstern, this meant "no one may assume that 'private initiative' will suffice, that a few tricks with 'stable money' and the like will do" — the latter point, at least, being a rare warning about dishonest government budgeting.

General George C. Marshall. World War II's organizer of victory who went on to serve as secretary of state and then secretary of defense. "His goodness put all ambition out of countenance," said Dean Acheson. *(Thomas McAvoy/TimePix)*

Dean Acheson. Undersecretary and later secretary of state in the Truman administration. Insouciant, temperamental, and effective. *(Leonard McCombe/TimePix)*

George Marshall, Lewis Douglas, and Ernest Bevin. Douglas (America's "most important diplomat") had pivotal ties with Bevin, perhaps Britain's greatest foreign secretary ever. To the surprise of many, Bevin was also a friend of Acheson's. *(Nat Farbman/TimePix)*

Albert Einstein, initially startled at the minimal postwar retribution against Germany, discussing the theory of matter with celebrated atomic scientist Robert Oppenheimer, who would be accused of disloyalty. *(Alfred Eisenstaedt/TimePix)*

President Harry S. Truman, the formidable banker/statesman Robert Lovett, and two very different stars of the foreign service, George F. Kennan and Charles "Chip" Bohlen. Both would be ambassadors to Moscow. (© *Bettmann/CORBIS*)

Stalin.
(*Chris Niedenthal/TimePix*)

General Douglas MacArthur, "American Caesar," greets Truman administration foreign policy adviser John Foster Dulles upon his arrival in Tokyo after a pep talk in Seoul, June 20, 1950. War started days later. *(U.S. Army/Truman Presidential Library)*

President Dwight D. Eisenhower and Secretary of State John Foster Dulles (left) meet at the White House with Prime Minister Winston Churchill and Foreign Secretary Anthony Eden (right), 1954. The visitors were being lectured on "appeasement." *(National Park Service/Eisenhower Presidential Library)*

Nikita Khrushchev contemplating a bust of Stalin, after a painting by Rembrandt. *(Herbert Orth/TimePix)*

The Soviet Presidium, later Politburo, 1958. Khrushchev is second from left, his successor Leonid Brezhnev is on the far right, with ideological enforcer Mikhail Suslov in between. *(Howard Sochurek/TimePix)*

"He had everything going for him but his skin," it was said of Paul Robeson. All-American football player, Columbia University Law School grad, world-renowned artist. The most widely admired African American at the start of the Cold War, he was hounded until 1974 by the FBI for leftist sympathies.
(Hank Walker/TimePix)

President John F. Kennedy, FBI director J. Edgar Hoover, and his nominal boss, Attorney General Robert F. Kennedy. Hoover had powerful sway over any politician with behavior to hide.
(Abbie Rose, National Park Service/John F. Kennedy Library)

President Kennedy, Secretary of Defense Robert McNamara (left), and Secretary of State Dean Rusk (middle). *(Cecil Stoughton, White House/John F. Kennedy Library)*

McGeorge Bundy, who moved from Harvard dean to national security assistant. He was quick to find the arguments of others "intellectually incomplete" as America entered Vietnam. *(TimePix)*

LBJ signing the Civil Rights Bill, July 2, 1964, after directing it through Congress. Dr. Martin Luther King Jr. is behind him. Racial justice was an issue close to Johnson's heart, and one improved by the Cold War. *(LBJ Library Photo by Cecil Stoughton)*

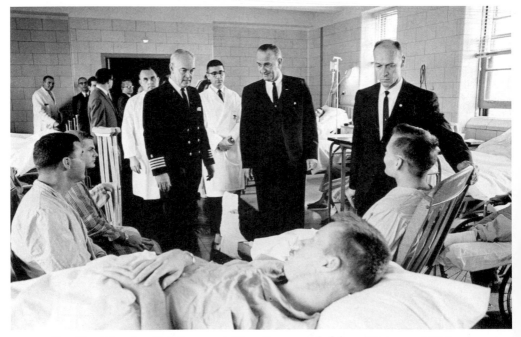

President Lyndon B. Johnson visiting the wounded from Vietnam, 1967. He failed to push back against the "best and brightest" defense policy advisers he inherited. *(LBJ Library Photo by Yoichi Okamoto)*

"Economic science can make a vital contribution in determining the exact nature of this sub-economy, this 'nucleus' or 'kernel' of our present economic system," wrote this brilliant man, whose own government contracts reflect some of the temptations that extended into so many callings throughout the Cold War.[102] Realizing that "the expected destruction would go beyond all bounds where the term and concept of 'costs' has any meaning," Morgenstern recommended "a simple shelter program" of $30 billion to $50 billion, "about 10% of one single year's GNP." A somewhat larger investment might save the lives of fifty million more people, he advised.

Critics might have pointed out that burying so much of America's population and even industry would be foolishly wasteful — directly so if peace held, indirectly if it panicked the Soviets into pre-emption. (The Soviets were well on their way with civil defense and war recovery preparations that dwarfed anything Americans ever implemented.) As for waste, Morgenstern responded, "So is the premium on every accident insurance wasted if the expected accident does not happen."[103] All this was not a vision of serious avoidance; it was one of a world anticipating disaster.

Thick manuals were rushed out on how to evacuate the cities along the unfolding interstates, a literature paralleled by the growing library about life in a postnuclear world. Europeans tended to think of World War II as the end. Period. Americans could for a while longer believe that some people would still be alive to rebuild after experiencing firestorms one hundred miles wide. Little was actually put into law, but studies and hearings continued. One designer drafted a plan to create a massive underground shelter to accommodate every resident of Manhattan. Civil defense officials proposed a relatively useful program of guarantees to construct home shelters: the Veterans Administration and the Federal Housing Authority would from 1960 on consider the value of a shelter in determining loans. Wasn't this "just as sensible as insurance on your car, and just as necessary"?[104]

Despite his nearly self-parodic writings, Morgenstern's brilliance shone in *Theory of Games and Economic Behavior*, coauthored with John von Neumann. What else might he have accomplished during those years spent consulting on strategy to Congress's Joint Committee on Atomic Energy, to the AEC itself, and to defense contractors, as well as toiling as coeditor of the long-forgotten *Naval Research Logistics Quarterly*? This also can be asked of von Neumann, who dutifully chaired the Strategic Missiles Evaluation Committee and who likely could have achieved even more.

Other well-received writings from respectable sources might not even have had their facts straight. For example, *Nuclear Weapons and Foreign Policy* was an influential book published in 1957 by Henry Kissinger, a thirty-four-year-old professor of government at Harvard, who had written it while serving as staff director of a Council on Foreign Relations study group. Among other arguments for devising a spectrum of capabilities to resist the Soviet Union, Kissinger noted that five-hundred-kiloton "tactical" nuclear weapons could be used on a European battlefield without causing vast collateral damage. However, the ratios of the blast and heat effects had been miscalculated, discerned Paul Nitze, former vice chairman of the U.S. Strategic Bombing Survey which, at the end of World War II, had been charged with discovering what kind of bombing had most damaged Germany and Japan. To him, such an error was one indication that "the picture Kissinger presents [was] oversimplified and overdrawn," and that "the book was disconnected from the elemental facts of geography and nuclear weapons."[105] Nitze, whom Kissinger initially threatened to sue for libel, was rare in not being buffaloed. As was the case so often, being shocking harvested greater reputation than being rigorous.

Congress, meanwhile, trustingly concluded that the AEC had publicly released all "significant" information about fallout, although such material was said to be beyond the average citizen's understanding.[106] In fact, as AEC scientists knew, highly incomplete data had been used to reach the official conclusion that radioactivity from weapons testing was not hazardous. Arizona's Stewart Udall, secretary of the interior before becoming an attorney for the people living downwind from the Nevada Test Site, would later refer to this minimizing as "the fox guarding the chicken coop." Government immorality, if not criminality, kept piling upon government secretiveness and deceit. It took about twenty years for the country to see what was inflicted on "a low use segment of the population," as one AEC memo described these citizens of Nevada and Utah.[107]

The AEC's Division of Biology and Medicine was also employing doctors in Washington state and Oregon to study the "effects of ionizing radiation on human spermatogenesis." To learn more about genetic effects, a preoccupation of the commission, prisoners were paid to have their testes irradiated. It was thought regrettable for science that vasectomies had to follow. "Since every effort will be made to prevent these subjects from breeding," lamented a senior scientist, "there will be no opportunity to observe any actual mutations."[108] Much of the academic research that the AEC funded in biology was kinder and gentler, such as using computers to simulate human genetic processes, and genuinely free of political interference. It was becoming clear, however, that what the apolitical were capable of coming up with by themselves in this environment called for the closest scrutiny.

Americans were not only anxious about the possibilities of incineration. The prospect of dreadful births also was making a bleak impression, not the least in fiction. Two examples are Walter Hiller's "Pope's Children," monsters whose lives the church protects, and the fish-shaped baby creature seen by a loving eye as entirely ordinary in "That Only a Mother." In 1959, the distinctly Tory *Spectator* of London carried a cartoon of one wolf warning another, "Lay off children's bones. They contain Strontium-90," reflecting the amount of potentially contaminated milk consumed by the young.

Government was doing a better job in protecting itself from fire and poison. At the elegant Greenbrier hotel in West Virginia, an underground office complex three stories deep and the size of two football fields was hollowed out of an adjoining hill, the construction being passed off as a new wing. Maintained, until its decommissioning in 1995, by a sixty-person staff disguised as hotel TV repairmen, this real-life 153-room catacomb was designed as an alternative site for Congress. Senators, representatives, and selected aides were expected to dash to the verdant mountains as Washington and their home districts were reduced to ruins. The bunker offered not only a hospital and a cafeteria equipped to serve the famous Senate Bean Soup, but also an underground TV studio complete with four portable photomurals of the Capitol amid appropriate seasonal foliage, against which a legislator could tape reassuring messages year-round for his irradiated but not unrepresented constituents. It also had a crematorium.

The Greenbrier redoubt, or Government Relocation Center, was supposed to be top secret to baffle Soviet targeting (if not an outraged American citizenry). Only half a dozen congressmen knew of its existence. Yet outside its four 25-ton blast doors, this bunker was widely gossiped about in the town of White Sulphur Springs from the day construction began. The secrecy that otherwise surrounded the center epitomized Washington's belief in the power of its own devilish cunning, whether used against foreign malice or an uninformed public.

The Greenbrier was just one page of Washington's doomsday portfolio. A web of refuges, known as the Federal Arc, surrounded the capital. Most were built by the ITT Corporation. Eisenhower and his cabinet practiced their escape to Raven Rock, the 265,000-square-foot "Underground Pentagon" near Gettysburg, or to Mount Weather in Virginia's Blue Ridge Mountains, under which was buried a 200,000-square foot refuge for senior federal employees. About seventy-five secret Presidential Emergency Facilities ended up being created, including an airborne command post and one aboard a cruiser permanently stationed at sea. Several would be used for real in September 2001. Doomsday planning in the decades ahead also involved the possibility of taking the president well out of the United States.

Other measures were implemented. Washington, D.C., is encircled by a chain of Cold War artifacts, less identifiable than, but resembling in purpose, the circle of Civil War forts that also still surrounds the capital. The remains of a ring of fifteen surface-to-air Nike missile sites set at a twenty-five-mile radius around the city commemorate Pentagon plans to clear the skies of Soviet bombers bent on decapitating the Republic. If a nuclear attack killed the president, or if he "or other persons empowered to act in his stead" could otherwise not respond, there existed "Instructions for Expenditure of Nuclear Weapons in Emergency Conditions." Starting in 1957, "pre-delegation authority" plans were in place for Curtis LeMay and other top commanders to fire at will. As head of SAC, he was asked to take care that such authority was "not assumed through accident or misinformation." Not just anyone should be obliterated in retaliation, his instructions continued, only "the enemy identified as responsible for the attack." (Presumably, the culprit could be fingered.)[109] Eisenhower also gave U.S. commanders in Europe advance permission to incinerate attacking Soviet forces should he not be reachable for a decision.

By decade's end, SAC had minutely targeted the Soviet Union, right down to obscure provincial cities, in what the Air Force by December 1960 began to call its Single Integrated Operational Plan (SIOP). Since only SAC had the necessary computer capacity to prepare this massive plan, bitter rivalries had to be overcome so that the Navy's Polaris warheads could be included in the SIOP's targeting. Several of Eisenhower's civilian advisers denounced such redundant means of destruction as the result of interservice jockeying; others detected a serendipitously invulnerable "triad" of ICBMs, bombers, and SLBMs that the Soviets would never be able to destroy as a whole. It was both, as well as an example of how haphazard even nuclear strategy could be.

And still "the country was starved for intelligence on the Soviet Union," according to *Corona*'s project manager. Even in the late 1950s, Nazi maps from World War II were being used to try to identify the topography around Soviet missile facilities.[110] LeMay's successor as SAC commander, General Thomas Power, a reputed sadist whom even LeMay believed to be unbalanced, could publicly state without fear of contradiction that Moscow was so far ahead in ICBM development that U.S. defenses could be wiped out in thirty minutes. An ingenuous press ran with the story, as Power took the opportunity to insist on $500 million more for an additional bomber wing. Other experts found it professionally useful to presume certainty. Professor Kissinger told the country there was no doubt that the missile gap existed.[111]

Actually, the doubt was immense. The Army believed it was a put-up job by the Air Force. The whole story of the missile gap epitomizes the stop and go, the overestimates swinging into underestimates, the infighting, and the alarms (false and otherwise) that became commonplace. U-2 reconnaissance of the Soviet Union had effectively come to a standstill; only two penetrations were flown in 1959. Above all, Eisenhower wanted negotiations with Khrushchev and feared that U-2 incursions would compel the Kremlin to cancel them. Yet he had to yield to the shrillness of Democrats and assorted academics who wanted more spending. The first overflight in sixteen months swooped above the Tyuratam missile test range in July 1959. In September, Khrushchev came to the United States and boasted of his new ICBM armory. The Democrats turned up the heat, as the bombastic Stuart Symington, senator from Missouri who had been Air Force secretary under Truman, cried that the gap was getting ever wider.

The events that followed have created yet another Cold War myth. "President Eisenhower," CIA director George Tenet insisted in the late 1990s, "knew for certain — *for certain* — that we had no bomber gap and no missile gap with the Soviet Union."[112] A bomber gap, however, was no longer the question. Even the Air Force had long acknowledged there was none. Tenet's real error concerned the much more controversial question of what was known about the missile gap at the time, and his mistake is significant.

Eisenhower allowed an additional U-2 flight in February 1960, covering the test ranges of Kapustin Yar and Tyuratam east of the Urals near Stalingrad. Excellent photography, now says the CIA, convinced the Agency, the Army, and the Navy that no missile gap existed. The Air Force remained skeptical. More U-2 photos were urged by Allen Dulles, as well as by a board of consultants (initially chaired by MIT president James Killian and including the president of Brown) that Eisenhower had established in 1956 to advise him on intelligence matters. So an additional mission was flown in April over Tyuratam, the nuclear test facilities at Semipalatinsk, and the early antiballistic missile test range at Sary Shagan. Still there were no signs of ICBMs, thereby supposedly confirming the CIA's "intelligence triumph," which Tenet now cites.

In fact, the U-2s were concentrating on Soviet R & D facilities, not searching out ICBM sites in the most likely places. Such evidence could have been found only west of the Urals, in European Russia. Eisenhower was rightly nervous about penetrating this heavily defended area. That would be permitted only on the ill-fated May 1960 mission. Had the CIA's most experienced pilot, thirty-year-old Francis Gary Powers, completed his flight, the missile gap would indeed have been disproved while Eisenhower was president.

Powers took off from Pakistan on May 1 at 6:26 A.M., attempting for the first time to cross the Soviet Union from the south to the northwest, a flight that would have covered thirty-eight hundred miles in nine hours. Navigating over the peaks of the Hindu Kush, then over Central Asia, his destination Norway, he was en route to take photographs of the SS-6 complex north of Leningrad. The CIA had thus far been unable to scrutinize more than just the test ranges (it would be several years before ICBMs would be deployed in Kazakhstan). But the Russians finally showed that they could knock out the U-2 at the edge of space. A surface-to-air missile exploded behind Powers's plane in the vicinity of Sverdlovsk. It flipped over, and both wings came off. He kicked free of the aircraft, and his parachute opened automatically. While at Mount Weather for an evacuation exercise, Eisenhower received the news that Moscow was claiming credit for the lost U-2. He had not been told that the plane's "self-destruct mechanism" had to be activated by the pilot and that it was unreliable in any event. The ejection mechanism was also unreliable, a point the CIA seems not to have shared with its pilots.

Not caring to use the poison pin that he and the other pilots carried occasionally, Powers was dragged before a people's court and tried for espionage. His Soviet attorney asked for mercy, noting that the young man had been driven to take the CIA's $2,500 per-mounth paycheck because of mass unemployment in the United States.[113] A New York lawyer worked behind the scenes to swap Soviet spy Rudolph Abel and bring Powers home seventeen months later — to widespread opprobrium as the man who had not killed himself rather than be captured. His U-2's wreckage (along with the poison pin) can now be seen in the Central Museum of the Soviet-Russian Armed Forces.

May Day, 1960, spelled the end for Eisenhower's summit with Khrushchev and for the U-2 bases in Turkey and Japan, given Khrushchev's threat to attack them. Nor would NASA continue to let the CIA use the cover story that the spy planes were doing weather research under its auspices. There would be no further flights over the Soviet bloc. The true nature of the missile gap thus remained a mystery for a while longer. Powers had gone on trial the same day that *Corona* went into orbit. The first usable film concerning the missile gap did not appear until December, and it was inconclusive. The Agency was nearly as wildly wrong about the gap as was the Air Force, projecting a ramp-up of hundreds of ICBMs in its key National Intelligence Estimate.[114] By year's end, all that could be agreed on was that the heavy, cumbersome Soviet ICBMs had to be deployed by rail before they could become operational. Not until 1961, months after Eisenhower left office, did *Corona*'s photos prove that the gap favored the United States.

Eisenhower's sound instincts gave him reason to suspect that there was no missile gap, although perhaps less cause to allow officials to perjure themselves in assuring Congress that he had no involvement with the U-2 flights. But he could not be "certain." Tenet's well-intentioned assertion shows how easy it is for any director to be misinformed categorically by one part or another of his bureaucracy. Curiously, he was speaking in direct contradiction to quiet public disclosures just the year before. At that time, Roland Inlow, former chairman of the director of Central Intelligence's

Committee on Imagery Requirements, had published the correct story of how *Corona* had finally put the issue to rest, but only in 1961.[115]

Khrushchev had been using the same tactics as in the mid-1950s to create the illusion of a bomber gap, which also had brought outcries from Symington and other Democrats. The Soviets had then led Americans to believe that they had built hundreds of intercontinental bombers. In reality, the Soviets had fewer than two hundred, although their hangars did hold about one thousand medium-range bombers, targeted against Western Europe and U.S. bases on either end of Eurasia. To create the illusion of a missile gap, Khrushchev had implied that hundreds of ICBMs were being built. What actually were mass-produced were hundreds of medium-range ballistic missiles (MRBMs), some six hundred of which were lined up along the Soviet border from Leningrad to Odessa like artillery pieces, each having a target in Western Europe.[116] As with the medium-range bombers, the CIA had not expected the Soviets to field more than a couple of hundred such missiles. NATO, for its part, had decided by 1958 to position U.S. missiles of a slightly shorter range in Britain, Greece, Italy, and Turkey. To the Soviets, these were indeed strategic missiles.

The Soviet Union did not orbit its own photoreconnaissance satellite until July 1962. As for the U-2, its next mission after May Day came five months later over Cuba. U-2s would keep flying right through the century — over Vietnam and Laos, in the 1991 Gulf War (where they provided 90 percent of all targeting intelligence), over Iraq and Bosnia, and during the Kosovo conflict. Invaluable intelligence has resulted. At least forty-five pilots have died flying these extraordinary planes, the highest casualty rate for any operational flight program in history.

In 1960, Eisenhower created the National Reconnaissance Office, soon to be the most expensive of America's secret agencies, whose existence remained unknown to the public and nearly all of Congress until 1992. Lyndon Johnson would remark that satellite photography had stopped the country from "building things we didn't need to build," claiming with pardonable exaggeration that this knowledge alone was worth ten times the $35 billion or $40 billion that had been spent on the space program. Perhaps. The CIA has yet to release any information about *Corona*'s own multibillion-dollar cost, even though so much else about the program has finally become known.

Corona and its successors also extensively photographed the American continent and the rest of the world. The results were the basis for many U.S. government maps, including those of the Geological Survey. Moreover, the wave of innovations behind the system aided the Apollo program and the creation of space telescopes. "Whatever we did had not been done before," its managers justly boasted — and it would likely not have been done then, but for the world struggle.[117] The Cold War imposed so many steps back that it is pleasant to recognize one that went forward.

U-2s were also flying over China, still considered a part of the Sino-Soviet bloc. This bloc, however, was crumbling, partly due to Khrushchev's refusal to share nuclear weapons with Mao, who was foaming about inevitable war with the West, partly to his refusal even to side with Mao in a showdown with the U.S. Navy over the shelling of Quemoy and Matsu, and very much to centuries-old rivalries. It is worth remembering, however, that the split between Russia and China was also over core strategies of how to destroy the West.

The U-2s could detect in China something that truly had not been done before — the inexplicable devastation of vast areas of Mao's realm. As many people died in history's greatest famine as would have been killed in a nuclear war. This entirely man-made, state-sponsored holocaust took somewhere between 20 million and 43 million lives between 1959 and 1961, perhaps more than the terrors of Hitler and Stalin combined. China was at peace when its rulers, adopting policies sufficiently disastrous in the Soviet Union, set out to remake agriculture in a country barely able to meet subsistence. Class solidarity would be imposed on nature. Among other superstitions, Trofim Lysenko's magical agricultural methods were forced on the peasants. The result was humanity's greatest single tragedy.

Had it not been for the Cold War, China would surely have been more tied to reality. Political and commercial connections with the world might have provided at least some reinforcement to common sense, some attenuation of Mao's cruelties. But Beijing's utter isolation left it far removed from the rest of civilization.

China's grain output had been about average when the Great Leap Forward was launched. Suddenly, provincial Communist Party bosses had to make it five to ten times better or convict themselves of sabotage. At first, Britain's economy was to be overtaken in fifteen years, then just two. Once again, a regime dedicated to "scientific so-cialism" passed by a natural progression into legislating fantasy — infant piglets to spawn litters, broken glass to fertilize crops. All was supposed to lead to unprecedented yields.

As human flesh was sold in the markets and enough "rightists" were herded into China's gulag to constitute a respectable Euro-pean nation, torture and execution were visited upon those already perishing for hoarding nonexistent grain. The usual parade of fawn-ing Western cheerleaders — including French socialist politician François Mitterrand, with the Marxist economist Joan Robinson applauding as well — glowed at a nation reborn. For thirty years, the world would not get around to examining what had occurred.

Fever dreams of counterrevolution helped Mao arouse an obses-sion with national self-sufficiency. He spoke casually of being ready to lose even more of China's population to war — perhaps half, or maybe a third. Some still see in this Great Leap Forward the linea-ments of a utopian quest, as in Leninism itself. True enough. "Man is neither angel nor beast; and the misfortune is that he who would act the angel acts the beast," Blaise Pascal said. Communist delu-sions in China exacted the supreme human sacrifice.

✪

A central principle of economics is that uncertainty is expensive. Uncertainty is imprecision; imprecision is waste and risk. During 1956 to 1961, so much was not only uncertain but also unknown. Eisenhower was able to face the fog of war with salutary caution; several of the men who came after him were less successful. A year-to-year standoff had been reached between Washington and Moscow by the end of his presidency. China remained beyond the pale. For the United States, the Soviets were becoming "more civi-lized," as John Foster Dulles hoped in the final months of his life.[118] Any national system of such evil has to moderate over time — although Beijing, for good reason, would see Soviet behavior as increasingly dangerous. In any event, the Soviet Union was becom-ing more prosperous in the late 1950s, although it was hardly the economic juggernaut many Americans feared. It was ever more like the antebellum South: an economic power running on principles equally repellent and inefficient. As for America's allies in Europe, they were becoming more politically and emotionally dependent, but rarely reluctant to offer criticism.

Eisenhower's singular achievement is that Americans were not in a shooting war when he left office, despite a close call in Vietnam. Without the stern audit of actual conflict, however, it was ever easier for layers of waste to keep accreting. A building boom in 1960 reflected Washington's increasing role in the world: the CIA began relocating from shabby temporary offices on the Mall into a sprawling 240-acre headquarters in Langley, Virginia; the State Department started extending its Depression-era Foggy Bottom offices into a new facility.

Throughout his presidency, Eisenhower was widely criticized because his military spending was said to be negligently insufficient, even though an amount equivalent to $304.7 billion today went to the Pentagon during his last year. His budget cutters nonetheless continued to struggle, and John Kennedy at his 1961 inauguration was startled by the skeletal appearance of Treasury Secretary Robert Anderson. Three days before retiring to Gettysburg, Eisenhower spoke, with archaic dignity, of pressures exerted on "the councils of government." He had wanted "to have something really significant to say," recalled one of his speechwriters, Johns Hopkins politics professor Malcolm Moos, who understood how entirely novel it was for America to support both a large military and its companion defense industry when not actually at war. Meanwhile, a colleague, Captain Ralph Williams, on assignment to the White House, was gunning for Curtis LeMay. "I wasn't worried about my precious Navy," Williams reflected about his motives for coining the now-famous phrase "military-industrial complex," "it was the Air Force we had to watch out for."[119]

Thus the term entered American discourse, characteristically on the spur of the moment, imprecise, incomplete, and local (not global) in its concerns. Only at the last minute did Eisenhower politely decide not to speak of a "military-industrial-congressional complex" in his farewell address. Less well remembered is that the president also warned of the "scientific and technological elite" who were making their hunts for taxpayer money "virtually a substitute for intellectual curiosity."[120] The agendas were becoming uncountable.

What had emerged by 1961 was a spending constituency — for national security and everything that might accompany it — that had fitted itself into the most dynamic parts of the nation. No longer were industrialists necessarily "people with something to sell," who were hostile or indifferent to military needs. They and every other interest group, from unions to universities, were eager to profit. This was no conspiracy in a corner, no attempt to hypnotize the nation into buying things it did not realize it wanted, as Madison Avenue was supposed to be doing on behalf of General Motors. The enthusiasts for arms outlays were in an open, noisily credit-seeking cabal. To the extent that all this money hastened some innovations that businesses would not otherwise have rushed into, its impact on the economy was (for the moment) at best neutral.

Eisenhower prevented the spending of billions of dollars that, we know today, would have been unnecessary. Several less attentive Republicans joined the Democrats' clamor for more money. After winning the governorship of New York from Averell Harriman in 1958, Nelson Rockefeller insisted, while being advised by Henry Kissinger, that "there must be no price ceiling on American defense." He promptly instigated a major fallout shelter program in his state.[121] By contrast, Eisenhower coolly dismissed as routine bluster Khrushchev's tirades over Berlin, in which the Soviet leader added that the city's defenders "will burn." Eisenhower had witnessed Russia's postwar devastation and correctly concluded that the Soviet Union was unlikely to be a direct threat anytime soon. The military balance, he suspected, was almost certainly lopsided. At the time, this was difficult to prove, given *Sputnik*, Khrushchev's posturing, and the shortcomings of reconnaissance. Eisenhower nonetheless sensed it, and he was wise to the ambitions of the services and other Cold War beneficiaries. History would prove him right.

Most poignant was his conclusion that the Cold War "promises to be of infinite duration." A generation before, there had been a joyous assertion of "America's coming of age." Now Murray Kempton, public radical and the most cultivated correspondent since H. L. Mencken, collected his columns in an account of the weary time, titled *America Comes of Middle Age*. It was dourly appropriate. Jules Feiffer drew a cartoon that conveys this sense of unending, tiresome imposed duty: "First I was told that I had a moral obligation to overcome the Depression," says a put-upon little man, "then I was told that I had a moral obligation to fight Fascism. . . . I feel as if I'm living in a moral debtor's prison." John Kennedy was to heap on much more responsibility.

The closest thing to a man on horseback during this half century was Kennedy as a 1960 campaigner, denouncing the five-star general in office for not spending enough, not being tough enough. During his first debate with Vice President Richard Nixon, he railed about immense "Soviet productivity," while insisting that the world could exist "half slave and half free" only if the United States was stronger than under Eisenhower. He set out relentlessly to milk public fears of a missile gap for political gain. Apart from 1980, this was the only election won by a candidate advocating a stronger U.S. military position. Contrast the 1948, 1952, and 1964 campaigns; that of 1968, which featured what journalists called Nixon's "secret plan" for peace; the "peace is at hand" campaign of 1972; and the 1976 race, with its rival platforms of retreat.

Kennedy's first three months would be, in the words of Arthur Schlesinger, Jr., who hurried down from Harvard to make history with a view toward writing it, "a thrust of action and purpose": a new generation would take charge after a "decade of inaction." There was private talk of winning the Cold War.[177] This was the generation that had been on the front lines in World War II, after an attack by Japan driven by the valor of ignorance.

The sense of possibility that can accompany such characteristics — in so many ways so admirable and so well-founded — passed readily into a confidence that zealously pushed into commitments wise and foolish. In the very speech in which Kennedy asserted that the country would put a man on the moon within the decade, he made explicit what Eisenhower had started in quiet drips, and he committed troops to Vietnam. Many who listened to him in 1961 must have doubted that the gulf of space could be crossed in that time, if ever. Yet that goal was achieved even sooner. A half dozen years after that "giant leap for mankind," however, Saigon fell before the eyes of a humiliated America. Such a disaster surely would have been even more unthinkable than a moon landing to anyone who even suspected the immensity of the effort that the United States was about to devote to Southeast Asia.

PART II

6

The Burden and the Glory

(1961–1963)

The cost of freedom is always high — but Americans have always paid it.

John F. Kennedy, 1962

H. G. Wells died in 1946, not long after publishing *Mind at the End of Its Tether*, a sketch of an era that had gone beyond the imagining even of the father of science fiction. What came next would have seemed still more far-fetched. The world of 1945 to 1960 was being shaped by people who were qualified biplane pilots (such as Robert Lovett) and military academy graduates from the horse-cavalry era (such as Eisenhower). Suddenly, they had to handle fission weapons (which Wells had put into a novel in 1912), delivery systems denying all security of distance and defense, and (in Maoism) a raging mass faith apparently expanding more rapidly than had any great religion.

Fifteen years after Wells, the United States had replaced the oldest president with the youngest elected one. The country was ready for the torch to be passed to a new generation. It also entered a new Cold War, one that offered at least a half dozen striking differences from the struggle as fought under Truman and Eisenhower. Fears that Moscow might indeed fulfill Khrushchev's promise to overtake the West catalyzed defense spending, propaganda, espionage, and covert action. Poignantly, John Kennedy spoke in his inaugural address of America's "burden." By the time of his second State of the Union address, he would acclaim the "burden and the glory" of the hour at which America had arrived.

The first and most apparent difference in this new Cold War was the incaution. The leadership under Kennedy's two predecessors had at least been aware of America's limitations, even to the point of exaggerating them. The youthful and vigorous men who came to power in January 1961 saw few limits and acted accordingly. The excitement of these World War II junior officers could now work on the institutions and practices that had settled in place over the preceding fifteen years. A handsome young president now challenged his fellow citizens to "pay any price, bear any burden, meet any hardship, support any friend, oppose any foe." It was a blank check tossed before the world, an immense change from the Cold War of Dean Acheson and John Foster Dulles. The most impatient of men, Kennedy, told Americans that they would have to be "patient in tribulation."[1]

A second difference in this new era was the exaggerated interest in foreign affairs. Martin Luther King, Jr., was marching. Much of Appalachia, the Mississippi Delta, and other forgotten pieces of America were barely more advanced than in 1900. Yet nothing on domestic affairs deserved mention in Kennedy's inaugural address. All the problems at home "pale when placed beside those which confront us around the world," the new president declared to a joint session of Congress after a week in office. He then let it be known how he remembered that the Federal Reserve dealt with monetary policy: it was because the surname of Fed chairman William McChesney Martin (who had been in office for ten years and was the world's most powerful economic figure) began with an *M*.

Third, this preoccupation with foreign affairs was accompanied by an astonishing militancy. Kennedy had spoken in the campaign about "a struggle for supremacy" against "ruthless, godless tyranny." It was a simplifying view in which, he said, Americans yearned "to be led by their Commander-in-Chief." To him, the Eisenhower years were "the days when the tide began to run out for the United States" and a red one began to pour in.[2] The stridency of the new administration surpassed anything proposed by other avowed anti-Communists. The consciously sophisticated, well-schooled people around Kennedy simply substituted the suave language of international conflict for the coarse rhetoric that Joseph McCarthy had made familiar. Kennedy's reputation has become that of a man of peace, but in fact he thrived on "neither war nor peace."

Misjudgment became inescapable as emergency moved further into a dramatizable, institutionally underwritten way of life.

Fourth, militancy would be backed by the serious-sounding social sciences, which had been growing in influence since World War II. Professors, who had previously been mostly advisers to the departments dealing with national defense, now became practitioners. They helped supply the analytic tools and the many social science certainties that would become the biggest and best casualties of the Vietnam home front.

A fifth difference was that by 1961, the Cold War seemed truly open-ended. What under Truman had been seen as something hopefully short and not too sharp, and what Eisenhower had tried to moderate with alliances and judicious spending, came to look indefinite. Kennedy declared at the start that there would be "a long twilight struggle year in and year out."[3] If this was peace, what might the next stage in the struggle be like? Probably not all-out war, but something harder, and correspondingly more thrilling.

Sixth, Kennedy made explicit that the Cold War was a "global civil war," one that would be waged in the "whole southern half of the globe." That half included some of the world's most morally treacherous terrain. The United States had certainly bribed and threatened before the Cold War — "We want Perdicaris alive or Raisuli dead," thundered Secretary of State John Hay in 1904 — but the years of the Kennedy administration settled such behavior into a system. What followed was a routine cultivation of "friendly dictators," a profligate use of covert operations, and an endorsement of assassination at the highest levels unique in the history of the American presidency.

During Eisenhower's last days in office, Walter Lippmann had written of the "vacancy" in American life, suggesting that the people had been put to sleep. Americans apparently yearned for more political direction rather than, say, more rewarding private activities. Clearly agreeing, Arthur Schlesinger had also written in 1960 of "heroic leadership." The country, he believed, was falling behind because of a national lack of purpose. Presumably, its citizens would answer only to "heroism," that quality in this politically oriented time to be found among politicians.[4] No need to specify names.

The Cold War brought forward a certain type of politician who presumed to give tone to American lives as the country tried to adapt to its new energies. These were men licensed to become overexcited, the kind of politician who fascinates intellectuals. There was no one better than John Kennedy for exalting the glamour and authority of the state. Kennedy, presented as PT boat hero, was the embodiment of fame won by going in harm's way. Conflict and danger might lift everyone into a larger scope of being as the nation faced what its president called at his inauguration the "hour of maximum danger." Such a view rationalized activities ever farther off the point of the original Cold War confrontation: "nation building" and more security assistance far beyond Europe; a cultivation of "world opinion" going well beyond the 1950s secretly funded "cultural Cold War"; contracting for weapons to an extent never before considered by Americans in peacetime.

The supposed aging complacency of the Eisenhower era was replaced with new orthodoxies held by men of young middle age. Those men in turn set themselves up to be blindsided by the upheavals of the late 1960s. The world's complexities made everyone in power more or less ignorant to some degree, but this was especially true of the cleverest men, those who were most eager to prove valor and vigor. All the accreting pathologies of the previous fifteen years came together, including secrecy, politicization, brinkmanship, and "situation ethics."

There are several ways to explain how all this occurred: first, by examining the men and their assumptions, along with the unprecedented peacetime enthusiasm over "national security" that they brought into office; second, by discussing the nuclear scares that quickly followed; third, by looking at the influences that were transforming the world, as more opportunities were lost to the Cold War; and finally, by trying to show why and how America entered what would prove to be fearsome involvements in the "southern half of the globe."

This period took its name from a musical, *Camelot*. Four hundred years before, old Dean Colet of St. Paul's had asked grimly, "What was it with King Arthur and his knights but bold bawdry and open manslaughter?" Likewise, with John Kennedy, there was no shortage of adrenaline, violence, or noble intentions. That was so much of the problem. In the words of the weary hero of the mythical *Camelot*, sailing into the shadows of Avalon, "Lest one good custom should corrupt the world."

✪

After the Cold War, Robert McNamara, the former president of Ford Motor whom Kennedy had brought to Washington practically sight unseen, confessed he "had always been confident that every problem could be solved." He specifically regretted that he, McGeorge Bundy, Dean Rusk, and so many others had failed to recognize that there just might be matters in international affairs that had no immediate solutions.[5] The press accounts of forty-four-year-old McNamara and the other prodigies of Kennedy's civilian general staff make today's *Vanity Fair* cover profiles seem subdued. Awed idealization of this brilliance and style was projected onto the man who served in the national security arena — onto those in the Office of the Secretary of Defense and on the National Security Council, less so onto the capable Paul Volcker, Robert Roosa, and others who served quietly under Treasury Secretary Douglas Dillon.

The crusty Sam Rayburn, Speaker of the House and longtime mentor to Lyndon Johnson, had it right. "I'd feel a whole lot better about them if just one of them had run for sheriff once," he told the new vice president in 1961, suggesting that none of these self-assured men had ever encountered the messiness of life.[6] Such naïveté is very much a reflection of America, but it is usually confronted by an Abraham Lincoln, an Elihu Root, or a George Marshall before it runs amok as national decision.

On the first page of Arthur C. Clarke's novel *Childhood's End*, as the United States and the Soviet Union race for the moon, there is a figure clearly based on Wernher von Braun. He recalls a friend from his days of working on rockets at Peenemünde, a man who in 1945 chose the Soviet Union. "Democracy, nuts," the von Braun character says to himself. "One Konrad Schneider was worth a million names on an electoral roll." A single overriding individual in authority, he is shown to believe, has so much more to contribute than do the masses.

Similarly, the Washington of these years also had a sense of there being great men with nearly masterly genius at the center. There was excitement over ennobling power, immense stakes, and decisive moments. "It is the President alone who must make major decisions on our foreign policy," Kennedy asserted.[7] This was hardly a vision of tyranny, rather an ominous one of star quality. The decisive and more prudent voices of the early Cold War were fading: Lovett, Lewis Douglas, Acheson. Robert Taft, Marshall, and John Foster Dulles were already gone. The jagged emergency that they were the first to confront was a younger man's proving ground.

The confidence of being able to change the world combined with Kennedy's penchant for the allegedly historic overview. His wife spoke of being married to "an historian." Schlesinger wheedled, "You are a writer and a historian." Kennedy biographer Richard Reeves explains, " 'History' was a trigger word for Kennedy." It was "the goddess Kennedy pursued with notes and short calls to [adviser Ted] Sorenson or Schlesinger."[8] It was not only the relatively applicable history of Barbara Tuchman's *Guns of August,* which it had been made known he had read, but also such dubious lessons as "Munich" and the "loss" of China. To Kennedy's mythologizing eye, history was being made where and by the same methods it had been crafted in the pages of his favorite book, Lord David Cecil's *Melbourne,* the definitive evocation of a skeptical, enlightened patriciate that he and his hyperalert cadre would emulate. The Cold War gave them their chance.

In Kennedy's New Frontier, the Council on Foreign Relations enjoyed an Indian summer, as more of its downtown partners and blue-chip board members felt the obligation to accept senior positions in an expanding government. Many were good men, to be sure, but still from a small world. Schlesinger's *A Thousand Days,* the first work that combined conventional history with the modern twist of politician as media star, presents the brilliant galaxy surrounding Kennedy, sparkling in their belief that the complexities of social relationships were finally yielding to science — an assumption so much more readily made then than now. He throws these almost Platonic young scholar-rulers into contrast with the overstuffed ornaments who obstructed the world's light under the somnolent Eisenhower — nice people, perhaps, but insufficiently tough-minded and realistic to understand, let alone undertake, what was necessary. "Intelligence," he boasts, "was at last being applied to public affairs."[9] Kennedy's first appointments had nevertheless been reappointments — J. Edgar Hoover and Allen Dulles. Both the FBI, as an instrument of unwholesome curiosity, and the CIA, turning the throttle as an engine of secret power, felt a firm pat on the back. All that new vigor that Kennedy's administration advertised was not about to threaten Hoover, whose personal files were rightly feared by any politician with behavior to hide, or, initially, was Dulles's far-reaching influence about to be challenged.

Kennedy was a frightening risk taker. During the campaign, he had warned Americans that they, too, would "live on the edge of danger" in the decade ahead.[10] Like many compulsive womanizers, he suffered from a deficiency of excitement. The British journalist Henry Fairlie wrote in *The Kennedy Promise* about how these new leaders lived off adrenaline: Americans were told repeatedly how little their president slept. They were what Jacob Burckhardt, a great historian and a burned-out radical, had long before called "emergency men," people whom the opportunities offered by the modern state tempt into an eternal trifling with danger and extremity. The talk and drama of "crisis management" played conveniently into these years. "Great crises produce great men," Kennedy had concluded in *Profiles in Courage*.

Without the Cold War, the United States would not have been so self-conscious of its dignity, of its real and imagined responsibilities, of the way it was perceived by the world. Not that this self-consciousness lacked good points. For instance, it worked as an all-too-gradual force for civil rights. Otherwise, America was not playing to its strengths. The cadences of Kennedy's inaugural address, with its dramatic inversions such as "Ask not," were either pretentious or substitute anachronism for the ability to communicate the future. He was, after all, the last president who wore a top hat to his inauguration, one followed by a parade with tanks and missiles. This was undoubtedly a new time for Americans, but it was being met on conflicted lines.

"A lot of people who yearn for a man on horseback still want him to have a textbook under his arm," novelist Paul Anderson once said. This was never more true than in 1960s America, where the thirst to marry "poetry and power" ran deep. The phrase was Robert Frost's, as he heralded "an Augustan age . . . with the emphasis on power." (Kennedy said of Frost, who read at the inauguration, that he was impressed by "his toughness.")[11] Here was the warrior/cultural combination that America has otherwise fortunately found unnecessary. Critic Alfred Kazin had little patience for it. He deflated the pretensions of Kennedy and his entourage in "The President and Other Intellectuals," where he subtly described a restlessly ambitious, would-be intellectual who was about to take the country on a convictionless crusade.[12] A fascination with outfits like the Green Berets, with the soldier/scholar Maxwell Taylor, and with "decision" and "courage" reflected the passions of the excited bystander rather than the somber practitioner. Kennedy was setting a muscular and stylish tone — the corollary of a patronizing lack of confidence in an allegedly doughy, aimless America.

Never had such power fallen so suddenly upon a nation, and at the back of many minds lurked some sense of national imposture. Washington, it was proclaimed, must become a place of civilization and grace, a federal Paris or Rome. The *New York Times* had recently equated the cultural standing of this modest city with so provincial a backwater as Tiflis in the Soviet Union.[13] Invidious comparisons were drawn with the refined splendors of Europe's capitals, which the United States was defending, while all the District of Columbia could show for itself was a baseball team (which did not stay). So it is no accident that these years also fostered all sorts of edifying ambitions at home, such as building the National Portrait Gallery. The museum was spoken of by its sponsors, "in this period of Cold War and revolutionary and national aspirations," as being the necessary "symbolic heart of American patriotism."[14] Patriotism, however, was a quality that had been able to flourish without such a perch to crow from in the days of Jefferson, Lincoln, and the Roosevelts.

A "national cultural center" and a "national endowment for the arts" also played into the sensibility of those strutting years. Detecting a "crisis in our cultural life," newly elected Senator Claiborne Pell (another un self-made New England millionaire) argued that America had to be seen to be contributing something loftier than the common sense that was the first line of competition with totalitarian materialism. The ideals of the American Century and the prosperity rising from U.S. capitalism did not seem enough to such men, although the American spirit was already showing vividly in Shriners hospitals and rural libraries, in contrast to corporatist cathedrals to "culture." This was a time when ever more ambitious politicians in Washington were incredulous that their fellow citizens might hesitate to pay $30 million for a showplace when "we waste more money than that in these trial shots of rockets and missiles that do not go off or explode two seconds after they leave the launching pad."[15]

The White House itself was to be turned into the "most glamorous house in the nation" — in implied contrast to the hayseed America of Truman and Eisenhower (and, again, a curious discontinuity with its role under Jefferson and Lincoln).[16] Such an effort to tart up the United States rang false, as it does today. America under the Kennedys felt compelled to prove that it had dispensed with its unsophisticated past.

Such attitudes, to be exercised through lives in "public service," helped open new lines of public spending. At other times in American history, all this silliness would have been ridiculed, but the sardonic American sense of humor, as best seen in Mark Twain, had at this stage of the coming to power been put on ice. The pretentious books of much-cited editor and former Eisenhower speechwriter Emmet Hughes, one of which has a fifty-nine-word subtitle, are self-revealing examples.[17] Jacqueline Kennedy was the first presidential wife to look like a European consort, talking French literature with a notably uninterested Charles de Gaulle, who got her number at her husband's funeral: "She will ultimately end up on the yacht of some oil baron," he predicted.[18] That generation had a deep thirst to show sophistication as well as strength. It fed into the Cold War's great pattern of short-term distraction and long-term disillusionment issuing in angry frustration.

Kennedy delivered his State of the Union address eleven days after the inauguration. It was a wartime speech without a war, asserting that the economy was in trouble and that the Russians might well be on their way: a fit and foolish prelude to the biggest U.S. peacetime buildup yet.

The embodiment of this penchant for toughness, grace, and brilliance was McGeorge Bundy, not perhaps known for his learning but certainly for his mastery of Harvard under a weak president. As Ward Just, the political novelist, has observed, Kennedy "wanted his own mandarin, an intellectual who knew something of the world and of government as well, the sort of man who could discipline other men and with whom you didn't have to finish every damned sentence you started because you spoke the same language."[19] Bundy was promptly appointed assistant for national security. He moved his desk from the Old Executive Office Building to the West Wing, whittled down the staff from seventy-four to forty-nine, to deal more flexibly with the departments, and added a "situation room." It was immediately clear to the world that there was a star closer to the sun than the ploddingly dutiful secretary of state, Dean Rusk.

A profile by Max Frankel in the *New York Times Magazine* (a newspaper Bundy believed to be "influenced by Zionists") described the national security assistant four years after he arrived in Washington: "He is a man of sharp — often acid — brilliance, lean and trim of body and mind and almost collegiate at forty-six, agile, combative and confident, on the tennis court and in intellectual volley. He eats, drinks, dances, plays, and, above all, speaks briskly: some say tartly." David Halberstam, then also with the *Times*, simply

recalls that "he was smarter than the average blue-blood WASP."
For Bundy, a favorite expression when casting doubt on a critic's
thought was that the idea was "intellectually incomplete."[20] He, and
the rest of America, would soon learn the price of connecting all
the dots.

Observers recall that Bundy was an early hawk on Vietnam not
just because of his intellectual analysis of the matter but because of
his "energy."[21] He was one of the confident elite articulators — a
Yale (Skull and Bones) mathematics major, wartime aide to an
admiral, and coauthor of the memoirs of Secretary of War Henry
Stimson, who had effortlessly swooped into a Harvard Junior Fellowship and then into becoming dean of Arts and Sciences at thirty-
four. Bundy was a man to whom little appeared too complex. He
invented the policy machinery intended to streamline the president's ability to make the toughest executive decisions.

A certain insobriety appeared. National security aides spoke
matter-of-factly about their power to inflict one-eighth "DOE" (death
on earth), of trading the wiping out of a half dozen American cities
for a half dozen Soviet ones.[22] There was a "bold" and "tough"
inner-sanctum secrecy among men such as McNamara and Bundy.
Neither had ever seen bloodshed, and now they were putting other
men's lives on the line.

One surreally insouciant example of "national security" decision making involves the thirty-six-year-old Michael Forrestal, an
engaging figure of the Cold War's middle stage and a man of
increasing behind-the-scenes influence as he grew his international
practice at Shearman & Sterling. His father was James Forrestal, the
first secretary of defense, who committed suicide in 1949. After his
father's death, Michael was adopted by Averell Harriman. Like Harriman, he was fluent in Russian. He was always happy to remind his
friends that he had barely entered college and certainly never graduated. (Harvard was the only law school that had accepted him after
he applied to a dozen.) He was Bundy's man for Far Eastern affairs,
although he genially admitted having no particular knowledge of
the Far East. Together, in 1963, he and Bundy would compare U.S.
casualties in South Vietnam to Washington, D.C.'s traffic-related
injuries and, for the moment, would find them insignificant.[23]

Despite these men's gifts of literacy and style, the details of war
and peace were not to be communicated clearly. So many of the
assumptions, so much of the reasoning, and more than a few of the

conclusions were veiled in language meant to conceal. However, there still had to be experts who, nearly as possible, could look directly into the nuclear sun. One such increasingly influential seer was Herman Kahn, the jovial, extra-large Californian who functioned for several years as the choreographer of Armageddon. His widely sold *On Thermonuclear War* was published in 1961, as he pursued a self-imposed task of "thinking about the unthinkable." A consultant at the Rand Corporation in Santa Monica, and a valued adviser to government, he went on to build forty-four "rungs" on the ladder to ultimate thermonuclear war, twenty-nine of which involved the use of nuclear weapons.

Not holding office, Kahn could be one of the supremely playful intellects of the age. He was also an unconsciously backward and glancing figure, in an epoch that was nothing if not backward-glancing. It was one that longingly aligned himself with Freud, Jung, and Toynbee against their rival peddlers of certainty, Marx and Lenin. In Washington, Kahn reiterated to the most senior generals and policymakers the opinions of earlier generations of untested military theorists.[24] The sheer intellectual satisfaction of his teachings shone through both the horror and the vagaries. So he pressed forward, explaining, as the decade proceeded, such ideas as how the Viet Cong (the Communist guerrillas in the South) could be smothered by draining the Mekong Delta, then turning his attention to another monument of eccentricity as he began to examine (amid almost everyone else's puzzlement) "the emerging Japanese superstate."

Kahn's intricate scenarios of how ever less limited nuclear war would be fought epitomized a whole class of the Rand Corporation's writings on strategy, the theme of which was to convey a sense of being in control to the Air Force chiefs who paid the bills. Only no one would be in control. From biblical times on, it had been all too well known that nothing went by plan once men were delivered to the battlefront. War after 1914 had merely reinforced the scope and speed of disaster. Now Rand and MIT models that presumed such military precision — and that shaped the flow of billions of dollars into ICBMs, bombers, and bases — were being applied to nuclear war.

Reporter and historian Theodore White proclaimed the emergence of "a new priesthood of action intellectuals," before going on to write a paean to John Kennedy as president, which further hyperbolizes the roles such people should have within American life.[25] A variation of this term was pleasing to bookish men in academia and the public policy institutes such as Rand. The term "defense intellectuals" came to describe a whole cadre not quite as provocative or lucid as Kahn, but every bit as entrepreneurial, as they accumulated contracts, consultancies, and tenure. They were able to win inordinate influence over policy because the actual decision makers who had to wrestle with questions of nuclear war (and soon guerrilla war) were walking in the dark. Not surprisingly, Pentagon-funded "nonprofit" think tanks — ANSER, IDA, and a host of others — proliferated on the example of Rand.

Even Carl Vinson was briefly taken aback by the whirlwind buildup. Within two months of Kennedy's inauguration, however, his Armed Services Committee authorized $808 million for new military construction at nearly eight hundred installations dispersed among all fifty states. Lockheed, in passing, received a special $1 billion jet transport contract reported to add two thousand jobs to its plant in — where else? — Georgia. Vinson could truly assure the House that "there is something in this bill for everyone."[26] Defense spending, which had always been in danger of being constrained even further under Eisenhower, instead kept draining an average of 9 percent of a larger GDP during 1961 to 1963. Contrary to the commonsense criticism of this notion within the Eisenhower cabinet, Kennedy proclaimed that the economy would somehow be invigorated by these defense dollars.

The full range of U.S. military power was enhanced, the purpose being to respond at any level of violence from any source, from jungles to space. The Joint Chiefs of Staff would be charged with preparing for protracted conventional combat, as in Europe, in addition to sudden, intense nuclear war. Nowhere is the buildup's scope better described than in a speech the president gave to the Fort Worth Chamber of Commerce three and a half hours before he died:

> In the past three years we have increased the defense budget of the United States by over twenty percent; increased the program of acquisition for Polaris submarines from twenty-four to forty-one; increased our Minuteman missile purchase program by more than seventy-five percent; doubled the number of strategic bombers and missiles on alert; doubled the number of nuclear weapons available in the strategic alert forces; increased the tactical nuclear forces deployed in West-

ern Europe by over sixty percent; added five combat ready divisions to the Army of the United States, and five tactical fighter wings to the Air Force of the United States; increased our strategic airlift capability by seventy-five percent; and increased our special counter-insurgency forces which are now engaged in South Vietnam by six hundred percent.

The boast included the standard demand for "sacrifice by the people of the United States," likely to be required into the next century.[27] The president knew soon after entering office that the threat was no more dangerous than it had been in recent years, yet he felt compelled to appear tough on tough issues. The missile gap itself was proving false and was soon ridiculed as the "mineshaft gap" in the black comedy *Dr. Strangelove*, the title role being that of a gutturally accented scientist-cum-presidential adviser fixated on mass destruction. After his inflated campaign rhetoric and all the denunciations of Eisenhower's lassitude, there was not much room for second thoughts.

In March, Kennedy called for $52.3 billion in military spending, with another $1.2 billion for the space program — 50 cents of every dollar in what that era judged a "mammoth" $106.8 billion federal budget.[28] The Defense Department, which in 1947 had had one cabinet secretary and three special assistants, besides uniformed officers, had expanded under Truman to include a deputy secretary and eight assistant secretaries. By 1960, there were also eleven deputy assistant secretaries. There would be twice as many in 1963, with the military's Joint Staff swelling accordingly. Gone were the modest, cost-conscious days when Lovett reused his old World War II stationery as "Assistant Secretary of War, Washington, D.C." by typing over two words to read "Under Secretary of State, Washington, D.C."

"The armed forces should have loved McNamara," observes his biographer, noting how he won big increases in their budgets.[29] This secretary of defense, however, had a personal staff that presented itself as possessing all the answers, and these at best deriving from simple cost-benefit comparisons presented as systems analysis. At the heart of this coterie, "the brains behind the muscle," according to *Time*, were bright young clones of the original "whiz kids" who had shaped Air Force production and targeting so efficiently during World War II. It was all much more riveting than teaching or practicing law, a point Joseph Califano made explicit when leaving behind a tedious corporate tax case to join McNamara as an aide. Their boss had more than a little "disdain for the military institutions and culture he was presuming to change."[30] For him, almost everything could be measured and then answered. The Office of the Secretary of Defense (OSD) built a myth of omnicompetence. It tried to underscore the belief that some problems, as Kennedy said at Yale in 1962, are so complicated and so technical that only a handful of people understand them — an unhelpful observation, as the best mathematicians remind us, because a sure sign of accomplishment is to be able to explain easily the most complex details of one's work to anyone.[31]

"Systems analysis" became the magic phrase, not just rippling through Pentagon budgeting but shouldering its way into strategy and tactics.[32] There was a search for precision that to McNamara as supermanager was merely "quantitative common sense," yet to his critics was often a device for hiding inexperience under a barrage of data. This outsize faith in the social and managerial sciences had been created during the 1950s by economic expansion and by the establishment of a set of vocabularies, if not of results, that seemed the equals of those in the physical sciences. "The whip-smart people who thought they could 'cost-benefit' anything," says policy analyst Robert Coulam about this generation of managerialists, "gave us rather few benefits and lots of costs." There are lesser-known analogues to their best-known debacle in weapons buying — squandering millions of dollars on McNamara's certainty that his TFX fighter-bomber could serve both the Navy and Air Force.[33] Among these was the secretary's belief that giant C-5 transport planes could replace ships in rushing U.S. Army divisions overseas.

The OSD turned into a "scientific-technological elite," composed of too many men who just did not know what they did not know. The Joint Chiefs drew together to resist the common enemy. Since the battle was to be fought on efficiency, the Chiefs simply offered higher estimates of what they construed was just about any program's operational minimum. The result of such game playing was that the necessary reform that McNamara tried to bring to the Pentagon — and that he went far in achieving — was given a bad name for decades to come.

A revolving door also began to turn between the Pentagon, Rand, and the universities. The types of analytical skills honed under McNamara might merit tenure. Former staffers who spun into the classrooms could pass off egregiously unctuous writings as scholarship: "McNamara has all the best qualities of a professional manager," gushed one new MIT professor with no background in management. "He doesn't worry over details or the possibility of making mistakes."[34] In a decade of shaky conglomerates, McNamara and his men became exemplars of the "big engineering" notion that a good manager could manage anything, no matter what the product. To "manage" is to run something well and otherwise does not mean much. "My entire life is an effort to exorcise the demon of Robert McNamara from society," says business guru Tom Peters today.[35]

Terrible results occurred when Kennedy's senior appointees saw themselves serving not only as tough defenders of their country but also as shapers of global progress. The futures of disparate third world countries offered fascinating problems and kept drawing in additional well-credentialed men with the spell of the Great Game. Social problems would be addressed through conscientious rigor. The study of international politics therefore also came to be characterized by gobbledygook versions of systems theory and simulation.

Walt Whitman Rostow, an MIT professor serving as Bundy's deputy on the NSC before running Policy Planning at State, explained that guerrilla war in general and Vietnam in particular were part of "the pathology of economic development." To John McNaughton, the personable former Harvard Law School professor who was McNamara's alter ego at the Pentagon, Vietnam was a problem that could be resolved "by simply dissecting it into all its elements and then piecing together the resultant formula."[36] Rostow's perspective was by no means false, nor was McNaughton's approach as simplistic as it sounds. But it is naive to try to include centuries of particular richness in such a vision or to think that war can be painted by the numbers. As was soon clear, it took more than economic pathologies and cost-benefit analyses to produce and to fight soldiers as brave as those urged on from Hanoi.

★

Renewed Soviet bluster over access to West Berlin made such hubris, nuclear philosophizing, and fuzzy math even more dangerous. After his dressing-down by Khrushchev during an impromptu June 1961 summit in Vienna, the president pulled the fire alarm. He was shocked into tears, as went unreported in the press, that

Khrushchev could be so "harsh and definitive" as again to issue an ultimatum. "I never met a man like this," Kennedy admitted to *Time* correspondent Hugh Sidey. "[I] talked about how a nuclear exchange would kill seventy million people in ten minutes and he just looked at me as if to say 'So what?'"[37] Having worked for Stalin had its uses.

As soon as he arrived home, Kennedy spoke to the nation as if *Der Tag* was only months away. The last cycle of Soviet threats to Berlin had coolly been ridden out two years before. Now a seriously rattled president went beyond his initial request to Congress and urged that defense spending return to the Korean War's constant-dollar peak. The situation in Berlin sounded terrifying, except that there were serious people who kept their nerve. For instance, Bernard C. Clarke, commander of the U.S. Army in Western Europe, refused even to consider the situation as a crisis. The president nonetheless called on every man in America to provide protection for his family, saying it would "be a failure of responsibility" if he did not know what to do or where to go in case of nuclear attack. Shelter would be a "kind of insurance to our families, and to our country."[38] Like any form of insurance — especially when it had to be available to "everybody" and "as rapidly as possible" — it would cost dearly.

By August, the Russians were again blocking the autobahn to Berlin. Because East Germany's economy had been hemorrhaging due in part to the escape of skilled young people, the East Germans erected around West Berlin the sixty-four-mile-long Democratic Anti-Fascist Protection Wall, which became the Cold War's most famous symbol. "If you send in tanks," Khrushchev thundered, "they will burn and make no mistake about it."[39] At month's end, Moscow broke a three-year bilateral moratorium on aboveground nuclear testing. It detonated fifty-nine more devices over the next two months, including one equivalent to 58 million tons of TNT — the largest man-made explosion ever. U.S. tests resumed fast. The times whispered through Robert Lowell's poem "Fall 1961": "All autumn, the chafe and jar / of nuclear war." The period 1961 to 1962 was the only other time during the Cold War when a majority of Americans did not say federal taxes were too high.

Sensibly, the European allies had no intention of rushing to "pay any price" along with America. The president pleaded with British Prime Minister Harold Macmillan to send a symbolic detachment to flout the blockade on the roads leading into Berlin, but the dwindling empire's military role was increasingly irrelevant and by now somewhat of an afterthought. Macmillan skeptically dispatched a small, reinforced column, which passed through unchecked. De Gaulle, after an initial roar to gratify West German Chancellor Konrad Adenauer, denied all assistance. As for West Germany, it was contentedly shipping bulk orders of large-diameter steel pipes to the Soviet Union to connect Azerbaijan's oil fields to Eastern Europe. Not until late 1962, and then more for symbolism than strategy, did the Kennedy administration persuade its highly reluctant NATO allies to impose an embargo on such products. "The West" was again a euphemism for the United States.

Kennedy's appeals went way beyond any previous talk from Washington on civil defense and shook up the nation. Until 1961, household bomb shelters had been resorted to largely by the eccentric and the nervous, who were prepared to invest anything from $13.50 up to $5,500. Most were sold in Southern California. The grandiose plans of the Morgenstern school had so far not gone much beyond theory: they were too expensive even for SAC and the liberal Democrats. "I don't think I would put that much money into holes in the ground to crawl into," LeMay commented. "I would rather spend more of it on offensive weapons systems to deter the war."[40] With alarms jingling, however, the country rushed to build and stock an entire underground nation of fallout shelters. The Federal Housing Authority offered a choice of three financing plans for "the average suburbanite."[41] Washington also promoted a warning system for fallout: a turbocharged smoke detector. More money was needed immediately than had been spent on civil defense throughout the 1950s. McNamara himself would head the effort, not the functionaries who under Eisenhower had been drafting plans about turning off billboard lights.

A genuinely capable statistician, McNamara had to caution Congress that it was financially far-fetched to think of hiding millions of people from thermonuclear attack.[42] But who really knew? Not the expert advisers. Edward Teller argued that shelters could save 90 percent of the nation; Herman Kahn spoke of forty million dead, which meant that at least 75 percent would live, although he entertained silent reservations about their long-term future. Probably all would die, said Nobel laureate Linus Pauling, who had refused to work on the Manhattan Project. Everyone seemed to understand that only the federal government was "in a position to make a sound judgment," so Morgenstern's visions started to be made real.[43]

Government shelters were to stockpile supplies for two weeks: a lean number of calories per person at a total cost of $1.25 per day; water at 2 cents a quart. Emergency medical supplies costing about $170 million were already being stored, and 1962 would be the first time in five years that enough money would be found to hoard plasma and penicillin. New public buildings were constructed in which to conduct two-week courses for the thousand or so architects and engineers needed to design nuclear-resistant structures. Not only was Washington to get busy surveying and motivating, but the president wanted $450 million so that schools and hospitals could double as shelters, reinforced by an additional $25 "incentive payment" for each person they could accommodate. Fifteen thousand schools already had radiation-monitoring kits, but even safer places were to be found. Planners in Walla Walla, Washington, discovered that the state's maximum security prison could offer maximum protection against blast and fallout. Sections were obligingly set aside for the public.

Scientists meanwhile offered a Chinese menu to Congress from which it could select how much to spend to save how many lives. For instance, 100 million people could be sheltered for roughly $30 each, 70 million more for $60 each, and the remaining 35 million for $300 each. With enough money, promised the director of the U.S. Naval Radiological Laboratory, 99 percent of the people in and around New York City could survive. The legislators were left to weigh a program costing anywhere from $22 billion to $115 billion out of a GDP of $568.6 billion. Little wonder that they refrained from tackling civil defense on such a gargantuan scale.

The State Department, however, still had no fallout shelter. By contrast, the Pentagon was pressing for $93 million to improve its own existing capacity to ride out the big one.[44] Every agency at least had its own elaborate doomsday plan; some are still in place today. The Post Office would forgo demanding stamps on letters sent to devastated areas; the Treasury Department would require banks to keep regular working hours; the Department of Labor would deploy a postattack economic stabilization program; the Federal Highway Administration would seek to protect motorists from fallout; the Department of Agriculture would ration the daily calories needed to survive; and the Federal Reserve designated banks for postwar check cashing, while stocking millions in shrink-wrapped dollars in a radiation-proof center in the Virginia countryside. Right until the Cold War's end, the National Gallery of Art depended on a private trust to keep armored cars at the ready to race its Leonardos, Vermeers, and Raphaels to safety.

American enterprise also proved to be up to the challenge. The National Concrete Masonry Association, the American Iron and Steel Institute, and the Douglas Fir Plywood Association all developed plans for family shelters available upon request. Dallas's Acme Bomb & Fallout Shelter Company, Sacramento's Atlas Bomb Shelter Company, and others designed prefabs. Wall Street expected shelters to be a $20 billion business in 1962, should that year come to pass. More or less reliable designs were circulated by the Pentagon, complete with recommended list prices.[45] IBM extended to its employees interest-free loans to build their own shelters. Reaching into his own pocket, Time Inc.'s finance committee chairman, Roy Larsen, sank a comfortable cost-is-no-object shelter under his new Fairfield, Connecticut, estate.

Little went as planned even at this pre-apocalyptic stage. Once the checks started coming in from what was expected to be a $320 million annuity, for example, local school officials were more inclined to put the money into, say, building gymnasiums than buying air filters and dried eggs. When fifty-five million wallet-size cards were distributed with instructions to follow in the event of an attack, the silliness got personal. Cabinet member Lawrence O'Brien recalls receiving special ones that his family (supposed to be left to themselves as he was whisked to one of the federal redoubts) was to put in the car window to give them priority in fleeing Washington. It would have been the equivalent of showing a complimentary pass in a subway fire. Chief Justice Earl Warren quietly let it be known that he would stay behind in Washington with his wife.

John Updike wrote a *New Yorker* piece about a recently built motel, appropriately in Massachusetts, offering an underground shelter (with a house machine gunner) large enough to maintain for six months the sixty motorists lucky enough to be visiting it on doomsday.[46] People also could read about those civilian shelters whose doors had rifle ports, vital should it be necessary to cut down one's pleading, too-long-complacent neighbors. (The ethics of such procedures were much canvassed in church discussion groups.)

Norwalk, Connecticut, forty miles up the coast from Manhattan, debated how to keep out neighbors from Darien and Westport were it to build public shelters.

All sorts of flimflam predictably arrived. Franchises proliferated, and shelters with no air intakes or that flooded after the first rain were sold. *Consumer Reports* warned that fraudulent builders might show up on the doorstep, insist that "the President wants you to have a shelter," take a down payment, and disappear.[47] The Federal Trade Commission quickly issued advertising guidelines warning that a substandard shelter could boil its occupants to a crisp.[48] The AEC's Willard Libby built a shelter near his house in the Los Angeles hills, around the time that he received a Nobel Prize for his work in chemistry. The shelter was incinerated by a summer brushfire.

All the commotion over how to protect 180 million Americans against blast, fire, and poison soon moderated, especially once Khrushchev that December withdrew what appeared to be, literally, his deadline over Berlin. In fact, only around 200,000 families actually built shelters between the late 1950s and early 1963. Even during the Cuban missile crisis in October 1962, family shelters sold poorly. Six hundred builders went out of business. Almost overnight, frantic effort went the way of some geostrategic hula hoop.

Academic entrepreneurs prospered more enduringly, but perhaps with even less substantial product. Seventeen million dollars was appropriated for "shelter management studies." For the sake of "post-attack research," one thousand hours of scarce computer time in 1962 and five thousand more in 1963 went to estimate the number of dead and dying who would be left by various forms of attack. The National Academy of Sciences saw fit to establish the Disaster Research Group and harnessed the considerable intellects of a number of its members to explore how people should be alerted to an attack. Sirens seemed too quaint. AT&T's Bell Laboratories evaluated using an override on the private telephone network that would ring as one last nationwide wake-up call, but it would have cost $40 per phone to change the central switchboards at a time when most calls still went through an operator. Philco proposed mass-producing cheap, special-purpose radios to ring the electronic tocsin and instruct people who were about to find themselves under mushroom clouds.

However the alarm might be delivered, Kennedy and McNamara learned that once the president decided to use the codes, what happened thereafter would be up to the Curtis LeMays of the country. "The chain of command was a gigantic and deadly snake with a life of its own if the Commander-in-Chief opened the cage," says Richard Reeves.[49] SAC intended to level Eastern Europe as well as the Soviet Union. Kennedy understood that this had to be corrected — fast. New doctrines began being entertained, hopefully to prevent the need for scurrying into shelters in the first place, but also to calibrate nuclear escalation should deterrence fail. Once the world caught fire, these entirely theory-based procedures were to be rocks of reason and restraint to which the terrified men underground might cling.

McNamara began the tradition of what Bundy called "authoritative public exposition of American strategic doctrine," as in discussing which Soviet targets would be nuked should the worst occur. The defense secretary suggested an alternative to all-out destruction or "massive retaliation." It would be more proportionate, and therefore more believable, he explained in a 1962 speech in Ann Arbor, Michigan, if U.S. missiles and bombers were aimed at Russian missiles and bombers, not at cities. Moreover, Soviet targets might be destroyed in a gradually escalating process, depending on what Moscow did to deserve it. An armored attack on Western Europe, for example, would be answered by a theoretically "limited" use of nuclear weapons. "McNamara's brief brush with counterforce," Bundy would astutely reflect, demonstrated "the tension which is inherent between the desire for forces that can be applied in a discriminating fashion and the danger that any such forces may become destabilizing."[50] The more playful Herman Kahn gave his lay readers headaches trying to imagine the possible iterations of move/countermove or strike/counterstrike.

There was no reason, however, to be comforted that all this would remain theory. The *New York Herald Tribune* quoted McNamara as arguing in the fall of 1961 that it was "absurd to think that we could have unbalanced the budget simply to strengthen a weapon we had decided to never use under any circumstances." Attorney General Robert Kennedy, at thirty-six the country's second-most-powerful man, said that he hoped Khrushchev realized "the President will use nuclear weapons" if pushed.[51] Although the United States in the early 1960s had an overwhelming intercontinental nuclear superiority, divided into its serendipitous "triad" of ICBMs, bombers, and SLBMs, Washington nonetheless believed that the Soviet Union had sufficient firepower to kill ten million to fifteen million Americans even after absorbing a U.S. first strike.

A voice from a more responsible era was heard. Dwight Eisenhower said that he found all this talk of general war "preposterous." He was right, and most Americans came to know it. When one thinks about American "militarism," it is telling that there were only three years between Kahn's *On Thermonuclear War* and the skewering of all this pretension and certainty in *Dr. Strangelove*, the 1964 Stanley Kubrick movie in which a berserk SAC commander (Sterling Hayden eerily looking like General Thomas Power) orders his bombers to attack Russia. Western Europeans, for their part, hoped that the missiles and B-52s would just fly over their heads. So why should they raise expensive armies? Yet they had reason to be nervous. Although the United States had agreements with Britain, France, West Germany, and other NATO countries, as well as Spain, concerning the diplomatic approvals necessary to launch U.S. nuclear weapons from their territories, there were no guarantees how "joint" such joint decisions would be on the world's last day.[52]

Weapons ground out of U.S. labs; plans were drafted, redrafted, and put into place. Nobody could know how anything would work unless deterrence failed. But surely, thought McNamara and his civilian advisers, the Russians were what economists call "rational actors": Soviet war planning could not be all that different from American war planning. Certainly, they would be sensible enough to subscribe to these cost-benefit analyses.

The defense intellectuals knowingly discussed the fine-tuning of nuclear war, just as their colleagues across campus were "extremely self-confident" of their ability to forecast economic fluctuations and to manipulate monetary as well as fiscal policies accordingly.[53] The irony was that only one side in the Cold War occupied itself with such refinements. Anyone who looked at a military organization dominated by Russia should have known that it was poised to go all out from the start — attempting to pulverize as much of the enemy's forces as possible, then laying waste to its society as the opportunities arose. The Russians, historically remarkable at both war and ballet, have retained their respective excellences by not seeking to combine the two.

A country so recently invaded by the Wehrmacht might not be inclined to stand about on day two of World War III subtly choosing which rung of the "escalation ladder" it might clamber to. Soviet doctrine always set out to maximize firepower and to be the first to use it should war seem imminent. On this the Soviet Union was "as open and candid as the most open of Western societies."[54] All too confident in believing that they knew more about the Soviet marshals' beliefs and motivations than did the marshals themselves, U.S. officials embarked on what became a stubborn misconstruction of Soviet military aims.

A few years after the Kennedy presidency, McNamara would explain regretfully to the Soviet ambassador that the United States had come to have more nuclear weapons than it needed.[55] However, it is solipsistic to believe that "American moves triggered the Kremlin's decision to seek nuclear parity" or to think that the Soviet ICBM buildup was "thanks to the McNamara-Kennedy increases and the U.S. entry into Vietnam."[56] Nor did the surge that would be all too clear by the late 1960s begin after Moscow's humiliating retreat from the Cuban missile crisis, as is commonly believed.[57]

In fact, it had started in 1959 with Khrushchev's Seven Year Plan, which began funding ambitious ICBM and SLBM programs, as well as a fractional orbital bombardment system. A permanent shift in Soviet spending priorities occurred. Nor could military outlays have been "on hold" before the missile crisis. The R & D timelines are impossible for these types of weapons, and new Russian sources report key dates that push the beginning of development farther back than previously understood. Moscow always followed its own plans, and the overriding priority, approved by Khrushchev in 1960, was to build a missile force intended to destroy America's own ICBMs and bombers. Except for when it discerned signs of weakness, the Soviet Union was unaffected by anything the United States did or did not do — a point on which Eisenhower had instructed the new president right after the Bay of Pigs.[58]

That the Soviets had already begun a deadly serious long-term buildup — of which U.S. intelligence was almost entirely unaware — does not mean that Kennedy's tremendous military expansion should be regarded as serendipitously prudent. Timing is everything, perhaps more so in a cold war than in anything else. Spending enormous amounts against an exaggerated threat, let alone crying wolf, is likely to ensure skepticism in a democracy by the time the wolf is really at the door. A huge letdown was certain to follow the binge of 1961 to 1963. Calm and continuity were called for in enhancing America's strategic capacity, just as they were needed in considering additional overseas commitments. A cooler, Eisenhower-like approach toward U.S. nuclear forces during Kennedy's one thousand days would have ended up costing much less if the forces could have improved in a more methodical fashion through the mid-1960s. Moreover, when the Soviet buildup finally became apparent later in the decade, there might have been a sense of urgency in the country to confront it seriously rather than to offer rationalizations.

For the moment, the United States was so far ahead in the numbers and quality of its missiles and bombers that there would have been no risk in being patient — not even a political risk from the tightfisted Republicans. Whereas Truman and Eisenhower had worked for a reasonably predictable America, the events of Kennedy's administration did nothing to stabilize U.S. attitudes and Soviet perceptions. For instance, at Cuba I (the Bay of Pigs), the president was timid, at Cuba II (the missile crisis), he was ready to go all the way.

Right up until Soviet missiles were detected in Cuba, the Kennedy brothers had been indulging in a chatty back-channel dialogue with Moscow through a congenial middleman, Georgi Bolshakov, who was based in Washington. (Unknown during the Eisenhower years, back channels would become commonplace in the Cold War's middle stage.) Of course, this ostensible journalist was from Soviet intelligence, but White House eagerness to "just get direct contact" let him broker, as Robert Kennedy said, "most of the major matters dealing with the Soviet Union and the United States."[59] It indicated to Khrushchev, as it would to his successors, how hemmed in the president was by his own government. The cumbersome State Department, which Kennedy ridiculed as a bowl of Jell-O, had been left on the sidelines. Such well-intentioned, ego-satisfying dialogues set the tone for equally chaotic practices in years to come, making it all the easier for the Politburo to trifle with U.S. policymakers.

The missile crisis is one of the twentieth century's defining moments. Like other Cold War events, such as the run-up to Korea, it is surrounded by misunderstanding, in this case assisted by conflicting Russian testimony. On a human level, it is a poor example of "a leader who led," as President Kennedy's special counsel today recalls. On a political one, it was hardly "the 'best managed' crisis of the last half of the century," as McNamara claims. Behind the fun of the 2001 movie *Thirteen Days* (overlooking Hollywood clichés of warmongering U.S. generals and soul-searching Russians) and the "maturing" of Robert Kennedy during his "finest hour" (in the eyes of his latest biographer) were significant costs to the country. The crisis was largely self-inflicted, its outcome would be bodyguarded by lies, and the consequences of the brothers' heightened obsession with Castro came to bedevil the nation for decades. Nor was the crisis even uniquely perilous, as has also come to be believed — an instance of "Soviet troops authorized to use tactical nuclear weapons against American forces," in McNamara's words.[60]

Documenting the episode may help clarify a tale that has become increasingly confused and may further strip away the myths of cool rationality. More than forty thousand Russians were already in Cuba, including four elite combat regiments and two tank battalions equipped with the latest armor. Khrushchev's decision in April 1962 to place 2,000-kilometer-range SS-4 nuclear-tipped missiles in Cuba stemmed directly from eighteen months of White House attempts to dispose of Castro. His ensuing statement to the Politburo that nothing he was doing would involve nuclear war, hardly lessened the recklessness.[61] Yuri Andropov, a rising secretary of the Central Committee, seems to have been involved in the adventure, intending to target America's underbelly.

Sometime during May, in a discussion with Marshal Malinovsky, Russia's minister of defense, Khrushchev apparently "gave" General Pliyev, the Soviet commander in Cuba, authority to use fifty-kilometer-range nuclear-tipped missiles should Americans invade the island or should the Soviet contingent otherwise lose touch with Moscow. However, that judgment was not relayed to Pliyev, and by September a Ministry of Defense directive specifically told him that control of "Soviet Armed Forces in combat actions in order to repel aggression" remained in the Kremlin.[62] Around the same time, Marshal Zakharov, chief of the General Staff, prepared a directive, per Khrushchev's prior order, to give Pliyev predelegated authority to launch those missiles, presumably subject to the conditions that Khrushchev had outlined several months before. Zakharov signed this, but Malinovsky did not.[63] Sometime in September or early October, Pliyev sent a message to the General Staff asking for instructions in case of invasion. He was told to fight to the death, but under no circumstances to use nuclear weapons. During these same months, the CIA concluded that it would make no sense for the Soviet Union to send any guided missiles or nuclear weapons to Cuba.[64]

Whether Soviet forces in Cuba were able on their own authority to launch nuclear weapons of any kind against Americans, even a

U.S. invasion force, is the critical question in assessing how close the world was to calamity. Contrary to impressions today, it is unlikely that these Russian commanders possessed the "predelegated authority" of their U.S. counterparts. Without Malinovsky's signature granting such emergency authority, the warheads could not be mated with the missiles. Nuclear war could be started only by a deliberate decision in Moscow. There were overwhelming reasons, though not understood in Washington at the time, why Moscow would be extremely unlikely to take that step.

The sky indeed darkened in October when the *Indigirka* arrived in Mariel harbor with 154 warheads for the missile launchers and 6 nuclear bombs and 4 nuclear mines for the planes that were also already in place. The deadly cargo was unloaded at night and stored in caves under KGB command on the same day a U-2 (under Air Force direction) first detected the missile sites' construction.[65] The famous climax came on October 22, when America imposed a naval blockade — personally commanded by George Anderson, now chief of Naval Operations — and the President went on television to tell the country, in a well-crafted speech, that it was on the brink of war. Less than three hours after Kennedy's announcement, Malinovsky ordered Pliyev to increase the alert level of his forces, but he still withheld the predelegated release order for the tactical weapons that had been drafted in September.[66] All three SS-4 regiments in Cuba then went on a higher alert, with one regiment of eight launchers being two and a half hours away from an actual ability to launch. However, warheads were never mated nor codes from Moscow issued. At the same time, the Operations Directorate in the Ministry of Defense began drafting orders to return everything to the Soviet Union, and by October 28 Moscow ordered all units to stand down. Russia went on to complete a much more important project in Cuba — one of the largest electronic eavesdropping facilities ever built.

Throughout this exaggerated Cold War drama, the Kennedys, Bundy, and other senior officials knew that the intermediate- and medium-range missiles in Cuba could not really upset the strategic balance. Even *Aviation Week,* the U.S. defense industry's trade journal, dismissed them as "PRBMs" — "Psychological Range Ballistic Missiles."[67] Yet they were a stark political threat right before midterm elections, and therefore the White House would take risks. President Kennedy valuably pulled the country back from danger (though unlikely from a nuclear exchange) by eschewing advice from the Joint Chiefs of Staff, Dean Acheson, Senator William Fulbright, and other advisers who were ready to bomb the missile sites and maybe invade Cuba as well. Paul Nitze, serving as an assistant secretary of defense, led the hawks. Perhaps doing his sums and knowing that the nuclear balance would not be upended, McNamara opposed these moves. The natural next step, he knew, would have been for the Red Army to snatch West Berlin. Behind the pretensions of "crisis management," however, the president's secretly made tape recordings of those meetings show terrible desperation.

The confidence Kennedy demonstrated during the crisis was generously assisted by a U.S. nuclear advantage that Malinovsky figured as fifteen to one and that neither Khrushchev nor anyone else in Moscow was going to trigger. Terrifying as the crisis seemed to be, it was not "the most dangerous nuclear confrontation of the entire Cold War," as it is often described.[68] That would come twenty years later when another president faced down the far more expansive ambitions of a cornered, equally well-armed Soviet superstate.

After the missile crisis was over, the White House firmly and falsely denied that any trade-off had been made to remove U.S. missiles of a similar range in Turkey — the ones that NATO had agreed to place in the late 1950s and that had just been deployed (already obsolescent) the previous summer. For years, only eight men (not including the vice president or director of Central Intelligence) knew the truth — a compromise, for better or worse, under threat. The deal's secrecy was imperative, Robert Kennedy told Soviet ambassador Anatoly Dobrynin, because the appearance of any record "could cause irreparable damage to my political career in the future."[69] As for damage to the country, that would come from the increased fervor to go gunning for Castro.

The missile crisis's only fatality was a U-2 pilot shot down on the morning of October 27, his plane's routine overflight of Cuba obligingly occurring at the "usual time," according to Castro.[70] Today, the plane's engine is displayed in Havana's Counter-Revolutionary Museum. In the aftermath of the crisis, the Emergency Broadcast System was developed to allow the president to address the nation on a moment's notice. The long, shrill tone over radio and TV, followed by the warning "This is only a test," became the Cold War's sound track. Also created was the hotline for direct communication between Moscow and Washington, although for five years

McNamara had no idea it ended in the Pentagon rather than the White House.[71]

Overall, the dashing years 1961 to 1963 were imposing a range of undashing burdens: the shelter mania; the belief that a nuclear showdown could be coolly managed; the beginnings of a U.S. conviction that the Soviets "thought like us" in the use of ICBMs; the practice of concealed back-channel dealings with Moscow spinning webs of deceit; and the glamorization conferred on secret operations of the sort which more temperate leaderships avoid, or at least minimize.

✪

At the same time that Americans were riveted by prospects of apocalypse, an ocean of economic and scientific wealth lay barely discovered before them. Yet the country's hyperpoliticization meant that too much time and energy kept being taken away from important developments not making the headlines — such as the arrival of the first integrated circuit in 1962 or what future Nobel laureate Dr. Earl Wilbur Sutherland was achieving alone in Nashville as he illuminated the working of the human organism. The brilliant Oskar Morgenstern, for his part, kept writing and consulting amid the unveiling of DNA and the discovery of pulsars, bacterial conjugation, and electron microscopy. Yet he would still wrongly assert that science's most important objectives were defense related.

Also overshadowed by the Cold War was the significance of how the country would pay all those prices about which the president spoke. Between 1955 and 1963, real federal revenues had increased more than 40 percent, by $26 billion. Although Kennedy respected the taboo against sustaining large deficits, familiar fiscal constraints were increasingly relaxed. Americans were becoming accustomed not only to prosperity but to budget overruns. During the next two decades, or until the immense deficits of the 1980s, a sense developed that public debt was an entirely weightless cost, obligations that the nation owed only to itself. That was true to an extent. Yet the fact that these overruns were likely to buy less and less that was worthwhile and to crowd out better investment had yet to be grasped.

Moreover, few people in what had been those thirty-plus months between Bretton Woods and the enunciation of the Marshall Plan had imagined the extent to which the world would remain dependent on America. The certainty of the international exchanges was still based on the value of gold being held in place by its ties to the dollar. In that sense, the world was on a dollar standard. Yet 1944's original good idea, that stable currencies would undergird stable politics, had long been eroding. Fearing amid the Korean War that Washington might freeze any dollar assets it possessed, Beijing had begun keeping its greenbacks in a Soviet bank based in Paris. The cable address was Eurobank. The term "Eurodollar" had been coined in 1957 to describe the expanding category of dollars held overseas and not fully mediated by the Federal Reserve. Their number tripled in 1959 and doubled again the following year.

The United States first went into balance-of-payments deficit in 1958, and Eisenhower, during his last year in office, had planned to withdraw some U.S. troops from Europe unless the allies helped stop the outflow of gold. The problem came to be seen as so severe that a senior White House adviser cited it along with nuclear arms as the two biggest issues facing the Kennedy administration.[72] Far more dollars were going overseas than were returning home, not because Americans were spending wildly on foreign cars or tours of Italy, but because those Bretton Woods parities were being maintained amid the Cold War. "The United States can balance its payments any day it wants," Kennedy asserted, "if it wishes to withdraw its support of our defense expenditures overseas and our foreign aid."[73] A nation's balance of payments, however, is generally an index of its currency's health, and Western Europe was pointedly making clear its diminished confidence in the dollar.

As a hugely successful merchant banker at Kleinwort Benson, George Kennedy Young would observe in his magisterial *Finance and World Power* how thoroughly this world had changed by 1961. At an International Monetary Fund conference in Vienna, a human face could be put on such criticisms. Vienna was a city whose citizens only seven years before had been counting the days to the "American month," when the Soviets rotated out of occupation. Now these pampered clients were reproaching U.S. "irresponsibility" and lack of self-control. They somehow overlooked the fact that America's balance-of-payments deficit was around $1.3 billion — roughly the same amount being spent on U.S. forces in Europe.

Kennedy started pushing forward an across-the-board tax cut, understanding that severe tax rates on the wealthiest Americans were dragging on the nation's growth. But the cuts were delayed in part by what he called the "burdens of freedom" — meaning that he did not dare risk a loss of "world confidence" in U.S. fiscal policy.[74] For a decade thereafter, an array of tangled manipulations were put into place to uphold the dated assumptions of Bretton Woods and to protect the dollar. Among these "fixes" were the interest equalization tax and the two-tier price of gold — all the ornamental waterspouts of a world financial system too complex for its own good but seemingly irreplaceable.

Another obligation Washington justified upholding for the sake of Cold War stability was the increasingly lopsided relationship with Japan. What the secretary of commerce called America's "anchor ally" in the Far East was still presumed to be backward as compared to the booming Atlantic world. For example, the administration matter-of-factly offered to send volunteers from its new Peace Corps — an organization mostly dedicated to helping the world's poor. Their presence was courteously declined. Construction loans going back to the Occupation were nonetheless renegotiated, with Washington agreeing that only a quarter of the $2.1 billion would be repaid, and then only over fifteen years at 2.5 percent interest. It also kept up the annual secret payments of $6 million to $10 million (funneled through the new ambassador, Harvard professor Edwin O. Reischauer), since the ruling Liberal Democratic Party insisted that it needed more "anti-subversion" money to confront the Japan Teachers Union and other suspect labor groups.[75] All this was paid for at a time when the size of Japan's economy had surpassed that of Britain's.

Not all Americans shared their government's concern with Japanese fragility. The Anti-Friction Bearing Manufacturers' Association, for instance, testified against Japanese "cartels" and dual-pricing; textile manufacturers urged Washington to emulate Europe's quota system; the Sulfur Export Association denounced Japan's non-tariff barriers. But against the stern demands of the Cold War, such special concerns seemed self-serving. Negotiations soon led to a "Trade Expansion Act" in 1962, from which some sort of "Grand Design" uniting co-prosperity with common defense policies was supposed to emerge. What did occur was modest. Until 1965, the United States could enjoy a persistent, though persistently diminishing, trade surplus with Japan. Then that reversed too.

At least Japan posed no technological challenge, or so it was thought. In fact, Americans were overlooking the most enduring implications of technology worldwide, in part, because the Cold War had been framed in the pre-computer era. For example, it was easy to ignore predictions that a technological revolution would inevitably undermine the Soviet order, as Hungarian emigre-scholar George Paloczi-Horvath already promised in 1963.[76] The think tank assessments about step-by-step nuclear escalation were deemed provident and rigorous. More subtle views about, say, computers becoming instruments of individual power and dominion, commercial advantage sounded outlandish, or even subversive in a world of "managed markets," "planned obsolescence," and, of course, "heroic leadership."

One or another military-technological upheaval had detonated at least every five years since 1945: Hiroshima; the Soviet A-bomb; both sides' thermonuclear explosions in 1952–53; the ICBM and *Sputnik* in 1957. By the time Kennedy entered office, the destabilization from this sequence of shocks was passing into a sullen equilibrium. But Kennedy's language canonized the alarmist vision. To him, any technological advance was only of interest for its politico-military impact. Space is an example, as the Soviets — within forty-three months of *Sputnik* — launched the first dog, the first rocket to hit the moon, and, in April 1961, the first man into orbit. With America's survival presumed to be at stake, the president concluded that "there's nothing more important" than to accept the stunning cost of landing men on the moon before the Soviets.[77] The ninety-eight-month "race" that followed became the most visible front of the technological Cold War.

"The real inspiration for the growth of NASA," Kennedy's press secretary was given to understand, "was a threat to the balance of power." The able James Webb, Truman's budget director and a man who "understood NASA's Cold War origins," was placed in charge.[78] From retirement, Eisenhower found the new White House assumption that America would turn into "a second-rate nation" if it was not first to the moon ridiculous.[79] Lyndon Johnson was similarly skeptical, preferring that the money go to medical programs, or even to foreign aid, but knowing that Congress would allocate such sums only for geopolitical competition. However, he was not going to be left out as the race quickly became a jumble of noble intent and pork barrel politics. Much of the latter rolled along the Dallas-Houston axis courtesy of Johnson and Congressman Albert Thomas, head of the relevant House Appropriations subcommittee.

By 1962, lobbyists and politicians from the rest of the country began complaining about a southwestern monopoly on NASA contracts. The word *moondoggling* came into use. The CIA, for its part, contended that the Soviets could accomplish a manned lunar landing somewhere between 1967 and 1969.

By turning space flight into yet another emergency, Kennedy helped send Americans to the moon perhaps a half dozen or so years sooner than would have happened anyway. That giant leap was a natural next step for a frontier people. The price of racing, however, went well beyond the inevitable waste and patronage. Because this was a race, getting men into space (as distinct from emphasizing the more rewarding aspects of space science) became the essential and ultimately disappointing purpose. Eisenhower got it right, telling astronaut Frank Borman in 1965 that this endeavor, which was drastically expanded right after the Bay of Pigs fiasco, meant that "costs went up dramatically, while the benefits of the space program were lost."[80]

Nor were NASA's ideals free from other compromises that naturally went along with bureaucracy and secrecy — for example, the tie to the AEC's testing on humans. Although the Oak Ridge National Laboratory acknowledges only having provided some data on high-level radiation experiments, there are hundreds of 1960s purchase order invoices from NASA to the AEC debited to "human studies," including those on men in prison. Probably many of these studies were benign, but at least a couple of now-famous NASA executives had seen far worse than even the AEC could concoct. Arthur Rudolph, Nazi war criminal and former project director for the underground V-2 death camp, had become manager of the Marshall Space Flight Center's Saturn V launch vehicle, the one that carried Neil Armstrong to the moon. Rudolph's close friend since the 1930s, Wernher von Braun, who quietly admitted that their tunnel factory, which had swallowed tens of thousands of souls, had been "hellish," was Marshall's director and elder statesman of the space effort. In 1963, the American press chose to ignore a typically heavy-handed but not inaccurate East German exposé of von Braun's SS work.[81] It was in no one's interest to acknowledge, let alone examine, the appropriateness of employing such people.

MIT received the first Apollo money. With its wartime research on microwave radar as a springboard, MIT used additional Air Force–sponsored projects on inertial guidance to lift its instrumentation laboratory to a budgetary orbit of $54 million by the end of the 1960s — a figure actually larger than all the rest of MIT's income. "We were the real war profiteers," genially recalls the director of MIT's microwave tube laboratory, "no question about it."[82] MIT remained the country's largest university defense contractor, although Stanford was coming on fast. Harvard, in turn, was receiving more income from federal research grants than from its endowment, which was among the country's largest.

The Pentagon's Advanced Research Projects Agency (ARPA) seeded its Information Processing Techniques Office in 1962 with $9 million, a figure that would rise to $230 million per year (out of a $1.36 billion budget) by the Cold War's end. The following year, MIT opened its famous laboratory for computer sciences, which would be funded for the rest of the century chiefly by the Defense Department. MIT also received a $2 million grant for Project MAC, which helped redefine the computing world by making it possible for many users to share a single machine simultaneously. Moreover, this office germinated computer networking — a driving industrial force of early twenty-first-century America — because ARPA needed to share information among its array of sponsored projects around the country. Neither IBM nor AT&T wanted much to do with packet switching, the innovative breaking up of data into small bunches before transmitting them along different lines. This gave Rand the opportunity to offer its own useful analyses of the problem, thereby fostering the myth that the Internet originated as a means of protecting military communications from nuclear attack. In fact, Rand was exploring ways to ensure reliable telephone, rather than data, communications. The phone monopoly, certain of its invulnerability against man and nature, spurned packet switching as the thinking of hypochondriacs.

Although researchers had reduced the production costs of a transistor from $45 to $2 and were mass-producing integrated circuits, complacent big business presumed that no one but a few bureaucrats or computer obsessives would ever use such networked communications.[83] At the origin of the Internet, the government was the only immediate source of funds. Contrary to what many people believe, however, Washington was hardly indispensable to the Net's creation. One way or another, computers were going to be networked and data shared. Yet innovation for the moment may have been accelerated by public money, as the budget of the

National Science Foundation, for example, went from $100,000 in 1951 to $100 million ten years later, with federal R & D spending going from $1.1 billion in 1950 to twelve times that in 1963. This spigot would not have been even halfway so loose without the Cold War. However, other opportunities were being lost amid the taxpayers' largesse. Engineering and physics research, to take two conspicuous examples, would no doubt have followed more socially and commercially useful paths had they not been so heavily shaped by military sponsorship.

Some businesspeople observed that the country's growth was being impaired. Kennedy may have come to understand this, too. He warned of America "[paying] a price" when around two-thirds of its scientists and engineers were preoccupied with defense, space, and atomic energy. In a preview of the trend that would become obvious by the early 1970s, the National Academy of Sciences concluded that technologies with any civilian value were spinning off of the country's military-related programs too slowly.[84] The example of how the B-52 bomber helped bring the 707 jetliner into being was already becoming tiresome. Nonetheless, MIT and Stanford started using defense money to serve as de facto incubators for high-tech companies that they pushed out into the larger economy — companies that helped commercialize navigation systems, semiconductors, computers, and much else in the dilating electronics sphere. The U.S. electronics industry had become particularly dependent on the federal budget's "national security" category. These and other achievements led to the unwarranted inference that military spending was the natural critical path toward scientific creation.

Frederick Terman, who helped build that Mecca of venture capital, the Stanford Industrial Park, always reminded his university colleagues that the Pentagon was not "trying to run a do-gooder program."[85] The Defense Departments's own ends, however, could often complement those of the university and, for a while, of commerce. For instance, solid-state physics had expanded so heftily since 1950 under the sheer pressure of money that the number of Ph.D.'s graduating into this discipline had quintupled by the early 1960s. The Defense Department and the AEC were the paymasters for nearly all academic research in physics. Careers of ambitious professors in a range of other disciplines blossomed, as they also became conduits for enormous flows of public money. Few complained. But where was all this heading, as government patronage and secrecy began to extend even into the humanities? Eisenhower's farewell address, after all, had also warned about "the prospect of domination of the nation's scholars by Federal employment." It is unclear who was using whom.

The cost of the colossal, barely audited transfers to the intellectual sector is still debated. Perhaps the pace of innovation was slowed, suggests one authority on the subject, as the large, immediately visible rewards of research money fostered "our scientific community's diminished capacity to comprehend and manipulate the world for other than military ends."[86] One certain price was paid as the imperatives of secrecy wrapped around the campus. Virtually all the faculty and a third of the students in Stanford's electronics program, for example, held security clearances in the mid-1960s. Anyone who has taught on the university level knows the invidiousness of classified work, as the contributions of students and scholars not cleared" become marginalized.

❇

The covert operators, not only of the CIA but also now of the White House — the sort of people John Le Carré calls "the global architects . . . the political charm-sellers and geopolitical alchemists" — did not have much time for those uncharted areas of economics and science. They heard life and death hammering on their doors. The administration saw itself being tested in its very first month, even before the bullying over Berlin, by Soviet talk of supporting wars of national liberation, or "holy wars" as Khrushchev labeled them. "It was a significant event in our lives," McNamara remembered years later. Others have called the administration's overreaction "strategic panic."[87]

For merely the price of training nationalist firebrands in Moscow and opening a couple of Asian- and African-language schools, the Soviet Union was able to stampede bewildered America into believing that it had to compete for the goodwill of a billion or two desperately poor people, or, more precisely, for the few thousand kleptocrats ranting in their name. Every rustle of a badly translated copy of Lenin's *Materialism and Empirio-Criticism* in Ayacucho or Jakarta could be drowned out by the thunder of planes hurling ambassadors, U.S. Information Service teams, Green Berets, CIA operatives, and, of course, money against the impalpable, but therefore more terrifying, threat. To be sure, there were teeth in Moscow's words. Its customer list for weapons expanded from 1960 to 1964 to include Algeria, Sudan, Ghana, Mali, Somalia, Tanzania, the Congo, Laos, and Cambodia. It also included India, where Khrushchev assured Prime Minister Nehru that whatever modest Soviet aid he accepted would immediately be multiplied by a fortune in U.S. assistance.[88] Sure enough, India had to rely on American food relief to feed itself while Nehru neglected agriculture, pursued a pro-Soviet foreign policy, and dragged his country down under the weight of malfunctioning, state-run, industrial white elephants.

"The great battleground for the defense and expansion of freedom," the president rhapsodized, lay in "the lands of the rising peoples." Billions of dollars were expected to relieve their misery in this Decade of Development, during which his officials anticipated poorly understood "traditional" societies to "take off," if only they were provided with enough cash and protection.[89]

Rather than one breakwater — Britain — there would now be an entire shoreline of well-banked and equipped regional allies with which Washington could work on the Cold War periphery. Americans went deep into "nation building," although the fashionable term should have been a reminder that many of the states springing up from what Churchill had called the "drizzle of empires" were as much nations as a lumberyard is a house. There was minimal concern about what kind of nations were being built or whether in the short term they could be. Third world surrogates were developed to help master this "great battleground" south of the Tropic of Cancer. The whole helter-skelter, confused, headlong business entailed endless nips and tucks of covert action, foreign aid, and even Peace Corps deployments, whose volunteers might be useful in battling Soviet propaganda.[90]

Money was now routinely going to places ever more remote, imaginatively as well as geographically, from official Washington. State visits and White House accolades were being extended indiscriminately. At least journalist Joe Alsop called these supposed friends what they were: "workable fixtures," something akin to plumbing. It was only the unworldly who spoke of democracy. Dictators were also easier to work with, as a national security assistant genially admitted in the 1990s, because "we only have to take one phone call."[91] Few, if any, of them would have been so materially supported by the United States had it not been for the Cold War. Nor were relations usually as expedient as they seemed — even before the chickens came home to roost. After all, such strongmen had already proved themselves on much more slippery slopes than had NSC staffers down from Cambridge or career officials at State and Defense.

Behind America's compromises and likely "strategic panic," however, were no mere terrors cast by firelight on cave walls. Small groups of ruthless, well-equipped men in Asia, Africa, or Latin America could get things done — fast. In the right places, they could bring about drastic political change to an extent not to be imagined in modern lands, where road and telephone networks, among other technologies, might work against such upheavals. Confronting these people and their Soviet friends could not be left to New England–style town meetings. Backing the bad against the worse often remained unavoidable. But what was troubling about the new, young American operators was how comfortable they were with having to make these moral adjustments.

At least some of their efforts played into "nation building" at home, although Kennedy, like Eisenhower, was largely dragged along by events when dealing with racial justice. Kennedy had made 479 references to Africa in his campaign, asserting that the United States had "lost ground" there under the Republicans and more than doubling development aid in his first year to $459.6 million. The Pentagon then began U.S.-based training programs for select African soldiers, as well as a five-year university related course for officers.[92] Relatedly confronting civil rights, if largely to impress constituencies overseas, became unavoidable. In 1962, however, Maryland's legislature voted to maintain segregation in the state's hotels and restaurants, a decision that received worldwide publicity. Moscow still had little need to propagandize. The White House also found itself ordering Major General Creighton Abrams to dispatch troops from Memphis to Oxford, Mississippi, where mobs had risen against attempts to integrate Ole Miss. The contradictions were obvious, but it would take another administration to push through the pathbreaking Civil Rights Act.

In quieter surroundings at Johns Hopkins University, McGeorge Bundy gave a lecture that focused directly on this administration's preoccupation — foreign policy, especially in the developing world. He titled it "The Battlefields of Power and the Searchlights of the Academy" and acclaimed the "big measure of interpenetration between universities with area programs and the information-gathering agencies of the United States" (read "CIA," and occasionally the new Defense Intelligence Agency that Kennedy created to consolidate Pentagon analyses).[93] The failure to distinguish between the purposes of universities and those of the secret parts of government was deepening. Harvard's mild and sensitive president, Nathan Pusey, was among the few beneficiaries of public (that is, defense) money to worry openly. Otherwise, skilled specialists who were by no means scientists or technologists were now expected to spring from the government-enriched environments of academia, with Washington getting a direct return. Actually on the ground in Vietnam, Stanford University's advisory group reported directly to the President — of the United States. A member of the Michigan State team argued that Saigon's future lay in a military coup against Ngo Dinh Diem. On more agreeable terrain, Penn State maneuvered to take responsibility for managing an anti–submarine warfare research center at La Spezia, Italy, in conjunction with NATO.

There was a steady growth of thinking, or at least paper circulating, in global or "area" terms about issues better approached at the micro level, and perpetual alarms about indistinct places whose languages no one spoke. (Communication between U.S. operatives and Ho Chi Minh in the mid-1940s had been in French.) It had taken the world thousands of years to bring Laotians and Montagnards, Sumatran farmers and Senegalese nomads, into being. Now resources greater than these cultures had ever amassed were being wielded among them like the scalpel of a blind surgeon, often by men who had not heard of any of these people six months before.

A particularly feckless example is Tibet, a land as large as all of Western Europe. It is also an ironic one, in light of Eisenhower's 1956 comparison of Hungary's revolt with the remotest spot he could suggest. Overrun by the Chinese in early 1951, its cause had been taken up energetically by C. D. Jackson, who urged U.S. backing for "this Dali Lama fellow."[94] The result was disastrous. "The covert action that George Kennan had levied on the CIA," says one student of Tibet, had turned by 1958 into an intense commitment of Agency support for the newly constituted National Defense Army.[95] Two hundred fifty tons of arms, ammunition, and supplies were airdropped to this bedraggled band over the next three years, with China claiming to have killed 89,000 Tibetans (out of a population of 4 million to 6 million) just by the end of 1959.

Beginning that year, several hundred guerrillas — mercifully not the "thousands" of myth — had been trained at a CIA camp in Colorado. Only one of the forty-nine instructors spoke their language.[96] Nor did the Agency know much about Tibet's geography.

Until the first accurate maps could be produced in 1959 from U-2 photos, it had to rely on British maps drawn well before World War I. Its operatives saw themselves in the adventure of their lives — one that could replicate the European resistance movements in which several of them had participated. The British, who did know something about this strange theocracy, rebuffed repeated U.S. efforts to enlist even their diplomatic support. Early failures should have ended the excitement, but CIA officials, recalled one rhetorical participant, would have regarded cancellation "as a personal failure."[97] Instead, haphazard paramilitary operations continued until 1974. Some 10 to 20 percent of the nation perished.

Tibet was just one tiny corner of Kennedy's "global civil war." Given the forlorn places in which it was being fought (and the fact that its most vexing manifestations, as in Korea and Vietnam, were civil wars indeed), the United States would require additional, bolder, finer-crafted military capacities if it wanted to play. All this fed into Kennedy's overinterest in men who were both elite and tough — a penchant for deadly crack forces that was common among a certain type of national leader, such as Churchill. This commando fixation ran parallel to his bringing down to Washington the Harvard dean (Bundy) to assume the role of national security assistant and the youngest-ever president of Ford (McNamara) to command the Defense Department. Both, after all, were successful (meaning rich) and reputed to be smart and steely. That was enough.

Newspaper articles about former Army Chief of Staff Maxwell Taylor would mention his fondness for quietly reading Greek or Latin when being flown into combat. This good-looking World War II paratrooper had also been a powerful critic of Eisenhower's constricted Pentagon spending and an advocate of what he called "heroic measures" to achieve an adequate defense. He touted U.S. Army Special Forces as the means to deal with third world conflict, as in Vietnam, without committing large conventional units. Eisenhower had not reappointed him. He retired to write his denunciation of the administration (for which Eisenhower wanted him recalled to duty and court-martialed) and to oversee construction of the Lincoln Center for the Performing Arts in Manhattan.

Not unsurprisingly, Taylor was the Kennedys' favorite soldier. Robert Kennedy named one of his boys after him. Taylor quickly joined the White House as military adviser to the president, soon chairing the interagency Special Group Counterinsurgency, which rapidly turned into Special Group-Augmented (SGA) to oversee covert operations. Its members included Bundy, Robert Kennedy, and Edward R. Murrow, the new director of the U.S. Information Agency. Development of U.S. super-units flowed naturally. Like the gun on the wall in a Chekhov play, it was highly unlikely that they would not be used. Yet the patience required in what the Communists called "people's war" was just the quality that Americans were least likely to display. Today, it is stunning to recall how valiantly ignorant Washington was of precedents, other cultures, and even geography.

"American frontiers are on the Rhine and the Mekong and the Tigris and the Euphrates and the Amazon," John Kennedy had declared during the presidential campaign. "We are responsible for the maintenance of freedom all over the world."[98] His administration then rushed onto some of the world's darkest and bloodiest grounds, concentrating on what he preferred to label "internal defense" rather than counterinsurgency — most fatefully in Southeast Asia, but also in Latin America and Africa. He took to quoting Sun Tzu, the ancient Chinese philosopher of war. What followed was hardly "a new type of warfare."[99] In fact, irregular war was familiar to Americans. Filibustering had been a diversion for a century, distracting the politics of the 1850s, titillating O. Henry's readers in the 1890s, and stealing Panama for Teddy Roosevelt in 1903. The distinction now was that Washington was no longer backing some freewheeling condottiere but building up its own versatile talents.

The Army Special Forces had been created on a small scale in 1952 with an eye to fighting behind enemy lines in a European war. In 1961, Kennedy allowed an expanding force of these soldiers to wear their distinctive European headgear to publicize his aim of going toe-to-toe with Communist revolution. His brother kept such a hat on his desk at the Justice Department. Fit young commandos would regularly be invited to Hyannis Port for weekends of games and exercise with the extended family. The president studied the training manuals and supervised the selection of new equipment. Before he showcased what became known as the Green Berets, the CIA had carried out such secret warfare. (In 1961, the White House still placed the first Green Beret units sent to Vietnam under Agency direction.) Soon enough, the other services had to match the Army.

One hundred million dollars was diverted from McNamara's first budget to reorient U.S. forces. The Navy formed its first two SEAL teams in January 1962. Air Force Chief of Staff LeMay scoffed at all the snake eating, later concluding that "the Army simply climbed on the bandwagon" of military spending's latest fashion.[100] Yet he would not let the Air Force be ignored. The Air Commandos were formed in 1963, building off the specialist glamour of SAC's security guards, with their custom stag-handled revolvers and white foulards. Robert Kennedy, among other senior civilian officials, would attend earnest interdepartmental seminars on "subterranean war" and guerrilla tactics.

The CIA, for its part, was beginning to acquire a reputation for omniscience at the same time that sophisticated veterans such as William F. Buckley were beginning to mock it. Already in 1958, for instance, Buckley wrote in his *National Review* of an assassination attempt on Sukarno that had all the earmarks of a CIA operation — everyone was blown up except Sukarno. It continued to act equally daft and no less cruelly. For example, a secret manual on "counter-intelligence interrogation," was printed in 1963 and remained standard for at least two decades. In the sophisticated, scholarly, and utterly cold-blooded style of the head of counterintelligence, James Jesus Angleton, this 128-page handbook explains the increasingly intense range of coercive techniques, including "electrical materials and methods," that might be used on defectors, spies, or anyone else engaged (or perhaps suspected of engaging) in clandestine activities against America. The Agency could be patient: "Until the source dies or tells us everything that he knows that is pertinent to our purposes, his interrogation may be interrupted, perhaps for years — but it has not been completed."[101] This was no mere theoretical perspective, as would be shown disastrously by the nearly five-year interrogation of KGB defector Colonel Yuri Nosenko deep in the Virginia woods.

Popular art had caught on to the curious backgrounds, peculiar methods, and frequent ineptness of America's secret operatives. In Alfred Hitchcock's *North by Northwest*, for example, suave adman Cary Grant is mistaken for an agent working for "the Professor and his Washington colleagues." "I don't like the games you play, Professor," exclaims this innocent caught up in the double-edged tactics of something very much like the CIA. "War is hell, even when it's a cold one," responds the spymaster. Unconvinced, and appalled that

Washington needs to ask "girls" like the patriotic Eva Marie Saint "to bed down" with the enemy, Grant tells the professor, "Perhaps you ought to start learning how to lose a few cold wars." The professor replies, "I'm afraid we're already doing that, Mr. Thornton."

A common belief that America was somehow "losing" in the jungles and *mercados* had helped propel Kennedy into office. Leftist national liberators, however, kept proving more corrupt in their absolute power than just about anyone backed by Washington. The "purification" that Frantz Fanon, Herbert Marcuse, and other radicals attributed to such pitiless contests might have started in justified rage and understandable illusion but swiftly followed paths that led into darkness. Cuba became an example. It had been Latin America's fourth most prosperous nation in 1959 when Fidel Castro ousted Fulgencio Batista, a "friendly dictator" who, though mild enough to have previously amnestied and exiled Castro after a failed coup, had become practically a recruiting sergeant for the Politburo. Washington promptly recognized the new government, and U.S. oil companies advanced Castro $29 million, since Batista had escaped with much of the treasury. (Sra. Batista ended up living opulently in Palm Beach.) Castro then expropriated almost $1 billion of U.S. property and introduced machine-gun executions of several thousand opponents in what his lieutenant Antonio Jimenez termed "The Year of the Firing Squad."[102] Much of this was televised. "I wasn't the vice president who presided over the communization of Cuba," Kennedy sneered at Nixon during the campaign. Diplomatic relations were severed three weeks before his inauguration. By April, Castro was openly declaring himself a Communist.

The first recorded mention of killing Castro is from December 1959, when the chief of the CIA's Western Hemisphere division listed a series of "recommended actions" for director Allen Dulles, the "elimination of Fidel" being one. Nothing was done, perhaps because John Foster Dulles's successor as secretary of state, the quietly authoritative former governor of Massachusetts, Christian Herter, simply dismissed Castro as "very much like a child."[103] In August 1960, Eisenhower's decision to approve a $13 million CIA plot to oust him was anything but child's play, and the Agency began creating a Cuban exile force. In his final State of the Union address, Eisenhower dropped a heavy (and misleading) hint that "Communist-dominated regimes have been deposed in Guatemala and Iran."[104] Although often contemptuous of the Agency, he had never forgotten how it had brought him such apparently dramatic returns on remarkably small investments. The man now called up to apply the "Guatemala model" (which was on everyone's mind) was Richard Bissell, Bundy's former economics professor, who had rapidly risen to head the Directorate of Plans, the CIA's arm for covert activities and espionage.

By the time of the Kennedys, secrecy trod upon secrecy within the Agency itself. Special action called for special procedures, with special "compartments" of information extending into the directorate so that a given plan might be known only to its assigned officers. Internal review and overall accountability became casualties of security. In addition, Kennedy and his key advisers had no time to pay attention to the invasion planning. For example, Robert Lovett, back at Brown Brothers Harriman & Co., the New York private bank, had been consulted during Eisenhower's last months about the wisdom of forcing Castro out and had quietly denounced it. Kennedy also admired Lovett, sought his advice during the transition, and had offered him his choice of State, Defense, or Treasury (each of which Lovett characteristically claimed to be too ill to fulfill). But apparently no one in the administration got around to letting the last Democratic defense secretary know what was being implemented. There had not even been an NSC meeting to review the scheme.

Sliding into the April 1961 invasion was easy. McNamara recalled, "We were hysterical about Castro" — this from a man whose international concerns six months before had extended little further than Ford's European market share. Such emotion found its outlet and proved, as usual, the enemy of sensible decision: there would be neither a full assault against Castro nor a retreat. "They've got the damndest bunch of boy commandos running around . . . you ever saw," Adlai Stevenson remarked to a friend after visiting the White House just before the invaders landed at the Bay of Pigs.[105] He did not know the worst. Although Eisenhower's own record in international meddling is less than admirable, it is hard to imagine him giving free rein to such people.

The budget for the Cuba venture jumped to $46 million. Sensibly, Kennedy initially doubted the Agency's ill-conceived paramilitary plan, which he had inherited. Invasion might look like "an American Hungary" should even one U.S. Marine end up being landed, he told his aides. "Do you want to be perceived as less anti-communist than the great Eisenhower?" Allen Dulles purred. Moreover, the CIA had a "disposal" problem: it had to do something with the well-armed exiles it had trained. That argument may have forced the president's hand. Neither Dulles nor anyone else at the Agency apparently told him that the Soviet Union had already learned the exact date of the attack, a rather germane point of which Dulles and Bissell were aware.[106] So Kennedy proceeded in a spasm of literally unthinking anticommunism.

Once events went wrong, he sounded "almost hysterical" to State Department Policy Planning director George McGhee and ended the day in tears. Vice President Johnson sounded "even more hysterical."[107] Bundy remained cool. "Well," he said flippantly, "Che learned more from Guatemala than we did."[108] John McCloy, of all people, was horrified at the invasion. Now chairing the President's Advisory Committee on Arms Control and Disarmament, while commuting to his New York law firm and serving as chairman of both the Council on Foreign Relations and Chase Manhattan Bank, this elder statesman told the White House counsel that the United States had no more right to attack than Khrushchev would have if he invaded Turkey. Allen Dulles, for his part, concluded a bit too late that the CIA should not be running paramilitary operations. At least it had attended to the details it found important: the pilots in its Guatemala-based exile force were all polygraphed to ensure that they were neither Communists nor, equally menacing, homosexuals.[109]

The 1,453 insurgents who hit the beach in Cuba were demolished. The 1,189 who were quickly captured were ransomed eighteen months later, but they were left to linger for four extra months in Castro's deadly prisons. So would say John McCone, millionaire shipbuilder from California and former AEC chairman, whom the president soon appointed to replace Dulles. Robert Kennedy, according to McCone, had worried that the Republicans might focus on the issue in the midterm elections.[110] The same lawyer who had extracted Francis Gary Powers handled the private negotiations with Castro at the attorney general's behest. Baby-food and drug companies, as well as shipping firms, were persuaded to cough up $53 million in tax-deductible donations in kind. As would be officially denied for seventeen years, CIA pilots also had perished during the invasion. Two unprotected, unmarked B-26s were shot down because no one on the CIA operations staff remembered that Nicaragua, whence they departed, is in the central time zone, whereas Cuba is in the eastern zone. An alternative excuse was that the Agency had used Cuban time, whereas the U.S. Navy had relied on Greenwich mean time.

Marine Commandant David Shoup had been appalled that the White House commandos and CIA operatives did not even know how long the island of Cuba might be. As the Cold War ground on, the sheer unpreparedness of so many of the men in power began to grate. Graham Greene (who had worked for Philby in SIS during the war) and other skeptics realized that such incompetence had come to characterize the secret agencies in general, especially regarding ignorance of elementary geography. "They won't know the difference," says Jim Wormold, the clever vacuum cleaner salesman in *Our Man in Havana*, as he defrauds his spymasters. They swallow his stories of secret installations hidden "in the snow-covered mountains of Cuba" as readily as the Agency believed that the swampy Bay of Pigs was the right place for an amphibious landing.

The CIA was at least blunt in self-criticism, although the postmortem was useless. For three dozen years, no outsider would see the one copy of the 150-page report by Inspector General Lyman Kirkpatrick, a truly honorable man. Kirkpatrick presented the Agency's performance as "ludicrous or tragic or both" and criticized its officers for having treated the exiles under their command "like dirt." If it could not work with Cubans, he asked, "how can the agency possibly succeed with the natives of Black Africa or Southeast Asia?" Any such future operations, Kirkpatrick concluded, should be conducted by the Defense Department.

Kirkpatrick showed that one of the reasons for the failure was that almost none of the officers involved spoke Spanish or had much experience in Latin America. When his report was declassified in 1998, Agency officials had to acknowledge that this lack of foreign language ability and of experience remained one of their severest problems.[111] But it was the administration's appointees, according to Roger Hilsman (himself a gung ho new arrival at State), who became "fundamentally responsible for making covert action a fad."[112] As in the aftermath of the missile crisis, for which this blunder was so largely responsible, lies (or artful constructions) were used casually. "There will not be, under any conditions, any intervention in Cuba by U.S. armed forces," Kennedy had told the press four days before he proceeded.[113]

Adlai Stevenson, sidelined by the Kennedys as ambassador to the United Nations, had faithfully repeated to the world that the

United States had nothing to do with this business. A cutting *Mad* magazine cartoon came a bit closer to the truth: Stevenson and the two brothers are in the Oval Office, with the Kennedys' friend Frank Sinatra expounding on foreign policy. When Stevenson meekly disagrees, he is slapped full in the face by Bobby, snarling, "Never interrupt Frank again!" Just as viciously, the president and his brother were ready to avenge their embarrassment by getting rid of Castro once and for all. In a case of life imitating pop art, they dove further into Mafia liaisons that the CIA had begun cultivating during Eisenhower's final months.

Nor was Cuba the only recipient of their toughness. Also during the first six months of Kennedy's term, the CIA was trying to remove Rafael Trujillo — "one of our sons-of-bitches," as FDR had referred to him. For thirty bloody years, this more or less friendly dictator was Benefactor of the Dominican Republic. He had just signed a nonaggression pact with Castro. The Agency whipped together another assassination plot, and one young aide, Richard Goodwin, drafted a follow-up plan for sending in the Marines. Robert Kennedy wanted a few boots on the ground after the hit. Cooler heads prevailed, and the Generalissimo was cut down instead by local gunmen who had been armed but not directed by the Agency. Washington still had to lever Trujillo's wastrel son out of his fiefdom, once he had taken six of his father's killers from prison and personally shot them. McGhee flew in to wrangle personally with this playboy heir over whether he would first accept $15 million, then $25 million, with the money ostensibly coming from the Dominican treasury but actually drawn from U.S. development funds.[114] The real-world analogue to *Have Gun — Will Travel*, the period's tough-guy TV western, was proving to be "have checkbook, will interfere." By the fall, it was the far more benign native-born socialist premier of Guiana (still a British colony, with 600,000 people) whom the president himself apparently determined had to go. Surely, this naive East Indian, who tried to explain his ideals in the Oval Office, was a stalking-horse for Castro. The CIA went to work.

Part of the problem behind the CIA's recurring failures, as can be seen by this point in the Cold War, is that there was always too much cash. "There basically wasn't a limit," observed Kirkpatrick. Seemingly anything could be approved. "Are you sure you're asking for enough money?" Bissell recalls Clarence Cannon, chairman of the House Appropriations Committee, asking Allen Dulles.[115] What was limited, however, was supervision. After 1962, CIA budgets would be free from U.S. General Accounting Office audits.

The Cold War was not just an oubliette of falsehoods; it was also a whispering gallery of the formally unsayable — an encapsulation of all the "unthinkables" bandied about by the intellectuals. How some human obstacle might be "terminated" in the Caribbean, Africa, or Southeast Asia was only to be discussed elliptically. The endless demand for tactical responses provided government with years of temptations to deceive, or worse. One reason Kennedy believed that the Bay of Pigs invasion stood a good chance of success was because Castro would be dead by the time the exiles landed, a CIA convenience begun under Eisenhower.[116] After the Bay of Pigs, the president appointed his brother as de facto head of all intelligence operations, including the Agency's. "From inside accounts of the pressure Bobby was putting on the CIA to 'get Castro,'" writes former Kennedy aide Harris Wofford, "he seemed like a wild man who was out-CIA-ing the CIA." After one of his tirades, deputy director of the NSC Walt Whitman Rostow urged him to calm down, then hinted privately to the president that his brother was going over the top.[117]

Thomas Finletter's long-ago disgust with operative Ernie Cuneo's cavalier talk of assassination was the mark of another time. Again life would imitate art. The president let it be known that he had enjoyed Ian Fleming's James Bond adventure *From Russia with Love*, an adolescent fantasy wrapped around the superagent's "license to kill." Jackie Kennedy had given a copy to Allen Dulles several years previously, and the CIA director would reminisce that "President Kennedy and I often talked about James Bond." Fleming himself had been a Kennedy houseguest in the spring of 1960, had outlined anti-Castro tactics to Kennedy (proposals very similar to those eventually acted on by the CIA), and had kept in constant touch with Dulles, who observed that he found the novels professionally useful. Robert Kennedy would engross himself with Fleming's latest, *Diamonds Are Forever*, while on government business in Djakarta.[118] This silliness was best addressed by *Private Eye*, the satirical London weekly. Lampooning Fleming, it depicted a somewhat feel-good-looking President Kennedy avidly devouring novels titled *Goldwater* and *Dr. Castro* (echoes, for those of a later generation, of Fleming's actual *Goldfinger* and *Dr. No*), and yodeling, "Attaboy, kill 'em all."

The first James Bond movie appeared in 1963. By the time "intelligence" dramas became popular on television, however, it was in the even sillier forms of *Mission: Impossible* and *The Man from U.N.C.L.E.* American commercial fiction, at least, did not yet offer the spirit-burdening visions of *The Spy Who Came In from the Cold* and *All Men Are Lonely Now*.

Seymour Hersh, winner of four George Polk Awards for investigative reporting, documents the unique intimacy of the Kennedy White House with Bond's methods as acceptable tools of statecraft — although a recent study of "Kennedy's wars" reminds us that there is no evidence, such as perhaps a writ of execution, that the president ever ordered anyone's assassination. Right from the start, as Senate hearings would begin to reveal fourteen years later, national security assistant Bundy discussed with Bissell the prospect of expanding the CIA's killing capabilities. He and many other men of Camelot prided themselves on having no illusions — a simple but dangerous vanity. Such pride breeds a competing vanity that anything goes. It was not too large a step from "nation building" (as defined by Rostow and other academics) to nation strengthening (using the Special Forces) to what Lyndon Johnson called "a goddamn Murder Inc. in the Caribbean." That cover-up would last for decades.[119]

It is not at all clear that Kennedy's penchant for stories about the hypersophisticated Commander Bond was merely a "publicity gag," nor can charges that the president fomented assassinations be dismissed as a "myth."[120] To be sure, the first crackpot CIA scheme to murder Castro surfaced in Eisenhower's closing days. (An exploding cigar was the weapon of choice.) But thereafter, efforts became personal, although three documented CIA attempts from those years (using an exploding seashell, a contaminated diving suit, and a poison pen) read like parody.

President Kennedy's chief regret was that he had not actually made his brother head of the CIA, in order to bring that murky outfit under closer family control. No matter, the attorney general "personally managed the operation on the assassination of Castro," according to Richard Helms (the smooth deputy to Richard Bissell), who would ascend to the top in June 1966. Thirty-five years after these events, Helms would finally admit what records were making ever harder to evade. He acknowledged that the effort could not otherwise have assumed such size and character: "It was Bobby on behalf of his brother. It wasn't anybody else."[121] Helms may self-servingly be spreading the blame, and the CIA's own written report on the subject states that Robert Kennedy did not approve any plot.

In the tough, no-holds-barred mores of this White House, however, it appears that the attorney general was cheered on even by McNamara, who insisted, two months before the missile crisis, that "the only way to get rid of Castro is to kill him . . . and I really mean it." In 2001, James Woolsey, the first post–Cold War director of the CIA, offered his straightforward conclusion: assassination was pursued with "the full knowledge and approval of the President, John F. Kennedy."[122] It is difficult to believe that the Agency was a rogue elephant, acting alone, during the heated one thousand days. Castro had to be gone by the 1964 election. The pressure from the Kennedys became even stronger after the missile crisis. Having taken the chair of the Special Group-Augmented when his brother appointed General Taylor to head the Joint Chiefs, the attorney general kept planning for yet another CIA-backed invasion. He "knew everything we were doing," recalls a key Agency official, and "the [exiled] Cubans got all the money they needed."[123]

Already by the fall of 1961, the University of Miami campus contained the world's largest CIA station, as six hundred case officers handled a payroll for around three thousand Cuban exiles. In January 1962, Robert Kennedy declared Castro the administration's "top priority. . . . No time, money, effort — or manpower is to be spared." His brother selected Edward Lansdale, now a brigadier general and known for his nips and tucks in the Philippines and South Vietnam, to run sabotage, propaganda, and infiltration. The president thought that Lansdale embodied the essence of James Bond. (He had already been disappointed to see that William Harvey, the plodding, overweight CIA officer who had established the "Executive Action [that is, assassination] Capability" at White House urging, was anything but Bond.)[124] All sorts of plans, from the sophomoric to the insane, were dreamed up in the Pentagon and at Langley. Perhaps they could fake a picture of a bloated Castro grasping two voluptuous women to destroy his reputation, or sink a boatload of Cuban refugees ("real or simulated") and pin the atrocity on him. Or maybe Castro could be blamed should the 1962 Mercury space flight carrying John Glenn crash. Or U.S. operatives might develop a "Communist Cuban terror campaign in the Miami area," maybe even "blow up a U.S. warship in Guantanamo Bay and blame Cuba."[125] "Remember the *Maine*" would pale in comparison.

It didn't matter that Lansdale had zero experience in Latin America or the Caribbean. The Joint Chiefs endorsed these ideas as "suitable for planning purposes," with the CIA adding thirty-three different plots of its own. Taking the Bond novels a bit too seriously, Agency operatives even asked British intelligence to become involved in a "hit" on Castro. "We're not in it anymore," replied a senior officer of MI5, the counterintelligence arm. "We got out a couple of years ago, after Suez."[126] Pushed on by the White House, America's would-be 007s nonetheless kept stalking Castro, and Cuban exile teams returned to hit-and-run raids that, the president believed, "were probably exciting and rather pleasant for those who engage in them" (except, presumably, for the twenty-five exiles recruited by the CIA who were killed or captured during 1963). There was no U.S. defense need for any of this. Insiders such as McGhee note that these measures helped bring on not only the missile crisis but, perhaps, gunfire in Dallas. Robert Kennedy seems to have suspected this, too.[127]

Ever since Castro's takeover, the United States has scrupulously paid its annual $4,085 rent check to Havana for Teddy Roosevelt's perpetual lease on the fifteen-square-mile naval base at Guantánamo. ("It's a really good deal," says a State Department desk officer today.) Four thousand Cubans from nearby towns kept working there during the Kennedy years, drawing seven million Yankee dollars annually into Castro's boycotted economy. For the next three decades as well, Cuban exile politics would embarrass U.S. officials, from the 1976 sabotage of a Cubana airliner that killed 73 civilians to the 1998 confessions from remnants of the CIA-trained clandestine military wing that it had organized a wave of bombings on the island the previous year. "When the Cubans were working for the C.I.A. they were called patriots," lamented one graying commando leader, "now they call it terrorism."[128] Castro, for his part, has stayed in place during the terms of eight more American presidents.

Perhaps a mess like Cuba could have been avoided if Washington had been better at controlling its collection of friendly dictators, of which Batista was by no means the worst. Building on the alliances beyond Europe, which John Foster Dulles had largely arranged, more than 100,000 foreigners had taken U.S. military training courses since 1950. An international military academy, the School of the Americas, had been established under U.S. auspices in Panama right after World War II. It would train 60,000 officers from every Latin American country by the time the Cold War ended, including homicidal gangsters such as El Salvador's Roberto d'Aubuisson and Panama's own Manuel Noriega. At least all these high-rising graduates could help soak up U.S. heavy weapons and materiel — the ongoing sales being justified as strengthening U.S. influence on generals who might otherwise have behaved even worse, as lowering economies of scale for U.S. manufacturers, or as preempting European and even Russian vendors. The School of the Americas also epitomized a central fact of the Cold War years: military relations were the key point of contact between the United States and some of the world's surliest, most overarmed regimes.

Iran would become another example of chickens coming home to roost, although at the time, General Taylor glowed over its U.S. military ties. "I stood on a hilltop . . . with the Shah," he gushed after a demonstration by Pahlavi's U.S.-equipped army and air force, and "sensed the influence of the American soldier in his role as teacher of the armies of freedom."[129] Seeing the Shah as a force of "freedom" was as foolish as believing that Guatemalan colonels understood the kind of liberty for which Jefferson had fought. The Shah, who had received $387 million in outright military aid since being plopped back on his throne, rebuffed U.S. attempts to make actual weapons sales conditional on his investment in Iran's civilian economy. So in Iran, as elsewhere, Americans kept reaching into their pockets to back bad means toward the long-term end: stable liberty. The trouble was that the end was often poisoned by the means.

One of the Kennedys' highest priorities in the "global civil war" was to go beyond just offering more military aid and training in the world's nether regions. Police assistance had to be expanded, and fast. Some forms of police instruction had begun in 1954 under State Department auspices, and since then they had been operating ad hoc. John Kennedy brought what he called his Office of Public Safety center stage, placing it within the new Agency for International Development (AID). Aid from this office went to some of the grossest violators of human rights outside the Communist world. Impatient in his aerie at Justice, the attorney general was annoyed that AID's top officials were more concerned with economic than with police development.[130] The CIA, for its part, had no time for "the horse-and-buggy type of police officers" and, in a spirit of true missionary generosity, wanted to see Washington's Interdepartmental Committee on Police Aid introduce "a group of J. Edgar Hoovers" into these countries.

Such cloning was difficult, and Robert Kennedy initially failed to accomplish it through the International Association of Chiefs of

Police, an essentially benign and far too tame trade organization. The association squandered its $275,000 contract on programs such as sending several Iranian police officers to work alongside Kansas City patrolmen. It then found itself helpless when these jaded guests were picked up within weeks by the FBI on various vice charges. Ethiopia had its own complaints: the quality of training its police were receiving in America was disappointing, perhaps because Haile Selassie expected more technique than could be delivered under the Bill of Rights.[131]

New, bolder institutions and deadlier procedures were called for. The president created by executive order the International Police Academy, next to Georgetown University, to train three hundred to four hundred of Tehran's or Manila's finest per year. Latin America's actual police forces — Somoza's or Stroessner's, for example — could already resort to the U.S.-sponsored Inter-American Police Academy, also in Panama, and be taught for thirteen weeks at around $13,000 per student in today's dollars. However, it was a bit much to expect graduates to make the distinction between military matters (much more inclined to violence) and police work (usually reflecting more moderate civilian norms). This distinction was certainly lost on the Guatemalans.[132] Some Americans were troubled. "Just what we think we can teach the Dominican police that they did not learn for themselves in Trujillo's days is hard to understand," observed Oregon Senator Wayne Morse.[133]

Instruction in Georgetown was backed by the sale of police equipment, rather expansively defined beyond caps and badges. Washington imposed a "Buy American" caveat on riot gear after Mali saw fit to accept $150,000 in unspecified police products and then turned to Moscow for actual lessons in how to use them. Alternatively, some foreign police forces took the courses, accepted U.S. equipment, and kept right on torturing. Training at the new International Police Academy began a month after John Kennedy's death. His brother gave the commencement address to its first class the following February.

It was in Indochina, however, where energy truly outstripped wisdom. There, all the fascination with counterinsurgency, covert operations, secret policing, defense assistance, and even nuclear threats came together. At his first NSC meeting, within ten days of his taking office, Kennedy had urged the CIA to launch guerrilla operations against North Vietnam. Within twenty-four hours of shouldering the blame for the Bay of Pigs, he had ordered a review of U.S. options in South Vietnam — his first major acknowledgment of that gathering storm, during a day that would be described in the Pentagon Papers as one of "prolonged crisis meetings at the White House." Four hundred Green Berets were to be quietly dispatched. After his humiliation by Khrushchev in Vienna six weeks later, Kennedy's first thought was again to demonstrate toughness in Vietnam.[134] The number of U.S. advisers was tripled once he returned to Washington.

Since 1954, the United States had spent the immense sum of approximately $250 million to build a 25,000-man army in Laos, a country with a population (which could only be estimated) of perhaps 2 million. The cash was to help defend a people barely aware of their government's existence, let alone of the conflict of superpowers.[135] Twenty-nine thousand rifles, ten tanks, heavy artillery, and armored personnel carriers were only part of the flow of steel into that moist land, which had not found it necessary to build a single all-weather road. By 1962, the "Kingdom of a Million Elephants" had consumed nearly a half billion dollars worth of aid (more per capita than any other country), of which about 2 percent was thought to have gone to improving the lot of the desperately poor villagers who were most of its people.

Laos was a white space on a map surrounded by white space. It was inhabited by delicate folk with melodious names — genuinely "a faraway people" about whom Americans knew virtually nothing. Eisenhower had left office with several hundred U.S. advisers already in place. Yet Arleigh Burke, chief of naval operations in 1961, already discerned that the Soviet-backed Pathet Lao, who challenged the somewhat Western-leaning Royal Laotian Government, in tandem with the North Vietnamese were a threat to America's "national welfare." He advocated U.S. air strikes to support the royal government "with all their faults."[136]

Three months later, following Soviet airlifts of small arms to the Pathet Lao, Kennedy had moved aircraft carriers into the South China Sea and landed five hundred Marines by helicopter in Thailand. A C-47 was shot down in March. The crew was killed, and the U.S. deputy air attaché was captured and interrogated by the Pathet Lao and their North Vietnamese allies, with the results going straight to the top of the KGB.[137] Skittish SEATO allies were dragooned to get ready to fight in Laos, with even the British promising a battalion from Hong Kong. The Joint Chiefs of Staff debated sending sixty thousand U.S. soldiers to Laos and recommended using nuclear weapons should China intervene. The nearly concurrent events at the Bay of Pigs checked these enthusiasms, and Kennedy sensibly warned that sending more Americans might lead precisely to such intervention by China. His caution in this instance was encouraged by Army Chief of Staff George Decker, a prudent man who went so far as to raise an unfounded threat of yellow fever should U.S. troops appear in Laos. As for secretly injecting small Green Beret units into Vietnam, Decker warned that there was no such panacea. Military involvement needed to be looked at as a major war. He was not reappointed.

With Laos still a battleground in 1962, McNamara wanted to inject forty thousand troops. Kennedy instead acquiesced to a coalition government. Perhaps another conference in Geneva could sort matters out, especially if the North Vietnamese and Soviets attended. The North Vietnamese chose to spend their days by the lake denying what everyone, including the Russians, admitted to be true: the presence of about five thousand of their soldiers not only in combat against the Royal Laotian Army but also improving the network of supply lines cutting through Laos into South Vietnam. Negotiations ended with Laos's neutrality formally reaffirmed. The use of its territory for military purposes was barred. Hanoi violated this agreement from the first.

The dollars kept flowing. Perceptive journalists saw Laos "ecstatically drowning in American aid." Most of the money was wasted from the moment of its arrival, as the Vientiane elite assigned the dollar an absurd exchange rate. The graft only began there.[138] Meanwhile, around $350 million ($2 billion today) went to Cambodia during Kennedy's thousand days. It did not take the chairman of the Senate Foreign Relations Committee to recognize that if Americans were offered any sort of referendum on foreign aid, they would soundly reject just about all of it. However, William Fulbright did not rise above the most repetitious mechanical endorsement: "All the paraphernalia of our international programs must be at least tolerated by the people during the long twilight struggle."[139] Congress reluctantly appropriated $4.75 billion in economic and military aid in 1962, heaping it upon the $32 billion already thought to have been spent on military assistance to sixty-nine countries since the Korean War. But the legislators were getting wise to the racket, and they slashed aid the following year to the lowest amount since 1947. The Peace Corps also lost a quarter of its budget.

If the United States had to make a stand in Southeast Asia, the president had argued privately after the 1962 Geneva conference, it would be better to do so over the South Vietnamese border than in Laos. Eisenhower disagreed, counseling his successor to place Americans astride what later became known as the Ho Chi Minh Trail. To him, the stakes remained immense: losing South Vietnam might result in "cutting the world in half."[140] An equally authoritative military presence until his death in 1964, Douglas MacArthur, quietly warned Kennedy against sending any troops at all: they weren't expert in guerrilla war. This advice must have rankled.

U.S. military advisers had already been training South Vietnam's army for a half dozen years, spending roughly $85 million a year since 1956 to supply it with uniforms, small arms, helicopters, and tanks. There were 692 advisers in South Vietnam at the start of the Kennedy administration, and 7,000 more were sent there in November 1961. Two years later, there were 16,700 Americans in place. When journalists and Republican politicians exposed the fact that this presence had become much more than "advisory," the embarrassed president insisted that they were "not combat troops in the generally accepted sense of the word." Whatever he was hoping, small numbers of armed Americans were not going to turn the tide against the people who had overrun Foreign Legion machine gunners at Dien Bien Phu. "Special warfare," however, was this administration's mantra. The Kennedy brothers and McNamara presumed that it was a sharp and quick way to pressure Hanoi, but playing by Hanoi's rules was easier said than done.[141]

The president was nonetheless correct in repeatedly expressing his revulsion for Hanoi's particular methods of "liberation." Even on its own turf, Ho Chi Minh's regime, during a single "agricultural reform" in 1956, had been responsible for around fifty thousand executions by its "people's tribunals." Ngo Dinh Diem's elder brother and nephew also had been murdered. Below the 17th Parallel, other executioners loyal to Hanoi had "taken the lives of four thousand civil officers in the last twelve months in Vietnam," the president stated before Congress. And that was said only in May 1961.[142] Contrary to revisionist memory, Diem's strong-arm tactics in rooting out South Vietnamese Communists in the late 1950s did not come close to this carnage.[143]

Americans had to face an ugly reality. It was impossible to impress Vietnamese villagers with U.S. economic assistance when the people who accepted it courted death at the hands of the Viet Cong, or to help build any properly functioning grassroots electoral system when hideous reprisals would fall upon every participating schoolmaster and village elder. Where massacre is a daily possibility, the prospect of establishing government legitimacy remains pretty remote.

As the *Washington Post* reflected in an editorial valedictory to McGeorge Bundy in 1996, "The American role in the Vietnam War, for all its stumbles, was no accident. It arose from the deepest sources — the deepest and most legitimate sources — of the American desire to affirm freedom in the world."[144] Actually, it was the commitment that was no accident; the "role" itself was far more stumble than affirmation. The important distinction is that the Cold War can be used to explain why U.S. leaders opposed Castro and backed Diem (for a while). Cold War reasoning, however, is not enough to explain why these men acted upon so many of their chosen commitments so rashly. The kindest explanation is that the confusion was characteristic of a country which had no interest in empire.

Today, McNamara blithely says that when Kennedy took office in January 1961, his administration failed to understand that the Vietnam problem — so recently one of the century's most dramatic wars, on which the United States had spent billions to back France — "already had a history of its own that antedated John F. Kennedy's presidency by many years." Bundy, for his part, was even vague as to when and how South Vietnam, a member of the World Bank and the UN, had come into being.[145] McNamara insists that the administration simply could not obtain sophisticated insights on Vietnam, a nation slightly larger than New Mexico. This argument has become conventional wisdom, with McNamara concluding that a major lesson of Vietnam is "know your opponent." Arthur Schlesinger, for one, laments that "the purge of old China hands in the State Department deprived Kennedy and Johnson of the expert diplomatic counsel" they needed. McNamara echoes that sentiment, saying that the legacy of McCarthyism kept him from obtaining sound advice, as China specialists such as John Stewart Service (the first U.S. official to have met Mao) had been run out of Foggy Bottom. Yet responsibility cannot be so easily passed.[146]

Far more expertise was available at that time than a decade before, but still nothing like what would have been considered adequate to deal with, say, Belgium or Switzerland. The problem was that even tentative inquiries (of a kind that previously would have been considered the merest beginnings of serious study) had become sufficient for world-affecting action in Southeast Asia.

It was not the McCarthy era that "cost us 58,000 lives in Vietnam," as legend now claims.[147] There were always able Sinologues at the State Department, such as Deputy Assistant Secretary Marshall Green and Edward Rice, who discerned an imperialistic appetite in Maoism. Kennan, who served briefly as ambassador to Yugoslavia, empathized, for the moment, with those who wanted to take the emerging war in Vietnam directly to Beijing.[148] Other experts detected much more of a civil conflict. Among these were men such as scholar Bernard Fall (remembered as a hero of moderation, but the first advocate of bombing North Vietnam in 1962); journalist Jean Lacouture, who had come to know Vietnam during the French disaster; and professors such as George Kahin and David Marr, who had studied Vietnamese nationalism. Even the victimized John Service, arrested in 1945 for passing hundreds of classified documents to a left-wing journal, had been returned to State in 1957, although the Kennedy administration chose to post him to Liverpool. However, nuanced advice, no less than raw information, must be evaluated to be useful. Closer to the truth is McNamara's equally casual observation that fateful steps were taken in Vietnam without having "investigated what was essentially at stake," that they were discussed "in only a cursory way."[149]

Kennedy was riveted by China's ambitions, particularly by its progress toward an atomic bomb. To him, the Chinese would be America's "major antagonists of the late '60s and beyond." Bundy was the point man for approaching Khrushchev about a joint effort to "strangle the [nuclear] baby in the cradle." (He would deny it in later years.[150]) Moscow was unresponsive. Kennedy encouraged the CIA and other government arms to explore preventive action, including plans to "take out" China's nuclear program. He suggested using "anonymous planes."[151] Taylor proposed some sort of paramilitary feat. Prudent opinion at the State Department stood in the way. Inevitably, schemes arose to make short work of China's weapons scientists, a thought apparently contributed by an Arms Control and Disarmament Agency official who also went on to teach at MIT.[152] This was the context for decisions concerning South-east Asia.

The greatest single wound that the Cold War chewed out of America — and America's greatest policy blunder in the twentieth century — might have been avoided by taking a leaf from Herman Kahn's book *On Thermonuclear War:* Just what was it that was "unthinkable"? Hanoi's takeover of South Vietnam? War with China? Losing an election in 1964? The unthinkability of ends got in the way of the unthinkability of means as America crashed into a war of murderous naïveté. "What does Graham Greene know?" Anthony Lake, a future national security assistant, would recall asking himself while reading *The Quiet American* en route to Saigon as a young ambassador's aide in 1963.[153] What could anyone in Washington learn from this portrait of a confidently parochial, gen-uinely naive, bravely dangerous super-amateur who imperils just those people whom he is relentlessly set on uplifting? "He was deter-mined," observes Fowler, Greene's seasoned foreign correspondent, in speaking of Payne, "to do good, not to any individual person but to a country, a continent, a world." Lake, too — with his president behind him — "was in his element now, with a whole universe to improve."

Payne is a metaphor for America's plucky attitude, combined with its sense of righteousness. Its leaders were ready to "do some-thing." Yet serious thought on Vietnam was foreclosed by all the noise of the Kennedy years. Leaving aside ideals, there was also the White House's deeply political motive — not wrong in itself, since democracies can hardly avoid the popular fervor of not wanting to appear "soft."

South Vietnam as another "wall of freedom" had a sandy foun-dation. Against it leaned ruthless ideology, genuine nationalism, and a warrior spirit that the United States could never awake in its own Vietnamese allies. To join with the Viet Cong, according to Hanoi's Institute of Military History, 21,533 North Vietnamese sol-diers were sent south from 1961 through 1963, a stream beginning to turn into a river. Opposing them was Diem — a remote, corrupt, patriotic bully, a Catholic amid a mostly Buddhist population, although with strong credentials in having opposed the French. But today's notion that he ran anything like a "tyranny" seems a studied insult to the memories of Khrushchev, Mao, and Ho Chi Minh.[154] Costly to history, if not to character, has been McNamara's late-1990s hand-wringing in Hanoi during visits in a "search for answers to the Vietnam tragedy" with former North Vietnamese officials. Throughout the meetings, he records himself as speaking of Diem's "brutality" and "violence."[155] Through all his contrition, however, there rises not a hint of the savageries of Ho Chi Minh and the men who came after.

By 1963, the Kennedys had joined those officials who believed that Diem, losing the confidence of his people, had become one more obstacle to efficient "nation building." Diem came to be regarded, with some reason, as an arrogant mandarin who had kicked the peasantry toward the Viet Cong and who was using his U.S.-trained forces against political opponents. He was also losing the war. Getting rid of him, and of his more sinister younger brother, Ngo Dinh Nhu (claiming to be in quiet negotiations with Hanoi about neutrality), might bolster popular resistance to Hanoi. Such machinations had become nearly second nature in Washington.

Until then, Americans could regard toppled leaders such as Mosaddeq and Arbenz in terms of shackled nations casting off their despots. (No one overthrown had that clean a record.) However, the ouster and murder of the brothers Diem — the first step, at least, problematic without Washington's approval — presaged deeper responsibility in a faraway country of which America was soon to know much too much. Lyndon Johnson sensibly opposed the coup, as did McNamara and Taylor. CIA director John McCone predicted disaster would follow. John Kenneth Galbraith, on leave from Harvard as ambassador to India, nonetheless preferred military rule.[156] In any event, the overthrow of an inadequate yet homegrown civilian cabal was likely to leave a vacuum that would be tricky to fill.

The alternatives to Diem at that moment were deplorable. It was neither the Vietnamese left nor right that deposed him: it was the American center. On November 1, 1963, a CIA operative working as liaison between the new U.S. ambassador, Henry Cabot Lodge, and Diem's top generals "swaggered into the plotters' headquarters, toting an ivory-handled .375 Magnum revolver and a valise bulging with the equivalent of $40,000, in case they needed funds."[157] No one would have been surprised if the White House had in fact ordered the next day's murders, as postmortem rumors alleged. But it had not. Whatever it wanted, it soon found that the unstable junta replacing Diem could not quell mounting Communist attacks.

That fall, Kennedy expanded his covert guerrilla war against North Vietnam. Skeptical of CIA ability, he turned "special warfare" of the Green Beret variety back over to a reluctant Pentagon. As violence and U.S. involvement increased, the Joint Chiefs of Staff believed that the only way to uphold the Saigon government was to wage war against the North. Yet the Chiefs also concluded that Kennedy would forbid such "overt action." They had no enthusiasm for the "special warfare" they were assigned and therefore pressed for more Agency operations. McNamara — who has since represented himself as a befuddled administrator, distanced from the makers of policy, forever seeking a way out, unable to get advice, and who says he already knew that the war could not be won — promised the men of the CIA whatever was necessary to accelerate their efforts.

With 145 Americans killed by that autumn, might upholding South Vietnam even be possible? It was Kennedy's belief, as in West Berlin, that "any dangerous spot is tenable if men — brave men — will make it so."[158] This was a kamikaze ethic in any locale, but such bravado was accomplished. "The cost is large," intoned the New York Times about defending South Vietnam, "but the cost of Southeast Asia coming under the domination of Russia and Communist China would be larger still."[159]

Reports from the battle zone by young journalists working for the New York Times and the wire services meanwhile recounted the ongoing failures of South Vietnam's army, despite the assistance of additional U.S. advisers. Unlike the more specialized war correspondents of World War II and Korea, these men — including Halberstam, Neil Sheehan, and Peter Arnett — were unencumbered by any particular knowledge of Asia or of military affairs. The small cadre of seasoned observers on the ground, such as the New York Herald Tribune's Marguerite Higgins — who dared to be critical of their unrelentingly pessimistic assessment of Diem at the same time they were urging total U.S. commitment — had little influence.[160] Recognizing the looming disaster, and regarding the increasingly unpopular Diem as better than chaos, she understood that any hope of military effectiveness could not survive the collapse of what there was of a political base.

No one knows whether John Kennedy would have kept going further into Vietnam had he lived. Probably so. He believed the threat from China alone to be immense. Had he intended to extricate the United States, there could be nothing more contrary to that objective than a coup. "President Kennedy," explains Harry McPherson, longtime assistant to Lyndon Johnson, "was as sure of

America's ability to impress its will on struggles such as the one in Vietnam as any wahoo congressman."[161] He knew that a war in Vietnam would be costly, but he also feared that there could be a huge political cost to him for withdrawing. His own aide Kenneth O'Donnell (the Kevin Costner character in *Thirteen Days*) writes of the president telling him several times in 1963, "I can't do it until 1965 — after I'm reelected." Since he feared political attack, only then could there be "complete withdrawal of American forces from Vietnam."[162] This is a chilling interpretation. It presupposes a president ready to benefit from allowing young Americans to die for another year for a cause in which he did not believe. And how much deeper were they going to get during another year?

In the speech that he brought with him to Dallas that final day, Kennedy was once again ready to extol the demands on U.S. power. His text was a mixture of statistics and implied derring-do. Again he trumpeted "an increase of nearly 600 percent" in America's special forces in Vietnam — men ready to meet "guerrillas, saboteurs, insurgents and assassins" on their own ground. Given how he had plunged ahead with the nuclear buildup even after the missile gap was disproved and how he had pursued Castro long after the missile crisis, this was not a man to retreat or to let himself be thought of as "chicken" before Congress and the press, especially after repeated denunciations of Hanoi's atrocities.[163] What is equally likely, however, is that he would never have allowed the war to be fought in the blundering and bureaucratized way that made "avoidance of defeat" the objective. He was too dutiful a student of history and combat, and too much a skeptic of the brass, to believe that the United States could ever win a distant contest of attrition with Ho Chi Minh.

✪

When John Kennedy was shot, Chip Bohlen, ambassador to France, was informed of the event by the stationmaster after his train was stopped at Nancy, and the fastest way of returning to Paris was in the prefect's car. Six years before the moon landing, this remained the ordinary pace of state affairs. Americans were shipped six thousand miles across the Pacific to pursue black-pajamaed peasants sowing the land with punji sticks, while others in the Pentagon were helping weave the Internet and sail toward the stars. The mixture of brilliant insight and of incantation masquerading as policy was bewildering.

A Cold War streak wove through the assassination itself — in the endeavor to murder Castro, certainly in Lee Harvey Oswald's vague contacts with Moscow, and most of all in his very real pro-Castro politics. Lyndon Johnson not only immediately worried "when would the missiles be coming" but also that "Castro got Kennedy first" and the Cubans would now be gunning for him.[164] He was convinced for the rest of his life that the Kennedys' plotting had backfired and that Castro had somehow beaten the young president to the draw. Yet neither he nor anyone else in authority wanted to expose the tragedy's possible links to Cuba, if only from fear of public reaction. While there was no conspiratorial cover-up, every facet of the Kennedys' social milieu, including the press and a deliberately limited Warren Commission investigation, quietly perpetuated a continued secrecy. The American people sensed something wrong. They considered the deceits, and, a generation later, half of them were convinced that federal officials likely had a direct role in the president's death.[165] White House plotting against Castro had ironically combined with the president's own assassination to begin inducing that wave of suspicion toward Washington from which the country will not soon recover.

By the time of Kennedy's death, around one million U.S. servicemen were stationed at more than two hundred foreign bases. The Cold War was by then so huge in its global range and its apparently ever higher stakes that it operated more on dangerous generalizations and less in pursuit of specific objectives. Vietnam, for example, was not treated as possessing the uniqueness of any other great nation, despite a population of nearly forty million and a history that stretched into the antediluvian mists. It was approached as if the United States were getting involved in one more third world shoot-out, as in, say, Lebanon or the Congo. All the ready comparisons to the past, especially to Munich, only brought out further ignorances. Sensible decisions were impeded by emergency, by looking backward, by power in too few hands. Consequences were increasingly unknowable. Finance, for example, became part of the confusion. War would soon combine with social spending to dilute the dollar, export inflation, wear at the public confidence underlying international trade, and energize OPEC along the way. Too many causes, too many effects.

Virtually Kennedy's last official act was to threaten Moscow with a grain embargo if it did not release Yale professor Frederick

Barghoorn, grabbed for some impenetrable reason by the police machine. This incident followed the success of the Partial Test Ban Treaty just reached in October, which finally outlawed all but underground nuclear detonations. Why such provocation, and then why so intense a reaction? No one knows. Nor did anyone besides a very few imagine that the tools of a thermonuclear apocalypse were being handled well outside democratic scrutiny, even beyond the oversight of the highest elected officials. The Pentagon was taking dangerous operational shortcuts, such as putting thousands of weapons on hair trigger alert, and men outside the legal chain of presidential succession would have been able to decide to launch them. So much was ad hoc and arbitrary.

Just as classic psychoanalysis, Keynesian economics, and manipulative advertising — all the applied social sciences of the postwar epoch — started to unravel by the midpoint of the Cold War, so did that strange profession of strategic studies as practiced by Kahn, Morgenstern, and their less gifted imitators. Confidently presented axioms of deterrence kept sounding weirder and proving ever less relevant. By this time, there was too much to think about and yet not enough knowledge; too much to hope and fear and yet no adequate perspective for either. The Cold War by November 1963 had been ticking long enough that the "unthinkable" could often be the first thing of which to think. Not just thermonuclear war, but mass lunacy (China), proliferation (perhaps everywhere), and alienation (on your nearest college campus).

Much of the excitement over President Kennedy, at least in retrospect, lay in seeing him as the last hope for the United States to change the antagonism with the East and to get off the treadmill. He would inspire hope, however, not fulfill it. Five more years in office would likely have diminished the promise. His final speech, on that sunny November morning in Texas, rested America's strength squarely on the willingness of the country's citizens "to assume the burdens of leadership."[166] He knew then of what he spoke. It was becoming easier for people to wonder whether so much of what was going on had anything to do with the "cost of freedom."

Some people believe that America was more focused and vital under the Cold War's great challenge, particularly during the Kennedy years, than it is today. This is an adolescent emotion that often surfaces after wartime. As president, Rutherford B. Hayes once said that the Civil War had been "the best years of our lives." Such a view of the thrill of battle renewed itself in those heady thousand days. It was dangerous then and is hardly worth mourning now.

Certain great issues such as civil rights were bound up with politics. Beyond a point, however, politics was a diversion of attention, and more than a psychological one, as decades of deficit-burdened budgets would attest. In the name of an ill-defined "new generation," John Kennedy's presidency pointed the country of Edison and Ford into vigorous archaism. There had been a president who was made for a new frontier: his name was Jefferson. Instead, the country got a veneer of Theodore Roosevelt: vibrant, long-term possibility running down into a set of exhausting divisive crises. It was becoming a strenuous life indeed for Americans.

7

The Burden Felt

(1964–1969)

*Start thinking about anything and, if you think long enough,
you find yourself thinking the unthinkable.*

Michael Frayn, *Constructions*

By the end of 1963, America was well on its way to being transformed from the nation of only twenty years before. With unemployment around 4.5 percent, the average hourly wage was $2.14
in an economy in which a family of six could be well fed on $30 a
week. For ten years, inflation had averaged 1.3 percent. Government spending, revamping a still-marginal South, was washing
over into the West. Segregation was finally being confronted. Cape
Canaveral, the Houston Space Center, the interstates, and mobility
between regions and classes were changing America for the better.

A generation bemused by its sudden postwar wealth found it
easy to pay for bold new ventures. An amazing 96 percent of Americans believed that their standard of living would keep improving, so
they were receptive to waging a war against poverty at home and
one against communism abroad. These, however, were the years
when the country started derailing on its speedy drive into the
twenty-first century. It did not tear itself apart, but it did endure an
exhausting family quarrel. Overseas, it was sucked into the chaos
caused by the deaths of Europe's empires. Toward the decade's end,
Americans would be shelling out weapons, money, or both to nearly
a hundred countries. And there was Vietnam.

At the start of Lyndon Johnson's administration, liberal opinion leaders worried deeply that Johnson, a graduate of a Texas teachers college, would revert to an emphasis on domestic priorities at the expense of foreign policy.[1] After all, he was much closer to the real problems of the nation's life — poverty, race, public schooling — than Kennedy had been, and he was not infatuated with commandos or other global excitements. Within three weeks of Kennedy's assassination, he ordered all plots involving sabotage and murder in Cuba to stop. Knowing that the United States would have to recognize China sooner or later, he wanted no "steps" against its nuclear preparations.[2] Yet Johnson soon faced choices in which he had less interest, and they would claw away at those closest to his heart.

Foreign and military aid had become an established diplomatic tool, but money was buying neither development for the client nor leverage for the donor. Instead, entire cultures of corruption were being created. As the United States grew more involved in the third world, it condoned the most abominable actions in the Congo, Indonesia, and a shadowy list of more forgettable places. What the country was doing and countenancing was well known in secret and often willfully unnoticed in public.

These were also the years that Western Europe drifted out of the consciousness of most Americans. Only once did Johnson visit, a quick courtesy for West German Chancellor Konrad Adenauer's funeral in 1967. Yet even when Americans realized that the original approach of relying on strong partners was going nowhere, they kept on literally trying to pass the buck — to pay for proxies, to plead with their allies to do more. They did not ratchet up the costs for opposing the United States — banging heads in NATO for greater cooperation, writing trade law for Japan, cutting corrupt generals in Guatemala City and Jakarta off at the knees, squeezing Moscow's access to food and finance, hammering North Vietnam. Instead, so much was done, but only partially and reflexively. It is unlikely that a United States less indulgent of its allies, less generous to its dependents, and more ruthless toward its enemies could have made matters worse. It was this diffidence that, once the country was embarked on whatever its leaders thought it was doing, resulted in vast losses in money, decency, and lives.

Johnson was fifty-five, although he tends to be remembered as much older. Counseled by his predecessor's advisers, he initially drew on early U.S. experiences in Greece, and in Western Europe with NATO, to explain that America could avoid "appeasement" without actually "sending men to fight in Vietnam."[3] Once men had been sent and the United States refrained from both ferocious bombing and closing North Vietnam's harbors, Dean Rusk offered an explanation for such constricted war: there was no need to use greater force because Hanoi could be pressured to relent, as had the guerrillas in Greece, the Soviets in Berlin, and even the Chinese in Korea.[4] These comparisons did not take into account the differences in time, place, and peoples. No one involved investigated what was at stake or worked out what American power could not so easily do.

It is Vietnam that frames these half dozen years, from the getting in to the getting stuck. Yet the same folks who brought the country Vietnam also brought it an even more peculiar thermonuclear relationship with the Soviet Union. About as many dollars were spent on U.S. ICBMs, SLBMs, bombers, and other weapons between 1965 and 1975 as went to Southeast Asia. Just as Washington refused to understand the North Vietnamese, so it failed to listen to Moscow. "There is no indication that the Soviets are seeking to develop a strategic nuclear force as large as ours," McNamara said before the Soviets unveiled a force far larger than anyone outside the Kremlin had imagined.[5] The blunders came because accomplished and well positioned men were talking loudest about complicated matters they knew little or nothing about.

This chapter approaches the growing Cold War burden in four ways. First, beginning with Vietnam, it examines the morass America was struggling through in the developing world, with a moral as well as a material toll. Second, it discusses the "guns and butter" trade-offs that help make explicit the opportunities being lost — a loss all the more embittering given the disappointing responses from U.S. allies in Europe and Asia. Third, we return to the rising costs of actual war in Vietnam, particularly to their ties with upheavals at home. Finally, and again at the other extreme of violence, the story starts tracking the accelerated nuclear arms competition that would dominate U.S.-Soviet relations to the end.

Much of the healthy skepticism that Americans once showed toward foreign entanglement — whether voiced by Will Rogers or Lenny Bruce — had been worn away by cries of emergency, by the sudden glory of it all. Once this early-1960s faith in America's world role ended, it was followed by an increasing suspicion that the country couldn't do anything right anywhere. The respect that Americans had for their government peaked around the middle of the decade, when the Great Society was legislated at home and intended to be emulated abroad. The collapse of that respect would be the most important influence on American politics for the rest of the century.

✪

Johnson retained his predecessor's entire national security cohort, telling McNamara, Bundy, and Undersecretary of State George Ball that they were individually among the "extraordinary people I could never have reached for."[6] Perhaps he was giving them his famous "treatment," but one man who knew the president for thirty years argues that Johnson was so convinced. For example, he could not bring himself to believe that he had lost the 1960 nomination through any fundamental defect of his own; he assumed Kennedy had marshaled better talent.[7] The corollary worked themselves halfway around the world, as the new president tragically did not push back against the sparkling, hardworking advisers he had inherited.

During his first months, Johnson repeatedly queried them for concise, clear summaries of U.S. objectives in Vietnam. "What is a one-sentence statement of what our policy is out there?" he asked McNamara and Bundy, as he worried that Americans would be bloodily committed to "hold Southeast Asia" before he could make a decision. "What the hell is Vietnam worth to me? What is Laos worth to me?" the president asked Bundy. He feared the country might be biting off more than "it was in the end prepared to chew."[8] Then things got worse. In January 1964, the junta that had replaced Diem was in turn overthrown by one led by a young officer trained at Fort Leavenworth.

"I don't think it's worth fighting for," Johnson said within six months of becoming president. "And I don't think we can get out." He despairingly recalled having "sat down with Eisenhower in '54." Johnson now insisted he would do anything to avoid "another Korean operation" and feared another Chinese intervention if the United States took harsher steps against the North.[9] As senator, he had asserted soon after Korea that U.S. military action, other than in response to something close to direct attack, should be pursued only as a multinational task. In the years since, however, the United

States had become bold enough to ignore that self-imposed principle at the first challenge.

It had also developed the dangerous habit of backdoor diplomacy. Staying on as attorney general into 1964 before continuing his political career as a senator from New York, Robert Kennedy was not helping matters. He reopened his channel with old friend Georgi Bolshakov, who had been hauled back to Moscow after the missile crisis. The Soviets were told by a go-between that the Kennedys (now meaning Robert and Edward, the senator from Massachusetts) regarded Johnson as a "clever time-server incapable of realizing [President] Kennedy's unfinished plans" and that RFK intended to run for president, probably in 1968.[10] Other men were more responsible, although their opinions were nearly as self-serving.

Redolent of the late 1940s, for example, Ambassador Henry Cabot Lodge cabled Washington that South Vietnam might have to be run by a U.S. "High Commissioner," having himself in mind. Georgia's Richard Russell was still chairman of the Senate Armed Services Committee and had known Lodge and Johnson for more than twenty years. He cautioned the president that Lodge "thinks he's dealing with barbarian tribes out there."[11] Maxwell Taylor, who temporarily replaced Lodge during 1964, was also deadly wrong on nearly every detail, even the terrain, which he thought was "not an . . . unpleasant place to operate for American soldiers." Vietnam could never turn into something as terrible as Korea, he vouched, but even on the bitter Korean peninsula "U.S. troops [had] learned to live and work without too much effort."[12] Vietnam, in brief, was the war that "wasn't to be Korea."

Anything that becomes a true American cause ends up being magnificently examined, deeply committed to, and grossly overdone. Korea had been terrible and divisive, but the dozen years of suburb building and middle-class mobility between its end and the entry into Vietnam had helped bury that sacrifice in the memories of many Americans. At least Korea had been dressed up as a UN operation. Now most people hoped that Vietnam also could be handed over to the UN, this time for real. Russell merely wanted Congress to spend whatever it took to install a government in Saigon that would promptly ask the Yankees to go home. That possibility was lost with Diem's murder.

By the summer of 1964, the Vietnam involvement was not yet calamitous. McNamara and Bundy were doing everything possible to "damp down the charge that we did not do all that we could have done." Bundy pondered the situation. "In terms of U.S. politics," he asked, "which is better: to 'lose' now or to 'lose' after committing 100,000 men? Tentative answer: the latter."[13] If the United States indeed ended up fighting the North Vietnamese on their own turf, it occurred to him one night, then perhaps that could be done just by committing volunteers. Perhaps there could be a public relations campaign saying "Only Americans Who Want to Go Have to Go." He knew that the Joint Chiefs of Staff might object to this rallying cry, but he thought his insight worth sharing with the president.[14]

Military aid had been tried as a means of avoiding deeper commitment and had not worked. But it was still central to U.S. hopes of minimizing the country's engagement elsewhere in the world. For example, the annual cost of maintaining a local soldier in countries on the Sino-Soviet borders, McNamara claimed (lumping together such allies as West Germany, Turkey, and South Korea), was $495, compared to $4,347 for putting an American in his place.[15] Development aid might also keep the Soviets at bay. So both forms of help were offered to other contested places, not just Vietnam.

For instance, dollars had been going to neutral Afghanistan since 1954, around the time that it first received Soviet credits. A country slightly bigger than France, Afghanistan bordered the Soviet Union on the north, Iran on the west, Pakistan on the east and south, and, for several dozen miles, China on the east. By 1959, when Eisenhower visited Kabul, the United States had begun a famously ambitious aid project, literally paving the way from the capital to Kandahar, Afghanistan's second-largest city. Once completed in 1966, the crushed gravel and asphalt "Eisenhower Highway" epitomized U.S. largesse toward the most unfathomable places. Afghanistan's prime minister, however, was playing a dangerous game: he bragged of lighting his American cigarettes with Russian matches. His countrymen joked that the U.S.-built road melted in the heat, while the concrete one from Kandahar toward Turkmenistan, which the Russians were building in a similarly grand project, was suitable for Red Army tanks. Today, both roads sprawl as ribbons of rubble across the shattered land, cemeteries of the great bidding wars, just like the towering U.S.-built hydroelectric dam that also lies in ruins beyond Kandahar.[16]

In addition to aid, another indirect means of world involvement could be found through the CIA. While continuing the subsidies (that is, bribes) to cooperative journalists and publishers that had been doled out since 1953, for example, the CIA, with President Kennedy's approval, had established a secret fund that ended up spending at least $3 million, or about $1 per voter, to help the Christian Democrats defeat socialist Salvador Allende in Chile's 1964 presidential election (compared to the 50 cents per voter that Johnson and Senator Barry Goldwater spent that year in their own contest). The next year, twenty-four thousand U.S. Marines and soldiers were sent to "clean up the Dominican Republic," as Johnson put it, after his staff completely misread supposedly Castro-instigated turmoil in the aftermath of Trujillo's assassination.[17]

Also in 1965, Washington's first deep involvement in black Africa got uglier. Today, the land known as the Democratic Republic of Congo shows the results of Europe's African past perhaps more than any other country and is still in the news for being at the center of that continent's largest war ever. In 1965, thirty-five-year-old Joseph Désiré Mobutu (not yet the carefully re-Africanized Mobutu Sese Seko) finally consolidated his rule after one of Africa's first military takeovers. He and his "Mobutuism" would flourish with U.S. and assorted other Western backing for thirty-two years. This was also the year that blood started to flow throughout Indonesia, where more lives were lost than in Vietnam over the previous twenty years. Indonesia and the Congo presented policy dilemmas carried over from the Eisenhower and Kennedy years, as America had unclean hands in both places.

A symbol of what was happening is the old colonial city of Kisangani, formerly Stanleyville, on a navigable stretch of the Congo River in the land that Mobutu renamed Zaire in 1971. V. S. Naipaul's 1979 novel *A Bend in the River* unmistakably describes this as a "place where the future has come and gone." That was true of the entire country of fifteen million, one quarter the size of the United States. Belgium had imposed a particularly virulent form of colonialism, without even a pretense of the moral vision about which Britain, for example, had boasted. Soon after Belgium quit the Congo in 1960, the highly intelligent Mobutu maneuvered to profit from the Cold War by offering stability. As the largest and richest of the newly independent colonies, let alone one bordering on nine others, the Congo was seen by Washington as a bellwether. The anarchy that followed Belgium's departure resulted in the largest UN peacekeeping operation of the Cold War (the UN operation in

Korea having been one of outright war), as twenty thousand troops from thirty countries were deployed there. During this tumult, the CIA recruited Mobutu, gave him $1 million via the UN to pay off restive soldiers, and thereafter found him useful in molding congenial governments. He began building a career as Africa's cleverest, most rapacious, and longest-reigning despot, and as Washington's closest African ally.

First, the CIA had to handle Prime Minister Patrice Lumumba, the charismatic, left-leaning, fiery figure who had led the Congo to independence. During Eisenhower's last months in office, the Agency bankrolled a $100,000 murder plot, which was, perhaps, murkily countenanced by the president. It did not matter that Lumumba was recognized by the newly arrived CIA station chief as "a bit of a Tom Paine" and "a loose cannon," but not a Communist.[18] What terrified Washington was the presence of one thousand or so Soviet "technical advisers.

Until being assigned to the Congo in 1959, middle-ranking CIA officer Larry Devlin had spent his years since Harvard doing what he describes as "Soviet work" in Europe and remaining "sort of behind the curve careerwise." He was probably not the most effective person to be mastering factional politics in the capital of Leopoldville or to carry out a hit. He recalls how Richard Bissell, fearing "another Cuba," despatched Sidney Gottlieb, traveling under the alias Joseph Braun. In late 1960, and serving as Bissell's assistant for scientific matters, Gottlieb carried a vial of the bacterial culture of a disease indigenous to that part of Africa ("something far out . . . it was supposed to cause paralysis"). He also brought hypodermic needles, gauze masks, and rubber gloves.[19] Devlin says he could never get sufficiently close to do the poisoning, and Lumumba was, in any event, soon beaten to death by his rivals.

Mobutu, for the time being, remained the army's commander in chief. Lumumba loyalists, however, were still being backed by Russia and China, with a cameo appearance from Che Guevara. Therefore, when Mobutu seized full power in 1965, he was enabled by American-financed Belgian mercenaries, CIA-acquainted Cuban exiles, and several pilots from Langley. No matter that U.S. officials knew almost nothing of central Africa, and American academia little more. (Dr. Newton Gingrich would soon fill some of the gap with a thesis on Belgian colonial education.) From then on, recalls a former assistant secretary of state for Africa, "Mobutu played us, and his environment, like a Stradivarius."[20]

Mobutu enjoyed formal visits to Washington, as at least $2 billion in U.S. aid and loans started flowing to help his new state of some 250 tribes seize its future. The main economic effects were to uphold the price of chateaus in France, Switzerland, and Portugal. His French patrons called him a "walking bank balance with a leopard-skin hat." Surprisingly, his former inland empire, today with around forty-two million people, still has only a thousand miles of barely usable roads — but at least the Russian ZIMs never barreled down them.

Nor would Russians or Communists of any sort be seen in Indonesia after 1965. Washington knew little more about Indonesia — a fourteen-thousand-island archipelago that possessed neither precise borders nor even a name for itself until German geographers coined one — than it did about the Congo. However, its size, resources, and population were by far the greatest in Southeast Asia. Always spluttering alarms, George Kennan in 1948 had identified Indonesia as America's "most crucial issue" in opposing the Kremlin. A Communist Indonesia, he had warned as the new country fought to free itself from the Dutch, would be an "infection" that "would sweep westward" through South Asia.[21]

In 1955, the CIA had spent about a million dollars in Indonesia to try to influence elections there. Most of the money was lost or stolen. By 1957, the CIA began spending $10 million in an astoundingly inept operation that supplied arms, ammunition, planes, and pilots to rebel colonels. Some of the cash was squandered to spread the rumor of an affair between Sukarno and a Russian airline stewardess. The work included using Bing Crosby, the most commanding personality in show business, to make a pornographic film starring a Sukarno look-alike.[22] As if that would do anything but enhance the reputation of a Malay dictator. Sukarno had to be placated once he busted these operations, quickly receiving thirty-seven thousand tons of rice and a million dollars in arms, ostensibly as part of a U.S. aid program. The CIA lost nearly all contacts and influence, which at least left it minimally blamable for what followed.

Throughout his brief presidency, Kennedy had worried that Indonesia might move from an annoyingly leftist neutrality toward outright alliance with Beijing, virtually bridging the gap from a Communist mainland to the shores of Australia. The prospect plagued him at least as much as Vietnam. In fact, the two seemed to fit together — as did almost everything in the Cold War. The $1 billion or so in military credits and $650 million in economic ones that

Jakarta received from Moscow in the early 1960s surpassed Soviet generosity to any other non-Communist country. And Indonesia's military men were likely to be decisive as the rest of the state teetered.

The State Department insisted on maintaining its own flow of money, whether or not it was used properly among Indonesia's 100 million people. Twenty Peace Corps volunteers were sent for good measure. Without this aid, it was thought, Sukarno might lean more heavily on what he began to call his "natural allies" in Moscow, Beijing, Hanoi, and Pyongyang. According to Washington, the ever-growing and increasingly popular Communist Party (PKI) was already the world's third largest. Sukarno, meanwhile, balanced between his anti-Communist Soviet-equipped army and his more loyal Soviet-equipped air force. There were at least two attempts on his life in 1962 alone, and the United States again came under (apparently unfounded) suspicion.

With war in Vietnam making Southeast Asia's future look steadily worse by late 1964, this seemed to be no time to sit idle as Sukarno nationalized U.S. property, took his country out of the UN, appeared to countenance mob attacks threatening the AID mission, closed what opposition press remained (saying it had collaborated in CIA murder plots), and, according to the Agency itself, was ready to aid Communist rebels in Laos, which the CIA-run secret army of Hmong tribesmen was already fighting. The country was a pressure cooker. To justify the growing U.S. commitment to Vietnam further, McNamara called Indonesia "the greatest prize" of Communist ambitions.[23]

In the early-morning hours of September 30, 1964, a hit team drawn from the Indonesian air force raided the homes of the army's high command in Jakarta, killed six generals, dumped the bodies down a well on Halim Air Force Base, and seized the radio station to announce that they were saving the country from a CIA takeover. A prominent soldier, General Suharto, commander of the army's strategic reserve, survived. He rallied the Army, and crushed the plot by sundown. Still, it had almost succeeded. A rattled U.S. Embassy judged that had Suharto been among the dead, "communism," whatever this meant in *Lord Jim* country, would have washed through Indonesia overnight, leaving Thailand and South Vietnam as the pathetic headlands of a reddening continent.

Army retribution would have been terrible in any event, but it was bolstered by not-so-subtle U.S. diplomatic support. Two years earlier, Washington had assigned a political officer to research the PKI structure, using methods he had found useful when posted in Moscow. Meticulous chart building and cross-referencing from all sorts of party publications yielded several thousand names, from the Central Committee down to the villages, including cadres of the Communist youth, peasant, and women's organizations.

"I'm 99% certain that [the Indonesian Army] did not know this stuff," recalled that officer   Suharto's army lacking a certain Germanic proclivity for record-keeping. To be sure, the army could have accumulated such names "eventually," but that would have taken "a massive research effort," and the Indonesian armed forces were better at a lot of other, cruder things. Marshall Green, the shrewd professional diplomat who had become ambassador, acknowledged that "the Indonesian Army had many people in it who were our friends," including Suharto. As an index of its faith, the embassy promptly supplied him after the attack with a dozen walkie-talkies for his bodyguards — the army not even possessing anything like these devices.[24]

The embassy also gave Suharto the lists so meticulously compiled. They dwarfed such trivial accumulations as the CIA's Guatemala roster and were put to deadly use. Steadily for weeks from the morning after the coup attempt, names and details were relayed from the embassy to Adam Malik, suavest of the new ruling triumvirate and soon to become Indonesia's foreign minister and vice president. As Suharto condemned the whole three-million-member PKI for the murders, names of the party members were published in the army newspaper. But "Communist," as Ambassador Green recalls, "was just a label" for all but the hard core of that sprawling party.

A CIA research report ranked what followed as "one of the worst mass murders of the 20th Century," comparing it to the Soviet purges of the 1930s and to Hitler's handiwork.[25] The body count was anyone's guess. Pressed for a number by Washington, the embassy pulled the figure 300,000 out of the air. Green later remarked, with a certain sophistication regarding third world statistics, that he should have added "give or take 250,000." Malik would say that 250,000 was about right. Everyone else trying to document the terror — a glimpse of which is offered in the 1983 movie *The Year of Living Dangerously* — estimates the number as being closer to one million, many of whom were children.

Despite the number of dead in central Java, Sumatra, Bali, and the farther islands, the United States did nothing as "the Indonesian holocaust" ripped across the country, killing not only PKI members, their families, and their friends but also any small landowner whose property might be better tended by local army commanders. "I probably have a lot of blood on my hands," reminisces the embassy's political officer, "but that's probably not all bad." Not everyone agreed. By the end of 1965, Americans were reading about corpses so thickly piled as to cause sanitation problems.[26] Robert Kennedy had visited Indonesia in 1962 for his brother (to help avert war with the Netherlands over what is now Irian Jaya) and again in 1964 as a reluctant emissary for President Johnson (to mediate a guerrilla war with the British-created Federation of Malaysia). Now he made explicit public comparisons with Communist and Nazi butchery, demanding that America "speak out also against the inhuman slaughter."[27]

While sopping up the mess, Indonesia at least cut its ties with Moscow and Beijing, invited in the Bank of America, and returned U.S. property, in addition to assuring Washington that Americans no longer had to compete for favor. At the same time, Washington urged the International Monetary Fund (IMF) to extend $200 million in credit and other nations — notably Japan, whose economy was beginning to be taken seriously — to welcome Indonesia's aid requests. The new military rulers allowed Sukarno nominally to stay in office for another year.

By April 1966, however, the American press was still reporting that "one of history's most vicious massacres has not yet ended." "PKI suspects" were still being rounded up for nighttime beheadings, with men being "slain together with their wives and children to reduce chances of later revenge."[28] Contrary to popular belief, it is wrong to conclude that "hundreds of thousands of Chinese were killed."[29] Ethnic Chinese were not singled out, this time, because the PKI did not accept them as members. Suharto would wait until 1986 to execute four of the remaining plotters of the coup attempt, whom he had left to contemplate their fate in prison.

The U.S. embassy collected $26 million in discretionary funds, which it relayed to Suharto in May. So many eager AID personnel from Washington began turning up on the embassy doorstep that Green complained to the State Department, while already warning about the new regime's rampant corruption. But its thieving was only pennies compared to what would occur during the following thirty-two years of Suharto's own rule.

Malik, meanwhile, glided across the United States later that year, explaining away the regrettable events to distinguished civic groups. He went on to serve on the UN's Commission on Humanitarian Affairs. Washington would explain the benefits of aid to Indonesia vis-à-vis Vietnam. Military aid before the coup had "paid dividends," McNamara told a Senate committee. Particularly valuable, he thought, was the program that had brought Indonesian officers to U.S. universities.[30] Perhaps these students of democracy were emboldened by the U.S. stand in Vietnam. Or perhaps their response to Sukarno's overtures to communism showed that the "domino theory" was invalid. In any event, America did nothing to stop the bloodbath. A rigidly anti-Communist government had emerged in this nation that was so populous, potentially rich, and pivotally located.

Good intentions continued to have messy results. The vast amounts of foreign aid that began being handed out in Indonesia and the Congo, whether dispensed directly or through the World Bank, rarely trickled down. Development aid bought few political or economic successes anywhere, and hardly any lasting ones. Much of the money, loaned on very easy terms, just evaporated. Senator William Fulbright dismissed voter grumblings about where this money might be going with the simple declaration, "There is no more waste in our foreign-aid program than in any other government function."[31] He was right: the waste was not at the American end, and tended not to be waste but plain theft on the other.

Leaving aside an extreme case like the Congo, some people would later point to Taiwan and South Korea, where assistance was conditioned on nothing but survival, as successes of a U.S. aid program with a budget that, its supporters argued at the time, was merely 0.5 percent of GDP — less than American women spent on cosmetics. However, these countries received mostly military help for fifteen and twenty years, respectively, and their economies boomed only after necessity forced them toward free-market reforms. In Argentina, U.S. development aid would do little to spur growth amid the chaos left by Juan Perón and the terror unleashed by the right. In Africa, only Botswana — with its small population, its diamonds, and the investment it received from apartheid South Africa — was a success.

Any attempt at useful assistance requires good sense, relative honesty, initiative, and outside governance. Otherwise, the gold runs back into the sand from which it was panned. Through the World Bank, the IMF, and AID, Washington during the 1960s came to follow a doctrine of third world development that was profoundly unsophisticated even for that time. The way that money was force-fed to the initially bewildered, highly centralized regimes had much to do with Cold War assumptions. Zambia, for example, would never have been able to borrow as recklessly as it did in any time of international tranquillity and sound-mindedness.

The World Bank, in which the United States has always been the largest and most influential shareholder, would measure its success by the amount of money distributed — which would shoot up once McNamara became the bank's president in early 1968 after leaving the Pentagon. The total would rise from $883 million per year when he arrived to $12 billion when he left in 1981. This money translated into effectiveness about as well as did the U.S. dollars he directed to Vietnam. Within the World Bank the process could nonetheless be career enhancing. Lending became inseparable from the ambitions of bank officials, who still hold on to their jobs by meeting ever larger, politically determined targets for disbursing money.

The few successes of U.S. aid to the third world, such as agricultural research and eliminating the disease known as river blindness (due significantly to Merck), show what could have been accomplished with all those payouts. But the more consciously political the aid, the more corrupt, bureaucratic, megalomanic, and environmentally destructive it was: the banana-boxing plant in Somalia so oversize that it could never be profitable; the Congo's Inga-Shaba power line, the longest of its kind in the world, four times over budget; the self-regenerating "consulting contracts" growing like a fungus over the world's biggest dam in Paraguay; all the bloated state-owned enterprises inflicted on all the developing continents. African nations in the early 1960s were widely considered more advanced than most East Asian ones. The World Bank did nothing to save Africa from today being tragically far behind.

Well after the Cold War, the World Bank would struggle to the conclusion, long obvious to any observer, that billions of dollars showered for decades on the poorest of countries had yielded no positive economic change whatsoever. Only among the few recipients who could already balance their budgets and had opened their markets did aid prove anything but waste. Yet bank officials had a ready excuse for half a century of self-absorbed activity: the Cold War had required them to shovel U.S. and other Western money into clumsy, not to mention filthy, hands, lest those hands grasp something worse.[32]

Indonesia, for instance, plunged into economic agony during the late 1990s after long having been extolled as an example of rapid, World Bank–assisted growth. Western donors were shown to have compromised mightily with the Suharto regime. Twenty-five billion dollars had been sunk into Indonesia since 1966, with the results being, the World Bank optimistically concluded, only "marginally satisfactory." The sad convergence of Indonesian criminality and, at best, bank neglect had actually institutionalized corruption. "Everyone is red-faced," the bank's president would say.[33] By winking at systemic looting among its government customers in Asia, Africa, and Latin America, the World Bank kept breaking the policymakers' version of Hippocrates' hard-learned admonition: "First, do no harm."

The IMF, in its turn, had originally been expected to help guard the world's currencies from balance-of-payments shortfalls. Again, Americans were the largest donors. But the fund turned into something else entirely — a lender of last resort to countries that got into financial trouble, and one that kept impeding economic growth in poorer countries. More than half of its borrowers between 1965 and 1995 would be no better off than when they started. A third would be worse off. Almost all would end up deeper in debt as IMF bureaucrats routinely aided pathetic examples of what passed as socialism. Whether in dealing with the World Bank or the IMF, and somewhat less so with AID, it was not the poor in villages and slums who took the loans, but bandit leaders who were enabled to borrow billions from the overeager West.[34] Today, it is unconvincing to place responsibility for repayment on those anonymous people whom Graham Greene called the "torturable classes."

When the United States tried to serve as a politicized banker on a supercolossal scale, it failed. It succeeded uniquely when it helped poor countries by doing what it was good at — showing and sharing its approach to private enterprise by opening its markets to exports and nurturing small businesses, as well as by not abetting the corruption of what was later called "state capitalism." Since development assistance of all sorts was more likely to be full of payoffs and politics, it is not surprising that Americans grew disdainful of such assistance and of the recipients. By the end of the Cold War, they would come to believe that foreign aid consumed a vast proportion of the federal budget. In fact, America would rank last among the leading twenty-five industrialized nations in the percentage of GDP devoted to aid.

✪

By 1964, Americans had spent nearly twenty years knowing that war with the Soviet Union was possible. The accompanying preparations were the single greatest force redrawing the lines that separated notions of public and private. As government's role expanded, there was license for social policies at least as ambitious as what the country was doing overseas. Good was no longer good enough. "The rich society and the powerful society," Johnson declared in 1964, had to become "the *Great* Society of the highest order."[35] Such exuberance was admirable. It was a time when Detroit was breaking all records, America's capital investment and corporate profits surged, and prices remained steady after that year's deep tax cut. Franklin Roosevelt's make-work programs during the Depression could even provide good debating points as Johnson tried to rein in military (and military-related) spending. "I am not going to produce atomic bombs as a WPA project," he scolded critics who still believed that defense dollars might have some economic benefit. His budget director noted, "The space program is not a WPA."[36] Yet so many Cold War dollars now involved patronage that comparisons to FDR's old Works Progress Administration were more apt than people realized.

With all his dreams for social betterment, Johnson had to juggle to keep the federal budget from passing what was then thought to be the dangerous height of $100 billion. But he was about to be faced with horrific open-ended spending that would make it impossible to keep all the balls in the air. Fiscally, it was not so much a slide into Vietnam as a sequence of eruptions. From July 1, 1964, to June 30, 1965, fighting there cost around $100 million. Then suddenly, $700 million was needed, followed in January 1966 by requests totaling $14 billion.

"We can do both," the president persisted in 1965, using that unfortunate term from the Third Reich, "guns and butter." He continued, "We are a country which was built by pioneers who had a rifle in one hand and an ax in the other." And then he added, for emphasis, "We *will* do both."[37] The 89th Congress churned out welfare legislation as if from an assembly line. Both Detroit and public entitlements would meet their reckoning, but meanwhile the 1966 State of the Union address promised a massive second round for the Great Society, including a GI Bill for Vietnam veterans and the pledge to "give our fighting men what they must have: every gun, every dollar," no matter that "the days may become months, and the months may become years." The country had become accustomed to both endless conflict and endless payouts.

Within months of the first major troop commitments in 1965, Johnson, McNamara, House Ways and Means Committee Chairman Wilbur Mills, and almost everyone else knew that both could not be sustained. The budget numbers were fantasy, as the president tried to preserve the image of a costless war — one that McNamara fatuously promised would be the "most economically fought war in history."[38] Without boosting taxes, the secretary of defense nonetheless concluded, inflation would hit hard. Johnson berated him for not knowing that a tax increase would be rejected on the Hill, while the Democratic Congress's elderly Southern bulls, seizing on the concession, would stick to the guns and throw out the butter.

Only constantly sustained growth (whose imminent slowdown was partly due to Vietnam) could have avoided the need for tradeoffs. America in the mid-1960s, however, departed from sound finance in the name of continuous international emergency, and the economic consequences would resonate around the world. Without the war, speculated Walter Heller, chairman of the Council of Economic Advisers, the price rises that followed from moving toward full employment after the tax cut would have been half as great.[39] It was that doubling that brought the country into a danger zone of self-reinforcing inflation. The economy was turning over nicely until the pattern of unsound finance, fueled by war, helped launch an inflation that would take seventeen years to subdue.

Under Johnson, the demand for action — the swift, confident, vigorous action that excited so many journalists and that had been the hallmark of Kennedy's foreign policy — came to represent authority and achievement on the domestic scene as well. Much of this government "action," whether in Harlem or Hue, would be accompanied by deception. This was the fraud as well as the force that Hobbes reminds us are the essences of war.

An important truth was discovered even before the Great Society's entitlements began to bite: vast sums could be appropriated and squandered without serious criticism. In his final meeting with Michael Forrestal, the first senior White House aide to be forced out over Vietnam, a weary President Johnson looked up from behind his Oval Office desk to speak privately not of the war, but of the astounding thievery that had accompanied the real achievements of the New Deal.[40] Only in 1968 would Congress be cornered into making budget restraint its top priority, by which time the war was consuming more than $20 billion annually (over $100 billion today) and defense spending had leaped in a year from 7.9 to nearly 10 percent of GDP.

By the mid-1960s, the bureaucracies of defense and social policy substantially converged — not that they were strangers. What was new was the degree of explicit mutual interest, the intensity of common purpose, and the sheer amount of money. As always, there were some benefits. For instance, James Webb at NASA let Alabama's governor know that segregation made it difficult to bring the best talent to Huntsville, hometown of Senator John Sparkman, Adlai Stevenson's running mate in 1952. Should policies not change, he said quietly, part of the George C. Marshall Space Flight Center might have to be moved to more civilized surroundings.

Though lacking Webb's abilities, McNamara was a fundamentally decent man completely free of prejudice. He tried using the armed forces as a tool for off-base desegregation, coldly but correctly presenting discrimination against men in uniform as a "military effectiveness" issue that even the thickest redneck or country club bigot could understand. He was saddened by the overall failure of this noble initiative, seeing it as far more serious than "the TFX [which] was only money."[41] More successfully, he had a program designed in 1966 that would annually induct into the Army 100,000 recruits otherwise ineligible because of low IQ scores, which were blamed (often rightly) on an impoverished upbringing and flawed testing. The men would now be helped by education. The first five years of his visionary Project 100,000 resulted in 340,000 recruits succeeding out of a specially inducted group of 500,000. The project was falsely reviled at the time for being a means of getting more blacks into combat — a charge made even by his biographer after the Cold War, but one debunked by studies that show the recruits came to surpass their peers who had not entered the Army.[42]

Meanwhile, the European allies had assiduously built up their welfare states, sacrificing, or so they claimed, their immediate defense spending to meet the challenges of social justice. Washington offered nothing like the benefits of a Western European social democratic regime, as most health care, for example, was delivered through private enterprise and philanthropy. Conflict in the federal budget between spending on defense and spending on social needs did not become fierce until the Great Society programs arrived. As arguments intensified, renewed attention focused on what more the allies could do to defend themselves. Despite their tariff walls, however, they were still being indirectly subsidized. If the choice was between guns or butter, the Europeans chose butter — protected by American guns. The likelihood of their aiding the United States in Southeast Asia was ni no matter what they thought of the war.

Americans were baffled by Western European resentments. They had not encountered Shaw's remark that he couldn't understand so-and-so being his enemy; after all, he had never done so-and-so a kindness. At least the allies could not push Washington too hard on the expanding balance-of-payments deficits, as one ready solution was still withdrawal of U.S. forces from Europe. Nor could they expect Washington to ameliorate the gold shortage by increasing the price: no one wanted to hand such a windfall to the world's second-largest gold producer — the Soviet Union.

Americans were building up resentments of their own. For example, the courtly Dean Rusk fumed over Britain's refusal to send even a token battalion to Vietnam, growling that next time, the United States would leave that supposedly special ally to defend the white cliffs of Dover alone. Bundy's ire on the subject was tougher because it was more specific, as Britain faced yet another financial crisis and wanted U.S. credits to fend off devaluation. "A British brigade in Vietnam would be worth a billion dollars at the moment of truth for sterling," he advised the president.[43] These officials only echoed, with a dozen years' extra dismay, the anger of Dean Acheson and Chip Bohlen from the early 1950s. Yet this time, there would be no strong-arming. Instead, they found themselves scurrying to Europe to buy back from the allies bombs that McNamara had hastily sold only a year or two before to help correct that payments imbalance.

The sole support from across the Atlantic for America's increasingly desperate fight in Vietnam might have come from the amazing number of Britons, five hundred or so each week, who volunteered for the war. A U.S. Embassy spokesman remarked, "We would have no trouble in raising a British division or two."[44] (At least twenty-five thousand Canadians also volunteered for Vietnam, in contrast to the ten thousand or so U.S. draft dodgers who fled there.) But Washington was not about to amend the old legal proviso that overseas volunteers must pay their own fare to the United States. Otherwise, it might appear that the Republic was recruiting a foreign legion, a notion already dropped around the time of Korea like a hot potato. The irony, of course, was that it had been Truman's Europe First policy that had originally pulled the United States into Indochina, while politicians and military men who emphasized America's Asian interests tended to oppose European imperialism there and were identified with reactionary politics. None of the players in Washington could take account of everything, let alone consistency.

Where "were Britain, Japan, and Germany?" Johnson agonized to his staff. Well, many Germans were busy pushing their government to back out of its agreement — compelled by Washington's anxiety over payment imbalances — to buy U.S. military goods and services supposedly equivalent to the costs of keeping American forces in place.[45] As for Japan's whereabouts, the president might as well have been talking to the wind. If Japan "got in trouble, we would send our planes and bombs to defend her," he told Prime Minister Sato, so now that America was "in trouble in Vietnam . . . how can Japan help us?" Oh, by moral support and building a strong Japanese economy, Sato replied, while urging "continued perseverance." Tokyo would not consider expanding its forces or doubling the $100 million it spent annually on U.S. military equipment. "It is not easy," added Rusk, to "draft a boy from a Kansas farm or a Pittsburgh factory in order to send him to Japan as a rifleman when Japan has a population of 95 million people." Tokyo smoothly countered that one by replying that the world was looking to Japan for commercial rather than military strength.[46]

Japan, moreover, was again about to profit big, earning at least $7 billion from 1965 to 1972 from sales of war-related goods and services. It thrived all the more by quadrupling its U.S. exports, which filled production shortages caused by war, as in the steel industry. Tokyo believed that it was doing quite enough to help, given that naval bases at Yokosuka and Sasebo were supplying the war, while "without Okinawa," according to the U.S. commander in the Pacific, "we couldn't continue fighting."[47] Nor were Americans ready to strong-arm Japan and demand open markets. It was still barely recognized as a formidable commercial rival.[48] One commentary of the time is Graham Greene's short story "The Invisible Japanese Gentlemen," wherein a young woman is shown to be so consumed by her lovers' quarrel as not to notice the sight of such an astoundingly rare presence in a top restaurant as a table of Japanese patrons. These men were about to reveal their extraordinary abilities throughout the world.

As America slid further into Vietnam, Johnson kept trying to get other Pacific allies to send troops, hoping to show Americans that they were not carrying all the weight. South Korea, which had finally deposed Syngman Rhee in 1960, shipped 45,000 men — but in exchange for lucrative procurement contracts, as well as for more money to modernize its army. (That was in addition to other money for equipping the arriving soldiers.) By 1967, Australia had 5,465 men on the ground (proportionately significant to its total armed forces), and New Zealand reluctantly delivered a 381-man artillery group. Philippine president Ferdinand Marcos demanded an average of $26,000 for each of his 2,200 soldiers, in addition to more "aid." Thailand was wrangled into offering 2,500 men, for which Washington paid $50 million a year, in addition to hundreds of millions more dollars between 1965 and 1971 for Thai soldiers who backed the CIA forces in Laos. That was it, each nation emphatically told Washington, and prospering Singapore turned Johnson down flat.

Yet the leaders of all these nations — the Australians and New Zealanders; the Filipinos; the Thais, Malaysians, and Koreans; the Japanese and Indonesians — told U.S. officials repeatedly, in public and private, that resistance to North Vietnam (and thereby to China, which sent in more than 320,000 troops from 1964 to 1973 to maintain the North's infrastructure and air defense) was vital. Always seeing the war as a proxy struggle between Americans and Chinese, Tokyo was suspicious of any hint that the United States might start negotiating its way out. It extracted assurances that no one in Washington favored overtures to Beijing. So why had no one else stood behind South Vietnam? "Because we have," concluded Harry McPherson, now counsel to the president. Even Australia's stalwartly loyal prime minister confided that he could not survive the inevitable deficits and casualty lists — at least as long as strong, rich America was carrying the fight.[49]

The alliance systems — NATO, SEATO, CENTO — had begun by assuming that most of the dirty work would be done from the allied capitals, themselves under U.S. protection. By 1965, NATO was an unplanned (therefore confused and expensive) system, bearing little relation to what had been envisioned in the late 1940s, when it was inconceivable that half a million Americans would be based for decades "over there." The coherent, if not always plausible, preference of George Marshall's generation had been for holding well-defined fronts: the wasp waist of Europe, the 38th Parallel in Korea. Yet something much more ambitious had evolved with the time and resources available. The 17th Parallel that divided Vietnam was not just itself vastly more penetrable; it ran out against Vietnam's porous western flank, Laos and Cambodia. No line in the sand there.

Moreover, several allies were happily conducting a steady seaborne commerce with North Vietnam. Eighty-five British vessels unloaded in Haiphong during the first five months of 1964, and 147 in the same months the following year. Thirty-five and then thirty-nine ships, meanwhile, sailed in from Japan; surprisingly, only one came from France. More than three times as many ships from the allies, including Norway and Greece, arrived than from China, Russia, and Eastern Europe. Japan, at least, cut off such trade by April 1965. So did all other U.S. allies, except Britain, as the war intensified.[50]

Among the disappointments, hostility focused on France. Fury at President Charles de Gaulle arose less from any specific sense of his ingratitude than of that ingratitude's Old World, high-nationalist roots. In 1965, the formidable stone-faced anachronism who instructed Elizabeth II on how to be a queen withdrew France's military participation from NATO. Why? In part because Gaullism is not an ideology; it is the pragmatic application of an almost pathological national egotism, "a way of behaving more than anything else," his successor, Georges Pompidou, said.[51] Americans raged at de Gaulle for practicing standard power politics from a position of unchallengeable weakness. But his assertion that the United States would never risk itself in the nuclear era to protect Western Europe spoke to the core suspicion of all the allies.

One of the weirdest reasons for being in Vietnam was to support U.S. credibility in NATO, an argument still being made today when reexamining the war.[52] If Americans had given ground in Quang

Tri, it has seriously been said, perhaps de Gaulle would have found more takers for his pitch that they could not be counted on in the Fulda Gap. NATO had, in any event, become a chore and a bore. That same year, Henry Kissinger published *The Troubled Partnership*, the focus of which was already a cliché. NATO was always said to be "in disarray" — as if it had ever been in "array." Lavish conferences in Berlin, at Ditchley, or at Airlie House were attended by frowning officials and wandering professors. Earnest seminars were held at bÿth and Park, books and articles were written — all with variations of the same interchangeable title, decade in, decade out: "NATO at the Crossroads: Problems and Prospects." Fifty years of political intimacy with Europe's airless statism would detract from American dynamism. One of the Cold War's central costs was that of Europe First, at the expense of a more discerning view of Asia.

Two years later, in 1967, a host of political and military forces came together in the Eastern Mediterranean, part of the region where the United States had first become engaged in the Cold War. What ended up colliding that summer was the self-perceived moralism of U.S. foreign policy, Britain's ever-contracting role "East of Suez," the discord of other European allies, hints of U.S. espionage, despair as the developing world clashed with modernity, and a superpower showdown.

Once the Arab-Israeli war started, France (until then, Israel's principal military supplier) immediately denounced not only Israel as the aggressor but also the United States, because its Vietnam intervention was supposed to have instigated, through example, the sudden Israeli air strike against Nasser's Egypt.[53] It did not matter that France, eleven years before at Suez, had instigated a much less urgent Israeli preemption.

With a war flaring in the Middle East, it was not surprising that a U.S. intelligence vessel, the slow-moving, lightly armed *USS Liberty* and its crew of 294, would appear off the Sinai peninsula in international waters. It appropriately flew a five-by-eight-foot Stars and Stripes in the midday sun. It did not particularly resemble any Arab ship. It displayed large white U.S. Navy letters and numerals on its hull. First came six hours of intense, low-level surveillance by Israeli photoreconnaissance aircraft. Then came a meticulous attack of more than two hours with unmarked Mirage jets using cannons and rockets, followed by slower Mystere jets with napalm and more rockets. The *Liberty*'s communications antennae were precisely severed in the first minute of attack; radios on both U.S.

Navy tactical and international maritime distress frequencies were jammed. Boats arrived to launch torpedoes and then to slowly circle the ship. They fired machine guns at close range at anyone topside helping the wounded, then machine-gunned the life rafts that the survivors dropped in hope of abandoning ship. Awaiting the arrival of Israeli commandoes to finish them off, the crew believed the attackers wanted no one to survive.[54]

Israel, of course, apologized quickly for killing 34 Americans and wounding 171 others. Modest reparations were extracted during the course of a thirteen-year struggle. Tel Aviv made it clear that the American ship, after all, was on an espionage assignment — one that would likely have overheard preparations for Israel's imminent invasion of Syria, or, according to the definitive, unclassified study, might have detected the execution of hundreds of Egyptian POWs a dozen miles inland. The highest U.S. officials, including the president, the chairman of the Joint Union of Staff, and the secretary of state, believed it "inconceivable" that the attack was anything but deliberate. The director and deputy director of the National Security Agency, which had been listening in, agreed. "There is no way they didn't know the *Liberty* was American," concludes the senior NSA official responsible for conducting that agency's still-classified investigation of the incident. [55]

Surely, said Tel Aviv, the Americans were at fault for not confirming the whereabouts of their vessel. Foreign Minister Abba Eban added, "It seemed inevitable that those who took risks might sometimes incur tragic sacrifice," thereafter refusing to elaborate on the cover-ups that the United States and Israel imposed for the sake of ongoing relations.[56] The *Liberty* had suffered proportionally more casualties than any U.S. naval vessel since World War II. Its captain received the United States' highest military tribute, the Medal of Honor, for bringing his remaining crew through the massacre, although it was presented out of sight. The dead are remembered among the 152 names chiseled on a polished granite wall at NSA headquarters under the words "They served in silence." This tragedy provides a glimpse of what would become routine in the 1970s: it looked as if America would tolerate anything from friends and foes alike.

✪

Vietnam became an example. Perhaps the United States should have stayed out; perhaps it should have broken the North. It ended up getting the worst outcome of all by doing something in between and by being manipulated by both its enemy and its ally. One of the best summaries of the war comes from Daniel Ellsberg, the radicalized former Marine and hawk intellectual who helped to compile the Pentagon Papers, the Defense Department's massive compilation of top-secret military, CIA, and other documents concerning the making of Vietnam policy from 1945 to 1967. These pages are replete with talk of "games," "models," "probabilities," and "options." Leaving aside the jargon, Ellsberg says that the story was simple: each president did the minimum necessary to avoid defeat. Tellingly, McNamara would never read the revealing work he had ordered to be written.

One interpretation of Vietnam is that it was "a war of no real consequence to the security of the United States," in which Americans died to prop up a corrupt regime that could neither reform nor defend itself. That is why, five years short of the century's end, McNamara's memoirs set off such a clamor. The atrocious outpouring of lives could only have been justified, say the proponents of this view, had Johnson and McNamara "possessed superior knowledge, not available to the public."[57] Of course, there was no superior knowledge from inside information, let alone the "secret stability" that John Le Carré's world-order men toiled for. The enemy's courage, adaptivity, and lack of strength (which is not the same as weakness) were obvious to casual observers. Yet nineteen-year-olds were now being sent from Stanley, Wisconsin, and Chandler, Arizona, to face the victors of Dien Bien Phu. That was the kind of tiger Washington had by the tail.

In his first book on the tragedy, McNamara rightly laments America's loss of "political unity" resulting from war in a distant country whose name he could never correctly pronounce (calling it *vit nam,* or "lying duck" in Vietnamese). He reflects that incalculable life and treasure might have been spared if only the United States had withdrawn after Diem's murder, or even a year later, "saving our strength for more defensible stands elsewhere." Where was "elsewhere"? Vietnam, after all, was John Kennedy's "elsewhere" for not having a showdown in Laos.

As the full horror began to hit home, *Doonesbury* would depict loyal, solid-between-the-ears B.D. crying from the heart: "But this war had such promise!" It was the promise of upholding a chaotic ally, with all its faults, against a Soviet- and Chinese-supplied assault by a regime for which mass murder was a means of governance as well as of war. From the first, there was a moral commitment to South Vietnam among powerful men "bordering on religious intensity."[58] It was foolish to see Ho Chi Minh as a puppet of Moscow or Beijing, but Communist terror was all too vivid.

The only people who believed that America had an imperialist eye for Vietnam's riches — rubber, exotic commodities, some oil — were the dimmest leftists and, tragically, the isolated men in Hanoi, who seriously thought that the United States was out to "replace France."[59] Only a trickle of goods was ever received from that lush land, and even by the late 1960s, barely $10 million of private capital was invested in South Vietnam. Instead, Lyndon Johnson argued repeatedly, America was "trying to allow these people a choice" to build their own prosperity. It was essentially the same argument John Foster Dulles had presented in Seoul before that earlier, less ambiguous invasion. U.O. protection could help bring widespread prosperity, democracy would eventually emerge in the South from wartime heavy handedness, and national unity could then evolve.

"Lessons of history" kept popping up in other ways — not only fears of being charged with "losing" Southeast Asia, as China had been "lost," but the conviction that withdrawing would only feed the aggressor's appetite ("Munich"). It did not matter that 90 percent of Americans wanted nothing to do with Vietnam, as Bundy told the president in 1964. Once pushed in by their leaders, they gave of themselves. "I accepted as completely as any man in the White House," reminisced McPherson, "that what we were doing in Vietnam might help to forestall the cataclysm of another major war."[60] Yet South Vietnam itself was about to be "lost" in early 1965.

The first extended involvements four years earlier had set the tone and presaged the war's end. One undertaking, still obscure today, exemplifies how the war would be fought and remembered. Since Kennedy's January 1961 initiative, the CIA had dropped hundreds of South Vietnamese commandos into the North. Some of them were killed, the rest captured. With the Agency being compelled to turn this operation over to U.S. Army intelligence in late 1963 or early 1964, the Pentagon simply wrote off all the prisoners as dead, declaring each "a nonviable asset." ("They were not the responsibility of the U.S. Government," John Singlaub, one of the colonels who was in charge, would later say in overlooking the fact that they had been captured on the Agency's watch.[61]) The CIA and the Pentagon also ignored basic security principles, suffering from rivalry and hubris. Men responsible for operations, for example, believed that they had no need to hear from those in counter-espionage. Hanoi was, therefore, able to "play back" every captive commando against the Americans — meaning that each one became a double agent who lured yet more unfortunates north to their doom. This went on until 1969.

Although perhaps not as tragically incompetent, the CIA was equally slippery in adjacent Laos, where it had begun mobilizing the Hmong in 1962. There was no need to depend on Laos's inept, if lavishly funded, army, Langley advised. This ancient Mongol race of about 350,000 people could be trained in low-cost, low-profile harassment of Laotian and Vietnamese Communists in the mountains dividing North Vietnam (a country half the size of Florida) from the Mekong lowlands along the Laotian-Thai border. As the U.S. military got directly involved in the widening war, the Hmong rescued American pilots, gathered intelligence, and held down tens of thousands of North Vietnamese troops. Enlisted as guerrillas, they began fighting so fervently alongside the Americans that some families were down to the last surviving male, often a boy of thirteen or fourteen, by the time the war ended.[62] Most were recruited and trained by the CIA paramilitary program in Laos under station chief Larry Devlin, his post-Congo career no longer "behind the curve." Of course, the Hmong were too weak to prevail should the North Vietnamese turn against them in force, whereupon the CIA would, it promised, find them sanctuary. But the war spread, and no sanctuary was ever provided, although the Agency considered the arming of the Hmong "one of the best operations ever."[63]

The same was true of the ethnic Nung, originally from China's Guangxi province, bordering Vietnam. Their men had fought in all-Nung units against the Viet Minh in the first Indochina War, then joined the exodus south, where they had formed a division in South Vietnam's army. In 1964, the U.S. Army Special Forces formed several Nung battalions, directly recruiting many sons of the original fighters. Once U.S. troops withdrew, the Nung would join South Vietnam's army and guard the remaining U.S. installations. They, too, were left to their fate.

It was with such unwitting treachery that Americans began fighting. There were ways to win, but Washington picked the certain way to lose. Everyone acted in character. The president was more than ready simply to buy off "Old Ho," as he called Ho Chi Minh, and thought the Communist leader might be softened with a Marshall Plan or Tennessee Valley Authority public works program for the Mekong Delta, if he would just abort his life's ambition. Bundy and McNamara presumed that they could apply the theories of graduated response in vogue with civilian strategists of the day. A civilianized, managerialized officer corps went along. Amid "dereliction of duty" on all sides, in the words of one historian, the Joint Chiefs of Staff could be manipulated to endorse policy decisions in return for McNamara's concessions on parochial disputes having nothing to do with Vietnam. Finally, the CIA remained its expedient self. It could offer a scathing analysis of the war's progress (one which remained uncirculated, if not smothered), while advising at almost the same moment that the Viet Cong were "getting tired of this war faster than we are."[64] So much was business as usual, and Washington politics could appear more real than combat in Vietnam — except to the people there.

McNamara, Bundy, and their staffs had a casual disdain for the Joint Chiefs, which by law must give military guidance to the president. From late 1963 to mid-1964, the White House and McNamara failed to seek professional direction on the war. The bipartisan Tonkin Gulf Resolution that Congress overwhelmingly passed in August gave the White House another blank check, but it was not until the following February that it was cashed. Bundy's first trip to Vietnam (or anywhere in Asia) coincided with a Viet Cong attack on the airfield at Pleiku, a city in the central highlands. Eight Americans were killed and 109 wounded. Of course, the attackers had no idea that this eminent person was in Vietnam, as Hanoi would explain decades later, but Bundy regarded the incident as arranged to coincide with his presence.

The U.S. commander in Vietnam was General William Westmoreland, class of '36 at West Point, tall and lean, a protégé of Maxwell Taylor. He recalled Bundy quickly taking charge in the Saigon operations center with a "field marshal psychosis." Bundy urged immediate retaliation against the North, then zoomed the 250 miles to Pleiku, where the carnage powerfully affected him.[65] Once back in Washington, he pushed "sustained reprisal," including more bombing. It would demonstrate U.S. willingness to use a "new norm in counter-insurgency," he averred, and "set a higher

price for the future upon all adventures of guerrilla warfare."
Johnson went along, and the Marines landed in Danang. Yet the
president also offered unconditional peace talks over Vietnam, although the offer was rejected by Hanoi, as well as by Beijing, which
preferred to announce a strategy of encircling the West through
"revolutionary warfare." *Time* magazine celebrated Westmoreland
as 1965's "Man of the Year."[66] By then, 184,300 men were committed in Vietnam, with more than 350,000 others following fast.
Although 1,636 Americans had already been killed, Bundy noted,
"Casualties and costs are to be accepted."[67]

There was no planning for failure, none of the worst-case analyses that characterized the nuclear effort. "We can't assume what we
don't believe," scoffed Bundy.[68] This was childish. Pilots do not
believe that they will crash. They know, however, that they can, and
they drill for it. Bundy was displaying not command confidence, but
narcissism. Nor could anyone in Washington (or elsewhere in
America) be expected to find their way through the briar patch of
Saigon politics, where a pivotal political faction, the Cao Dai — a
syncretic religion with well-organized bullyboys — believed that
Victor Hugo was a demigod (something that no one had previously
recognized, except perhaps Hugo himself). The United States ended
up choosing a strange form of caution as it fought a highly limited
war. At the same time, it kept wrapping itself around the Vietnam
tar baby.

Except for the politically attuned General Taylor, the military
never shared Bundy's and McNamara's belief in controlled escalation. Given the chronic inability to transcend interservice rivalry,
however, the Joint Chiefs were short on helpful advice. At least they
were clear on one crucial point: if the United States was to commit
itself, it had to pay the price of seriousness. They warned in the summer of 1965 that the country could "win if such is our will" — the
"will" entailing mining North Vietnamese ports, attacking supply
lines in Cambodia and Laos, perhaps invading the North, and dispatching 700,000 to 1 million men for a seven years' war. They
urged Johnson to call up the reserves, which would provide leadership cadres for the expanding forces.

This was the year that Moscow decided to provide massive mili-
tary backing to North Vietnam. Eisenhower now added his opinion.
He wanted to "swamp the enemy with overwhelming force."
Haiphong should be mined immediately and the world told to keep

away its shipping. There should be no sanctuaries. War should be declared against North Vietnam. In brief, the country should "take any action to win." No weapon should be precluded.[69] Johnson, however, refused. Such steps would torpedo the budget, the balance of payments, and the Great Society. Draft calls more than tripled during 1965 and 1966, ending the likelihood that conscription would have been phased out by the mid-1960s.

The president's persuasive civilian advisers preferred "graduated response," since this offered "the greatest return for the least risk" (especially, as they learned, for North Vietnam).[70] They not only punctuated their highly restrained approach by sixteen attention-getting bombing pauses, but they also injected such senselessness as prohibiting U.S. jets from attacking surface-to-air missile (SAM) sites when the Soviets began building them, preferring to wait until the sites were completed and truly deadly. Even economic operations, such as creating havoc with North Vietnam's fishing fleet, were regarded as unacceptable. What was occurring on the ground was equally misguided. If the civilian leadership tied the military's hands, these bureaucratized chiefs did little to complain about the pinching ropes. No general or admiral resigned in protest over how the war was being fought.

Just as the armored caravan roared into high gear in the South, Geoffrey Household wrote an extraordinary novel of Latin American politics, *Thing to Love*, in which the wicked but crafty elder statesman dooms the dashing modernist regime by ensuring that the Americans give it energetic support in a civil war. "I *want* them to send more troops," Ho Chi Minh reportedly said to the astonished Soviet premier Aleksei Kosygin (one of the duo who replaced Khrushchev in 1964) when he was warned about the consequences of not settling with the Americans.[71] The subtlest and most malevolent enemy, with the most powerful friends at court, could not have devised a better strategy to cripple his opponent.

Almost every part of the U.S. government, as well as every military branch, grabbed its own piece of the war: seven full Army divisions, sixty-three artillery battalions, heavy battle tanks, two large Marine divisions, jets from the Sixth Fleet (although there was no lack of cheap airfields for the U.S. Air Force), advisers from the Departments of Agriculture and Transportation, and men from the CIA, NSA, and Defense Intelligence Agency all arrived. Telling self-indulgences were further encouraged, such as carrying on the tradition of issuing a special .32-caliber pistol to generals alone. This pistol, in true band-of-brothers spirit, was engraved "General Officer's Pistol" and required ammunition different from the standard issue .45 automatics. This was an army, after all, in which every combat colonel could type, a navy in which carrier pilots with scores of flights over North Vietnam had to make way for their brave but untested seniors from Washington who also wanted action.

As in a tropical version of the DEW line, the giant tractors, bulldozers, and cranes of Army engineers and private contractors worked around the clock to carve out roads, build bridges, and dredge rivers. Washington was linked to Saigon with submarine cables. Six new deep-water harbors were created, including the $2 billion complex (roughly $15 billion in today's dollars) of five thousand buildings at Cam Ranh Bay. Prefabricated piers were towed across the Pacific.[72] Long Binh became the biggest U.S. military base in the world. Vast overlapping inputs of fighting men and equipment crowded into a rather small country. By 1967, a million tons of supplies per month, averaging a hundred pounds a day for every American, were needed.

Each armed service would set out to prove its indispensability, keeping to the goal of maximizing "production": bombing sorties, shells fired, highest body counts, documents captured. McNamara acknowledges that he was lulled by the industrial doctrine that the larger the investment, the larger the return — an old-fashioned concept even by mid-1967, by which time he concedes that he knew "no amount of bombing can end the war." In fact, McNamara was bayoneting smoke: a determined low-technology adversary can take a great deal of the kind of punishment meant to break more developed societies.

North Vietnam's leaders were too savvy to make a practice of frontally attacking U.S. forces. Yet Westmoreland kept pursuing his strategy of big-unit attrition warfare. When we look back on this terrible war, Westmoreland is usually remembered as a man of Eagle Scout qualities who became trapped in a quagmire. Yet he is a much darker character and, oddly, a senior officer who did not graduate from the Army Command and General Staff College or the Army War College (or one of its equivalents). He had served in World War II and Korea, but he possessed no decorations for valor. Of the four generals President Johnson considered for commander in 1964, Westmoreland was the only one who proposed using his men to wear down an enemy who had been at it for twenty years. "We have more guts," was his meaningless refrain. By definition, "search and destroy" operations did not hold and secure territory, or foster development. Instead they enveloped civilian inhabitants in the war.

There were 1.3 million Americans under arms in that part of the world, but only between 50,000 and 60,000 were put into offensive combat even at the war's height, when nearly 550,000 troops were in Vietnam. South Vietnam's stumbling army was nonetheless shoved aside in 1965. The Vietnamese would have fewer helicopters three years later than at the start. There would never be a joint command. Americans did the planning, coordinating, and supplying but never wielded operational control over South Vietnam's forces — with the authority to dismiss officers — as they had along in Korea. Not until 1968 would South Vietnam's soldiers start receiving compact M-16 assault rifles, decisively easier for them to use than bulkier M-14s and equal in performance to the North's AK-47s. U.S. tactics swung between doing too much (the amount of firepower and hardware blasted into the South) and doing too little (waiting several fateful years to develop Saigon's own forces and to actually defend the villages).

The convulsive transformation of South Vietnam turned into a war of impatience. "We should have cut two-thirds of the size, and we might have increased the efficiency 50 percent," said one White House aide.[73] However, by 1966–1967 overkill had become endemic, with power being concentrated as well as conflicting. For instance, a pivotal, top-secret intelligence-gathering base in Laos, Lima Site 85, was linked directly to the White House. The president received daily reports on enemy force dispositions, weather patterns, and the safety of specific roads.[74] He boasted that the Air Force could not bomb a chicken coop without his say-so. Yet the administration would only go so far.

During 1966, 5,008 Americans were killed in Vietnam. From his Gettysburg farm, Eisenhower publicly urged that U.S. troops be allowed to cross the Demilitarized Zone along the 17th Parallel, which meant invading the North. Already campaigning for president in late 1967, Richard Nixon disagreed but privately argued that North Vietnam's harbors should be mined. Texas Governor John Connally, who had been shot alongside Kennedy in Dallas, asked Johnson why he didn't just use nuclear weapons.

The deference to civilian experts that so characterized this part of the Cold War meant that the opinions of anyone with establishment credentials were taken seriously. Political scientist Hans Morgenthau wrongly insisted that the war was neither created nor sustained by Hanoi. Historian Howard Zinn chimed in that maybe a total of twenty-three infiltrators had arrived from the North during 1964, by which time units of the People's Army of Vietnam were operating effectively in the South. Arthur Schlesinger, Jr, wrote a critical volume, *The Bitter Heritage*, in late 1966 that nevertheless argued unhesitatingly against abandoning Vietnam. Within months of publication, as Robert Kennedy's presidential campaign took off, Schlesinger reversed himself to advocate a coalition government in Saigon — that is, a short-term cover for the Communists, with no guarantee of what might become of all who had resisted. "Neutrality" was synonymous with imposing an irreversible totalitarian system on the South. As for neutrality in the North, that was unacceptable, explained Hanoi, since there were no foreigners in the North.

Twenty-one years after the Communist threat in Greece had precipitated the Truman Doctrine, and twenty-one years before the Berlin Wall came down, the Tet Offensive in 1968 was the hinge of what proved to be the "middle stage" of the Cold War. The nerve of many U.S. opinion leaders was broken by Hanoi's ability to strike so fiercely despite Westmoreland's assurances that the tide had turned. McNamara writes that the war's greatest cost was the shattering of America's "political unity," a judgment that illuminates little unless turned upon the costs of the Cold War as a whole. For it is Vietnam that distills so much of what made the Cold War so demanding.

The offensive begun in the early morning of January 31, 1968, with an attack on the U.S. Embassy. Tet was a military disaster for Hanoi, which incurred around forty-five thousand dead and disabled and saw the Viet Cong crushed. Intended to destroy South Vietnamese officialdom and spark a popular uprising, Tet ironically had more of an effect in turning South Vietnam's people against the North. Three thousand eight hundred and ninety-five Americans were also killed in what a West Point textbook describes as an "intelligence failure to rank with Pearl Harbor."[75] Now 53 percent of their countrymen wanted to slam North Vietnam hard, even at the risk of China or Russia entering the war, with 70 percent saying that the limited bombing of the North should at least continue.[76]

The most prominent U.S. correspondents thought differently and declared a Communist victory. "Crisis journalism," says Peter Braestrup, who covered the war for the *Washington Post*, had rarely "veered so widely from reality."[77] British combat photographer Donald McCullin sums up one result. "By making it so easy for us to go to Vietnam," he says of the ever-helpful Pentagon officials, "they were digging their own grave. . . . The American military never forgave the press."[78] They had their reasons.

The West essentially ignored the twenty-eight hundred South Vietnamese whom the Communists buried alive or otherwise butchered after overrunning Hue, the country's third-largest city and one in which there had been no U.S. combat presence. Instead, a defining moment of the war became Eddie Adams's Pulitzer Prize–winning photo: South Vietnam's national police commander raising his pistol, extending his arm, and firing a bullet through the head of a prisoner standing with his hands tied behind his back. A horrible picture, to be sure, but a spontaneously emotional killing that could not hold a candle to Hanoi's terror. The doomed man had just killed a policeman and knifed the policeman's wife and children. Yet the photo of this execution is credited with helping to turn public opinion against the war. Twenty-five years after Hanoi's victory, *People* magazine would feature it in a poignant profile of this Viet Cong officer's widow.[79]

Now back in Cambridge watching what was already called "the living-room war," John Kenneth Galbraith could knowingly insist during Tet that anything resembling a South Vietnamese government would disappear "within the next few weeks."[80] What would disappear was the Johnson administration, as the weary president announced on March 31 that he would not seek a second term and as McNamara stepped down in tears. Yet throughout the 1960s, the war was more popular with Americans than the Korean War had been, even if Washington was not revving up the country by choosing to "wrap the flag" (as Bundy had put it) around the dead. Why the relative popularity? Not only was the Vietnam draft calling up fewer men than had been conscripted during the Korean War, but there had been a shift in attitude among many Americans: they had come to assume that they had interests worth fighting for ten thousand miles away.[81] Not until 1969 did more than 20 percent of the country express support for withdrawal, by which time Nixon had started bringing troops home.

In the late 1940s, support for the draft had been strongest among white males under age thirty-five. So, too, during the Vietnam War, when polls consistently showed that eighteen- to twenty-four-year-old men were the most hawkish segment of the population. Most of them wanted to escalate the war, although three years of ghastly "search-and-destroy" combat was slowly eating into the rest of the nation's commitment. The only group steadily hostile to the war, reported pollsters, was what they indelicately called "the Jewish subgroup" — a provocative insight that FBI agents in the field would pick up as a working assumption of their own during the later 1970s.[82]

However, part of America will every so often go into crusade mode. Farsighted advocates of containment, such as Dean Acheson and Robert Lovett, had warned against precisely that. Now the crusade came from the left, as it offered its own appeal to U.S. idealism. But the youth convulsions of those years did not have their roots in Vietnam, as is commonly thought, and connections to the war were more complicated than they may seem. Such upheaval hit other countries even during their piping times of peace: de Gaulle got France out of a hated war in Algeria in 1962 but was much closer than Lyndon Johnson to being overthrown in 1968. Japan (characteristically, for that time almost unnoticed) had been undergoing almost a decade of similarly wracking events, which were beginning to simmer down. Mexico had it bloodily. A youth rebellion was rolling around the globe in the late 1960s, including, in a terrible way, China with its Cultural Revolution, a Cold War–related agony exacting around one million dead and also driven by adolescents. These movements dissolved, eroded, or totally withered by the mid-1970s.

It was in Czechoslovakia that upheaval against real imperialism drew unusual courage from the young. "Brezhnev's bottom line was that we were his country's colony," Alexander Dubček, first secretary of the Czech Communist Party, would recall about his Soviet counterpart.[83] In that ebullient early summer of 1968, Czech students were routinely amazed to encounter backpacking Americans who believed they had a friendly audience for tales of oppression at home. In August, Soviet tanks, around forty-six hundred in the first wave, arrived to silence such tragicomic dialogues. The invaders killed only ninety people, mostly in Prague, and Leonid Brezhnev fumed at the injustice of Czech radio calling him (very briefly) a

"Stalinist."[84] There was no question of U.S. assistance of any sort to Dubček, reported the Soviet ambassador in Washington. America's "rather restrained reaction," he concluded, was due to its resources being "tied up in Vietnam" and to a preference for not jeopardizing "the preparation of Soviet-American talks" on arms control.[85] Western European governments were equally placid. Britain's socialist prime minister argued back and forth with his foreign secretary over whether to send a Christmas card to Mr. Brezhnev that year; the full cabinet finally decided yes.

In America, revolt was overdue against the "big engineering" rigidities, with all their 1950s notions of deference to large institutions, as well as against the other overblown costs of the Depression–World War II–Cold War sequence. It partly reflected much older American anger at establishments and elites. Revolt was further energized by reaction against all the Kahn-like visions of the "unthinkable." That heated protests broke out amid the psychodramas of the Vietnam experience ensured the maximum amount of posturing and ill will. This was a time when the *New York Review of Books* diagrammed a Molotov cocktail on its cover and the president of Yale (the university being on strike to support the torture-slayers of an African-American suspected of being a police informer) questioned whether U.S. courts could give black militants fair trials. The babble of rival emergencies distorted the whole context of public life. This was a huge price of war, entirely behind the lines. From 1965 on, Vietnam increasingly became less a place and more a handy looking glass for innumerable American preoccupations — not just war and peace, but race, class, political power, and, above all, the opinions, passions, and loudly proclaimed ideals of so much of the generation chanting its way onto the world stage.

When political philosopher Harvey Mansfield called the late 1960s and early 1970s "a comprehensive disaster for America," he was saddened by the sight of a country, fit to engage in everything from exploring Mars to overcoming the eye-rotting rivers of Africa, instead becoming lost in theatrical self-absorption.[86] For example, most of the 1960s counterculture had its wires crossed about technology, further wasting possibilities that might have been. Computers were invariably seen as tools of the centrally powerful. But political fireworks were not affecting people who were really changing the world. Stephen Crocker, one of the fathers of the Internet, was a graduate student at UCLA, as was his high school friend, Vinton

Cerf, soon to be head of the Internet Society and today an architect of electronic commerce. Part-time university employment came from Defense Department money as these young men tested the limits of interface message processors. The campus radical demonstrations, Crocker recalls, "all looked pretty superficial to us."[87]

As for the New Left of those years, more than a few of its adherents positioned themselves as Marxist purists who rejected what strains of compromise and alliance building there had been in the earlier post–World War II radical movements. The result was further fragmentation of any potentially reformist/social democrat–type movement in America. Also involved in that era's upheavals were many principled critics of the war, such as Navy Lieutenant JG John Forbes Kerry (now a Massachusetts senator), who testified forcefully before the Senate about his own combat experiences while a skipper on the Mekong River, and recent Harvard College graduate Robert Klitgaard, who, along with other Divinity School students, refused the draft exemptions available to them. However, real revolutionaries and courageous opponents were the exceptions at a time when many of America's privileged or well-connected spoke of "loathing" their country's military.

Today, some people still argue that the war was unrelievedly pointless — useless and immoral, its whole terrible consumption of lives and spirit to no purpose — but they at least acknowledge the sacrifice of the veterans. They also speak of "another set of heroes — the thousands of students who returned the nation to sanity by chanting, 'Hell, no, we won't go.'"[88] Anyone who was within earshot of those chants recalls that equal time was given to thousands of people bellowing out, "Ho, Ho, Ho Chi Minh, the NLF is sure to win." Equating the white, privileged minority who demonstrated a few yards from their dormitories with the men who went out to seek a brave and deadly enemy in the clammy jungle shadows shows how foolish much of today's informed opinion on Vietnam still is. After 1968, there were few antiwar demonstrations in the United States, let alone those by Americans in London and elsewhere abroad, that did not include waving the flags of North Vietnam and the Viet Cong — a detail about today's leadership generation that college students are appalled to discover.

Given the uncritical assumptions that got the United States into the war, as well as the bizarre way it was being fought, an impassioned opposition was inevitable. But the rage went further.

For instance, in 1967 a Marine corporal, twenty-one-year-old Richard F. Sutter, was shot through the head near Khe Sanh. As he was brought home to Atlanta for burial, reports the *Washington Post*, "antiwar protesters were phoning the house to tell [his parents] they deserved what they got for sending their son to Vietnam." His family remembers these "telephone calls coming in like hot rounds."[89] There are other examples, other testimonies. Not just the war was being opposed, but also the young men who fought it.

Johnson chose to ignite a firestorm of middle-class wrath by tightening student deferments and raising draft calls. The antiwar fury exploded. "Don't worry, men," joked Bob Hope when entertaining GIs in Vietnam, "your country is behind you fifty percent."

In the days of Joe McCarthy, too many guardians of academic freedom had cowered to political noisemaking, newspaper demagoguery, and trustee arrogance. At least they had the excuse of being buttered by real, if not serious power. Now came the not very comic reversal. In the name of foreign policy, students were disrupting calculus and home economics classes. In the late 1960s, as in the early 1950s, faculty and administration capitulated, while "liberalism rolled over on its back like a turtle awaiting its end."[90] The American Association of University Professors refused to consider the occupation of classrooms an abridgement of academic freedom. Everything that was wrong — whether corruption in Washington or a cut in the English lit department's budget — could be blamed on Vietnam. The difference in university life from fifteen years earlier was that then the compromises to political bullying had been as much as possible dirty little secrets.

What occurred by the late 1960s was often a highly public exercise in intellectual dishonesty and self-humiliation. It might also be regarded as an understandably desperate attack on government and academic authority after two decades of deceptions going well beyond Vietnam. In either case, the consequences became enduring. Today's radical counterculture notions — that so much that is established is probably illegitimate, and that distinctions between high and low or good and bad are subjective — began penetrating schools, foundations, churches, the art world, and the professions.

As student protests grew fiercer, Johnson wanted government agencies "out of the university business," slashing graduate study programs. Support for university research (particularly biomedical)

fell away, in part because of the war and the related budget strin-
gencies. Seeing military influence as troublingly pervasive, Congress
insisted that no classified work be performed on campus. This, at
least, was no great loss.

Like the ethnic anticommunism of the 1950s, the divisions of
the time ran along class lines. Although the citizen-soldiers who
fought the war were not disproportionately from poor or minority
backgrounds, as myth concludes, they were mostly young men from
the middle and lower-middle classes who volunteered, or were
drafted, after they left high school or dropped out of college. They
were not people who sang Malvina Reynolds songs about "little
boxes made of ticky-tacky," meaning the housing tracts of the early
postwar boom. The well-meaning, self-pleased young who were par-
roting such views were largely the children of more successful parents. These protesters were usually too self-conscious to use the
word "class" themselves, although they felt the fact all the same.
That was nothing, however, compared to how those below the suburban divide felt it. There grew the poisoning sense that high views
walked arm in arm with hypocrisy, and it is with us still.

Before long, it dawned on almost everyone in the country that
Vietnam was becoming the first major American war in which the
top socioeconomic stratum was not fighting to any degree proportionate to its numbers. The 1970 Yale valedictorian spoke of how
many of his college friends would be dead in Asia before twelve
months were out. Stewart Alsop, class of '36, checked: one Yale
draftee had fallen in the previous five years. Only nineteen Harvard
alumni of any sort died in Vietnam, fewer than were lost by several
high schools in working-class neighborhoods, and no one from the
classes of 1969 to 1972. Among those nineteen, which included
civilian officials, only one may have been a draftee.[91] Yes, exemptions could be bought during the Civil War, and that war had been
reviled as "a rich man's war, a poor man's fight." But it was the
institutionalized deliberateness of the way the Vietnam draft was
conducted that finally made it unendurable.

Draft records were destroyed or looted in Rhode Island and
Delaware. The director of the Selective Service System and other
officials were threatened with death. Many hundreds of amateur
draft counselors knew more about the law than did volunteers on
the country's four thousand local boards. Although the draft boards
and courts were strained by noncooperation and protests, the flow

of young men into uniform was never really disrupted.[92] Nor did it ever cost much to administer the draft. The few attempts to focus on its dollars and cents — to determine how much higher total U.S. defense spending would have been without the draft — cannot begin to illuminate conscription's burden over twenty-five years. Such compulsion was being besieged from left and right. Economist Milton Friedman described conscription as a "tax-in-kind," and a "regressive," "discriminatory," and "hidden" one.[93] The draft had become a system, and thus manipulable, rather than a grim emergency measure to distribute sacrifice. Eventually, a real price kicked in — undercutting legitimacy, goodwill, and national spirit — which would linger in attitudes toward public service to the present day.

Without the antiwar movement, might there have been a push to intensify the war, with people crying with Barry Goldwater, "Why Not Victory?" That is unlikely. The most sensitive political antennae — those of Republican presidential hopefuls — detected no such groundswell on the right. Not many called for Goldwater in 1964. Four years later, Curtis LeMay, ready to bomb North Vietnam "back to the stone age," became only a feeble addition to Alabama Governor George Wallace's presidential ticket. Richard Nixon had a "secret plan," journalists said, and it was rightly assumed not to involve any kind of Inchon landing. Losing in Vietnam might involve heavy consequences for America, but winning big was of no particular interest to the public. People knew that victory of one form or another would by this time settle nothing outside a few fetid jungles; they just wanted Vietnam to go away. It never would.

Like the victim's heart in the guilty imagination of Poe's murderer, the war would not stay dead and buried in the cellar where America keeps most of its history. Today, some scholars argue that the opposition not only failed to stop the war but actually prolonged it, as the protests escalated from 1965's "Hell no, we won't go!" to the later "Smash the glass of the ruling class!" and its accompanying violence. Maybe disengagement would have been compelled by the "utterly normal contours of American politics," but there is no real parallel to cite.[94] The Korean War at least restored South Korea.

Other costs of Vietnam are more speculative. Given the weight of gender stereotyping in those days, how many mediocre, draft-avoiding male applicants to graduate schools shut out promising young women? Compounding such unfairness, the pattern of grade inflation took hold in those guilt-ridden times of the academy. Universities such as Yale changed their grading systems to pass/fail in case draft boards should use grade point average as a criterion for deferments. Nobody was going to be flunked out, except at Faber College. Adding to these enduring impressions of injustice was the curious role of the National Guard, which was never mobilized. Many men served honorably, although only 8,728 did so in Vietnam, of whom 97 fell. The Guard ended up with a waiting list of around 100,000 draft-eligible applicants by the end of 1969, finding itself 45,000 men understrength two and a half years later once conscription ended.

Certain steps were especially characteristic of the Cold War, to the extent that they have continued for decades after they ceased to be useful. There were 174 campus bombings and serious bombing attempts during the 1969–1970 academic year alone. Today, midshipmen still stand watch at their naval reserve buildings on campuses, a holdover from such days at Berkeley and the University of Wisconsin. Yet that sort of violence was water pistols compared to the racial upheaval. "Each war feeds on the other," said William Fulbright, comparing burning American cities to Vietnam.[95] Indeed, the previous hundred years' great race riots had also been tied to war, in 1863, 1919, and 1943. Antiwar sentiment, however, was not now conspicuous amid the rage. It would have been surprising if African-American defiance during these years had not been accompanied by disorder in any event. Yet George Kennan knew whom to blame: the "cities in question did not invite the enormous influx of Negro residents that has occurred in recent decades."[96]

J. Edgar Hoover was on the case. Vietnam-era radicalism combined with racial unrest to offer him new vistas of employment. His enthusiasm was hardly "the war coming home," as some now argue. He did not need anyone's instruction on bringing it back. That rare creature, a high official actually born in Washington and one who lived his entire life without leaving the United States, he was indeed the "Compleat Bureaucrat," as journalist Joseph Kraft portrayed him — often useful and efficient. However, vendettas continued, and new ones were added. As attorney general, Robert Kennedy had wanted to discover whether Martin Luther King, Jr., was under Moscow's influence. He did nothing to limit FBI wiretapping and had found it important to share with his brother salacious FBI recordings of King, gossip about the "old black fairy"

Bayard Rustin, and other civil rights heroes.[97] Kennedy had none-theless tried to get Hoover to document the money being spent on infiltrating the minuscule American Communist Party. The director rebuffed him, replying that any such accounting would compromise Bureau informants.[98]

One of Dan Ackroyd's *Saturday Night Live* skits looks back cruelly on this era: Jack and Bobby at Hyannis Port giving Martin Luther King a PT 109 tie clip (containing a tiny microphone), and cajoling him as to whether he slept with white women. "In fifteen years we'll all be laughing about this," the brothers agree.

FBI offices, meanwhile, kept updating their Security Index of people meriting arrest should the president invoke the Emergency Detention Program, solidly in place since Congress had authorized it in 1950. For instance, farm labor leader César Chávez was added to the index and pointlessly investigated as a Communist by hundreds of agents for more than seven years beginning in 1966, with the FBI involving the military, local police, and the Secret Service. "I was just amazed at how dumb and what a waste it was," said the United Farm Workers' general counsel upon reviewing the 1,431-page file extracted from the FBI in 1995, the year when Chávez posthu-mously received the Presidential Medal of Freedom.[99]

But it was King whom Hoover hunted as Ahab hunted Moby Dick. Sixteen thousand pages of files were accumulated before 1968. He used columnist Joseph Alsop as a tool for his obsession, simply reminding Alsop that the Bureau had compromising photos of him with male KGB "swallows." Within a month of King's assas-sination, the FBI began a six-year investigation of his successor, Ralph Abernathy, vainly looking for the same "promiscuous activ-ity" that it had hoped would discredit King. Hoover wallowed in the titillation of interracial sex. His St. Louis office used the U.S. mail to send deliberately semiliterate diatribes signed "A Soul Sister" to tor-ment one married white activist. Also in the field, agents enjoyed repulsive pranks such as putting itching powder into hotel tampon dispensers at Communist Party gatherings.[100]

More refined, but no more law abiding, the CIA and the NSA joined in the surveillance of those deemed radical, looking for links between dissidents and Soviet provocateurs. No one in the White House or at Langley worried about statutes against domestic spying. The CIA was, in fact, so busy monitoring the activities of radicals and black militants that Director Richard Helms complained that "the backlog of undigested raw information" had become "a formidable obstacle" to the Agency's work.[101]

For most people, of course, life went on quietly amid increasing prosperity. The 1960s were less trauma than the "happiness explosion" Tom Wolfe describes in "The Intelligent Coed's Guide to America," a time when "the post–World War II boom had . . . pumped money into every level of the population on a scale unparalleled in any nation in history."[102] Few of the boomer generation had anything to do with demonstrations, combat, or even coeds. Consider, for instance, the admirably unremarkable journey of America's first baby boomer, one James Otis Sickler, Jr., who arrived in St. Louis just after midnight on January 1, 1946. First in a generation of seventy-six million born between the end of 1945 and 1964, he never went to Vietnam, although he spent four years in the Navy after graduating high school, never protested the war, never tried drugs, and never grew his hair long. Surviving the shrinkage of the defense industry, he still is employed as a machine operator for the McDonnell aviation plant in the city where he was born. His wife works part-time; they have four children. Describing himself as "a typical average American," he notes, "I never had much respect for those people who burned our flag."[103] It is this generation of Americans, and particularly families like the Sicklers, for whom the country could be so much better had it not been for the Cold War, and for the way it was fought.

❂

Report from Iron Mountain on the Possibility and Desirability of Peace was concocted in 1967 by a group on the left as a satiric, and possibly commercial, venture. At first glance, this supposed top-secret document was a good enough imitation of Vietnam-era think tankese that the debate over its authenticity was front-page news in the *New York Times*, with no less than Henry Kissinger ultimately denouncing it. The "premise" was that the most important duty of government is to provide stability and that a stable U.S. society requires war. This argument was not far-fetched, based on what the popularizers of "military Keynesianism" had been whispering all along, and it drew the corollary that an outbreak of prolonged peace would be an economic catastrophe.

The frame: A study group of just the sort that Morgenstern, Kahn, and Kissinger had sat in countless times has been convened.

It meets largely at one of the government's bunkers, not unlike that inside Colorado's Cheyenne Mountain or the one cut into the super-hard greenstone of Mount Weather. The proceedings exhibit a whiz-kid fixation with planning, plausibly affecting the value-free style cultivated by the defense intellectuals, lamenting that nothing will match the "war system" for delivering social cohesion, price stability, and population control. And now this document is exposed.

Given what the oracles had been saying at least since the Air Force created Rand in 1948, the parody was persuasive. And life kept imitating art. For instance, a real bunker lay buried three hundred feet beneath Hudson, New York, the well-appointed refuge-designate for the executives of Standard Oil of New Jersey. Here, White House emergency planners joined these corporate chiefs for a 1970 exercise — not unusual given government coordination of recovery plans with industry. Standard Oil's hospitality ended when it learned that Washington wanted to take over the company in the event of war. As with most events concerning the Cold War, there would be a truly ironic consequence: nearly thirty years later, reprints of *Iron Mountain* energized not the left, but the right, once pathetic self-described "militias" seized on the book as a heroically leaked truth that substantiates their own discovery of government conspiracy and the "new world order."[104]

Iron Mountain stemmed from a long unease with the secret world of defense thought. The real think tankers and their sponsors nevertheless had a true apocalypse to ponder, as the Soviets by the late 1960s began building missiles of a size and number that seemed to emphasize destruction without mutuality. China, in turn, was again disemboweling itself in an ideological frenzy, but it demonstrated its nuclear weapons capacity by 1964 and its thermonuclear one by 1967. Moscow came to reverse its position from the early 1960s: given the faintest encouragement from Washington, it would do the whole white race a service by taking out China.[105]

About as many people in Washington understood Soviet perspectives on nuclear war as understood Vietnam. In fact, America's own views on nuclear matters could be whimsical. In 1964, McNamara elucidated, with deceptive precision, a concept of "assured destruction" far different from his "brush" with the counterforce/ no cities approach he had outlined at Ann Arbor. In what his critics termed "mutual assured destruction" (with its Strangelovian acronym, MAD), deterrence would not rest on U.S. ability to destroy Soviet military targets incrementally. Rather, it would depend on the certainty that, even after a Soviet attack, SAC would be able to erase the Soviet command system, one-fourth to one-third of the Soviet population, and two-thirds of Soviet industry (figures thought in 1968, with eccentric realism, to be more accurately reduced to one-fifth to one-fourth of population and one-half of industry). The deterrent McNamara envisioned would emphasize cities although SAC always had enough warheads to keep a range of Soviet military resources on target as well.

Understanding that reciprocally inflicted deaths in the scores of millions would be militarily senseless, reasonable men in the White House and the Kremlin would presumably not choose to behave like scorpions stinging each other to death in a bottle. Turning beliefs of assured destruction into policy meant doing little or nothing that would inhibit that desirable condition, such as building defenses against ICBMs or building ICBMs designed to preempt and destroy the opponent's missiles. It was all very logical in theory, but the problem was that the Soviets did not want to behave as it was then thought scorpions behaved. They had an altogether different, and not entirely unreasonable, agenda.

Although the CIA did not accept the facts until a fateful decade later, Soviet views of nuclear war remained clear. They had been explained in the secret documents passed on by Oleg Penkovsky in 1959 and had surfaced in the three editions of Marshal V. D. Sokolovsky's *Military Strategy*, published between 1962 and 1968 — essentially unclassified syntheses of what Penkovsky had stolen and for which he had been shot.[106] The types of Soviet missiles that began being seen in the late 1960s embodied the alarming conclusions of these materials. "While rejecting nuclear war and waging a struggle to avert it," summarized the Central Committee's V. V. Zagladin in the empire's final days, "we nonetheless proceeded from the possibility of winning it." Around the same time, the Soviet defense minister would offer his own confession. "Until Chernobyl," said General Yazov, in speaking of the 1986 nuclear disaster in the Ukraine, "I was convinced that we could fight a nuclear war and prevail."[107] McNamara nonetheless kept thinking he knew better, as did many inward-looking U.S. theorists. On the basis of flawed intelligence reports, McNamara declared, with characteristic Cold War certitude, that "the Soviets have decided that they have lost the quantitative" strategic arms race. Lest the point be missed, he added that they "are not seeking to engage us in that contest."[108] Only his arguments on Vietnam were as categorical — an unsettling precedent.

Several boldly iconoclastic analysts, conspicuous among them CIA veteran and Sovietologist William Lee, nonetheless offered warnings that came down to three points: (1) the Soviets were not going to taper off their missile development until they achieved their targeting objectives; (2) they were building their ICBMs to destroy U.S. missile sites in a preemptive attack if war appeared inevitable, with cities being secondary; and (3) they were placing ballistic missile defense, not just civil defense, at the center of their military effort. In fact, they had their own answer to that timeless Cold War question, How much is enough?

"Enough," or what Rand called "strategic sufficiency," to the Soviets simply meant building what was necessary to produce, should the heavens fall, a world in which the motherland endured, however scarred, and the enemy had gone the way of the Third Reich. It did not mean the ability to exact genocidal retaliation after one's own society was obliterated. It meant a strategy of striking first, should attack seem imminent, to limit damage to one's own country. Rather than laying the Russian people open to the greatest slaughter, it also meant building a nationwide antiballistic missile (ABM) system, as well as a means of shielding the *nomenklatura* (that network of Soviet citizens more equal than others).

In 1962, Lee and a counterpart at the NSA had predicted the arrival of heavy-payload ICBMs designed to destroy America's Minuteman missiles and launch control centers in a preemptive attack. Deployment began in 1966, as U.S. theorists and decision makers (categories now often blended) were confounded by the several hundred SS-9s with 18- to 25-megaton warheads that the Soviets deployed over the next four years. Russia "seemed to be rejecting the American experience," according to *New Yorker* staff writer and future Arms Control and Disarmament Agency counselor John Newhouse, who interviewed U.S. officials and their advisers. "It made no sense, at least not to American scholastics," he went on, judging the giant SS-9 "an aesthetically contemptible Russian missile. . . . Its destructive power is out of all proportion to any rational strategic mission" — at least as defined by Americans recently smitten with arguments of mutual vulnerability.[109] The problem was important because only ICBMs then combined the speed, accuracy, and payload needed for a disarming surprise attack against an opponent's long-range, land-based missiles.

William Lee was a sharecropper's son from the Missouri Ozarks, who had learned Russian in the Air Force and then been sent to graduate school to prepare him for the CIA in 1951. A master craftsman rather than a "scholastic," and anything but an ideologue, Lee even in his mid-forties was a cantankerous yet thoroughly focused analyst. His objective was not to prove the essential wickedness or aggressiveness of the Soviet system, but to establish from the labyrinth of newspapers, journals, academic texts, stolen documents, and classified technical information just what was happening in both the Soviet Union's military and its economy. His work was like reconstructing Jurassic dragons from bone fragments scattered through the rocks. Just as paleontologists are sometimes startled into new conclusions, so the data for Lee began to take strange, and not welcome, shape. He simply called it as he saw it, having left the CIA in 1964 for the Stanford Research Institute, then still a university-affiliated think tank with ties to Army nuclear missile programs. Only later, in the 1970s, when the internecine battles became particularly vicious, did he receive the backing of a far more publicly formidable dissenter from the prevailing wisdom, Paul Nitze.

Since his first years in office, McNamara had been faced with the decision of whether to develop the Nike defenses from the late 1950s (posed against bomber attacks) into a nationwide exo-atmospheric anti-missile defense system. The cost for defending forty to fifty cities was estimated at $40 billion over five years. It might buy a rough means of curbing the slaughter from Soviet warheads. For another $10 billion or so, defenses could also be built to protect America's ICBMs from a preemptive attack — ensuring that, in the heat of some future crisis, there would be no advantage in striking first, and thereby minimizing U.S. retaliation.

Could something be done for a reasonable price that would reduce the number of American dead from between 100 million and 120 million to about 20 million to 30 million? McNamara's people argued that any missile defense system sophisticated and dense enough for this just wasn't worth the cost. For every dollar Americans might spend so that more of them could survive, it was argued, the Soviets could counter by paying only one cent to build an offsetting armament of warheads and missiles.

A second issue, and, for McNamara, a troubling one, concerned Soviet military thinking. Was the intention to hit American cities should war break out? Or might Soviet leaders, as Lee insisted, preempt what they might fear to be an American attack by striking first at U.S. "hard targets," such as ICBM silos, bomber bases, and submarines in for repair? If so, it would make sense to defend both those categories. Should the Soviets decide to devote most of their megatonnage to attacking hard targets, that fact might be a further argument for defending cities as well. The point was that the majority of Soviet warheads would be directed at hard targets, with only the leftovers going against population centers — and many of those warheads could be intercepted. The hitch was that any ability to defend U.S. cities would pull the rug out from under McNamara's concept of mutual destruction and allegedly undermine deterrence.

To explore these bizarre problems further, McNamara had funded an independent think tank study under Army supervision. The Army, after all, was by Cold War tradition responsible for protecting the country from those Soviet warheads. The think tankers included men from AT&T's Bell Labs and Stanford Research, whose analyses soon punctured the 100:1 ratio that McNamara had initially assumed. The analysts emphasized — as do advocates of ballistic missile defense today — the revolutionary improvements in U.S. technologies: much simpler, perhaps more reliable, technologies than would be debated over the decades ahead.

These outside experts, including Lee, who would receive the Army's Distinguished Service Medal for his contribution, reported in the fall of 1966 to the conference room adjacent to McNamara's office. The secretary was flanked by Harold Brown, a prominent physicist recently appointed Secretary of the Air Force; John Foster, another physicist, who had replaced Brown as head of Pentagon R & D; and Cyrus Vance, deputy secretary of defense, formerly secretary of the army, and long a partner at New York's Simpson Thacher & Bartlett. Using the customary flip charts, one of Lee's colleagues argued the cost-effectiveness of a nationwide ballistic missile defense that would protect cities as well as military assets. It was feasible, explained Richard B. Foster, head of Stanford Research's missile defense practice, to defend both. No pretense was made that a "box," or a perfect defense, of America's ICBMs or its cities could be created. But defenses would vastly complicate Soviet plans for a preemptive attack and might also save tens of millions of lives.

Furthermore, he argued, the Soviets already possessed their own crude defenses against missiles — ones that had the dual function of also defending against bombers. What was not known at the time, but what could have made the argument for such a U.S. defense stronger, was that Russian scientists had begun, in 1964, to engineer what would be known as MIRVs. These were multiple reentry vehicles (a multiplicity of warheads that could soon be targeted independently) atop an ICBM.

Soviet missiles were of immense size compared to their American counterparts. They were much heavier and capable of lifting more destructive payloads. Rather than an ICBM carrying a single twenty-five-megaton warhead, a MIRV might soon allow a given missile to deliver eight or more autonomous warheads, which, once they separated from the booster in space, could each seek out a separate target. Such warheads, designed to strike precisely and devastatingly each Minuteman silo, were well within Soviet capabilities and it was argued in this presentation, would probably be fielded by the mid-1970s. Combined with what Soviet military leaders were saying about their own nuclear doctrine, this seemed convincing evidence that they were going after America's ability to retaliate, perhaps making the entire land-based part of the U.S. nuclear triad vulnerable to sudden attack within a few years. These were not the type of forces, argued Richard Foster, needed just to incinerate St. Louis and Los Angeles.

That was too much. McNamara ripped the pointer from Foster's hands and slammed it against the charts. "No, no, no!" he shouted, coloring dangerously. "As a Red marshal, I'm going to put them all on the cities!!" A stunned silence followed, in which no one said, "Well, Mr. Secretary, but you're *not* a Red marshal."[110] To McNamara, nuclear war was the end of his world, to be treated with fitting millenarianism. To real Red marshals — Sokolovsky, Malinovsky, and others — who had fought from Stalingrad to Berlin against the best army in the world, twenty million to forty million dead was experienced historic fact. This did not necessarily make them aggressive. It might indeed give them second thoughts. But it did make them grimly confident of enduring in ways that the civilized secretary was fortunate in not being able to imagine.

For the survivors, life goes on. Was not the motherland stronger than ever? Nuclear war was not hopeless — build more missiles, dig deeper holes, erect more defenses, impose more coercion and fear.

Meanwhile, the Soviet leadership would construct its military in ways that made the most sense. Any treaty arrangements with the West should compromise neither core assumptions nor the building plans needed to follow through on them. Negotiations, however, could be valuable for cementing Soviet advantages. McNamara once yelled at some student demonstrators that he was "tougher" than they. He learned the hard way — though not as hard as that of so many grunts — how tough Ho Chi Minh and General Vo Nguyen Giap were. He never seemed to learn how tough those who had survived Stalin were likely to be. In this instance, he refused to approve the defense of American cities. To him, all of these people had to be held hostage in order to uphold stability.

The Joint Chiefs of Staff united against this visionary moonshine — if only, in part, because, as heads of large procurement enterprises, they could see that such a doctrine of assured destruction would inevitably place a ceiling on the development of new ICBMs, SLBMs, or ABMs for the Air Force, Navy, and Army, respectively. Along with civilian theorists less enamored of McNamara's latest views on nuclear war, however, the Joint Chiefs also believed that ABMs protecting cities made sense because of the potential for saving lives. Their allies in Congress had the usual full range of motives. For instance, Charleston, South Carolina, a city of about 66,900 people, was always first or second on the construction list for ballistic missile defense. Whether or not Charleston was America's most vital metropolis, even with its naval facilities, it certainly was in the district of Mendel Rivers, chairman of the House Appropriations Committee.

In December 1966, McNamara and the chiefs trooped to the LBJ Ranch outside Johnson City, Texas, to thrash out the whole dour business before the president and Bundy's recent successor as national security assistant, Walt Rostow. McNamara insisted that defending cities would just provoke the Soviets into building more missiles and that Moscow had "been wrong in its nuclear defense policy for a decade" — apparently meaning that they had been putting too much money into air and civil defense and, he thought, into just researching missile defense.[111] The Chiefs persuaded the president to overrule McNamara, at least for the moment. In true Cold War fashion, half a glass was being poured. Cost was now paramount, much more so than when the question of missile defense was considered in the early 1960s, again in the 1980s, and again

today. For it was during this time at the ranch that McNamara
had to acknowledge the financial squeeze from Vietnam: the war's
drain for the current fiscal year was not the $10 billion or $12 billion he had earlier insisted, but $20 billion — pushing the budget
into a then-shocking $9 billion deficit. Since Kennedy's buildup,
overall defense spending had jumped, had plunged, and was rising
again.[112]

Though opposing a national missile defense and standing by his
notion of assured destruction, McNamara had to hedge his bets
should deterrence fail — if only because of pressure from Congress
and the Joint Chiefs. In addition to accepting a limited ABM system,
as would be announced later in 1967, he asked for money to build
MIRV warheads for Minuteman ICBMs and for the new strategic
missiles on the equally new Poseidon submarines. However, neither
he nor other advocates of assured destruction were comfortable
making U.S. missiles as accurate as was technically possible. MIRVs,
explained Newhouse, could be good or bad. Good MIRVs were not
particularly accurate, carried relatively low-yield warheads, and
were appropriate only for the indiscriminate destruction of people
and cities; therefore, they were "stabilizing." Highly precise missiles
with MIRV warheads were bad and "destabilizing" because they
could be used to launch a theoretically disarming first strike. Obviously, the Soviets had a different view. In any event, it took them
eleven years to make MIRVs operational (after commencing in
1964), by which time U.S. developers, despite having started a year
or two later, were much farther ahead.

Contrary to common belief today, this U.S. concept that both
societies should be mutually vulnerable, and that their mutual ability to retaliate devastatingly should not be infringed, was not just a
crude method of measurement and force planning. It affected
actual policy, although McNamara ran out of time and personal
forcefulness before his latest beliefs could penetrate the closely held
targeting plans of the Chiefs. Policy was influenced in three ways.
First, the Navy was directed not to put stellar navigation systems
into Poseidon missiles, which would make them exceptionally accurate for the time. Believers in MAD worried that Moscow, which
monitored U.S. test data, might be alarmed if it appeared that such
invulnerable submarine-launched missiles could imperil Soviet
ICBMs. Second, the Air Force's new ICBM, which it began testing in
1968, was deliberately not as threatening to Soviet forces as it easily

could have been. Each Minuteman III carried three low-yield (0.17-megaton) warheads, in contrast to the large, heavy-payload ICBMs with six to ten warheads each (of 0.5 and 0.75 megatons, depending on the ICBM model) that the Soviets chose to deploy. Third, the Army never developed a serious ABM capability. In the continued absence of a nationwide missile defense, the Army and Air Force naturally found it pointless to maintain their surface-to-air missiles and jet interceptors to defend against the small proportion of Soviet nuclear strength carried on intercontinental bombers. So the country had no active defenses of any sort, nor was it making any serious attempt at civil defense. The consequences of this approach to Armageddon are still with us.

It was at the Glassboro, New Jersey, summit with Premier Kosygin in June 1967 that Johnson (in addition to seeking Soviet help with ending the Vietnam War) had to revisit the mind-numbing topic of ABMs. He was desperate to avoid spending that anticipated $40 or so billion, a sum that he knew would have to come from "the peaceful development of the country," meaning the Great Society.[113] Moscow was puzzled why anyone would want to limit missile defense in the first place. Four months earlier, Kosygin had told Britain's prime minister and foreign secretary that the Kremlin regarded such U.S. proposals as "obscurantism and misanthropy," arguing that antimissile systems could let mankind "live in peace because nuclear war would be neutralized."[114] Once in the United States, he said that "defense is moral" and suspected McNamara of taking a starkly "commercial approach" in opposing ABMs because such a system was so expensive, no matter how many lives it saved.[115] (Shreds of Marxism could surface even in the burned-out cases of the Politburo.) He also had no qualms about identifying a particular missile, the SA-5, as one that Moscow's Strategic Rocket Forces depended on for ballistic missile defense.[116] Its increasingly sophisticated successors would be the SA-10 and, today, the SA-20.

Throughout the Cold War, the American conceit was that the Soviets should be imitating U.S. plans and theories and could be persuaded to do so. The degree to which McNamara believed that the Soviet Union functioned more or less like the state of Michigan is shown by his fantasy that U.S. and Soviet military spending could be lowered in tandem. The two countries, he suggested, could exchange budget documents every year — an utterly loopy view of how the Soviet Union worked.[117] In this atmosphere, it is not surprising that U.S. estimates of the types and numbers of ICBMs that Moscow was building went awry. From then until nearly the end of the empire, the Soviet weapons procurement bill would grow at an annual average rate of more than 10 percent.[118] There was nothing inadvertent or reactive about such intensity.

Despite Washington's sanguine appreciation of Soviet intent, the search for actual protection from the Red Army's bombers and Strategic Rocket Forces never ceased. It had gone from Thomas Finletter's ridiculed "Maginot Line" in 1948 and the DEW line and Nike-Zeus initiatives of the 1950s to arrive, in September 1967, at what McNamara announced as the Sentinel ABM. He thought this latest defense to be demonstrably useless against an assault of Soviet magnitude, but it might close out the possibility of a Chinese attack on America for the next twenty years. The Sentinel was not what the Army or the Joint Chiefs wanted, but it was at least a nose under the tent. Moreover, McNamara had retreated from his original belief that an attacker would have a 100:1 advantage over even a determined high-tech defense. Given the arbitrary assumptions underlying most of these calculations, he came to accept publicly that attackers had only a 4:1 advantage and admitted privately that the ratio was about even for defending up to 80 percent of the population.[119]

The Chiefs hoped that Sentinel could soon be expanded into a comprehensive means of defense against Soviet ICBMs. Bitter argument over price, effectiveness, and safety forced Sentinel to be radically downscaled by 1969, with the Senate approving its first phase by a single vote. Once the political economy of the Vietnam War made it impossible to go much further in building this system, the Army came up with yet another justification: rather than protecting cities from Chinese missiles, a limited ABM effort could be undertaken just to protect eight hundred Minuteman ICBMs in South Dakota and Montana from Russia. By 1970, this approach would be renamed Safeguard, and it went on to consume about $24 billion (in today's dollars), although it operated for less than a year before being deactivated in 1975.

Not racing forward with a much more robust missile defense program in the late 1960s might today be seen as a rare and fortunate saving. After all, the country was spared from spending tens of billions of dollars more on a nationwide complex of radar, computers, technicians, and nuclear-tipped interceptor missiles, which (we now know) never would have been used. However, the conclusion is more complicated. If the United States had pushed ahead in 1967 to defend not only its largest cities but particularly its ICBM silos (using the same missiles and types of radar to do both), the whole purpose of the Soviet Union's sweeping strategic buildup — with the numerous, heavy-payload ICBMs — might have been trumped before Moscow's truly dangerous deployment started in 1975. Although cities could never be shielded completely nor every ICBM made invulnerable to a surprise attack, a powerful protective system with Nike-X's radar, missiles, and computers was at hand. Soviet missile building, on the scale undertaken, might well have been nullified. U.S. means for responding immediately and relatively precisely to an attack (meaning ICBMs, in contrast to bombers and SLBMs) might then have remained relatively secure.[120]

If the Soviets wanted an arms race, it can be argued, here was the time to give it to them, at technology's leading edge. The more warheads and heavy ICBMs they chose to build, the better. The United States could probably have added more defenses more efficiently just with the integration of proven technologies and commercial computers, let alone with what would follow. The hardened, concentrated Minuteman silos were defendable with Sprint ABMs, just the start of a revolution in high-acceleration intercept technology. McNamara's 4:1 ratio favoring the offense was the worst case. It was just as likely 1:4, and probably much better for the defense of ICBM silos. In 1965 dollars, it cost the Soviets at least $5 million to add one more warhead to their attacking force; it cost the United States about $1 million to add another Sprint missile for defense. In any such race, the United States would have held its lead by constantly improving in technologies where the Soviets never came close. Perhaps Americans could have played that game forever — a risky one, to be sure, but perhaps no more so than what followed, and with a higher upside. The United States instead chose to try to ban ballistic missile defenses on both sides — again ending up with something in between and the worst of both approaches.[121]

Once more, the politics of the time, combined with McNamara's faith in assured destruction and in intelligence (which would prove flawed), may have made this moment one of the great lost opportunities of the Cold War. For the United States to have proceeded with a national missile defense would have cost more in the short term than did going without it, but it might have cost much less in the longer term given what would unfold. Unlike the Americans, the Soviets were not looking for perfect solutions. "The best is the enemy of the good" has long been an axiom of Russian defense, and was often emblazoned on banners hanging in military plants. To conceive of a moment in time when Soviet ABMs would have been used in practice is truly to ponder the end of history. This was not necessarily so for Marshals Malinovsky, Ogarkov, and Akhromeyev.

At the time, some people also spoke of reviving a national shelter program. The Office of Civil Defense, for instance, urged Congress to approve new tax incentives for homeowners. However, the basement refuges of Kennedy-era franticness were now storing bicycles, snow tires, and vintage wine — if they were being used at all. Even an executive at defense contractor General Dynamics acknowledged that the emergency rations in his own home shelter had gone stale.[122] Americans were not going to buy into this again. The prospect of arms control, building upon the initiatives broached at Glassboro, appeared to offer better hope for survival. In 1968, two achievements offered convincing evidence: the Nuclear Nonproliferation Treaty and an agreement to ban nuclear weapons from space.[123]

Nonetheless, nearly every policy issue, whether of arms control or Great Society entitlements, was by the end of the Johnson administration being framed by Vietnam. No one in government could even determine how much the war was costing annually in terms of dollars being spent. Nor was anyone thinking long-term — meaning a year or two ahead — during 1968, Johnson's last full year in office. That decisions kept being made in ignorance was bad enough. That there was an overall absence of purpose, other than "avoiding defeat," not only in Vietnam but in the core competition with Moscow, was what made everything the Cold War touched on so terribly costly.

✪

"Nobody had it straight at the time, hawk or dove, what was going on," says Douglas Pike, the State Department's leading analyst on Vietnam for fifteen years. He could have said the same thing about the arms race or foreign aid. Or he might have said it about the deadly suspicions between the two Communist giants: Was China insane, as the Soviets hinted, and Russia the next U.S. ally, so long predicted by pundits, or was China to be the next ally, the enemy of my enemy?

These years were ones of an incoherent sense of great change, rather than of change itself. There was a distrust of leadership, which Assistant Secretary John McNaughton, just before he was killed in a 1967 plane crash, summarized to McNamara — "a feeling . . . widely and strongly held that 'the Establishment' is out of its mind."[124] And that is from where defeatism would come. Clark Clifford, a lawyer who epitomized the politically potent, technologically null understandings between big government and big business in post–World War II Washington, was McNamara's replacement. He lacked the rectitude of George Marshall and Robert Lovett and the boardroom gravitas of Charles Wilson and Thomas Gates, but he did know a losing proposition when he saw one. Whether they wanted to leave or to escalate, the American people were increasingly soured with the investment in Southeast Asia, so Clifford told his clients to cut a deal. But even "the granddaddy of influence peddlers," as Business Week called him, had little to swap with Hanoi — except South Vietnam.[125]

George Kennan, who had considered leaving the United States altogether after being pushed out of the State Department in 1953, concluded that American civilization had failed. "I do not think that our political system is adequate to the needs of the age into which we are moving," he wrote without visible distress. "I think this country is destined to succumb to failures which cannot be other than tragic and enormous in their scope."[126] It was this authoritative despair that dragged on the country, and he was only one of the curious figures who thrived in the Cold War's dizzying alternations of hyperactivity and hopelessness. In 1968's presidential election, the United States did not need a "Manchurian Candidate"; it already had a couple in Richard Nixon and Robert Kennedy. There were serious observers who thought the new senator from New York was dangerous enough. George Ball, who as adviser to Adlai Stevenson and as undersecretary of state saw him close-up, claimed to have felt a surge of relief upon hearing of his death.[127]

Politics is rarely an uplifting exercise, except for those who love the game for itself, and the Cold War imbued American life with politics. The drive for personal security — the eagerness to be embraced by big organizations — was reinforced by the extension of hard-times attitudes into postwar prosperity. Yet Cold War dangers had not dimmed people's confident belief that "if it's new, it's good, and it will be newer and better next year." That was the promise that had served America well into the 1960s. At least for a moment longer, the United States followed through on possibilities that no other country could achieve.

No one doubted that Americans were racing to the moon because the Soviets had thrown down the challenge. If the Soviets astounded the world with a space walk in 1964, for instance, NASA had to interrupt its Gemini program to do the same within five months. The 1969 Apollo landing, involving at least 300,000 workers at around 20,000 companies in all 50 states, finally represented a form of short-term Cold War victory. All through this decade, some people valued NASA not only as a "wave of the future" but as "an alternative to the 'military-industrial complex,' a dynamic, positive aggregation of public and private power."[128] It was absorbing a stunning 25 percent of the nation's civilian R & D dollars. NASA and the space race were driven by politics during the excitement of the early 1960s, and it would be hard to untangle the venture from politics later in the decade once "the anti-Russian theme," as Senator John Glenn would reflect, "had worn out."[129] Without the Cold War, of which the Apollo program was only a small part, might Americans have benefited from more scientific discovery in space? So it looked by NASA's fortieth anniversary when the seventy-seven-year-old Glenn was shot into orbit for the second time.

By the end of the 1960s, the combination of technologies, entrepreneurial flexibility, and venture capital that would transform the U.S. economy was moving into place. The next generation of innovation was embodied neither in the moon landing nor in military funding. The subtler initiatives of microelectronics were making their own case in the market and cutting government strings. For example, Fairchild Semiconductor came to avoid military contracts, with their long development cycles, noncommercial specifications, and fixed profits. So would the efflorescence of other companies that would drive the information revolution. Around this time, many informed people also stopped seeing the Pentagon as a source of positive change, whether moral (the draft, say, as noble public service) or material (the interstates, nuclear power, or aeronautics). The requirements of American society were diverging at ever sharper angles from those of the military.

The successes of computing and molecular biology were spinning around the oblivious assistant secretaries, station chiefs, political science professors, journalists, and campus radicals who were wearing themselves out trying to rearrange a suddenly aging old order. America's world leadership today has nothing to do with the celebrated public policy makers of that time, let alone with their counterparts on the (always imaginary) barricades. It is due to the likes of the software engineer who heard the demonstrators chanting for Ho Chi Minh and said to himself, "Information power doubling every eighteen months! *We're* the revolutionaries." Yet it has become close to orthodoxy that "American power declined steadily from the 1960s" and that the late 1960s were the "crest" of the American Century — a formalist conception of power indeed.[130]

8

Blight on the Battlefield

(1969–1975)

The years like great black oxen tread the world . . .
And I am broken by their passing feet.

William Butler Yeats

In 1968, the American economy stood proud: industrial production was 34 percent of the world's total, a peak matched on Wall Street, where the Dow stopped just short of 1,000. A dozen years later, adjusting for inflation, it would be down to 300 — a gauge of a real loss of confidence in America's economic prospect. A similar situation existed in the space race. A decade before, one of the country's foremost scientists, Lee De Forest, had said, "Man will never reach the moon." In 1969 the "Eagle" landed. But by 1975, the attitude was "So what?" This says a good deal about the nation's disappointments.

During the 1970s, Americans became more European in their attitudes than in the previous two hundred years. This was evident in the decay of confidence in public leadership, in the anxiety that scientific developments were likely to be personally threatening, and in the suspicion of overseas engagement, which makes for insularity and close horizons. Roughly by the end of 1969, it was no longer widely assumed that consumer miracles or technological breakthroughs worked to the good of all or that going beyond the moon would enlarge America's spirit, as the costs appeared vastly to outweigh any returns. No one expected good news from abroad, especially as Americans were shocked at being challenged commercially from Yokohama rather than the Ruhr, a surprise less racial than cultural.

The country was soon hit with peacetime inflation, unprecedentedly combined with high unemployment. The Cold War was among the causes, not only because of more than two decades of money and talent lost, but also because the United States was simultaneously conducting the ongoing war in Asia and creating immense entitlements at home. How different America might be today had the sustained period of growth that the country enjoyed during the 1960s not been grievously interrupted. Many attempts to lessen the burden quickly appeared at the time, and weapons buying fell by more than a third between fiscal years 1970 and 1975, while overall defense spending declined nearly 20 percent in real terms during the decade. Yet Pentagon budgets were still in the $300 billion range (in today's dollars), consuming 6 percent of GDP, although with ever less to show for the money, whether in upkeep, stimulus, or return on power.

At a time when Americans could reach for the stars, they also heard their leaders acclaim great new achievements in the "balance of power," a concept from the days of the Borgias. This entailed not only some supposed "equilibrium" with the Soviet Union and China but also an elaborate "pentagonal balance of power" involving Western Europe and Japan. The standing of the Soviet Union as the world's co-superpower became sufficiently fixed as to appear a fact of the indefinite future. Anyone resorting to President Kennedy's rhetoric about Russia and China would have been met with ridicule, just as Barry Goldwater's "Why Not Victory?" passed from alarming chauvinism to an amusing eccentricity.

Americans were tolerating much from the dyspeptic industrial democracies, from Moscow, and most of all from Hanoi. They also watched North Koreans snatch a spy ship, the USS *Pueblo*, from international waters in 1968, imprisoning and torturing its eighty-two-man crew for eleven months after killing one; shoot down with equal impunity an unarmed Navy communications plane ninety miles over the high seas in 1969 (in daylight and with no possibility of mistaken identity), killing the entire crew of thirty-one; and hack to death two U.S. officers in the 38th Parallel's Demilitarized Zone in 1976. All this, Americans swallowed. And there continued to be demands from the Somozas, Marcoses, Mobutus, and Pahlavis. The demands themselves were not all that expensive, but it was dispiriting, and ultimately dangerous, to nurture such people. Not just neo-isolationists welcomed George McGovern's plea at the 1972 Democratic convention: "Come Home America."

These years start with the moon landing, when so much seemed possible, and end with South Vietnam's fall, by which time more disappointments than had ever occurred between 1947 and 1968 were taking their toll. This chapter first examines the efforts to reduce the Kennedy era's open-ended commitments and to take new approaches to Moscow and Beijing. Second, it explores why détente, as conducted by Richard Nixon, was so misguided, worsening rather than relaxing tensions. Third, it discusses how the Cold War played into these years' turmoils in finance and trade. Fourth, it explains why Vietnam opened into an even deeper wound than could have been imagined at the height of combat in 1968. Finally, we consider the secret manipulations, each justified by "national security," that were brought into the light by 1975 and the impacts of which live on.

Blaise Pascal warned that "all human evil comes from . . . man's being unable to sit still in a room." The Cold War produced plenty of people who could not sit still anywhere. Nixon, like John Kennedy, delighted in emergency — something that cannot be said about Vice President Hubert Humphrey, whom he narrowly defeated in 1968. Nixon and Kennedy were men who had to be *doing* something, and, unlike Johnson, they felt compelled to do it overseas. The more extreme things were, the richer the flavor. As with Kennedy, the presidency for Nixon was a means for displaying planetary ambitions. Like Kennedy's, Nixon's accomplishments abroad appeared worthy at the time but proved fleeting. Also like Kennedy, the shortening of Nixon's presidency was framed by the Cold War: Cuban burglars, assertions of presidential power for "national security," and subterranean dealings with secret agencies. If one triangulates back from any of these events, one finds long-term unintended consequences of a very long-term unintended conflict.

✪

Nixon was the first twentieth-century president to enter office without a majority of his party in either house. He arrived on a platform of reassurance and a "driving dream" of hope — Nixon's own phrase. So had every president since World War II, with the possible exception of Truman. But Nixon's dream was shadowed by his invocation of Stephen Vincent Bénet's "young men listening to trains in the night," the picture of lonely ambition. He had been raised in a reserved family, then fought his way into that hyperexcitable culture of political power, of which the Cold War was the ghastly routinizer. The title of the book he wrote before his presidency (*Six Crises*) and of the ones that followed it (*The Real War* and *In the Arena*) document these febrile impulses. In the first, it is extraordinary how often he shows himself on the point of losing his head. It is impossible to imagine George Marshall, or Dwight Eisenhower, or John Foster Dulles having his staffers tell the Soviets that they had a borderline madman on their hands, as Nixon once directed his own people to do for negotiating advantage. He was exorcising his private demons; the Cold War provided a public outlet. A science fiction story of the 1950s had posited the late-twenty-first-century Republicans running an "abnormal man for an abnormal world." He had arrived ahead of schedule.

Throughout his years in executive office, Nixon was obsessed with that international theater for which he asserted the United States really needed a president. While awaiting inauguration, he appointed another clever man who tragically interpreted every great change — social, demographic, technological — in terms of state power. Henry Kissinger, Nixon later concluded, was among the people who would foment crises to "earn attention for themselves," adding that Kissinger would cause one over someplace like Ecuador if Vietnam had not existed.[1] A country that incubates such careers is in store for unpleasant surprises and expensive repairs.

Less than a decade after Kennedy's thrilling confrontations with Khrushchev, now known largely as the "Crisis Years," such drama was already becoming the stuff of parody. In 1971, Woody Allen captured these times in a short film titled *Men of Crisis*, which mockingly celebrates a nation's self-important "men of power" battling self-inflicted emergency. The film is funny, but the increasingly prodigious cost of such conduct was a distancing of the government, and the American elites, from a public whose lives might lie in their hands. Nixon believed that "people need to be caught up in a great event and taken out of their humdrum existence."[2] This piece of wisdom he offered during the year that the memory chip arrived and a journalist coined the term "Silicon Valley." Here was the basic assumption of the Kennedy era — that to a nation in which people were trivially occupied, public stress comes as the only worthwhile challenge. This is a bizarre view of any democracy, let alone America.

A month after his inauguration, Nixon's joy was palpable as he met Charles de Gaulle in Paris, part of a five-nation jaunt through Europe.[3] He again dashed off overseas after only four more months in office, this time on a trip around the world. His first stop was Guam, where he shared impromptu thoughts with impressionable reporters. In what Nixon himself termed the "Nixon Doctrine," he observed that Americans would not "conceive all the plans, design all the programs, execute all the decisions and undertake all the defense of the free nations of the world."[4] What had started to evolve against the backdrop of Vietnam was not retrenchment but an attempt to return to some sense of limits against which Cold War policy had originally been framed.

Through several elaborations, the Nixon Doctrine reflected the country's growing sense of the prosperity of its allies, as well as its suddenly discovered doubt of sustained American will. Like the Truman Doctrine, it presumed that other nations would be carrying most of the weight for their own defense and was similarly vague and contradictory. By whatever name, the Nixon Doctrine would guide policy well after its author passed from office.

Nixon announced in his first annual "State of the World" declaration (reports generated by Kissinger echoing the constitutionally required State of the Union address) that he would apply more constricted criteria for determining defense needs. No longer would the country try to build ships, jets, and divisions for such a "2½-war" capability as had been crafted by the Kennedy and Johnson theorists, in which Americans were simultaneously supposed to fight a three-month non-nuclear contest in Europe, a full-scale Chinese attack in Korea or South Asia, and some doctrinally "minor" shootout elsewhere — as in, say, Vietnam. Now Americans were merely to prepare themselves to fight "1½ wars."[5]

With revived appeals to "unprecedented [if unspecified] urgency," foreign military assistance had to be boosted to fill the gap. Mantras were repeated: manpower would come from allies, hightech weaponry and support from the United States.[6] This was a variation of the concept scorned by NATO at its start and not much more appealing to clients in Asia, down whose throats the Nixon Doctrine was originally to be forced. Getting even modest cooperation from America's closest allies was often tricky. For instance, 114 British merchant vessels had docked at Haiphong during 1968, with 74 slipping in to bear helpful trade the following year.

Other reasons for elevating allied self-defense included benefits to America's balance of payments. In 1970, the United States sold $952 million worth of weapons abroad. Eight years later, this had increased more than tenfold in nominal dollars, but it still fell behind what the Soviet Union and France were cumulatively selling by the end of the decade. The results of America's expansive share of such commerce could be ironic. When two NATO allies went to war with each other in 1974, for example, Turkey's U.S.-supplied bombers sank one of its own cruisers, mistaking it for a Greek naval vessel of the same model, also bought from America.

Once again, Washington discovered that it was not easy to use more money and materiel to avoid direct entanglements. Whether in South Korea or Iran, political ransoms essentially ended up being paid to hard-bargaining clients who demanded large gifts, sophisticated weapons, and ever more explicit U.S. commitment in consideration of their loyalty. For instance, to withdraw a single U.S. division from South Korea in 1970 entailed comforting Seoul with the permanent basing of a U.S. fighter-bomber wing there and a special $1 billion appropriation to help South Korea modernize its forces — in addition to the $700 million it already stood to receive in regular military aid. In Iran, some twenty-five thousand Americans were soon involved in tending the Shah's new U.S.-supplied arsenal. Israel could not be left out. In 1970, Nixon agreed to a long shopping list of armaments previously denied Tel Aviv in the interest of dampening the Middle East arms race.[7]

Returning to a greater reliance on countries with supposedly common interests was overdue. As for the risk of nuclear war, it seemed most likely to occur between the two Communist giants. By 1969, deadly border skirmishes made Moscow consider the prospect of going it alone and initiating a nuclear attack on China. Beijing became convinced that "those arrogantly dangerous people in the Kremlin were ready to do anything," recalls one of China's foremost students of this era.[8] Perhaps the Brezhnev Doctrine of no country being permitted to leave the Socialist camp applied to Mao as well. China's leadership had good reason to anticipate Soviet attack. They had just enough of their own nuclear weapons to terrify their recent patron.

Nixon's inauguration ended the increasingly strained justification that the United States was in Vietnam to contain China's ambitions. No matter who was president, attempts at rapproachment with the world's most populous country were inevitable. Yet many people in Europe and the United States, including the new arrivals in Washington, seem barely to have registered that China's overtures to the West represented the most seasoned judgment of Soviet malevolence. Travelers through Siberia in January 1971 encountered soldiers fully expecting to go into the line against China. The city of Khabarovsk on the Amur River was periodically out of bread as people braced themselves for siege and famine.[9]

No U.S. official, and essentially no private citizen, had entered the People's Republic since its founding. Kissinger's secret arrival in Beijing that July (slipping in through Pakistan, which had also served as an intermediary) elicited the desired invitation for a presidential visit. Back-channel communications, in which the White House short-circuited the State and Defense Departments, had become second nature in this administration. All the care surrounding the China initiative was good fun for those involved, but gratuitous. Secrecy was essential, the public would be told, so that right-wing critics would not sabotage such bold diplomacy. Of course, the chief right-wing critic, had he not been president, would have been Nixon. The invitation once received, he sprang this grand gesture on the nation in an evening television address. California Governor Ronald Reagan was delegated to go to Taiwan to explain.

The New Yorker ran a cartoon of a slab-faced figure in a fur hat scrawling "Unleash Chiang Kai-shek" on the Kremlin wall. The world was coming full circle: now it was Chiang that the United States was setting aside, Beijing growing real again in American eyes. Taiwan faded even more after its expulsion from the UN later that year. Nixon's "opening to China" the following February is so much less than conventional wisdom acclaims — "a great moment," the brilliant work of a "creative global strategist" — with the Shanghai Communiqué (deferring the issue of Taiwan to the indefinite future, seeking to curb Soviet "hegemony," moving toward normal relations) being "one of the most sophisticated [agreements] in American history."[10] Reinforcing the weaker of two main enemies is hardly a masterstroke, however, nor is echoing an assertion equally acceptable in both Beijing and Taipei. The design for identifying one China of which Taiwan is a part had originated in a position paper for John Foster Dulles.

As for the communiqué that Nixon and Kissinger negotiated personally, it contained a fundamental flaw, at least until handed to Marshall Green, who had become assistant secretary of state for East Asia. Though excluded from White House deal making, Green zeroed in on the blunder: all U.S. security treaties and commitments in the Pacific except one had been reaffirmed in the final document. Missing was the Mutual Defense Treaty of 1955 with Taiwan, entered into by Eisenhower and ratified by the Senate. Not surprisingly, the Chinese insisted it was too late for the U.S. delegation to change even this self-inflicted, politically catastrophic oversight. They at least agreed, after U.S. imploring, that the entire section regarding Washington's ongoing treaty commitments in Asia be dropped. The text was then released.

The costs of the Nixon Kissinger performance with China were several, including not just the slighting of Japan (uninformed of the overture), but also essentially countenancing helpful Pakistan's extermination, at the time of Kissinger's secret trip, of at least half a million Bengalis. ("We had to demonstrate to China we were a reliable government to deal with," recalled Kissinger aide Winston Lord. "We had to show China we respect a mutual friend.")[11] Moreover, at a time when Americans were being killed with China's assistance in Vietnam, the sudden "opening" got deliriously out of hand. None of this was necessary to deter the Soviets from attacking China or, by this point, to prevent China from intervening further in Vietnam. The hope that embracing China would induce Mao to cut off support for Hanoi was also fanciful. U.S.-Chinese relations of some sort would have emerged anyway during the 1970s. That they came about as another of Nixon's grand architectural gestures — as if Oceania's leader were visiting Eastasia that week — was unfortunate. Overexcitement inescapably brought disappointment.

Nixon had been among the strident critics of Truman and Acheson for "losing" China in the first place. He had urged MacArthur's reinstatement, as well as the bombing of the mainland. Now this supreme would-be realist acclaimed Mao as one of the century's greatest men. Nixon's presence was broadcast as genius by a political-press complex of astounding archaism. James Reston, Arthur Hays Sulzberger, and Joseph Alsop all still worked as insiders and self-censoring amateur statesmen more than as newsmen. The highly anti-Communist Alsop's sudden enthusiasm for Chou En-lai, his trip to Yunnan on a Chinese military plane, and his unctuous praise of the hospitable tyranny in a two-part *New York Times* series, right in the wake of Nixon's visit, demonstrate that little was more important to the era's most powerful journalists than influencing foreign policy — that is, being in the know. Network computing and DNA sequencing waited in the wings, but what was that compared to having lunch on the seventh floor with the undersecretary?

The China craze swept the accepted periodicals like a prairie fire — the marvels of acupuncture, the acclaim of barefoot doctors, the awe toward those wise and subtle old men in Beijing who had seen it all. Not to mention John Kenneth Galbraith's star struck *A China Passage*. This eager prostration before Mao's stultifying autocracy illustrated the difficulty America had in calmly pursuing any sustained political objective during this phase of the Cold War. Rapprochement was seen as a sign of enlarged peace instead of what it primarily was: Beijing's deep, reasonable fear of Kremlin vengeance — an intensification of the Cold War on another front.

U.S. leaders subjected to criticism at home look enviously at despotic states and the diplomatic fireworks they can lay on. No one was ever given precise appointments with Mao, and the president of the United States would be no exception. In this case, Nixon had to wait to be summoned because of the Chairman's ill health. Once granted an audience, he went so far in trying to ingratiate himself that he explained that America was working to contain not only the Soviet Union in Asia but also, incredibly, Japan. He offered effusive toasts as the bloody Cultural Revolution ground over the Chinese people and munitions rolled steadily south to Hanoi.

Nixon was immensely pleased and wanted a White House publicity effort to underscore his role as "a big-league operator," with the encounter to be spun as "a classic battle between a couple of heavyweights."[12] This contest in Beijing was slugged out with all the enthusiasm of the 1919 White Sox, as Nixon and Kissinger fawned. Had de Gaulle been president, the cynics carped, Mao might instead have been scheduled for a breakfast at the White House. What is frequently lauded as "geopolitical wisdom" followed the celebrated reconciliation and may be one of the modest benefits to emerge. Although Congress was kept in the dark, Beijing would begin receiving highly sensitive U.S. intelligence on Moscow's military capabilities in exchange for letting the Americans use its territory for electronic monitoring of Soviet missile testing. Valuable information was collected, but it did not notably help the performance of top U.S. officials during the arms control negotiations that followed. These became the centerpiece of superpower relations.

After Beijing, Nixon staged his next summit three months later in the Kremlin, which no sitting U.S. president had previously entered. The Soviet oligarchs reached the same conclusion as the Chinese: his eagerness in election year 1972 could give them leverage. On the eve of Nixon's flight to Moscow, Foreign Minister Andrei Gromyko described "the real situation": Washington was afraid that the United States would be defeated in Vietnam because of weakness in the "economic and social rear."[13] Its leaders were hungry for deals, and deals would follow. The Russians, of course, could move in and out of détente as tactics dictated, their maneuverability helped by the now commonplace back channels that skilled often more capable U.S. delegations and departments.[14]

American hope and Soviet ambition were reflected in the arms control minuet of the 1970s — notably, the ABM treaty and the SALT (Strategic Arms Limitation Talks) I interim agreement in 1972, the ceilings agreed to during 1974, and the unratified SALT II agreement in 1979. At first glance, U.S. zeal seems admirable. A closer look finds countless illusions, including a dangerous way of perceiving the Soviet Union. The difficulty of determining some level of equivalence between the two sides' highly dissimilar forces was among the least of the problems.[15]

The year after the Cuban missile crisis, Dean Rusk had told the Senate that he favored maintaining "a very large overall nuclear superiority," such as the United States then exercised, over the Soviets. Within six years, the rough equality that Moscow instead achieved made the Nixon White House talk about a "new balance of power in the world" — a balance that would become more curious still within eight months of SALT I, as flight testing began for the fourth generation of Soviet heavy ICBMs. A couple of years after that, Moscow would forthrightly admit that "the purpose of détente is to make the process of international change as painless as possible."[16]

Strategic arms talks had begun in 1969 after a brief mourning hiatus for Czechoslovakia. Whereas Kosygin had ridiculed the idea of limiting ABMs, by 1970 that was exactly what Moscow wanted to talk about. It was frightened into negotiations by U.S. high-tech headway with the prospect of deploying a national missile defense. Amazed that U.S. leaders, whether Republican or Democratic, preferred to forgo ABMs and to entrust their nation's future to a pledge of joint suicide, the Russians embraced SALT. The White House at the time was hardly in the best position to negotiate. People expected a "peace dividend" once the Vietnam War ended, with Congress reluctant to fund more missiles.[17]

The delegations sat down for the first round of talks in Helsinki during 1971. Throughout, the Soviet Ministry of Defense dominated its side's agenda, backed by the KGB — the Politburo's omnipotent intelligence and secret police nation within the state — which since 1967 had been headed by Yuri Andropov. For the United States, negotiations were handled by distinctly milder organizations: the State Department and the Arms Control and Disarmament Agency (ACDA). There was also input from the Joint Chiefs of Staff and secret orchestrations by Kissinger. The ostensible chief negotiator in dealing with the Soviet marshals and the hard men of the Lubyanka was ACDA director Gerard Smith, a genial aristocrat out of Yale Law School who had been at State under Eisenhower, working initially on atomic matters. He had a deft touch in establishment politics, closing down *Interplay*, a glossy European oriented international affairs magazine that he had founded, the day he got the new job. Such subtlety was scarcely matched by his understanding of Soviet military thinking.

U.S. officials and academic advisers, Smith recalls, "expended a great deal of intellectual capital to educate the Soviet leadership" about what they regarded as appropriate nuclear policy, offering a "sort of tutorial" on U.S. theories of mutual vulnerability. "Management," he recalled, was one of "the watchwords by which those of us on the delegation lived."[18] In regarding the Russians as students, there was an arrogance no less brazen than seeing the Japanese as children or the North Vietnamese as buyable. From the start, Smith says, he "tried to get some idea of their views on basic strategic concepts" — as if the marshals had not been laying them out for at least ten years. He emphasized that "assured destruction capabilities are the basis of mutual deterrence" and notes with satisfaction that "no American academician could have put the matter in simpler terms."[19]

This was the same patent universal formula proposed by McNamara to scoffing Soviet officials at Glassboro. But now, explains

Ambassador Dobrynin, who was still serving in Washington, the KGB's Andropov had become "a cosponsor with Gromyko of major foreign policy proposals."[20] So why not tell the Americans what they wanted to hear? After all, Moscow's natural purpose, according to one of its key players, General N. N. Detinov, was "preserving and strengthening Soviet military might which, in this case, included weakening the potential chief enemy — the United States — by means of negotiations."[21] The Americans faced position papers written by General N. V. Ogarkov, first deputy chief of the General Staff, who headed the Operations Directorate responsible for Soviet war plans, and by General N. N. Alekseev, deputy for arms procurement at the Ministry of Defense.

Smith and Secretary of State William Rogers, Eisenhower's attorney general and an eminent New York lawyer, at least could anticipate how Congress would react: it would have little tolerance of the numerical edge that the Soviets were being given in ICBMs and SLBMs, albeit one counterpoised by U.S. advantages in warheads because of America's ongoing edge in R & D. Nixon and Kissinger thought they knew better. For reasons of bureaucratic slyness they eschewed the assistance of U.S., as opposed to Soviet, interpreters in private meetings with the Russians. As they secretly cut Smith and his delegation (which included Paul Nitze) out of the final decisions, refusing to let them come to Moscow from Helsinki, the Politburo likely concluded that Nixon and Kissinger were a softer touch.[22] Moreover, Kissinger again could not get his facts straight. For instance, one professional U.S. negotiator on the delegation, a serious student of Soviet military affairs, later noted that Kissinger never really understood that the word *dimensions* had been substituted for *volume* in the final document, thereby permitting the Soviets to increase the size of a missile silo by nearly a third, rather than the agreed 15 percent — not insignificant when introducing new generations of missiles.[23] Within four months, irritated senators of both parties approved an amendment requiring "essential equivalence" in any future deals.

The ABM treaty was also signed. The superpowers agreed that neither would build a comprehensive (or "national") defense against the other's long-range nuclear arsenal. Each was initially permitted two ABM sites: one around its capital and another at a place of its choosing. (Only a single site would be permitted after 1975, which the Soviets would openly devote to Moscow.) There would also be strict curbs on the construction and location of ABM-connected radar powerful enough to track incoming missiles in space — a vital component of any nationwide missile defense. Each side would be the judge of the other's violations.

Amid the treaty signing, one of Moscow's top priorities was a thousand-word U.S.-Soviet code of conduct concerning the "Basic Principles" of superpower relations. Each would renounce "efforts to obtain unilateral advantage at the expense of the other" promising not to exploit regional tensions or to claim spheres of influence. It would be the road map to detente. Kissinger considered the mutual pledge, prepared behind the back of the secretary of state, to be a major achievement. He enlisted General Secretary Leonid Brezhnev in springing it upon the startled Rogers.[24]

None of this was strategy. For in strategy those who presume to craft it must make the results of their wisdom comprehensible to friend and foe alike. In its secretive imprecision, U.S. weapons diplomacy was serving the country poorly. Moreover, whether this diplomacy was pursued through front channels or back channels, Americans were left to provide all the information and data — for the Soviet negotiators as well as for their own side — as to the numbers, types, capabilities, and locations of *all* the weapons to be discussed. This is a point barely mentioned in memoirs of that era. Until several observers from the U.S. Senate, including Ohio Democrat John Glenn, had enough of this nonsense, Moscow's negotiators simply let the United States proudly lay out its idea of the Soviet order of battle. They would then indicate their assent to U.S. estimates of their own forces by remaining silent.

Since it was up to U.S. intelligence to provide every detail to be discussed, the Soviets could easily assess Washington's skill at collecting information on their capabilities, thereby enabling General Ogarkov to spend the next three to four years improving his concealment measures — a tactic at which the Soviet Union excelled.[25] And since Moscow would never permit on-site inspection, all verification had to be done solely by "national technical means" (that is, electronic detection by satellite and other distant methods). Only in 1978, after intense U.S. lobbying, would the Soviets agree to share their information.

"What in the name of God is strategic superiority?" Kissinger asked his critics in understandable exasperation. The marshals had an answer. To them, "mutual assured destruction," which one

Russian military writer would call that "odious formula," was the essence of instability. Actual stability would instead rest on the capacity massively to preempt any attack, while meeting whatever counterstroke might be launched with one's antiaircraft and countermissile defenses, as well as unrivaled civil defense and recovery capabilities.

The Soviet national missile defense system that emerged was not intended to create a perfect, or impermeable, "box," particularly since such defenses would be swamped by a U.S. attack against the Strategic Rocket Forces' ICBM fields. The purpose of the ABMs was instead to provide a degree of effectiveness, after a successful Soviet preemptive strike, against a ragged U.S. retaliation. The Soviets knew these dual-purpose systems (the SA-5s and their radars, for starters) were relatively ineffective, but deployed them on a massive scale anyway. The United States accepted revised explanations that they were not intended to be used against missiles. In sum, there was no reason at all to believe that the men who had fought from Moscow to Berlin had recently been socialized to the hypermodu lated contingencies of U.S. professors.

Only after actual deployment in 1975 of the whole disturbing range of new Soviet ICBMs (the SS-17, 18, and 19, with four, ten, and six warheads, respectively) could an amazed CIA bring itself to concede that these missiles possessed a size, accuracy, and technical sophistication that made them uniquely appropriate for launching a counterforce/first strike. These were weapons capable of pounding Raven Rock, Mount Weather, Cheyenne Mountain, Minuteman silos, and anything else on the face of the earth (or beneath the surface, for that matter) to rubble. The United States had nothing like them.[26] These behemoths could loft much heavier payloads than America's ICBMs or SLBMs, with warheads three times the yield of the three carried by the Minuteman missiles and ten times the yield of the ten relatively small warheads carried by the comparatively inaccurate Poseidon missiles. These were not city-busting tools of retaliation.[27] All the forecasts that the Agency and McNamara had rejected, and that those "scholastics" could not stomach, began to appear conservative. How much was enough? Enough was what was needed to minimize damage to oneself by first destroying as much of the enemy's forces as possible — not a very original posture. It has even won wars.

Some opponents of SALT called it a Soviet "war-winning" doctrine. Senior Soviet officials did not disagree. As intelligence official

General V. M. Milstein blurted out to me sometime later, "Of course we have a 'war-winning' doctrine! What do you expect it to be, a 'war-*losing*' one?"[28] Few of the administration's critics ever believed that Moscow was plotting a bolt-out-of-the-blue attack. But it was not too difficult to imagine some horrific showdown several years hence in which desperate and isolated men in the Kremlin might see some form of advantage in launching first. To them, the concept of "winning" presumed that espionage would detect Western preparation to strike (most likely in a sudden lunge out of ostensibly routine NATO maneuvers) and would provide enough warning to preempt with these first-strike ICBMs. A missile defense network would then mitigate retaliation. As in 1945, Russia would emerge the stronger.

At the same time Moscow was expanding its strategic nuclear forces, it was strengthening its divisions in Eastern Europe. Meanwhile, Nixon and Defense Secretary Melvin Laird let slip such phrases as America's "adequate [nuclear] warfighting capability." Their critics would mistakenly cite such terms in trying to show that, when it came to nuclear reasoning and preparation, the superpowers were essentially working down parallel paths. And sensible steps were being considered (though not yet taken) to emphasize again the targeting of Soviet military, rather than civilian, assets. Laird had been the ranking Republican on the House Defense Appropriations Subcommittee and was a shrewd bureaucratic player. Like McNamara, he had to reassure Congress that U.S. missile accuracies would not be made too precise.[29] Throughout the Cold War, the United States never combined its offensive and defensive capabilities (let alone its armored divisions) to the extent that anyone could honestly call "war-winning."

To have a strategy intended to "win," as the Soviets conceived that possibility, would have required doing all the things that the United States was doing to shape its nuclear forces and all that it was not doing, or doing halfway. It would have entailed nationwide ABM defenses, air defenses against the relatively few Soviet bombers, and a national policy also emphasizing antisubmarine warfare. (The Soviets had a huge antisubmarine effort. By contrast, there were no actual policy directives behind U.S. efforts, which were left to the discretion of the Navy.) It also would have meant pursuing more than a halfhearted counterforce capability, meaning that the Soviet leadership, as well as Soviet missiles in their silos, would have been threatened by numerous large, accurate-as-possible ICBMs. And it would have included civil defense on at least a fraction of the Soviet scale.

The survivors of Stalinism understood this sort of "victory." They knew more about horror than anyone at the top in Washington, and they had learned from Stalin and the Great Patriotic War that, however bad events turn out, life goes on, preferably with oneself in charge. To them, destruction was not a theory. Not for a dozen years would their belief be shaken in the capacity for recovery possessed by the great Russian land and people — the timeless, earthy strength to which Stalin had ascribed victory in the last ordeal.[30]

Ironically, all the arms control hoopla never constrained either side from building what it had planned to build anyway. But trouble lay in at least three false assumptions framing the first SALT agreement: (1) that if Washington negotiated general limits, such steps would stem Russia's impulse to build missiles particularly constructed to destroy that part of the U.S. retaliatory force most capable of wiping out the Soviet leadership and their remaining ICBMs, (2) that SALT would somehow curb the overall military outlays highlighted in Moscow's panoply of force improvements, and (3) that the Soviets could be held to their treaties. For example, the ABM treaty, thwarted from the start with U.S. acquiescence, would linger on into the next century, still widely championed as the reason U.S. missile defenses could not be built in an entirely different world.

From the early 1960s until 1975–1976, the CIA's National Intelligence Estimates showed that Soviet strategy was more or less of the American sort, if slightly backward. From 1963 to 1971, the Agency even concluded that the Soviets would not seek parity, much less try to jeopardize America's ICBMs.[31] Year after year, Langley would assert that "we do not believe that the USSR aims at matching the U.S. in numbers of intercontinental delivery vehicles" (1964); that "the Soviet leadership must be reluctant to face the prospect of additional heavy arms expenditures" (1970); or that the building of dual-purpose antiaircraft/antiballistic missile capabilities was "coming to an end" (1971). Such missiles would nearly double by 1980. The CIA still insists that it was correct in predicting the numbers and sizes of ICBMs that Moscow introduced. It refuses to address seriously Moscow's end run around the ABM treaty, one that likely results from integrating big radars and nationally dispersed dual-purpose interceptors.[32]

Some of these errors may not appear significant today. After all, the worst nightmares were never realized. Nevertheless, two heavy costs were levied over and above the likelihood that an all-out U.S. effort to build ABMs (had it been possible politically) might have diluted the Soviet ICBM challenge in the first place. One is that the illusory settlements of the 1970s would be replaced by the expensive, headlong U.S. compensations of the 1980s. The second is an intelligence community — in fact, not a community but a set of organizations — still mired in a culture of dealing with its serious mistakes by denial.

✪

Reflecting toward the Cold War's end on this decade of accommodation and steady armament, Michael Howard, a widely respected British defense thinker, wrote approvingly of Kissinger's "success in managing the Soviets."[33] Here the notion of "management" is carried to an extreme. One might wonder, with Montaigne, whether Mr. Kissinger was playing with the cat or the cat was playing with him. Whatever transactions occurred between the superpowers by the mid-1970s, they hardly involved a degree of U.S. control at any level deserving to be called "management." But the vision of some sort of "geopolitical" mastery of great-power relations had become the core delusion of this administration. In the months before the 1972 presidential election, the unarticulated entente with China and the novel arrangements of détente with the Soviet Union were presented to the country as a new start, a historic emancipation from an odious pathology, rather than as further moves in the same old game.

All that this high-toned statesmanship finally offered was a legitimized Soviet Union, an impression in Beijing that the People's Republic was indispensable, and the dangerous notion at home that the Cold War was fading, if not quite "officially ended," as *U.S. News and World Report* described the position of Nixon and his aides that autumn.[34] Today, we hear that all of détente's enthusiastic bargaining was a careful deflection from the threat of war, or the next thing to it. Kissinger reminisces that it was undertaken primarily to preempt the Politburo from using "its conventional superiority to spark a crisis" in Europe while the United States was hamstrung in Vietnam. This rationalization presumes that the Soviets would find aggression more tempting as that war was running down in 1972–1973, rather than when it was at its height in 1967–1968.[35]

It might appear to some as if the Cold War indeed had "ended" in the early 1970s, with Kissinger bragging to the president about continuing "to have our mao tai and drink our vodka too."[36] After all, China, more fanatical than Russia and ruled by an even greater tyrant, was being acclaimed as practically an ally. Ironically, the Soviets could therein find protective coloration. If the United States could embrace the likes of Mao, surely it could keep moving closer to the well-intentioned General Secretary Brezhnev, a man who had not shed serious blood for years.

The Soviets had been paying a far harsher levy than the United States for the Cold War. By now, anyone could see that the West had won the economic competition. Russia and Japan, for instance, had been comparably poor in 1905. Each lay devastated in 1945. By 1970, they were different worlds. What no one in Washington was anying, however, was that the Soviet economy was stagnant and vulnerable to U.S. pressure. The Kremlin asserted convincingly that it would accept any sacrifice to ensure that "no world deul slon . . . [could be] decided without the Soviet Union or in opposition to it." The people (if not necessarily their leaders) would "live on potatoes," it was declared in 1968, or would "eat grass," as it was put a dozen years later, to remain the superpower equal of America.[37] Through its diplomacy and looming forces, the Politburo realized that it could avoid being overtaken by history at a time when everyone else was rushing to compromise: Western Europe by its own reconciliations with the East, known in Bonn as Ostpolitik, which also meant doing nothing to irritate Moscow; China by swallowing its pride and aligning itself with the United States; the United States itself by rushing into détente. All this was suddenly life-affirming.

The Politburo, not just propagandists, spoke seriously about the "deepening of the general crisis" in America and pointed to failures in Vietnam, turmoil from assassinations, racial upheaval, devaluation, the oil crisis, Wall Street's slide, and soon the saturnalia of Watergate.[38] Many eminent Americans of otherwise diverse opinions agreed.

For instance, Admiral Elmo Zumwalt, the most widely admired leader of the U.S. Navy since World War II, had what he believed to be an entirely friendly conversation with Kissinger on a train to the Army-Navy football game. America "has passed its high point like so many other civilizations," Kissinger remarked, according to notes that Zumwalt made minutes later. "The American people have only themselves to blame because they lack stamina." Since Americans refused to stay the course against the Russians, who played "Sparta to our Athens," Kissinger explained, he could only try "to persuade the Russians to give us the best deal we can get." Kissinger would denounce this recollection of his worldview as a "fabrication" by a "dovish, doltish admiral," other times insisting that he had been misunderstood.[39] But the texture of U.S.-Soviet relations during these years shows this attitude at work. From Princeton, George Kennan apparently offered his own map of the tides of time: "I recognize in the theory of Soviet communism (in the theory, mind you, not the practice) certain elements which I think are probably really the ideas of the future. I hate to see us reject the good with the bad . . . and place ourselves in that way on the wrong side of history."[40]

Even more than it knew, the United States was assisting the Soviet Union. Between the summers of 1972 and 1974, the two countries made twenty-nine treaties, agreements, and interim agreements covering trade, finance, the arts, and arms control. U.S. industries signed more than forty specific protocols on which to base the sale of technology to Soviet state-controlled entities — "technology," in these cases, meaning not just products but also design and manufacturing know-how. With White House encouragement, Congress cut the list of products embargoed from thirteen hundred to two hundred, although Moscow soon boasted that it had long been skirting export controls anyway through the overseas subsidiaries of General Motors, IBM, Honeywell, and other U.S. multinationals.[41]

Moscow even paid part of its Lend-Lease debt stemming from the Roosevelt era in return for long-term loans. It also accepted a three-year, $750 million credit to buy American grain. Ineptly, Kissinger had thought the Soviets would buy only $150 million worth. Instead, they quietly cut deals with U.S. companies to spend an enormous $1 billion at subsidized prices. Eagerly helped by an export subsidy (an unnecessary gift to the grain traders), Moscow secured its 20 million tons at even lower prices by intercepting these same traders' bidding calls to the Department of Agriculture — all of which added to inflated bread costs for Americans.[42]

Within a year of the 1972 summit, Chase Manhattan became the first U.S. bank to open in Moscow, after financing the first manufacturing deal of this new era, the giant Karma River truck plant;

IBM's System 7, the best computers and software at the time, would control automated forging equipment. (No trucks were to be used for military purposes.) David Rockefeller, the bank's chairman, and younger brother of the governor, was one of the world's foremost business statesmen. He deeply believed that commercial bridge building would lead to ever closer cooperation. Nixon's secretary of commerce, Peter Peterson, recently head of Bell and Howell, glowed about large East-West gas deals, seeing oil and gas as the "most important product of this new commercial relationship." In the spirit of interdependence, the CIA briefed corporate executives on investment opportunities and encouraged them on specific deals. [43] The whole history of U.S. interaction with the Soviet Union during the 1970s gives the impression of intelligent, well-meaning men generally oblivious to the Soviet belief that détente's purpose was to codify a shift in power.

Organized labor had an altogether different view. "Some American businessmen are developing a vested interest in downplaying the repressive and inhuman character of the Soviet regime," the AFL-CIO's George Meany testified before the Senate Foreign Relations Committee. As with almost everyone, his principled stand nonetheless had elements of self-interest: the unions feared that cheap goods made by Soviet "slave labor" might pour in.[44]

Grave misinterpretations of the Soviet Union otherwise led to hopes of "managing" all these encounters. Although the United States could no longer count on having more missiles, its segue into MIRVs (with Moscow following close behind) showed that it retained a qualitative lead. However, the first ICBM, the first satellite, and the ensuing space program showcased the originality of Soviet engineering and the brilliance of Soviet mathematicians. The trouble for Moscow was that it fell short in applying laboratory successes (or stolen technology), largely because of its command economy. Most of all, the Soviet Union kept lagging in computers and microelectronics.

By contrast, the United States was on the verge of leaping into the next century. One unequivocally justified plus at the Pentagon was support for the research that produced the memory chip, or microprocessor — the "brains" of a computer. Its arrival would hasten the movement of initiative and control away from government (any government) and, eventually, would help doom totalitarianism. But the Politburo did not have to reconcile itself to facing the

full clout of U.S. innovation, and this part of the story has never
fully been told.

During 1970, Andropov had established a new unit within
the KGB intended to ensure that the West would unwittingly be
doing R & D simultaneously for him and the Soviet General Staff.
The State Committee on Science and Technology, as well as the
Military-Industrial Commission, gave the KGB's newly formed Directorate T and its operating arm, Line X, a shopping list. Détente provided perfect cover, something far beyond the mutual "trade and
investment" and the "degree of interdependence" that Kissinger
envisioned.[45] Soviet spymasters had long practice in ferreting out
science secrets, going back at least to the Manhattan Project and, in
the 1960s, having agents in place within General Electric, Sperry
Rand, DuPont, RCA, Brookhaven National Laboratory, and certainly
IBM. Détente gave the KGB astounding new scope.[46]

As with William Lee's seasoned analyses of Soviet forces and
doctrines, there was one key official who was the first to discern
what was going on, although in this instance, the conclusions were
offered in the cuttingly smooth manner of a Harvard-trained economist from Nashville. Gus Weiss became a colleague of that strange
visionary, Herman Kahn, soon after Kahn left the Rand Corporation
in 1961 to found his own think tank in a former sanitarium along
the Hudson. Weiss also taught economics at New York University
before joining the Nixon White House, where he became responsible
for exports of militarily significant technologies. Notably, this was
done under the small Council on International Economic Policy, not
within the powerful NSC staff, bloated under Nixon to hover around
140 people. He would stay in government through the Ford and
Carter years, departing only after making a pivotal contribution
under Reagan.

In late 1972 and during the following year, the arabesques of
visiting Soviet trade and cultural delegations, as well as the experience of the recent grain purchase, indicated to Weiss that there
might be an overarching KGB plan for technology theft. He met with
the chief of the Soviet/East European Division of the clandestine
service at Langley, with his staff, and with the CIA's National Intelligence Officer for Economics. One of the officers snorted at the existence of any such threat, describing infiltration of this sort as "not
usual Soviet practice," and he assured Weiss that there existed "no
evidence and no sources" of such a strategy. The national intelligence

officer for the Soviet Union and other key players would reiterate this view. Years later, after the Cold War, when Weiss had become legendary in this secret world, he would quietly write for the CIA's own *Studies in Intelligence* that "it seem[s] to have escaped these authorities that having no evidence does not mean it is not true."[47] Weiss became the first outsider to receive the Intelligence Medal of Merit.

The higher ranks of the CIA are much like the White House staff, with many contending interest groups and personal intrigues. After a particularly discouraging meeting at Langley, Weiss was contacted by Helen L. Boatner, an officer who was then a manager of the Agency's operations center and later would receive the Distinguished Intelligence Medal. On the deepest background, and saying that she could be fired for making the call, she explained a startlingly peculiar change in the itinerary of a group of Soviet scientists and technology directors. Visas had been obtained for the specific purpose of visiting the innocuous Uranus Liquid Crystal Watch Company of Mineola, New York. Three days before the group's arrival, Moscow requested an expansion of the itinerary. It was to include tours of key U.S. computer and semiconductor facilities, including those of IBM and Texas Instruments.

Although Soviet agricultural, aviation, and other delegations had been making regular visits throughout U.S. industry by 1973, Boatner agreed with Weiss that someone in Moscow had studied U.S. regulations for the newly formed joint technical commissions enough to know precisely what was allowed by the legalistic Americans. Such a last-minute change was both permitted under the rules governing friendly exchanges and timed deftly enough so that the Defense Department would be unable to object. Moreover, an entirely unscheduled Soviet scientific delegation could pop up at a major corporation, such as Amdahl in Sunnyvale, California, and, in the spirit of the time, be genially led around with questions dutifully answered. Line X was parasiting these excursions with its own experts and strongly augmenting existing sources. At this juncture, no one within the U.S. intelligence community was responsible for impeding theft in the worlds of technology and science.[48] What resulted was a Great Game on the front lines of innovation, at first played by only one side.

There might be an utter lack of official interest at Langley, but William Krieger, the astute FBI assistant director for counterintelligence, began taking the threat seriously. Thwarting technology theft, however, was not his division's core function, nor did it possess particular expertise. Around the same time, Weiss began creating an informal group of about twenty sympathizers dispersed among the executive departments and coming from the CIA, NSA, Defense Department, State Department, and Air Force. Calling themselves the American Tradecraft Society, these mid-level intelligence professionals began to collaborate on their own, conducting increasingly sophisticated blocking maneuvers. No records or files were kept. The society remained active until the end of the Cold War, and several of its members rose to the heights of responsibility.

By 1975, at least seventy-seven agents and forty-two trusted contacts were working for the KGB's Directorate T within American companies and laboratories, including defense contractors McDonnell Douglas and Westinghouse. The expensive dikes of industrial security procedures were proving amazingly porous. Extremely valuable material on reconnaissance satellites drained out of TRW, and telecommunications from Boeing, Fairchild, Grumman, Lockheed, and General Dynamics were routinely intercepted to provide Moscow with the inner details of nearly all new weapons systems. Even a nuclear warhead fusing device, which controls sequencing and height of burst, was stolen around this time — an immensely significant, unsolved, and still classified loss.[49]

Riding the wave of détente, more powerful computers were allowed to be exported to the East. Even during the 1960s, Soviet efforts to catch up with the West had depended largely on espionage, and not until 1974 was there any U.S. framework to associate computer power with Soviet military use. A few sharp officials who understood the value of civilian information technologies came to see why Moscow was so hungry for them: command and control not only of ICBMs but of anti-ballistic missiles and battle management radar (which had to pass complex data to the missile batteries) required the Soviets "to *upgrade their entire civil and military computer industry.*"[50] In the past, the Soviet military had been able to rely on rudimentary, specifically designed computers. As the amount and sophistication of its requirements increased, as in tying its dual-purpose ABMs to its radar grid, it would have to depend on a much wider base of expertise, production, and use.

That level of sophistication could come only from a thriving civilian industry indispensable to a modern society in the information age — let alone to the armed forces of a late-twentieth-century superpower. Andropov and several other astute Soviet officials recognized this; so did Weiss. He ended up chairing an official interagency study to examine what the Russians wanted to buy. His study's highly restrictive recommendations became National Security Decision Memorandum 247, "U.S. Policy on the Export of Computers to the Communist Countries," a decisive document of the Cold War, given that it circulated amid the information technology upheavals of the mid-1970s. Détente's penchant for selling ever-stronger machines would at least be restrained.[51] With no U.S. policy for confronting the still-unseen operatives of Line X, however, U.S. resistance would otherwise remain ad hoc for more than a half dozen crucial years.

Well below the level of great-power respectability, other dangers were gathering. Particularly during the Cold War's final two decades, fads characterized the discussion of nuclear issues. For a year or two, one topic or another — ICBM vulnerability, ballistic missile defense, proliferation, tactical weapons in Europe, terrorism — would benefit from a flurry of articles in *Foreign Affairs, Foreign Policy,* and *International Security* by senior officials and defense intellectuals, with accompanying conferences in pleasant places and a spate of Ford Foundation grants and Pentagon research contracts. The topics would then fall out of fashion, only to roar back a few years later.

In the early 1970s, for example, the chance of a nuclear weapon passing to criminals or political terrorists came briefly to enjoy elite attention. For ten years, the U.S. arsenal had developed extremely lightweight devices, including a shell that could be shot from a 52-pound recoilless rifle handled by a single soldier. In 1972, that weapon, the Davey Crockett, was withdrawn from Army units in part because it could not be kept sufficiently secure. Although largely ignored by government until these years, imaginative people had been writing about the prospect of nuclear explosives being used for sabotage or anonymous attack for decades. In 1939, for instance, Einstein had warned Roosevelt that a single atomic bomb could someday arrive by boat to destroy a great city and its surrounding territory. In "Top Secret," a short story from the early Cold War, the bombs being assembled by Russians right on American soil were to be delivered to various destinations precisely at the same time the next day. That would be done by the U.S. Post Office (an operational detail not yet considered science fiction).

The practical result was that shipping nuclear weapons around the country required new procedures. The atomic energy industry also began to transport fissile material more carefully, having previously relied on contractors (often in flatbed trucks) carrying shot-guns.[52] Although further discussion of nuclear terrorism essentially evaporated until after the Cold War, the Transportation Safeguards Division was established in 1975 at what would soon be named the U.S. Department of Energy. Ever since, the division's convoys have journeyed over eighty million miles without any personal injuries or more than scratches to its eighteen-wheelers. Specially built $1 million Safe Secure Trailers with bullet-proof cabs, each capable of carrying two dozen warheads and driven by an antiterrorist-trained "nuclear courier," began traveling at night with escort vehicles made to look like passenger cars. The trucks are so designed that even a crash engulfing one in fire would not damage the cargo or permit the dispersal of uranium or plutonium. Tracked by satellite, these secret concentrations of force thread the interstates like hog consignments rumbling to Chicago. Invisibility remains part of safety — in regard to the imagination as well as to the land itself.

✪

With few exceptions, such as deciding to handle computer sales case by case, the U.S. approach to strategy was surprisingly one-dimensional, with Nixon and Kissinger indifferent to economics. Kissinger would modestly admit that this had not been his "central field of study."[53] Of the more than 140 National Security Study Memoranda (choices generated for the president's consideration) prepared during the first three years of this administration, about 4 dealt with economic matters. Roger Morris, a member of the NSC staff, recalls that economic policy "enjoyed equal rank with U.S. policy in Haiti" but less than that in Peru. Another NSC staffer contends that discussing economics with Kissinger was like discussing military strategy with the Pope.[54] To the president and his national security assistant, power meant military.

The sole presidential candidate to bear down on international economics in 1968 had been Minnesota Senator Eugene McCarthy, as he competed for the Democratic nomination. Apart from balance-of-payments questions, practically no one in Washington was paying much attention to the economic implications of a world-wide, eternally unfinished, impossibly interconnected echo chamber of finance, industry, demography, and defense. A world system less constrained by the Cold War would surely have been more alert to the expanding range of possibilities.

By late 1969, America was annually producing $1 trillion worth of goods and services. The Commerce Department wanted to celebrate this milestone, but White House political advisers feared that cheering about this inconceivable number might bring attention to creeping inflation.[55] In London, *The Economist* ran a cover article titled "The Neurotic Trillionaire" because its editors were astounded at the unease of many Americans amid prosperity of this magnitude. The seers were discussing entire economies in terms of the big picture, with the illusion that whole systems could be run from the political center. Meanwhile, the economic framework hammered out in the 1940s to avert a recurrence of the 1920s and the 1930s was breaking down. The dollar did not have a chance of keeping its value. The rising cost of living that resulted largely from financing the real bombs-and-bullets war (and Nixon's easy-money policy) began to be pumped into the world economy through fixed exchange rates.

John Connally's arrival as secretary of the treasury in January 1971 at least restored the department's voice. Son of a tenant farmer, he had been president of the University of Texas student body, earned his law degree in Austin, saw combat in World War II, and was a long time adviser to that other larger-than-life Texan, Lyndon Johnson. He made his money wheeling and dealing until Kennedy appointed him secretary of the navy, where he served for eleven months before going on to win three terms as governor of Texas. Nixon thought of him as his successor.

Connally was entirely different from Nixon's first treasury secretary, a staid Mormon commercial banker from Chicago who had been appointed two years earlier with no attention whatsoever from the president. When skeptical reporters asked Connally about his qualifications for a post normally held by a banker, he quipped, "I can add." Coming in with a fresh mind — one, that is, no more than a few years out of date, given the transformations in just about every market — John Connally understood that (as in Vietnam) inescapable problems could not be handled incrementally.

Under the Bretton Woods system then in force, the dollar was the key currency by which all others were measured, and the United States was pledged to convert those dollars held by foreign governments into gold at $35 an ounce (or $150 today). Everyone knew that Fort Knox did not contain enough gold to meet U.S. obligations at such a price. Each foreign holder of U.S. dollars realized that it might precipitate a "run on the bank" by going up to the window and asking. Should the United States close this window and decide no longer to pay out in gold or to meet the established price, the dollar's value would (alarmingly) be determined by supply and demand.

In the summer of 1971, Connally thought that the United States was a victim of other countries' arbitrarily floating their currencies and leaving the Americans hanging. Because of yet another financial emergency argument, it was the British who finally asked during August for bullion to the value of $3 billion. If Washington agreed, others would almost certainly follow. If it refused, the impression would be unavoidable that the United States lacked the gold margin to maintain the dollar-centered system. In any event, it was a crisis, and not the kind that Nixon enjoyed.

In early August, the president gathered his advisers at Camp David. The dollar's convertibility must be suspended; there was no point in letting other countries stampede America and in so doing pull down the currency. Would they be upset? "So what?" asked Connally. Arthur Burns, William McChesney Martin's successor as chairman of the Federal Reserve, feared retaliation. "Let 'em," snapped Connally. "What can they do?"[56] What indeed? Not all the last twenty-five years of U.S. power were being repealed. As occurred so frequently in the use of that power, however, few of the Camp David decisions had been thought through.[57] Connally launched an overt attack on Europe and Japan, not only repudiating fixed exchange rates but adding a 10 percent surcharge on imports for good measure. This Nixon *shokku* (as the Japanese called it) was arguably the relatively greatest overnight default since Edward III broke the Florentine banking order six hundred years before. It was succeeded by the brief Smithsonian regime, which agreed to realign currencies with a new higher price for gold — truly a last-chance work of devotion to an older era, and a way to buy time for the new structure of free currencies to establish itself.

Nixon felt that one of the risks of closing the gold window was that "*Pravda* will headline this as a sign of the collapse of capitalism."[58] He was saying, in effect, that capitalism was a function of governments, not of their societies. Why should any president entertain such a strange opinion? Because the Cold War, and the "big-engineering" corporatism it fueled, had helped make that the prevailing view. This view had been trumpeted loudest by Galbraith, who happily announced that Nixon's unfortunately named New Economic Policy (a phrase originated by Lenin) of accompanying restrictions on the domestic economy could now never be lifted.

The upending of the old order from Bretton Woods to the China Strait was a dazzling electoral success in 1972, at least for Nixon. To some today, the burial of Bretton Woods looks like Atlas shrugging, the weary evasion of "an America no longer willing, and increasingly less able, to bear its burden."[59] Emotionally, this has some truth; practically, it is unconvincing. The terror of the unknown, should government take its hands off the value of its currency, proved unfounded. Robert Roosa, partner at Brown Brothers Harriman & Co. and former undersecretary of the treasury, had testified before the Senate that if the dollar were devalued, world currency markets would not open the next day. But the dollar was devalued, and panic did not sweep Japan and Western Europe. No longer was gold the foundation of modern currency and international trade. The dollar remained paramount, not just a totem carried over from an entirely different time.

The practical Mr. Roosa was articulating the general judgment of the wise and informed, but it is a sign of how deeply fragile the international economy was still perceived to be. Few recognized how a communications revolution and a vast advance in worldwide financial sophistication would strengthen free markets. Why were expectations so gloomy? In part because international economic matters were implicitly compared with the instabilities of the world military system. Still preoccupied with the Cold War, U.S. decision makers were looking wider, not deeper. More attention was paid to hostile French central banking and the price of an air base in Maastricht than to Japanese competition or the implications of flattening productivity.

Despite new wage and price controls, inflation was rising higher than at any time since the end of World War I. Eighty percent of Americans, according to Gallup, identified economic problems as the most important ones they faced. Yet public conversation was mostly about war, the Soviets, China, and even NATO, as in Kissinger's feeble designation of 1973 as "The Year of Europe." In all of Nixon's press conferences that year, there was not one question about the nation's budget. The priorities were Vietnam, followed by Watergate. Since 1947, productivity gains had averaged 3.3 percent a year. Now recession and inflation hit hard in tandem.

Thus began the second-worst bear market of the twentieth century, comparable only to the Depression's first three years.

The Japanese ascribe their own forbearance in not following the Europeans in requiring the exchange of gold for dollars to a concern for maintaining U.S. military power. They still stress their sacrifice during those days in 1971 as gold prices rose — without discussing the possibility that a more aggressive attitude would have triggered a trade war. Nor had Japan been required to revalue its currency in spite of its trade surplus.[60] Washington did not hold the Japanese to their repeated promises since the early 1960s to remove trade and investment barriers, even as their annual exports soared. The consequences were beginning to be felt throughout America. A telling insight on social change is John Updike's Harry "Rabbit" Angstrom, suddenly enriched by his Toyota dealership. One exception to the flood of Japanese goods, however, was textiles. For the good of the Republican Party in South Carolina, Nixon compelled Tokyo to accept "voluntary" quotas. The amazingly heavy-handed method chosen was to threaten to invoke the Trading with the Enemy Act passed during World War II. After sufficient upheaval, Connally, in 1973, was succeeded at Treasury by Secretary of Labor George Shultz.

At least the CIA's covert aid to the Japanese Liberal Democratic Party was dwindling. The powerful men of the LDP, tied to the vastly rich *keiretsu*, could hardly be mistaken for pathetic pensioners still needing tax dollars from the barber in Lincoln, Nebraska, or the stoker in Erie, Pennsylvania. For as much as it mattered, the CIA was by now well positioned in all of Japan's government departments. It apparently had penetrated the prime minister's office and the agriculture ministry to the extent that Langley knew Tokyo's fallback positions before any trade negotiation even began. But this was a pointless presence. Japanese officials, especially junior ones, were never particularly secretive in discussing their bargaining approaches with American counterparts. Moreover, essentially no one at the CIA spoke Japanese. Even in the early 1980s, as Japan became increasingly muscular, there were only about five officers with that capability.[61] Meanwhile, the succession of currency and oil shocks during the 1970s encouraged Japan toward even greater protectionism, aided by the quasi-corrupt political machine the United States had long nurtured.

America's economic grievance in the early 1970s, however, was more with the cost of oil than the predations of Japan. Since the

1950s, U.S. oil companies, seeking protection from foreign competition, had successfully insisted that quotas against barrels from overseas would ensure more domestic drilling, and therefore more secure supplies in the event of war. After the record-setting cold of the winter of 1969–1970, demand quickly began to outstrip supply. As the dollar kept inflating, the Shah, that faithful ally, worked to persuade his fellow oil-exporting countries in the Middle East to restrict production and raise prices. Following the lead of Colonel Qaddafi with Occidental Petroleum in Libya, the first jolting OPEC increase was set in Tehran during 1971. It lay the groundwork for the embargo and the quadrupling of prices in 1973–1974.

The Vietnam War weakened both the dollar and the standing of the country that issued it. Without the war, it is hard to imagine OPEC having found the nerve to cartelize the world's most vital commodity. The sudden courage to use embargoes and price squeezes in 1973, after thirteen years of sullen complaint, was mustered not in the conference rooms of Caracas or Tehran, but vicariously in Vietnam's jungles and paddies. Strong-arming the cartel was out of the question. Pressure from the United States, such as it was, elicited reminders that OPEC could also do business with Moscow. No one dared call the bluff.

The immediate costs of this first peacetime shortage of a critical resource were financial. Energy shortages also proved to be a terrible blow to self-confidence, which is essential in times of enormous change, and helped pave the way for additional emergency-driven spending. The Cold War did not cause the oil shocks, but OPEC's maneuvers certainly let Moscow, as the world's second-largest oil producer, raise its own prices and obtain new customers in Western Europe. The Soviet economy was thereby further granted "a stay of execution."[62]

Suddenly, all the experts, many of whom could not have found Riyadh on a map the year before, were predicting exhaustion of the world's oil supplies by 1990. Their alarms combined with Britain's determination to withdraw its small but experienced forces in the Persian Gulf. Having no intention to replace the British presence with men and money, as it had more or less been doing since 1947, Washington urged London to maintain its historic "East of Suez" protectorate arrangements for the sake of stability. "Our pleas went unheeded," remembers one NSC staffer.[63] The British insisted that they could no longer afford it; presumably, the Americans could.

Instead, the Nixon Doctrine kicked in big. Might Iran help to police the Gulf? "That, of course, was music to the Shah's ears," recalled George Ball, who had become a partner at Lehman Brothers, the New York investment bank.[64]

U.S. policy, Ball explained, came to rest upon a fantasist who had just recrowned himself in a spectacle of comic excess, which dramatized a previously indiscernible succession from the great Oriental dynasts Cyrus and Darius, and who had given himself a 2,500th anniversary pageant, with feasts and jewels provisioned from Paris. It might have been noticed, perhaps by the CIA with its longstanding ties to SAVAK (the Shah's secret police), that such a pseudo-emperor was unlikely to be the most enduring of friends — particularly in a country with a per capita income of $250 and a strict Islamic tradition. Moreover, since the appetite grows with the eating, the Shah imposed conditions before he would allow the Americans to fulfill his dreams.

First, the United States had to assist the Kurds in their revolt against his enemy, Iraq. Until 1972, these ten million or so nomadic, tribal, stiff-necked Muslims had been backed by Britain and Israel, as well as by Iran. But why should any of these countries continue their aid when the United States could step in? So from 1972 to 1975, Washington provided the Kurds with around $16 million, funneled through SAVAK, to pay for weapons — just enough to give them the illusion of full U.S. support and to allow them to fight Saddam Hussein's army to a standstill. "I trust America," declared one of their leaders. "America is too great a power to betray a small people like the Kurds."[65] Of course, once the Shah struck a deal with Saddam in 1975, that is exactly what happened.

Second, the Shah had to be able to buy U.S. weapons on an unprecedented scale. Not wanting to precipitate a regional arms race, Washington had held down its Iranian weapons sales to a mere $1.2 billion over the entire nineteen years since the Shah had been returned to his throne. The often-prescient George Ball could see it coming: giving the Shah such access to the U.S. arsenal was like handing the keys of the world's largest liquor store to a confirmed alcoholic.[66] America was abetting the megalomania that would tear Iran to pieces as the Shah started ordering $19.5 billion (nearly $80 billion today) in U.S. hardware, including the newest, most advanced plane in America's arsenal, as well as laser-guided bombs only recently available to U.S. pilots in Vietnam. The Pentagon protested that the Imperial Iranian Air Force had no conceivable use for the F-14s and that selling them to the Shah might imperil the plane's secret technologies. Instead, Nixon exempted Iran from regular U.S. procedures for evaluating foreign military sales. Nor would he abuse Iranian friendship by driving too hard a bargain on price. The immediate benefits to America appeared self-evident: "A continuing and growing supply of oil from Iran appears as certain as anything can be in an uncertain world," reported the CIA.[67]

For better or worse, at least OPEC's profits fell into the hands of Western banks. To head off a supposed asphyxiation of the world economy by the hoarding of Western buying power in oil-state vaults, the petrodollars were hastily pumped into third world loans. Seventy-five billion or so went to countries (or kleptocrats) with no particular intention of repaying them and promptly vanished. This included more than $6 billion to Indonesia before its predictable default, and some $3 billion to Zaire (or rather Mobutu's accounts in Europe) by the end of the decade. The international economic order was compromised for a dozen roller-coaster years after 1973. The ensuing disruption showed how unready America was for this new world, as petrodollars did harm in two ways: by further increasing inflation and by generating a body of global debt that has dogged international transactions from that day to this. Mexico's crash in the mid-1990s, for example, makes one wonder how and why that country was ever able to incur such vast obligations to so many U.S. banks.

☆

It says something about the American ordeal in Vietnam that one of the people who unequivocally distinguished himself was John Paul Vann, a former Army lieutenant colonel who became an insightful adviser on what was called "pacification." He had been appointed, as a civilian, in effect to command all U.S. forces in the Central Highlands. Neil Sheehan's Pulitzer Prize–winning book on Vann's life and times devotes 725 pages to the war through Tet in 1968. It tags on only 65 pages to cover the entire rest of his life, even though Vann fought in Vietnam for four more years, American involvement continued for five, and the war ground on for seven. This also was true of most of the other influential writings on the war, notably Frances FitzGerald's *Fire in the Lake*, David Halberstam's *The Best and the Brightest*, and Stanley Karnow's *Vietnam*. FitzGerald won her own Pulitzer as she looked forward to a Communist victory and "one of those sudden historical shifts, when 'individualism' and its attendant corruption gives way to the discipline of the revolutionary community."[68] As was characteristic of so many Cold War episodes, once Americans felt they had had their fill of a problem, they would set out to ignore it.

Vann is worth remembering because of his long experience on the ground and because he has been used so lucidly to explain the first half of America's experience in Vietnam. The belated pacification efforts that followed were meant to extend and deepen Saigon's presence in the towns and countryside. Vann believed by 1971 that Washington's willful optimism until 1968 had been replaced by an unnecessary despair. Improvements in South Vietnam's forces were not being considered, as the 543,400 men of the Kennedy-Johnson buildup were steadily being brought home. Most of all, he helped show that after Tet, perhaps the United States did not have to pony up the dreadful price that it had been paying: more than one-third of the U.S. Army deployed in Vietnam, American fatalities between January and June 1968 higher than during any comparable period in the Korean War or even in World War II's Pacific theater, and no end in sight. The casualty list had been sufficiently devastating for the U.S. Marines to turn to the draft and to demand (in vain) that the secretary of the navy order 40 percent of all Annapolis graduates be commissioned in the Marine Corps.

Vietnam was the most researched war in American history during the years it was fought, but it was the U.S. government through the early 1970s that was the sole sponsor and consumer of all the field studies. One of the few exceptions is a book published in 1972 by a former Army lieutenant who had returned to South Vietnam to conduct interviews for his Ph.D. thesis at Berkeley. In *War Comes to Long An*, Jeffrey Race explains how a violent social movement, led by a ruthless Communist Party, used the technique of a people's war to win and run a key southern province — and how the U.S. Army offered the worst response possible. "Although I can get thousands of dollars shot out of tubes," he quotes the province's senior U.S. military adviser as saying about his ability to call in artillery and air strikes, "it's very difficult . . . to get thousands of piasters shot out of the bank" for local development.[69] The entire rural construction budget in 1968 amounted to approximately $1 million, or just half the sum spent on artillery fire used for harassment and interdiction

(H & I). This in turn accounted for only 10 percent of all artillery rounds used and only a small fraction of the entire U.S. military effort in Long An.[70] Whereas severe limits existed on which targets could be struck in the North (where no ground combat ever occurred), American forces had too free a hand in the South, the territory they sought to protect.

In March 1968, U.S. infantrymen under the nominal command of a bottom-of-the-barrel lieutenant massacred at least 150 South Vietnamese men, women, and children at My Lai. Only in late 1969 was Seymour Hersh able to expose the abomination. The murderous lieutenant was court-martialed and sentenced to long imprisonment, although he was quickly released by Nixon. In an unrelated incident, the Army jailed the colonel commanding Fifth Special Forces — a dashing product of Exeter and West Point — for giving the order to kill a suspected "double agent" being held by his men. Nixon overrode Army demands to court-martial him. Nineteen seventy-two was the year that the secretary of the army flatly asserted that continuing the war would be a function of U.S. casualty rates and dollars.[71] It was hardly that simple. One way or another, America would be paying a moral price as well.

There is no evidence that the My Lai atrocity was repeated elsewhere, which is surprising in such a war. "The men who were at My Lai knew there were aspects out of the ordinary," according to Daniel Ellsberg. "That is why they tried to hide the event, talked about it to no one."[72] Between 1965 and 1973, in less grievous incidents, 201 soldiers and 77 marines were convicted for serious crimes against the Vietnamese. Hanoi is hardly known to have conducted similar prosecutions. The death and destruction visited by U.S. forces on civilians largely arose from murky decisions in a murky war, as in the confession of former Navy SEAL and U.S. Senator Bob Kerrey, which would make headlines thirty years later.

The gratuitous ruin that occurred was due largely to the way Westmoreland chose to fight. Westmoreland, whose clippings before Tet noted his management training at Harvard (that is, the Business School's quickie Advanced Management Program), did more damage to his country's purpose than just squandering four years of public support. His war of "search and destroy" and of attrition meant a fixation on the statistical scorecard of "body count" with insufficient regard for whether the Vietnamese bodies being counted were the enemy's. Westmoreland's deputy, Creighton Abrams, replaced him in May 1968 and immediately began to impose change. They had been in the same class at West Point, and each had graduated into the horse cavalry. But as a commander and a human being, the stocky, plainspoken Abrams was the antithesis of Westmoreland, whose methods he had been trying to redirect, if not moderate, for eighteen months. "Tactics changed within fifteen minutes," said General Frederick Weyand, the last U.S. commander in Vietnam — an acknowledgment of the dreadful practices that had gone before — though not fast enough, as the Ninth Division's notorious six-month Operation Speedy Express demonstrated in the province of Kien Hoa.[73]

"My problem is colored blue," Abrams once shouted, referring to friendly forces (including the anything-but-chivalrous South Koreans) who were customarily depicted in blue on battle maps. Backed by his own deputy, Lieutenant General Andrew Goodpaster, Abrams used persuasion and discipline to shift the war away from how it had been fought under Westmoreland. He insisted that it made no difference how many losses the enemy suffered, emphasizing civilian security over body count. He began by severely reducing the viciously random H & I artillery fire, going as far as withholding rounds for the guns.

Under Abrams, the U.S. Army would "clear and hold" territory, repelling Communist terror by protecting the villages and hamlets, rather than flailing about the deep jungle trying to hunt an elusive enemy. Counterinsurgency capabilities that had made U.S. intervention conceivable in the first place would now be used with a hard-learned effectiveness.[74] Most of all, the gross Americanization of the war that had taken place from 1963 to 1968 was being successfully undone. Once thousands of Americans were no longer vainly fighting a war of attrition, pacification began to receive the resources and support it should have had all along. For the first time, for example, South Vietnam's People's Self-Defense Force received M-16 automatic rifles to replace a hodgepodge of firearms. (Freely arming one's citizens is not a notable feature of a tyranny.) In addition, around 200,000 of Hanoi's forces switched sides during the war, many during the early 1970s — one of the details overlooked by "crisis journalism."

The often mindless U.S. destructiveness never approached the Communists' relentlessly deliberate terror. Hanoi was never going to agree to any solution other than total control of the South. So the

Nixon administration could accept the momentary sham of a "coalition government" and turn over millions of South Vietnamese who had tied their lives to the U.S. commitment, or it could keep fighting. If it kept fighting, it had to conduct what military historian Lewis Sorley calls "a better war," meaning one that would finally be pursued without dependence on attrition, U.S. forces, the phony measure of body counts, and the free-fire zones of the preceding years. As for the South Vietnamese, many of them naively held to what one of their officials later called an "investment theory": no matter what happened, it was presumed, the Americans had put too much blood, money, roads, buildings, and bases into the country ever to let it fall.[75]

Nixon, whose presence in the White House may have been due to his secret undercutting of the Johnson administration's 1968 peace talks with Hanoi, would later reflect that his worst decision as President was not to have crippled North Vietnam during his first year in office. At a minimum, this would have required intense renewed bombing of the North and a naval blockade, as would happen three years later, and probably the harsher steps against agriculture and population that McNamara today melodramatically tells Hanoi would have involved "genocide."[76] In the summer of 1969, Nixon sent a secret ultimatum to Ho Chi Minh warning that something terrible was about to happen. Ho called Nixon's bluff, and Nixon instead tried to finesse an end to the war by fruitlessly eliciting help from Moscow and Beijing. He was not prepared to ignore the already outraged Europeans, let alone to rattle the American public, whose shifts in mood might jeopardize his reelection. Here again, the steps he took were the minimum ones to avoid defeat. Whether or not the war really could have ended in 1969, as Nixon later argued, it is hard to imagine what he might have done that would have turned out worse.

The story of these final years of the Vietnam War is anything but an account of how South Vietnam's army of 1.2 million was "rendered powerless by America's departure," as dispirited officials of the Kennedy and Johnson years prefer to remember the aftermath of their own failed efforts.[77] At this point, the terrible outcome was by no means foreordained. The key to the "better war" of the latter years was the development of strong territorial forces (both regional forces and popular forces) that, in conjunction with South Vietnam's army, could effectively provide local security. For what it was worth, "Asianization" in general and "Vietnamization" in particular formed the core of Nixon's self-styled "Doctrine." For most of the war, it had been understood among U.S. civilian and military leaders that the United States would leave a residual force in South Vietnam once the war was over, as it had in Europe and in South Korea. Attempts to buy time explained the decisions that followed.

Once the United States had decided to intervene in Vietnam, the excitement of going in had overcome nearly all common sense. Now, if the U.S. role was to be restored to one of support as South Vietnam's forces improved, hitting northeastern Cambodia was one of many actions that were long overdue. Except that no one in Washington had any political or even geographic understanding of Cambodia.[78] There had been no diplomatic relations with the country for five years. What was clear, however, was that around 300,000 North Vietnamese, including four permanently based divisions, used nominally neutral Cambodian territory as a sanctuary. They could reach out into Vietnam, killing more than 1,000 Americans during Nixon's first six weeks in office, and then fade back into Cambodia. Nixon began bombing Cambodia in March 1969.

Indochina as a whole was always a single battle zone for Hanoi. Yet Cambodia's Prince Sihanouk was sufficiently emboldened to restore relations with Washington a month after the bombing started and even to ask Nixon to visit. His subjects had mostly fled the territory occupied by North Vietnam. For reasons not central to the war, and to Washington's surprise, he was deposed the next year by the government he had appointed — a pro-American regime promptly demanding that North Vietnamese troops evacuate. They instead pushed inward. The United States quickly sent an initial $40 million or so worth of equipment, mostly small arms, to Cambodia. Despite U.S. requests, no aid of any sort would come from Britain, France, the Philippines, Australia, or New Zealand. Pol Pot had built Cambodia's Communist Party, called the Khmer Rouge by the Sihanouk regime which it had been battling. When Sihanouk fell, Pol Pot was grudgingly backed by Hanoi in the interest of winning a decisive communist victory throughout Indochina.

In the spring of 1970, the United States undertook its last ground offensive. In response to articulate opinion and public clamor, the president announced the precise distance that thirty-two thousand U.S. troops would go into Cambodia (twenty miles). He also said when they would be withdrawn, and promised that they would never return. Abrams recognized this restraint as another lost opportunity. The president distractingly boasted about destroying an elusive North Vietnamese headquarters and that Cambodia represented "the Nixon Doctrine in its purest form." Significantly, Saigon's army performed impressively; the real work of building territorial forces and expanding rural security in South Vietnam could continue. The United States would spend a total of $1.85 billion, most of it on military aid, to help Cambodia's new government rid itself of the North Vietnamese, plus billions more trying to bomb shut the Ho Chi Minh Trail, a nine-thousand-mile network of jungle roads and paths that ran through Cambodia and Laos. Some people insist that the United States destabilized the country and was "largely responsible for Pol Pot's rise" — and for much of what followed. This makes as much sense, one notable participant rightly says, "as blaming the Holocaust on the British bombing of Hamburg."[79]

Perhaps the fighting of a "better war" led to its being won by 1971, although Hanoi kept attacking and would achieve total victory four years later. Whether or not South Vietnam was on its way to the long-predicted victory depended on what happened in the villages and hamlets, the real battlefield. If they could be made safe, the objective should be achieved. By 1971 the heroic will and persistence of North Vietnam's soldiers (now nearly exclusively North Vietnamese army main-force units rather than Viet Cong guerrillas) were not enough to prevent the war from going steadily against them. Long An, for example, had by then been freed from essentially any armed Communist presence. In the Mekong Delta, where 60 percent of the population lived, U.S. officials could routinely ride around South Vietnam's largest province on motorbikes, a suicidal gesture only a few years before. Despite its shabby politics, Saigon had become a safer place to live, it could be argued, than most large American cities.[80] With South Vietnam relatively stable, Hanoi wanted no part of a coalition government.

The war had been "won" to the extent that the word applies to the Cold War's other ambiguous victories — certainly to South Korea, where two U.S. divisions were still stationed twenty years after an armistice, and to Western Europe, where six U.S. divisions sat. By 1972, South Vietnamese forces were carrying the entire fight on the ground, although Hanoi's manipulations effectively exploited America's doubts. With the "people's war" thwarted and

the Viet Cong crushed — but with its army having slowly recovered — North Vietnam had no alternative to outright invasion.
Washington chose to do nothing other than "protective reaction"
air strikes during a clearly visible nine-month buildup in "off-limits"
territory right across the border in North Vietnam and Laos.

In April 1972, Hanoi's soldiers crashed south through the
Demilitarized Zone and plunged in from the west out of Cambodia.
Fighting was more intense than even during the Tet Offensive in
1968. The equivalent of twenty divisions were equipped with new
long-range artillery and antiaircraft weapons from the Soviet
Union, on which Soviet advisers had trained twenty-five thousand
men for two years. Soviet-made rockets and around five hundred
tanks gave a mailed fist to the attack, with China contributing clothing, food, ammunition, and small arms. For more than ten weeks,
South Vietnamese units held at the province capital of An Loc, only
sixty-five miles northwest of Saigon, under ten thousand incoming
rounds of artillery a day — a bombardment of an intensity never
experienced by U.S. troops. Not by coincidence, this all occurred
weeks before the SALT agreements were to be signed in Moscow.
Given the massive supplies involved, an assault of this magnitude
could not have happened without hands-on cooperation at the
highest Soviet levels.

This was a straightforward conventional invasion on multiple
axes. South Vietnam's ability to resist was a fundamental achievement — a U.S. ally (backed by U.S. air and naval power, as well
as logistics) able to stand up against a powerful army of invaders
backed by Russia and China. U.S. advisers were serving only at senior levels. The most prominent adviser, John Paul Vann, forecasted
the outcome before he was killed in a helicopter crash. "It is quite
predictable," he wrote of the North Vietnamese, "that their regular
forces will be . . . defeated and will suffer such heavy casualties and
losses of equipment as to be ineffective for the next one to two
years." Abrams told his commanders that ten times the U.S. air support would not have stopped that army had Saigon's forces been
unable to stand and fight.[81]

What had been accomplished was the distanced approach to
world problems (if there was no way to avoid them) that Americans
had yearned for since 1940. Ironically, it was in South Vietnam, not
in Europe or Korea, that the United States momentarily achieved the
self-reliant resistance it had long wanted from its allies: indigenous

soldiers buttressed by the U.S. Air Force and Navy. Better still, there was no need for U.S. nuclear weapons to be placed in South Vietnam, as they were in South Korea, in Taiwan, and in several NATO countries. By this stage, South Vietnam was a democratic partner (given the steadily improving standards of the region) with a multiparty system, its own feisty press, and a popular land-reform program.

The Saigon government had been elected more cleanly than those of at least two NATO members, let alone the government in Seoul. To be sure, its politics were drenched in corruption. But it was only the scale of corruption among South Vietnam's elites that was unique in this squalid war. There was corruption all around. Having covered the war in the 1960s, *Time* magazine's former diplomatic editor recalls that "many of the best and brightest American journalists added thousands of dollars to their paychecks" by submitting expense accounts at the official exchange rate, then paying their bills with black market currency. With Saigon condemned in the American press for corruption, this is just one insight into the hypocrisy of those tragic years.[82]

Bucked up in his belated decision by Connally, Nixon finally began hitting North Vietnam in April 1972, three and a half years after Johnson had declared a halt to the bombing. Polls showed that the U.S. public approved by wide margins. Knowing that only the severest force would bring results, American prisoners of war recall being overjoyed at the sounds of bombs falling on the outskirts of Hanoi. Major North Vietnamese ports were at long last mined, as the Joint Chiefs of Staff had been urging. Finally, the main conduits for Soviet weapons and supplies were cut off, and new laser-guided munitions blasted the land routes with unprecedented accuracy. These minimal steps were warranted because, despite Nixon's deal making in Moscow and Beijing, there is little evidence that either power tried to pressure Hanoi by even threatening to reduce its aid. As for the imminent arms control summit in Moscow, the Soviets had no reason to cancel: they had too much to gain.[83]

To an extent, Nixon and Kissinger ratcheted up the hopeless Johnson-McNamara tactic of "measured response." For Kissinger to recall the home front of 1972 as having "the character of a civil war" is rationalization for holding back.[84] A majority of the population had supported the foray into Cambodia, three out of four Americans opposed the demonstrations against the government, and even bombings of this still-limited magnitude produced minimal protest. Nixon was about to be reelected with the largest plurality in U.S. history, and only 15 percent of Americans considered the war the most important issue facing the country. Campus upheavals had wilted. Characteristically cynical, Nixon understood that, as the draft wound down, so would the political concerns of these "other heroes" and of a huge proportion of their parents, girlfriends, and vicarious admirers.

Only after the invaders were bloodied and North Vietnam itself pummeled did Hanoi stop demanding that the Saigon government be dismantled before negotiations could begin. Nixon and Kissinger scrambled to reach an agreement with Hanoi before the U.S. election. Initially, however, they failed to force South Vietnam's President Thieu to concede to having about 150,000 North Vietnamese soldiers from the Easter invasion remain within his borders, primarily in the Central Highlands, the country's least densely populated region. Their presence reflected the difficulty of defending large areas against an enemy who can decide where and when to concentrate his forces. They were a grave threat, but arguably one that could be dealt with as long as they could be kept out of the South's populated areas, as was happening. After a breakdown in U.S. negotiations with Hanoi, around-the-clock bombing resumed between December 18 and 29, 1972. There was no bombing on Christmas.

For the first time, B-52s were used over Hanoi. Again the POWs cheered, their guards suddenly becoming nervous. The North Vietnamese immediately claimed fourteen hundred civilian dead, a small albeit tragic number for the war's severest air attacks. And one undoubtedly exaggerated. Nonetheless, the West German newspaper *Die Zeit* called it "a crime against humanity," and Sweden's prime minister compared it to the Nazi death camps. The tons of bombs dropped on the North over the years were said to be more than the United States had used against Germany in World War II. Yet they caused no comparable damage. Only one side was conducting total war in Vietnam.

By the end of 1972, there were around 27,000 U.S. troops remaining in Vietnam, the last of some 2.6 million who had served there at one time or another and of the approximately 700,000 who had participated in the war from elsewhere in Southeast Asia. Six hundred and forty-one Americans were killed in action that year. Fifteen B-52s had been downed over Hanoi.

There was a lot about which Congress was not being informed, including two years' worth of Kissinger-conducted U.S.–North Vietnamese peace talks, parallel to the public peace process, also in

Paris. The secretaries of state and defense were in the dark as well. Hanoi's negotiator, Le Duc Tho, kept insisting that the United States impose a new government on Saigon. A decade behind the times, he specified that one means to this end might be for Washington to assassinate Thieu, by far the most able of Diem's successors.[85] Instead, Thieu was compelled to accept the U.S. position. The Paris peace accord that finally resulted in January 1973 was silent on the matter of Hanoi's forces in the South, not requiring a reciprocal withdrawal when all U.S. and supporting forces were removed from the country. That deal, and the ensuing communiqué in June, did not compose an actual treaty; there was nothing to place before Congress. Like the Geneva accords of 1954, it constituted a short military recess in Hanoi's long struggle. What had been bought since 1968 at a cost of an additional 20,552 American lives was a stronger South Vietnam. Ultimately, it would be the only Cold War ally left to defend itself alone.

Nor did anyone, including the Joint Chiefs, know of the promises Nixon and Kissinger made to Saigon to return to war should the settlement be breached. Far surpassing publicly acknowledged guarantees, the president conveyed these promises in a series of detailed letters. "You have my absolute assurance that if Hanoi refuses to abide by the terms of this agreement it is my intention to take swift and retaliatory action," read just one of the Kissinger-drafted letters from Nixon to Thieu.[86] At least Nixon was skeptical of any diplomatic solution. Kissinger seems to have hoped that new friends in China and Russia (co-guarantor of this ceasefire-in-place) would uphold compliance and that Hanoi might prefer U.S. financial assistance to pushing for victory. Beaming over a lasting peace, he insisted that the 150,000 troops in the South would go home once they realized they could not be reinforced.[87] Secret assurances, however, drowned in the swamps of war weariness long before Watergate reached its crisis stage. Pol Pot's Khmer Rouge in Cambodia never accepted a cease-fire. During the six months beginning in February 1973, the U.S. Air Force dropped some 250,000 tons of bombs on Communist forces there. Once Congress learned of this, it was fed up with what the defeated George McGovern called "secret wars, secretly arrived at."

The North Vietnamese simply maintained the Orwellian fiction that they had no troops whatsoever in the South. In a variation on Lenin's slogan "neither war nor peace," Hanoi immediately adopted what it called a "half-war, half-peace" strategy, which morphed into a "peace in war" approach, and finally an "attack in peace" directive by the end of 1973. One embittered U.S. official compared the ostensible settlement in Paris to "a 1938 [Munich] scrap of paper."[88] Kissinger and Le Duc Tho shared the 1973 Nobel Peace Prize for their achievement; only one of them accepted.

As the last U.S. troops departed in the early spring of 1973 and 591 POWs were finally released, a cold indignation ran through public opinion. It was comparable only to the emotions felt when prisoners had returned from North Korea twenty years earlier. Americans were angry "as never before" once they learned of tortures and murder, although other details, such as gruesome interrogations of 19 POWs by visiting Cubans during 1967–1968, would long be kept secret.[89] The months after the Paris accord, which Hanoi immediately began to violate by bringing surface-to-air missiles into the South, offered another reason to hit North Vietnam so hard that it would have been unable to conceive of supporting, let alone sending, its soldiers anywhere for years. Such retaliation could have been exacted by air. It was not. In any event, the draft was ending. Only 646 men were called up in 1973, and one Dwight Stone, an apprentice plumber from Sacramento inducted on June 30, became the last of the 4 million men conscripted since 1948. (He recalls his Army experience as worthwhile, as he went on to receive two years of college at government expense and a Veterans Administration home loan.)

As an inducement for a nervous Saigon to sign, South Vietnam had been given so many weapons and so much materiel that Abrams believed the country might choke. If the United States had thereafter done what it had pledged to do in Paris — enforce the agreement, replace the equipment on a one-for-one basis, and provide further financial support — South Vietnam might have been able to defend itself in the fashion of South Korea (while not even requiring U.S. soldiers). In June, however, Congress sealed the fate of South Vietnam's eighteen million people by deciding to deny any funds "to finance directly or indirectly combat activities by United States military forces in or over or from off the shores of North Vietnam, South Vietnam, Laos or Cambodia." The bill was debated while Brezhnev was in Washington for Nixon's second U.S.-Soviet summit, and it passed the day after he left. Never before had money for any ongoing military action been denied a president. Yet South Vietnam and Cambodia fought on for nearly two more years.

Those were the years during which the North Vietnamese Ministry of Defense admits to having sent 263,691 more soldiers south, including superbly equipped divisions and armored columns, and during which its backing of the Khmer Rouge became unrestrained. Nonetheless, elements of South Vietnam's army held fast against division-strength attacks in 1973 and division- and corps-magnitude follow-ups the next year. Repulsing an all-out invasion without U.S. money even for fuel, ammunition, and maintenance was another matter. The chief of staff of North Vietnam's People's Army recalls, "The decrease in American aid had made it impossible for Saigon troops to carry out their combat and force-development plans."[90] By the end of 1974, Hanoi's Soviet-supplied divisions had clear-cut superiority, and the chief of the Soviet General Staff, Viktor Kulikov, went to Vietnam to participate. The CIA foresaw no general offensive for the following year.

It is surprising that there was not even more desertion, graft, and fear among South Vietnam's forces. The newly elected congressional class of 1974, full of McGovern Democrats, set about terminating what little U.S. support for those forces remained. It demanded "compromise" and the dismantling of Saigon's government. Gerald Ford — protégé of Senator Arthur Vandenberg, Minority Leader of the House, successor of the disgraced Spiro Agnew as vice president in the fall of 1973, and ultimately president by default in August 1974 — summed it up this way: "U.S. unwillingness to provide adequate assistance to allies fighting for their lives" was by this time undeniable.[91]

By early 1975, Hanoi knew that it finally possessed overwhelming strength. It also knew that "the Americans would not come back even if you offered them candy," as the North Vietnamese premier told his politburo. The scale, starkness, and effectiveness of the final assault against its outgunned and outsupplied opponent can only be compared during the Cold War to North Korea's June 1950 invasion.[92] These were not little men in black pajamas. The entire North Vietnamese army was totally exposed as its trucks headed south, bumper-to-bumper, by daylight. Incredibly, France offered to mediate.

Having received no replacement equipment for two years, the South Vietnamese pleaded for money to meet the catastrophic new prices of petroleum products. Congress concluded that they had already received enough and had not spent it wisely. Congress banned the use of American-supplied Vietnamese piasters to pay for soldiers and police, even for fertilizer. As the country strangled, its minister of economic development rushed to Washington, taking with him copies of the original reassuring letters to Thieu from Nixon and Kissinger, as well as several newer ones from Ford and Kissinger. No one on the Hill or in the press cared to look. He dashed to the World Bank, from which South Vietnam (though one of its older members) had never borrowed. Bank president Robert McNamara would not entertain a loan. All he cared to talk about were breakthroughs in creating "miracle rice."[93]

The South's army, meanwhile, fought desperately in the central Vietnamese town of Xuan Loc during early April until hit by three of Hanoi's divisions. The Senate Foreign Relations Committee told Ford that there would be as much money as was needed to evacuate the roughly six thousand Americans still in Vietnam, but not a nickel for anything else. Nor were congressional leaders inclined to save many Vietnamese, although eventually visa requirements were waived, as had been done on behalf of Cuban refugees in 1960. The CIA station chief in Saigon, for his part, recommended a coup.[94]

As South Vietnam stumbled to the graveyard, a strange echo of earlier times jarred the few Americans who knew of it. Washington had felt certain enough about South Vietnam's future in 1962 to have included it among those nations to receive nuclear fuel under the Atoms for Peace nuclear energy program. A canister of plutonium and some highly enriched uranium for a research reactor in the Central Highlands had been shared at the time of McNamara's first visit. During the false desperation that followed the Tet Offensive, the plutonium had been hurriedly returned to the United States. But AEC officials were angered, charging the Pentagon, of all places, with dangerously undermining a symbolic commitment. So back the plutonium went to its reactor in the mountain city of Dalat amid intensified war. Once Hanoi's forces began closing in that final spring, two American volunteers dashed into the beset city — and took the wrong canister.[95] Somewhere in the Socialist Republic of Vietnam lurk these small quantities of the strange metal sent under John Kennedy in another era.

Also left behind in the rout was an entire warehouse overflowing with NSA's most important cryptographic machines and other supersensitive cipher materials, all in pristine condition.[96] Still classified, this incident may be the most staggering loss of intensely secret coding gear for either side during the Cold War. Undoubtedly the machines went to Moscow. Even worse, treason assured that the Soviets would, for another decade, keep having the updated U.S. crypto devices needed to stay abreast of NSA changes to its lost machines.

Agonizingly, President Ford realized there was nothing more that could be done to save South Vietnam. Many people, including the South Vietnamese, were incredulous that the world's greatest military power would just walk away after ten years and more than fifty-five thousand American dead. But Ford knew it was over; he seemed to order the war's end, although he later recalled that "Henry Kissinger had urged me to tell the American people that Congress was solely to blame for the debacle in Southeast Asia."[97] There was more than enough ignominy to go around. Remnants of South Vietnam's army continued to fight. "Why don't these people die fast?" Kissinger moaned to White House press secretary Ron Nessen. "The worst thing that could happen would be for them to linger on."[98] Saigon finally fell on April 29. In a spasm of disorganization two weeks later, it was eighteen Marines who died trying to rescue the American crew of the *Mayaguez*, who were already being released by Cambodia's Khmer Rouge. The world did not get "cut in half," as Eisenhower had feared not so long before — at least not the world beyond Indochina. But much had changed during the years in between.

At the Oscar ceremonies in Los Angeles, the audience gave a standing ovation to the producers of the vicious documentary *Hearts and Minds* when they read a telegram from Hanoi that announced the "liberation" of South Vietnam. Not only South Vietnam, but Vietnam itself then disappeared from people's view. Now the "discipline of the revolutionary community" could truly be felt. Slammed into place were variations on the familiar twentieth-century story of Soviet gulags, Nazi concentration camps, and Chinese reeducation. Feeling betrayed that all of Hanoi's talk of reconciling the nation proved to have been propaganda, one North Vietnamese colonel made the obvious comparison to Ho Chi Minh's land reform campaign in the 1950s.[99]

Nearly 2 million people were thrown upon an irritated world, beginning with the rush of 130,000 fleeing Saigon by helicopter, boat, and airplane. The liberators began "many thousands of executions" (65,000 is one respectable estimate), including those left behind after working for the CIA. Many more people simply died in confinement.[100] Then came the flood of boat people, perhaps 10 to 15 percent of whom died at sea, and the land people who fled on foot through Cambodia. The Montagnards — several hundred thousand isolated mountain tribesmen whom U.S. Special Forces had first encountered in the 1950s — had allied themselves with the Americans and (reluctantly) the South Vietnamese, also were abandoned to their fate when Saigon fell. Deep in the forests, some fought a long, fruitless rebellion. The United States began admitting them as refugees only after 1986.

When small nations and quickly forgettable peoples commit their fate to a great power, they stand to win, or more usually to lose, big. Americans were too preoccupied with their own humiliation to consider the agony of those they had promised to protect. Laos also went under in the hurricane. Its new Communist regime singled out the Hmong for slaughter and internment. In Cambodia, U.S. Marines had frantically evacuated Americans from Phnom Penh in early April as totalitarianism approached down the country roads.

Confident American experts and associated journalists explained that the Khmer Rouge were OK. Sydney Schanberg of the *New York Times* noted their "concern for the peasants" and observed that things could only be "better with the Americans gone." His colleague Anthony Lewis found "the whole bloodbath debate unreal."[101] The Khmer Rouge bureaucracy of death then devoured at least a million and a half of its own people between 1975 and 1979, starting with stoic government officials who refused to flee abroad, and with their wives and children. While economically bashing in many of their victims' heads to save bullets, the Communists nevertheless invested in keeping meticulous execution logs of the thousands of people they killed every day.

Indochina, the world's last region to be fully communized, was struck by a coven uniting the qualities of "all the little Stalins and Maos who appeared elsewhere in the world during the Cold War: Kim Il-sung, Ho Chi Minh, Pol Pot, Fidel Castro, Haile Mengistu, Babrak Kamal, and many others."[102] The twenty professional political intellectuals heading the Khmer Rouge, all of whom had studied in France, had been forthcoming about plans for "total social revolution," a grand vision of compressing what Mao had done to China over a generation into one bone-splintering surgery for the new Communist man. Given what such language had meant in China and Russia, especially when it came directly from the mouths of Leninist intellectuals, there was little reason to be surprised at what followed. Pol Pot believed that Mao had erred by not sufficiently cleaning away the old regime in China. He resolved to eliminate all vestiges of the past more successfully.

Americans still keep trying to explain their relationship to that singular catastrophe. Today, people write of Cambodia's noon of darkness as a hubristic hiccup, "a radical Maoist philosophy that quickly slid into madness," noting that "no one could imagine the devastation, the ruin, the mass killings that were about to begin."[103] But the Great Leap Forward, the Cultural Revolution, indeed the Soviet collectivization and the Great Terror had given more than enough warning. There is reason to believe that Leninist dictatorship does not portend the possibility of madness as something new, but simply raises the question of what new form the criminal lunacy will take.

Other innocents were killed by a Southeast Asian friend of America much more powerful and experienced than those just liquidated. President Ford and Henry Kissinger, by now elevated to secretary of state, visited Jakarta in December 1975 on their way back from another summit in Beijing (China's rulers not deigning to visit Washington while an official Taiwanese presence remained). The day after they left, sixteen hours after Kissinger discussed the matter with General Suharto, Indonesian forces invaded and then annexed what had been the Portuguese colony of East Timor. A green light may have been given. Still in office, Foreign Minister Adam Malik would this time concede a body count of between fifty thousand and eighty thousand Timorese civilians in just the first eighteen months of occupation.

Once back in Washington, Kissinger erupted in front of his staff: "Can't we construe [stopping] a Communist government in the middle of Indonesia as self-defense?"[104] Leave aside the facts that this Connecticut-size speck of an island, the easternmost in a chain from Asia to Australia, is remote from Indonesia's main islands and that its 600,000 mostly Roman Catholic people were seeking independence, not communism. Indonesia had broken American law by attacking with U.S.-supplied weapons. Congress was again misled. As a former CIA operations officer in Indonesia notes, Suharto might not have been able to pull off his occupation without U.S. logistical support.[105] A quarter century and $1 billion in arms sales to Indonesia later, at least one-third of the Timorese were dead as the succession of massacres continued. What happened over those years, as the United Nations would document in the late 1990s, could well be the worst slaughter in proportion to population since the Holocaust. It might also have been the easiest to prevent.

Trying to determine the mere dollar cost of the American war in Vietnam seems nearly beside the point. About $5 billion in U.S.-supplied equipment and facilities were captured with Saigon's fall. One overall tally discerns an incremental U.S. government budget cost at $128.4 billion. Other direct costs, mainly veterans benefits, are said to have added up to $304.8 billion. Costs to the economy imposed by the war, but not carried on the budget, are perhaps $70.7 billion. And indirect economic costs possibly attributable to the war, such as recession, inflation, and loss of exports, might even be $378 billion. All of this adds up to a total of $882 billion — in 1976 dollars — or several trillion today. A provocative sum to be sure, but one that pushes us to consider the full scope of the calamity.[106]

Of course the most searing cost was the 47,205 Americans dead in combat; the 10,420 who perished otherwise; the 153,312 wounded, and the 6,655 who lost at least one limb. Much would be made of chronic post-traumatic stress; one physician identified a quarter of a million veterans as sufferers.[107] Hollywood helped to exaggerate, but the coldest estimates still reflect an ocean of agony. Affirming their sacrifice, two out of three men who had served in Vietnam said they would go again even if they knew how it would turn out.[108] At least 1,564 of their comrades remained missing in action, and from there arose what was to become another burdensome legend of Vietnam: the belief by some two-thirds of Americans that the Vietnamese held on to hundreds of POWs in secret jungle prisons. By not acknowledging for twenty years that those missing in action were nearly all men who had been killed in combat, their bodies not recovered, Washington itself would help make the case for movies such as *Rambo: First Blood Part II* and paperback series such as *M.I.A. Hunter.*

The stories of abandoned fighting men infected many people's faith in the honesty of their government. There were reasons. No earnest search was made for missing Americans until the 1980s — no serious debriefing of refugees, no involvement of the military attaché's office in Bangkok, nothing. Not until 1983 would U.S. "augmentation teams" arrive in Thailand to begin collecting evidence in the refugee camps. Not until December 1983 would anyone bother talking with the French about their valuable experience in tracking soldiers missing in action in Indochina.[109] Hanoi, for its part, ignored its promise in the Paris agreement to help locate

America's dead and missing. It first wanted the United States to hand over about $3.25 billion in reconstruction aid that Nixon and Kissinger had promised in Paris, presuming the North Vietnamese complied with the peace accord.

Silly words such as *militarism* and silly numbers (100,000 veterans supposedly committing suicide by 1988) have flourished since the war. The *Harvard Guide to Contemporary American Writing*, for instance, reflects on the fighting in Vietnam, as well as in Korea, and then absurdly concludes that "American casualties in both wars together far exceeded World War II figures."[110] Hundreds of tales of assorted war crimes have been falsely conveyed by self-styled "veterans" and echoed by the press for more than a quarter century. *The Wall Within*, a 1988 CBS documentary with its make-believe confessions of butchery, and the shameful CNN/*Time* magazine story in 1998 accusing U.S. soldiers of using nerve gas against their own are only two of the more easily refutable.

The original memorial to Americans lost in Vietnam was finally dug into the Mall in 1981 and dedicated the following year. There is no inscription, just the names. Did the price that these men paid in fact "buy time" for anti-Communist forces elsewhere in Southeast Asia and the Pacific to escape totalitarianism? No one can know. What is known is that the Stalinist reality that descended on Indochina was every bit as evil as had long been predicted.

As the greatest single Cold War outlay of lives and money, Vietnam has become the most painful episode of these years in the memories of many Americans. Some of us still regard it with shame and guilt; others view it with pride as one terribly lost battle. The war marked a defining passage for America — from a power perhaps too ready to seek control without thinking into one unprepared even to contemplate the range of disorder that still afflicted the world.

☆

A truly Old World cynicism leached into American life during the middle part of the Cold War: a dripping corruption, ranging from the politicization of the nation's most somber commitments to the knowledge that all over the world money from AID, the World Bank, and the UN was being shipped to Zurich; to public belief that elected officials were allowing secret agencies to run rampant at home. The country, as George Ball argued, seemed to have "thrown away one of our great assets" — a certain purity of intent, the city-on-the-hill quality handed down from the early Republic — by trying to fight communism on its own terms and on its chosen terrain in the gutter.[111] Inevitably, dishonest assertions of "national security" penetrated into the Oval Office, adding to the many betrayals.

Americans of the Depression and World War II generation took it for granted that part of the business of the CIA overseas was to shake filthy hands and that the FBI probably routinely felt obliged to violate the Constitution at home. Before the 1970s, the wailings of eccentric malcontents like intelligence colonel L. Fletcher Prouty, who wrote of such unbelievable behavior as mid-level government workers in the Northern Virginia suburbs concocting poisons, could be dismissed as cranky.[112] But perhaps they should not have been. What the press and Congress brought before the country between 1974 and 1976, however, was a blend of farce and viciousness, as if P. G. Wodehouse had been forced to write a serial for *Soldier of Fortune* magazine.

Of course, there were significant differences between what the United States was doing in the shadows and what its enemies were up to. Most informed people took something like John Le Carré's views of the great powers' back-alley treacheries. While offering no favorable impression of the Western intelligence services, his novels showed the men on the other side to be dangerously different from the rest of us by another order of turpitude. For artistic reasons, he might have found it interesting to portray the Soviet Union as the more wronged of the two. But he could not write fiction he found believable if he presented the Soviets as anything but callously frantic for power. Similarly, Ross Thomas, suspicious of U.S. institutions including the CIA, makes clear in his own fiction that the business of the West is to keep faith with some level of decency that the other side cannot feel. Without excusing the Soviets, he nonetheless shows, as in *The Cold War Swap,* that there were plenty of people on our side who would have been equally comfortable working behind the Iron Curtain.

Decades of Cold War and the growing sense of secret government offered more than enough material to resupply "the paranoid style in American politics." It was finally becoming public, for instance, that the federal budget invisibly included a barely answerable entity the size of a major corporation.

Nixon insisted that he heard nothing from the Agency that he had not read three days earlier in the *New York Times.* When, for instance, television news announced around noon on November

22, 1971, that India had attacked Pakistan, the White House was unable to get any confirmation of that fact from any part of the U.S. intelligence network for the rest of the day.[113] Nixon concluded that the $5 billion going into intelligence was essentially useless and wanted it cut across the board by 25 percent. Believing that no country had ever spent more and gotten less for its overall defense, he also wanted Pentagon personnel cut by 5 percent, AEC personnel slashed (incongruously to let "the scientists go back to MIT [to] steal documents") by 25 percent, and the nondefense agencies axed by 10 percent. "This is the pleasantest morning I've had in years," he said to his budget director.[114]

He did entertain a sour admiration for the well-bred Ivy League sorts who until then had shaped the CIA. The last of the "daring amateurs" were in their fading years, although — gratingly to the president — several of them were still in charge at Langley. By the 1970s, even their sons (and daughters), whom the Agency has always preferred to employ, began to find that the CIA had become a troubled place. "Oh, running agents in Africa," one of Kermit Roosevelt's boys airily replied in the mid-1970s when I asked what he had done between graduating from Harvard and entering business with his father, who was by then brokering deals with Iran.

To be sure, creative people were still making their lives in the Agency, such as Dr. Lansing Bennett, who was shot by a terrorist outside CIA headquarters in 1993 and whose duty it had been to perform long-range health assessments on foreign leaders. But the CIA was no longer passing the "ambition test" in the quality of its people, meaning that gifted individuals now rarely considered such a calling, let alone stayed in should they try it. With some impressive exceptions, there were generally two types in the clandestine service of that time: the weary, sunken-eyed, chain-smokers who spoke (only in the outside parking lots or cautiously at the Joshua Tree restaurant, later Charley's Place) of how dirty it all was, of people being hanged "over there" for the work they themselves had lured such unfortunates into; and the chirpy bureaucrats in ties and short-sleeved shirts relishing the sheer fun of it all, "the chance to travel."[115]

Not only second-generation slump was affecting the CIA. It had been performing a slow mutilation on itself, more painful than any sanctions Congress would ever inflict, due to the paranoia of a man too ideally adapted to the Cold War — its own James Jesus Angleton, since 1954 head of counterintelligence. Except for

J. Edgar Hoover (dead in 1972 after forty eight years running the FBI), no one in the U.S. government had held the same senior position for so long. Angleton could have been invented by Le Carré: Yale class of '41, where he had founded the poetry magazine *Furioso;* Harvard Law School; a friend of Ezra Pound, for whom he took the cover photo for *Selected Cantos;* the young orchestrator of OSS operations in Italy; and a meticulous hobbyist who cultivated orchids, tied flies, and crafted gold jewelry.

By the 1970s, distorted traitors were leaping at him from every corner of his hall of mirrors. His friend Kim Philby had betrayed him once; never would he be deceived again — except, as always happens to obsessives, by himself. Respectable careers withered under his cross-eyed alertness as he sat in a darkened office — a single table lamp failing to dispel the gloom, stacks of folders on his desk. Tall and thin, he looked like an impeccably tailored T. S. Eliot. He would invite the occasional favored, highly cleared visitor to receive "The Briefing," a dizzying full-hour lecture. It was the world turned inside out by a demented genius.

KGB cadets in Moscow would be taught how Angleton had come to exemplify Lenin's theory that fervid, high-ranking anti-Communists would inevitably do more harm than good to their own cause. "He was our best asset," lectured one gray-haired colonel, explaining how Angleton had demoralized the Agency beyond Andropov's wildest dreams and how he had ruined counterintelligence to the extent that the Agency would end up having to pay compensation for his capricious firings.[116] To make matters worse, Angleton had unwittingly deterred unknown numbers of defectors by his imprisonment of Yuri Nosenko, whose fate was apparent to all within the KGB. For the CIA to believe that Nosenko's plea for asylum was a sham also revealed to Moscow that the KGB itself had not been penetrated. Had Angleton done more harm than good? To answer this question, once he was pushed from office, the Agency undertook a six-year study in a vaultlike room that contained an even more secure inner vault. The public will never see the eleven volumes that resulted.

Discrediting of security and counterintelligence by self-parody was opening the door a little further to tragedy. For instance, after leaving Burma, the undistinguished Carleton Ames had ended up in Washington as an analyst doing busywork on Angleton's increasingly distended counterintelligence staff. His equally undistinguished son, Aldrich, had begun working for the CIA as a clerk-typist in 1962 after dropping out of college and eventually joined the Career Trainee program in 1967. Nearly twenty years later, Aldrich would begin causing more damage than even Angleton could have conceived.

The Agency's internal troubles did not inhibit its worldwide reach, including proprietorship of an airline and a string of bases from Arizona to Thailand. Its real mystique was an apparent omnipresence, no country seeming too far or too small for its attention. Did Che Guevara descend on Bolivia in 1967 to win peasant support for Fidel by promising planned terror?[117] The Agency was there before him, and he did not live long. Less dramatically, Radio Free Europe and Radio Liberty were also backed by the Agency until the 1970s, by which time this fact became public, to no one's great surprise. Despite public impressions, covert activities never claimed more than half of the CIA's budget, and that only at the height of the Vietnam War. How well all the money was being spent was another matter, as Chile came to exemplify in the 1970s.

The charming, hard-living cardiologist Salvador Allende was a more disturbing presence than Che Guevara, because he had a serious following in a significant country. Despite Kennedy's and Johnson's attempts to undercut Allende, he was once again the left's presidential candidate in 1970.

Neither the CIA, the State Department, nor the Pentagon saw U.S. interests threatened. Yet the Nixon White House impulsively disbursed several hundred thousand dollars, channeled through the CIA, for "spoiling operations." Another part of its plan was to incite Chile's military into a coup, which caused even the CIA officer in charge to pause, given Chile's fully functioning democratic tradition. The Agency proceeded to grossly mishandle its preelection mischief and was shocked when Allende emerged as the first democratically elected Marxist head of state anywhere. Nixon and Kissinger feared a Castro-style dictatorship and worked, as Kissinger recalls, "to preserve democracy in Chile."[118] It was Kissinger who chaired what was then known as the 40 Committee, the secret interagency group responsible for supervising U.S. covert action.

Skirting the State and Defense departments and reporting only to the national security assistant, CIA director Richard Helms was then famously ordered to "make [Chile's] economy scream." He in turn instructed his station chief in Santiago to do anything "your imagination can conjure which will permit you to press forward toward our [deleted] objective."[119] This was Operation Chaos. From November 1970 until the September 1973 coup that put General

Augusto Pinochet in power, the CIA used $8 million more (about $27 million today) against Allende. Warning that it would boomerang like the Bay of Pigs, the astute U.S. ambassador in Santiago ordered CIA and military officers in his embassy to stop their plotting. With the still-classified approval of an undisclosed "interagency committee" driven by Kissinger, the CIA nonetheless supplied the money, machine guns, and tear gas grenades for a plot that ended up killing the constitutionally minded commander of Chile's army. Thirty-five thousand dollars were then paid to the people who shot him, and the weapons were returned. The U.S. ambassador, whom Kissinger tried to blame as a "Democratic appointee," justified his own mild opposition to Allende by seeing himself as a "fiduciary" for the money that had already been invested in Chile under President Kennedy's Alliance for Progress.[120] Whether or not the Agency had a direct hand in the coup, Pinochet hardly needed encouragement from its "street case officers" with their so-so Spanish. Nixon and Kissinger kept denying any U.S. involvement.

Surrounded by Cuban advisers, Allende had been doing enough damage to himself. His nationalization schemes isolated Chile from world trade, and he found himself squeezed between his party's Leninist wing and an outraged middle class. Nixon hoped to make matters worse by flooding world markets with copper to force down the price of Chile's main resource. The World Bank approved not a single loan to Chile, and Allende finally perished as the military took over the presidential palace. He ended up, like John Brown, being more trouble dead than he likely would have been alive. It looked as if Washington had a mirror image of the Brezhnev Doctrine.

The Soviets (always shrewder the farther they were from home) had seen how Washington could be made to work against itself, and despite Allende's warm relations with the KGB, they refused to bail him out of the economic breakdown he had inflicted on his country. Had he been allowed to serve out his term, his Socialist-Communist coalition would likely have been swept away in 1976 — in so doing making once-prosperous Chile a worldwide example of Marxism in practice. Patience on the part of Washington might also have resulted in less violence and just as much prosperity as Chile would enjoy under Pinochet. Yet these were not times for taking chances.

Pinochet's security services instead began killing at least 3,197 leftists, a spree that did not catch up with him until his arrest twenty-five years later in London on human rights charges. (At least 100 police were also killed during this crackdown.) Two young

Americans who applauded Allende, a filmmaker and a writer, were put to death early on, their fate dramatized — and U.S. complicity strongly implied — in the 1982 movie *Missing*. Washington would not press for prosecution of the killers until 2000. In 2001, the FBI finally received subpoena powers to examine Kissinger's sealed personal papers in the Library of Congress. The Bureau was finally investigating ties between the highest U.S. authorities and the Chilean intelligence operatives who, soon after the coup, blew up the exiled Chilean opposition leader, along with an American assistant, in the middle of Washington, D.C. At the time, the FBI had tried tracking down dissident Chileans in the United States, as requested by Pinochet's new regime, and may have fingered one of those two Americans in Santiago on whom it had a dossier. Such undiscriminating cooperation with foreign enforcement agencies had become routine.

Ten years after being founded, John Kennedy's Office of Public Safety (OPS) had schooled in the United States about 10,700 policemen from 77 countries, placed around 400 advisers abroad in 52 countries, and had spent roughly $1.6 billion (in today's dollars), much of it in Latin America.[121] By 1973, when the Costa-Gravas movie *State of Siege* brought before the public the murder of OPS official Daniel Mitrione by Uruguayan guerrillas, it had also become routine in Latin America for the United States to be identified with almost every act of police oppression. Through such movies, many Americans with no particular interest in these events were introduced to a harshly muddled history of their country's foreign policies, although based on a disturbing amount of fact.

Beyond all the "global nips and tucks," some truly imaginative technical work could be found at Langley, including the satellite reconnaissance programs. One of the Cold War's classic swords-to-plowshares stories, as well as one of the CIA's most expensive creations, is that of how the Agency in the early 1970s commissioned the extremely complex, 618-foot *Glomar Explorer*. This was a ship built to lift surreptitiously an entire Soviet submarine — larger than a football field and containing three nuclear missiles, communications codebooks, and the remains of seventy men — from a three-mile-deep ocean grave. The eccentric billionaire Howard Hughes provided the cover for an estimated outlay of $300 million (more than $1 billion today) to employ six thousand people to create a vessel supposed to scour manganese nodules from the Pacific floor. Part of the Soviet sub was raised in 1974. The technological feat chilled the Russians.

When the mission was over, the head of the Directorate of Science and Technology, Carl Duckett, held a reception at headquarters for the families of people who had labored on this venture. He said it had been a failure. But who really knew? Thereafter, the *Glomar* was mothballed until the late 1990s, when Texaco and Chevron were permitted to spend about $250 million to convert it to an oil drilling vessel. The audacious effort would be recalled in 2001 when the United States demanded that China return a downed Navy surveillance plane. If the plane represented a sovereign extension of U.S. authority, as Washington insisted, what about America's own Cold War escapades? Hadn't a CIA director once acknowledged that, given the traditional sovereignty accorded sunken warships, raising that submarine constituted theft?

Other such operations that required secret budgets during these years were not as ambitious as the *Glomar*, or as messy as Chile. Most seem to have been routine spy-vs-spy games or expensive hobbies. Starting in the 1970s, for example, the Agency began spending what would add up to $20 million on developing a presumptive psychic ability called remote viewing. Part of its work was to commission a report as to whether government-employed psychics could describe unseen objects — such as the location of Soviet missiles or North Korean tunnels under the Demilitarized Zone — with greater accuracy than might be explained by chance. Langley, as well as the Defense Intelligence Agency, felt compelled to take such techniques seriously: weren't the Soviets supposed to be betting on them? In the words of the chairman of the Clinical Psychology Department of the Uniformed Services University of the Health Sciences, "people were talking about an ESP gap."[122]

There was a wackiness to the manipulations of these years, whether at Langley or in the West Wing. Intrigue, after all, was the Nixon administration's hallmark. Kissinger fit right in. For example, it was a time of so many deceits, large and small, that the chairman of the Joint Chiefs of Staff felt compelled to infiltrate a spy into the NSC staff — a Navy yeoman who would make copies of sensitive documents not intended for the Chiefs, then have them smuggled across the Potomac. As defense secretary, Melvin Laird was using the National Security Agency to intercept Kissinger's concealed back-channel communications with China and Moscow, as well as to read North Vietnamese reports of what he called Kissinger's "sniveling" in the secret Paris negotiations.[123] Kissinger, whose own phone was tapped by the attorney general, helped expand White House wiretapping, recalling that he did so to assist the peace process. He had also persuaded Nixon to try stemming Daniel Ellsberg's mammoth leak of the Pentagon Papers (taken from a vault at the Rand Corporation) to the *New York Times*. Such publishing of state secrets, Kissinger has explained, might have made Beijing conclude that "our government was too unsteady, too harassed, and too insecure to be a useful partner" — as if the Republic had to prune its liberties to justify itself to Asian tyrants. Moreover, the *New York Times*, as he insisted directly to Mao, had long had "a vested interest in American defeats."[124]

Domestic skulduggery is even harder to keep secret than derring-do overseas. FBI abuses under Cointelpro — "counter-intelligence probe" shortened, as Hoover had explained, "for economy" — also became public during these years. The still-unsolved burglary of an FBI field office yielded stolen files showing that during the previous decade, the Bureau had lavished $300,000 on 1,000 or so informers connected with the 2,500-member Socialist Workers Party. This Trotskyite sect characteristically mixed acumen and aberration. It had been practicing Harvard Business School enterprise at its sharpest by giving the Bureau 7,000 party documents in return, while letting 10,000 more be photographed in 173 break-ins and yapping through 36,000 man-days of wiretapping and bugging. Even in 1975, General Accounting Office audits would show a fifth of all FBI resources still going to the struggle against a pathetically burned-out radical left.[125]

Such foolishness will thrive when efforts continue for so long. During a war, the tension, artifice, and license end after three, four, or perhaps five years. In the Cold War, they were able to drift on for decades, less acutely examined but usually better funded, more fully staffed, and increasingly weird. A telling passage in *Eighteen Acres Under Glass* by Robert Gray, secretary to the cabinet under Eisenhower, describes a beam of light falling on the polished, room-long table during a meeting. One official had learned at a security briefing that certain light rays could function as sound carriers, so the Secret Service is sent pounding off to check the beam's source, which of course proves to be the sun. Such hypersensitivity to "security" can be funny for a few thousand readers of a political memoir, but when millions of suspicions are loose, a happy ending is unlikely.

By the 1970s, once-unattainable high- and low-tech security capabilities were seeping into the larger culture. Even the white-shoe law firms of which novelist Louis Auchincloss writes were (discreetly, of course) coming to retain their own G. Gordon Liddys. Document shredding became routine and a cottage industry of its own. Had a ruthless businessman at the beginning of the century, such as John D. Rockefeller, thought to have his underlings perform wiretaps or sieve garbage, he would undoubtedly have done so. But it is usually risky for private corporations to be the first to develop expertise of this sort. Apparently, such practices first had to ooze out of Washington, and before long, the spiral of private initiative and reaction surfaced in Main Street's specialty electronics shops.

Not only were certain characters shaped by the excitements of the Cold War; certain otherwise unacceptable temperaments become specially valued, even at the top of government. Such an atmosphere was required to enable someone like former FBI agent Liddy, the man who held his hand in a flame to demonstrate his will, to work at one remove from the president. Can Liddy, an intelligent person without any semblance of judgment, be imagined two steps from the elbow of Coolidge or Herbert Hoover or indeed Eisenhower? It would have been difficult for Grover Cleveland even to find someone like that.

Most of the other Watergate burglars had CIA ties — certainly career officer and spy novelist E. Howard Hunt, as well as the Cuban operatives. For some reason, Nixon expected the Agency's help in the cover-up. As he said on the famous "smoking gun" tape of June 23, 1972, "we have protected Helms from one hell of a lot of things." Unfortunately, he did not specify, although Helms had been a key follower of Robert Kennedy's lead in the Castro assassination plots. There was a labyrinth of secret tunneling that seemed to reach out from American government, and people were coming to believe that it was undermining their own house, darkening their sense of how they were ruled. Paranoid suspicions of what else these "things" and their descendants might include today bounce among the websites.

At the heart of Watergate lay a combustible mixture of Cold War politics and Nixonian paranoia. The president rails on the tapes of crushing the Council on Foreign Relations, about White House "hanky-panky" being vital to national security, and about tying the Watergate burglary to the Agency's Bay of Pigs fiasco. Even his dismissal of the first Watergate special prosecutor was necessary, said his press secretary, because Archibald Cox had pressed "for further confrontation at a time of serious world crisis," during the October 1973 Arab-Israeli war.[126] Accounts of a White House floundering in scandal, then joyfully reborn by that war with its accompanying U.S. nuclear alert, are much more cautionary about the dangers of trying to turn private desperation into public urgency than is any tale of a "third-rate robbery."

It came naturally to Nixon, the international dreamer, to invoke "national security" as his enemies closed in: this explanation was the dignified exercise and excuse of power. It might also be argued, if one remembers South Vietnam, that in the enthusiasm to ruin Nixon, Congress and the press cast aside considerations of principled defense. Willy Borowy, a character in Ward Just's *Echo House*, has the notion that Nixon is "Washington's Jew." He says, "If only they get rid of Nixon, Washington will be sound once again." But the times had gone beyond scapegoating. Gerald Ford made an unconvincing exorcist. After being sworn in as president, he would pronounce, "Our long national nightmare is over" — except that the nightmare was not the burglary and its cover-up; it was the overall destruction of trust.

Ross Thomas's novel *If You Can't Be Good*, set in Washington just before Nixon's fall, is pervaded by the sense that anything could happen. James Schlesinger, who had succeeded Melvin Laird as secretary of defense in the late summer of 1973, says that he was prepared in those final days for an attempt at something like a military coup, even claiming to have prohibited troop movements around Washington that he had not personally approved. It sounded like Chile.

The standard recurring hysterias were amplified in "an age of anxiety" by the impression that there must be worse secrets than Watergate. And, of course, there were — older secrets, such as nuclear testing on unsuspecting citizens and White House ties to assassination. The suspicious unanimity of the Warren Commission fell ever more in doubt as rumor filtered out of "Murder Inc. in the Caribbean." Ford hoped to deflect congressional investigations of the CIA and FBI (arising from press reports on Chile, Cointelpro, and all that surrounded Watergate) by establishing the Commission on

CIA Activities Within the United States under former New York governor Nelson Rockefeller, whom he had appointed vice president. "Intelligence oversight" on the Hill had been an oxymoron nearly from the start. At this juncture, the accumulating scandals made the CIA ripe for attack and even more so for fantasy. Not to be overshadowed by the White House, the Senate set up its own investigating committee, deploying 135 mostly young staffers and $750,000. Eager to participate as well, the House also began investigating.

The type of documentation that started to appear in 1975 may not have been surprising to the already cynical, but the quantity of embarrassments was astounding. Public exposure tended to confirm what people had feared: the standard combinations of sordidness and incompetence that come together in the dark. Ross Thomas, for instance, began another novel by playing off the apparently true story of a CIA team trying to attach its polygraph equipment to the electric system of a Singapore hotel and blowing it out.

The CIA director at the time was the subdued, scholarly appearing William Colby — World War II resistance hero in France; head of the Phoenix Program, which had identified Viet Cong for death and (mostly) capture; responsible for conducting the political side of the Vietnam War; devout Catholic. He had made it to the top nearly two years earlier, soon after Helms had been packed off as ambassador to Iran.[127] Colby had then begun moving to oust Angleton. In this wilderness of mirrors, the head of counterintelligence himself had finally come to be suspected of treason, although there was already reason enough to fire him for recklessness.

Colby is best remembered for making public some of the CIA's worst secrets, even though some others, such as CIA payoffs in Japan, were successfully concealed. The reasons he disclosed so much to Congress, and seemingly to anyone else who asked, remain puzzling. The most persuasive explanation may be this: if the Agency was to endure, it had to share responsibility for its predicament, not just take it.[128] With the old interrogator's knowledge that one is at greatest advantage with people when they are terrified or relaxed, he packaged some of the most horrific high-level transactions and their presidential complicity, then ensured that they were broached with President Ford in the disarmingly wholesome surroundings of Vail during Christmas, 1974.

The new president inadvertently found himself locked into the amorality of what had been done by his predecessors in the Oval

Office. Ford had been somewhat of an Agency insider in the hands-off Congress of earlier days, instrumental in having slipped money through the Navy budget from his seat on the Appropriations Committee.[129] He had also been a member of the Warren Commission and had at the time declared himself dissatisfied with its investigation of foreign connections. Now he faced nasty ramifications, as senators on the first day of hearings displayed a silent, electrically powered poison-dart gun, made by the Pentagon but dutifully sent over from Langley, where it was called the "Nondiscernable Micro-bionoculator." Three million dollars, the Agency confessed, had been spent over the past eighteen years to develop poisons. Some had resulted in that LSD-induced death of a CIA officer in the early 1950s. President Ford apologized to the family, the government paid them $750,000, and the details remained hidden.

The even less disciplined House investigative committee zeroed in on the CIA's secret budget, trying to revive authority over how "*all* public money," as mandated by the Constitution, was being spent, not "*some* public money," as the committee chairman acidly reminded Colby. The committee discovered that the Agency had been escaping General Accounting Office audits for a dozen years. The CIA was, as one member concluded, "an open spigot without accountability."[130] Sensationally, the three parallel investigations turned up several inconclusive documents of the attempted murders of the Congo's Lumumba and Cuba's Castro. McGeorge Bundy artfully skirted perjury on the subject by quickly amending his testimony to the Rockefeller Commission: "There is no doubt that Bundy lied to me," recalls the commission's executive director. McNamara claimed total amnesia, insisting that his "memory of those years is very bad."[131]

In early 1976, George Bush, former congressman and recent U.S. representative in Beijing, replaced Colby as CIA director, with Colby disappearing into the background before the ceremony was over. The next day's *Washington Post* described the event as "an ending that would have done justice to George Smiley . . . understated and not without its ironies."[132] Perhaps the self-aware Smiley, with his sadly wise perspective, would have known that little was going to change. "When all is said and done," scoffed Helms after the investigations' fleeting drama, "what did [they] achieve?" He was right, to an extent, as he reflected on the nation's hypocrisy. "We like things to be done," he added, "but we don't want to have the blood on our hands."[133] No one, however, asked him who "we" might be and what "things," exactly, Americans should be pleased about.

In true Cold War fashion, Congress preferred to scrutinize events that lent themselves best to publicity. It did not address CIA shortcomings in analysis or specific intelligence failures, such as concluding that the chances for war in the Middle East were remote a day before it erupted in 1973 or that the prospect of a nuclear test was far-fetched a month before India's first detonation in 1974. Knowing how to defend itself, the CIA increased the number of attorneys in its Office of General Counsel from two in 1974 to sixty-five by the end of the Cold War, and it added more than a dozen lobbyists to deal with the Hill.

The CIA benefited from patriotic sympathy after the 1976 machine-gun slaying of Athens station chief Richard Welch. He received a hero's burial at Arlington National Cemetery, and his alma mater, Harvard, named a fellowship in his honor. Welch's identity had been revealed by Fifth Estate, an outfit founded by Norman Mailer, author of the swollen, demagogic *Armies of the Night: History as a Novel/The Novel as History*, about the 1967 march on the Pentagon. Mailer and friends were now dedicated to exposing the Agency's officers and activities. The country had had enough of that sort of irresponsibility, too.

One worthwhile result of the hearings was Ford's executive order in 1976 banning assassination. Curiously, nearly all the plotting had occurred between late 1960 and November 1963, with none of the targets ever being suspected of sponsoring violence against the United States or its citizens. As renewed in 1981, the prohibition states that "no person employed by or acting on behalf of the United States shall engage in, or conspire to engage in, assassination."[134] However, Congress never adopted the ban, it is not enforceable by criminal law, it can be revoked or suspended by any president at any time, and it remains ambiguous about what constitutes assassination — significant details when the practice was not only revisited after the Cold War, but essentially reversed after September 2001.

What the *New York Times* called "the year of intelligence" — roughly the eighteen months covered by the investigations — was characteristically Cold War: brief hyperdrama, emotionally intense, user of national energy, then back to hidden, increasingly expensive business not altogether different from usual. Congress's recommitment to oversight meant a modest tug on the reins for the CIA and FBI. Helms was fined $2,000 for how he had incompletely explained operations in Chile to Congress. New guidelines cut the Bureau's domestic security investigations during six months in 1976 from 4,868 to 626, then half a dozen years later to 32. The Senate and then the House set up separate, permanent intelligence oversight committees. Yet CIA officers responsible for all sorts of wrongdoing, including performing drug tests on unknowing Americans from 1955 to 1966 and assembling a database of around 1.5 million potentially "subversive" fellow citizens, blamelessly served out their careers.

The Senate finally released six thick volumes of reports. From this disgorgement on, the CIA would rarely be given the benefit of the doubt by increasingly skeptical Americans, as it often did little to inspire renewed confidence. Meanwhile, entire livelihoods would continue into the twenty-first century, wrapped in the comfortable employment of cataloging, maintaining, defending, and (following the 1974 Freedom of Information Act) slowly declassifying secrets. These were secrets collected not only by the CIA and FBI but also by other government organizations, which kept storing vast categories of material deemed incommunicable to the public until proven otherwise.

In a characteristically good-natured insight on the dilemma of secrecy in a free society, President Ford remarked that he would be glad to share the nation's deepest confidences with 214 million Americans — if no further exposure would occur. Should any such openness ever become possible, it would have two results: Americans would be uninterested in the pointless paperwork that the bureaucracy deems classified; and they would have no inclination to keep paying for any but a fraction of the secret activities once they knew how useless most of them are. Until well into 2001, counter-terrorism was by no means an exception.

✪

Looking back, it is painful to think how differently America might have approached its bicentennial without all the Cold War weight it had been carrying for thirty years — including the promise snuffed out with the ninety thousand American lives claimed by the Pacific Rim since 1950. Absorbed with a narrow definition of national security and how to obtain it, Nixon and Kissinger added to the burden by trying to rearrange an old order of "power balances" and "equilibrium" amid short-term accommodations. They were at home in the Cold War. They were not the men to discern how the world was changing. Their apparently clever approaches to Moscow and Beijing quickly proved to be more of the same. This was no time to think of doing business so ebulliently with China or to chase negotiations with Moscow that combined the complexities of chess with the verifiability of poker.

Strategy is the longer-term deployment of resources. The hallmarks of mastering it are far more likely to be clarity and predictability over great distances of time, geography, and institutional complexity than they are to be day-to-day elaborations on television. The excitements of 1970s *Grosse Politik* distracted the great practical American nation from the fundamentals and left it with a headache when the dream processes with Russia and China evaporated at decade's end. No one, after all, was able to "manage" primitive dependents such as Iran and Saudi Arabia. It was silly to think of "managing" the Communist giants.

There were farsighted men in the nation's service during these years who had neither a fondness for the limelight nor time for intrigue, ones also perhaps better informed than the national security cohort on the matters with which they dealt: George Shultz, previously dean of the business school at the University of Chicago; California entrepreneur David Packard as deputy secretary of defense; the somber Herbert Stein, heading the Council of Economic Advisers; the courtly industrialist and lawyer Kenneth Rush as ambassador to Bonn. There were many other men, and a few women, who similarly owed their public prominence to Richard Nixon's unusual ability to identify talent of various kinds. Yet this was a time when steady, quiet accomplishments were easily pushed aside by "national security" — a term soon revealed as a rhetorical device to conceal activities that were at best ineffective.

Until the 1970s, the whole patriotic, optimistic, bipartisan, victory-forged establishment was still generally united in support of internationalism, military strength, and ever-higher government spending. The habit of victory needs the repeated fact of victory to refresh it, however, and this was hard to find in that anticlimactic decade. Its absence rusted the confidence of so few years before. The growing list of disappointments was being justified ever less convincingly. "Covert action should not be confused with missionary work," Kissinger instructed Congress in 1976 when explaining America's tactical callousness as the Kurds died abandoned and alone, the chief policymaker for this affair even refusing them emergency food and medical aid. The remark was one display of "geopolitics" Kissinger later regretted. Yet he went on to insist that, during these years, there were no alternatives to such necessities that included placating the Shah, abetting dictatorship in Chile, indulging Indonesia's generals, or adjusting throughout to the Soviets. But, of course, there were.

George Meany, head of the AFL-CIO, asked at the time whether détente (which he concluded to be "a fraud") did not expose Nixon as "an opportunist without deep beliefs or large ideals."[135] To Nixon, almost any concern was about tactics and short-term gain. His dealings with Moscow had nothing more to do with anticommunism than his regulatory and price control policies had to do with conservatism. Both the unmourned Chiang Kai-shek and the bemused Democrats had one experience in common during these years: a president turning against his long-declared beliefs.

Americans rarely idealize their government, although they occasionally celebrate a president. The course in applied patriotism that had been going on since the beginning of World War II was long overdue for correction. When this came in the 1970s, the correction was reinforced by a despair that went so deep because it was based on so deep a disillusion. Faith in their leaders — not just in the policies but also in the principles to which the nation had committed itself before the world — was waning.

The most valuable potential players were regularly turning away from the Great Game. With the rise in professional salaries, there was even less incentive to spend time in Washington, except for well-placed appointees who could launch themselves into more lucrative careers. By the mid-1970s, "public service" — the nobility of devoting one's life to it having been extolled in Senate hearings by no less a practitioner than Nixon's self-identified "chief executioner" H. R. Haldeman — was losing its glitter for the truly ambitious and its challenge for the dedicated. Americans from now on would widely assume that people who went into government did so for the wrong reasons. Military service was the exception.

Young men would still be called on to make sacrifices. British military historian John Keegan remarked after the Cold War that he did not understand how the American aversion to casualties had come about. "It didn't used to be the case," he observed, taking the tone of a seasoned European as opposed to an emotional Yank. "The American Army took terrible casualties during the Second World

War, and it was the price you paid for fighting Hitler. The British and French are much more bloody-minded. If you join the army, you can get killed, can't you? The [British] public doesn't really buy it in the way the Americans do. It's more: 'poor chap, dreadful for the family,' isn't it? But then you go on."[136]

There are reasons, however, Americans came to "buy it" in the first post–Cold War decade. Many were a result of skepticism toward the boundless demands of "national security," decade after decade, not to mention decades of assuming outsize burdens to protect the British and French. Moreover, only twenty years before the Soviet collapse, the United States had endured the longest war in its history since the Revolution. Britain and France had not fought an outright war lasting more than ten days in a generation and had never watched their kids reduced to bloody heaving rags on television.

In the summer of 1949, George Marshall reflected about World War II. One of the most important lessons he had learned was the fact that a democracy "could not indulge in a seven years' war" — precisely the duration of the American combat experience from 1965 through 1972.[137] Today, no one knows how a closely informed modern democracy would respond to the casualty list of Alamein or Guadalcanal. Or how the United States will endure in a new type of open-ended war.

9

In the Hollow of the Wave

(1975–1981)

If I'm not for myself, who is?
But if I'm for myself only, what am I?

Rabbi Akiba, circa 1200

The confidence of Americans in their economic and military strength was corroding. As the world drew closer together through trade and technology, they sought to pull back politically. It appeared as if the country had run through three hundred years of quasi-European experience in thirty: the flag had been taken boldly forth, encounters in Asia and Africa were found drainingly dangerous, and the weary nation wanted to cut its losses and come home fast.

The intellectual patrons of the age were not called from the profound (such as French political philosopher Raymond Aron) or even from the profoundly perverse (such as Jean-Paul Sartre or Marxist Herbert Marcuse). Instead, they were obscurely experienced novelists, among them John Le Carré and Graham Greene, who wrote their intricate stories in shades of gray. During the late 1970s, an Argentine military dictatorship, with backing from the Soviets, nearly came to blows with a U.S.-aided Chilean military dictatorship backed by China — a contretemps finally resolved by a Polish pope. In Indochina, America looked to be supporting Pol Pot against an invasion by Hanoi, which then found itself both attacked by China and stuck in a ten-year quagmire in Cambodia, where it lost fifty-five thousand soldiers of its own. Such combinations were odder than just the strange bedfellows of politics and would not have been believable if presented as fiction.

For the Kremlin, everything was, as usual, tactical. Soviet leaders had been content to pursue their ends through racist parties in the colonial world and were as happy working through right-wing barracks as with Marxist cells. Sadly, much was being seen in no more than a tactical light by Washington as well. At the same time, many influential Americans were blaming their own country for much of what was wrong in the world, specifically giving it at least half the guilt for the arms race. Early-1970s illusions of entente, détente, equilibrium, and power balances (curious objectives in so fluid a world) were followed by well-meant preaching about human rights — helpful, to be sure, but also the traditional substitution of "moral leadership" sloganeering for power and purpose.

During the Russian quarter century between the end of Khrushchev's brief international thaw in 1960 and glasnost's onset in the late 1980s, the bloody Stalin era was officially not mentioned. A similar silence descended on the West during the 1970s. Many people seemed to have forgotten what terror Stalinist Russia had so recently aroused, and were oblivious to the trembling caused by Brezhnev's regime even in hardened Maoist China. A substantial part of the American elite had come to assume that these plain truths could be presented only with dishonest intent.

"We want to be number one once more," was the plaintive summary of the public mood around the time of the bicentennial, "but we want to attain that goal with a measure of caution and without the excess of commitment that resulted in Vietnam."[1] This was a difficult path to follow for an impatient democracy, and it would become an expensive one, because Moscow mistakenly assumed that accommodationist U.S. officials and pundits were long-term predictors of America's behavior.

Following upon the illusory successes of the first half of the 1970s, this chapter initially focuses on deteriorating U.S.-Soviet relations — specifically, on how the "arms control process" was dragging out the struggle, while not making it any safer. Second, it looks at the new Soviet adventures in the third world and how U.S. responses were palsied by dread of "another Vietnam." Throughout, there were anxieties about overseas oil supplies, which, in the usual Cold War fashion, opened entire new lines of spending in the name of "energy security." Meanwhile, the complicated dealings with allies, the blundering of the intelligence agencies, and the ongoing diversion of talent kept adding to the burden.

Jimmy Carter echoed the good sense of Democrats such as George Ball and Thomas Finletter when he said, within months of being elected president in November 1976, that America had lost something once it "fought fire with fire," including being too eager "to embrace any dictator" thought to oppose communism. Yet he described the Vietnam War as an example of "moral poverty," and his first official act was to pardon, en masse, all those who had been or could be charged with draft evasion. He spoke of an "inordinate fear of Communism" as he urged further cuts in defense, then let it be known toward the end of his term that SAC would "deny Soviet war aims" by specifically targeting these apparently not-too-threatening people directly in their command centers. He tried to constrain U.S. weapons sales but ended up approving the largest deal ever.[2] He vowed not to "ass-kiss [the Chinese] the way Nixon and Kissinger did," then normalized relations with the mainland, sold advanced technology to Beijing, and barely mentioned human rights. He ordered the first comprehensive study of U.S. technology flows to the Soviet Union but only distantly addressed the immensity of KGB theft.[3] It is not surprising that when rearmament finally did come at decade's end, it came as a shock.

✪

Creighton Abrams tried to repair the spiritual and material damage that Vietnam had wreaked on the U.S. Army. It had been "destroyed as a fighting force" in Europe by drug use and demoralization, according to his classmate General Bruce Palmer.[4] After Abrams had again replaced William Westmoreland, this time in the summer of 1972 as Army chief of staff, he had made changes as abrupt as those he had imposed in Vietnam. Seven major Army headquarters around the world were done away with, saving millions of dollars and thousands of personnel. He had inherited a black Cadillac limousine, then symbolically replaced it with a Chevelle from the Pentagon motor pool.

"We have paid, and paid, and paid again in blood and sacrifice for our unpreparedness," Abrams repeated in looking back on World War II, Korea, and Vietnam, "we've paid because we wouldn't prepare to fight."[5] Before he died in office in 1974, he had been able to redesign the Army in a way that would make it nearly impossible to go to war without involving a much broader segment of Americans in the military reserves — a reasoned response to what had occurred in Southeast Asia. However, repair was slow and did not fit with the official temper of the times. The post-Vietnam Army was the smallest in numbers since before Korea, and the Navy's reenlistment rate was the lowest in memory. Even in 1980, Chief of Staff Edward C. Meyer would still warn of America's "hollow army," unconsciously echoing George Marshall's description of the senior service back in 1947.

By 1975, the Soviet Union's transformation from a continental to a global power was obvious. People spoke about the "legitimacy" of the Soviet regime (meaning that it had grimly endured until so many of those who might have remembered its founding were dead) and of its undeniable defense concerns. There was a desperate eagerness in the 1970s to negotiate and to be statesmanlike before the cameras. Driven by wishful thinking, Moscow had reason to presume that the United States was no longer competing for influence. As one astute State Department analyst concluded, the country was "reaping the costs of our prior extravagance" in having expended "enormous public relations efforts" to oversell détente.[6]

During the two months following North Vietnam's victory, Defense Secretary James Schlesinger had ordered U.S. commanders to "tighten up everything," even scrutinizing the 38th Parallel that divided the two Koreas as well as other lands for signs of attack.[7] He feared that what the Soviets called the "correlation of forces" could suddenly become infinitely worse and dreaded what he labeled "simultaneous" or "geographic slippage." This vision of a self-reinforcing momentum of defeat combined the domino theory with what today some call "contagion" — the idea that if one country's economy is permitted to implode, an uncontrollable chain of failures may be set off around the world. In mid-1975, it was not far-fetched to think that a rout in Korea might detonate even more war in Asia at the same time that Soviet pressure on the border with Turkey increased, or that disaster might cascade through all of Eurasia and perhaps across the oceans, until the whole Western defense structure yielded to a kind of institutional chaos theory.

Portugal, NATO's least appealing founding member, was poised to leave the alliance. The CIA had failed to predict the previous year's overthrow of that country's clerical-fascist regime. The new governing group included some Communists, who prepared for a takeover by a months-long campaign of assaults on press freedom comparable to those that had accompanied Castro's advance to absolutism fifteen years before. In Portugal, there was a classic Communist boring from within. U.S. officials said it resembled that in Czechoslovakia in 1948 and seemed all too likely to succeed just as totally. Kissinger suddenly appeared "almost paranoid," spouting academically defiant talk of fomenting, once Portugal was surely lost, an independence movement in the Canary Islands and Azores. At least that step might let the United States keep operating the Lajes Air Base, a way station that had proved vital for resupplying Israel in 1973 when nearly every other NATO ally prohibited U.S. overflights.

On November 25, the Stalinist boss of Portugal's Communist Party made his move, using leftist paratroopers. But strategic aid in deutschemarks and services (such as phones and copying equipment) had been arriving through anti-Communist West German political foundations.[8] Acting on his own, the zestful U.S. ambassador, Frank Carlucci, helped disperse the relief through a newly emancipated Portuguese body politic, which was prepared to save itself given the remotest encouragement.

While Kissinger — who, from 1973 to 1975, had for the first time united the posts of secretary of state and national security assistant — was consumed by the drama of the moment, such as overreacting to the situation in Portugal, Schlesinger was more anxious about the wider range of Soviet initiative. He understood the radical differentness of the men on the other side, occasionally quoting William Yandell Elliott, with whom he and Kissinger had both studied at Harvard, on the historic "line of cleavage" between political systems based on compulsion and those allowing for the vagaries of individuals and small groups. Defense policy in the Ford administration (and into that of Jimmy Carter) was being shaped less on the merits of the arguments than by clashes of personality — in contrast, say, to how issues of trade or taxation were addressed. Surprisingly diffident, Schlesinger did not play this game remotely as well as Kissinger. One reason was that in his role at the Pentagon, he was the retrograde bringer of bad news, cast against Foggy Bottom's promises of reconciliation and further world-changing settlements with Moscow.

Schlesinger — serious economist, Rand analyst, professor at the University of Virginia — was an easy target because he refused to share fully the alarm he felt about the intensity of the Soviet challenge. No leaks to sympathetic reporters of secret information about Soviet missile construction. No briefings to congressmen on Cuban exploits in Central America. No long, intimate talks with powerful journalists. He would not up the ante against Kissinger. "I don't have the stature to go to people like Reston. People like Paul Nitze can do that, I can't," he told his aide Scott Thompson, referring to Thompson's formidable father-in-law.[9]

Schlesinger had also been chairman of the Atomic Energy Commission and, briefly, director of Central Intelligence, where he had started dropping the deadwood from the Directorate of Operations (known until 1973 as the Directorate of Plans, and throughout as the Clandestine Service). But he was infected by Washington's ghastliest disease of judgment. A rumpled, white-haired, pipe-smoking forty-five-year-old who was most enthusiastic when watching birds, he knew that he lacked star quality. He sold short both his message and his clear public responsibilities. In a capital where personal jockeying had come to count more than ever for so dangerously much, Schlesinger's low impression of himself — ill concealed behind its consequent bluster — buried his intellect and subverted his mission.

In November 1975, he was replaced by a more confident player, one not prone to such brooding. "You can be provocative by being belligerent," summed up forty-two-year-old Donald Rumsfeld, former Navy pilot, congressman, and White House chief of staff under Ford. "You could also be provocative by being too weak and thereby enticing others into adventures they would otherwise avoid."[10] He was amused by Kissinger's machinations, such as excluding Defense Department officials and the uniformed military from strategy sessions concerning U.S. proposals for a SALT II treaty. Rumsfeld skillfully made the case for higher defense spending, cruise missiles (a staple in today's arsenal), and new bombers and ships. He also cautioned against Kissinger's enthusiasm for coaxing another arms control deal out of Brezhnev. During Ford's final fourteen months, however, he was opposing both the conventional wisdom and a combative Democratic-controlled Congress seeking to slash the Pentagon's budget.

The previous year, when *The Gulag Archipelago* was published in the West, Aleksandr Solzhenitsyn was promptly exiled from the Soviet Union. In early December, he argued in the press that the

United States had given up. He had come face-to-face with the official timidity of this era, as the State Department and NSC staff had
kept him off the Voice of America so as not to offend Moscow, and
as President Ford's schedule was suddenly too heavy to receive him
at the White House. Perceptive as Solzhenitsyn was about Russia, his
conclusion that the quivering fatalism of the time went straight to
the core of America showed that he never understood this country.

Other men with access to the audiences that Schlesinger hesitated to address, and with conclusions less fatalistic than Solzhenitsyn's, were equally alarmed. In the first weeks after Solzhenitsyn so
publicly conveyed his gloom, Nitze published an unsettling essay in
Foreign Affairs. Using research from Boeing, he demonstrated that
Moscow's new generation of heavy-payload missiles might well give
the Soviet Union a "theoretical war-winning capability."[11] Whether
or not a possible capacity to destroy most of America's ICBMs in a
first strike might encourage greater Soviet willingness to take risks, at
least the denials about Moscow's likely intentions were increasingly
being challenged. This was partly because the Politburo was finding
it hard to contain itself, in everything from missile building to third
world adventurism. Nitze's concerns, of course, were augmented by
Boeing, Northrop, and other contractors. That was no more than the
usual Cold War mixture of self-interest, habit, and experience, but
with some alarming new facts whipped into the mixture.

Views of Soviet military matters had never been so polarized,
and critics were openly questioning the CIA's own interpretations.
In early 1976, President Ford's Foreign Intelligence Advisory Board
recommended that a consciously contrary "Team B" should review
U.S. intelligence assessments. Chaired by retired Admiral George
Anderson, the board urged that the outsiders be given access to the
same highly classified raw materials available to the Agency. The
most influential of the three committees in this exercise, the one
that became synonymous with Team B, was led by Richard Pipes,
Baird Professor of History at Harvard, and included Nitze. Approximately $500,000 was designated for this unprecedented effort — a
small sum that would have seminal consequences. Team B was not
necessarily "worst-casing," but its members pictured an alternative
that jarred Langley, the whole arms control establishment, and certainly Congress.

Scholars such as Pipes — together with historian Oscar Handlin,
Sovietologist Adam Ulam, and a few others on the faculty — repre-

sented a different element at Harvard than the one of equally learned men who had committed so much of their time to the Arms Control and Disarmament Agency (ACDA), to SALT, or to justifying détente in *International Security* and other journals of record. Those on the faculty with a more sanguine view of U.S.-Soviet relations were appalled by CIA director George Bush's disclosure of the existence of such a "team" and particularly by the appointment of Professor Pipes.[12] Once staffed and assembled, Team B set out to produce a parallel draft of the annual assessment of Soviet offensive missile power formulated by the Agency's analysts (Team A). When the drafts were exchanged in November, Langley's conclusions could not withstand reasoned contradiction. The decade-long interpretations of Soviet nuclear capability and objectives were revealed as acts of ever more obstinate faith. "It was like putting Walt Whitman High against the Redskins," observed one CIA official.[13]

By the time the CIA submitted its own penultimate draft assessment of Soviet behavior to the White House a month later, it had conceded all essential points on Soviet nuclear war strategy to its harshest critics. Of course, some face-saving was necessary, and Bush loyally claimed that Agency analysts had come to these sudden and seismic changes of mind on their own.[14] Whatever the reason, National Intelligence Estimates declassified from then through the early 1980s began appraising Soviet intentions through even more hawkish glasses than Team B's.

Such a competitive exercise remains unique in the experience of any nation's intelligence service. To be sure, Team B's alternative National Intelligence Estimate contained its own mistakes, including exaggerating the mission and the production run of the Soviet Backfire bomber and misconstruing at least one type of Soviet "directed-energy" weapon (lasers and particle beams). However, Russian sources now show that the Team B analysts were fundamentally correct on all the key issues: the accuracy of MIRV-equipped Soviet missiles; the scope of Soviet civil defense, including the existence of entire underground cities, as in Sevastopol; the ABM treaty violations; and, certainly, the emerging Soviet capability to wipe out U.S. ICBMs in a first strike.[15] Indeed, sometimes Team B underestimated. A study of this sort was healthy and long overdue. The costs involved did not lie in the duplication of the original CIA efforts or in the chagrin of professional analysts, but in the inability to systematize such reality checks. The CIA proceeded to take almost every legal step to avoid any repetition, a poor show of confidence in its own advice.[16]

Soon after entering office in January 1977, Jimmy Carter abolished the Foreign Intelligence Advisory Board, a useful expert panel from the Eisenhower era, which would promptly be revived after Carter's departure and maintained by every president thereafter. Part of Carter's purpose was to stigmatize the fear of communism as "inordinate." A competent nuclear engineer, he knew enough to be frightened of the thermonuclear demon. However, the man who set aside time to draw up the White House tennis schedules believed devoutly that the fitting response to the Politburo was to get it to understand truly and exactly Washington's eagerness for compromise. His campaign manager and consequent chief of staff, Hamilton Jordan, had said that victory at the polls would mean failure if such usual suspects as Cyrus Vance and Columbia University professor Zbigniew Brzezinski became secretary of state and national security assistant — which they did, to an accompanying pavane of back channels and rivalry that replicated that of William Rogers and Henry Kissinger.

Brzezinski had earned his doctorate at McGill University, taught for several years at Harvard, and then expanded his belief that the Prague Spring of 1968 was the beginning of the end for the Soviet Union. He was among those astute critics of détente, often Democrats, who concluded that Nixon and Ford had been out-traded in almost every instance by the Russians. Specifically, he was uncomfortable with what he regarded as Kissinger's static view of the world.[17] With the exception of Brzezinski and a few other senior appointees, this well-meaning administration was drawn from the same familiar faces out to do business as usual with Moscow — men yearning to "break through" at one more summit, concerned that one more honest effort would at least get the Soviet Union to "understand." But the Soviet Union understood, or thought it did, already — and very differently.

The Carter administration toiled for an arms treaty, although it was too often guided by the assumption, in the words of Secretary Vance, that "Leonid Brezhnev is a man who shares our dreams and aspirations." This insight illuminated only the dreams and aspirations of Vance and his decent friends. Much of the growing opposition to arms control negotiations during the 1970s had little to do with the significance of one or another number of warheads, the range of such and such a Soviet bomber, or even the vulnerability of Minuteman missiles. It arose from amazement at the behavior of many of the U.S. officials who were cutting the deals, including Vance's predecessor, who had commiserated with Brezhnev that American critics of SALT were mostly "dishonest people."[18]

Arms control presumed that money could be saved and the world made safer through treaties. The irony, however, was that arms control actually required more money and weapons in order to gain a strong negotiating hand. Writing checks was seen as valuable for its own sake; cuts might otherwise send the "wrong signals" to Moscow.

All the major fault lines of nuclear calamity were creaking. The flight testing of the surprisingly accurate SS-18 during 1973–1975 had appalled U.S. negotiators. Paul Warnke, Clark Clifford's law partner when not acting as President Carter's new director of ACDA, spoke of the "dishonesty" of the Soviets building such an instrument and lamented over how this missile "broke the spirit of SALT."[19] Above all, it was the combination of accuracy and warhead megatonnage that put U.S. ICBMs at risk from a first strike, not just the possible number of warheads that might be crammed atop one of these behemoths.

The CIA had concluded that the Soviet Union could not achieve so accurate a missile within ten years. It also had grossly underestimated the Soviet nuclear stockpile. Whereas U.S. intelligence estimates would not go above 30,000, we now know that Russia possessed 45,000 to 60,000 bombs and warheads. Nor could the Agency bring itself to admit, despite warnings from Pentagon analysts, that the Soviet Union was going so far in its post–World War III planning as to be producing plutonium deep underground in three reactors buried beneath a mountain some 25 miles north of Krasnoyarsk. The diversion of water from the Yenisey River, which emerged from the mountain radiating heat in winter, showed something was happening — but surely not that.[20] The expensive steps of accumulating warheads and of hardening processing facilities should have been further indications that the Kremlin expected the next world war (and its aftermath) to be something very different from what U.S. arms control negotiators conceived. It would be fought (and won) over days or weeks, rather than suffered in a single, mutually suicidal spasm.

Intelligence projections of what Soviet missile forces *might* have looked like in the absence of SALT would prove unconvincing.

Moscow, after all, had its answer to "How much is enough?" "Enough" could be achieved by mounting about 10,000 warheads on its ICBMs, about 90 percent of which were dedicated to destroying Minuteman missiles in their silos, as well as other hard targets. Preemption did not require the 20,000 to 25,000 warheads that the National Intelligence Estimates were "worst-casing" in a world without arms control. There was never any evidence that Soviet planners would use their heavy-payload missiles to create such a shower of multiple warheads.[21]

By this time, Soviet factories were busy spitting out an average of five fighter planes, eight tanks, eight artillery pieces, and at least one ICBM every day.[22] Meanwhile, the Soviets kept casually circumventing the ABM treaty, commonly seen as the hallmark of SALT.[23] Moreover, the ability of their divisions to blitz into Western Europe remained daunting. "Enough" for the Politburo also meant immense efforts to protect scores of thousands of the party elite: a 217-mile-long second subway system deep under Moscow's famous metro, huge concrete bunkers, underground shelters as deep as two thousand feet, and much more. It also included detailed preparations to recover from nuclear war. The United States never went a fraction of this distance.

Of course, the United States also kept improving its nuclear forces, as well as repairing its conventional ones. A third stage was put on five hundred Minuteman ICBMs, increasingly accurate SLBMs arrived with ten to fourteen warheads each, B-52s were rebuilt, an entirely new Soviet-size ICBM (the MX) began being developed, and war plans de-emphasized civilian targets to focus on military ones. But U.S. construction did not approach the Soviet surge.

Less than two years into the administration, Carter's secretary of defense, Harold Brown (who had returned to government from his presidency at Caltech), explained the consequences: "[I]f the present trends continue, the situation five years down the road could be a serious one." Some observers thought it already looked plenty serious. Brown himself laid out the realities of an arms race in which only one side was racing: "When we build weapons, they build; when we stop, they nevertheless continue to build."[24] A half dozen years of negotiation was proving to have ratified, rather than restrained, Moscow's expanding forces across the broadest of fronts. There is no evidence that U.S. restraint persuaded the Soviets to forgo any developments they pleased.

An abiding faith in arms control nonetheless ran deep in the

Carter White House and the post-Watergate Congress. There had been some modest accomplishments since SALT I, including the Threshold Test Ban Treaty of 1974 and the Peaceful Nuclear Explosions Treaty of 1977. Enthusiasts, however, wanted much more.

Right after the election, Vance continued the early-1970s tradition and tried for another ambitious strategic arms deal that might somehow simultaneously save money, reduce Soviet arsenals, and make the world safer. He rushed to Moscow, presenting a grand vision whose problem was that it presumed the Soviet Union was not out for unilateral advantage. Many of the defense intellectuals who had embraced arms control also reached for ways to rationalize further efflorescences of Soviet ICBMs, as well as of the ground warfare and airlift capabilities that imparted new offensive capacities to any conventional option and that, therefore, would force a nuclear response on the West. They strove to justify whole new classes of vessels which also made the Soviet Union (a Eurasian landmass, still lacking all but a few noncontiguous clients) a world naval power. Perhaps Moscow was only reacting. If so, it was reacting to weakness, not strength.

Some people explained the buildup's magnitude as simply reflecting Russia's old-fashioned view of international relations. Or perhaps the Politburo was a victim of its own "bureaucratic politics," succumbing to the defense industry which was the force driving Soviet modernization. Or maybe the Soviets really were entitled to such versatility because they had to police Eastern Europe, deter China, face Western Europe's two nuclear powers, and balance the United States. Such opinions were close to the mainstream of these years' rationalizations, as serious students of the subject kept citing reassuring Soviet statements eschewing any notion of advantage in nuclear war.[25] To stem U.S. provocation, officials on ACDA's Social Impact Staff spoke seriously about trying to impose "arms control impact statements" on the Pentagon. Such provisions, were they introduced, would follow Washington's new model of "environmental impact statements" and would have to be reviewed by regulators before the services would be allowed to acquire new weapons.[26] America was strong and rich enough to indulge in such willful self-preoccupation for a little while longer.

Arms control also meant more than the control of nuclear weapons. Until 1969, when Nixon directed a unilateral halt, the United States had had a highly secret "black biology" program for germ warfare. In 1972, the year of SALT I, the United States, the

Soviet Union, and more than 70 other countries signed the Biological Weapons Convention, which barred the possession of deadly biological agents except for such purposes as vaccine research. Almost immediately, in 1973, the Soviet Union set about defying it. Biopreparat, the pseudocivilian pharmaceutical agency, was established that year to provide cover. In 1979, Yuri Kalinin, an army engineer from the Soviet chemical weapons directorate, took over (and still remains in charge). Biopreparat became an empire of forty laboratories and production facilities producing the world's most horrendous stockpile of bacteria and viruses. The biological war machine reached its heyday in the twenty years *after* the treaty, employing some thirty-two thousand people, as well as another ten thousand in the Defense Ministry. The Soviets were stockpiling hundreds of tons of anthrax, as well as dozens of tons of smallpox and plague microorganisms, which could be loaded into bombs and missiles for use within days. No other country has ever had anything like it, and none of this would be known until after the Cold War.

This could not be happening, insisted U.S. experts on the subject, just as technology was not being stolen or the ABM treaty being violated. Surely bioweapons could have no strategic value for the Soviet Union. And yet, somehow inevitably, it was the Soviet Union that was struck by the severest outbreak of anthrax ever recorded, arising from a germ laboratory in Sverdlovsk, as the once-and-future Yekaterinburg was then named, during 1979. Until communism's collapse, the Kremlin indignantly maintained that the disease originated from contaminated meat. So did many Western experts who were invested in the current practices of arms control. Nor was the city's party boss, Boris N. Yeltsin, about to speak out.

A curious cross section of skeptical and increasingly influential Americans, however, kept alert to the ways of Stalin's successors. They were Republicans, Democrats, Social Democrats, conservative Catholics, Jewish neoconservatives, union leaders, and industrialists. In November 1976, a critical mass of them formed a lobbying organization, the Committee on the Present Danger, taking the name, in a true Cold War recycling, of a pro-defense ginger group of the early 1950s. Its founders contributed $10,000 each to urge more military spending and to warn that the Soviet buildup was, in part, "reminiscent of Nazi Germany's rearmament in the 1930s."[27] The committee included top officials from every administration since Roosevelt's: Paul Nitze and Chip Bohlen, the latter of whom insisted that the Soviets should still be seen as Bolsheviks; former congresswoman and ambassador Clare Boothe Luce; Dean Rusk and Maxwell Taylor; Yale Law School's Eugene V. Rostow (brother of LBJ's national security adviser, Walt Whitman Rostow) and Henry Fowler, who had been undersecretary of state and treasury secretary, respectively, in the Johnson administration; recent Chief of Naval Operations Elmo Zumwalt; Herbert Stein, James Schlesinger, David Packard, and George Shultz. They were joined by Harvard's Pipes, Handlin, and Ulam, along with other academics; by the fiercely anti-Communist leadership of the AFL-CIO, including its new president, Lane Kirkland; and by a collection of intellectuals previously on the left, such as Norman Podhoretz, Irving Kristol, and Saul Bellow.

The chief of the Social Impact Staff, which was part of ACDA during the Carter years, today dismisses this unusual concentration of talent as "all white middle-aged males . . . most relatively wealthy" — an illuminating technique of discredit.[28] One reason that the clout of this unofficial body, unknown to the general public, would be more enduring than any previous or more famous public policy group, was that Ronald Reagan soon became a charter member.

Reagan's intuitions were already taking him along different paths and lines of sight from those of even such distinguished realists. He had narrowly lost the 1976 Republican nomination to Ford, whom Carter had then squeaked past. Soon after the inauguration, Reagan began positioning himself for 1980, traveling with several aides to Western Europe in 1978 to discuss foreign policy. But Europe was not ready to play. In Britain, Margaret Thatcher, leader of the opposition, was the only senior politician who wanted to see him. He was otherwise condescended to by the pompous foreign secretary. A journalist was prompted to ask Reagan the setup question: what would his "Soviet policy" be. The answer was immediate and matter-of-fact: "Very simple. We win. They lose." This was a total vision whose implications virtually no one dared to examine, let alone articulate, during these years of riots, Watergate, OPEC, and the fall of Saigon, when the whole postwar order seemed to be shaking dangerously.

During the summer of 1977, the divisiveness and sterility of argument that characterized most discussion of the nation's defense was made evident at the annual Aspen Arms Control Seminar.

Aspen was one of many arms control forums, and by no means the most lavish, then benefiting from Ford Foundation funding. Since 1966, McGeorge Bundy had been the foundation's president. Robert McNamara soon joined as a trustee. Paying generously for defense intellectuals to advance arms control became a key priority, with the Ford Foundation disbursing $4,270,028 just in 1977. That was in addition to the $6.1 million that had already been handed out over the previous half dozen years, mostly for research and advocacy by a small group at Harvard. Over $35 million more would be spent in the next decade to put arms control on a systematic footing with permanent centers at a number of universities and research organizations — a total of around $132 million in today's dollars. The Ford money was distributed by the sister of Harvard's president, who had a Ph.D. in defense studies from MIT. Ford's grants, moreover, ran on a curious roller coaster: a 50 percent decrease one year, a 3,300 percent increase the next, then a 25 percent drop, and so on.[29] Like almost everything else in the Cold War, the process was arbitrary and personal. Henry Ford II saw fit to resign from the board of the foundation, letting it be known that he was unhappy with what he deemed a drift to the left.

That summer at Aspen, leading theorists from Cambridge, senior executives from the national weapons laboratories, and Carter administration and Ford Foundation officials confronted the familiar issues of deterrence, the power of nations, and the balance of terror. Paul Nitze, with his discordant views on these matters, also attended. He had initially not been invited, but since he owned much of the Aspen Skiing Company at that time, there was little alternative. I served as rapporteur. Teaching at MIT since serving in the Kennedy and Johnson administrations, and about to return to ACDA as an adviser, the same expert who had been ready to terminate China's weapons scientists spoke passionately for a wider embrace of arms control. Everyone's arguments provided a case study of the mixture of zeal and hubris in high places that is so often the prelude to disaster. Significantly, no one from the armed forces was included in that or most similar conclaves.

With nearly a psychoanalytic faith in the efficacy of talk, Aspen consumed days of fruitless argument, endless speculations about Soviet intentions and capabilities. The topic of the moment was Minuteman vulnerability to Soviet ICBMs. Harvard's Thomas Schelling offered a cogent insight: the United States was not factor-

ing into its threat assessments the appalling technical and managerial problems that Moscow would face in making any practical use
of its raw strategic power. By ignoring them in general debate,
Schelling sensibly concluded, the admittedly real dangers of the
terrible new Soviet capabilities were being vastly magnified.

He was correct, even without knowing the extent of the Soviet
failings that would be exposed after the Cold War. U.S. policymakers,
for their part, were steadily losing touch with these facts of power
and control in real war, and not only as such concerns applied to
Moscow. The decision to launch would have reflected the greatest of
human failures: why assume greater efficiency in its execution?
After his service in World War II, Schelling had spent years at Rand
and Harvard analyzing the patterns of threats and bargains. A
wiry and disciplined man who wrote about the economics of "self-
command," he was the scholar who, in the 1950s, had established
the conceptual structure of nuclear deterrence by applying game
theory to international politics. Now he grew irritated with his
friends' assumptions that the use of these weapons on either side
could operate with any serious precision amid the shock of doomsday. What emotions would prevail in that last half hour? It was ever
more unrealistic, he insisted, to believe that even the U.S. effort
would work in some remotely rational way, despite the past decade's
technological leaps in computers and communications.

George Lee Butler was that same year a colonel who commanded a SAC bombardment wing at Griffiss Air Force Base outside
Rome, New York. The task of this fast-rising officer was to ensure
that scores of thermonuclear bombs could be dropped on a range of
targets across the Soviet Union. Even at the time, the practicality
looked doubtful to him: Eighteen bombers were to be sent, each carrying at least four bombs, at nine- or ten-second intervals even in
the middle of a snowstorm. Then the pilots were to fly for at least
five hours to Eurasia, descend almost to ground level while zooming
through Soviet fighters and surface-to-air missiles, hit a target they
had never seen, and return to some surviving recovery base. No one
would know what would be functioning at home — whatever functioning meant — after those ten convulsive hours. Nonetheless, all
this was exhaustively planned and painstakingly pondered not only
in Washington and SAC's Omaha headquarters but also in Cambridge, Santa Monica, and Aspen.

Studies of how a nuclear war might actually be fought entailed some of the most arcane and unrealistic calculations imaginable. There could be no real simulations (using 1970s computers) of what monstrosities blast, fire, fallout, electronic disruption, and plain terror would beget. Into the Single Integrated Operational Plan (SIOP), so shrouded in secrecy that it had its own classification code, were programmed bizarre mistakes. It would take years to discover, for example, that a 1974 directive from Defense Secretary James Schlesinger requiring that strategic forces be able to destroy 70 percent of Soviet industry was instead taken to mean 70 percent of every industrial facility rather than 70 percent of Soviet economic-industrial capacity as a whole. To be sure, that was no big difference, and the Soviet Union would be ruined in either case — if it could be done. But the fact that such a miscalculation could slip through is revealing. "The idea that somehow we were in charge, that somehow all of this was infallible and manageable and we could make it work," acknowledged Butler, the four-star general who eventually moved SAC to a world without Cold War, "is fatally flawed."[30]

Also in 1977, as another example of Americans perhaps not quite getting what they thought they were paying for, the Soviet Union launched a surveillance satellite, *Cosmos 954*, with its radar and signals powered by a nuclear reactor. By early January 1978, it became clear to U.S. observers that the satellite was dying and that its wavering orbit meant an imminent crash, perhaps in North America. Allies were notified, as were congressional leaders and federal emergency response teams. The public was not. Secrecy held until January 24, the day of reentry.

CBS News got wind of the drama. Soon after *Cosmos 954* hit the snow and ice of Canada's Great Slave Lake, but before the public was informed, anchorman Walter Cronkite had his Pentagon correspondent chase down the facts. The breaking story became thoroughly tangled: CBS let it be known to senior Defense Department officials that network management was "about to be tipped off" that recent "sonic booms" heard in New York had really been ABM attempts to shoot down an errant Soviet satellite, one with a reactor on board. No, was the patient response from Gus Weiss, who had been charged with fielding the call, the United States did not possess missiles able to hit something nasty reentering the earth's atmosphere. The one U.S. ABM site had been shut down two years before, whereas the Soviets had many and were adding more.[31] It did not take long for the press to note that, had the satellite survived two more flattening orbits, it would have fallen, reactor and all, somewhere on the U.S. East Coast.

By now, the Cold War was for most people — even those who discussed it for a living — a matter of airy conversation. In Washington, civilian NSC staffers debating force deployments had no idea how many troops constituted a battalion. Pentagon consultants, advising on plans for using tactical nuclear weapons to close the passes in the Alborz Mountains in case of a Soviet drive on the Iranian oil fields, did not know the size, let alone the distribution, of Iran's population. Language standards at Defense and especially at the CIA (where recruits could be certified as fluent in French after spending a half hour in schoolboy patter with two elderly *Parisiennes*) remained disappointing. The State Department's desk officer for South Africa had never heard of the Great Trek.

The whole game was being played in a truly opulent gymnasium, but by an ever narrower group of people. Many of the same men who had been overstimulated in the early 1960s about competing with the Soviet Union — Bundy, McNamara, and Arthur Schlesinger, for instance — were by the late 1970s arguing that to deal with Moscow required merely a deeper sympathy for Soviet dreads and difficulties.[32] Adequate American strength and firmer purpose were nearly beside the point.

Had they themselves not failed in countering Moscow, and was it not unsparingly clear that where they had failed, no one could succeed? As public opinion swung back to quietism, these men and their friends roamed through the campuses and foundations, always surfacing in the editorial pages, yet never really accomplishing anything to diminish Soviet malignity. As they aged, they reveled in their supposedly intimate contacts with Soviet grandees, whose amused attention they took for leverage on world events. Moscow capably played into this, sending scores of supposed defense intellectuals of its own to endless meetings around the Ford-sponsored conclaves.

Moscow's men would travel individually or in small groups, chair panels, explain away Soviet policies, and bend influential ears. Bertrand Russell, dealing with similar visiting propagandists in the late 1940s, got to the heart of things in one line: "Tell your employers . . . !" he shouted, in emphasizing that such putative scholars were tools of the state. Now, however, well-meaning greeters were all too welcoming at Harvard and MIT, at Stanford, and at Ford itself. The mischief was usually nothing more harmful than sowing the Communist Party line at Pugwash meetings of disarmament-oriented scientists or dropping well-crafted opinions to meet preconceptions at the Brookings Institution or Carnegie Endowment. Of course, back home these visiting firemen's helmets often bore Soviet intelligence insignia. Away from the think tanks and campus policy centers there were agendas that some of them also had to fulfill for Line X. The Soviet system allowed little of the contact between its citizens and the outside world to be spontaneous, even sixty years after the revolution.

The FBI, its wits sharpened against dissident 1950s schoolmasters and impressionable 1960s coeds, braced itself to try to distinguish the mild academic boondogglers from the KGB hard cases. Despite its best efforts, the Bureau was way out of its league. For example, it lacked matching counterintelligence manpower in both numbers (except in New York City) and quality. In the Boston field office, about a dozen good-natured agents were assigned to monitor the interesting and subtle types visiting MIT, Harvard, and the rainbow of laboratories, research centers, and spin-off businesses. With no special competence in anything international, these G-men could not be distracted from the cutting-edge Bureau observation that many leaders of the radical left in America were Jewish.[33] Locally, Brandeis University remained the terrible example. There, in 1970, two students had been sufficiently enthusiastic about public policy to get themselves on Hoover's Ten Most Wanted list for committing armed robbery. Thus defended, the nation slept.

Appealing to patriotism and thrills, the Boston office at least found that it could leverage itself by asking selected university faculty to entertain, and thereby delicately to interrogate, particular Soviet visitors, even to introduce them to certain assignees — an occasional undergraduate being recruited so that her off-campus apartment might be used for undisclosed purposes. By 1979, the FBI's presence became sufficiently commonplace at Harvard's newly dedicated Kennedy School of Government that a rule was imposed: any regular contacts with the U.S. intelligence agencies had to be approved by the dean. (Nothing was said, chuckled the academics, about registering ties that one might have with *foreign* intelligence agencies.) These relationships inevitably became tricky for the counterintelligence people as well. From developing connections with questionable Soviet visitors, it was a seemingly small step for

General Creighton Abrams (right), who fought a "better war" in Vietnam, consults with U.S. Ambassador to South Vietnam Ellsworth Bunker, 1970. This was a significantly higher level of ability than the men who had preceded them in these roles *(Patton Museum Library)*

National security assistant Henry Kissinger sharing a joke with North Vietnamese negotiators in Paris, 1972. *(Dirck Halstead/TimePix)*

President Nixon and Texas Democrat John Connally, whom he appointed Treasury Secretary in 1970 and envisioned as his successor. *(Byron Shumaker / National Archives)*

President Gerald R. Ford, a good man who came to office upon Nixon's 1974 resignation and faced the collapse of South Vietnam the following year. Here he comforts a refugee and her child. *(David Kennerly / Courtesy Gerald R. Ford Library)*

Ford also encountered the superpower arms control minuet of the 1970s, an effort well summarized by U.S. negotiators standing out in the cold at Vladivostok so as not to be bugged by the KGB. *(David Kennerly / Courtesy Gerald R. Ford Library)*

Ford with chief of staff Dick Cheney (right) and Secretary of Defense Donald Rumsfeld (left), 1976. *(David Kennerly / Courtesy Gerald R. Ford Library)*

President Jimmy Carter, man of peace, with Israeli leader Menachim Begin (left) and Egyptian president Anwar Sadat (right) at Camp David, 1978. Efforts with the Soviet Union met with similar disappointment. *(Bill Fitz-Patrick/Jimmy Carter Library)*

Successor generation: Bill Gates (lower left) and friends in 1978. America and the world were being ever less affected by what was happening in Washington. *(Courtesy Microsoft)*

President Ronald Reagan and William P. Clark, the one man whom he considered his friend. During nearly two crucial years as national security assistant, Clark helped implement a five part strategy that would make "the Soviets cry uncle." *(Jack Kightlinger/Courtesy Ronald Reagan Library)*

Reagan chairing a National Security Council meeting, 1983. Vice President George Bush is on the left, Secretary of State George Shultz on the right. Coldly impressive. A man who knew exactly what he believed and wanted. *(Terry Arthur/Courtesy Ronald Reagan Library)*

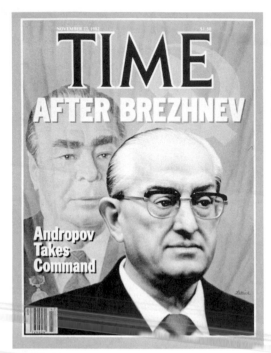

Yuri Andropov, head of the KGB since 1967, who became General Secretary in 1982. This was a man whom Secretary of State Shultz believed was "ready to take us on." *(TimePix)*

President Reagan in the Oval Office with leaders of Afghanistan's anti-Soviet resistance. The United States responded by helping start a holy war in 1981, leaving behind weapons, warlords, and religious zealotry once the Soviets retreated in 1989. *(Michael Evans/Courtesy Ronald Reagan Library)*

Reagan and Vice President Bush in New York with Andropov's eventual successor, Mikhail Gorbachev. Gorbachev's room for maneuvering was cut off. *(Pete Souza / Courtesy Ronald Reagan Library)*

The end of Big Brother. Stalin in the street, 1991. *(Arnold H. Drapkin/TimePix)*

Children cycling home from school in Hanoi during fall 2000 pass a billboard advertising U.S. personal computer giant Compaq. "All power to the masses." *(Kevin Lamarque/Reuters/TimePix)*

One terrible cost of the Cold War. *(Cartoonists and Writers Syndicate)*

the Bureau to ask its friends to go to the Soviet Union to develop such leads, if the attorney general approved. And he did.

These were the late 1970s, after all, the years between détente and the realization that accommodation had gone too far. The value of such Bureau-financed excursions into Moscow officialdom is unknown, but they further abraded relations with the CIA, particularly when the FBI would not share what it had learned. The nursery battle of rivalries made the career of an Aldrich Ames inevitable by default. Not yet a traitor, he was working during these years in the CIA's fifty-seven-person operation in New York, trying to suborn Soviet diplomats at the UN.

Overall, U.S. intelligence during the late 1970s was itself in further decline — not that this set the intelligence community apart from the government as a whole in its confusion on defense matters. The FBI's counterintelligence division had highly sophisticated electronic surveillance capabilities, with the old Elliot Hotel on Boston's Commonwealth Avenue (frequented by Soviet delegations) being wired up like a Christmas tree. As usual, however, there was a domestic price to be paid. Counterintelligence "was adamant about not giving an inch to the criminal division's needs" for such eavesdropping equipment in fighting the Mafia. The technology and techniques marshaled against the KGB, said the FBI's counterintelligence agents, might otherwise have to be revealed in common criminal court.[34]

Squabbling over turf also meant that the FBI failed to meet the wave of Russian organized crime that swept into America with the gangsters who accompanied Jewish dissident émigrés during the mid-1970s. The KGB had seen to the departure of these "anti-social elements" as well. Not until 1994 would the Bureau set up a Russian organized crime squad in New York, by which time this new *mafiya* was thoroughly entrenched.

Time and again, the costs of the Cold War were ones of misplaced effort. Another recurring example was the wheel spinning of "security clearances." Whereas KGB specialists had barely impeded access to critical military technologies, such as large-scale integrated circuit manufacturing, millions of staff-years and billions of dollars were being wasted on the ways Americans scrutinized each other.

Eisenhower's original sweeping executive order from 1953 on internal security had become a basic document of the investigators' trade, giving canonical authority to what these busy people should be looking for. By 1974, however, the Justice Department's list of subversive organizations — with puzzled Marine Corps NCOs still quizzing young officer candidates as to whether they had ever been members of the Abraham Lincoln Brigade — had gone the way of the Alien and Sedition Acts. Three years later, the requirement that applicants for government employment disclose any involvements with the Communist Party was also dropped. Equally outgrown was the insistence that homosexuals be excluded from sensitive positions. One result of all this was that the Bureau insisted it had become hobbled and that "the loyalty provisions . . . are in complete disarray at the present time."[35] How were investigators to know, for instance, whether someone might make a reliable GS-12 within the bowels of the Commerce Department?

So the investigating had to be done on a massive scale, and there were other agencies besides the FBI to help. In 1979, for example, the Pentagon's Defense Information Service (DIS) processed 950,000 security clearance cases, mostly for the armed services. All but around 3 percent inevitably passed, although approximately 150,000 required "special attention." The Civil Service's Office of Personnel Management (OPM) was annually going through 25,000 other background checks. All sorts of agencies and departments had become involved in the process since the early 1950s, with the FBI, Civil Service, and Defense Department — not to mention the CIA — operating their own security clearance mills.[36] Only the OPM was charged primarily with investigating aspirants to the Civil Service, but the DIS and the FBI were available when called upon to hit the streets and quiz neighbors, previous employers, friends, and lovers.

Each agency complained that the recent Freedom of Information Act further undermined its work, since the act permitted, in theory, someone who had been investigated to discover what those neighbors, employers, friends, and lovers had said. Millions of government and contractor employees kept being put through these processes, many unnecessarily, as the General Accounting Office (GAO) testified.[37] Defense contractors who depended on quick investigations for urgent projects were especially hard hit. The Rand Corporation huddled trailers into its Santa Monica parking lot to house the desks of the ever-replenished legion of analysts awaiting clearance. The GAO estimated that the logjam in defense-related positions alone cost $850 million annually during these years.[38]

No one could really know what level of security all this investigating, with its inevitable abuses, was buying. Apparently not much. In 1977, William Kampiles walked out of CIA headquarters with one of the most secret documents existing — the operations manual of the KH-11 satellite — stuffed under his jacket. At Langley, unlike, say, the Smithsonian, there is no bag check for employees.

The political economy of defense wrought another strange effect, tying into both the search for talent and the sodden business climate of the 1970s. More than a few extraordinary young people saw a career in public policy as far more exciting than one in enterprise. These were the Bundy, Kissinger, and Brzezinski wannabes, who had superb academic credentials, no particular beliefs, and an orientation to action (or, more likely, to decision). They were men and women at least a generation younger than the powerful figures they sought to emulate, who anticipated careers that would allow them to move between the Ivy League and the think tanks, the State Department's seventh floor and the Pentagon's E-Ring, with intermittent stops on Wall Street and corporate and foundation boards.

While the information revolution and the late-twentieth-century bull market were on the point of exploding, this successor generation of defense intellectuals committed themselves to Rand, arms control institutes, and academic specialties in strategic studies. After the Cold War, it was clear that most of these bright, high-energy types had developed few skills that were transferable to the more creative arenas of a world remaking itself under strikingly little state direction.

✪

Among the instances of being unable to get matters right, there was the problem of rarely being able to buy the right tyrant. Too many of the leaders Washington chose ended up being smothered under their moneybags — Pahlavi in Iran and Somoza in Nicaragua being prime examples. The Soviets, meanwhile, were ready to try to profit from both opposition to the thuggish regimes to which Washington often was tied and from America's post-Vietnam fears of further involvement. The equivalent of about $34 billion in rubles for military aid, an immense chunk of Soviet annual production, went to the developing world from 1974 to 1979 — hardly a sign of a withering regime resigned to losing an empire. The military, one Kremlin insider recounts, knew that these flanking movements would be an easy win. "The Americans will swallow it," the marshals are said to have argued.[39]

Such expectations of retreat were not unrealistic. Within three months of taking office, for instance, Jimmy Carter announced his intention to withdraw all forty thousand U.S. ground forces (and thereby U.S. nuclear weapons) from Korea. Major General John Singlaub, now chief of staff of U.S. forces in Korea, was forced to retire for protesting such myopia. Various academic experts, after all, were detecting "opportunity costs" in America's failure to develop better relations with a supposedly mellower North Korea. The "corrupt and repressive government" in Seoul, they insisted, could take care of itself. (The North's Supreme Leader, Kim Il Sung, would not get around to blowing up half the South Korean cabinet for another few years.)[40]

As always, Washington had to keep dealing with non-Communist dictatorships as facts of life. Yet it rarely had an appropriate posture toward them — a stance, say, between the firm correctness that it had usually displayed toward Eastern bloc nations earlier in the Cold War and the genuine cordiality appropriate to constitutional governments. U.S. diplomats, especially when they were politically appointed ambassadors, were traditionally gung ho for the strong-armed host regime. Moreover, military juntas and assorted satraps were well equipped to "wabble" (H. L. Mencken's marvelous word for *co-opt*) visiting American columnists or bankers. So the United States kept offering unpleasantly quotable commitments to thugs, who accepted its support with embezzlement and smug assurance that Washington had nowhere else to turn. It was not so much a question of there being no alternatives to the likes of the Shah, Mobutu, or Suharto as it was that none was imagined.

Some of the world's most despicable regimes were ensconced in Africa. For fifteen years, the United States and the Soviet Union had not jockeyed there. In the mid-1970s, Africa became by default the center of the Great Game. The dark mischief of Angola is a case study of U.S. aimlessness. About twice as big as Texas, with around six million people, this ancient Portuguese colony was mutilating itself as competing, tribal-based factions struggled to succeed the old order. Washington, as usual, knew little about any of them. It had assiduously avoided encountering the nationalists in order not to offend their overlords in Europe. Nor had it complained when Portugal had diverted American-supplied napalm, expected to be used only for NATO purposes, on to African villages to make up for the metropole's lackluster fighting qualities.

Fidel Castro, of all people, had long been supplying and training the Soviet-sponsored Popular Movement for Liberation (MPLA) in Angola. As Portugal shrugged off its last colonial claims, he began using Soviet aircraft to transport and provision what would soon be upwards of fifty thousand Cuban soldiers to serve as the power behind the throne of Angola's new regime. In response, U.S. officials became all the more attentive to the odious Mobutu, to whom they had already handed over more than $1 billion in aid (read "Swiss holdings") during the previous ten years. His adjoining Zaire would be the staging area for any attempts to supply an indigenous opposition to the MPLA. The immensity of his larceny and his ingratitude did not matter. Washington took it as only a minor discourtesy when he momentarily expelled the U.S. ambassador as being guilty of the meaningless crime of sabotaging Zaire's economy.

Around this time, a Harvard faculty and fellows seminar on third world contingencies (some of whose members would assume high government positions in the new Carter administration) searched for Angola on a map of Africa, finding it with difficulty. A Council on Foreign Relations study group on Africa would soon discover itself similarly at sea about the region's borders and population. As a participant in both, I was as geographically impaired as anyone.

In early 1975, Kissinger had approved a CIA outlay of $300,000 for covert assistance to Angola's National Liberation Front (FNLA), which the deluded thought to be the strongest of that country's contending parties. It was led by Mobutu's brother-in-law (long on a CIA retainer), who had just received, via Zaire, 450 tons of supplies and 112 military advisers from America's new friends in Beijing, in addition to North Korean military instructors based in Zaire during the summer of 1975. The third faction fighting for independence and succession, the National Union for the Total Independence of Angola (UNITA), appeared to be the weakest. Originally a Maoist organization and forever signing pacts with the devil, it was initially supported only by South Africa (no great advertisement).

The final choice between the two anti-Soviet groups had been arbitrary. Washington initially joined with Beijing to back the FNLA, then drifted over to Jonas Savimbi's UNITA once that faction was discovered to be stronger than initially assumed. Neither the head of the FNLA nor Savimbi ever condescended to be sufficiently cooperative as to tell Washington about their other sources of support — whether they be China, South Africa, or even shadowy Portuguese interests.[41] Smart people at Harvard and the Council on Foreign Relations were not the only ones who were perplexed.

Only twelve individuals who spoke Portuguese reportedly could be found among the CIA's fifteen thousand or so employees. Nor did anyone in Langley know much about the interior of Angola. Once Portugal gave up in November 1975 and the Soviet-backed MPLA regime took power in Luanda, covert operations nonetheless became "the biggest thing in Africa Division since the Congo."[42] Heading that part of the Directorate of Operations was the irrepressible Larry Devlin, his earlier connections with Mobutu and the long-dead Lumumba having been inflated into legend. He would soon retire and follow the consulting path common to high-level former operatives in this case maintaining ties with Mobutu as the representative of Maurice Tempelsman, the New York diamond and metals magnate.

Angola had become promoted to "crisis" standing in the weeks after Saigon's fall. Given Soviet involvement, it looked like a test of America's ensuing will and commitment. All cables were labeled IMMEDIATE. It was beside the point that the few people in Washington who knew anything about Africa doubted the effectiveness of such secret support — both because of the picayune amounts committed, which meant that America would try to fight "an economy-size war" on a continent ready for self-destruction, and because there was no attempt even to try to mobilize public opinion against Soviet neocolonialism.[43]

Kissinger had detected some sort of "African balance of power" that he was determined to maintain against a Soviet attempt "to tilt the African equilibrium."[44] This statement is otherworldly. There is no realistic way to apply "balance of power," a concept developed in Renaissance Italy, to postcolonial Africa. Only if adventurers from outer space had occupied the lands of Palmerston and Bismarck, defined frontiers for their own convenience, then pulled out overnight, proclaiming each of their brief holdings a historic sovereign state, would Europe and Africa have been comparable in these terms. Unfortunately, the Cold War, during the Kissinger years no less so than during those of McGeorge Bundy, was characterized by such slapdash thought. Unfortunately, the full extent could not be seen. Upon leaving State, Mr. Kissinger was able to install the most important of his papers (meaning government documents accumulated while in office) in the Library of Congress under a deed that made them inaccessible until five years after his death. Only his staff and lawyers had access.

By July 1975, Air Force C-130 transports had carried obsolete National Guard and Army Reserve weapons from CIA warehouses in San Antonio to Charleston, South Carolina, for reshipment on C-141s to Kinshasa, with the Agency being billed $80,000 per flight. The Navy hauled amphibious vehicles, trucks, and trailers, as well as five thousand M-16s and forty thousand other rifles, for $500,000 more. To get French help in hiring mercenaries, the CIA had to give Paris $250,000 as "proof of the United States' good faith in Angola," according to the disaffected CIA officer John Stockwell, who headed the operation at the African end. The actual gun men cost extra, around $500,000 being paid (in advance) to one shrewd entrepreneur for twenty-two of them in what would be a very short-lived venture.

That initial $300,000 in secret assistance was seed money. Soon $31.7 million was flying out of the Agency's Contingency Reserve Fund. Of this, $2.75 million in cash was sent to Mobutu, who had let it be known that he needed more personal incentive for arms to be passed through his country. Two million dollars more slid through the hands of each of the men leading the two anti-Soviet guerrilla groups, supposedly for operations. The Reserve Fund ran dry in late November, by which time Moscow had decided to supply the MPLA government in bulk.

In response, the post-Vietnam Ford White House was not about to let the CIA "borrow" $28 million more from the Defense Department. Even as the money was running out, the Agency sent more advisers to Angola, just as regular Cuban army units were pouring into the country with tanks, helicopters, and eventually MiG-21 jet fighters. Another "covert" disaster loomed. "In a penny-ante war," fumed Stockwell, "the Soviets had opened their wallets and put real money on the table." Estimates ran as high as $225 million.[45]

Nevertheless, critics of the executive branch's diffident steps once more spoke of America provoking Communist intervention. Since much of the U.S. reaction was secret, the White House had not been able to lay out the sequence of the MPLA's longtime backing by Castro and Moscow, which it could easily have done. In early

1976, the Democratic Senate prohibited any U.S. military role in Angola whatsoever. Before the CIA could extract itself, additional bills had to be paid: $600,000 more to Mobutu for the loss of one of "his" planes; $353,600 to another mercenary recruiter to meet the entirely unproved claim that he had induced 126 men still in Portugal to quit their jobs for the great aborted adventure. ("The agency never bargains hard in dealing with agents," recalls Stockwell.[46]) Finally, Mobutu pocketed another million-plus intended as a solatium to UNITA. The operation safely rolled up, Stockwell put in weeks back at Langley helping to prepare commendations for 26 medals and certificates, 140 letters of appreciation, and 1 salary increase for the people behind the mess.

Angola's civil war has continued wretchedly into the new millennium. In 1999, astute African observers reported that UNITA has used the Internet to buy weapons.[47] Castro's soldiers stayed in Angola until 1990. Throughout, Gulf Oil, later part of Chevron, contentedly pumped away. Once the United States pulled out, Gulf's operations were guarded by Cuban soldiers from remnants of CIA-backed rebels in Northern Angola. Eventually Gulf would be joined by most of the Western giants, its taxes helping Luanda finance those Cuban forces. Never would Washington demand the company's departure. Influential lobbyists and lawyers, mostly schooled in the city's ways through previous public service, argued from the mid-1970s on that withdrawing from this profit center would only increase U.S. dependence on Middle Eastern oil, and that European or Japanese firms would simply step in anyway.

After the U.S. retreat from Angola, the emboldened Soviets went deeper into Africa, supplying a quasi-Marxist regime in Ethiopia with four hundred tanks, fifty MiG fighters, and an airlift of at least ten thousand Cuban troops from Angola. At least one thousand Soviet military advisers directed the Cubans and some four hundred East Germans in a war against Somalia, a country usefully situated on the Horn of Africa, the southern choke point of the Red Sea and the Suez Canal beyond it. Increasingly uninhibited, Moscow was on a path that would lead it right into Afghanistan. At the time, such ambitions looked to be anything but ruinous. Indeed, they need not have been if the United States had continued to stumble and concede.

Again, Washington acted halfway between serious involvement and doing nothing. And again, it was getting the worst results. It was not even prepared to take an ideological offensive denouncing, for instance, expansionist Soviet tyranny. By the Ford administration's last year, such talk was coming from Beijing. "Our experience has been that it means nothing to the Soviets when they sign a paper," China's ambassador to the United States insisted, as the *People's Daily* openly questioned Washington's value in resisting the "Social-Fascists" and their "dictatorship of the Hitler type." Mao himself had recently spoken of America's Insular "Dunkirk" approach to security in Western Europe, while Vice Premier Deng Xiaoping — amazed that the United States was not using its "strong points to make up for the Soviet weakness" — compared U.S. policy to that of "Neville Chamberlain" and "appeasement." Both deplored Washington's "Munich-like" mentality.[48]

With anti-Soviet friends like Communist China, it was tricky for the White House to speak too expansively about human rights in scoring points against Moscow, valuable as Gerald Ford's intervention was in first internationalizing the question at Helsinki in 1976. Recent spurious miracles of Cold War diplomacy sprung by Nixon and Kissinger in embracing Russia as well as China, and these men's accommodations in Chile, Iran, Indonesia, and elsewhere, had put the country in a poor position to talk in terms of "evil" or "empire." As for black Africa itself, raising the topic of morality was regarded as impolite, as long as the dictators there were aligned with the West — meaning they were accepting more money from Washington than from Moscow.

For its part, Moscow had a far stranger collection of allies than the United States' array of friendly dictators. The barely literate Marxist-Leninist colonels of Benin, the swaggering Jew baiters of Argentina, the manic Fidel, and the enigmatic word spinners of New Delhi together reflected how nihilistic the Soviet Union had become in the decade of its last great reach for power. Argentina's Communist Party, under the military-fascist junta of the late 1970s, openly gave "critical support" to the men in dark glasses and field boots. Local Maoists and Trotskyites were eagerly fingered. Most Americans, for their part, wished to believe that their allies were not just business partners of the state but fellow dreamers of freedom. As the world grew closer, however, their government's intimacies with tyrants, whether of the left or the right, felt slimier.

On a rainy afternoon in June 1978, Aleksandr Solzhenitsyn spoke at the Harvard commencement, where he was to receive an honorary doctorate for his writings and his witness. His words were not what his hosts had expected. He ridiculed the maladroit U.S. response to Cuban forces in Angola and reminded the West that, in allying with Stalin to defeat Hitler, it had raised up a worse and more powerful enemy — a fact it was trying to whitewash away around the world. The rest of his thunder was even more terrible. He forced his polished listeners to address the forbidden — Vietnam, something barely spoken of in Cambridge amid all the conferences, consulting, and teaching about U.S. foreign policy during those years. It was a topic like incest, something horribly felt and never discussed. Yet it had been inflicted on the country in part through the efforts of some men once very close at hand and had been applauded in its inception not so many years before by a number of people actually present that day in Harvard Yard.[49]

The grim, bearded figure insisted on rubbing into the uneasy crowd spilling into Quincy Street the fact that the consequences of defeat would not go away. He demanded a review of judgments made. "All along," recalls the eminent historian Oscar Handlin, who was there, men like "George Kennan, Hans Morgenthau, and [Handlin's colleague] Stanley Hoffmann had linked policy to cost/benefits." Now Solzhenitsyn addressed this head-on, dismissing Kennan by name and letting his listeners know that such "political wizards" were something of a joke among Soviet officials.[50]

He raised the even more intensely unsettling question of responsibility. "Members of the U.S. antiwar movement became accomplices in the betrayal of Far Eastern nations, in the genocide and the suffering today imposed on thirty million people there." Here was cost indeed, though falling at its hardest — as usual — far outside America. It was starkly evoked, and the West did not even know the worst.

The indignation of the unreflectingly free quickly descended on Solzhenitsyn. The *Boston Globe* wrote that he sounded like Joe McCarthy. The *New York Times* editorial board noted his "obsession" with communism. The *Washington Post* accused him of trying to revive the "boundless cold war," which everyone knew had ended.[51]

As for America's allies in Europe, Solzhenitsyn simply wrote them off as spineless. Altogether, NATO members were spending about $100 billion on their non-nuclear forces. The extent to which Americans carried a disproportionate share of the burden, given that they were paying overall about four times per capita more for defense than the major allies, kept being debated in official and academic gatherings. Washington repeatedly heard the same detailed, philosophical explanations: It was overridingly important for the common security, said these prosperous allies, that they give primacy to reinforcing their welfare states. Social cohesion, after all, was their first line of defense. Moreover, their societies were benefiting tangibly from détente, since they were exporting five times more to the Soviet Union than was the United States.

Toward the end of the decade, however, opinion among Western European governments became hagridden by a sense of a strategically ascendant Soviet Union assuming true global status — and of several of the world's primary producers asserting a monopolizing claim to vastly larger shares of the developed world's industrial wealth. "In order to fill the vacuum that a faltering United States has left in matters of European and Western security," concluded one spokesman of mainstream alliance wisdom, Europe would have to look "within itself" for leadership.[52] Yet any form of leadership has to be exercised in some direction. No one knew what that direction might be without strong U.S. backing, unless it was retreat toward some resigned acceptance that "the barbarians might also be a solution."

Respectable opinion among the allies began casting Europe as a "civilian" rather than a military power. To Kennan, by now an ardent détentist who argued for NATO's unilateral nuclear disarmament, Western Europe's proper defense was to offer passive resistance once occupied or perhaps, at best, guerrilla war against the Red Army.[53] Although that notion was laughed at even in West Germany — so enthused with its own opening to the East — an entire chapel of influential voices in Europe tried to turn military weakness into a virtue, attempting to seize the moral high ground always available to the ineffectual. They rationalized their countries' impotence except in marginal roles and positioned themselves to draw passing advantage from the conflicts of others, or at least to limit the damage from such clashes. The sequel to this would be seen in Western Europe's asserted capacity to "settle" Bosnia during the 1990s.

The chance of Western Europe being even an intermediary force among the superpowers was conceivable only if America remained the leader. The United States, which could hardly pursue similar dreams of irresponsibility, was expected to remain on guard, less the ally than the unpaid mercenary of what Europeans asserted was their indispensable contribution to world prosperity. Not Bismarck himself could have envisioned this lingering arrangement that parodied the urgencies and resolutions of only thirty years before. Western Europe, so impossibly richer than had seemed attainable at the time, had become comfortable enough to be as graspingly hypochondriac as Japan.[54] One consequence was that more and more Americans felt themselves being used. The price in resentment and suspicion continued to grow.

At the same time that he called on the allies for some modest increase in defense spending, President Carter asked NATO as a whole to improve the effectiveness of its sixteen armed forces. The alliance was a military museum, and one with a poorly run endowment, given the chaotic variety of its equipment. In contrast, Moscow's heavy hand was thought to have imposed standardized rules and weapons within the Warsaw Pact. It is said that the government-owned railroad system in France had been built to carry votes, not passengers. Similarly, allied arms buying seemed to maintain the front line less against the Red Army than to uphold nationalistic military manufacturers.

The allies had long-standing fears of American "technological colonialism," and the United States could never outright decree what weapons its partners should buy — just as Congress would never allow U.S. forces to adopt significant amounts of foreign equipment, such as West German tanks, no matter how superior. Questions of who would make and use what "system," ranging from radios to armor to air transport, had been bitterly argued at least since Truman and Churchill had wrangled at the White House during 1952 over which rifle caliber NATO should accept. Not surprisingly, it had proved to be the American one.

Even in the late 1970s, the alliance possessed thirty-one types of antitank weapons, both sample and symbol of the operational incoherence that lay behind the high-toned alliance communiqués. Similar destructive redundancies were to be found in combat aircraft, warships, antiship missiles, naval communications, and surface-to-air missiles, as well as in communications gear employed purely within the U.S. armed forces.[55] An Army helicopter on which I was flying was forced down by weather near Ramstein on a flight back from the Eleventh Armored Cavalry in Fulda. It could communicate with that nearby U.S. Air Force base only by getting patched through Washington.

So often the Western alliance was less than the sum of its parts. Rarely was a decision final, especially when subject to Soviet propaganda. In 1978, for instance, rallies by Communist-front groups in Western Europe, as well as sympathetic press coverage, abetted by about $100 million in Soviet disinformation, convinced Carter to back off from deploying the "neutron bomb" (in fact, an artillery shell uniquely effective against tanks).[56] No public opinion in the Soviet Union, however, constrained Moscow from replacing its fixed, and therefore vulnerable, intermediate-range ballistic missiles targeted on Western Europe. The arrival of movable, multiwarhead SS-20s that year seemed to offer more evidence of the Red Army's belief in some form of victory through the earliest direct application of nuclear force, which was entirely in keeping with its overall "maximum deployment at the outset" doctrine.

Whatever Russia's motivation, in 1979 the allies became sufficiently scared to ask the United States to deploy nuclear missiles of a similar range in West Germany (Pershing IIs), as well as to post far-reaching yet subsonic ground-launched nuclear cruise missiles on the territory of three other NATO members — provided that removal of the Soviet missiles could not be negotiated within two years, by December 1981. (U.S. planners cut back the Pershing's 2,200-kilometer reach so as not to jeopardize the city of Moscow, a detail that an incredulous Politburo never believed.) West Germany Chancellor Helmut Schmidt compared the situation to the eve of World War I, when one false move could bring catastrophe.

In addition to immediate and often Soviet-financed protests from the left against even the prospect of new U.S. missiles in Europe, the allies faced more virulent opposition — threats sown in the East to help raise the price of social tranquillity. Urban terrorists drew strength from Cold War ideology. Building on clandestine cells, these mostly young, middle-class killers had grown out of various 1960s radical movements. West Germany's Red Army Faction — with training, weapons, and funds supplied by East Germany's secret police — was now showing itself to be Europe's most deadly terrorist group, and one that was not formally dissolved until 1998. East Germany, according to its last minister of the interior, had become "an Eldorado for terrorists."[57] Other Soviet satellites were also assisting, most likely with Andropov's encouragement. Czech intelligence, for instance, was supporting Italy's Red Brigades, which in March 1978 kidnapped Aldo Moro, leader of the Christian Democrats, and murdered him fifty-four days later. The

Soviet Politburo itself authorized KGB training in covert operations for picked Italian Communists.

An international network stretched from the Soviet bloc to the Middle East and beyond. For example, one of the witnesses at the Lockerbie airliner sabotage trial in 2001, a terrorist already serving a life sentence in Sweden for a bombing campaign against American and Jewish targets in Europe, confessed that he learned to use surface-to-air missiles in the Soviet Union during the 1970s.[58] Andropov was also thinking ahead, as the KGB scattered weapons caches (including suitably worn cloths obtained from railway workers, forest rangers, and other locals, as well as radio transmitters) around Western Europe for wartime use behind the lines. Meanwhile, the KGB was assisting the American Communist Party, comically sending the unrehabilitated Gus Hall about $40 million between 1971 and 1990.

Perhaps more insidious than terrorism for average Europeans was the damage being caused by inflation, which the United States was commonly blamed for exporting. This was a case of damned if you do, damned if you don't. The latter years of the Bretton Woods system had seen the United States buying goods and commodities (especially such relatively long-contract ones as oil) with depreciating dollars. Once currencies were generally free to float without necessarily coordinated central bank intervention, U.S.-caused inflation was blamed for diluting the rewards of hardworking allies. This was destabilizing for the world economic order, argued the West Germans, among others, because such irresponsible market influences were undermining their solidly responsible monetary policies. However interpreted, inflation was combining with the oil shortage to inflict a devastating one-two punch on all the industrial democracies. With inflation in America approaching 12 percent, the price of an ounce of gold leaped to $850 (or the equivalent of $2,300 today).

At the same time, the United States was going to pay for its support of the Shah, going back at least to the 1953 coup and extending through his 1977 Rose Garden appearance as "a champion of freedom" and Carter's ingratiating reciprocal visit to Tehran the following year. As late as August 1978, the CIA would conclude that there was not "even a pre-revolutionary situation" in Iran, as Carter observes wryly in his memoirs.[59] Reza Shah was predicted to be securely enthroned for at least another ten years. He fell within months, to be replaced not by the pro-Soviet Tudeh Party (which

Washington had long seen as the likely threat), but by something much stranger. At least it was strange to American officialdom, if not to Iranian peasants.

The victory of Ayatollah Khomeini's fundamentalism increased the oil squeeze that Carter called "the greatest challenge that our country will face during our lifetime." With the nominal-dollar price of crude oil rising almost fifteenfold in less than a decade, all sorts of measures were rushed into place in the name of the "energy crisis." Few policymakers bothered to think of oil as a resource that expands as technologies (in this case, sourcing and extraction) improve. Energy experts were themselves certain that oil would imminently soar to $100 a barrel. Carter let the excitements of politics overcome his good sense as an engineer. He warned Congress that, at current consumption rates, the United States and other countries "could use up all the proven reserves of oil in the entire world by the end of the next decade" (1990).[60] The CIA, for its part, discovered that the Soviet Union also was running out of oil and gas, although Soviet output of crude oil increased by one-half in the 1970s, thereby displacing the United States as the world's largest producer. Today output keeps growing.

Legislation was rushed through to provide generous subventions to independent power producers. For instance, the Public Utility Regulatory Policies Act of 1978, a $40 billion boondoggle of subsidies in the name of lower electricity prices, obligated utilities for more than two decades to buy electricity above market costs from hundreds of alternative energy plants.[61] Congress even invested $35 million in guayule plantations in the hope that this hydrocarbon-rich desert plant might offset the depletion of the oil fields. Waste became endemic, as "security" was multiplied by the urgency of "energy," even before taking into account government's unquenchable propensity to roll the pork barrel through every emergency.

The Strategic Petroleum Reserve was another supposed battlement of freedom, with more than 600 million barrels of oil being pumped into holes along the Gulf Coast since 1975. Another cry for "energy security" resulted in the 1978 tax subsidy for ethanol, the inefficient gasoline additive typically made from corn. Conceived as a short-term incentive to develop alternative fuels, this was easy to get into but has proved impossible to get out of. The roughly $600-million-a-year subsidy to produce ethanol-based fuel — a poster child for corporate welfare — continues into the twenty-first century, having already drained more than $20 billion from the U.S. Treasury on behalf of agribusinesses, albeit ones heavily positioned in the presidentially pivotal state of Iowa.

Stockpiling affected other commodities. For instance, the national helium reserve — thirty-two billion cubic feet of the buoyant gas stored in Amarillo, Texas — remained sacrosanct as a relic from the 1920s vision of battling blimp armadas, and still costs about $24 million a year to maintain, with no plans to privatize it before 2005. Also being stockpiled with gusto, were scarce materials used in military hardware: platinum, natural rubber, cobalt, and diamonds. Started in 1939 and valued at $11 billion forty years later, that stash still contained $6 billion worth of stuff in the late 1990s — even though the Pentagon says that it can make do with just three of the items (iridium, tantalum, and quartz crystal), worth about $24 million.

While the nation focused on an oil shortage that the president called "the moral equivalent of war," the civilian nuclear industry was coming undone. In the late 1970s, there were 64 nuclear power plants in operation, 72 under construction, 84 on order, and 8 more firmly planned. Just 103 would be functioning by the century's end, with none being licensed nor ordered after the victimless accident at Three Mile Island in 1979. One reason for the industry's twenty-year demise is the fact that the civilian value of nuclear energy was presented for decades in the same breath as the military value of nuclear weapons. The rest of the world marched on as a majority of Americans mistakenly came to believe nuclear power to be the most dangerous and environmentally damaging energy source of all. Visions of the mushroom cloud made it difficult to distinguish, say, the Nevada Test Site from a malfunctioning electric plant. Emotion came to dominate hard science, at least until 2001, when alarms over global warming combined with fears of the worst energy shortage since the 1970s. [62]

George Kennan predictably elbowed his way into the despair: Environmental matters were being handled better in the Soviet bloc, because they were under the central authority of responsible officials. "In this day of technological complexity," he argued, knowing nothing of technology, the average man had become incapable of usefully shaping his surroundings. In addition to Vietnam, Watergate, and "the stupidities of the CIA," he found the environment another example of how a self-indulgent America had little to offer the world, particularly to the developing nations where trying to introduce democracy was pointless.[63] By now, in the words of Kennan and others who shared his beliefs, the United States, with its pollution, pornography, and materialism, was barely worthy of containing anyone, let alone of being emulated.

Many of the less lucid among these critics also tended to see "the decline of the United States as an economic and industrial system," in the well-received words of Columbia University professor Seymour Melman. The country was said to have been operating a parasitic "war economy" for thirty years, and that economy was rightly pulling America under.[64] In the politicized intellectual climate of the time, views of the consequences of Cold War spending had changed 180 degrees from those of the early 1950s. Of course, the overall pattern of military spending had never had a special position as driver of domestic advancement. But the doomsaying ecstasy behind "Come Home America" — and the belief that defense budgets were ruining the economy — was just as wrongheaded.

Equally far-fetched were arguments tying the undeniable hardships of the industrial heartland in the 1970s (soon to be called the Rust Belt in the boom-arrogant 1980s) to the dramatic drop in the share of defense spending going to that area since the Korean War. There were many more reasons for Detroit's reckoning, as there were for the collapsing mills on the Monongahela. However, if there was one reason why something had gone badly, it was the Cold War, or America's self-reinforcing failure therein. By the late 1970s, this explanation offered a big, safe label to slap on a multitude of disappointments.

Sometime in late 1977, the Pacific basin overtook Europe as America's foremost trading region. As the trade deficit grew in 1979, it became easier for many Americans to conclude that the more impressive of their long-defended clients (Japan, Taiwan, South Korea) were stacking the deck. Japan seemed to be able to drown U.S. markets with products that were anything but flimsy, while having minimal willingness to import from those markets. Though difficult to see, Japan's hypercompetitiveness was also doing much to make U.S. industry leaner. Instead, it was easier to write books, such as *Japan as No. 1* by Ezra Vogel, or to insist, as did future Labor Department secretary Robert Reich, who soon joined Vogel on Harvard's faculty, that the United States was politically and economically "not organized for change."[65] Americans began being told, by an elite that envied the power conferred on the rigid government mandarins of Japan and Europe, that not only had the U.S. world role been warlike and threatening to all, but the country's future well-being looked deservedly bleak.

Japan was no more adept at making digs at the United States than was Western Europe, but often these were more surprising when they came. And there were a number of ways for the Japanese to remind themselves and everyone else of the injustices they had to endure. In 1975, for instance, that unfortunate fishing trawler, the *Lucky Dragon* (whose crew had suffered from fallout in 1954), was discovered abandoned at a garbage dump on the shores of Tokyo Bay. A group of private citizens enthusiastically set about restoring the boat, and the Tokyo metropolitan government built a huge steel-and-concrete museum around it. About 300,000 people a year visited this monument to national ambivalence, where one of the survivors was retained to describe the horror.

Inevitably, the Soviet Union could be relied on to ensure that even the most painful memories and visceral disputes among the allies would recede. As the 1970s wore on, the need at least to finesse an alarming range of pressures tempted the Politburo to offset its problems by highly believable threats. On the one hand, Soviet leaders could feel their own economy faltering and see China getting away with a tacit alliance with America (helped by 1979's transfer of U.S. diplomatic relations from Taipei to Beijing). On the other hand, Western Europe's ties to America might be loosened, while third world opportunities appeared exploitable as Marxist-Leninist parties seized power in more than a dozen countries over the decade. The actual value of these governments, which often consisted of little more than a barracks and a foreign office, was being no better assessed in Moscow than in Washington.

Once again, many thoughtful Americans explained the Soviet Union to their fellow citizens as more or less well-meaning. In August 1979, for instance, Edward Kennedy told *The New Yorker* how "open" he found Brezhnev. Eighteen years after his brother's inaugural, this highly experienced U.S. senator believed, and pressed upon the educated public, that he had just encountered a bluff, genial grandfather with big eyebrows. Meanwhile, Ambassador Dobrynin in Washington was reporting President Carter to be confused and inconsistent, with a public image of weakness.[66] Such impressions of American uncertainty could not help but encourage overreaching.

Whereas conservative Republicans and a few Truman Democrats, such as Washington senator Henry Jackson, had talked earlier in the 1970s of Soviet danger, by late in the decade this looked very real to an ever-wider cross section of the country. Although a SALT II agreement was signed in the summer of 1979, it was quickly shelved in the face of objections from the Senate Foreign Relations Committee. Powerful men on the Hill and in the executive depart-ments also were coming to fear that Iran's Islamic revolution might play into Soviet hands. Nothing comparable to Tehran's seizure of fifty-two U.S. diplomats as hostages in November, it was quietly said at the time even by anxious Western European officials, would ever have been inflicted on a Soviet embassy. No regime anywhere, they murmured, would have dared flout Russia to that extent.

Ultimately, it was a Democratic Congress, pushed by a public annoyed at the naive acceptance or Spenglerian doomsaying of elite managers and negotiators, that grew impatient with the pressures of Soviet armed power. By 1979, U.S. defense spending as a percentage of economic output had fallen to its second-lowest level in the Cold War (4.7 percent). For fiscal year 1980, it increased 15.2 percent, to $134 billion, a leap some mistakenly cite to show how fast such spending was rising. In reality, however, adjusting for the vicious inflation of the time, the increase in the months before the December invasion of Afghanistan was only about 3 percent.[67] What then followed was a powerful reaction to the 1970s indulgence of the Soviet Union. Only after the invasion was a truly galvanized revival championed by a president horrified that Brezhnev had "lied to me."

Passing from the obvious to a renewal of Cold War hyperbole, Carter described the skillful airborne and armored assault on Afghanistan as the greatest threat to peace since World War II. Something nasty had certainly been brewing for months. Kabul had signed a detailed twenty-year "friendship" treaty with Moscow exactly a year before, yet there were worrying trends of what the Soviets called "political reorientation to the West" within its revolutionary Marxist cabal. In an unprecedented Cold War event, U.S. ambassador Adolph Dubbs had been kidnapped in February 1979, and then killed in an exceedingly suspicious shootout involving his Russian and Afghan would-be rescuers. Carter ordered the two thousand or so Americans living in Afghanistan to depart, and nearly all had left by June. Some seventy-five hundred Soviet advisers were already in place; should more arrive, they would not have to worry about American civilians getting underfoot.

Senior Soviet diplomats attended "Spike" Dubbs's funeral in Arlington National Cemetery. Columbia University's gentlemanly Marshall Shulman, on leave as the State Department's top Soviet expert and a former student of the murdered ambassador's, gave the eulogy. Shulman urged, in the interests of peace, against blaming anyone. The State Department accepted Kabul's incredible explanation that antigovernment mujahidin resistance fighters were responsible — despite strong circumstantial evidence of KGB complicity. There would be no serious investigation.[68]

The Politburo had hesitated to take the next step. Its chief ideologue, the perennial hard-liner Mikhail Suslov, insisted that any westward drift in Afghanistan would endanger pro-Soviet regimes everywhere. The KGB's Andropov pushed the case for intervention, dangling before the chronically ill Brezhnev the scenario of having quislings "invite" Soviet assistance to crush counterrevolution. The plan had succeeded in Hungary. However the invasion was conducted, Afghanistan could not be lost. Right after Christmas, two KGB commando units shot their way into the national palace and summarily executed the inconvenient president, his son, and several of his closest aides. In private, Soviet officials also cited their Cold War experience in Czechoslovakia as evidence that world indignation would be short-lived. Brezhnev, in addition to well-informed people in Washington, expected the fighting to "be all over in three or four weeks."[69] But Vietnam had not been Czechoslovakia 1938, and Afghanistan was not to be Czechoslovakia 1968.

Carter's alarm was justified to the extent that the attack followed a string of seemingly successful third world adventures. But the President was wrong (as would be known only when Soviet archives were partially opened) in seeing this invasion as the first step toward the Persian Gulf. James Schlesinger had just been fired from the cabinet again, but in the eyes of horrified U.S. decision makers, the former defense secretary's notion of "global slippage" appeared to be grinding on. Whatever the intention, here was the first time in the Cold War that forces of the Soviet Union had crossed what the world still considered a neutral border. It was the first war they lost, and the last they would fight. Afghanistan was also on its way to war, first with the Soviet Union, then with the United States.

"For peace," Brezhnev liked to say, "it is necessary to pay a price." Carter resolved to make Brezhnev's definition of peace "as costly as possible."[70] A grain embargo was imposed on Russia, although Washington's purchase and storage of the 17 million tons not exported would cost around $5 billion, worsening the balance of payments. Computer sales were canceled, and the IBM system was shut down (by not supplying spare parts) at the Karma River truck plant, from which the trucks were now hauling Red Army supplies into Afghanistan. U.S. military ties with China grew closer. The allies considered economic sanctions, but Moscow threatened to block energy deliveries to Western Europe. Chancellor Schmidt proceeded with a trip to Moscow, while his country — along with France, Italy, and Japan — scrambled for new trade talks and began picking up the large trade deals canceled by U.S. companies.

Kennan denounced the U.S. reaction as foolishly provocative.[71] On the other hand, a suddenly antagonized Marshall Shulman asked himself what "would really sting." He persuaded his chiefs that this would be a boycott of the 1980 Olympics in Moscow, where it was anticipated that the Ministry of Sports would give the Soviet Union a world-resounding triumph on its own turf. (Western tolerance of flagrant cheating every four years was yet another bizarre sign of habitual diffidence.) In addition, truly to rattle the Soviets, Carter revived the Selective Service System. Outliving the Cold War, the rebirth of draft registration would cost about $23 million a year until 2000.

In January 1980, Carter also authorized supplying small arms and artillery to the mujahidin. They would be conveyed through Pakistan, with which the CIA had a long working relationship going back to the early basing of U-2 spy planes in Peshawar, near the Afghan border. The operation was to be done with extreme discretion: money would come from America and Saudi Arabia; the Chinese (again doing no favors but genuinely fearful of what Moscow might do next) would provide obsolescent Soviet-type black market equipment. Everything could be deniable for Washington. The purpose was not to defeat, but merely to harass. No one was about to poke the bear directly.

The invasion, however, had set off what would become the largest refugee movement in history. Americans were soon gripped by the Afghans' plight, particularly after forty million viewers watched a *60 Minutes* segment in April. National indignation pressed on Congress, where several legislators from both parties were inclined to do much more than harass. What was about to unfold was the largest U.S. covert operation ever, into which secretly flowed somewhere around $5 billion before the last Soviet forces formally withdrew in February 1989. Yet contrary to the belief of *60 Minutes'* savviest producer, the alacrity with which the Pentagon and the CIA pursued this mission would be anything but the "one brief shining Camelot moment" of the Cold War.[72]

White House interest in reassessing long-held commitments elsewhere quickly waned. The administration worried that South Korea might become the "next Iran," or perhaps an Afghanistan. (Harold Brown and Zbigniew Brzezinski had already convinced Carter in June 1979 that U.S. troop withdrawals were a terrible idea.) So there was no objection in May 1980 when officials in Washington and at the U.S. embassy in Seoul heard of South Korean plans to use brutal elite brigades to put down disorders directed against the harshness of martial law — the soldiers going out to bayonet, beat, and kill at least one thousand people in the southern city of Kwangju. For too long, America's clients had presumed that their patron's uninformed goodwill would overlook violence against every "subversive" who disagreed with them. By this time, however, television was creating a world in which injustice of all sorts could not hide.

In his 1980 State of the Union address, Carter promised that America would go to war against any "outside power" trying to gain control of the Persian Gulf — the protection of Kuwait and Saudi Arabia, governed by their own forms of despotism, being much in mind. This was easy to say, although U.S. forces, as General Meyer had been warning, were less than ready. A glimpse of this fact was seen in April. The courageous Army Special Forces attempt to rescue the hostages in Iran ended with three out of eight helicopters malfunctioning, costing eight men their lives. An investigation discovered that there had been no rehearsal to integrate all military elements of the complicated raid.

The day after this Desert One tragedy broke cold and sunny along the Charles River in Cambridge. A conference of some one hundred people was starting at the Hyatt Hotel. The conference, put together by the private Institute for Defense Policy Analysis and working closely with the Pentagon, involved the usual crowd from academia and the foundations, as well as senior Army officers and their aides. As the overnight news arrived from Iran, the gathering, ironically focusing on U.S. military "power projection," curdled. Couldn't America do anything right?

The kaleidoscope was turning fast, and in 1980, "foreign policy" worried Americans more than any other national issue for the first time since the 1950s. It even surpassed inflation, which rose at 13.3 percent in 1979 and another 13 percent in 1980. Looking back, the University of Virginia's Whittle Johnston still sees in that year "nothing less than [its] incipient disintegration." [73] By September, the Iran-Iraq War, which would kill at least 375,000 combatants during the next decade, broke out as Iraq tried to seize Iran's oil fields and bring down Khomeini. Washington found itself a new ally in Saddam Hussein.

In as near a mea culpa as a President has ever offered, Carter submitted a budget, one week before Ronald Reagan's inauguration, calling for spending $1 trillion on defense over the next five years, an average real increase of 5 percent annually over the already-expanded budget for that fiscal year. Yet it was the arrival of a new president, and of a Congress often skeptical of how three previous administrations had supposedly been "managing" the Politburo, that brought the Cold War into its final stage. The alternative to the steps America began to take would have been anything but costless. The Soviet Union might have been economically stricken, but this made its masters all the more desperate, and by now it was armed to the teeth.

✪

The United States had felt a challenge in the late 1940s. The 1950s made the Cold War a habit and brought the country to the middle stage of this story with the advent of the Kennedy administration. The 1960s got out of touch with the Cold War's original purposes, as once-useful slogans turned into epitaphs. During the bewildering 1970s, a soaring sense of hope contracted into sullen resignation. The Nixon, Ford, and Carter years were ones in which so much more had been expected and so much went unachieved. Yet they cleared the field for the endgame.

By 1980, America, the confident world leader of less than twenty years before, seemed cornered. In the previous decade alone, the country had given up in Vietnam; stepped out from under the dollar-denominated price of gold, which had anchored the world economy; behaved not once but twice like a lamb toward OPEC;

urged and adopted both sides of the argument in arms talks with the Soviets; and took the first steps to bring its forces home from Europe and Korea. Ultimately, the United States could no more pull back from the world after Vietnam than it could have after World War II. A West Germany reduced to being "defended" by French and British nuclear weapons would have been a strange target for Soviet diplomacy. An Israel relying on European goodwill would have been even edgier in facing Arab bluster. Whichever one of the strange triad of China, Russia, and Japan that might have been left apart after two of the others had cut a deal would have been a terrified and ruthless odd nation out. These were the years when the bill for America's earlier ambitions was coming due.

After more than thirty years of the Cold War, Americans faced the prospect of having to spend immense sums all over again, just to stay in place. No one any longer expected dramatic breakthroughs. At times in the mid-1950s and perhaps under President Kennedy, people had fleetingly believed in "winning." Now the only good news for Americans was that they were on friendly terms with the People's Republic of China — an even bigger tyranny than its better-armed former blood brother. America's pessimism about itself and its involvements ran deep and wide. As much as in 1960, the slogans of international conflict (missile gap, third world reversals, a timorous incumbent) were being used as blunt weapons in presidential politics.

Sixty-eight years before Jimmy Carter and Ronald Reagan faced off for the presidency, Speaker Champ Clark had nearly been washed into the White House on the waves of a trivial but eloquent ditty:

Ev'ry time I come to town
The boys keep kickin' my dawg aroun';
Makes no diff'rence if he is a houn',
They gotta quit kickin' my dawg aroun'.

The emotion behind these lines was remote from the high purposes with which the United States had entered the Cold War. The rhyme itself would have grated on the ears in Cambridge, Aspen, or Berkeley. It is nonetheless a reminder that continuing frustration will bring intense reaction. Patience had been ebbing against Viet Cong flags in the street, OPEC extortion, Cubans in Africa, months of televised humiliation as hostages were pummeled in Tehran, and more than a decade of balancing acts with Moscow. Many Democrats felt their dog kicked, too, as Carter was swept from office, losing forty-four states. The next few years were a period of incandescent improvisation, distraction, furious initiatives, and neglect — as well as one in which America set a new and formidable pace.

"War is the health of the state." However, there is, as anyone who has known a cocaine addict can testify, a big difference between health and short-term hyperactivity. The jump into sudden, heavier defense spending would compound many familiar Cold War habits of waste and indirection, even as it helped bring victory.

PART III

10

Hard Pounding

(1981–1985)

It is fever, not fight,
Time ~~~ the battle, that kills.

Rudyard Kipling, "The Years Between"

In its last decade, the archaism of the Soviet system — able to legitimize itself only through military menace abroad and police omnipotence at home — maintained the archaism of the Cold War. By 1980, that struggle had changed again. It was no longer a contest between two relatively matched and motivated powers. Now it was one between a state decaying in just about everything but political appetite and armed strength, and a Western world grown tired of the conflict. Japan was never really a player, although it was economically a crucial secondary participant. That unusually hardworking nation was able to move steadily forward, transforming itself from wartime predator to scarcely visible free rider to exaggerated threat. For several years at the Cold War's end, many Americans would see Tokyo as more ominous than Moscow.

Of course, the real danger, until the hammer and sickle came down at the Kremlin on Christmas, 1991, was the Soviet Union. The fiercely armed yet sclerotic giant might not have been long for this world, but no one knew what convulsions, fatal to far more than itself, might disfigure its last moments. The longer the Soviet Union survived in this condition, the greater the chance that something might go horribly wrong. Time was by no means on the side of the West, as conventional wisdom has it. Nor was it inevitable that those final moments would span only another decade. As in World War II, a few pivotal differences could have given events a less felicitous turn. The Soviet Union had nearly perfected the art of muddling through: its eagerness to undermine the West was surpassed only by its ability to feed off it.[1] What had to be done was to deliberately raise the "costs of empire."

"Reagan was the first postwar President to take the offensive both ideologically and geostrategically," Henry Kissinger acknowledged after the Soviet collapse.[2] The risk in doing so, however, was not fully to grasp how close the "best-case scenario" of pressuring the Soviet Union at its most vulnerable points came to the Politburo's sense of its own "worst case" — a collapse that was indistinguishable from the collapse of world order. One fault of the Reagan administration was that it ended up walking closer to the edge than it required. It barely considered the lack of self-awareness among aggressors: when resisted, they feel unjustly threatened. It would not have been difficult in the early 1980s for the Cold War, having smoldered for so long, to have ended in fire.

Reagan came to office saying nothing about communism's threat that John Kennedy had not declared twenty years before. He omitted only the Chinese peril from otherwise startlingly similar rhetoric. The differences between eras (the buoyant confidence of the early 1960s and the disillusioned early 1980s) and between the youngest-elected president and the oldest were nonetheless astonishing. In 1961, the United States dwarfed the Soviet Union in most measures of military capability except ground forces and medium-range ballistic missiles. By 1981, there was parity at best, including a global Russian navy (less aircraft carriers) and an impressive range of weapons, many of which were as sophisticated as anything possessed by the West.

Unlike Kennedy's windmilling, a key purpose of the U.S. buildup during these final years was to exploit the failings of the Soviet economy. Moreover, U.S. spending was part of a much larger response, as the country for the first time confronted its opponent in each mode of power: political and ideological assertion against tyranny, as well as military competition. To that end, the administration, with intermittent bipartisan help from Congress, designed an integrated set of policies and strategies specifically directed toward the Politburo's defeat. It was mapped out during the first two years in a series of presidential "decision directives" and pursued.

Significantly, foreign policy was not Reagan's preoccupation. Nor really were politics. From his inaugural on, he made clear that the country's future depended on ensuring a new economy in which individual energies could be unleashed. Real power had to grow out of Silicon Valley and the world-feeding soil of the Great Plains. The creativities of entrepreneurship combined with information technologies were moving to center stage. The larger part of government's responsibility would be to get out of the way. Reagan knew that this dynamism also worked against Big Brother overseas. At the same time, the editorial-page vision of foreign policy, as embodied in conferences and treaties, was shrinking in relevance before the transformations of whole societies. Little that was pivotal was going to be shaped by small groupings of great men in front of television cameras — the national security assistant of the moment, some headlong star cabinet appointee, or the latest wizard from Rand.

Unlike Kennedy, Reagan's disrespect for conventional wisdom was more than the junior officer's impatience with the brass. Reagan took the long view of almost everything. He was an extremely effective negotiator, which is not the same as being tough. He did not rattle, and his faith in America's strengths rested on an utter indifference to social class. A self-made man, he surrounded himself with self-made men, more inclined toward market competition than to the big-engineering, big-idea repetitiveness of earlier Cold War business and academic elites. He was the first president inaugurated on the west side of the Capitol, consciously looking out across the country toward the Pacific. There was no alliteration, hyperbole, or anaphora in the plainspoken address that he largely wrote himself.

Another contrast with Kennedy's years of "burden and glory" was not only that Reagan was oblivious to the glory but that he was going to make the burden a lot less heavy by working to transcend communism permanently. He saw the Soviet Union dying — as long as his administration helped with the euthanasia. He believed that Americans were under no long-term obligation to be "watchmen on walls," if they ever had been. Instead, they were going to be instrumental in tearing down the walls of communism. "Balances of power" and "spheres of influence" — let alone accepted notions of arms control — had not worked. This was a struggle of ideas first, territory and weapons mastery second. From the start, as he put it, Reagan intended "to break the deadlock of the past." The cost would be made unendurable for the Soviet Union not in some excitable spasm, but with a steady deliberation.

As for China, Reagan in his first year adopted a plan that involved selling offensive weapons to Beijing. He was not about to do anything that would ruin relations with the mainland at the same time that he focused U.S. energies on the Soviet Union. He dropped his campaign pledge to re-recognize Taiwan, yet he also sold jets to this old ally. If Beijing wanted to explore arrangements about future arms sales, that would be fine, he said, but if they did not, that would be fine, too. U.S. protection of its longtime friends in Taipei would be underlined, at the same time that Beijing would be used for U.S. ends against Moscow. There would be the customary photo ops at the Great Wall, but the president rebuffed Deng Xiaoping's request that Taiwan be pressured to discuss reunification.

Toward the developing world, there was no Kennedy-era fascination with the mystique of the guerrilla, nor any particular excitement about exotic, beleaguered places. It is as difficult to imagine Reagan studying the works of Mao, Che Guevara, or Vo Nguyen Giap as it is to think of FDR reading *Mein Kampf*. Nor did the tone that Reagan set evoke those well-publicized sleepless nights where men were always "in a constant hurry, taking last-minute decisions to last-minute meetings, making last-minute corrections to last-minute statements, as if they were always trying to catch up with events" — Henry Fairlie's sardonic encapsulation of the Kennedy administration's heated atmosphere.[3] It was much cooler yet more conclusive. The United States would no longer be frantically reactive to the Kremlin's whims.

Nor did Reagan and his closest advisers show any joy in risk and crisis. Lines were nonetheless drawn: Poland would not be a repeat of Hungary and Czechoslovakia; the Western Europeans would not conduct business as usual with Moscow; Soviet totalitarianism would be called what it was, rather than being granted legitimacy as a global partner. This was not a Kennedy-like contest of great hyperpersonalized powers, but something refreshingly redolent of John Foster Dulles's identification of "evil." There was no longer any inclination to subsidize and assist, let alone strive for that "degree of interdependence" that Kissinger had hoped would add "an element of stability" to superpower concord. Interdependence between the dying and the living usually implies that the living get sick, too.

The Reagan years cover most of the Cold War's third and final stage, even though the Soviet regime was able to hang on for just a little while longer, after he left office. This chapter looks at the key ways that the "costs of empire" began being raised, particularly during Reagan's first term. It opens by showing how and why America finally took the offensive and weighs the hair-trigger dangers as well as the successes. It tries to explain the opposition at home to what finally was under way — which was to be expected, given the vacillation, at best, of previous years. Then it discusses other parts of that offensive strategy, including how Soviet access to hard currency and technology was jeopardized. Much of the story has not been told before, including discussion of the longest and most complex U.S. counterintelligence operation ever. Ultimately, American cash, innovation, and salesmanship combined to rip into Soviet confidence and help bring the struggle to a close.

★

Some people believe that the Soviet demise was an event sealed off by itself, that the unraveling of communism was endogenous to the Eastern bloc, or that it was due to the arrival of Mikhail Gorbachev and only marginally resulted from renewed U.S. resistance, let alone to Reagan's determination. Somehow the bloodless implosion is willed to hang in the air, remote from what America was doing in the Cold War's last decade. There are four reasons for this.

First, the years since the Korean War had shown consistently that Washington could expend money and rhetoric without changing much. Such was the wisdom distilled from decades of accumulating frustration. Various commentators chose to deny that, whatever its efforts, the United States could significantly influence the Soviet Union. Détente's failure was the most recent example, and perhaps (as some people still think) America's fault.

Second, and even more important, Reagan was not reckoned to be a primary player, just as Truman and Eisenhower had been patronized in their day. At a time when the country's self-confidence seemed to have evaporated, there arrived this apparently charming elderly person — an actor, unapologetically dismissed by establishment wise man Clark Clifford as an "amiable dunce." Neither word went deep. Reagan could be so misread because he was not a Cold War obsessive, nor indeed a power obsessive. This was not the sort of leader that Americans had been used to since 1961.

Third, because each of the country's defense buildups has been less visible than the one before it — fewer men in uniform, greater technological complexity, and just plain less public interest — it became easy for Americans to regard the resurgence of military spending in the 1980s as simply more of the same. It was difficult to see how these dollars might be pressing Moscow over the final threshold of self-ruin. This time, there were no Green Beret ballads, televised warnings from the White House to head underground, or battle-for-the-world figures like the Dulleses, Lansdale, LeMay, or Vietnam's heroic Captain Pete Dawkins (who called in an air strike on his own overrun position) to pull attention away from the start of a bull market that would shoot the Dow Jones average from 1,000 to 11,000 between 1982 and 2000.

Fourth, today we are eager to forget that many influential Americans during the Cold War's final twenty years had hoped to settle the Soviet problem by redefining it. Particularly after Vietnam, they responded to failure by hurrying to discover how much American leaders might have in common with Soviet ones. For America to take the ideological offensive, let alone a political-military one, was regarded as fanatical, stupid, or doomed. For a president actually to speak of Soviet "evil" or of a Soviet "empire" would immediately be deplored as "primitive," "smug," and, worst of all, "judgmental."[4] Historian Henry Steele Commager described the address in which "evil" and "empire" were joined as "the worst presidential speech in American history, and I've read them all." Today, such critics insist that they, too, understood that the Soviet Union was not "just another form of government."

Born in 1911, Reagan — an inheritor of the FDR optimism, only twenty-seven years younger than Truman and thirty years younger than Marshall — was of the generation that believed that America was a country whose essence was that it could do anything if only it believed in itself, and that such a spirit should come naturally to upend so primitive a system as one arising from Marxism-Leninism. Behind Reagan's pleasing manner, shaped by the profession whose goal it is to please, lay the cold calm that had carried him unscarred through a hard childhood and a struggling youth. He was a throwback to the resourceful resolution of the startled but undismayed 1940s. He had the same sense that this was a contest between the natural and the unnatural and that the Soviet Union was so irrational that its survival was contrary to human nature.

Like Marshall and Truman — patient men who did not cast them-selves as specialists, who had no passion for summitry, and who were oblivious to their legacies — he saw the oppressive structure as preposterously unworkable, held together by police power and terror hardened into habit.

Reagan's upbeat good sense about resolving the world's most dangerous specific problem — about how to consign the Soviet Union, in Trotsky's phrase about Bolshevism's democratic oppo-nents, to the "ash heap of history" — was shared by few others. To him, that system was not an entity capable of enduring. He had no yearning to placate, to search for joint efforts and a specious "equi-librium." This vision of a world without the Soviet Union would unlikely have possessed even the chastened, suddenly pugnacious post-Afghanistan Jimmy Carter (had he been reelected) or the diplo-matically inclined George Bush, Reagan's rival for the Republican nomination.

At the 1980 party convention, Reagan asked for a moment of silence and evoked a force more frightening than noise as the gath-ering was stilled to a common awe. This was a strength in Reagan hard to ascribe to the choppy, gesticulating Nixon, who seemed to have to vibrate all the time, or to the frenetic Kennedy. Reagan instead had the ability to make most people feel as if they were sit-ting at the same table. Yet behind this, Reagan, like British prime minister William Gladstone, was "an old man in a hurry" — a hurry to make things new.

The country did not elect Reagan out of a serious belief that he would change things (in fact, it was weary of things changing), but because it felt cornered. If its embassies could be seized with impunity, if OPEC could gear up to new heights of effrontery, if the United States was behaving as if its liberties depended on the People's Republic of China, then America was indeed looking like "a pitiful helpless giant" and perhaps well on the way to becoming one. Reagan's victory was channeling anger and frustration rather than a wish to restore early postwar attitudes, which had drawn on rest-less confidence. This required new methods. As he archly reminded his first secretary of state, the 1980 election "was about not doing things just because that's the way they were done before."[5]

The greatest of all Reagan's underestimators were the Soviets, confidently convinced well into the first months of his presidency that cutting deals with him would be like working with Nixon: the defiant, conservative rhetoric would drop away as the new president acknowledged the obvious — that the Soviet Union was at least an equal enduring superpower. Moreover, Moscow was certain that Washington would keep inflicting on itself the same costly bureaucratic intrigues presented as world policy.[6]

Thus, in early 1981, Moscow assiduously tried to rebuild the 1970s labyrinth for transacting business, seeking to establish another back channel to the President. In this case, the NSC and State Department were both to be bypassed; Edwin Meese, counselor to the president, was to be the Talleyrand of Moscow's subtlety. Such an attempt highlights the lost-in-time quality of America's adversary. To Reagan, the United States was "the A Team among nations" and would not be buffaloed. He ordered that there would be no immediate high-level contacts at all with Moscow.

Nor would there be a U.S. ambassador in Moscow for the next ten months, once Carter's appointee, IBM chairman Thomas Watson, departed in January after serving two years. In Washington, Anatoly Dobrynin, Soviet ambassador for two decades, was affronted at no longer being given special treatment, such as losing his parking spot in the State Department garage. The president, in no hurry to mouth courtesies in which he did not believe, would not meet with him for two years. The new stance was not solely Reagan's. In 1981, with powerful symbolism against the Soviet police state, Congress assured that the long-lost Raoul Wallenberg was named an honorary U.S. citizen, the only person to receive that honor aside from Winston Churchill.

In Moscow, the British ambassador, Sir Curtis Keeble, also had time on his hands, as did almost everyone in that frozen-in-place diplomatic ghetto during the late winter of 1980–1981. His calendar had left him sufficiently idle to invite me, while visiting Moscow, for lunch in his sitting room overlooking the river. The observations were chilling: Soviet fears and gun-toting paranoia were ever more a substantial fact of life, perhaps of survival. He warned that the Soviets were vastly more isolated, inbred, and parochial — and therefore more subject to frantic, unpredictable anger — than the new men in Washington could suspect.

George Kennan also showed up in Moscow — as a private citizen, but one regarded by the Soviet elite (characteristically behind the times) as the preeminent authority on his country's foreign policy. He met with a cross section of officials, including Georgi Arba-

tov, who directed the influential Institute for the Study of the USA
and Canada and was believed to advise Leonid Brezhnev. Characteristically emotional, reddening as he spoke, Kennan denounced the
new leaders of his country as "dangerous," "stupid," "childish,"
"reckless" people who "might do anything."[7] His discovery of this
second great peril of his career was to help set off alarms in the
Soviet Union far more dangerous than those he had raised in America thirty-five years before.

Most of the people who thought of themselves as defense intellectuals were more circumspect. By 1981, influence on public policy
enjoyed far greater pride of place in parts of academia than did
dusty, dutiful scholarship. Immediately after the election, for instance, the dean and much of the faculty of Harvard's John F.
Kennedy School of Government hastened to retain political standing by the timely revelation that the institution's title should simply
contract to Harvard School of Government. After all, no other Harvard professional school bore an individual's name. (Learning of
this attempt, the outraged mayor of Cambridge promptly renamed
the venerably WASP Boylston Street, on which the school fronts,
John F. Kennedy Street.) Edwin Meese would be singled out by the
school for a public service award.

Stanford, for its part, was no longer in the defense business, having severed its ties with the Stanford Research Institute during the
campus upheavals. Thanks to the Ford Foundation, the university
had since created the Center for Arms Control and Disarmament.
Sensitive to political winds, the center added "International Security" to its name and dropped the quixotic "Disarmament," later
becoming simply the Center for International Security. Other organizations benefiting from Ford Foundation largesse similarly trimmed
their sails, though still deriding anyone extremist enough to suspect
the Soviets of violating treaties.[8] No matter who was in power, these
men and women wanted to be at the center of the action. Henry
Kissinger contributed $100 to the Committee on the Present
Danger.[9]

Reagan had long been denouncing "pseudo–arms control,"
while also saying, upon entering office, that he would "negotiate as
long as necessary to reduce the numbers of nuclear weapons."[10] To
him, it made eminent sense to expand the nuclear arsenal if that
would push Moscow toward accepting actual cuts. "Arming to par-
ley," Churchill had called it. Senator Edward Kennedy, among many

other Democrats, said he rejected such an "absurd theory." That was not unfair: excuses for greater military spending had been a part of arms control for more than a decade. The difference was that this time the spending would be just one approach to undercutting Moscow.

The early 1980s reaction to the Soviet Union, most visible in the defense budgets, was a levelly conveyed promise of an all-out, peaceful, and inconceivably expensive high-tech arms race, combined with a policy of calculated economic pressures whose scope and determination, as well as their dangers, are only now coming to light. In May 1981, as Yuri Andropov maneuvered to secure his position as the ailing Brezhnev's successor, the Politburo determined that the KGB would collaborate for the first time with the General Staff's intelligence arm, the GRU, in the largest peacetime espionage operation in Soviet history. East Germany's superb intelligence arm, the Stasi, was given its own collection tasks. "Not since the end of the Second World War," Andropov informed his foreign *rezidentsii,* "has the international situation been as explosive as it is now."[11] His global forces would spend the next two and a half years trying to collect evidence on Reagan administration plans to launch a nuclear attack (it still being assumed that the run-up would be camouflaged by NATO maneuvers). Hopefully, a seven- to ten-day warning could be established, affording Soviet forces time to preempt.

To Carter's irritation, Reagan had not even accepted a full briefing on the release procedures for pushing the button — the steps that would enable launch crews to fire their ground, sea, and airborne nuclear weapons. He would not get around to it until his seventeenth month in office, delegating the task of knowing the details to aides. The thought of being responsible for the button "sent shivers up his spine."[12] Kennedy, of course, had been fascinated by such mechanics and drilled deeply. Reagan found the prospect sickening.

Nonetheless, he wanted U.S. nuclear and conventional forces "modernized," which, to him, involved a quieter version of spending the Soviets to their knees, as contemplated by those very different architects of the Cold War, Curtis LeMay and John Foster Dulles. He also understood from the start that the country would have to depend heavily on "a reinvigorated NATO" and on a "close partnership among the industrial democracies." It was telling (and a sign that economic power was central in an age when West Germany and Japan had moved to the fore) that the discussion was of generic "allies."[13] There was essentially nothing in the president's deliberations to identify Britain or France, the two other Western thermonuclear powers, as full partners of the United States.

The role of the allies was nonetheless particularly sensitive given NATO's 1979 request for new U.S. intermediate range nuclear missiles. With most of its SS-20s already deployed and the U.S. missiles not yet in place, the Politburo naturally had little reason to bargain with Washington. Instead, it could play directly to Western Europeans in its search for "peace." Moscow was certain that, should America and its allied governments nonetheless proceed in the face of well-orchestrated popular outrage, NATO would be torn apart. That would move Western Europe toward conceding to Moscow an implicit protective role.

It could not be known in the spring of 1981 that the Conservative Party's Margaret Thatcher, elected British prime minister two years before, would last. Or that socialist President François Mitterrand, just elected in partnership with the French Communist Party, would take anything like the uncompromising stand he did against Soviet power, to the extent of wanting to bring French forces back into NATO planning. Or that West Germany's Helmut Kohl would defeat the Social Democrats. Whoever held the chanceries, the initiative seemed to be in the hands of the European left. "Labour rules, OK?" ran graffiti across the British inner cities.

It was around this time that Arbatov, reflecting Politburo opinion, fulminated that the Russian people (or most of them) would "eat grass" if that was to be the price of a military standing second to none. Alternatively, Reagan and his top officials believed that steady, long-term growth in U.S. defense was the most important way to demonstrate the country's staying power. To that end, the United States accelerated a military buildup of a scale not seen since Kennedy.

From 1981 to 1989, the Pentagon budget doubled from $158 billion to $304 billion. Reagan approved a $6.8 billion add-on to the Carter budget for fiscal year 1981 and then a whopping multibillion-dollar addition to Carter's final proposal, which had itself exceeded 5 percent growth in spending. Money devoted to R & D doubled between 1981 and the buildup's apogee of 1985–1986. With the economy expanded by nearly a third in real terms by 1989, however, Americans could spend $2.7 trillion for defense during the Reagan years while never sacrificing more than 6.5 percent of GDP.

The political hitch was that Americans had come to expect dramatic near-term "breakthroughs" — as in immaterial but telegenic summits — and had no appetite for sterile, long-term confrontation. The challenge was for the president to present this arms buildup as ultimately constructive. No Congress, however, would appropriate the much greater amounts needed to match the Soviet effort. Moreover, spending peaked early and, after 1985, continued to decline right until the end of the century.

The spending was not rigorously thought out, however. For instance, pledges for a "600-ship Navy" (an arbitrary number generated by President Ford's Foreign Intelligence Advisory Board) was more of a slogan than a strategy. The actual NSC document guiding the buildup would arrive a year after Congress had been asked for the money. The ten-warhead MX/Peacekeeper ICDM, at $189 million each, was finally deployed in the mid-1980s, but it would be vulnerable to a Soviet first strike unless it was made mobile. So between 1979 and 1984, $14 billion was spent trying to come up with a survivable basing mode — putting the new missiles on trains, underwater, or in subterranean desert rail yards — before they were simply stuck in the fixed silos evacuated by their Minuteman III predecessors.

Yet even such misdirection might be made worthwhile. "Brezhnev got us into an arms race that we could not afford," Eduard Shevardnadze, Soviet foreign minister from 1985 to 1990, would confess about the eighteen-year rule of that "fighter for peace."[14] The Soviet Union had got the bit between its teeth arming against a war-weary United States in the 1970s. When America recovered its spirit in the 1980s, Moscow continued to try to go even faster, and its whole system cracked.

After the Cold War, one of the Senate's more thoughtful members, Daniel Patrick Moynihan, would remark that the United States had been "spending more and more even as it was clear that the Soviet Union was coming apart."[15] He had early on detected many of the vulnerabilities within the USSR that might lead to collapse, whereas most of the experts had not. But knowing that the Soviet Union was eventually likely to pitch onto its face was no guarantee of any inevitability to the process; rather, it was an even better reason to maintain the pressure. After all, the self-mutilating Soviet

Union of 1934 to 1940 had rallied to destroy the world's strongest army in 1941 to 1945. There was no date certain for its "coming apart." One more cycle of Western concession could have brought the last and deadliest adventurist thrust. These were not people with whom America should seek "honorable accommodation," as *Washington Post* editorialists urged.[16] Accommodation had been tried, and it had failed.

So the Reagan administration persisted in what the affronted mandarinate thought was plain self deception, as Arthur Schlesinger described doctrines he might not have scanted twenty years before.[17] Not surprisingly, it also came to be asserted by McGeorge Bundy, Robert McNamara, and others — with an air of disappointment at their own incapacity to have remade the world the heroic way — that the new boys were uninformed, simplistic, crude, and dangerous. All this was delivered in the most confident of tones and reverently received by many capable listeners. Among the critics, this was also a time for mellower reflections on Stalin.[18] In his final testimony before Congress, the aging Democratic eminence Averell Harriman insisted that Americans should be sitting down and bargaining with Moscow no matter what.

In a book published in 1982, Kennan added to the terrible fears already sown in Moscow by insisting that America looked to be "in a state of undeclared war — an undeclared war pursued in anticipation of an outright one now regarded as inevitable."[19] He blamed the "military-industrial complex." In fact, Reagan's strategy was measured. The president would cross out contentious phrases in drafts of NSC directives, insisting to senior aides that he wanted nothing put in even these highly classified papers that could not be told to the Russians directly. He kept insisting that his purpose was "quiet diplomacy" and reminded overeager staff not to use terms such as economic "warfare."[20] He was speaking softly and growing a big stick.

He had ended the grain embargo (onerous for well-connected American producers) and, while in his hospital bed after the assassination attempt of March 1981, written a four-and-a-half-page personal letter to Brezhnev. Within months, he nonetheless ordered the neutron artillery shell into production and announced the buildup's details, which were to include one hundred new MX ICBMs, one hundred B-1 bombers, a follow-on "stealth" bomber, and larger Trident Ohio-class submarines. He also reiterated Carter's targeting requirements against Russia's missiles and leaders, while improving command and control procedures. The success of "building up to [make them] build down" might be best seen in his decisions about the missiles in Europe. The country was warned by diligent *Time* magazine Soviet expert, Strobe Talbott, that "the Kremlin will hardly be in a negotiating mood."[21] Who cared?

The venerable Paul Nitze had been appointed in the fall of 1981 to negotiate the issue of nuclear missiles in Europe. He despaired over the president's instructions: Pershing IIs and cruise missiles would be withheld, he was told, only if Moscow actually eliminated the SS-20, SS-4, and SS-5 systems it already had in place. Surely, Nitze insisted, the Soviets would never retreat in this regard, especially when it was clear that should America proceed, the North Atlantic alliance might shatter.[22] Almost everyone followed this conventional wisdom, including Talbott, who would be Nitze's biographer. All the foxes know the millions of little things that are the stuff of diplomacy; the quiet hedgehog Reagan knew the one big thing   that the world was ready to change.

Nobel Prize–winning novelist Günter Grass's comparison of the Pershing missile deployment to the Nazis' Wannsee Conference, which engineered the Final Solution, characterized the temper of the times. Some on Europe's hard left went further than hyperbole and street demonstrations. The Red Army Faction in West Germany launched a new terror offensive in the early 1980s, with training, weapons, false documents, and money from East Germany's secret police — impossible without KGB countenance. Among its actions were a 1981 car bomb attack at Ramstein Air Base, followed by a rocket attack in Heidelberg, which led to another terrorist offensive in 1984–1985, with an attempt to blow up a NATO school, a bombing of the U.S. air base at Frankfurt am Main, and an attack on GIs at Wiesbaden. In Paris, a U.S. official was assassinated in 1982 during one of three attacks there. Someone was engaging in real warfare.

In the United States, the quiescent "peace movement" reawakened. Seven hundred thousand people gathered at a June 1982 rally in New York's Central Park, far surpassing any anti–Vietnam War demonstration. Tales of thermonuclear catastrophe moved from the shelves of science fiction to the cathode glow of much-advertised network specials. Powerful Senate Democrats looked at U.S. military resurgence and demanded, as had Senator Ralph Flanders in the atomic monopoly year 1948, a U.S. pledge of "no first use" of nuclear weapons (the possibility of "first use" having since become the core of NATO's deterrence against a conventional blitzkrieg). In the House, Democrats forced through a resolution that would have frozen Soviet SS-20s in place and frozen the new NATO missiles out. The real enemy, it was said amid this vote of 204 to 202 in August 1982, was not the Politburo but nuclear weapons, and the president was being blinded by his anticommunism. Many academic specialists, such as Georgetown University professor Madeleine Albright, helped push the "nuclear freeze." Moscow played well to this passion, loudly committing itself to "no first use" before the UN — a propaganda move that the marshals, as one former Soviet defense official recalls, did not take seriously, "to put it mildly."[23]

During their hibernation since Cambodia 1970, protesters in the United States had changed. Believers in a "nuclear freeze" offered no sentimentalization of the Soviets as a polity, as there had been of the Viet Cong. Yet there was an ever deeper distrust of any argument citing "national security" as a reason of state. This attitude — sown by Vietnam and ripened by Watergate, FBI/CIA abuses, and countless deceits coming to light — began to reach far. Raw-edged survivalists in Idaho would come to have one thing in common with well-dressed antinuclear activists in Connecticut: a hatred and fear of Leviathan.

"Instead of a sober and balanced discussion of nuclear issues," John Newhouse concluded at the end of the Reagan presidency, "society has been confused, hence victimized, by shrill and polarized debate."[24] Such analysis slipped into characteristic Cold War phrase-making. How exactly did this "shrill and polarized debate" victimize society? Less than three years later, America had won.

It is important to distinguish between the laments of some intellectuals and the fact that the rest of America was pushing forward with increasing confidence and prosperity. George Orwell once wrote of the fury of the literary man toward the scientist, dutifully creating and building, who was stealing the writer's thunder. Many people were by now stealing the thunder of the Cold War mandarinate. Newhouse was correct only to the extent that knowledgeable Americans were wasting time battling among themselves rather than standing together against the Soviet Union. The quarrels even within government were by now among the worst of the Cold War. For instance, the State Department and the CIA had no inclination to cooperate with the new appointees on the General Advisory Committee on Arms Control and Disarmament (a group established by Congress to advise the president) in its first review of Soviet treaty compliance.

In the years since Team B, Harvard's Richard Pipes had involved himself valuably in framing public debate. He wrote about Soviet military appetites for *Commentary, Foreign Affairs,* and other magazines, although he had at least once allowed himself to be goaded at a faculty club dinner I attended into insisting that there was little significant difference in usability between thermonuclear weapons and those of the past, such as, say, dynamite.[25] In fact, Pipes possessed a much more nuanced view. He had been brought to the NSC staff at the start, to direct Soviet and Eastern European affairs, which was a key reason the Soviets wanted to skirt it. Pipes was soon reporting to former California Supreme Court Justice William P. Clark, a longtime Reagan adviser who was pivotal in advancing a many-front strategy and who became national security assistant in January 1982. These men and their colleagues began shaping a policy that might have been tailored to meet Yuri Andropov. The KGB chairman became general secretary in November, keeping a firm grip on his worldwide network of spies, informers, and agents provocateurs. At Brezhnev's funeral, George Shultz, appointed secretary of state eighteen month's into Reagan's presidency, sized him up immediately as a man who would not hesitate to take on America.[26]

No one should have been surprised that Andropov, the most formidable Soviet leader since Stalin, immediately proposed a new East-West summit, nuclear-free zones in Europe, a ban on arms sales to the developing world, and much else that his adviser Georgi Arbatov described as parts of "a crucial breakthrough." Other propagandists let Western journalists know of Andropov's appreciation for American jazz, fine white wines, and the decade of détente. Between July 1982 and January 1983, however, Reagan signed three National Security Decision Directives (NSDDs) that laid out the institutional arrangements and component parts needed to push the Soviet Union to the wall. Culminating in NSDD 75, one of the Cold War's pivotal documents, a sustained approach was created to bring the struggle to an end on America's terms.

The "costs of empire" would be raised severely as the United States moved not only to "reverse Soviet expansionism" but to diminish "the power of its privileged ruling elite."[27] Arms control would no longer be the centerpiece of U.S.-Soviet relations. New military technologies would be pushed into use, and the export of civilian ones would be tightened; economic ties would now serve strategic ends; Communist rule of Eastern Europe would be contested; aid would be used as "a most cost effective means of enhancing the security of the United States." Cultural, educational, scientific, and other visits could continue, but only if they contained "a strong ideological component" and, not incidentally, were secured against technology theft. Both America's specific interlocking steps and its overall effort to encourage "anti-totalitarian changes within the USSR" were novel. NSDD 75's nine single-spaced pages also acknowledged the value of dialogue, particularly in "driving home to Moscow that the costs of irresponsibility are high." It concluded that "important benefits for the Soviet Union" might greet a wise restraint, while "unacceptable behavior will incur costs." What was and was not "acceptable" would be unsympathetically judged in Washington.[28] This was much different from the "linkage" of the Nixon years: what mattered was not only Soviet actions but the nature of the Soviet system, including its hold on Eastern Europe.

It was not expecting too much to force this point after some thirty-five years of American endurance. Conversely, it was worth sacrificing more to that end rather than face further decades of increasingly dangerous Soviet power. The next five to ten years, roughly 1983 to 1993, were expected to be fraught with risk. What could at least be predicted were escalating appeals from important segments of domestic opinion for a more "normal" relationship with the abnormal. Today, the funniest of all conclusions about this era — as in CNN's international literary and television effort *Cold War,* which was advised by top historians and archivists — is that Andropov "saw all his hopes for peaceful coexistence shattered."[29]

Critics at the time gravely misread the Reagan strategy's cumulative effectiveness, but when it came to assessing its dangers, they were more accurate. There was much to fear on both sides. Everything Moscow touched seemed to be corroding — except the instruments of war.

N. V. Ogarkov, promoted to marshal, and chief of the General Staff since 1977, bragged of exposing "the historical futility of the capitalist system," while he privately despaired of the longer-term consequences of Moscow's lag in microelectronics. Nonetheless, the gap between Soviet weaponry and that of the West was much smaller than in any other area of production, due both to the enormous emphasis on defense and to the success of Line X. Soviet submarines could run truly silent, and those in the Typhoon class were the world's largest. The MiG-27 was second to none in aerodynamics and maneuverability, along with look-down/shoot-down radar. Soviet tanks were numerous, with excellent guns and armor. The nearly seven hundred SS-18 and SS-19 ICBMs leapfrogged in deadliness, size, and accuracy anything in the U.S. arsenal except for the newly arriving MX, which Congress (mostly concerned about upsetting mutual assured destruction) cut in number from one hundred to fifty. The United States always counted on a qualitative edge to offset Soviet quantity, but the maintenance of technological superiority across the board was by no means inevitable.

The U.S. nuclear strategy that Moscow faced, however, was not so ambitious that America could hope to "prevail" or "win" by any definition. For instance, U.S. preparedness to continue national life after a nuclear war was minuscule compared to what Moscow had steadily committed itself to in doctrine, practice, steel, and concrete since Stalin's day. U.S. mobilization plans barely touched on relocating population and much of everything else that could be moved, and only a fraction of U.S. military assets were hardened against a nuclear blast (or able to be relocated rapidly), compared to some 70 percent of all military and industrial targets in the Soviet Union. With a week's warning, the Soviet Union was ready to get through a nuclear war with "only" twenty million dead — a wound that it had endured before, once from Stalin and once from Hitler. The United States would not take any steps such as planning to evacuate cities or to shelter most of its leading citizens and would have lost half its population overnight had deterrence failed.[30] However, incautious talk in Washington about having "a capability to sustain protracted nuclear conflict" made it appear as if this administration had come to share longtime Soviet behaviors. Despite the saber rattling, at least everyone agreed that U.S. nuclear weapons would "not be viewed as a lower-cost alternative to conventional forces," as the budget obsessives of Eisenhower's day had seen them.[31]

"The peak of [Cold War] tension came in 1982–83," concludes the former Soviet commander of ballistic missile and space defense troops.[32] This period coincided with Andropov's brief supremacy. That terror-hardened man (like Stalin, he had never seen the West and was profoundly ignorant of it) was haunted by apocalyptic visions as he died from kidney disease, denouncing the "outrageous military psychosis" that he saw taking over the United States.[33]

There had been moments before in the Cold War when one side or the other had mistakenly concluded it might be under attack. Around this time, Moscow discerned a sequence of events that it believed implied that, in Washington, outright war "was now regarded as inevitable." In response, during June 1982, the Soviet Union conducted unique strategic nuclear exercises that simulated a preemptive assault by coordinate ICBM, SLBM, and SS-20 strikes on the United States and Western Europe and were self-described as a "seven hours' nuclear war which the Soviet Armed forces started."[34] For the first time since Korea, Soviet wartime military command structures were activated on a permanent basis. Andropov interpreted what became the Strategic Defense Initiative (SDI) as Reagan's next move to put the American people into a fitting frame of mind for nuclear war.[35]

Then in June 1983 came a real flash point: a satellite, the Soviets' only reliable means of detecting a U.S. launch, went defective and registered missiles pouring out of the silos. Solely because the duty officer of the day came from the algorithm department and could sense that the alert was inauthentic, it was not relayed to the Politburo, whose dread of attack by mid-1983 had "reached fever pitch."[36]

That was hardly the only perilous moment. On September 1, an SU-15 fighter pilot "flew up one side and down the other" of Korean Airlines Flight 007, as Assistant Secretary of State Richard Burt observed, and blasted this civilian plane just seconds after it had left the Soviet airspace into which it had strayed. Two hundred and sixty-nine people, including a U.S. congressman and sixty other Americans, plunged thirty-four thousand feet into the Sea of Japan. Moscow denied having found the plane's black box, and the instrument would not be returned until after the Cold War. Today, the former Soviet fighter pilot claims he is still convinced that the Boeing 747 was a U.S. intelligence probe. He regrets only that the 200-ruble bonus he received for his actions, nearly a month's pay, was half that of the radar officer who first detected the flight.[37] (That the United States had revived the 1950s psychological warfare practice of allowing air and naval probes of Russian borders went unreported.)

Years later, Russian president Boris Yeltsin would brand this incident the greatest tragedy of the Cold War. At first sight, in the light of so many other millions gone, that seems a poor judgment, but in another way he was right. For the West, the die was cast. Whether or not Soviet air defense knew Flight 007 was a civilian one, the shooting seemed to combine predictable cold-bloodedness with inconceivable inefficiency. It rallied the Western publics at a critical moment. It also laid the groundwork for the uninterrupted 1987 sports-plane flight of nineteen-year-old Mathias Rust across 450 miles of Soviet territory to Red Square, a jaunt that humiliated the Red Army at a decisive moment. Flight 007 was a tragedy for the old order.

A month after the incident, the European allies finally accepted U.S. deployment of Pershing IIs. Burt received the news at dinner with Scott Thompson, now associate director of the U.S. Information Agency. "This is the final turning point of the Cold War," he concluded emotionally.[38] A turning point perhaps, but unto an extremely treacherous street. On November 23, the first Pershings arrived in West Germany. The Soviet delegation that had been sitting with Nitze in Geneva promptly walked out, vowing not to return until the missiles were withdrawn. For the first time in twenty years, the superpowers were not engaged in any arms talks at all. "They'll be back," said Reagan phlegmatically.

And so during 1983, the United States went about its business. It was barely noticed — amid the President's equanimity, the disintegration of OPEC, the beginning of the stock market's seventeen-year roar, and the popular reaction against two overpoliticized decades — that the Soviet Union was on the brink of initiating nuclear war. Faced by the dissipation, one after another, of its dreams, the already-stressed but by no means militarily weak Soviet order began to lose touch with reality. It was indeed a "scared and furious" dictatorship. The entire system was in a frenzy: gas mask and air raid drills, civil defense preparations, classified Communist Party briefings in what one former foreign ministry official calls an atmosphere of "pre-war." Now it was Ogarkov who was comparing the likelihood of war to the 1930s.[39] Excerpts were broadcast of Stalin's famous 1941 speech to troops parading through Red Square to face the Nazis twenty miles away. In November 1983, Moscow marched just about as far as possible to the point of no return as second thought permitted. Never had the Cold War been like this.

Around the same time that a NATO exercise was practicing the command, control, and communications procedures that would authorize the release of nuclear weapons in combat, the Politburo came to surmise that U.S. forces might have begun the countdown to nuclear war. The Soviets may have come very close to launching an all-out preemptive strike. The fear was no longer that conscious wickedness might wreck the world, but that the far more common dangers of fatigue and confusion would. But not even Andropov could quite find the advantage in lighting the match, knowing that Soviet preemption would only substitute barely imaginable catastrophe for complete annihilation. What was terrifying was the isolation and sense of failure turned into outward alarm that made the Kremlin so violently suspicious in the first place.

The greatest of all Cold War "crises" did not so much come into focus in those few minutes in 1983 as over the whole gear stripping years of 1981 to 1984. By then, "crisis" was more than just one nuclear panic or journalists and politicians clamoring excitedly over a showdown in Berlin, Laos, or the Middle East. It was endemic, eroding judgment, real resources, and even the cautious preservative habits on which security from such extraordinary dangers rests. In insurance terms, civilization in the early 1980s was a bad life risk. Thereafter, pressure on the nuclear trigger eased, helped by Andropov's death in February 1984, by the slowing of a vicious cycle in which the Politburo expected to receive dire warnings from KGB and GRU operatives abroad, and by the realization in both Washington and London that the men in Moscow had become desperate.

The CIA undertook two Special National Intelligence Estimates to explain what appears to be a near-apocalypse, saying after the fact that there might have been some "abnormal fear of conflict," but concluding that Soviet leaders did not perceive "a genuine danger of imminent conflict or confrontation." For the CIA not to have realized what was afoot during this time is one of the Cold War's great intelligence blunders.

Thirteen years later, the Agency offered an open, scholarly study of the 1983 war scare, appropriately titled "A Cold War Conundrum." The interpretation no longer regarded Soviet preparations as having been disinformation and propaganda, although it concluded that the events were "not comparable to the Cuban missile crisis, when the superpowers were on a collision course." Yet it also noted that no top Soviet leader since Stalin had told his people (as did

Andropov) that the world was on the edge of a nuclear holocaust, let alone had taken several specific steps toward that end. It did not mention another evaluation of the "conundrum" — one that remains highly classified. The 1989 assessment by the president's Foreign Intelligence Advisory Board is said to be terrifying.[40]

Dobrynin would describe Moscow's perspective of events as a "paranoid interpretation."[41] It had much to be scared about. As former KGB General Leonid Shebarshin reflects, Americans during the Reagan years "did everything to destroy the Soviet Union economically and politically." His colleague in retirement, General Oleg Kalugin, concludes that "American policy in the 1980s [became] a catalyst for the collapse of the Soviet Union." There were about forty-five men and women on the NSC staff; some were by now talking privately of "takedown." Whether or not Reagan's tightening of the noose was more dangerous or virtuous than what had been tried by Nixon, Ford, and Carter in the 1970s, its effectiveness was soon evident.[42]

While squeezing the Soviet Union on all fronts, Reagan offered a constructive path out of old conflict. Conciliatory overtures in January 1984 publicly blazed the trail for his next steps. This was more than a year before Gorbachev came to office. In the words of Foreign Service veteran Jack Matlock, who served as ambassador from 1988 to 1991, "Anyone who says that Gorbachev started the process is ignorant of history."[43] Reagan had grasped the essentials; this enabled him to set the pace with the Soviets — not to "manage" them or to seek "equilibrium." Other than pushing into further confrontations even costlier to itself, the Soviet Union had no alternative but to concede the starkest compromises. The United States was deliberately blocking it from the capacity to make other choices.

The Politburo was already positioning itself for change by the time Foreign Minister Andrei Gromyko first visited the Reagan White House in late September 1984, his appearance offering a curious endorsement right before an election that was supposed to be anything but a landslide. Immediately after winning forty-nine states, the president instructed Shultz to resume the U.S.-Soviet dialogue.

The alert and vital Mikhail Gorbachev had been groomed by Andropov as the only Politburo member likely to be able to contend with Reagan. As second secretary, he bided his time during the decent interval between the indefensibly old and the relatively new provided by the moribund Konstantin Chernenko's nominal thirteen-month stewardship as party boss. Gorbachev's critical role in ending the Cold War, however, would be to lose it.

In March 1985, Gorbachev vowed in his initial speech as general secretary to maintain a firm grip on the "socialist camp" — meaning, at a minimum, continued domination of half of Europe.[44] The Soviet Union had the military power to follow through on such a promise — perhaps incompetently and irrationally, but still heavily. Gorbachev clung tenaciously to Leninist orthodoxy. Before glasnost (openness) came *uskoryenii* (acceleration), in which he spent his first year and a half vainly invoking old means to dynamize faltering tyranny: military spending was boosted, neighbors were threatened, the war in Afghanistan was intensified, and Washington was accused of promoting terrorism, in such time as it could spare from creating the AIDS virus at Fort Detrick in order to annihilate Africans. His first action was to invest billions of rubles into heavy machinery, which in Russia was essentially applied to military purposes. He attempted to change the Soviet system only upon realizing that the economy was too far gone for business as usual.

Having drilled into the proposed SALT II treaty during the late 1970s, Reagan understood the arcana of arms control — MIRVs, Minuteman versus MX missiles, SLBMs, mobile launchers, and so forth. The first summit, held in Geneva in November 1985, yielded few concrete results. "You can't win the arms race," he said privately to Gorbachev, "there is no way you can win it." No previous president had seen fit to say this directly, let alone to bring a Soviet ruler up-to-date on the history of Communist aggression starting in 1917, then simply to sit tight. Gorbachev described the president to his delegation as a "caveman, a dinosaur." Yet in his reactions, Reagan discerned someone with whom he could "do business."[45]

Between Geneva and the Reykjavík summit eleven months later, the old order heard a dingdong of doom of the sort that had never sounded before. In April 1986, the meltdown of a Soviet-designed reactor in Chernobyl created a radioactive cloud that drifted north and west over the rest of Ukraine, into present-day Belarus, and then into Poland and Scandinavia. Hundreds of thousands of Soviet citizens were evacuated, probably too late, and poison finally wafted over a flabbergasted Western Europe. The disaster, and Moscow's response to it — complete with frantic attempts at a cover-up — showcased the system's ineptitude, pushing the Soviet Union farther toward the end.

"Chernobyl will be with us forever," would say the health minister of independent Ukraine a dozen years later. Five times as many children in the years ahead would be stricken with radiation sickness than in the preceding poisonous decades of Soviet rule. The disaster that helped make his nation independent had also helped transform the dying regime's core strategy. As minister of defense General Yazov would confess, it upended prevailing military views about being able to "win" a nuclear war. Leaving nothing to chance, the National Security Agency embarked on its single most exhaustive operation ever. According to William Crowell, the powerful deputy director who had been at NSA since 1962 (and a member of Weiss's Tradecraft Society), every detail of Moscow's handling of the horror was monitored by satellite and electronic intercepts as a case study of the regime's likely responses should war ever occur.[46]

George Shultz discerned one more "turning point," as did Margaret Thatcher, in the Reykjavík summit of 1906.[47] Gorbachev's purpose, according to Foreign Ministry aide Sergei Tarasenko, was to catch the president off guard and "to kill SDI," his ambitious approach to a national missile defense.[48] To that end, and accompanied by Marshal Sergei Akhromeyev, the new chief of the General Staff, Gorbachev proposed eliminating all offensive missiles, if only Reagan's vision of SDI's development could be confined to the laboratory. The world's immediate hopes went out to Gorbachev, but Reagan set them aside and walked away from the table. "No Deal: Star Wars Sinks the Summit," *Time* reported in the sort of florid commentary that inevitably chronicled that notional disaster, the "collapse" of a "summit." Even today, partisans insist that the president's refusal to limit R & D meant "dashing any hope that *all* nuclear weapons would be eliminated within ten years" — as if there was any such chance.[49] A more balanced judgment comes from Zbigniew Brzezinski: it was at Reykjavík that the Cold War was won.

Neither the press nor Reagan's critics on the left appreciated his acumen in understanding that there was no reason to yield to Soviet bargaining. And his critics on the right, hungry for tactical victories, missed the larger possibilities ahead. From the perspective of the late 1990s, the Public Broadcasting Service's *American Experience* would simply call Reykjavík "his finest hour."[50] For Reagan and Gorbachev (and very few others who knew about it) the two days at Reykjavík contained a fitting symbol of the dangerous disorder surrounding the discussions, as well as of Soviet technological shortcomings. Somewhere, a U.S. submarine was accidentally rammed by a Soviet one, just one of many undisclosed incidents that kept the world on the brink.

After Reykjavík, the nuclear dialogue was repitched at almost bewildering speed: Reagan had forced the choice back upon the Soviet rulers to go on spending and walk into the abyss without his assistance, or to preserve the husk of power for a little while longer. It was too late for them to escape the logic of force; they tried to keep up just long enough to sacrifice both hope and maintenance. Absent SDI, Matlock believes, it is unlikely that Gorbachev could have convinced his military to accept the prospect of 50 percent cuts in heavy missiles that Reagan, nearly alone in Washington, had believed it reasonable for the United States to seek at Reykjavík.[51] At least this summit showed something surprising: in a little over three years since SDI had been announced, a general secretary was prepared to halve his country's strategic forces, asking in return only that the United States forgo a highly speculative goal. That was an unusual return indeed on a new investment so far of around $6 billion.

A year later, Gorbachev finally came to Washington to sign the INF (intermediate range nuclear forces) Treaty, eliminating all Soviet SS-20 and NATO Pershing II missiles. There was no reference to SDI. "The Soviets blinked," Reagan wrote in his diary, a telling document that his renowned biographer describes as "coldly impressive, the work of a man who knew exactly what he believed and wanted."[52] For the first time ever, arms control passed from promises for the future to destruction of existing armaments — four times as many warheads on the Soviet side as on the American. For the first time also, Moscow agreed to on-site verification. "Billions of rubles had been wasted," Dobrynin laments in his memoirs, "because of our own hasty decision to deploy the missiles in the first place."[53]

Reagan's critics nonetheless insist that the aspect of his strategy that embraced "building up to build down," let alone SDI, actually "delayed the eventual end of the cold war." To prove otherwise, they insist, would require demonstrating that "Soviet military spending (either actual or as a percentage of overall government spending) would have had to have shown regular increases, evidence of attempts to match or exceed U.S. expenditures."[54] That, of course, is exactly what happened.

The final swelling of Moscow's self-consuming outlays had begun with an amazing 45 percent increase in military spending initiated before the 1980 presidential election. Moreover, from 1981 to 1985, virtually all the increase in machinery output — the only fast-growing segment of the Soviet economy — was simultaneously assigned to the military, a shift unprecedented since the Korean War. The military share of Soviet GDP rose from approximately 21 to 22 percent in 1981 to 26 to 27 percent in 1985. The Politburo boosted military spending again in 1983, increasing it to about 55 percent above the 1980 level. After coming to power in 1985, Gorbachev promptly approved another 45 percent increase for the last half of the decade, with little of that going to manpower. Although military spending ceased to grow after 1988, Gorbachev ensured that spending during the Soviet Union's last five years equaled or exceeded what had been lavished on the military by Brezhnev, Andropov, and Chernenko from 1980 to 1985.[55]

Gorbachev also signed, in his "characteristic scrawl," according to the deputy director of the Soviet germ warfare program, a five-year plan, for 1985 to 1990, that brought the Soviet Union to its high point of developing an arsenal of deadly pathogens, including plague, brucellosis, tularemia, anthrax, and smallpox. (Unfortunately for Biopreparat, the AIDS virus's long incubation period prevented it from being used as a weapon.) Under Gorbachev, there was no limit to the resources Moscow was prepared to invest. In 1990, $1 billion and more than sixty thousand skilled workers would be devoted to match deadly germs (often in vaccine-resistant strains) with missiles aimed at New York, Los Angeles, Chicago, and Seattle. At the same time U.S. scientists were collaborating with Russian counterparts to eradicate any trace of smallpox in the world (from which some 300 million people died during the twentieth century), the Soviet Union was secretly hoarding twenty tons of the germ for military use.[56] New strains were being created. All this during glasnost.

The most demanding of totalitarian powers, which since 1959 had devoted ever greater amounts to its armed forces, was not going to hold back just to please an aging actor. This was especially true of Gorbachev, who was so determined to keep his grip on the "socialist camp" and to placate the military, an ever greater estate of the realm.

An index of the Kremlin's willingness to live with the rest of the country "eating grass" is embodied in the ratio of military spending to GDP: 10 to 12 percent in 1960 versus about 30 percent in the 1980s. The particular demands of Moscow's nuclear-war-fighting posture made the burden all the heavier. Shevardnadze, who succeeded Gromyko as foreign minister, priced the incremental cost of "confrontation" (that is, pushing beyond the requirements of nuclear parity) at 700 billion rubles, just for the years 1977 to 1988 — a sum perhaps equal to the country's entire GDP in 1983.[57] Suicidal as it was in the long term, this money was still buying alarming capacities in the short term.

Ultimately, arms control did not end the arms race; armaments did. The rest of the strategy was similarly effective, but as usual, the cost of effectiveness was high. One cost was the sheer size and expense of the effort. Another was confusion, for the determination to constrict, perhaps to end, the Soviet Union was not expected to show returns so soon. A third cost was fatigue, for the work had to be done fast while the energy was high.

✪

During the late 1970s and into the 1980s, Andropov's KGB had been running a huge endeavor to quantify the "correlation of forces" — the entire balance of political, economic, military, and cultural trends between the Soviet Union and the West. The Politburo took that analysis extremely seriously, and it was likely a cause of Andropov feeling cornered. The CIA learned about its existence through "blue border" sources, meaning well-placed moles. The Russians had more or less reached the McNamara stage of primitive confidence in basic techniques of systems analysis without understanding the significance of the data. Correctly, however, all trends — military, economic, technological, and political — were shown to be going against "progressive" forces worldwide.

If even emphatically "garbage-in, garbage-out" secret police social science had to concede approaching disaster, the bemused but not stupid men at the top could begin to consider what happens when a state uses more than a quarter of its production for military purposes, while collectivized agriculture wastes another 10 to 15 percent. As his increasingly gloomy speeches show from the mid-1970s on, Andropov understood the consequences. So did Reagan.

Nonetheless, many influential Americans not only misgauged the extent of Moscow's vulnerability but also were unable to accept the possibility of U.S.-assisted Soviet economic implosion. They even reported the system's buoyancy. The Soviet economy was making "great material progress," the ineffable John Kenneth Galbraith wrote in 1984, citing the cheery faces on Moscow's streets. All this was made possible, he said, because Soviet methods, unlike Western ones, made full use of manpower. "Those in the U.S. who think the Soviet Union is on the verge of economic and social collapse, ready with one small push to go over the brink," snorted Arthur Schlesinger, "are . . . only kidding themselves."[58] As in the late 1950s, it remained difficult for some otherwise well-informed people to imagine that collectivism made no practical sense.

The price of maintaining great-power standing on the resources of an irrational economy increasingly drove the Soviet Union into the role of a pirate state. In 1970, it was believed to be about fifteen years behind in computer electronics. By 1981, the gap was said to be narrowing: America was only three to four years ahead, according to NSC analysts; perhaps ten, suggested the Defense Department. In any event, the U.S. lead was grievous for Moscow. Ogarkov continued to worry about the "serious consequences" likely to stem from the "fast pace" of U.S. technological development.[59] His system could be remarkably good at conceptualization, as well as at applying laboratory or pilot program innovations, but it often failed in scaling up. One among many examples is "stealth" technology, conceived in the early 1960s by Pyotr Ufimtsev, chief scientist at the Moscow Institute of Radio Engineering but developed by Lockheed with a Cray 1 supercomputer for the B-2 bomber.

An estimated 100,000 people were working in the Soviet Union just to translate stolen documents. Access to Western technology was a lifeline for the regime. There was no reason not to snatch it away, nor was there any reason to let Moscow continue to have access to hard currency. NSC decisions made explicit that the garrote would be twisted while "forcing the USSR to bear the brunt of its economic shortcomings." Indeed, it was Russia's shortcomings in technology and hard currency earnings, as well as the prospect of the United States squeezing further, that made Reagan's announcement of SDI "a horror," as the deputy foreign minister put it.[60] Those shortcomings were also why Line X's mission was more vital than ever and why the Soviet future rested heavily on access to foreign finance.

In 1979, Roger W. Robinson, Jr., son of the FBI agent who had arrested Judith Coplon for espionage thirty years earlier, was a vice president in the USSR/Eastern European Section of Chase Manhattan's International Division. Trained in Soviet economics, Robinson also worked as a personal assistant to David Rockefeller, the bank's chairman. Natural gas exports by this time were supplementing, if not yet replacing, oil as the Soviet Union's principal hard-currency earner. Even given his other responsibilities at Chase, Robinson was struck by the curious financing under way for the seventeen-hundred-mile Orenburg pipeline — the largest East West deal so far — which would link the Soviet Union to the Western European gas grid.

Previously, such oil and gas projects had been financed by barter. There was no reason for Moscow to be in the syndicated loan market for funds to purchase wide-diameter pipe, compressors, turbines, and other equipment. It was all the more puzzling to Robinson in light of a conversation with a deputy minister of the Soviet gas industry, who had made it clear that his ministry would finance the procurement of Western equipment and technology via gas deliveries to Western Europe, as had been done in the past. He apparently had no idea that the Moscow-dominated International Investment Bank (an institution including the Eastern European satellites in financial ties) was finalizing the raising of some $2.4 billion, ostensibly for pipeline construction, via four syndicated loans led by Deutsche Bank, Dresdner Bank, and Chase. Robinson had uncovered an elaborate double-financing scheme that involved the unwitting participation of Chase. He reported it to the CIA; a mid-level officer thanked him for his concern.

No one in 1979 had any idea as to how Moscow would use the extra few billion in borrowed money. Since its *total* annual hard-currency income was only around $32 billion, this was a significant amount of discretionary cash. The loan drawdown from Chase, for example, had seemingly been transferred to Crédit Lyonnais in Paris and subsequently disappeared. The Western lending strangely coincided with surges in Soviet military spending; with generosity to Angola, Vietnam, and Ethiopia; and with well-financed terror in Europe and the Middle East. Oil, gas, guns, and gold accounted for around 80 percent of the paltry Soviet hard-currency income, with the first two accounting for some two-thirds. A sizable percentage of this income was going to meet the "costs of empire"; the gap was being financed by Western governments and commercial banks.

The sinew of war is money, they said in the Renaissance, but these were modern times. Trade worked for peace, right? Washington had never before regarded the diversion of large-scale Western loans as a national security problem. The eminent German bankers likely knew of the Orenburg scheme, but virtually no one on the U.S. side had been much concerned. The deal was essentially complete, and the CIA and the NSC staff were apparently unable to recognize its significance. In Washington, "national security" still barely involved economics and finance. No one on the NSC staff possessed a background on Wall Street, and probably no one at the Agency did either.

In 1980, Moscow announced a far larger venture — the twin-stranded Yamal gas pipeline, which would extend thirty-six hundred miles and require multibillion-dollar Western loans to reap Moscow $10 billion to $20 billion a year once the two pipelines opened. The Soviet Union's biggest-ever construction project was to bring Siberian natural gas to the Czech border, where it would be drawn into German and Austrian energy systems. So the issue was not just that the Soviets were double-dipping into Western financial markets on the same project revenues, but also that Western Europe was likely to become dependent for at least 60 percent of its total gas supplies on a state quite capable of playing with supplies and prices for political ends — perhaps, for starters, to undercut the development of Norway's Troll gas field. Meanwhile, Western companies bid against each other for pipeline contracts, thereby enabling Moscow to negotiate credit at below-market rates.

Then, in 1981, for the first time in the Cold War, a U.S. administration began looking at the Soviet Union from the perspective of cash flow. From his vantage point at Chase, the otherwise apolitical Robinson offered seminal congressional testimony and a provocative series of articles, urging that Western Europe avoid dependence on Soviet energy in favor of more secure sources such as Norway, and that financial transactions with the East be more disciplined. The NSC's Norman Bailey, recently a professor of economics at the City University of New York (CUNY), was the first to launch a "follow the money" initiative (Watergate's overdue contribution to strategic thinking) toward Moscow, as would later become commonplace in dealing with drugs and terrorism. The Reagan administration's initial approaches to Western Europe and to the Japanese (concerning the parallel Sakhalin gas and oil project with Moscow) revealed no willingness to cooperate in opposing the Soviet Union on the issue. NATO's forum for arranging alliance-wide export controls was explicitly limited to dealing with primarily military technologies.

In December 1981, the Soviets' enforcement of martial law on Poland provided the "pretext" for the United States' next steps, according to Bailey, who served as the NSC's new senior director of international economic affairs.[61] Rather than retaliating by throwing Poland into default on its debts, the administration would go directly after Moscow's hard-currency. Reagan imposed wide-ranging sanctions against both Poland's military regime and its puppet masters. The NSC estimated that it would cost Moscow the crippling sum of roughly "ten billion dollars annually for several years" if all Western equipment and technology were denied.[62] That, however, was not about to happen. Once U.S. companies were forbidden to sell tools vital to Yamal, Western Europeans saw even more opportunity. But their companies were largely operating under U.S. licenses or were U.S. subsidiaries, since it was the United States that exercised a near monopoly on specialized drilling and other equipment originally developed to cut into Alaska's North Slope.

Robinson left Chase in March 1982 for the NSC staff, where he worked closely with NSC colleagues and senior Pentagon officials, as well as with the CIA director. An entrepreneurial lawyer steeped in financial services, William Casey also understood how much could be accomplished by curtailing Soviet access to subsidized Western credits and windfall energy earnings. Reagan vainly hoped that the allies would rally behind these Poland-related economic sanctions. As he delivered his impassioned plea at a NATO summit in June, recall Americans who were present, Chancellor Schmidt pointedly looked out the window. Quickly thereafter, the president calmly used an NSC meeting to prohibit all subsidiaries of U.S. companies abroad, as well as foreign licensees of U.S. technology, from shipping pipeline equipment and technology to the Soviet Union. Even equipment that had already been delivered to Europe was covered. The British, French, Italians, and Germans reacted with "hysterical opposition" and chose to abide by their contracts with Moscow.[63] This time, however, in contrast to twenty years earlier, the U.S.-compelled embargo would be much more than symbolic.

For Reagan, the short-term maximization of exports, as well as of NATO harmony, was a secondary concern. Dollar diplomacy was going into reverse. The overbearing Alexander Haig, a former Kissinger aide and supreme commander in Europe who served as Reagan's first secretary of state, adamantly opposed these unprecedented extraterritorial restraints. He privately assured allied leaders, such as West German Foreign Minister Hans-Dietrich Genscher, that he would deal with the problem — that is, dilute the president's simpleminded intransigence.[64] Reports of these conversations went to the White House and arrived in the hands of William Clark.

This quietly thoughtful man, the antithesis of Haig, was a major but still barely known figure in ending the Cold War. According to Reagan's biographer, Edmund Morris, he was the only man the president considered a friend. His casual lack of interest in Washington, as well as his disdain for the frantic vocabularies of "crisis" and "emergency," reflected an older, more confident America. A West Coast rancher rarely yearns to cut *bella figura* as a world statesman. He was also entirely different from the ambitious college professors who had run the National Security Council staff in nearly every year of the Cold War's middle stage. Although he served in that role only until October 1983, he helped shatter the Soviet Union before briefly taking over the Interior Department, then returning to his cattle. His reaction to Haig's intrigues and bluster was not ideological but constitutional: using back channels of this sort was a challenge to presidential authority. General Haig promptly departed from office on June 25 following one final outburst in front of Clark.

"I expect that firm allied commitments will emerge," the president predicted after European companies that tried to thwart his embargo — Britain's John Brown Engineering, Dresser France, Germany's AEG Kanis, Italy's Nuovo Pignone — were shut out of the U.S. market.[65] Since the Ford administration, George Shultz had worked as the highly effective president of Bechtel and (before replacing Haig) had visited Western Europe, at Reagan's request, to report on the feasibility of stopping the Yamal pipeline. With his business school and Fortune 500 regard for contract sanctity, and after encounters with angry allies, Shultz found the sanctions as feckless as had his predecessor. So did most CIA officers working on the issue. But after what had just happened to Haig, no one was about to force the question in the Oval Office, despite fevered protests also under way in Europe against Pershing missiles. Reagan held firm as projections of lost U.S. revenue appeared to be crippling the wayward European companies.

Reagan's personal approach to the allies was measured, even humorous, as when he smilingly held up the telephone receiver so his staff could briefly hear an extended scolding delivered by Margaret Thatcher. He wanted to permit nothing that would further the Soviet military buildup or improve Moscow's position in the world, but not necessarily to restrict all useful commerce. He reminded his senior officials not to compromise his "quiet diplomacy" with Moscow.[66] The handwritten notes, marginalia, and addenda to the NSC paperwork of the early 1980s show a president thoroughly engaged in shaping a strategy that reflected his convictions.

A long-overdue instrument was created in July 1982. Institutionally, a cabinet-level apparatus was needed to help implement this complicated, unprecedented strategy — particularly to assist the NSC in "discharging its responsibilities for international economic policy."[67] Clark established, under the president's direction, the Senior Interdepartmental Group–International Economic Policy. It was the only time during the Cold War that the heads of the CIA, NSC, and Department of Defense belonged to a top policy-formulating organization mandated to integrate international economic and financial affairs with national security. Although the group was chaired by the treasury secretary, with the secretary of state as vice chair, it reported through Clark to the president, with Clark ensuring that all government agencies would execute its policies in a manner consistent with Reagan's goals.

Reagan refused to modify his decision on extraterritoriality despite intense pressure from allied governments, U.S. industry and its friends in Congress, David Rockefeller, and his own cabinet. This led to negotiations with the allies in La Sapinière, Canada, in October, setting in place an export regime with the East that allowed Washington to relax its pressure on the allies by November. La Sapinière's significance was outlined in December's NSDD 66, "East-West Economic Relations and Poland-Related Sanctions," a document composed to ensure that the State Department did not cease twisting the arms of both Western Europe and Russia. Its conclusions were ratified at the Williamsburg economic summit the following May. Measures included lessening of export credit interest rate subsidization by the West, tightening of technology export controls, and exploration of alternative gas supplies for Western Europe.

The payoffs were an increase in the cost of the first strand of the Yamal pipeline to closer to true cost (plus a maiming two-year delay, during which world oil and gas prices fell), effective cancellation of the second strand (it would not be completed until 1999, ten years later than planned), contraction of European and Japanese credit relations with the Soviet Union and its satellites, curtailment of the Soviet financial lifeline, and a deepening of the Soviet economic and financial crisis. Moscow paid at least $1 billion extra in hard currency just to offset the denial of pipeline parts, not to mention the cost of having to divert much of its talent to making substitutes.

In addition, the Organization for Economic Cooperation and Development, which comprised the world's seven most industrialized countries, moved the Soviet Union (at U.S. insistence) from a Category II standing of "less developed country" to a Category I standing of "relatively rich country." This was a compliment the Soviets could have done without, for it eliminated taxpayer subsidies on official credits to the Soviet Union. Irreparable damage had been accomplished by the time Robinson left the NSC in 1985 and a new team at the Treasury Department finally became involved in what should have been attended to well before the 1980s. Perhaps understandably, memoirs of several senior officials who opposed the sanctions dismiss their effectiveness. The final results show otherwise.

"Certainly it was economic warfare," recalls Richard Perle, an assistant secretary of defense who had been Senator Henry Jackson's arms control adviser, "although we had to deny it at the time."[68] Matters were dangerous enough without publicly acknowledging the deliberate constricting of cash, technology, and energy markets. Dealings with the allies also had to be firm but correct, capable of withstanding the light of day. As Reagan said repeatedly, NATO was an indispensable shield of democracy. His disdain for Western Europe's left-leaning elites was sedulously kept off the record.

By 1983, products assessed as "high technology" composed merely 5.4 percent, or $39 million worth, of U.S. manufactured goods sold to the Soviet Union, in contrast to one-third (of a much greater volume) only eight years before.[69] Stolen technology nonetheless helped the Soviets keep going a little longer, not only providing the base for perhaps half of all major Soviet defense industry projects, but also helping the Soviet economy to advance in metallurgy, power generation, engineering, and much more. Line X's existence, so insistently denied by the CIA during the heyday of détente, was conclusively demonstrated half a year after Reagan came to office.

Here there was opportunity for deep allied cooperation. France's counterintelligence arm acquired a defector in place (designated "Farewell") who supplied more than four thousand documents, including lists of what needed to be stolen and of the Soviet organizations that were expecting the goods. The documents also contained the names of more than two hundred Line X officers stationed in ten KGB *rezidentsii* in the West. Mitterrand handed the material to Reagan. It was irrefutable that a system of thefts comparable to the 1940s "super Lend-Lease" of Soviet espionage was in full operation. Line X had by then fulfilled more than two-thirds of the shopping list drawn up a decade before. This exposure of perhaps the KGB's greatest secret helped stiffen allied leaders. Once in its victims' hands, the list cast a timely backlight on precisely which areas of the Soviet military and economy were most technologically deficient and, by implication, what rewards might come from denying the East any technology that could help this rigid regime adapt without changing.

Since the early 1970s, the KGB had obtained so many thousands of American blueprints and products "that it appeared that the Soviet military and civil sectors were in large measure running their research on that of the West, particularly the United States," recalled Gus Weiss, who had gone back to the White House from the Pentagon after Reagan's election. "American science was supporting Soviet defense, whether in radar, computers, machine tools, or semiconductors."[70] U.S. industry would create elaborate systems, while Line X provided the Soviets with the information to build countermeasures nearly in parallel. Some Soviet weapons crafted from U.S. blueprints, such as the Kirov-class cruiser, debuted sooner than the American models from whose plans they were copied.

Moscow had gone so far as to dedicate three thousand people in its Lithuanian republic solely to try to reengineer stolen Digital Equipment Corporation VAX series computers. Even the Soviet space shuttle proved to be a replica of a (rejected) NASA design. Nor was agriculture neglected; the KGB stole high-quality seeds from Western laboratories. Moreover, the new ABM system (the one permitted by treaty) that became operational around Moscow in 1987 was a carbon copy, save for more powerful computers, of the U.S. Nike-X system that McNamara had persuaded Lyndon Johnson not to install twenty years earlier.[71]

Reagan relayed "Farewell's" hoard to William Casey, the first CIA director to be in the cabinet, and asked him what to do with it. As a figure literally from the past, that presciently capable OSS veteran emulated the tradecraft and mystique of his mentor, "Wild Bill" Donovan, another New York lawyer and corner-cutter. Casey also understood what "Farewell's" thefts indicated about the Soviet economy. "It's going to implode," he was already muttering in April 1982 — provided the United States applied appropriate pressure. This is the intelligence community opinion that mattered to Reagan.

With characteristic Cold War urgency — rebounding from equally characteristic neglected warning in the 1970s — the technology hemorrhage forced its way into the highest-secret priorities. The CIA immediately established the Technology Transfer Intelligence Center. The Pentagon set up damage assessment committees and tightened controls, then spent $400 million more to protect private phone lines in New York, San Francisco, and Washington from Soviet eavesdropping. Soviet wanderings through research centers and universities under the guise of "educational, scientific and other cooperative exchanges" were gravely narrowed.[72] The FBI redoubled its efforts around campuses and laboratories, as "Farewell's" documents reflected how KGB operatives developed contacts at major American universities such as MIT. After several of these visitors were caught stealing secrets, according to Jan Herring, who helped run the CIA's counterintelligence thrust (before setting up Motorola's corporate intelligence unit), there was even serious thought given to expelling all foreign students. It was Japan, with more than four thousand industry- and government-sponsored researchers quietly working away in the United States, that screamed the loudest against such overreaction.[73]

Inevitably, certain officials and interested organizations were in no hurry to change the status quo. Some people in the FBI insisted that the losses were overstated. (It had been the Bureau's responsibility to prevent them.) Some CIA officers feared that expelling Soviet scientists and assorted guests would impede Agency operations in the Soviet Union. (They hadn't recruited a "Farewell.") The National Academy of Sciences argued that unimpeded ties with Soviet researchers, many of whom were given collection tasks during their U.S. visits, promised peaceful relations. More than a few defense technologists argued that curbing such openness might hinder U.S. development of new weapons. "Some people, especially the R & D people, liked the arms race," recalls the former Pentagon official in charge of technology security policy.[74] Competition, after all, is the secret of efficiency.

Yet even then, Line X had barely attained its full powerful pull. There could not have been a more enticing moment for a sting.

In January 1982, Weiss, on his own initiative, proposed to Casey that some of the technologies the Soviets were targeting be "altered." In part through Weiss's Tradecraft Society irregulars, key officials within the CIA, FBI, NSA, and Pentagon collaborated with a seamlessness never before encountered. Products were modified and exposed to Line X collection channels. The Americans could not lose: even if the KGB should discover that stolen technologies had been doctored, it would not know which ones to trust in the future.

For example, there was another dimension to the pipeline equipment embargo. As at the Karma River truck plant, U.S. software for the pipeline was vital, and the Soviets contrived in this case to obtain it illegally through Canada. The FBI doctored the coding to cause destructive power overloads once applied in Russia, inducing surges and causing sundry destruction. At least one immense (and deadly) pipeline explosion could be seen from space. In another instance, the president of Texas Instruments allowed one of his company's chip-testing devices to be made available for Soviet interception in Rotterdam. The machine was modified to work initially as expected, but after a few trust-winning months, it would salt its output with defective chips. (Only later did it register that some of the chips might end up in the Soviet strategic missile program.) Other technologies, such as gas turbine designs, were elegantly deformed, mostly in a laboratory at the Pentagon, as Line X swallowed whatever leading-edge tools and methods seemed available.

To make matters worse for Moscow, those two hundred operatives were rounded up. Farewell, for his part, was uncovered by the KGB after a murder in Gorky Park. He was then shot. In any event, Soviet collection crumbled. It was unable to distinguish the kosher from the unclean, just at the time when Reagan confronted the USSR with the most immense technological challenge of all.

Reagan's understanding of the depth of Soviet technology deficiencies combined with his romantic vision of a nuclear-free world. He knew that the right mumbo-jumbo about committing the United States to an unprecedentedly ambitious venture on the space frontier would torment Moscow, but also that something might work. Since anything was possible with American ingenuity and wealth, who knew what would shake out? Although such an attitude was more characteristic of the 1940s and 1950s than the burned-out

1970s, it seemed applicable here. Hence, in March 1983, Reagan announced the decision to "embark on a program to counter the awesome Soviet missile threat with measures that are defensive," but with no promise that this would be accomplished even by the end of the century. The words were chosen carefully. It was simply "reasonable," he said, "for us to begin this effort."[75]

U.S. plans for this final instrument of strategic defense, also shaped by Clark, were unveiled two months after NSDD 75. Even though all the planning around SDI never involved using nuclear warheads to intercept ICBMs, as has been the Russian practice, the fact that U.S. officials were moving to protect their country worsened the Kremlin's nightmare. "Reagan was clearly struck by the fact that we had spent billions on national defense," recalls his first domestic policy adviser, "yet we were totally helpless" should the Soviets launch.[76]

Robert McFarlane, who with gently ambitious background soon replaced Clark as national security assistant, described SDI as more of a battle of resources than a military concept. "It was really about how we could reorient our investments strategy," he has reminisced.[77] The mere possibility of America preparing to spend $30 billion to $40 billion or more on creating the ultimate "box" of science fiction finally overstretched Moscow's capabilities — if not in the immediate moment, then in the way the Russians saw the future. In fact, SDI was most powerful as a play against the Russian imagination, prompting science fiction wizard Robert Heinlein to applaud missile defense as "the best news I've heard since V-J Day."[78]

The Soviets, chilled by Western triumphs in computing, the life sciences, and space, were ready to assume that their rivals had found yet newer worlds to conquer. SDI might be mocked as "Star Wars," but the designation had its own appropriateness to the times and stakes involved. One eminent British diplomat, a former high commissioner to both India and Pakistan, had a simple description of the invasion of Afghanistan: "The Empire Strikes Back."[79] Of course, Moscow's own immense futuristic strategic defense efforts were under way, many of which had started well before Reagan's speech.[80] Impressive prototype hardware was being developed, including a large airborne laser, two multimegawatt lasers, and large (one-to-three-meter) beryllium mirrors, to list only publicly known examples. To supplement its already existing national ABM system — the one formed by large battle management radars integrated with nuclear-tipped dual-purpose interceptor missiles — the Soviet Union was probably spending as much as the United States on a space-based initiative, at least through the mid-1980s.

To an extent, McFarlane was correct about SDI ultimately being a competition of resources. But as the dangers of late 1983 show, the Soviets saw it as part of a military environment that was far more unpredictable than anyone in the administration realized. Not only did fears unrecognized in Washington keep mounting, but a critical distinction separated the Soviets' sense of vulnerability from Americans' parallel perception of theirs — one that would have appalled U.S. decision makers had it been better understood.

In recent years, a flood of material has been published in Russian concerning all sorts of Soviet weaponry. Technical studies and program histories of tanks, aircraft, ships, and missiles are available to the casual reader or hobbyist in Russia and can be shipped by mail to curious Americans. "We spent around $10 billion trying to get the information just on that shelf," said strategic analyst William Lee, as he pointed to a dozen or so poorly bound volumes. Meanwhile, the United States has declassified many of its National Intelligence Estimates. For the first time, comparisons can be drawn to illuminate once-bitter controversies over Soviet capabilities. What the NIEs called "gaps" in this information can now be filled in.

For example, the Soviets judged their ICBM silos to be five to ten times more vulnerable to an American surprise attack than U.S. analysts believed. (The Air Force had no interest in hearing of Soviet anxieties about insufficiently hardened silos. That would undercut arguments for buying the MX.) In the nightmare world in which men spoke of a "theoretical war-winning capability," the Soviets had all the more reason to assume that it was they who needed to launch first should nuclear war seem imminent. Meanwhile, they were intent on being able to destroy America's ICBMs in a first strike, as U.S. explainers of a "window of vulnerability" had been insisting to mixed effect since the mid-1970s. This fact could not be proved conclusively until today, although a handful of perceptive analysts saw it coming at the time.[81]

Ballistic missile defense was one way for the United States to respond. Using the hyperbole customary in these years, the usually thoughtful George Ball denounced the president's call for SDI as "one of the most irresponsible acts by any head of state in modern times," which would "seriously jeopardize the confidence and support of our NATO allies."[82] He was ridiculing the president for upending two (often contradictory) core assumptions of U.S. policy: that stability depended on mutual vulnerability, and that the United States would respond with nuclear weapons against any Soviet attack on Western Europe, thereby ensuring a Soviet counterstrike and "trading New York for Bonn," as the saying went.

In its own way, SDI was a descendant of Thomas Finletter's 1948 "Celestial Maginot Line," which had originally tormented the Europeans. They now bewailed "a Maginot Line in space" as the technological embodiment of America's untrustworthiness to defend the Old World. De Gaulle's suspicions lived. Official complaints, however, could be assuaged in Britain and West Germany by promises of billion-dollar research agreements. As for the de facto allies in Beijing, they welcomed SDI as one indication that the United States was no longer a power "on the decline," as Mao had described it in 1973. Instead, Washington was seen as having "resolutely taken a number of steps" against the Soviet Union. Beijing may also have concluded that China was therefore less important to U.S. calculations, with its freedom of action more limited than in the 1970s.[83] It ended up playing a minimal role in the Cold War's last stage.

SDI itself sprang in part from frustration over SALT's inadequacies. But a modernized version of America's previous attempt at ballistic missile defense — one that had depended on fast nuclear-tipped interceptors — was not going to be deployed instead. First, such a step would be a clear U.S. violation of the still-popular ABM treaty, whereas the standing of a space-based defense was at least ambiguous. Second, Americans were not about to let their cities be ringed by warhead-carrying missiles, as had been done against bombers in the late 1950s and as had been contemplated against ICBMs in the late 1960s. Unlike the Russians, Washington would try to use elaborate non-nuclear means to defend its continent.

No one but Reagan dreamed of SDI becoming a bullet-proof shield — except, perhaps, Marshal Akhromeyev and General Makhumet Gareev, head of analysis in the Soviet Ministry of Defense. (As chief of staff, Akhromeyev helped convince Gorbachev that SDI could work, and Gareev saw no way to come up with countermeasures.)[84] A real-world version of the "box" written about by James Blish was neither technologically feasible nor affordable. The practical imperative, as in the ABM debates of a dozen years earlier, was to defend America in a way that ruined any Soviet confidence in the efficacy of a disarming first strike. If building a worthwhile defense was altogether impossible, as its American critics claimed, one wonders why the Soviets did not ignore SDI or urge Reagan to spend all the more on such folly.

Call it what one would, this last lunge in America's Cold War pursuit of shielding the nation sums up the costs as well as the winnings of the endgame decade. An arms race is a competition in imposing burdens, as well as in augmenting one's own strengths. The United States, therefore, redrew the lines of 1970s arms control. To the horror of the original architects. To them, missile defenses were destabilizing — in contrast to the less expensive, if equally unreal, theory of mutual assured destruction. Of course, over the longer term, it was the Soviet Union that SDI helped destabilize, not the nuclear balance.

"Star Wars unnerved the Soviets, the New York Times science correspondent would write, "making them amenable to arms negotiation at a time when they were engaged in a large expansion of their nuclear arsenal." Genrikh Trofimenko, longtime professor at the Soviet Union's diplomatic academy, Foreign Ministry adviser, and occasional propagandist, personalizes this observation. As he concludes about Gorbachev, it "was the most effective single act to bring that old *apparatchik* to his senses."[85] Furthermore, SDI brought some peace and quiet to the home front. Within months of Reagan's speech, the nuclear freeze movement fizzled.[86] Just as antiwar protests had evaporated with the end of the draft, Reagan's dream of multinational invulnerability removed a central rallying point of his opponents.

SDI "was probably oversold with the American public," recalls Matlock, "but to get money for anything you have to oversell it."[87] There was a price to this, however. Missile defense was pursued in so casually unfocused a fashion that scientific principles were regularly bypassed in favor of political content. That SDI was the "largest" or "most expensive" military research program ever was elided into the suggestion that it was the "most effective" or "most necessary" ever. The first head of the venture, an Air Force general who was a fine executive, would understandably use that superlative of size as a business credential upon leaving the Pentagon for Silicon Valley. At the time, it was the rigorously inclined George Shultz who worried about the hype. For his trouble, the Pentagon questioned whether he had the proper clearances for a top-secret SDI briefing.[88]

The total amounts that might be needed for a national missile defense were anyone's guess. Pentagon estimates began at a high of

$100 billion in 1983 and by 1986 had been compelled to dwindle to $56 billion. Meanwhile, SDI became "a scientific free-for-all, a license to spend tens of billions of dollars as creatively as possible." Some of this creativity issued in allegedly high-minded deceptions acclaiming breakthroughs that were never achieved. Time and again, physicist Edward Teller, popularly known as the "father of the H-bomb," insisted that "the X-ray laser works" — always categorically and always falsely.[89]

This would-be counterweapon that originally launched SDI was cheerfully succeeded by other approaches. A billion dollars would be sunk into just one, Brilliant Pebbles. One hundred thousand tiny electronic interceptors (or perhaps just one-tenth the number of Pebbles) might provide a space-based means to shred attacking missiles — at "an eminently affordable strategic defense system cost of $30 to $50 billion," according to Teller's Lawrence Livermore National Laboratory.[90]

By then, the desire to uphold the conventional wisdom of arms control had also gone to extremes. "The opponents of SDI did not want us to aggressively pursue the research because, Lord forbid, we might be able to do it," concluded Colin Powell, Reagan's last national security assistant before being appointed chairman of the Joint Chiefs of Staff. That would mean "all of their thinking about mutual assured destruction would be down the tubes."[91] Congressional Democrats were much more concerned about endangering the ABM treaty than they were about waste, and in 1986 they threatened to cut off all the money.

One of SDI's most gifted opponents was experimental physicist Richard Garwin, a designer with Teller of the first hydrogen bomb, longtime Defense Department consultant, holder of the prestigious title "IBM Fellow" at that still-dominant institution, and Kennedy School of Government professor. Garwin preferred the notion of "city mining," whereby the United States would allow the Soviets to place thermonuclear weapons beneath all major U.S. cities in return for the Americans being able to mine all major Soviet ones.[92] This seriously entertained, more than Strangelovian alternative to SDI merely took mutual assured destruction to its logical conclusion, while eliminating the costs of missile silos, submarines, and bombers — as well as such second thoughts as time might allow during a nuclear alert.

A similarly imaginative critic of Reagan's defense policy is Frances FitzGerald, who in 2000 brought the same keen insights to examining SDI as she had showed in writing about the North Vietnamese. Her *Way Out There in the Blue: Reagan, Star Wars and the End of the Cold War* may be as full of major factual errors as is any discussion of the Cold War's last stage. Among the ones most easily refuted by Russian sources are the claims that Soviet weapons spending had been frozen at the 1976 level; that Soviet ICBMs posed no first-strike threat to their U.S. counterparts; that the Soviets had not deployed national missile defenses; that Soviet military spending was a relatively modest part of overall production; that the Soviet Union had anything but a massive civil defense and war recovery apparatus; that Moscow's supposedly nonexistent SDI effort never produced anything anyway; and, predictably, that U.S. "right wingers" and "hardliners" prolonged the Cold War, which Gorbachev toiled to end.[93] She insists that Reagan found the inspiration for SDI in a 1966 Hitchcock movie, *Torn Curtain*. Where FitzGerald is moderately helpful, however, is in chronicling how this latest chapter in ballistic missile defense went beyond its original anti-Soviet purposes to become embedded in national spending right through today.

SDI would remain forever scattered between symbol, deception, and real power. Rules eventually imposed during the Reagan years, and carried through thereafter to satisfy Congress, ensured that it would never be put on a working basis. No part of the system was to be built until every technical problem raised by hundreds of complex devices was solved. SDI first had to demonstrate that a solution could not be cheaply offset by an opponent's new round of offensive weapons. Because of both SDI's science fiction technologies and the requirement to fit all tests within the framework of the ABM treaty, achieving such offense/defense ratios was far more difficult to demonstrate than in McNamara's day, when Sprint interceptors with nuclear warheads had made the task easier.

The set of regulations governing R & D alone took Congress and the Pentagon tens of thousands of man-hours and millions of dollars to draft and enforce. SDI fast became a parable of the Cold War — as did hopes of missile defense in general: race forward, slow down, speed up, then drag slowly along because everyone has forgotten the time when the program in question did not exist. In effect, SDI allocated another $1 billion for simulations that, having pitted nonexistent offenses against nonexistent defenses, then churned out unrealistic assessments of notional performance. Other fortunes went into supercomputers in a bizarre bid to centralize the management of the thousands of elements of a hypothetical system. In short, SDI fulfilled the staunchly Republican senator Malcolm Wallop's prediction at the start that it would become "a welfare program for well-connected scientists."[94]

America was spending billions on SDI, with no tangible missile defense in sight. Here was the Cold War's essence: Congresses and administrations of both parties pumped out fortunes in the *name* of something (in this case, missile defense), while in fact financing a grab bag of pet projects. Perhaps this time, the range of all these scientifically alluring, never-aggregated possibilities added up to a stunningly successful bluff — in fact, a multiple bluff: the Soviets pretended to have more wherewithal than they possessed, and the United States pretended that SDI was imminently achievable. Congress, too, was bluffed, as the Air Force initially doctored the results of test firings to fool Moscow.

By and large, Moscow was fooled. The United States "adopted the form of SDI and the inflation of military budgets," concluded one of the first high-level public critiques to emerge under perestroika, "and we naturally tried to follow suit."[95] This is an apt summary of only a fraction of what was befalling the Soviets. SDI was an inspired step in the war of attrition, whether or not Moscow tried to match it. At the start, about $13 billion was rounded up from existing parts of the defense budget.[96] Then the usual momentum gathered. Over the next fifteen years, a total of around $50 billion would be spent exploring every conceivable technology without ever focusing on a few of the more feasible ones that might have been translated into a workable ABM defense: these were forbidden by the 1972 treaty.

From 1981 to 1989, federally funded research in general grew larger than ever, guarded by bloated bureaucracies and careers too often open to mediocrity. In the following decade, that offspring of SDI that came to be called the Ballistic Missile Defense Organization kept asserting its importance to America's economic competitiveness. It issued glossy illustrated brochures summarizing vital contributions through "matchless expertise" to both business and the country's commercial technologies. However, this way of justifying military programs had already grown old and was used solely by the government organizations and nominally private ones that would themselves benefit. Only the impressionable would be persuaded after the Cold War into seeing these military bureaucracies and their affiliated national laboratories as powerhouses of resourcefulness.

✪

Nearly fifty movies were made about the Soviet Union during the early 1980s. These are not heartwarming ones such as 1966's *The Russians Are Coming! The Russians Are Coming!* (in which sailors from a grounded submarine befriend villagers in Maine). Instead, they reflect the obsessions of the time and some misguided energies. In 1984, *Red Dawn* showed a class of rural Colorado high schoolers taking to the mountains as a partisan band, the Wolverines, to battle Soviet and Cuban soldiers who had invaded the United States. Within days of the movie's opening in Washington, "Wolverines" was spray-painted in enormous red letters on the high white wall surrounding the new Soviet embassy.

Vandalism aside, much of the effort undertaken between 1981 and 1985 was probably unavoidable if the Soviet Union was to be cornered as quickly as possible. It would have taken an entirely different United States to have accomplished the task without the usual pork barrels, bureaucratic archaism, and vagaries. Beyond putting an unprecedented strategy in place, as encapsulated in NSDD 75, the vital contribution of the first Reagan administration was to reenergize America's innovative, open society. It was the American ability to do thousands of things and get a lot of them right, in contrast to the Soviet ability to accomplish relatively few things (such as unscalable technological innovation) superbly. This is what carried America less to victory than to a level of development of which victory was one of several consequences.

Throughout the Cold War, the United States proved least successful when it emphasized the political in its contest with the Soviet Union. The more centralized and *realpolitische* its efforts, the messier and more despairing they were — as became evident in the 1970s clutter of misguided summits and deceitful webs of would-be statecraft. When the superpower antagonism was shaped as a contest of political elites, the Soviets — whose power elites were more professional (to the happy exclusion of economic competence) and vastly more cynical — could nearly always take tactical advantage.

The Cold War was won by people who did not make it their life's purpose. Much less was contributed by the secretaries, deputy secretaries, undersecretaries, assistant secretaries, deputy assistant secretaries, professors and think tank denizens, global architects, or directors of Council on Foreign Relations study groups. The men and women who were preoccupied with the Cold War, who lived the drama daily and who tried distilling it into "lessons," strategies, and equilibria, had ways of getting it horribly wrong.

For the twenty years after 1961, a "new class" had been putting its imprint on the struggle — experts who were very different from the late-middle-aged men present at the creation, such as Truman and Acheson, Eisenhower and Dulles, who, for instance, all disdained summits. These were the younger politicians, defense intellectuals within government, generals with their MBAs, and celebrity commentators for a handful of media outlets. The Cold War had become a trellis on which they could grow careers. Sophisticated people believed that it would never be over — not that they consciously wanted it to go on forever, but military men had budgets to defend; politicians had tax dollars to spend, and, when out of office, lucrative foreign clients to represent; and those professors fascinated by power could find ways to escape the classroom and thereafter front for well-paying clients, too. It was a wonderful way of life for hundreds of thousands of people, not even counting the arms manufacturers and defense-subsidized scientists.

The more the United States consciously committed to the Cold War, the more statist the result, and therefore the easier it became for the un-American influences of secrecy and elitism to become part of the system. Those consummate Cold Warriors John Kennedy and Richard Nixon contrived to make the contest part of America. They each insisted before the nation that there was nothing more important, and they encumbered the country's response with a sophisticated pessimism. The entire middle stage of the Cold War witnessed a fascination with America the state. Not surprisingly, the public increasingly became disdainful of expert wisdom. Vietnam, conceived as a clever man's war with its escalation ladders and the certainty that it would not be Korea, was only the most ghastly example, to be followed quickly by détente's hazardous triangular dealings and then by Carter's idealist trustfulness.

During 1981 to 1985, Reagan applied a winning policy based on fundamental beliefs about the Soviet Union. He was confidently being guided by common sense. He knew the Soviet system was both evil and inept, whereas America's was good and (potentially) fabulously productive. So when he turned his administration to confront Moscow, the approach could more or less be focused powerfully. When, however, his policies were aimed at tangential Cold War targets, particularly in Central America and the Near East, he was without those core insights. Government practice could then too easily revert to type and go awfully wrong. Much more so than in dealing with Moscow, there was a price to be paid for Reagan's hands-off leadership style when it came to having to choose among evils on the margins of the U.S.-Soviet battle.

11

Shaking Loose

(1985–1989)

Nothing except a battle lost can be half so melancholy as a battle won.

Duke of Wellington

Ronald Reagan understood the acute vulnerability of the Soviet economy at a time when that opinion was hardly commonplace. Among his favorite reading during his first years in office was the two-to-three-page collection of anecdotes, backed by raw intelligence, that the NSC staff prepared for him every Friday, which carried stories large and small about the sort of economic chaos that only Leninism can produce, particularly when abetted from the outside.

The Soviet Union could have saved itself, or at least endured for a while longer, had it been able to take at least five specific steps: (1) export more oil and gas, thus sharply increasing its hard-currency earnings; (2) eschew the ruinous compulsion to devote so staggering a percentage of its total resources to military preparations; (3) meet America's final Cold War thrust for missile defense with a deserved skepticism; (4) withhold its worthless commitment of scores of billions of rubles from third world quagmires; (5) win wider legitimate access to Western technology and credits. In short, it would have had to make radically tactical, truly Leninist adaptations.

Yet the system was too old and brutalized to maneuver deftly. In each instance, moreover, U.S. decisions taken between 1981 and

1985 pushed the Politburo further into making the worst possible choices for itself. As Mikhail Gorbachev later remarked, Reagan genially led him to the edge of the abyss, then calmly asked him to take "one step forward."[1] But he was a proud man raised in a formidable school, and his surrender was anything but inevitable.

As Leninist self-confidence withered, the thuggish assertiveness that passed for Soviet domestic legitimacy was undercut and the last ideological veneer of Soviet adventurism abroad peeled off. In 1981, Secretary of State Alexander Haig had blustered about "going to the source" (meaning Cuba) to stop the flow of arms to Central America. Reagan was not about to enter that time warp of superpower showdowns over a ragtag Soviet client state. His focus had been on economic recovery and on using recovery as the means of squeezing Moscow directly. By 1985, the U.S. economy was booming. What became known as the Reagan Doctrine — backing ostensibly democratic forces against Soviet-supported regimes — replicated the liberal outlook of the late 1940s, including the belief that countries around the world would adopt free enterprise if given the chance. But the doctrine, such as it was, emerged slowly. The term became popular only in the mid-1980s.

Upping the ante on what U.S. officials unashamedly called "imperialism" initially focused on Eastern Europe. What a quarter century earlier would have been seen as a manic attempt at rollback began to be applied in those places where it was most likely to succeed. All initiatives beyond Europe, however, were shadowed by Vietnam. Even on the highest tides of the 1980 and 1984 elections, Reagan, unlike John Kennedy, could not have pledged to "pay any price, bear any burden." America's roles in Africa, Afghanistan, and Central America were instead characterized by almost excessive caution. They were tangled by Washington lobbying, indifferent allies, routine interagency turf battles, and, over Central America, divisions on Capitol Hill truly reminiscent of Vietnam. Success, however, was measured not just by the absence of defeat but by the possibilities of victory. There would be a conscious ideological thrust against Moscow. The moral leadership that Jimmy Carter had spoken about began to pay off once U.S. power was reasserted.

During the 1980s, the CIA helped bring kindling in many of these places to the Soviet Union's pyre, and the flames were initially fanned by William Casey's personal enthusiasm. The overall effort was nonetheless becoming ever more encrusted by failures. Intelligence analyses continued to fall short. They were as grievously mistaken on the four biggest issues of the 1980s — the Soviet economy, Soviet military spending, the nuclear crisis of 1981 to 1984, and the ICBM "window of vulnerability" — as they had been on the two comparable ones of the 1970s, the Soviet leaps in technology theft and strategic forces. Part of the problem was that intelligence budgets had been on a roller coaster for ten years — immense during Vietnam, slashed once U.S. troops withdrew, edging up in 1976, rising by the end of the Carter years, and jumping even further with Reagan. This stop-and-go-go pattern rarely translates into effectiveness in any organization.

Reagan understood another decisive point better than his critics. It was not "the era of big government" that had "succeeded for a long time" after World War II, as some people conclude today. Nor would "big government" bring Cold War victory.[2] What "succeeded" over the long haul was the enormous growth in productivity during the Cold War decades, the technological component of which has probably been underestimated for the final stage. Specific public projects contributed usefully early in the conflict. Since the late 1960s, however, government had at best been riding along. In R & D, the country received few if any benefits that would not have arrived more cheaply through nonmilitary efforts. By the 1980s, it was undeniable that dispersed initiative (from the garages more than the corner offices) and less supervision from above could propel the economy ahead even faster. A large chunk of the mandarin, big-institution system — that of muscle-bound IBM quite as much as, say, the Department of Housing and Urban Development or the world of the defense intellectuals — began being pushed aside during the Reagan years. It was the Cold War that had helped put that increasingly creaky system in place and that had kept it going.

This chapter initially looks at the administration's (often troubled) efforts to raise the "costs of empire" by ensuring that propaganda and popular resistance were part of the overall offensive — starting right away in Poland and then stretching into a "doctrine." Unlike during the busy 1990s, let alone during the 1960s, there were few instances in which U.S. forces entered combat. Second, the story again turns to the CIA, that useful gauge of Cold War cost. Finally, we explain why the popular impression arose toward the end of the decade that all the exertion had finally crippled the country. "Imperial overstretch" was often said to be the main reason, and unprecedented trade and budget deficits were among the consequences. America at the moment of victory would not really be exhausted, but it was encountering Wellington's hard-earned wisdom about melancholy. There was no denying the terrible strain that had occurred.

✪

Through most of 1981, Soviet officials queried nearly every knowl-edgeable American they encountered about what the White House might do if they cracked down on Solidarity, the trade union move-ment from the Gdansk shipyard that had become a ten-million-member national platform against Poland's Communist regime. Reagan, after all, had vowed to prevent a repetition of Hungary and Czechoslovakia, even implying a military response. Early that year, Richard Pipes had sent a two-page memo to the president describing Poland (the place of his birth) as "the single most important state in the Warsaw Pact," making the case for helping Solidarity survive, and again emphasizing the price to Moscow.

Once more, George Kennan urged his country to understand the Soviet need to use force for the sake of the status quo. To him, demands for freedom by the unruly Poles were "inevitably self-defeating." He discerned a useful step toward stability in the imposi-tion of Soviet-inspired martial law during December.[3]

It was after Solidarity was driven underground that the further involvement of U.S. companies in Soviet pipeline development was prohibited, that grain sales were once again denied, that Aeroflot's U.S. landing rights were pulled, and that a sophisticated effort began, for a time, to countervail Soviet-related transactions in world financial markets. Sanctions against Warsaw's new military regime were accompanied by humanitarian assistance from a secret Catholic Relief Services program, by medical help from Project HOPE, by CARE food relief, and by farm assistance and secret cash subsidies. Lane Kirkland played a vital role, believing that the AFL-CIO could be as instrumental in forcing change as it was in working for democracy in South Africa. Actually within Poland, Casey expanded electronic intelligence operations to assist Solidarity and along the way created new CIA guidelines for recruiting agents, reducing the old 130-page handbook to a few paragraphs.

That was the least he could do. From the early 1970s through most of 1981, the CIA had crucial sources on the Polish General Staff that were monitoring Red Army preparations to intervene. A month before the crackdown, senior officials at Langley had even been handed the details of a Soviet-Polish collaborationist contingency operation to impose martial law. Yet the secretary of state did not learn of it. Solidarity could not be alerted. U.S. silence may have been interpreted in Moscow as Kennanist acquiescence. The Agency had simply found it "extremely implausible" that Poland's soldiers would be forced to turn against their fellow citizens. The warnings just spun away into the recesses of Langley's bureaucratic "machine," recalls a still amazed Pipes.[4]

Solidarity at least had bipartisan support in the U.S. Congress, as did Reagan's personal initiative for creating the National Endowment for Democracy in 1983. Its initial budget of $13 million would openly fund democratizing movements worldwide. The third world clients that Moscow had accumulated in the 1970s were to be turned into millstones. They were already heavy for Yuri Andropov, who had suggested to the Central Committee that they might be too expensive to keep carrying. The U.S. objective was to use a combination of economic assistance, "private sector initiatives," diplomacy, and covert operations to help make them heavier still.[5]

That Reagan did not regard even Europe's division as immutable was a crucial new fact. Practically no one else in Washington agreed: it had been inconceivable since Hungary's revolt in 1956 that the democracies would adopt their own policies of expansion. One means for doing so now became "public diplomacy" — directly trying to persuade a nation's people without necessarily dealing with its government. Voice of America (VOA), the U.S. Information Agency, and Radio Liberty received more money than ever before. Radio Free Europe, acclaimed as so helpful during détente, returned to its aggressive original purpose, and Radio Martí was created to broadcast into Cuba.[6] Reagan believed that the United States was as far behind the Soviet Union in international broadcasting as it had been in space at the time of *Sputnik*. He ordered that the same priority be given to rebuilding the sleepy VOA as Kennedy had placed on putting a man on the moon. Eighteen languages were added. The Soviets spent the equivalent of some $1.2 billion annually on electricity alone to jam Western broadcasts, even well into Gorbachev's years of glasnost.[7]

Reagan also revived U.S. willingness to use force. In August 1981, two Soviet-built Libyan fighters were shot down by two U.S. Navy F-14s. If Libyan jets again opened fire on U.S. aircraft conducting training exercises in the Mediterranean, he said, American pilots should not only shoot back but feel free to pursue them. How far? "All the way into the hangar."[8] There would be no second-guessing as over Vietnam. It was more difficult, however, to apply such operational good sense to so-called peacekeeping missions, where U.S. involvement (in a preview of the mid-1990s) could be open-ended and dangerously undefined.

In the Middle East, this administration proved no more adept than any other. For the second time, Americans were killed in large numbers. Multilateral ventures, as envisioned originally in the early Cold War, had come full circle. In 1958, for example, the United States had essentially acted unilaterally in Lebanon. Twenty-five years later, it deployed its forces only alongside the flags of France, Italy, and Britain. This was definitely a preferable procedure, although the Beirut that the Marines encountered was no longer a tranquil port. It was a ruin devastated by civil war, a lawless Palestine Liberation Organization (PLO), and continuous Israeli bombing, the civilian dead of which Reagan described to Prime Minister Menachem Begin as "a holocaust."[9]

The massacre, by Israel's Phalangist partners, of around seven hundred Palestinian women, children, and old men in Lebanon's Sabra and Shatila refugee camps, supposedly under Israeli control, became the occasion for relanding Marines. Given America's minimal influence over its most heavily subsidized ally, let alone over the fratricidal Lebanese and the Soviet-backed PLO, the Joint Chiefs of Staff were desperate to avoid this snake pit. Furthermore, according to their chairman, General John Vessey, almost any intervention "would detract from our ability to deter the Soviet Union" in Europe.[10] American forces had not previously encountered the region's most characteristic modes of violence, opening the gate for a bomb-laden suicide truck to kill 241 Marines.

The first actual combat for U.S. forces since Vietnam, however, came with the invasion of the small Caribbean nation of Grenada on October 25, 1983, after a bloody intra-Marxist coup. This was also the first such operation in the region since Lyndon Johnson had put the Marines in the Dominican Republic. About six thousand U.S. servicemen and military units from six Caribbean states hit the island. They booted out thirty Soviet military advisers and several hundred Cuban combat engineers involved in completing a ten-thousand-foot landing strip that Washington saw as ominous.

A new government took office, the people said they were elated, and 740 American medical students at St. George's University were rescued, or at least evacuated. Ousting the revolutionary military council was "a message to the Soviet Union, and to Nicaragua, and to Cuba," according to Vessey.[11] Nineteen men were killed sending it.

The *New York Times* depicted this adventure as Gilbert and Sullivan gunboat diplomacy. Activist professors such as Georgetown's Madeleine Albright denounced it as bullying. But the administration was not addressing them. Eight years after Saigon fell, the point was to let Andropov, Castro, and their friends know there were limits to how far the United States could be pushed. Within months, the Soviet navy responded with a major deployment in the Caribbean.

America was again selectively ready to resort to force, but welcome changes in attitude alone were not going to overcome routine stumblings. "Our intelligence there was primitive," former national security assistant Robert McFarlane says of Grenada, "there was virtually none, really."[12] The U.S. Navy, for example, had to use a chart prepared by the British in 1898 and an old map from Exxon. So much for the billions that had gone into the Defense Mapping Agency. The invasion was "a sloppy success," said Colin Powell, and "hardly a model of service cooperation."[13] Nor was anyone prepared for the quantity of Soviet arms and ammunition uncovered. As in Vietnam, every service was mindful that it had to justify its budget on Capitol Hill; therefore, none could afford to be left out. A CIA yacht used to monitor the operation was shooed away by the Navy along with other civilian craft; with all the different radios being carried, it was rumored at the time, an Army officer trying to contact Fort Bragg had to use one of the island's pay phones; and Vessey wrapped up the operation by sending a list to Casey of allegedly grievous CIA deficiencies in providing tactical intelligence.

These telling details of late–Cold War disharmony were obscured by the vast public support Reagan was able to garner. Although the *New York Times* also complained that "the cost is loss of the moral high ground," the rest of the country was as tired of that contentless posturing as it was of European reproaches — let alone of comparisons to Moscow's invasion of Afghanistan. There was even bipartisan support in Congress for lifting restrictions on armed involvement in Angola, to back Jonas Savimbi's UNITA guerrillas who were still fighting against the ruling Marxist regime.

The contenders in Angola hired Washington lobbying firms, each paying about $600,000 a year, to argue their cases. The MPLA government used one headed by Robert Gray, recently chairman of Reagan's inauguration committee. To enlighten the Hill, Gray & Co. hired a just-retired admiral who had been deputy director of Central Intelligence. One of the lobbyists' contributions, when their clients flew in from Luanda, was to ensure that they were dressed for success in Brooks Brothers suits, occasionally with such accessories as scholarly looking horn-rimmed glasses. (Savimbi favored fatigues when in Washington.) "Their image problem," the admiral nonetheless complained, "is that they're a bunch of Communists who have a bunch of Cubans there."[14] Despite his efforts to ingratiate them with a wavering Congress, U.S. assistance finally went to Savimbi once the ten-year-old restrictive amendment was repealed in 1985.

Shipments were given hesitantly — in the beginning, only non-lethal aid, followed by a modest total of $15 million in covert assistance around year's end. Savimbi's Washington friends were finally, in January 1986, able to engineer an Oval Office visit. Spurred by Reagan's enthusiasm for these "freedom fighters in Africa, at the same time that he condemned apartheid, the bureaucracies began to shake off dismal memories from the mid-1970s. In this instance, general cooperation among the Pentagon, the NSC staff, and Langley followed. Stingers proved valuable. Fifty of these $26,000, state-of-the-art, thirty-five-pound, surface-to-air, shoulder-fired missiles were in Savimbi's hands by the early fall, and antitank missiles soon followed. Manifesting little sign of imminent collapse, Moscow showered an estimated $1 billion in new weapons on the MPLA the following year, and one and a half times that amount between 1988 and 1990, under the on-site supervision of a Soviet general. U.S. backing of Savimbi helped drain the Soviet Union, but it also perpetuated a pointless civil war that is still going on today.

Other abscesses from the 1970s, and earlier, kept oozing. In May 1984, after a ten-year interruption, the Soviets started to provide military supplies to North Korea, including MiG-23 fighters and surface-to-air missiles. That same year, weapons also started flowing to the New People's Army in the Philippines. Anything that involved Southeast Asia, however, chilled Americans to the bone. The tiny amount of aid directed to Cambodia reflected the trauma of the war just passed. "Having abandoned the decent Cambodians in 1975 and being still unwilling to back them decisively," reflects former Policy Planning director Peter Rodman, "we found that the remnant was barely able to hold its own."[15] During the 1980s, the United States publicly gave them $5 million a year for medicine, tents, and the like. By 1989, some $20 million to $25 million was being funneled in for such items as training, uniforms, vehicles, and overseas political offices. Essentially no one in the United States had the stomach actually to send weapons. Cambodia became a case study in the agony of trying to square strategy and morality.

It was in Afghanistan that these two elements seemed most to coincide. About $100 million worth of U.S. supplies had been committed for resistance during the year and a half since the Soviet invasion. Nine months into the Reagan administration, the Pakistani conduit was solidified with a six-year, $3.2 billion agreement for economic aid and arms credits, including forty F-16s. Pakistan's military government, headed since 1977 by General Mohammad Zia ul-Haq, who happily pursued a nuclear weapons program while showing no interest in ever holding elections, became a fellow "freedom fighter," as Congress demanded more than the "harassment" that Carter had introduced.

Already in December 1981, a bipartisan Afghanistan Task Force was formed, first under Democratic senator Paul Tsongas, then under Republican Gordon Humphrey. A memorable Texas Democrat, Congressman Charlie Wilson — Naval Academy graduate and member of the House Appropriations Committee — played a pivotal role, as did Michael Pillsbury, a Republican staffer and former Rand analyst fluent in Mandarin. "There were 58,000 dead in Vietnam and we owe the Russians one," Wilson told the press.[16] Pressure increased in early 1982 on a White House so far from being crusadingly anti-Soviet on this issue as to raise questions among true believers. It was one thing to sell military hardware to a frontline ally such as Pakistan but quite another to arm a guerrilla movement facing Soviet forces. For the CIA, applying U.S.-made weaponry would violate the "plausible deniability" principle of covert action. Meanwhile, Moscow's Fortieth Army settled in for the long haul, mining the Pakistani border, dividing Afghanistan into seven military districts each headed by a Soviet general in Kabul, and shipping in about 120,000 troops.

In September 1983, Reagan spoke at the UN of Soviet atrocities in Afghanistan, such as violations of the Biological Weapons Convention. This was not enough for the mujahidin's friends in Congress, who began calling publicly for the delivery of decisive military assistance. Defying CIA orders in the field, leaders of several of the many mujahidin groups set out from their mountain strongholds, aided by congressional staffers, to storm Capitol Hill with painfully clear accounts of how peasant patriots with bolt-action rifles were being cut down by Soviet jets, gunships, and, tanks.

Casey ordered Milt Bearden, deputy director of the Soviet/East European Division, to "go out and kill me 10,000 Russians until they give up," as he dispatched Bearden to manage the arms flow to the mujahidin.[17] At the working level, however, the Agency hesitated to raise the stakes, in part because it was still shaken by the investigations of only a half dozen years before. It cautioned against too much aid, which could be both provocative and corrupting. Never before had the CIA provided U.S.-made weapons to support anti-Soviet insurgency, and it was not about to start now. It was supplying Stingers to UNITA around the same time, but that task was being handled by a different group at Langley and was not a direct encounter with the Red Army. Tsongas, a soft-spoken liberal from Massachusetts, soon called CIA reluctance and interdepartmental bickering "criminally irresponsible." The following year, he demanded that the resistance be given the means to attain "victory" and not simply be used to "fight and die" — in implied contrast to what had happened to the Kurds, the Hmong, and so many other brave, misled peoples.[18]

Congress passed the Tsongas-Ritter resolution, previously blocked by the State Department, in October 1984, calling on the president to "render effective military aid to the freedom fighters." Only in March 1985 did Reagan sign NSDD 166 to increase aid to a level that might maim Soviet forces. As covert backing apparently doubled after 1985, Moscow was hit with a substantially different war. Then came the president's order that "all necessary means" be thrown into Afghanistan, which included Stingers. In a rare display of unity, senior CIA career officials joined with the Joint Chiefs to resist. The chiefs were alarmed that missiles were being withdrawn from West Germany. What if the Red Army should blitz through the Fulda Gap? At Langley, the excuse was that Stingers were too complicated an instrument for illiterate Afghans, although the more likely danger was that their deployment would involve the Pentagon in what had been an exclusively Agency operation.[19]

Meanwhile, Pakistan was cooperating, encouraged by U.S. supplies of increasingly sophisticated air-to-air missiles. In August, Congress approved money for humanitarian assistance within Afghanistan. Now in power, Gorbachev described the war as a "bleeding wound." He had ways to close it. Although the invasion had been Brezhnev's gift to his people, the war's brutality was mostly Gorbachev's. He was the one who kept Soviet forces in the longest and under whom most of the one million Afghan civilians died. He immediately increased the scale of the war, tried to cut off supply routes from Pakistan with the KGB's elite *spetsnatz* commandos, and intensified the policy of devastating the areas outside the control of Kabul's puppet government — about 80 percent of the countryside and 40 percent of the towns. Gorbachev was throughout a man of force and drive, only secondarily and lately — by default — a man moved by new ideas.

Not even the Washington bureaucracy could hold out forever against congressional anger and presidential orders. "Leading the charge to stop the Stinger idea dead in its tracks was the Directorate of Operations at the CIA," concludes one (CIA-sponsored) study of the subject. In fact, the ranks were divided, roughly between older cautious personnel and younger officers who expected to accomplish more than just avoiding defeat.[20] Factions within the CIA were able to delay the deployment of Stingers by about a year. There were also conflicting opinions among the military, with General Colin Powell, then gatekeeper at the Pentagon for the secretary of defense, pivotally allowing the Stinger issue to be reintroduced. Finally, in the summer of 1986, the State Department decided to push ahead with getting the missiles transferred. They were first used in September, immediately destroying three MiG-24 helicopter gunships. This marked a turning point, as the effectiveness of Soviet close air support plummeted.

Like the U.S. Army in Vietnam, Soviet forces were suffering ever more from trying to ram the long-practiced methods developed for war in the North German Plain into a very different place. Moreover, U.S. assistance mounted in 1987. The CIA went so far as to work with Pakistan's Interservices Intelligence Agency (ISI) to help the resistance carry out strikes across the Amu Darya River into Tajikistan, still a Soviet republic. Nothing like this had been done against Moscow since Kennan had embarked on "political warfare" forty years earlier. This time, there was a purpose behind the violence.

Albeit belatedly, the White House had again robbed the Soviets of a choice, as the cost of their war headed to somewhere above $100 billion, with at least fifteen thousand Russian dead. For Moscow, which so tightly controlled public information, it was the money that hurt, not the blood.

U.S. aid plunged once Gorbachev announced troop withdrawals in early 1988, but nothing was ever final in the Cold War. At the worst possible time for the Soviet Union, when economic frostbite was cracking so many institutions, Moscow reportedly saw fit to leave behind about $1.5 billion in supplies, while propping up Kabul with cash and material estimated at an astonishing $300 million per month. Moreover, Moscow introduced SCUD missiles with a 170-mile range — thousands fell on tribesmen in the hills despite the official absence of Soviet forces.

The Directorate of Operations gave itself a party right after the final Soviet columns retreated across the frontier. Almost everyone associated with Afghanistan received commendations and promotions. Yet the Marxist regime in Kabul fought on, backed by Soviet air support and troops in mufti, not to collapse until four months after the Soviet Union itself caved in. By that time, a new crop of fundamentalist fighters was emerging, many raised and trained by religious schools in Pakistani orphanages and refugee camps. Within five years, a movement of Pathan students — the Taliban — would sweep the country to impose order and their own form of civil government.

Afghanistan ended up as an imploded state heaped upon an eviscerated nation. The jihad that America and Saudi Arabia underwrote had included about twenty-five thousand non-Afghan Islamic militants from some thirty countries. No one in Washington worried at the time about potential repercussions of religious zealotry, although at least one seasoned observer saw trouble ahead. Gratitude from the mujahidin was short-lived. Once the Soviets departed, and with a lot going on elsewhere in the world, recalls Bearden, the CIA "got the hell out of there." The Agency and, more excusably, the rest of the U.S. government, were blind to the danger caused by political disintegration. CIA operatives stayed long enough to buy back — for $200,000 each — those Stinger missiles that could be found. Ten million landmines were also in the country, buried in the mountainous terrain and making Afghanistan twenty years later the most heavily mined place in the world. As for the non-Afghan militants, "they're a real disposal problem" remarked one Western diplomat in Peshwar.[21] He had no idea.

The very notion of holy war had barely been seen in the Moslem world for one thousand years. The Soviet invasion had caused the United States to stoke a pan-Islamic movement that would soon reach out to the Gulf, to Israel, Egypt, and Algeria, and eventually to New York and Washington.

The process of ousting the Soviets from Afghanistan, no matter how rancorous and terrible the consequences, benefited from strong Democratic support on the Hill — to the extent that Reagan was criticized for doing too little. It was another story in Central America, where the White House was attacked for doing too much, even though assistance to the Nicaraguan rebels was a fraction the size of the Afghan program. The goals were murkier in Central America and many of the allies even less savory.

One significant change arising from the mid-1970s CIA hearings was that certain stipulations in the 1947 National Security Act had to be taken seriously. Anytime the Agency was set to work on such operations, said that faded statute, the President must first "find" — hence that curious term of art "finding" — that the purpose is in the national interest. He must so notify Congress, though not necessarily in writing. This requirement would be at the core of the Iran-Contra scandal.

In Central America, more so than anywhere, the U.S. anti-Communist presence in the 1980s was often a case of backing the bad against the worse. In 1966, when commandoism still aroused Kennedy-era excitement, "The Ballad of the Green Berets" by Special Forces Sergeant Barry Sadler was a number one pop hit for five weeks, selling nine million records. In 1989, Sadler died after being shot in the head during a domestic dispute outside a squalid Guatemala City bar, a sour metaphor for the arc of U.S. involvement over these decades as it went from glamorous good intentions to sordid choices between lesser evils.

In El Salvador, the smallest of the five Central American states, it was not just the eminent centrist José Napoleon Duarte with whom America dealt during a twelve-year civil war in which roughly seventy-five thousand people perished. It was also with Duarte's defense minister and senior officers responsible for the network of death squads that killed, among thousands of other innocents, four American churchwomen in 1980 — the truth of this not being confirmed until the convicted guardsmen pointed up the chain of command many years later. The United States had not tried to force change in El Salvador. For instance, Washington never used its full clout, such as impeding World Bank and Inter-American Development Bank loans, until outrages like the 1976 torture/slaying of Ronald J. Richardson, a twenty-four-year-old African-American tourist, were seriously addressed by the Salvadoran National Guard. This was just one of the murders upholding "stability" there.

In neighboring Nicaragua, the largest of the five Central American states (about the size of Michigan), the forty-three-year reign of the U.S.-supported Somoza dynasty finally collapsed during the summer of 1979. U.S. intelligence had predicted in May that Anastasio Somoza's National Guard would crush his opponents.[22] Cutting off aid, because of theft as well as brutality, proved to be the mortal blow. Policymakers could not believe that whoever followed could be worse. They proved to be wrong, as Cuba's polished intelligence director, Manuel Pineiro, slipped in to advise the National Liberation Front.

Recent perspectives can be useful. On the twentieth anniversary of the 1979 Nicaraguan revolution, former Sandinista leaders readily admitted to what they had until then denied before the world — that they had promptly begun funneling Soviet arms and ammunition to guerrillas across the border in El Salvador. Looking back from the late 1990s, the Public Broadcasting Service's *American Experience* put the U.S. reaction in perspective: "It is by now a matter of record that Reagan's assessment of the Sandinistas was largely correct, and the American public was in fact duped."[23] The duping was abetted by generally well-intentioned critics in Congress and the press who were appalled by years of indulging murderous U.S. allies in Central America and who insisted that President Daniel Ortega was something other than a ruthless opportunist aligned with Cuba and the Soviet Union.

As had Eisenhower with Castro, the Carter administration initially hoped for the best. Nicaragua's new regime received $120 million in aid between 1979 and 1981. The Sandinistas nonetheless shoved their non-Communist rivals out of the government in a way that still brings comparisons to Czechoslovakia in 1948.[24] Elections were canceled, as thousands of Cuban advisers were welcomed. The usual weapons-intensive "friendship" agreements were signed with the Soviet Union and other Warsaw Pact members. Money and moral support arrived from Western Europe's socialist parties.

Carter's final aid budget for Latin America was $440 million, or about $1 per person for the hemisphere. He also authorized CIA covert action against Nicaragua during his last months in office. In 1981, Reagan nearly tripled aid to Latin America. The first question in his first press conference as president was how he intended to avoid having Central America "turn into another Vietnam." One answer was by increasing military aid to El Salvador by $24 million and sending in another two dozen military advisers, for a grand total of fifty-five, a number that Congress then decreed could not be exceeded. At the same time, the White House worked with mixed success to quell the death squads, culminating in a 1983 visit to El Salvador by Vice President George Bush, although massacres by American-trained and American-armed military units in the region were another story.

The first two years of the Reagan administration were busy ones in Central America, with Pineiro working hard to repeat Nicaragua's revolutionary experience in El Salvador, Guatemala, and Colombia, as well as in Honduras and Costa Rica. The Sandinistas would provide weapons and training, although Ortega kept denying any ties whatsoever. A vicious contest emerged, in which the United States would spend at least $4 billion during the 1980s to support Salvadoran security forces against Marxist rebels, with roughly $3 billion being more directly deployed against Nicaragua. Western Europeans were startled when visitors from Washington spoke of these efforts as occurring "in America's front yard," which all sensible people knew lay in the Mediterranean, in Kent, or along the Rhine.[25]

On December 1, 1981, Reagan signed his own authorization for the CIA to "support and conduct" paramilitary operations against Nicaragua and to spend nearly $20 million to train and arm an existing exile force — which became known derisively as the Contras, for counterrevolutionaries. No matter what they were called, the Contras came to include the first genuine peasant revolution in Latin America backed by the United States. That fact was obscured by the passions of the time, and is still generally unrecognized. The vast majority of combatants in the main Contra army were peasants backed by a mass popular movement of tough, independent inhabitants of Nicaragua's central highlands. Starting in 1979, their reaction to government expropriation and intimidation grew swiftly. Only in 1982 did the United States offer of weapons persuade them to enter an alliance with the former Guardia anti-Sandinista exiles —

those the rest of the world called Contras. Officials in the State Department, Defense Department, and CIA never saw the resistance as more than a means of forcing a negotiated solution, rather than as an alternative to Ortega's rule. This perspective was not, however, shared by these men on the ground.[26]

Assisting the Contras led to political turmoil in the United States. The White House also paid a price for the program's initial secrecy. When Reagan asked in 1983 for military aid to El Salvador to fight Communist guerrillas, the nationally televised Democratic response was predictable. "The United States," said Connecticut senator Christopher Dodd, had "to move with the tide of history rather than stand against it."[27] The Soviets were supplying weapons to Nicaragua, insisted Indiana Congressman Lee Hamilton, only in response to U.S. covert action — a reversal of sequence all too common in the Cold War. Canada, France, Sweden, and the Netherlands extended new trade credits to Nicaragua to offset the effects of a U.S. embargo.

George Shultz recalls "a Communist movement that was entrenched in Nicaragua and was actively trying to spread itself." Believing Mexico to be "a very flaky place," he sensibly worried about that movement propelling chaos up the isthmus, eventually "having to do with our Pacific coast."[28] The word *domino* was notable only by its absence. Further, the Sandinistas had created an army as well as a secret police force, each around ten times larger than anything Somoza had possessed. By 1985, they were supported by Soviet artillery and helicopter gunships.

In December 1982, the Democratic House passed an amendment, named for Intelligence Committee chairman Edward Boland, prohibiting the CIA and Defense Department from supplying any further military support or advice to anyone for the purpose of overthrowing Ortega. Meanwhile, the Sandinistas were well counseled by American friends, including members of Congress, and free to raise money in the United States.[29] The Boland amendment was full of loopholes, and here is where the administration began to overreach. Nine months later, in September 1983, Reagan signed a finding authorizing CIA action against the Sandinistas for the following fiscal year. Limpet mines, for example, were to be attached to Nicaraguan freighter hulls; the (minimal) damage caused by the mines would make the ships uninsurable.

Senator Henry Jackson, a strongly anti-Communist Truman Democrat, proposed "a Marshall Plan" for Central America; the president recommended $8 billion in aid. As John Kennedy had said of the original Marshall Plan, however, aid in any amount was moot without U.S. protection — in this case for places such as El Salvador and Honduras. To Reagan, protection included backing the Contras against the Nicaraguan regime he held responsible for spreading violent revolution. When the Agency's covert operations inevitably became messily public, a second Boland amendment was passed in October 1984. "It clearly ends U.S. support for the war in Nicaragua," crowed its sponsor. Nonetheless, Boland's amendments were obscure. The law changed five times between 1982 and 1987 regarding the permissibility of U.S. assistance.

To keep resistance alive against Ortega and his Soviet suppliers, the White House had to solicit money and materiel from South Africa, Israel, and Taiwan. Beijing offered to help the Contras by shipping surface-to-air missiles via Guatemala. By the spring of 1985, Saudi Arabia had contributed $32 million and Brunei around $10 million. Today, all this desperate panhandling to thwart a Soviet client in Central America sounds strange, yet such were the times. Reagan remained consistent in working to undermine this particular "little Stalin," and although it was Congress that offered support one year, only to withdraw it the next, it was the president who came to pay a severe penalty for the secrecy of his assistance and for coming very close to breaking the law.

In part because of the president's detachment, by early 1984 a cowboy ethic had installed itself in a part of the NSC staff where men saw themselves as global operators rather than analysts and pencil pushers. William P. Clark's two immediate successors were out of their depth. The problem was not only due to the fantasist Lieutenant Colonel Oliver North and the people who worked for him, such as Felix Rodriguez, leader of the CIA team that had helped hunt down Che Guevara. (Rodriguez kept a piece of Che's last cigar embedded in the handle of his revolver.) It was also a result of the sort of grandiosity among poorly supervised functionaries that led the director of the newly formed Crisis Management Center to boast to me of his being head of the "the NSC's NSC."[30] Although such men were small fry compared to the "boy commandos" of the Kennedy era and the damage they created was hardly the Bay of Pigs or Vietnam, the deceits that North was all too easily able to practice would wound the administration.

One reason this particular tangled web could be spun for so long, according to former Joint Chiefs chairman William Crowe, was that "everything was so highly classified."[31] In addition, Reagan was attempting to advance democracy and even liberal capitalism in Central America at the same time he was secretly trying to obtain the release of hostages taken in Lebanon. The combination of these two passions dramatized an escalating quarrel with Congress over the proper powers of the presidency.[32]

In the summer of 1985, Reagan compared Iran to the Third Reich. But perhaps it could be helpful in returning kidnapped Americans, including the CIA's station chief, William Buckley, who would be tortured to death. To that purpose, Reagan ended up proceeding with a bizarre arms deal that sent 4,508 antitank missiles to Tehran to make more deadly its merciless 1980–1988 war with Iraq. By flying in a cargo of 18 Hawk surface-to-air missiles from Tel Aviv during November, moreover, the CIA had let a covert mechanism be used without first receiving a "finding." Congress came to see the flight as an illegal operation, specifically a violation of the Arms Export Control Act, while North attempted to dissociate himself from it. He tried to convince Congress that these weapons and their deliverymen had no connection at all to the U.S. government.

Iraq's Saddam Hussein, in turn, was throughout the 1980s receiving billions of dollars in loans through the Agriculture Department and the Export-Import Bank. In the course of his half-trillion-dollar war with Iran, he was also running up other debts (for a total of around $80 billion by 1990). Contrary to recent claims by U.S. policymakers, Iraq was viewed as an ally.[33] To them, Ayatollah Khomeini was the greater danger in the Gulf. So during the most desperate period of his war, Saddam became an intelligence partner, receiving vital U.S. satellite downloads. Iraq was dropped from the State Department's listing of known terrorist nations. Oilmen rushed to develop its substantial energy resources. Unfortunately, years of having received U.S. intelligence meant that Saddam had a substantial knowledge of American capabilities in the region once friendship faded.

Saddam was already using chemical weapons and was likely developing biological ones, even before he got around to shooting and poisoning some 100,000 Kurds in his own country in 1988. True to the Cold War pattern, he was a moderately friendly dictator — for the moment. At the same time the NSC's McFarlane and North (themselves ironic victims of secrecy) were trying to establish their own channels with Saddam's archenemies in Tehran, the CIA was

attempting to initiate a relationship with him, which even Iraqi officials thought "insane," according to Duane Clarridge, chief of the
Agency's Latin American operations during the pivotal years 1981
to 1984.[34]

At the heart of the Iran-Contra scandal was the attempt to
use profits from secret arms sales to Iran to supply the Nicaraguan
rebels. North's own ignorant chatterings were fittingly conducted
through a veritable caravan of Iranian rug merchants. Less excusably, ignorance also permeated Langley's Directorate of Operations.
The Iran desk chief could neither speak nor read Farsi. Further, neither at that time nor during the rest of the Cold War did a single
Near East Division chief know Arabic or Turkish, let alone Farsi.
(One was said to be able to get along in French.) The Near East officer sent to debrief Manucher Ghorbanifar, the Khomeini regime's
go-between in dealing with the United States, neither knew the language nor had any background in the region. Ghorbanifar had to
spell out for him the names of the prominent Iranian officials
involved.[35]

Iran had paid $30 million for U.S. weapons, and part of the pro-
ceeds was channeled into a Swiss bank account. Money from arms
sales was commingled with money for the Contras. Private investors
solicited by North who had essentially provided bridge loans to the
government on the Contra's behalf were ready to make the questionable transactions public unless they were repaid. The fact that
the "missing" cash sat in Switzerland for nearly a year, with little
ever getting to the Contras, might be the best evidence that neither
the president nor Casey knew the scope of North's arms-hostages-
Contra scheme.[36] Since a "finding of necessity" had not existed for
the November shipment of weapons to Iran, the transaction was
probably illegal. So believed Edwin Meese, who had become attorney
general. If Reagan had known of the shipment and had approved it
in violation of the law, he had laid himself open to impeachment.

The inquiry into the affair was not as agonizing as those into the
actions of Nixon and Clinton, who both found "national security" a
timely distraction from their own imminent impeachments (Nixon
in trying to involve the CIA, Clinton in helpfully timed cruise-missile
strikes). Reagan himself called for the appointment of an independent counsel. He refused to assert attorney-client or executive privilege. Had it been proved that he had countenanced the sale of
weapons to Iran, and the diversions of the profits to Central Amer-

ica, the charges might have been theft of government property — stealing and using government funds for unauthorized purposes. The entire controversy is a reminder of how contrary to common sense the whole way of Cold War life had become: the moral compromises, the ideological antagonisms with Congress, the secrecy, and the accompanying CIA blunders. North escaped conviction on a technicality. Reagan survived an investigation.

In June 1986, Congress after all approved a bill restoring aid to the Contras. Some months later, General Powell best distilled the issue in which the scandal was rooted. "We're talking about whether men who placed their trust in the United States are going to live or be left to die," he told Democrats on the Hill.[37] Too many trusting peoples had found America's back turned to them when the going got rough. This was not going to happen now.

Reagan ended up ordering a review of all covert operations. He also prohibited the NSC staff from undertaking them. Richard Neustadt, scholar of the American presidency who had served in the Kennedy White House, soon added perspective about Iran-Contra: "It dominates this chapter in a way it will not dominate [Reagan's] history. For Reagan recovered from it. Indeed, the recovery is a success story."[38] During the two years after the Iran-Contra disclosures, Reagan's foreign policy began showing its most valuable results. In Central America, Oscar Arias, President of Costa Rica, put together the peace plan that would win him the 1987 Nobel Peace Prize. He opposed the Contras, yet he also implied his dismay that U.S. politics stood in the way of directly removing the Sandinistas.[39]

Undoubtedly, many influences worked toward uplifting Latin America. At the start of the 1980s, only about 10 percent of the nearly half billion people in those thirty-four countries south of the border lived in anything that could be called democracies. Eight years later, around 90 percent did, with some countries, such as Chile and El Salvador, still in positive transition. Moreover, Reagan's North American trade accord led to the creation of NAFTA, the liberalizing Free Trade Area, by his two successors. Given the amount of blame, some of it gravely deserved, that was heaped on the United States for the earlier state of affairs, it seems just to apportion it some of the credit for the reversal.

By the summer of 1988, Soviet foreign minister Eduard Shevardnadze admitted that "the adventures in the Third World were costly failures."[40] For instance, Moscow had reportedly sunk about $29 billion into Vietnam since 1979 and somewhere over $8 billion into Angola since 1975. It had spent about five times what Americans had invested to raise communism's "cost of empire" in the third world.[41] Moscow's outlay was another wound and would not have been so severe had the United States not responded in these backwaters. For example, the Politburo felt compelled to subsidize Nicaragua until 1990 to the tune of almost $1 billion a year in money and weapons. All these tyrannical little "states of socialist orientation" were no more likely to go quietly than the Soviet Union. They first had to be robbed of choices. A decade of U.S. military and economic pressure helped push Nicaragua to elections that year. In those elections, a center-right coalition finally ousted Ortega, who nonetheless still clings to the private estate he requisitioned as the presidential palace. By 2001, he was running for a third time, finally insisting that he had come to believe in free markets.

Elsewhere in the world, Ferdinand Marcos was eased out of office in the Philippines in 1986 by popular demand, with the United States pulling the rug out from under him. South Korea enjoyed its first free election in 1987. The following year, Pakistan's military rule retreated until 1999. Market economies came to be equated with stability and democratic reform. Aid dollars, said Shultz, would now be used to hasten third world efforts to decentralize, deregulate, and denationalize. Americans who would have been happy, say, to contribute to victims of floods in Bangladesh finally had had enough of the aid programs that they suspected kept Mexican mistresses in Mercedes, and recollections of the waste linger today.

In the autumn of Reagan's last year in office, an array of well-known officials from previous administrations convened with a group of Soviet wise men such as Georgi Arbatov to announce the results of an ambitious study that they had been working on for three years. It called for far-reaching steps to demilitarize superpower competition in the third world, recommending, for instance, that Moscow end its traditional support for "national liberation movements" and that the United States cease military activity under the Reagan Doctrine.[42] Although those Americans who enjoyed such conferencing believed that bargains still had to be struck, the Soviet Union had, in fact, already lost — and lost big in the "lands of the rising peoples," where Leninism's power of liberation, or at least of transformative terror, had most alarmed the West.

✪

The successes of the Reagan Doctrine were accompanied by what the intelligence world calls blowback, the harmful unintended consequences of operations. Plenty of it appeared in the 1980s, if only because of the scope of these activities. Much more arrived thereafter, as from Afghanistan. For example, it should have been no surprise that drug-related charges involving the CIA boiled up from Central America in the 1980s, then, a half dozen years after the Sandinistas fell, pointed falsely into the heart of Los Angeles.[43] Had not Panama's Manuel Noriega received $160,058.10 from the Agency at the very minimum, despite his anything-but-concealed involvements with drugs and money laundering, for a spectrum of Cold War services such as providing a back channel to Castro and training Contra units?[44] Ends were being invoked to justify means all over.

It took almost a decade after the close of the Nicaraguan war for the CIA to disclose that it had done little or nothing about the allegations of drug trafficking brought against other people with whom it was working. Some Contra leaders even argued that they had to stoop to criminal activities to feed and clothe themselves while fighting the larger Nicaraguan criminality. "We fell down on accountability," reflects a CIA inspector general. "There was a great deal of sloppiness and poor guidance in those days."[45] In Guatemala, where the military ravaged entire Mayan villages during the 1980s, the Agency was at the center of a decades-long U.S. role that, in the recent words of that country's independent Historical Clarification Commission, "lent direct and indirect support to illegal state operations" during Central America's most brutal civil armed conflict.

Much of this and more occurred during Reagan's watch and is the tragic shadow to his style of leadership. Congress, of course, was denied the details despite diligent bureaucratic responses arising from the mid-1970s investigations, with the Agency dumping five thousand reports of all sorts on Capitol Hill during 1986 alone. Langley had done worse than wink at drug deals among the multiplex corruptions of the small republics. For example, Tegucigalpa station — in the 1980s, the Agency's largest station anywhere and a clandestine command center — knew very well that the Honduran military (still described by a former station chief as "a very benign kind of military") operated death squads. However, its prevarications misled Congress about the extent of the brutality.[46] Only two senior officers would be dismissed for their roles in managing the Agency's relationship with the Guatemalan military and for keeping gross human rights violations secret from Congress. One of them, a successor to Duane Clarridge for Latin American operations, was issued the Distinguished Career Intelligence Medal at a closed ceremony in Langley.

The Agency had all along been recruiting some of the worst thugs on that continent and paying them to promote certain political undertakings, even when those actions ran at cross-purposes with policy as articulated by a U.S. ambassador on the scene.[47] The habit of odious compromises grew with their making: Salvadoran guerrilla defector Pedro Andrade was settled in New Jersey with $10,000 to start anew; his only blemish was the likelihood that he had directed the Zona Rosa machine-gunning of four U.S. Marine embassy guards, two U.S. businessmen, and seven of his fellow Salvadorans in 1985.[48] With stern impartiality, the Agency in 1989 relocated to Miami the Salvadoran defense minister complicit in the 1980 murder of the American nuns, as well as his death squad cousin.

One lesson a century of totalitarian terror and treachery has taught us is that somehow glimmers of decency always break through. From New York, the private Center for Constitutional Rights ended up suing former Guatemalan defense minister Hector Gramajo. As he graduated from a mid-career program at the Kennedy School of Government in 1991, it placed in his hands, during the ceremony, the court papers charging him with responsibility for thousands of Mayan deaths in the early 1980s, as well as for the more recent rape and torture of an American nun. By the time a federal judge wrote a one-hundred-page opinion granting the plaintiffs $47 million in damages, Gramajo had fled the country, along with his diploma.[49]

As if to highlight such moral sinuosity, the Agency had distributed in the early 1980s one more of its embarrassing how-to manuals. Although *Coercive Techniques* may have enlarged the capacities for mental torture and coercion of at least five Latin American security forces, the times were changing. By 1985, the CIA had repudiated the ripe advice of only two years before. A separate manual also had to be prepared for the Contras. As in the Middle East, there was a language problem. The text first had to be translated from English into Spanish. Adolfo Calero, who headed the largest of the

Contra groups, immediately knew that some of its terminology would be misinterpreted — particularly the term "to neutralize," which could be read as "to kill." Yet too much money had gone into the manual for it to be revised, so the Agency had to pay in further damage to its mission when that document also became public.[50]

All across the weary decades, the unnecessary ignorances kept appearing. For instance, Duane Clarridge worked closely with Argentine military advisers collaborating against the Sandinistas on Nicaragua's border with Honduras. His memoirs, however, show that he was clueless about Argentina's just-ended "dirty war" of 1976 to 1979. "Tragically," he writes of his new brothers-in-arms, "they may also have killed associates of the Montoneros with less evil intentions" — a mild way of describing the more than ten thousand Argentines who were vaguely deemed "leftist" and were kidnapped, tortured, and disappeared during these years *after* the military had wiped out the actual Cuban-backed terrorists.[51]

Events in Latin America reflected only a small part of CIA shortcomings. For example, the United States needed new embassy facilities in Moscow, having expanded beyond the ones used since the 1930s. Soviet construction crews would be allowed to build them. No problem, CIA experts repeatedly insisted in the early 1980s; they could easily sweep out the sensors that the KGB assuredly would place in the new eight-story building. Unfortunately, the electronic devices that the KGB embedded in the structure proved astoundingly sophisticated — "the kind of things that are only on the drawing boards here," according to one CIA expert. The proud tower could never be occupied, at an utter loss of $400 million to $500 million to U.S. taxpayers.[52] Nothing had been learned from experiences with Soviet construction crews in the 1950s. Yet it was the Agency's core analytical failures during the Cold War's last decade, and the ramifying consequences, that were the most grievous and that continue to hurt.

William Casey served as director of Central Intelligence until his death in 1987. As with every recent director, his influence could barely penetrate the bureaucracies within bureaucracies that had grown in the dark for nearly forty years. A more involved president might have been able to induce reform, although none of Reagan's predecessors or successors were able to have much impact either.

From about the mid-1960s through the final days of the Cold War, the CIA consistently underestimated the magnitude of the resources that Moscow was devoting to the military by a factor of two to four. This was particularly dangerous at a time when U.S. strategy was based on upping the ante. The failure also is one that the Agency has worked hard to explain away. Fortunately, Langley's reporting did not affect Reagan's decisions. Its numbers were largely ignored. Reagan based his decisions on intuition and common sense. He put the CIA's top presidential briefer on his schedule only three times in eight years, preferring to hand the daily briefing over to his dutiful vice president.[53]

The validity of the Agency's method of determining the Soviet burden rested on its being able to estimate both the extent of military production and the prices of individual Soviet weapons. Immense amounts of money were spent on satellite photography, communications intercepts, and other technical means. Such tools were only marginally useful. Moreover, the Directorate of Operations also was unable to develop the "blue border" sources necessary to fill in the enormous information gaps. Even the most successful human collection efforts could not provide the data required by what the CIA called its "building block" model for estimating Soviet spending. After two decades of expensive effort, Langley could identify only about thirty-five Soviet prices (mostly of components) for the five hundred military hardware items it needed to track.[54] Moreover, insights that depended on what could be seen from space, or learned through electronic intercepts, meant that the Agency underestimated Soviet production of most weapons, such as nuclear warheads, usually by 50 to 100 percent or more.

Installed in the senior executive service at the Defense Intelligence Agency, William Lee, meanwhile, kept working with unclassified books and periodicals, newspaper clippings, state documents, and other official printed minutiae (as well as with the usual secret materials). He continued to establish, for example, the value of total machinery production, subtracting out the amount conceded to the civilian sector, and thus arriving at a general estimate of the Soviet resources being devoted to buying weapons. Whenever new evidence concerning military spending fell into the CIA's hands from human sources within the Soviet Union, the Agency inevitably had to raise its estimates. Each CIA revision, first in 1976 and again in 1982, confirmed Lee's numbers for Soviet procurement and military R & D. After each upward revision, Agency analysts would slide back into more comforting underestimates, in part because they simply did not have the data required — neither accurate production numbers nor Soviet prices for the weapons — and in part because they refused to admit that Lee's methods worked.[55]

After the Cold War, and with nothing left to hide, Genrikh Trofimenko as well as a former Soviet military intelligence colonel, would identify the "very few American analysts who long ago came to the realistic evaluation of the genuine size (amount) of the military expenditures of the FSU [former Soviet Union]," and who understood the "monstrous degree of militarization of the Soviet economy." Trofimenko clucked that even these analysts underestimated it. William Lee, the University of North Carolina's Steven Rosefield, and émigré economist Igor Birman. In connection with the "new" Soviet military budget published for 1989. Trofimenko recalled hearing Gorbachev admit that the "real aim was to produce a 'presentable' figure that would look 'realistic' [to US intelligence]," while of course being grossly below reality.[56] On the one hand, Gorbachev announced to the world unilateral cuts in Soviet forces and invited all nations to beat their swords into plowshares. On the other, even Lee's estimate of the military burden at about 28 percent of Soviet GDP in 1988 (when the CIA had it at 14 percent) was still well short of the real magnitude of Russia's effort.

The CIA sought to rationalize the numerical discrepancies as being due to "hidden inflation" — the result of factory management defrauding the Ministry of Defense by vast overcharges, which the ministry supposedly swallowed year after year. Yet Agency analysts had previously concluded that no such factor existed.[57] When Gorbachev, during his final years in power, reported a figure for military procurement that was 30 billion to 33 billion rubles *less* than the CIA estimate, the Agency alleged that the factory managers had instead received that amount in official subsidies.[58] And so, by a synthesis that makes Marx a piker, the same expenditures in the same year yielded *both* 33 billion rubles in subsidies and 35 billion rubles in "hidden inflation." Even so, the CIA still insists that Soviet military spending remained more or less constant throughout the 1980s.

Again, the CIA's conceit was that its own artifacts and interpretations were superior to anyone else's, and it entirely ignored unsupportive statements even from within the Soviet Union.[59] In 1991, as the Soviet dream dissolved and the chief of the general staff said that the military consumed one-third or more of GDP and at least

60 percent of the Soviet budget, the CIA ignored these figures from General Lobov. It advised the Pentagon, State Department, and White House that only about 12 to 14 percent of GDP (merely 25 percent of the state budget) was going down the armed forces' gullet.[60] The CIA could not, however, explain where the money was showing up in the standard of living of the Soviet people, let alone in health care, on which the Soviet Union spent a minuscule amount compared to the West.

All this occurred despite one of the most expensive social science projects ever attempted anywhere — the Agency's study of the Communist economies overall. During the Reagan years, this venture employed scores of analysts, millions of megabytes of computer memory, and untold fortunes in satellite reconnaissance. But the CIA was still getting results very wrong at a time when a cornerstone of the nation's strategy was enormously wasteful.

Langley's failure to determine the viability of the overall Soviet economy, in addition to the patterns of military spending, cannot be brushed away as mere faults in financial technique. They were signs of something much graver and more consistent, marching in step with misreadings of the Soviet Union during the 1950s, 1960s, and 1970s. It was a patronizing discounting of the other side similar to that which allowed Robert McNamara (who had waged World War II usefully enough from behind a desk) to think himself into the boots of a Red Army marshal. Year after year, the CIA would delineate every Soviet "barrier to intensive growth," from labor to energy, except colossal military spending — the great hole at the center of Soviet society into which was shoveled the difference between life and death.[61] And how ferociously personal Langley becomes when anyone disputes its conclusions.

Once the Cold War was over, George Shultz concluded that the CIA was "usually wrong" about Moscow.[62] The Agency's refusal to face these failings has serious implications today. Many of the people responsible for them during the 1980s are now in authority and are not about to admit to errors of any sort. In fact, the CIA's inability to resolve its track record of economic misinterpretation is the key issue to be raised at a time when it is expected to collect international financial and business intelligence on terrorist networks.

The Agency says that its critics are thin on specifics and that these differences in data are insignificant. That is incorrect, if only because the failures of these years are today quietly cited by intelligence analysts as reasons for altogether avoiding interpretations, let alone projections, of China's military effort.[63] First, the CIA wasted a lot of money getting so much wrong during the Cold War's middle and final stages. Now, it is wasting more money trying to convince the country that it got it right. For instance, well-publicized conferences are sponsored to examine topics such as the "CIA's Analysis of the Soviet Union, 1947–1991." Many of those conferences include panels of impressively credentialed professors and think tankers, many of whom have themselves enjoyed CIA funding.[64]

Princeton sponsored one such gathering in 2001 in conjunction with the CIA's Center for the Study of Intelligence. Missiles, budgets, and much else were addressed. Except for a former deputy director calling the Agency "a W.P.A. project for economists" and admitting a few errors, mostly from the 1940s and 1950s, Langley's employees and the other panelists concluded that, all in all, the CIA had done a splendid job.[65] Every myth was repeated. The CIA still knew better than former Soviet officials themselves, such as Trofimenko or Georgi Shakhnazarov, once a Gorbachev adviser, who a few months previously had expressed his belief that "military spending reached stunning levels — as high as 40 percent of the national income."[66] Virtually nothing was said about the vast amounts of information that have been written in Russian since 1991, including memoirs and technical manuals, that undercut the conventional wisdom about a range of Soviet military issues. As tax dollars were spent on conferencing, the core questions were ignored: What might have been the CIA's most important analytical mistakes? What can we learn so as not to repeat them today?

Focusing on getting out its story, the CIA entered into a cooperative agreement with Harvard's Kennedy School of Government, which has so thoroughly adjusted itself to the times that one of its annual academic appointments became "CIA Officer in Residence." Even Melvin Goodman, the senior CIA officer and Soviet analyst who managed the initial Kennedy School ties, calls this collaboration "ethically questionable." As the Kennedy School "continued to receive millions in research contracts from the CIA," he writes, its scholars started offering generally favorable assessments of the Agency's track record. Goodman, once he left the CIA to teach at the Pentagon's National Defense University, compared the school's studies to those "on the tobacco industry, funded by the tobacco industry, based on a small number of documents carefully selected by the tobacco industry, with a preponderance of the testimony taken from senior officials from the tobacco industry."[67] The CIA and Harvard's Intelligence and Policy Program each reject the comparison, of course, noting the amount of declassified material that is being shared.

Langley indeed continues to offer well-policed quotations from its work of the time to show that the CIA understood in what direction the Soviet Union was moving. It publicizes, for example, declassified documents and congressional testimony to prove that it foresaw Gorbachev's demise. Such grace notes have to contend with other less helpful CIA conclusions as the Cold War and the Leninist order ran down together, ones that speak to Soviet stability.[68]

On February 18, 1988, Gorbachev revealed to the Plenary Meeting of the Central Committee that Soviet growth had been stagnant for twenty years (if the oil price rise and Brezhnev's artificial stimulation of the vodka industry were factored out). Right up until the Soviet collapse, the CIA saw the economy as growing snappily, anywhere from 1.6 to 3.5 percent per year through 2000, despite Gorbachev's despair and the insistence of some of the most acute Soviet authorities that it was dead in the water.[69] As late as the first Bush administration, Duke University Kremlinologist Jerry Hough quoted CIA estimates before Congress to argue that the Soviet economy had actually become stronger — a gross national product of $2.8 trillion, "bigger than [that] of Japan and the two Germanys combined." Today, former CIA director Stansfield Turner still shakes his head over what he has called "the enormity of this failure to forecast the magnitude of the Soviet crisis" — ensuring that the CIA fires back at him by publishing reams of unprioritized writings to the contrary with which he was provided in the late 1970s.[70]

The Agency was merely reflecting the conventional wisdom of foreign policy elites, although some people thought it had been set up to do better than that. Undoubtedly some individual analysts at Langley were more prescient, but their opinions were not the ones that came to the fore. Experts with even less basis for judgment offered their own certainties. "What counts is results," instructed Paul Samuelson, who also insisted until the end that a socialist command economy could thrive. The twelfth edition of his influential text *Economics* pondered what he saw as the "profound dilemma" of whether Soviet political repression was "worth the economic gains" — a strange question to ask in the age of Microsoft, Genentech, and Oracle, after the tens of millions of lives taken by Communist rule.[71] All of these mandarins were clueless about the growth of the military burden at the expense of consumption, let alone the overall stagnation and the drain from socialized agriculture.

Flawed intelligence estimates concerning particular events might be excused by noting that they should be treated merely as informed guesses. The truly valuable intelligence product, it can be claimed, concerns the spotting, tracking, and interpreting of trends and patterns. What is striking about the CIA, however, is how often it was wrong about particular events, as well as about general trends, decade after decade. Surprising gaps in intelligence about the Soviet Union, not just estimates of missiles and money, had become as customary in the 1980s as in the 1950s, when there was better reason for ignorance. For example, little was known of Yuri Andropov, even after he had headed the KGB for fifteen years and had thus been one of the pivots of the Soviet state. The Agency wrote up a full personal profile, but it had no idea of such significant details as whether his wife was alive until she appeared at his funeral. Or whether he spoke English.

One reason for making so checkered an intelligence product was the Agency's dependence on satellite collection systems, which cost billions of dollars a year to run and interpret. What is expensive must be accounted valuable. As George Smiley explains to an initiate in *Tinker, Tailor, Soldier, Spy,* expensively purchased information, even if spurious, is eagerly welcomed at the heights of government, whereas accurate information, perhaps gathered openly through diligent research, is often casually dismissed. "Ever bought a fake picture, Toby?" he asks. "The more you pay for it, the less inclined you are to doubt its authenticity."

The fetishism of information harvested by "national technical means" — the most exorbitant way possible — occasioned a revealing joke within the intelligence world of the 1980s: the entirely apocryphal, ultrasecret "KH-84" (KH for "keyhole," the designation for a spy satellite, and "84" taken straight from George Orwell), a Cold War–winning device to photograph *unclassified* Soviet writings, but in the most expensive, attention-getting way. Such expensive material could be adorned with the "special compartmentalized intelligence" stamp (far more rarefied than plain "top secret") and thus capture the attention of policymakers.

So much failure could have been avoided if the CIA had done more careful homework during the 1950s in the run-up to *Sputnik;* during the 1960s, when Soviet marshals were openly publishing their thoughts on nuclear strategy; or during the 1970s and 1980s, when stagnation could be chronicled in the unclassified gray pages of Soviet print. Most expensively, the CIA hardly ever learned anything from its mistakes, largely because it would not admit them.

It is not as if the Agency's men in the field were extraordinary either. The end of the Cold War would reveal how much "humit" (human intelligence) activity had been of little or no value — and how poor these abilities remain. Somerset Maugham and Graham Greene had braced any literate person for this eventuality for seventy years. Every CIA agent in East Germany during the 1980s had been doubled, with CIA officers themselves being so bumbling that Moscow worried that Washington was no longer taking the militarily formidable East Germans seriously.[72] A former deputy assistant secretary of state for intelligence and research draws these implications: "Literally thousands of intelligence reports, the expenditure of hundreds of millions of dollars and hundreds of successful CIA careers were based on information fed to us by our communist enemies."[73] In 1988, the Iranians eliminated nearly every CIA agent in the country. In 1989, a worldwide headquarters cable from Langley announced that every Cuban turncoat had probably been a double agent.

Toward the Cold War's end, the Directorate of Operations, with its several thousand men and women, turned dangerously dysfunctional. Nearly three-quarters of the case officers from the junior officer class of 1985 quit within ten years. By 1993, the number of CIA employees was around sixteen thousand, down from a peak of about twenty-two thousand a decade earlier — a decline due not only to post–Cold War retrenchment but also to personal despair with the entire organization.[74]

The most public catastrophe so far has been the CIA's nine-year failure to catch Aldrich Ames, who began spying for the KGB in 1985. Despite poor performance reports, being assessed for alcohol abuse, and facing both marital and financial troubles, he had risen to a vital position at the heart of the Agency's purpose. Still a mid-level bureaucrat, he headed the counterintelligence branch of the Soviet/East European Division, responsible for all CIA operations against the KGB and Soviet military intelligence outside the Soviet Union itself. How did this come about? "There are so many problem personalities," one frustrated investigator recalled after the Agency's lackadaisical efforts had finally uncovered Ames in 1993, "that no one stands out."[75]

The information that Ames sold to the KGB led to the executions of nine of the best agents the West ever possessed, including a legendary one quietly retired in the Soviet Union. Dozens of arrests occurred and scores of clandestine initiatives were ruined in what may be the most serious operational disaster to have ever befallen the Agency. The KGB kept staging successful double-agent operations against Langley, with the CIA submitting reports that included this false information to the White House and the Pentagon.

As "blue border" sources suddenly disappeared, discovering why this occurred was not a high priority. "If you find a mole," confided one intelligence official who was responsible for analyzing the Ames case, "you have to deal with him. It becomes embarrassingly public."[76] The scandal eventually arrived, all the worse for the delay. The inspector general listed the operations officers he wanted dismissed, punished, or reprimanded. Not much occurred. Several who had supervised Ames ended up with career achievement awards. As Ames burrowed away and spent lavishly, there had been no scrutiny as to the source of his sudden wealth, assumed by his bosses to be from an inheritance. Showing how clueless this closed world is about business, several colleagues asked Ames about his amazing acumen in the stock market and for the name of his broker.

Other deadly failures fell upon U.S. intelligence during these years and thereafter in Latin America, Africa, Europe, and the Middle East — blunders just as well hidden (from the American public anyway) as the secret successes to which the Agency regularly refers.[77] Vietnam had turned espionage from a cause into a career, as station chiefs in Saigon demanded a minimum of three hundred intelligence reports a month. The Civil Service Reform Act of 1978 compounded the problem, with its emphasis on a (non-entrepreneurial) business school philosophy of "objective criteria" in "performance appraisal systems." Case officers ever after were evaluated and promoted based solely on the number of agents they claimed to have recruited, which also determined whether they would receive coveted bonuses of $500 to $2,000. By the time CIA director James Woolsey vainly urged a semblance of quality consciousness right after the Cold War, there had been a series of scandals in which top-producing case officers were discovered to have invented agents and intelligence reports. Aside from the tens of millions of dollars wasted here and there, the lasting damage is that a significant part of the CIA is practically reform-proof. The

10 percent or so of the people who have made it to the top of today's clandestine service are those who excelled in this at best undemanding system.[78]

So many of the failures in the 1980s and afterward — in both analysis and operations — have stemmed from the core problem of personnel, which in turn arose from the way the CIA recruits its officers. This wilderness of failure remains among the CIA's deeper secrets and is one of its most troubling Cold War legacies.

In a 1986 interview, for example, Casey explained that by then candidates were coming "from state universities, from Catholic colleges, et cetera" rather than from "East Coast Ivy League schools" as during the Agency's heyday. No harm in that whatsoever. He then noted how applicants passed "the toughest screening test anywhere — a fifteen-year background investigation, psychiatric and psychological tests, IQ tests, aptitude tests of all kinds, polygraph tests." Yet, in an extraordinary backtrack, Casey revealed that "we disqualify, on security grounds, 90 percent of the people." Why? "The investigation doesn't disclose the problem; the polygraph does. Disqualification is usually because of drugs, alcoholism and sexual deviations, as well as theft, petty theft and the honesty of the individual."[79]

The polygraph, then uniquely required for hiring by the CIA and NSA, had become the last hurdle for a prospective officer. Its use remains one of the CIA's most cloistered and unaccountable arcana. Casey was asserting that after the most intense and expensive investigation in the world, such vices could only be uncovered by a machine, whose efficacy is far more a matter of institutional faith than scientific proof.[80] The CIA's confidence in this practice, which rests on a device that is least effective against the most professional spies, opened the Agency to tragedy. For instance, Larry Wu Tai Chin steadily worked for China undetected. So did Aldrich Ames for the KGB, passing three tests while in the full soaring flight of his betrayal. Finally interviewed in prison by a reporter, Ames said that his Russian handlers had laughed at his worries about the polygraph. Nonetheless, the CIA responded to this disaster by stepping up its efforts.

American bureaucracy was again placing too much reliance on technology. Moreover, this particular technology in the hands of the CIA quietly causes further havoc within the Agency, where an undisclosed number of employees who have had "difficulty with the process" sit in limbo. No part of government depends more on the polygraph or uses it more frequently, even though CIA officials responsible for its use know of its unreliability, according to prominent neuroscientists who consult under contract to create real biometric security solutions.[81] Equally pernicious, people entering the CIA recruiting process unknowingly expose themselves to grievous risk: applicants who surmount the full-field investigation but fail the polygraph soon discover that the Agency routinely shares its entirely polygraph-woven suspicions with any government department or corporation requiring security clearances to which these people might apply.

Hartford Courant editorialist Norman Pattis described how he underwent polygraph vetting after applying to the Agency during graduate school in the mid-1980s. Two four-hour sessions (always secretly taped, sometimes filmed) proved inadequate to convince his interrogators of his sexual preferences. He reminded them that they were not "an army of Sigmund Freuds" and that one could, amazingly, spend several years in New York City, and even at Columbia University, without trying cocaine. Polygraph results are exempt by law from disclosure to the individual examined, but, he learned, "according to an agency attorney, the CIA may share the information in my file, including, presumably, the polygraph exam, with other federal agencies."[82]

The Cold War ended at different times and on different fronts, one all too close to home. James Schneider graduated in 1991 from Georgetown University. He joined the Navy and served as an officer on a guided-missile carrier for three years before being honorably discharged with an unblemished record in June 1995. As his next career step, he had applied to both the CIA and the Foreign Service, making the extremely difficult cut for the latter and surmounting the State Department's intense background investigation. However, he was one of the 90 percent who had failed the CIA's routine polygraph test.

Schneider was sworn in that November by State, and by mid-1996 was awaiting assignment to Athens as a counselor officer. But the consequences of his CIA application were lurking. The Agency had originally turned his polygraph results over to its counterintelligence office, which includes several FBI agents — a spokesman later commenting that "the threshold for reporting cases is not all that high."[83] In summer 1996, nearly a year after the CIA test,

State Department officials learned of the failed polygraph from the Bureau. Schneider was immediately denied access to most anything concerning his work. Notification had not been made earlier to State because FBI officials had concluded that Schneider's questionable results were "eminently resolvable." The Bureau suddenly saw fit to administer its own polygraph — the CIA probably realized that Schneider had become a Foreign Service Officer — and he supposedly failed that one too. The issue, the FBI later said, may have been that he had "merely spoke[n] too loosely about classified material with non-Navy personnel" while in uniform.[84] Or it may have been nothing. There was no elaboration from Langley: it just helped draw the most destructive, disqualifying insinuations, eventually including unspecified ties to Moscow.

These persistent, career-threatening calumnies were sufficient to drive the twenty-seven-year old Schneider to suicide. It is unlikely that he was the first to be marched by those means down that bleak road — or that he will be the last.

Reagan signed the Employee Polygraph Protection Act of 1988, which prohibited industry from using the device to screen applicants. Shamefully, federal employees were exempted. For the CIA, the price of such peculiar vigilance can be seen in the quality of people it recruits: pleasantly accommodating types whom corporate human resources departments would have deemed useful in the 1950s, ones ready to be defined by the institution. Homosexuals, for instance, are today permitted to serve, as long as they are "out." The measure is that parents must have been told.

For the most part, these are the men and women whom the Agency chooses to carry it into the future, and so much of what it desires for its future is extrapolated from its past.

Camp Peary, occupying nine thousand acres of barbed-wire-encircled woods outside Williamsburg, Virginia, has long been the college of craft where career trainees prepare for clandestine service. During the 1980s, the course lasted a year and cost about $150,000 per recruit. Even today, much of it remains rooted in the nation-juggling paramilitary years: training at the pistol range, practice in infiltrating a hostile frontier's girdles of watchtowers and guards, midnight terrorist raids on dorm rooms, hijacking of the camp bus. Walter Mitty would kill to get in. It says much that someone with the unimpressive credentials of the traitor Harold Nicholson should have been considered a valued instructor into the 1990s.

Working relations between diplomats and case officers at U.S. Embassies became increasingly strained as the Cold War wore on. One reason was that the generally astute official commentaries from Foreign Service Officers and U.S. Treasury representatives overseas were commonly repackaged by less gifted CIA operatives and sent back to Washington (with tantalizing classifications), a practice that still goes on today. In 1982, the resentments had become so burdensome that the State Department and the CIA attempted something never tried before or since. In a strange bureaucratic vision of bringing these two cultures closer together, a recently schooled FSO and a just-graduated counterpart from the CIA's Directorate of Operations career trainee program were exchanged, to start anew through the other institution's learning process. Perhaps a precedent could be set for better cooperation of the two global services, beginning with the young.

The FSO surmounted all of Langley's hurdles, effortlessly concealing high school drug use from the polygraph. After mind-numbing months of career training, he emerged first in his class, finding his counterparts short of intellect and character. The language scores that had earned him a 2 (out of 5) at State were ranked 4.4 (fluency) at the Agency. What he recalls most from the many months at Camp Peary is the casual exposure to corruption. Senior case officers would boast in private of the opportunities for skimming the cash secretly disbursed to agents, though cautioning that it was prudent to take retirement before facing the whims of the polygraph, which employees were then exposed to about every eight years.[85]

Decrepitude of this degree is often best captured by fiction. In *A Firing Offense* by David Ignatius, foreign affairs correspondent and columnist at the *Washington Post* who knows whereof he writes, Rupert Cohen, a burned-out, bitter, and entirely convincing ex-CIA officer, says, "These guys had been on a 20-year losing streak. They were so mired in failure that a whole generation of them had done nothing but spin their wheels. They were collapsing of their own weight, in Washington and around the world. Most of what they did nowadays was make-believe."

Of course, some indisputably capable individuals have served the country nobly. One was Robert Ames, no relation to the traitor. Fluent in Arabic and with a distinguished record in South Yemen, Kuwait, and Iran, he was finally posted as station chief in Beirut, only to be killed with six other Americans in the 1983 bombing of the U.S. Embassy. There have been other similarly resourceful men and women, such as China hand James Lilley going on to become ambassador to Beijing. They may all have achieved spectacular successes still unknown, although the odds seem slim that the CIA would continue to hide profound achievements that might offset so continuously documented a record of failure.

Duane Clarridge, who left the Agency in 1988 as head of the new Counterterrorism Center, offers from retirement an anthology of that decade's most wildly misguided clandestine operations: "My staff both in headquarters and overseas was proof positive that the CIA was no longer attracting America's brightest. Every time they opened their mouth their ignorance showed."[86] Presumably, his own years in service, before being tarred by Iran-Contra, meant that the Agency contained many of the paragons that he laments. East German spymaster Markus Wolf recalls that by the 1980s, the CIA was "seedy."[87] Yet, we are told, much has since changed. That, too, has been heard before.

Just as the CIA may have been recovering from the damage done under James Jesus Angleton in the 1960s and early 1970s, Aldrich Ames began eviscerating its core Soviet espionage operations for cash. Angleton's ghost, as well as the smoke from the feuds between Langley and the Hoover Building, kept undermining the most basic security. At least since the mid-1970s, for example, the CIA had been routinely unable to gain access to local police records when needed. It certainly was not about to ask the FBI for help. Edward Lee Howard, formerly in the Agency's Soviet/East European Division, defected to Moscow in 1985 while under FBI surveillance in the United States, using his TWA charge card for the flight to Helsinki. As had not been seen since the early Cold War years, all sorts of treason floated to the surface. The *New York Times* called 1985 "the year of the spy," not even knowing of other recent cases (such as Soviet intelligence having obtained vital submarine secrets in 1978) that had been concealed. Also discovered that year was a hideously damaging espionage operation deliberately inflicted by an ally: the consequences of the Jonathan Pollard case still reverberate through U.S.-Israeli relations.[88]

Nineteen eighty-five was the same year that the Agency boasted to the Senate Intelligence Committee that it had never been penetrated by a Soviet agent and that Ames began his profitable second career. The 1980s were the KGB's heyday, and, in terms of espionage, it went strong right up to the end.

As for FBI counterintelligence, the quality of its personnel during the 1980s was neither better nor worse than its hated rival's. Aldrich Ames had worked closely with the Bureau's New York office. FBI agents who knew Ames still recall him as impressive by their lights.[89] Another traitor, Edward Pitts, with a lackluster record at Central Missouri State, taught at the FBI Academy before being plunged, wholly unprepared, into counterintelligence work in Manhattan.

New York was an embittering, underpaid, overworked posting in the 1980s. But it was also the main espionage battleground, in part because Russian visitors could not be as closely monitored as in Washington. The Bureau had nonetheless turned down the cost-of-living increases recommended by the Senate Intelligence Committee at the same time that FBI officials estimated that one-third of the Soviet bloc diplomats in New York were spies. "This place has entire squads of Richard Millers," said one experienced hand, referring to a traitor arrested in 1984. He must have thought that he was speaking for effect. Not only was Pitts burrowing away in New York, but agent Robert Hanssen had already begun his cataclysmic treachery.[90] Neither would be caught until well after the Cold War.

When the Justice Department finally concluded after Ames's arrest in 1993 that the FBI had been derelict in unmasking him, the Bureau's head of national security cried foul. "Twenty-twenty hindsight is terrific," he said, as if talking of another century, "but back in the mid-1980s we didn't have very good [Agency-Bureau] cooperation."[91] This was equally true of the mid-1990s, when CIA and FBI counterintelligence efforts were at loggerheads, with the Bureau threatening at one point to arrest a CIA station chief in Germany for refusing to cooperate on an espionage case. One step that increased cooperation, oddly enough, was the FBI director's 1997 decision to follow the CIA lead: all job applicants would be polygraphed, on the curious grounds that exhaustive investigative methods were insufficiently "capable of detecting national security risks."[92]

The past refuses to be buried. Altogether, more than eighty employees of the federal government or its contractors have been convicted of espionage since 1982. Belated discoveries of crimes by Ames, Pitts (who before his arrest was responsible for security clearances), and Nicholson have been followed by other revelations. David Boone, a former NSA cryptologic analyst was arrested in

1998 for selling secrets to the KGB in the Cold War's last years, and George Trofimoff, a former high-ranking employee of the Department of the Army, whom the KGB listed in the 1970s as their number one spy, was convicted in 2001 for selling secrets over a period of at least twenty-five years.

Also in 2001, it was Hanssen who was brought down, having progressed from counterintelligence work in Manhattan to being the FBI's chief representative at the State Department. He was unearthed after at least fifteen years of providing Moscow with some of the most sensitive, highly compartmentalized documents America possessed — and three years after Pitts told FBI interrogators he suspected Hanssen of being a spy. Mediocre in his day job and socially awkward like Ames, Hanssen became the Bureau's analogue of the most destructive CIA mole of the late Cold War and beyond. There in another comparison Hanssen told his Russian handlers how, as a young man, he had been thrilled by the memoirs of that original Janus-faced genius of the era, Kim Philby.

★

Essential to the defeat of communism and the revival of the American spirit was the economic expansion that started in 1983 and continued, except for a seven-month recession in 1990, into 2000. The military buildup of the 1980s was as near a painless rearmament as the world has known. That was due to a policy mix of tax cuts, deregulation (building on Jimmy Carter's good record), the hammering down of inflation to 5 percent by the end of 1982, and the expansion of free markets.

It is as schematically ideological to call the 1980s a "military decade" as it is to call those years "the decade of greed."[93] U.S. citizens at no point thronged to watch tank parades. People never said that they could not buy something because they had to pay their taxes to support defense, as did man of letters Edmund Wilson in the 1950s. Of course, the national debt increased, as at the height of any war. The $1.4 trillion that was added to the debt helped buy the end of the Soviet Union, as well as the twentieth century's longest wave of prosperity. Deficit financing was appropriately used to escape the gloom of excessive taxation and bureaucratic control that the country was wallowing in by 1980, when the Dow hovered around 900 and when marginal tax rates were 50 percent on so-called "earned income" and an even steeper 70 percent on investment income.

Over six years, in a bipartisan effort, Reagan reduced the top rate on all income to 28 percent. The explosion in national wealth dwarfed the additional debt and helped bring about the 1990s' characteristically Reagan policies of welfare reform and free trade. The economy of entrepreneurship, venture capital, and compounding innovation was given freer rein, resulting in a wave of tax revenues that helped finally make a balanced budget unavoidable in 2000. In fact, during the Reagan years, America's ratios of debt to assets, and of interest expense to total revenues, was indistinguishable from a corporation with a conservative balance sheet.

Critics nonetheless insist that Reagan's endgame with the Soviet Union and his prescriptions for ending the mini-depression of 1978 to 1982 came at too high a price. "Reagan's military spending nearly wrecked the economy," reflected Arthur Schlesinger in the middle of the booming 1990s, with the national debt somehow "t[ying] down the American government so wretchedly today." Columnist Anthony Lewis also obsessed about the debt of these years, saying, "We are continuing to pay it, and our children are going to pay it," around the same time that it began to shrink.[94] The large deficits about which they were properly concerned, however, arose less from tax cuts than from the bipartisan support for entitlement spending that had been set in place during the late 1960s and early 1970s. "Once the defense slide stopped," explains economic analyst Robert Samuelson about the end of the military buildup in 1986, "the basic cause of big deficits became clearer: Americans' inconsistent demands" — meaning their acquired taste for expensive government services and their persistent opposition to European-size taxation.[95] Although "big" for the United States, the budget deficits between 1981 and 1990 were exactly the average level for the world's other six leading industrial nations.

Many people in academia, the press, and business during the early 1980s were no more aware that lower tax rates would energize the country than they could imagine that a U.S. "ideological and geostrategic offensive" might fatally compound the self-inflicted economic and moral disaster that was Soviet Communism. They were still preoccupied with the Cold War's "big picture" of "big engineering" and state power. Upheaval caused by microeconomics and diffused initiative was something their careers had never had to encounter. In Cambridge seminars, for instance, John Kenneth Galbraith would scoff at the notion that people would work more, save and invest more, and take more risks should they be taxed less.

Mandarin hopes for management as a central discipline that combined academic rigor with worldly authority had not yet fallen away.

From Western Europe, as well as from their own savants, the people of the United States were berated, as they had been in the 1950s, for their "overindulgence" and "overconsumption" once they were again making their economy (and those of much of the world) hum. "Why won't Americans pay the same taxes as Europeans?" complained learned men foolishly certain that their country was in "a race to bankruptcy" (a mindless phrase from Reagan's first budget director) with the Soviet Union, of all places.[96] Many critics during the 1980s also admired Japan's approach to command-and-control capitalism, in which banks, corporations, and government operate hand in glove. Such people understood neither their country in the late twentieth century nor the failings of central planning as they were showing themselves in a land so potentially rich as Russia — and so soon in Japan.

Reagan's view was entirely different. His first act as president was to eliminate price controls on oil and gasoline. Another step was to break the power of an illegally striking public sector labor union. That quick and uncompromising decision had already begun to worry the Soviet officials I encountered at the time. He was for constrained budgets in the abstract, but he was, as usual, an enthusiast where it came to causes close to his heart — tax cuts to foster enterprise, as well as military "modernization." Under any circumstances, a Republican administration of this persuasion would have sought to cut back on a federal fiscal burden that by 1981 had reached its highest level since World War II.[97]

The Republicans conceded (by their votes, not their sound bites) that pay-as-you-go was as obsolete as the Democratic South. Tax cuts began to pull one way, federal spending the other, and an ever-widening gap opened, steadily replenished by debt taken up by foreign investors. Ironically, foreigners into the mid-1980s might have been even more eager to buy American securities because of a mounting sense of the rest of the world's dangers, a fact that was already becoming out-of-date. Reassertion of the dollar's value by the huge overseas deficit-covering sales of public paper incited Americans to keep buying more and more imports, and the trade deficit soared.

Finally, there came the backlash against Japan as a longtime free rider. America's former single-minded focus on protecting the limitrophes of China was blamed for an apparent shift in economic power. Japanese products seemed to flood U.S. markets as Tokyo's 4 percent annual growth through the decade overshadowed even the 3 percent of the Reagan expansion. Japanese buyers acquired such trophy properties as Rockefeller Center and, much more troubling to some, began acquiring leading-edge U.S. microelectronics companies. But it would not have been a Cold War story without opportunistic side changing. The slogan of "national security" became a cry for long-complacent U.S. industries, notably including computer manufacturers always reluctant to restrict their shipments to the East, to urge protection against Japanese imports.

During Hungary's uprising in 1956, Andy Grove had fled Budapest as a child, going on to earn his doctorate in engineering at MIT. As president of Intel, destined to dominate world microprocessor markets, he predicted the collapse of the entire American industry before Japanese cherry-picking. He urged Congress to restrict Tokyo's American investments, perhaps to require "impact statements" (a fashionable political device of the later Cold War era) before permitting majority holdings in U.S. information technology companies. This was an overreaction, but Japan was playing rough.

Between 1985 and 1989, according to Laura D'Andrea Tyson, who would head President Clinton's Council of Economic Advisers, Japan's carefully targeted, government-driven focus on several U.S. industries may have cost them around $100 billion in lost sales. Further concern arose from the "spin-on" phenomenon, in which Japanese manufacturers exploited shared U.S. military technology for unexpected civilian purposes — for example, modifying the disc brakes of U.S. F-104 jets, then rolling them out as better brakes for Japanese cars.[98] Worst of all were the unambiguously destructive activities of one Japanese firm, Toshiba. Since 1982, it had been selling sophisticated computer programs and machine tools to the Russians, suddenly enabling the Soviet navy not only to quiet its own subs but also to better detect and follow American ones.

By the 1980s, few people remembered the U.S. role in creating this state-led, *keiretsu*-dominated economy. When American capacity to compel Japan toward open markets had been greatest, in the 1950s and 1960s, U.S. willingness to twist arms had been least — given that Japan was part of the "outer fortress." As American capacity to compel Japan in the 1970s and 1980s waned, U.S. desire to twist arms intensified. Where the United States had legitimate complaints — that is, the U.S. machine-tool industry's charges that its Japanese counterparts were dumping — no retaliatory action followed. Japan, after all, was still regarded as too important to U.S. foreign policy to submit to any demarche, and Japan's entirely derivative machine-tool industry was thought to be too important to its economic stability for a president to take any steps that might strain the relationship. Washington's market-opening agreements with Japan, covering thirty-two sectors or products between 1985 and 1992, yielded few results.

In the Cold War's last year, one of the *New York Times* correspondents in Tokyo confided to me that his time there had convinced him that any American hope of ever regaining business competitiveness with Japan was forlorn.[99] The latest wave of experts additionally asserted that the prowess of Japanese software factories spelled the doom of an independent software industry in America or that Washington had to pick winning industries. "cold fusion" initiatives, to use one example, were said to need taxpayer money if only to prevent losing out to Japan.[100]

For more than forty years, "national security" had been the sun around which the U.S.-Japanese relationship revolved. What followed was characteristic of the Cold War: facts whose implications had so long been obvious (in this case, about trade and investment) were suddenly acknowledged and reconfused. Again feeling threatened by a juggernaut (now it was Japan), Americans continued throwing money at the problem and hoping it would go away. Only a handful of people in Washington tackled these complicated trade issues during the 1980s. This reflected a dilettantism of the sort that had long been apparent in facing the Soviet Union and in building America's intelligence capabilities. Committing added effort would have entailed more study of hard languages and more proficiency in economics.

Meanwhile, America's premier instance of industrial policy and centralized economic authority — the Pentagon — was hardly a reassuring example of dirigiste efficiency. By the late 1980s, the Pentagon's inability to master its own finances had inflamed such pertinacious civil servants as A. Ernest Fitzgerald, the whistle-blower who in 1969 had disclosed the first billion-dollar weapons buying overrun. Yet even when more billions in waste became undeniable — so familiar that everyone knew why newspaper cartoonist Herblock always drew the secretary of defense with a $600 toilet seat around his neck — it was seen as more of the same.

Waste hardly had to be thievery; it was part of the Cold War military-spending roller coaster, and it accompanied each Cold War buildup. Toward the end, however, the rush for sales brought the inevitable — the largest defense corruption scandal in the country's history. Dozens of consultants (meaning middlemen) took the term "Beltway Bandit" literally. More than ninety individuals and companies, including eight of the fifteen largest contractors, were convicted of various felonies, some of them grave. Much that was obsolete, unnecessary, or overpriced was foisted on taxpayers during the 1980s. The military's rote reaction to scandal and waste on this scale was to promise reform, pledge self-policing, and speak of "a few bad apples," then return with soldierly resolution to writing checks, often for highly questionable undertakings.

Against the backdrop of all the spending and misguided "expert" opinion, it was no wonder that in the last two years of the Reagan administration, the country found itself yet again ready to hear of its inadequacies. In 1987, Reagan appointed an early supporter of his presidential campaign, Alan Greenspan, to succeed Paul Volcker at the Federal Reserve. Volcker recalls a wry observation at the time by one of his overseas friends that the departing chairman's career had been "a long saga of trying to make the decline of the United States in the world respectable and orderly."[10] The ambitious work of Yale's Paul Kennedy, a diligent British scholar of early-twentieth-century military history, brought this sentiment into the open. It hit a nerve that year and furnished the pop-historical vision of the decade in *The Rise and Fall of the Great Powers: Economic Change and Military Conflict from 1550 to 2000*.

Kennedy set out to compress forty years of Cold War history around the planet into a single Western Front, explaining how it was consuming lives and treasure. All this the Cold War had done, beyond reckoning, but the forty years bought by this effort had created a world unrecognizable from Professor Kennedy's one-dimensional perspective. Brandishing his pointer of decline, he guided his readers along the same downward slopes followed by proud Spain, the assiduous United Provinces, spirited France, and, culminatingly, the pioneer industrial-strategic "super power," Britain. He attained his one-size-fits-all conclusion by refusing to compare the evolution of the earlier societies' economic bases with America's or with those of its enemies. He failed to distinguish between undoubted waste and incoherence on the one hand, and fatal overextension for territory's or glory's sake on the other. He tried to crowd bourgeois ascendancy into the same deathbed as imperial pride.

And why neglect the place of technology? It was beside the point that the United States was by this time producing only 15 percent of the world's steel, instead of the two out of three tons it was making right after World War II, or even that manufacturing, as a share of GDP, had shrunk from a postwar peak in 1953 to just over half that share by 1989. Like George Kennan, Paul Kennedy overlooked inconvenient facts, as information technologies forced decentralization and demanded the sort of adaptivity made for America. The mythic roll of his thesis was akin to that of another English historian at the Cold War's very beginning, Arnold Toynbee, who had lectured and sold amazingly widely to anxious Americans trying to find some perspective for their sudden prominence. He had offered a vast, synoptic, and bleak view of the rise and fall of civilisations. Now it was Professor Kennedy talking another worried generation through the cycles of empire. In neither was there any good news for America. Surprisingly, some critics believe that his warnings are still apt.[102]

As the Cold War was just about to be won, many influential people awoke, in the undistressed phrase of Gore Vidal, to "the day the American empire ran out of gas." For four decades, apocalypse had been a possibility. It was easy to bring such terms to bear on the country's economic future. This was no way for a democracy to think its problems through. For instance, former commerce secretary Peter Peterson, who had become a banker in New York, foresaw an inevitable "Argentining of America," whose day of reckoning — crumbling infrastructure, dwindling productivity, meaner quality of life — lay close at hand. The United States, he argued, had inflicted incalculable damage on its own economy, above all by consuming rather than investing, as well as by piling up debt abroad. Defense spending and the tax cuts of "Reaganomics" only made the damage worse. Carried to a fever of alarmism, Peterson invoked the likelihood of the United States being driven into "pawning off our Third World financial leadership onto more solvent economies" and predicted that the country would be doomed to remember the 1990s bitterly, as the time "when we took the British route to second class economic status" — except that the United States would have declined far more swiftly.[103] Here indeed was America as banana republic.

The lost leadership then being lamented was that which had come from being the sole large, prosperous country in the Cold War's first stage, among nations morally wounded and physically impoverished. America had to put this zero-sum perspective behind it, the faster the better. An increasingly dynamic world economy entailed that, at least in the short term, the country had to be in one form of imbalance or another. The trade deficits of the Cold War's final stage proved worthwhile because they helped revitalize often-bureaucratized U.S. industries more than they hurt the economy. Unintentionally, they accelerated the integration of global commerce. As for the empty phrase "Third World financial leadership," Americans had by now sunk quite enough money into the Congo, Indonesia, the Philippines, and scores of other places. The far more important leadership of economic example, which the United States as a nation was exercising for the developing world, instead paid off in the freeing of once-statist realms such as, well, Argentina. Ultimately, the imperial overstretch was the Soviets', and it was Reagan who reached out a decisively unhelping hand.

Simultaneously with Peterson, management guru Kenichi Ohmae, director of McKinsey & Company's Tokyo office, asserted Japan's "right to share world leadership." "Americans have mismanaged not only their own economy but the world's," scolded Ohmae. "Now, as your problems are becoming critical, you want us to bail you out. You want us to carry a heavier share of your burden."[104] It did not even merit notice what the United States had been carrying for Japan. America was being told that it had selfishly taken too much upon itself — and it was listening as closely as it ever does on such subjects.

The University of California's Chalmers Johnson soon concluded that "the Cold War is over, and Japan won," an elegiacally defeatist epigram widely parroted by journalists and politicians.[105] So it may have looked when Emperor Hirohito died in January 1989. Many third world nations, eager to obtain Japanese loans, were obsequiously reverent. Johnson's conclusion, however, was just a final example of the confidently delivered judgments that over the years had wasted so much effort and twice had led to the loss of so many lives. It reflected the perspectives of bankers, management consultants, professors, and reporters, but not, for instance, software entrepreneurs and small businessmen, who might have hesitated to speak of such inevitabilities. For many Americans to have taken this promise of decline so seriously, however, shows that something had been lost in the country's spirit by the distractions of the Cold War. After all, just the costs of real military purchases in the forty years since 1948 came to around $10 trillion, not including the hundreds of billions more in retirement pay, real estate, and the whole apparatus of the Atomic Energy Commission, Department of Energy, and intelligence agencies.[106] Who knew what had been forgone? The loss could only be felt.

✪

The story of the 1980s proved not to be that of the triumphant advance of communism after the fall of Saigon and a suddenly immense expansion of Soviet military power. Instead, it was one of the Soviet Union cracking from within, at the same time room for maneuver without was being blocked by a reinvigorated America. Dying societies have ever more things to be paranoid about. The question was whether this one would take the rest of the world with it or just crumble into the social and ecological deserts it had created.

What won the Cold War was the transformation of the United States. By the end of the Reagan administration, the country was no longer what it had been in 1980, whereas the Soviet Union that staggered dangerously on for three more years was essentially the same collectivist tyranny it had been not only in 1980 but ever since Khrushchev. The United States was ready for a different world; the Soviet Union was incapable of fundamental change. If America changed — with a new economy combined with a comprehensive offensive — it would win against a stagnating opponent. Reagan recognized the direction of history from 1964 to 1980, and he knew that all that was required was leaders who did not despair of the American promise of individualism and enterprise. He understood that the United States possessed the resources that the Soviet Union was denying itself.

To Reagan, the Cold War was not a set of problems to be fixed, but a situation to be ended. It would be a contest between two societies, one good and the other evil. Cold war did not preoccupy him, although he confronted the Soviet Union most directly. His years included the usual confusions of war, but this was as much as possible subsumed by the American vibrancy that he embodied. No other president since World War II has left office with an astonishing 82 percent approval rating among young voters. Reagan communicated a sense that the Cold War, which had been created in their parents' day, was part of the overhead as long as the Soviet Union existed, but that the United States had much to do otherwise.

When personality was uppermost in the Cold War, it did not necessarily harm. The two genial chairmen — Eisenhower and Reagan, each being operationally ruthless while outwardly kind — were, all things considered, the most effective presidents. They were able to focus relatively sustained efforts toward sufficiently enduring ends because less adrenaline (a substance of short-term effect) was being pumped into the "game of nations." Reagan revived Eisenhower's vision that the United States was in fine shape — neither lethargic, faltering, nor burdened by malaise — and that the Soviet Union was doomed. In fact, the somewhat dreamy quality that reminded his critics that he was an entertainer made him the only president since World War II to be truly lifted by imagination and to foresee the likelihood of ending the Soviet menace peacefully.

Truman, for whom Reagan had campaigned in 1948, is the president who may come closest to him in imagination. He had a touch of crankiness (not unusual in the founder of a great undertaking) that let him take initiatives as issues arose, undismayed by lack of precedent, and, as in recognizing Israel, he was not necessarily speaking for the foreign policy establishment in doing so. Eisenhower had the wisdom of big experience. He had a superb ability to follow up, which is by no means a put-down. But it is difficult to see those same qualities of imagination in him. (It is hard to place him in the White House circa 1940 considering what to do with Germany and Japan on more than military terms.) He was not a founder, but a defender, of cities. If civilization is "hope and maintenance," as Eric Hoffer believed, Truman was the former and Eisenhower the latter.

Lyndon Johnson, a man of great energy and creative power, was caught at a turning point in history. He treated Asia as being as important to the United States as Europe — which hardly looks like a foolish attitude today, although his moves were less sound than his perspective. He embodied intuition, but he was intuitive about the present and the immediate future and had not picked up that the New Deal was dead.

Nixon, a corrupt Quaker, believed that he was a realist. His hero was de Gaulle — not a man whose idealism, except about France, could be trusted. Nixon believed that the American redemption of the world — the Marshall Plan, the rescue of South Korea, the confrontations with evil — was over. America had to cut deals. He was a man who saw life as win or lose, and he felt, in his condescending way, that he was schooling America in a reality that actually was swiftly falling into the past.

Reagan understood that America had won the Cold War even before he took office. Perhaps the only other leader so perceptive by 1980 was Andropov, who would likely have been a deadly opponent had he lived. The standard talk in government, academia, and the press at the time of Reagan's inauguration was how Americans had to be "realistic" about accommodating Soviet power, how Western Europe might be "Finlandized" under the advances of "Eurocommunism," and how the democracies, as showcased by America's economic despair, might have become too complex to govern. By the time he left, the totalitarian bogeys had slunk back into the dark, the transformative power of markets and technology was blasting forward, and the confident pessimists of the 1970s had to try to explain themselves away to a world that barely remembers them today.

Reagan's vision of the world he was inheriting antedated the Reagan strategy. He recognized this as an age of revolution, and in that sense he was not really a conservative. Since his days as an active Democrat, he never lost the Wilsonian commitment to the spreading of American democracy. He despised the routine bullies passing themselves off as revolutionaries and a Soviet Union not all that different in 1981 than when Lenin died in 1924. Cut from the cloth of the small-town Republic of his boyhood, Reagan was nonetheless a figure from the new America: a harbinger of today's communications upheavals; the first divorced president; the first president to adopt a child; personally untroubled by homosexuality (having allowed homosexuals to teach in public schools when governor and permitting the highest security clearances for the first openly gay defense official). He knew he was part of a global revolution, while realizing that the Soviet Union had already driven its class-ridden one into the ground.

The tactics were secondary, and almost entirely worked out by aides, as they should have been. Here Reagan had much in common with FDR, who insouciantly let it be known that what he knew about the world came from his stamp collection. Reagan was similarly the intermediary between the American people and the experts, whom he directed. Both men did much more than substitute one set of policies for another; they shifted the general philosophy of the country. Like FDR, a man whose intellectual security lay in his intuition, Reagan did not share Carter's concern that others might be more capable than he, Ford's uncertainties, or Nixon's obsessive refusal to delegate on the issues that he deemed central. Eisenhower would have found Reagan's way dangerously visionary and gravely unstaffed.

Perhaps the Soviet Union could have careened dangerously on until today, trying to adapt as in the manner of Deng Xiaoping's China — although with armored divisions leaning against the rest of Europe and Asia and with ICBMs ready to preempt the United States. Astoundingly, its demise proved relatively peaceful. Fighter jets were used only for a matter of hours to intercept the fleeing Achille Lauro terrorists in 1985 and to strike Libya in 1986; the Marines were withdrawn quickly (though, tragically, not quickly enough) from Beirut; and the Grenada invasion lasted only a few days. Yet Reagan "made [the Soviets] cry uncle," recalls Oliver Wright, British ambassador to the United States during most of the 1980s and a Foreign Office professional with little patience for American partisan politics.[107]

Reagan had a sign on his Oval Office desk: "There is no limit to what a man can do or accomplish if he doesn't mind who gets the credit." America's other twentieth-century "organizer of victory," George C. Marshall, had always used that phrase. Both men preferred that papers presented to them be no longer than a page. Neither had much interest in the press and none in political gossip. Both had an uncanny ability to explain a subject lucidly. Like Marshall, Reagan cared little for his place in history. Official biographers had to be urged upon both men, and both treated them with courteous indifference (so unlike the yearnings of Kennedy, Johnson, Nixon, and Clinton). Like Franklin Roosevelt, there was an iciness at the core of Ronald Reagan's being, streaking the general warmth of his nature.

Reagan was another excellent example of the man and the hour meeting. He coincided with the communications revolution and saw what it meant for the Cold War, eventually walking through the streets of Moscow in the spring of 1988 as crowds of people chanted, "U.S.A.! U.S.A.!" At a time when extremely few politicians, professors, or CEOs understood the significance of twenty-first-century information technologies, he held up a microchip to students at Moscow State University as a symbol of freedom's power and material abundance. He invoked the "continuing revolution of the marketplace," telling them of ideas catching fire and the right to dream, while helping to legitimize the changes under way. "You're on the right track," he asserted, and, when asked about the "evil" he had denounced only five years before, he cheerfully replied, "That was another time, another place."

Gorbachev merely put a better face on the changes he was forced to accept. He was one of the great adapters of the late Cold War. He headed the Soviet Union at a point when it could no longer even pretend to embody a cause and had become merely an increasingly disconnected military superstate with an impossible economy. Gorbachev in highest office still had the Leninist arrogance to believe that the complexities of modern technologies and economies could be handled by ideologues. He at least had the wit to give up and would soon be doing a Pizza Hut commercial on television as America became Emerson's "country of tomorrow."

The Reagan strategy might not have succeeded before 1975, although Reagan's steadiness would have been salutary during those "crisis years" of the early 1960s and it is unlikely he would have played into the Soviet manipulations of the 1970s. Squeezing the Soviet Union to such an extent when it still thought itself on a roll might have been more dangerous still. Reagan wanted to be president in 1968, and a change of three votes in Mississippi's delegation would probably have set off a landslide that could have carried him to the nomination — and if not to repudiation as another Goldwater, probably to a presidency swiftly spoiled by the letdown of a decade not ready for Reaganism. Those were years in which the aura of big government and big engineering peaked. An inappropriate rebel in 1968, Reagan was perfect for 1980, because anything that was not working for individuality — Soviet and other socialism above all — was under siege in a post–World War II system that had outlived its time.

Reagan also had the advantage of dealing with the third generation of Soviet rulers, who had become worn-out, had lost their faith, and were grimly turning the wheels of a wheezing, blood-splattered machine. In dealing with the allies, he reasserted the obvious: Western Europe and Japan were clients. Yet he could do this while embracing even the most ideologically different sorts of people, as in being strongly backed in his international causes by the AFL-CIO, of which he was a lifetime member. Just as Ernest Bevin had drawn the line against totalitarianism, so ultimately did another socialist, François Mitterrand, who unequivocally endorsed Reagan's nuclear rearmament program from the first. Both knew that they needed to be championed by the United States against a Soviet Union that they believed had pushed too far, and both had the self-confidence not to feel humiliated. Mitterrand would sum up the power behind Reagan's determination as "primal: like a rock in the Morvan, like plain truth."[108]

"We meant to change a nation, and instead we changed a world," Reagan said in his farewell address. He was the only president since Teddy Roosevelt to step aside for a chosen successor, with his vice president being able to win a landslide victory. It is beyond the laws of probability to believe that this was all coincidence or a matter of being lucky. The worldly historian Sir Robert Ensor once observed that when Napoleon Bonaparte chose his marshals "for their luck," the word "'luck' here probably implies some final felicity of judgment." Like Eisenhower, Reagan had the cunning and the apparently effortless ability to get himself into place after desired place. The lack of surface arrogance should not conceal his force of will, nor should his modesty in details obscure a confidence in his contribution to the heart of things such as only great men or fools possess. The hypothesis of foolishness becomes weaker by the day.

As the Cold War wound down, however, Americans also could see that the costs kept going on. Debt, distrust, cleanup, nuclear weapons, and vicious little wars would keep breaking into a future whose landscape would remain less welcoming because of all that had been endured since 1945.

12

Unintended Consequences

(1989–)

The war is won, but the peace is not.

Albert Einstein, December 1945

In June 1988, one of America's more mischievous commentators crafted for Washington, D.C.'s distinctly alternative *City Paper* an "alternative history" of that year's summit in Moscow between Ronald Reagan and Mikhail Gorbachev.

The world is awed by the revolutionary changes under way, as the strongest and most feared of totalitarian states finds itself being transformed by a new and youthful leader astonishingly impelled toward reform. An amazed network anchorman reports from beneath the glittering chandeliers of a vast baroque hall whose opulent carpets disappear into the distance. Ceremonial banners nod against the walls. Fanfare rises and fades. "This is CBS World News," he intones, "live from inside the Reichstag."

And thence unfolds the imaginary "Berlin summit" between a young, energetic Reichsführer and an aging president of the United States. The very fact that American television is allowed to broadcast from this arcanum of the Reich reflects the changes sweeping the no-longer-so-evil empire. The two leaders are chronicled sitting on a couch before the meeting in which they will discuss arms control, the Reichsführer — flashing the smile that has shone from the world's front pages for three years — pushing sharply for a reduction in strategic weapons. The president, as *Time* magazine's foremost commentator on the empire recounts, seems fatigued, and the hosts are impatient to deal with a new American leadership.[1]

CBS presents a background report on the changes afoot. No one is so tactless as to mention Adolf Hitler, whose place in history has been unsteady for some time. In 1956, only a few years after his sudden and still mysterious death, his successor, who addressed the Reichstag in soon-pierced secrecy, accused the Leader of "excesses." But these were never officially acknowledged until now, when their existence is quietly deplored.

Looking back fifteen years to the actual summit in Moscow, one is startled to note how, even today, few of us recall the history of communism and the Soviet Union in terms comparable to Nazi Germany. For instance, people who deny Hitler's genocide are rightly shunned. But somehow, the Soviet experience has undergone a reverse process. Scholars who deny Stalin's holocaust, reburying immense crimes such as the Katyn Massacre, are considered respectable for publication even by a major university press.[2] That is because, by the 1980s, the Union of Soviet Socialist Republics had become only an oligarchic tyranny rather than a genocidal abattoir. It is still considered an act of churlishness in many quarters to bring up its enduring criminal record. Although many European and Israeli socialists, let alone Chinese Communists, had always found it possible to speak clearly, when even conservative Americans talked about Soviet evil, especially during its last twenty years, it was often seen as evidence of reaction and militarism. One consequence is that the reasons behind America's immense Cold War effort can appear unconvincing, at best part of the story of two hungry superpowers driven at each other's throats by imperial appetite.

Yet even National Socialism never quite communicated its full criminality to the wickedest of the states that aligned themselves with the Reich. But communism was able to arouse monstrous emulation in society after society, as tens of millions of people were swallowed from the dark Polish woodlands by way of the cellars of Moscow to the fields outside Phnom Penh. Nazis destroyed to create an ethnically "purer" society. Stalin, Mao, Pol Pot, and many of the other "little Stalins" destroyed to create a purer, or at least a more unqualifiedly subordinate, "proletarian" society. The difference lies largely in words.[3]

As Truman and Marshall recognized, and as Reagan was not embarrassed to say, Americans first had to exert themselves to defend civilization, then had to confront the appalling vestiges of the slave order after 1953. Today, it is less foolish than callous to conclude that had it been the Reich and Hitler's successors who were tossed on history's ash heap after decades of struggle, "the doves in the great debate of the past 40 years [had been] right all along."[4] The Cold War's end was predicated on the end of the Soviet Union. That did not come about by harmonization or convergence, but by the application of some fraction of the relentlessness that the Soviets had tended to regard as their own.

The Soviet Union was, of course, as repressive and expansionist as Gorbachev would admit to a joint session of Congress in 1992. It never got beyond its Leninist beginnings, passing effortlessly from revolution to reaction. The most avowedly revolutionary (and therefore intolerant) party could not keep up with the most revolutionary (and therefore unpredictable) century. Until the end, the Soviet Union remained a state organized in the name of unattained absolute ideals for extreme purposes, mercilessly pursued.

The disintegration of Communist Europe that began in 1989 was like that of a vast but archaic fortress that at the first serious earth tremor dissolves from towering menace to dust. The Berlin Wall, not only a symbol but a truly bloody fact of power, was torn apart literally overnight that November — twenty-nine fateful months after Reagan had ignored State Department and White House advisers to stand at its foot and demand that Gorbachev "tear [it] down." Solidarity came to power in Poland, with Czechoslovakia following. In December, Ceausescu, the Romanian dictator with his pathetic train of phony degrees and a British knighthood — an emblematic mixture of Leninist pseudoscience and demoralized Western accommodation — went out in character. Appearing on his balcony, he saw the crowds below turning on him, found his army in mutiny, and fled by helicopter, only to perish with his wife before a firing squad on Christmas Day, showing how much his gimcrack order (like most of the Soviet bloc) really was part of the third world. Germany was formally reunified one year later.

There were learned people who, even in the moment of the East's collapse, hoped matters could stay the same. The eighty-four-year-old George Kennan, for example, recommended in 1990 that Washington agree to a "binding moratorium of at least three years' duration" that would freeze Europe's post–World War II arrangements in place.[5] There should be no changes in the Warsaw Pact, no "alterations" of states. But the world was not about to be stuck in any "moratorium." The Pact was dissolved. Then the three Baltic republics that had disappeared with the 1939 deal between Hitler and Stalin — Lithuania, Latvia, and Estonia — reclaimed their independence, after Gorbachev's initial bloody crackdown. Suddenly, all seemed for a moment to hang in the balance during August 1991. The prime minister, the KGB chairman, the ministers of the Interior and Defense, the Party secretary, and other reactionary conspirators demanded that Gorbachev either declare a national state of emergency or hand over authority. The tanks of the Red Army foundered among an aroused people "standing up" in Moscow. The failed coup was the real end of the Cold War. Yet the Americans, whose commitment had bled the regime dry, were tellingly unimpressed. They gave as little attention to the end of the Soviet Union as they did that December to the fiftieth anniversary of Pearl Harbor.

This chapter addresses the Soviet Union's final three years and then discusses the peculiar post–Cold War decade, from late 1991 to September 2001, a time for America not so much apolitical or cynical as flippant. During that decade, it seemed as if the world had come to acknowledge the American example, at the same time that Americans gave increasingly less weight to experiences of the past. Perhaps the touchstone of the era was a mid-1990s *New York Times* advertising spot that intended to appeal to the average reader by asserting, "The only foreign country I'm interested in is one where it's 85 degrees and where I can get to on a big boat." That sentiment was the antithesis of bearing any burden and paying any price.

We begin by explaining how the old Soviet order tried to stay afloat after so much had been done between 1981 and 1989 to make its "costs of empire" unbearable. What did the United States undertake thereafter both to uncock Russia's nuclear hammer and to begin cleaning up the Cold War's poisons? Second, we probe America's combat operations during the ensuing decade, several of which were repercussions of the original conflict, as was the stubbornly enduring structure of the U.S. military. The most unequivocal case of genocide since Hitler's war against the Jews is used to show that much about U.S. policymaking was not about to change either. Third, we shed some new light on how terrorism was addressed during that peculiar decade and on how it should be considered now. As at the start of the Cold War epic, alert people soon recognized in the 1990s that winning a war would not bring several decades of peaceful development. It would bring further troubles. As it had taken disaster in Korea to become serious about confronting those troubles — often to the point of overreaction — something similar occurred in September 2001. Before that sunny late summer morning, terrorism was treated within government as just another national security fad, while to the public it was just one more emergency among an infinite number of alarms. Finally, in the chapter's last part, we reflect on several of the unsettling facts and ironies of the fifty-plus-year journey.

Security is achieved at a price — one that often cannot be assessed for decades. Whether the price is reasonable can be reckoned only from what has been made secure. The twentieth century was never more the American one than in its final decade. The good fight had been won. It would not be easy, however, for the United States to shake off the bad habits that had evolved during the years of "neither war nor peace."

Sometime after Appomattox, a Union major standing in a cemetery overlooking the ruins of Charleston was asked the way "to Mr. Calhoun's grave." "Madam," he answered, "the whole South is the grave of Mr. Calhoun." A hard commentary, but he spoke for the aroused power that had made it so. And so, too, is the whole post-Soviet sphere the grave of Lenin.

Reagan used the word "crusade" before Parliament in 1982, when he promised that the Soviet Union was finished, although his years in office were characterized more by moderation than the heat and upheavals of the crusading experience. His successor dealt more cautiously with Gorbachev. "Bush," recalls Jack Matlock who stayed on as ambassador to Russia into 1991, "was uncomfortable with change."[6] It is fairer to say that diplomacy was the politics of the first Bush administration.

The coda from George H. W. Bush's inauguration in January 1989 to Christmas, 1991, when Gorbachev left office, saw the Soviet Union give out. Yegor Ligachev, the number two man in Gorbachev's Politburo, argues that even toward the end, Soviet leaders might have been able to dam the cascade.[7] As late as 1989, perhaps the essence of the system could have been saved for a dozen or more years. Henry Kissinger offered his wisdom. He suggested that the new administration introduce a framework of accommodation to the Soviets, perhaps advanced by an august secret envoy yet to be named: Moscow would permit Eastern Europe to liberalize, and the United States would pledge not to exploit. As soon as this notion leaked, Zbigniew Brzezinski, teaching again at Columbia and eventually helping Poland to rebuild, denounced it as a "new Yalta." The White House brushed it off. Prospering as a business consultant with an array of ties to China, Kissinger returned to work explaining just why Beijing had no choice but to crack down bloodily in Tiananmen Square.[8] Meanwhile, the Soviet Union was losing control of its debt and going beyond the point of return.

Moscow kept raising untied, general purpose, loans from Western banks. The banks, as they had in making loans to the third world in the 1970s and as they would in making loans to Russia in the 1990s, saw easy profits. It did not matter that the government was abysmal; the money would be going to a government nonetheless, with presumably no risk of default. For the most part, Western loans flowed to all the unproductive purposes of this intensely militarized state. There were no identifiable sources of repayment, such as hard-currency-generating projects or import-substituting savings. Western bankers were among those people who toiled to keep the Soviet Union afloat.

By the mid-1980s, the Soviets had been forced to acquire considerable financial sophistication to play the world's debt markets. For example, Moscow was able to create an inexpensive, nontransparent, cash-reserve checking account of roughly $10 billion through an elaborate shell game. It tapped Western interbank deposits by using its seven subsidiary banks abroad — banks that were legally incorporated as institutions of the countries in which they operated. Western bankers were thereby unable to develop a full picture of their credit exposure to the Soviet Union or know the full extent of its debt, as Moscow deftly practiced this and other deceptions.

The West Germans, longtime bankers to the Soviet Union, grew anxious over the scale of debt they could discern. In addition, Moscow had to keep finding more creditors, and in 1985, it began borrowing heavily from Japan. In 1986, for the first time since the Romanovs, Moscow went to the bond market, quickly raising about $1.8 billion by offerings in Germany, France, Italy, Japan, Switzerland, and Austria. Once it turned to securitized debt, the exposure shifted away from Western governments and banks to individual Western taxpayers and depositors.

On the one hand, this step vastly expanded Soviet sources of borrowing by luring underwriters, insurance companies, and pension funds into supplying money for purposes that no one required the Soviets to explain. Moscow sought to establish vested financial interests on the part of these politically influential new constituencies, thereby ensuring that Western governments would not allow it to default. On the other hand, securitized debt opened the Soviet Union to more scrutiny, both because more people now held the loans and because bonds are extremely difficult to reschedule.

By 1987, Moscow expected to have access to the mother lode — the New York bond market, which processed the bulk of available world capital. Had it succeeded, the empire might have garnered a new lease on life. Working with New York's endlessly inventive investment bankers, for example, it might have been able to collateralize bonds against oil and gas in the ground. But a bipartisan effort in Congress, spurred by public-spirited lobbying, helped ensure that the Soviet Union would never be permitted to float a bond in the United States. Debt service requirements instead became more onerous.

Yet the Department of Agriculture's taxpayer-funded Commodity Credit Corporation, about to lose some $5 billion on loans guaranteed to Saddam Hussein, was allowed to help fill the breach. More than $3 billion in loans were guaranteed to the Soviet Union. These, too, would be lost. Otherwise, enough political pressure had built up to keep painting the Soviets into a cash-flow corner.

Ultimately, a half dozen reasons stand out among the many for why the Soviet Union was so vulnerable on this front: (1) in 1988, Japan simply stopped lending to Moscow; (2) bankers increasingly understood the scope of Soviet debt and the lack of hard-currency earnings, then refused new commercial loans; (3) the rollovers of Soviet lines of credit and interbank deposits slowed as bankers also realized that such practices were de facto medium-term lending; (4) the Soviets were blocked from fully exploiting world bond markets; (5) they were subject to ever more scrutiny once private Western investors became overexposed via government loan guarantees; (6) they could not collateralize with their gold reserves, because it was known that they had largely sold off or pledged what little remained. Gorbachev's attempt to "reform" communism largely on hard currency borrowed from the West made matters worse.

Western lenders would have detected Moscow's plight sooner had they insisted on more transparency and collateral. The Soviets were burdened by some $90 billion in debt at the end of 1991. Their potential financial exits, such as oil and gas sales, had previously been bricked off. Some two days before Christmas, Moscow publicly announced its inability to service this debt. In brief, the Soviet Union defaulted. Those in the West, particularly European governments, who had desperately sought to prop it up in the name of "stability" deservedly lost billions. The end had been predicted during Reagan's first term: once Soviet leaders had to face serious U.S. military, political, and economic pressures, the contest would largely come down to cash.

Soon after the great implosion, Russia's new president, Boris Yeltsin, compared his country's condition with the immediate aftermath of World War II. The question of what to do elicited the usual cycle of romantic rhetoric with which the United States greets mighty events. Talk of "shock therapy" (with the patient too weak to endure it), of "irreversible change" (death is the most irreversible of changes), and of "strategic partnership" (against whom?) served at least to prepare the American public to pay for some market-oriented and democratic reforms. What emerged was the nightmarish Russian economy — replete with recycled apparatchiks as tycoons, gangsters and fixers surfing on a toppling GDP, and a retrogression to barter. Here remains one of the more enduring monuments of the first post-Soviet decade, as reflected in the dire musings of Aleksandr Solzhenitsyn's slim volume *Russia in Collapse*.

Russia continues to try to pay off billions in pre-1991 defaulted loans and more recently defaulted Finance Ministry bond offerings. Ten years after the Soviet collapse, it still carried billions more in debt. Moscow pressured the IMF throughout the 1990s for money, while burying $50 billion or more in central bank funds offshore to avoid the prying eyes of creditors. Funds were then denied. From 1999 to 2001, however, a slowly improving economy permitted Russia to pay official creditors more than $30 billion. Yeltsin had succeeded in at least freeing Russia from its crippling state-owned holdings. Yet the real squeeze arrives in 2003–2005 when scheduled maturities of $45 billion in debt from Soviet days come due.

The "final price," some well-meaning Americans said, should have been a "Marshall Plan."[9] Yet attempts to stimulate Russia's dormant economy right after the Soviet collapse encountered deal-breaking realities: hundreds of billions in assets were smuggled overseas, and at least 40 percent of the economy under Yeltsin was controlled by criminal syndicates, with much of the country's wealth (particularly its oil fields) privatized into the hands of a few men who moved payments directly into privately controlled foreign accounts. The amount of capital flight during that decade dwarfed foreign loans and investment. George Marshall had built on a continent frightened into order, even in Germany. In Russia, any such initiative would have had to be erected on a swamp.

Americans were nonetheless generous. At one of the first academic conferences to address the impact of the Reagan presidency, Genrikh Trofimenko, while noting that Reagan had "raised the cost of potential victory for Moscow so high that it collapsed from the strain," chortled at the notion that Soviet victors would have offered their hands to help a defeated America to its feet or lobbied the World Bank and the IMF to extend credit.[10] The reform efforts for which the United States did help to pay were mostly outsourced to Harvard, Goldman Sachs, the IMF, policy wonks at think tanks, and other well connected intermediaries. For example, the taxpayer-funded Central Asian–American Fund blew through more than $100 million in salaries and preposterous investments while accomplishing zero for Central Asia. I received my own small share of the spoils, being paid $35,000 by the U.S. Information Agency to write about the elements of entrepreneurship. Better articles on the subject could have been reprinted and translated from any worthwhile business magazine.

Ultimately, this aid contributed little if anything. Since 1990, Russia's death rate has risen almost one-third, to the highest of any major nation, with the birth rate plunging almost 40 percent, making it among the lowest. Outside of AIDS-plagued Africa, only Haiti reports higher male mortality rates. A cumulative $66 billion from the United States, Europe, and the leading international lending agencies failed to generate sustained economic growth, as Russia today produces one-third less than it did at the start. Money was distributed rashly, which was just one of many unfortunate old habits.

Harvard's Institute for International Development received $57 million in Agency for International Development (AID) contracts intended to help the Russian government restructure its economy and its political institutions. This latest boondoggle ended up with the Department of Justice suing the university for alleged self-dealing involving several academics on assignment in Moscow. Triple damages were demanded. In 2000, Harvard's provost disbanded the institute after twenty-five years of operation and taxpayer funding of some $30 million a year.

The Cold War left Americans wise to the development business overall. For example, a handful of large, specialized Washington-based companies, inevitably run by former AID officials, benefit handsomely from the $7.5 billion budgeted by the United States for annual programs, and particularly from the labyrinthine way the money is awarded. To Americans, foreign aid is likely to be popular only when conveyed through specific charitable organizations, such as those addressing population issues and children's health, in contrast to government and its friends tackling the world's big social problems.[11] In the 1990s, the biggest problem was Russia.

As the post-Soviet economy crumbled, resulting today in a GDP the size of Holland's, there was finger-pointing over the question "Who lost Russia?" Some blamed the White House, which, during the Clinton administration, supported an ill-considered "big bang" approach to change. Prodigies of embezzlement resulted in Russia.[12] In the United States, former government officials from both parties also made money. They lobbied, opened doors, and provided various unspecified assistance for oil companies and other investors trying to do business in the new republics. Once the easy-money schemes began to dry up, Washington ties were valuable as well to the indigenous players in Russia's rough-and-tumble new capitalism. The biggest U.S. lobbying and law firms were retained in the hunt for loans. Such engagements have become customary in a capital where, upon leaving office in 2001, the former secretary of defense, secretary of state, and national security assistant (none having previously been in business) each started companies to offer "strategic advice" based on their recent public service.

Today, Russia is no more reconciled with its present than with its past. It has a third world economy and a government that considers itself a first world power. In 2000, the statue of Felix Dzerzhinsky, founder of the Soviet secret police, was reerected before the sufficiently notorious Lubyanka Prison, after having been torn down in 1991. Stalin's national anthem has been revived, though given new words. Lenin's mummy remains enshrined in its Red Square mausoleum. Whatever the future, Moscow still possesses what remains of one of the two greatest total armaments in all of history.

The radar at Krasnoyarsk, the location of which was the most unambiguous of Soviet ABM treaty violations, finally closed in 1989. Its construction had been ordered directly by the Politburo and explained away by U.S. arms controllers as a site for tracking satellites rather than ICBMs. The following summer, Bush and Gorbachev signed a treaty climaxing what Reagan had insisted on calling the Strategic Arms Reduction Talks (START). Fifteen months later, the president signed the START II treaty with Yeltsin, which then languished in the Duma. That treaty finally abolished land-based MIRVs, the warheads long identified as the most destabilizing.

Also during the Soviet Union's final year, the Red Army shrank to 2.7 million men, about 3 million less than in 1989, when it had begun withdrawing from Eastern Europe — something for which the General Staff had never planned, in contrast to "the eventual occupation of all of Europe."[13] Yet the arms reductions of these last days left alive the Soviet Union's germ empire, history's most pestilential arsenal. And there were other reasons for the first Bush administration to be cautious. "We keep telling them to knock it off," concluded Condoleezza Rice, a Russian-speaking specialist on the NSC staff, "but the Soviets are still putting military equipment into every nook and cranny of the Third World."[14] Nonetheless, Gorbachev was anointed Time magazine's "Man of the Decade," having previously been its "Man of the Year," for all those changes that had so largely been forced upon him. A Nobel Prize followed.

After the collapse, well-spent U.S. payments induced the former Soviet republics of Belarus, Ukraine, and Kazakhstan to transfer to Russia the nuclear weapons within their borders. Humpty-Dumpty was put back together to the degree that there would at least once again be only one thermonuclear power, however rickety, between NATO and the Chinese frontier. But more had to be done.

During the rest of the 1990s, Robert McNamara, still dashing between academic conferences on disarmament, sensibly argued that the United States cut its strategic weapons whether or not Russia ratified START II. Russia could no longer afford to maintain what was left of its once-unsurpassed arsenal, he argued, and must by any means be induced to diminish it further. Not only were these weapons in tremulous hands, but, for internal political reasons, Moscow warned that it might rescind its 1983 pledge not to be the first to use them. Although McNamara was naive to give any weight to that original sham renunciation, he was grimly right in recognizing that nuclear armaments may lose one form of menace only to engender others. Here, indeed, the unburied Cold War keeps hacking more pounds of flesh.

By the time of the failed coup in August 1991, the KGB had

tried to humanize itself by anointing a buxom young woman as "Miss KGB" and posting her photo around the disintegrating empire. It had also opened itself to meet in Moscow with CIA officials to discuss liaisons against terrorism. A year later, about 200 of the Russian Republic's leading atomic weapons scientists signed a contract with the U.S. Defense Special Weapons Agency (a Pentagon unit overseeing the U.S. stockpile) to write a detailed, 2,000-page history of the 715 Soviet nuclear tests since 1949. The fee for directly conveying much of the information that the United States had been trying for decades to ascertain through billions of dollars in balloons, U-2 flights, and satellites was $288,501.

Approved by Russia's minister of atomic energy, this insiders' account traces the long path from the first Soviet atomic and hydrogen bomb tests, documents the history of weapons making, and unveils the ten "closed cities" that were the plexus of Soviet nuclear armaments development. Only around $500 dwindled down to each of the 200 participants. The whole deal came not only amazingly cheap but most opportunely for the nearly destitute authors. Western intelligence feared that some of them, as well as others among the former Soviet Union's key 2,500 to 3,000 weapons scientists, might put themselves on the market to such unstable countries as Libya, North Korea, and Iran.

The proliferation of knowledge, however, no longer entails disaffected savants having to move to faraway deserts. Unsupervised talents can consult via the Internet to various anonyms. Beneath this core group of experts were thousands of penurious subordinates responsible for the day-to-day security of Russia's nuclear materials. U.S. officials worried that one or more of Moscow's weapons might be lost or stolen, maybe winding up in the hands of an international outlaw group, one perhaps employing expertise from former KGB officers. The FBI director was among those arguing that America faced a greater danger of a nuclear attack from such a source than it had ever faced from the Soviet Union. Witnesses before the Senate Foreign Relations Committee described Russian "loose nukes" as "a clear and present danger to national security," in the words of a well-funded National Academy of Sciences panel. Hollywood paid more attention than did people in San Jose or Trenton, who were too busy to notice. The Foreign Relations Committee itself was no longer a prime theater of national concerns where the ambitious heirs of Senators Nixon and Kennedy could perform.

Between 1992 and 2002, the United States spent more than $4 billion to help destroy Soviet-era nuclear weapons, improve safeguards, and work with the Atomic Energy Ministry to control uranium and plutonium. Russian customs agents have been trained at the Pacific Northwest National Laboratory and provided with X-ray detection vans to uncover fissile materials and to track technosmugglers. Less publicized was the fact that Russia's inability to pay its electric bills brought frequent power outages, which deactivated sensors at its plutonium reactors. To further constrain dangerous possibilities, the United States bought bomb-grade uranium from Kazakhstan and conventional weapons from other former Soviet republics. For example, twenty-one MiG-29Cs (the most advanced Soviet-era fighter jet) were scooped up for around $40 million, dismantled by Pentagon teams in Moldova, and air-freighted to Dayton, Ohio. Within a year or two of the collapse, however, any chance that the core assets of the Soviet strategic arsenal could be bought was lost. Nor can it be assumed that skeptical American taxpayers might have been persuaded to pay for them.

The embodiments of the momentous buildup of the 1970s and 1980s — the aging SS-18s, the corroding Typhoon-class ballistic missile submarines, the Blackjack bombers that were not lost to Ukraine — remain Russia's last claim to its old status. The weapons are as deadly as ever and perhaps under more lax command. In 1995, for instance, Russia misread a Norwegian scientific rocket as a possible nuclear attack by a Trident submarine — a ghastly few minutes that may have been among the more dangerous of the nuclear missile age. As a result, U.S. military technologies were put to work, necessarily at U.S. expense, to prevent Russia's defenses from setting off a mindless assault. This was a small step, yet reminiscent of Reagan's ridiculed vision of a world in which Americans and Russians might develop antimissile systems together.

Two decades ago, the Soviet Union's great Northern and Pacific fleets demonstrated the drive for global power. Today, the submarine graveyards of the Kola Peninsula in Russia's far northwest are among the unresolved legacies of the empire, with Americans paying for giant Typhoon subs to be towed into port and dismantled. What also remained of the navy included perhaps 72,000 spent-fuel assemblies. Nearly 2 million tons of liquid and half a million cubic feet of solid radioactive waste will cost *somebody* billions to clean up. All these obligations may be only the beginning. For example, the United States and Germany are helping Russia dispose of the world's largest stash of chemical weapons — 40,000 metric tons of mostly nerve and blister gas. By 2000, Washington had contributed $200 million or so to the effort. A lot more effort is unavoidable, given that the cost of destroying America's own 32,000 tons of chemical weapons will add up to about $13 billion.

As for the Soviet biological arsenal, its tens of thousands of personnel were not about to disappear. The United States has also paid to compete for the allegiance of these former germ scientists. Still run in 2001 by General Yuri Kalinin, Biopreparat re-created itself as a state-owned drug company, while maintaining its secrecy. In 1992, President Yeltsin disavowed biological weapons, and dozens of Biopreparat production facilities have since been converted to make pesticides or to carry out civilian biotech projects. Yet the military plants remained off-limits to outsiders.[15]

As for America's own cleanup problems, fourteen plutonium production reactors bred about 100 metric tons of that revenant element during the Cold War, not to mention 2,700 metric tons of spent fuel that is stored in aging containers and facilities.[16] Merely the cleanup of conventional weapons involves more than 15 million acres that need to be surveyed for unexploded ordnance (UXO), mostly bombs and shells. If just 5 percent of that acreage requires UXO removal, the Pentagon places the cost at around $15 billion. The Department of Energy added up as many of the sums as it could collect. It calls the cleanup ahead the "Cold War Mortgage" and prices it at about $350 billion until around 2045.[17]

In August 2001, there was a small ceremony in Petersburg, South Dakota, as the Air Force blew up a Minuteman III silo. It was the last in a series of demolitions required by START I, the final arms reduction treaty between the United States and the Soviet Union. Several hundred other Minutemen missiles are still maintained in silos located in the state and in Wyoming and Montana.

Ellsworth Air Force Base remains South Dakota's largest employer, even though its ICBMs have finally been disassembled and ranchers have been able to buy back the one-acre parcels that were taken for missile sites during the Kennedy administration. Some prosaic returns stand out. The National Park Service preserves a single silo and launch center as a museum on the desolate high plains. In Marin County, north of San Francisco, the Golden Gate National Recreation Area offers the country's only restored Nike missile site — one of the three hundred that, into the 1960s, surrounded major cities to defend against Soviet bombers. Some of the thousands of visitors who watch the forty-one-foot missile slowly emerge from underground ask why it was named after a sneaker.

The end of the Cold War did not stop America's fifty-plus-year debate over whether to build one or another sort of shield for itself. Nor did European allies stop insisting that creating such a shield would destroy the concept of shared risk. Russia was no longer the danger. So-called "rogue nations," a disparate group of states assessed as irrational or nihilistic, were said in the 1990s to be a threat of ungaugeable magnitude. Once North Korea launched a three-stage rocket with international potential — a capability in 1998 that the CIA had just determined lay fifteen years in the future — Congress was prepared to designate billions of new dollars for ABM research, testing, and construction.

In the spring of 2000, Vladimir Putin, a former KGB lieutenant colonel, succeeded Yeltsin as president of Russia. He sensibly, if incompletely, stated that it had been the "unrestricted stockpiling of weapons" that had led to the "disintegration of the Soviet Union" and endorsed the nearly ten-year-old START II treaty.[18] Yet Putin began warning that all nuclear, conventional, chemical, and biological arms control agreements would be canceled if the United States took further steps he deemed contrary to 1972's ABM treaty — the artifact of a different world. He also threatened to repudiate Moscow's old pledge of no first use. After September 11, Russia's role in America's popular front helped put such familiar quarrels in the background.

Disputes over nuclear weapons between the former rivals are unlikely to remain quiet forever.

One story reflecting Moscow's longtime approach to its military requirements tells of the need to develop a writing instrument that would work in the weightlessness of space: the Americans spent a fortune on R & D to create such an exquisite pen; the Russians decided to use a pencil. Whether or not one believes that the United States should build a national missile defense (NMD) system today, the least convincing argument is that it would violate the 1972 treaty. Russia already possesses such a system (crude as it is) consisting of some eight thousand missiles, many of which have nuclear warheads, backed by twelve huge battle-management radars that provide early warning as a by-product, and by the command

and control abilities that tie it all together. This is in addition to the one ABM site around Moscow, permitted by the treaty, which uses a different type of missile from those deployed around the nation.

What Russia has created is hardly an impenetrable shield, rather, a roughly adequate means (in Russian eyes) consistent with a traditional approach to defending the motherland. There are several reasons this is not acknowledged by U.S. intelligence.

The first concerns key information "gaps" about capabilities that could not be filled in until the latest untranslated material became available — "gaps" still very sensitive but ones acknowledged by the twenty-year-old National Intelligence Estimate (declassified in 1966) addressing those issues. During the 1980s, it could not be known whether the Soviet Union was cheating because the difference between a national missile defense system and a nationwide air-defense network depended on capabilities invisible to U.S. spy satellites. Second, the Russian system was put into place over time, piece by piece, and upgraded as new technologies became available. Third, a top DIA official recently claimed that technical analyses by U.S. intelligence show that the latest dual-purpose interceptor missiles are just too slow to use against ICBMs. Moreover, the argument goes, the Soviets might have wanted originally to integrate the interceptors into an NMD network but never demonstrated that they could. Recent Russian source material confirms how Soviet designers worked around the slow speed. These sources also document how the Soviets installed the national command-control system that tied it all together and demonstrate that the system worked without detection by U.S. satellites. This is what Russia has inherited.

There is another reason for America's misunderstanding. That official, the defense intelligence officer (DIO) for strategic forces, asserted in 2001 that he had not read the new Russian material. Nor did he know anyone in the intelligence community who had.[19] (Such material, after all, was both in a foreign language, easily available without high-tech reconnaissance, and *un*classified.) Acknowledging this capability would require the intelligence community to acknowledge many other mistakes. Meanwhile, Russia proceeds with the fifth in a series of interceptor missiles that are arguably part of a national missile defense structure. The United States, in turn, preferred in 2001 to justify its own much more technically elaborate NMD aspirations by emphasizing threats from "rogue states" while not raising questions of Russia having violated the original treaty. Especially after September 11, it was no time to rock the boat. Perhaps that treaty could be negotiated into oblivion.

The language surrounding national missile defense is familiar: President George W. Bush asked the country and its allies to "rethink the unthinkable," playing on the 1959 phrase of Herman Kahn. A "Maginot Line?" critics asked once again.[20] Also familiar is Russian propaganda to constrain the United States from proceeding with its own plans. In 2001, the deputy secretary of Russia's Security Council traveled "from Harvard to Stanford and from Senate hideaways to West Coast mansions" telling sympathetic opinion leaders about Moscow's grave concern that America might disregard a nearly thirty-year-old treaty that, he insists, has been the pillar of arms control.[21]

The fall of a great power releases its neighbors not to the ways of peace, but to the alarms of succession. Thus the Cold War originated in 1945. More than ten years after the end of Soviet Communism, the enigmatic greatness of China can look troblingly familiar.

During the 1990s, Russia sold old Kilo-class submarines and guided-missile destroyers to China. Aircraft carriers built in the 1970s sailed down the dialectic to become tourist attractions in Guangdong and Macao. China's military became Russia's best customer, purchasing fighter aircraft, modern submarines, and new destroyers outfitted with Russian missiles. In early 2001, Russia and China signed a treaty on friendship and cooperation, the first since 1950. The nuclear face-offs of the Cold War's middle years seem gone forever. Before September 11, it even appeared as if Russia would be urging China (and India) to join it in countering America's plans to extend its power. "The Next Cold War?" asked a bright red cover of *Time* magazine as an Asian eye peered from behind a cutout of a star from the Chinese flag. "Getting Colder" blared another one. Then the kaleidoscope turned as China, like Russia, found practical reasons to collaborate with America. Yet China's sense of wounded nationalism and its historical grievances endure.

Focusing on China during 2000 and into early 2001, espionage scandals were widely compared to the early spying of Theodore Alvin Hall, David Greenglass, and other traitors who had also been connected to Los Alamos. An FBI interview with nuclear scientist Wen Ho Lee offers a glimpse. Lee was the subject of a rash fifty-nine-count indictment arising from Bureau suspicions that he was a spy for Beijing. "You know what happened to [the Rosenbergs]? They electrocuted them, Wen Ho," the interrogator threatened. After decades of jousting with the Soviets, as the ham-fisted Lee case shows, U.S. counterintelligence was unprepared to face China's subtle, at least equally effective methods.[22]

Thirty years ago, the Nixon entente with China was a useful, if grossly overhyped, measure to redistribute the pressures of the Cold War. Once formal relations were broken with Taipei and switched to Beijing, more than a few U.S. policymakers hoped that the problem of Taiwan would go away — perhaps after only a slightly more decent interval than had the problem of South Vietnam. Instead, Taiwan democratized, and this state of twenty-three million people is America's fifth-largest trading partner. In the twenty-first century, China has as usual outlasted the urgencies of its rivals and friends alike. It wants Taiwan back. Not everything changed after September 11.

By routinely playing on competing factions in the U.S. government, by hiring former top American officials as consultants, and by offering investment opportunities, today's most potentially dynamic nation, containing a fifth of the earth's population, moves to take advantage of a world that Cold War quarrels have made.

✪

The 26,000 U.S. troops finally thrown against Panama's Manuel Noriega in 1989, bringing him to imprisonment for the drug trafficking that Washington had indulged during his years of power, also showed that the Cold War was just about over. So did the fight in early 1991 to end Saddam Hussein's grab of Kuwait, an aggression that would have given him control of the region's oil wealth, of which his $80 billion debt would have been a rounding error. At his diplomatic best, President George H. W. Bush gathered a 28-member coalition centered on 697,000 Americans. The one-hundred-hour Gulf War was fought not only with the muscle of the Reagan buildup but with a revitalized military that had, since the later 1970s, corrected deficiencies across the board: planning, training, leadership selection, historical study. This was nothing like the improvisations of Korea or the gradual responses of Vietnam. Filming of news footage was controlled by the military.

On the one hand, the war was exceptional in almost every strategic respect, particularly in the freedom of action that the approaching fall of the Soviet Union conferred on the United States.

On the other hand, the wearying practices of earlier years re-asserted themselves. The CIA had failed to anticipate Saddam's invasion. Once it occurred, the question of how to respond was permeated by the public's memories of the previous war, both in the intense, largely Democratic opposition to a war resolution passed in the Senate by only five votes and in Saddam's gleeful evocation of a "second Vietnam." Various defense intellectuals warned of terrible U.S. casualties in opposing his "battle-hardened" troops.

In part reflecting a lack of confidence in the country's abilities since the mid-1970s, the Pentagon prepared body bags by the thousands. It fought hard against Bush's decision to battle a massacre maker he compared to Hitler. To garner domestic support, the White House was careful to explain that one of America's goals was to promote democracy in Kuwait — then, as now, (with modest liberalization) run by the al-Sabah family.

The Vietnam experience is one reason the Gulf War victory was initially overestimated and Norman Schwarzkopf and Colin Powell were celebrated as the equals of Marshall, Eisenhower, and MacArthur.[23] The allied armies did not go beyond the UN mandate to expel Iraqi forces, and the Republican Guard, which has upheld Saddam ever since, was able to escape. Among the reasons for restraint were the beliefs that Saddam's worst weapons had been destroyed; that occupying Bagdhad would compel the United States to administer a dangerous succession; and that the CIA could finish the job. The unanimous conclusion at Langley was that Saddam would fall anyway. Instead, a new type of cold war evolved, one that has included more than ten years of economic blockade, recurring threats against Iraq, and America's longest air campaign.

With Saddam still in place three months after the Gulf War cease-fire, President Bush authorized the CIA to develop ways to oust the dictator. Congress's intelligence committees appropriated $40 million for this first year of intimate political involvement with one of the world's most complicated and violent societies. Upon entering office twenty months after the victory, President Bill Clinton reaffirmed Bush's "finding" for the CIA. Building on a Cold War relationship as a pillar against the Soviet Union, Saudi Arabia would meanwhile serve as one against Iraq — as well as a source of chronic concern in Washington that its royal family might one day go the way of Iran's shah.

Results against Saddam were familiar. In the tradition of Radio

Free Europe and Radio Liberty, more than $23 million of the initial cash outlay was spent on propaganda. Concorde-flying CIA contractors, according to one participant, had difficulty culturally adapting to London (where they were based), let alone the Middle East.[24] None of the CIA officers working with the motley resistance movement in Iraqi Kurdistan during 1994 and 1995 spoke Kurdish; only one spoke Arabic. And Saddam's spies penetrated the operation. An alert senior case officer in northern Iraq warned Langley of this fact and was ignored. When prospects for broadening the insurgency failed, the Agency tried to foment a coup in Baghdad. Once that plan was detected in June 1996, Saddam's execution squads went to work, but not before a gloating radio message was transmitted to CIA officers working out of Jordan.

According to a serious analysis of Saddam's resurrection, the Baghdad conspiracy was one of the most colossal failures in the Agency's history.[25] So complete was the disaster that the officials responsible could hope to evade condemnation only by pretending that nothing much out of the ordinary had occurred — which in a way was true.

Saddam then turned murderously on the Kurdish resistance in the north, ostensibly a safe haven that Washington had been upholding for five years. The U.S. presidential campaign in 1996, in which foreign policy had no role, meant there was little American response. Sixty-five hundred members of the resistance and their families ended up being airlifted to Guam, as had Saigon's evacuees twenty-one years earlier. This time, it was the dispirited officer in northern Iraq who chronicled the blundering, while the operation's overall director at headquarters was promoted. A lot of Iraqis had been killed for about $110 million, but they were on America's side. Thereafter a vaguely defined policy of "containment" was adopted. By 2001, Saddam was rebuilding his chemical and biological military capabilities.

Several Gulf War allies, such as Britain, helped the United States maintain the cold war against Saddam. Tactical success misread as strategic triumph in 1991, however, plus the recurring U.S. fear of getting "bogged down" in unknown places, raised a wider question: what role would America's strongest allies take in a world without the Soviet Union? The answers are still emerging. Post–World War II Europe had been the original theater in which Americans had dreaded getting bogged down (as indeed they did for decades) and where 100,000 troops still sit in the middle of a peaceful united

Germany, the country with the world's third-largest economy. From 1991 into 2001, old arguments smoldered about "burden sharing," fanned by wars in the Balkans.

NATO's fiftieth anniversary saw Hungary, the Czech Republic, and Poland inducted into an enlarging and ever less North Atlantic alliance. One Defense Department estimate showed that it cost each American only about 67 cents, "the price of a candy bar," to bring them aboard.[26] Otherwise busy writing a genealogy called *An American Family: The Kennans: The First Three Generations*, George Kennan was still around to denounce, no matter how minor the cost or lame Moscow's reaction. To him, "expanding NATO would be the . . . beginning of a new cold war." He explained that Russian democracy (meaning the regime that Yeltsin described as "the biggest mafia state in the world") was more advanced than the new, struggling liberal polities being embraced by the alliance. As for his views of his own country, they were, as usual, bleak. Kennan believed America to be coming apart, "partly because of its susceptibility to immigration."[27]

Within five years, nine more countries would apply to join NATO, including Bulgaria, Romania, and the three Baltic republics that had been part of the Soviet Union. Russia suggested that it also be included. Few, if any, Americans had expected the end of the Cold War to involve more, rather than fewer, obligations to Europe, let alone nine major U.S. troop deployments around the world during the 1990s. Nor could anyone have imagined that it would be eighteen NATO allies that would stand up once it was *America* that was attacked, invoking for the first time since 1949 the treaty's Article 5 on mutual defense, which binds the signatories to regard an attack on one as an attack on all.

In writing about the Balkans, "Saki" observed that the citizens of this region make more history than they can consume locally. When Yugoslavia fractured in 1992, no longer having to fear the Soviet Union, they went for each other's throats. War in Bosnia was a cost of the Cold War's disunifying end. It was also the first disastrous test of Europe's ability to take care of itself. The worst fighting since 1945 could not be prevented. Nor could the slaughter of more than 7,000 people on July 17, 1995, despite the presence of UN peacekeepers. The United States sent thirty-two thousand troops and upwards of $10 billion, with the president believing that "the source of the problem" was the wicked leader of Serbia. Then came war in Kosovo. Thirty-eight thousand U.S. troops were drawn in, along with other NATO forces, and a U.S.-dominated air war was launched against Belgrade's dictator. President Clinton compared the fight to World War II. Meanwhile, perhaps up to $1 billion in foreign aid was evaporating in the name of rebuilding Bosnia.[28] With the dictator gone, the American presence remained.

Among America's allies, Japan (the country with the world's second-largest economy) took a new role amid the rapidly changing political landscape following September 11. It vowed to permit its Self-Defense Force to provide rearguard support for U.S. forces. Its army, navy, and air force have incrementally expanded, although they are still restrained voluntarily from fighting except in self-defense. Asian neighbors remain worried. As if to underscore its decades of ambivalence about its role in the world, Japan revived the rising sun and a national hymn to the Emperor as the legal symbols of the nation. In 2001, a prime minister paid homage at the shrine that honors the hanged leaders of Japan's World War II war machine. Forty-seven thousand American service men and women remain in Japan — the largest element of the approximately 100,000 soldiers, sailors, and Air Force personnel based in Asia — with a U.S. division across the straits committed to the defense of Seoul.

The numerous U.S. combat actions from 1993 through 2000 were described at the White House as humanitarian or peacekeeping operations. The Pentagon called them "Operations Other Than War." Whatever the name, they were draining and their purposes ill defined. The partially U.S.-created commitment to Somalia, for example, squandered the lives of eighteen U.S. Army Rangers in 1993 and around $1.7 billion. The following year's "Operation Uphold Democracy" in Haiti required twenty-two thousand troops (four were killed) and $1.1 billion similarly to accomplish nothing. With America's help, thugs in suits replaced those in uniforms. They soon opened up a lucrative commercial relationship between their monopoly-owned telephone company and well-connected political players in Washington. Although Haiti remains the same murderous dictatorship, the White House at least upheld one of the five freedoms: voodoo symbols could not be used in leaflets calling on Haitians to remain calm during the U.S. intervention, the CIA was instructed, because that would show support for one religion over another.

Combat on two fronts, the 1960s standard used in the 1990s to calculate force requirements, no longer seemed far-fetched.

Discussion of foreign policy in the 2000 presidential campaign at least meant competing sound bites about the pros and cons of "nation building," that portentous phrase of the Kennedy years. In trying to save nations, however, let alone build them, Americans could still blunder dreadfully. Exhibit A of the post–Cold War era occurred amid world-class ethnic cleansing in a corner of Africa from which Belgian colonialists had bailed out thirty-five years before.

Rwanda may be the one instance among the world's upheavals between 1991 and 2001 where the slightest serious attention by the United States could have quelled the grisliest of crimes. The murder of some 800,000 Tutsi (an ethnic group originally privileged by the colonists) and politically moderate Hutu during one hundred days in 1994 was the fastest, most efficient killing spree of the twentieth century. There, too, the warnings had been clear. The White House had been stung by losses in Somalia and was cowed by a Pentagon leadership fearful that any African involvement — even as a UN supplier — was unlikely to be backed from Pennsylvania Avenue if peacekeeping got rough. America led a successful effort to remove most of the small international (non-U.S.) deterrent force actually in Rwanda and worked diligently to block authorization for UN (non-U.S.) reinforcements. The killers were by no means as well armed as those in Bosnia.

Frank Wisner Jr. was undersecretary of defense for policy, a superb professional diplomat and son of the CIA legend. A memo by him to the NSC staff testifies to the administration's reluctance to risk even the smallest responsibility. Who would pay shipping costs for any U.S. armored equipment sent to those peacekeepers in place? In a business-as-usual tone, Deputy Secretary of State Strobe Talbott searched for a "more manageable" way to respond. During three months of genocide, an utterly disengaged president never thought to assemble his top advisers to discuss the killings. "Failure to fully appreciate the genocide," concludes the best examination of the disaster, "stemmed from political, moral, and imaginative weakness, not informational ones."[29] Alone among the powers involved, the United States would refuse to investigate its part in the tragedy.

One defense intellectual serving on the NSC staff attributed the obstructionism to the fact that "there weren't any visuals" to clarify the problem.[30] Refusing to acknowledge that genocide was under way for weeks after denial had become ridiculous, the White House

spokesman had to chose his words carefully: it wasn't exactly genocide that may have occurred, only acts of genocide. President Clinton's first secretary of state, who had held the Talbott position
during the Carter administration, still knew little of Africa. He
pulled an atlas off his shelf midway through the holocaust to help
him locate Rwanda. Africa experts throughout the government had
minimal influence. Significantly, the NSC person responsible for
peacekeeping affairs and hence for Rwanda policy, was an experienced bureaucratic infighter eager to shield the president from con
gressional and public criticism. Today he concludes that, all in all,
he and his colleagues did everything right. "Would I have done the
same thing again?" he asks. "Absolutely. . . . I don't think we should
be embarrassed."[31] He went on to become the czar of U.S. counterterrorism policy — until replaced in mid-September 2001.

Half a century of involvements somehow never coming out right
on the ground, decades of unaccountability among national security
experts, and the usual inattention to the details of faraway places
combined to palsy the United States' ability to head off one of the
twentieth century's most extreme challenges to human solidarity.

The Clinton presidency, moreover, depended to an unprecedented
extent on public opinion polls, if not "visuals." It was an administration in which a *Time* magazine cover article would use the
same phrase once used to describe John McCloy at the height of
his power — "the most influential private citizen in America" — to
describe Dick Morris, a political consultant on the verge of being
caught in a sex scandal.[32] The Morris disgrace became a reminder
that although science flourished and the nation's material promise
was ever more fulfilled over the Cold War decades, the quality of
government had not comparably advanced.

To some critics, the impression was that the Clinton administration was composed of pie-eyed idealists intent to right wrongs
around the world. In fact, the priority was trade and an integrated
planet, issues which interested journalists much less than gunfire
and refugees.

For a half century, Americans had heard almost every issue
touching their lives described as one of national security. During the
1990s, AIDS and global warming were added to the mix. Most
people were unconvinced and felt ungenerous (or suckered). An
indicator is the drop in federal spending for international development, which fell about 20 percent over twenty years, although more

than $4 billion has been spent since 1989 to try to build democracy in Nicaragua.

Big military forces have meanwhile been maintained to address big problems, as in Korea, the Taiwan Strait, and Europe — a continent Washington has come to see as including much more than the influences of Britain, France, and Germany. Ten years after the Soviet Union disappeared, U.S. spending on the military was greater than the next twelve biggest spenders combined, most of which are U.S. allies. America outspent Russia more than five to one, although there are fewer Army divisions, warships, Air Force tactical wings, and uniformed personnel than when the Cold War ended. Following September 11, the boost in defense budgets was more reminiscent of that after the 1950 invasion of Korea.

Right after the Cold War, base closings and the elimination of defense manufacturing jobs were accompanied by dire warnings. A strange grouping of local politicians and "warfare state" theorists insisted that thousands of people would be consigned to unemployment. Yet the California aerospace workers who led the military boom through so much of the Cold War — the machinists, assemblers, engineers, and managers — prospered along with everyone else. Despite defense cutbacks, employment jumped in communities that had traditionally depended on military spending, as in aerospace-heavy Long Island and in Charleston, South Carolina, once the naval base there was shuttered. A large civilian market for talent and effort appeared in nearly every locale from which defense complexes disappeared. Sadly, it had been there all along.

Not until a new administration in 2001 would there be a comprehensive review of U.S. defense practices, one which eschewed the "two war" assumption and began by emphasizing new challenges in Asia and in space. It immediately clashed with the bureaucratic interests of the three services. Through the 1990s, decades of Cold War behaviors had helped prevent U.S. forces from taking full advantage of the new post-Soviet environment. There was minimal adaptation to the electronic age — tailoring task forces, recasting U.S. military power into new joint forces, and calibrating war plans minute by minute instead of just adopting electronics for traditional force structures. Capitol Hill added to the rigidities. A Connecticut delegation of liberal Democrats compelled the country to buy *Seawolf* from the New London shipyards — only the first of three $2.4 billion nuclear attack submarines begun in 1985 and now ready to use against . . . what? A Republican Senate majority leader insisted that the Navy buy a half-billion-dollar amphibious assault ship made in his home state. Each party and service has its examples.

Nor was there any remodeling of the post–World War II policy-making architecture, which brought into being the Department of Defense, the independent Air Force, the CIA, and the Joint Chiefs of Staff. To date, these institutions have remained largely as they were during the Cold War: mostly reactive, highly compartmentalized, and inwardly focused on their own missions. During eight years in office, President Clinton was "too handicapped," according to the *Washington Post,* by his Vietnam-era draft avoidance to lead a national effort to restructure the country's armed forces.[33] Moreover, in an era when the Pentagon is Microsoft's largest customer, the Department of Defense has had trouble learning how to be an astute participant in the marketplace.

Not until the mid 1990s did the federal government prepare consolidated financial statements subject to independent audit by the General Accounting Office (GAO). Billions of dollars could not be tallied up at the Pentagon, partly because of 122 separate and unreliable accounting systems. Resources the size of a small country's economy had vanished.[34] At the National Reconnaissance Office, a part of the intelligence community so secret that even its existence was not declassified until after the Cold War, about $1 billion went missing in a "fundamental financial meltdown."[35] This was an inadvertence roughly the size of the FBI and State Department budgets combined, yet only brought to light in the course of Senate curiosity about a lavish new $300 million four-building headquarters complex in the Virginia suburbs.

Also locked in time has been much of the federal R & D apparatus. Despite its penumbra of talented scientists, it has flocculated into a grossly inefficient arrangement hampered by layers of staff and rising mediocrity. "It's a disgrace," former National Science Foundation director Erich Bloch says of the system that had stumbled into being during the Cold War. Looking at the Energy Department's contracting practices, the GAO concluded that they remain "much the same as they were in the 1940s." Even the original centerpiece of the military "techno-empire," the Naval Research Lab, has become an exemplar of waste.[36] None of this has prevented the leaders of American science from keeping an abiding faith in the expansion of government funding.

Accompanying such funding are billions of dollars in corporate welfare. Unlike the old days, not just the giants get to participate.

One example is the Defense Department's effort to create a domestic flat-panel liquid crystal display industry, despite impressive commercial leads by Japan, Korea, and Taiwan. Hoping to serve both commercial and military markets, the Defense Advanced Research Projects Agency since the late 1980s has committed close to a billion dollars playing venture capitalist with just this industry. U.S. market share remains zero, with a trail of small-company bankruptcies resulting from this pork. Political influence routinely affects decisions when government assumes the de facto role of equity investor. The one positive exception, ironically, may be In-Q-Tel, the actual venture fund of the CIA.[37]

Defense dollars not only disappear but end up in surprising places. In 1998, as if a ghost from the Cold War past, Che Guevara's corpse (the hands having been cut off to prove his death) was uncovered in a hidden grave at a provincial airport in Bolivia. The local battalion that killed him had benefited from U.S. "foreign internal defense" assistance. Such "Fid" missions involving U.S. special operatives multiplied in that decade, circumventing a 1991 law intended to limit cooperation with countries accused of corruption or human rights abuses. Ten years later, these missions had ties with at least 110 nations amid minimal civilian oversight. The millions of dollars involved, in a Pentagon budget of hundreds of billions, make "Fid" programs appear costless and may prove particularly well spent against terrorism. However, training has been against "instability" — a credible objective when battling South American criminal cartels or worse, but a potentially troubling one when backing some third world friends. As one Indonesian general explains, the United States "teaches us how to stop civilian disturbances."[38]

Contrary to what was expected a generation ago, neither insurgent revolutionaries nor U.S. counterguerrilla forces played much of a part in transforming the world. In the post-Soviet era — and galvanized by the assault on America — special warfare is in its heyday. After adamant resistance within the services earlier in the 1990s, the following outfits are finally consolidated under an independent command: Army Green Berets, Rangers, and the covert Delta Force; Navy SEALs, Special Boat Units, and the covert Team 6; and Air Force special operations and internal defense squadrons. Even before the September atrocity, the Pentagon had begun taking the right steps. For the first time, an Army officer who served most of his career working in Special Operations became chairman of the

Joint Chiefs of Staff. These forces are central not only to "Operations Other Than War," but to the real war that began being fought ten years after the Soviet collapse.

✪

Never have so many people seen so many others die, and in real time, than on that stunned morning of September 11, 2001, when the terrorists struck. More people perished than at Pearl Harbor. Congress quickly proclaimed what amounted to a planetary state of war. The president promised a crusade and called reserves to duty. Americans rushed to give blood, but there were few to give blood to: almost none survived the towers' fall. It was by far the country's greatest intelligence failure.

Truman had used the message of "terrorist activities" to rally the country at the Cold War's start. Kennedy marshaled similar words about terror as special forces entered Vietnam. The frantic responses of the first post–Cold War decade were shot through with official outcries against terrorism. Rhetoric grew increasingly careless after the deadly bombings of the World Trade Center in 1993, of an American military apartment complex in Saudi Arabia, after destruction of embassies in Kenya and Tanzania in 1998, and following the deaths of seventeen sailors on the USS *Cole* off Yemen. Increasingly, think-tank seminars and the departments resounded with calls for "fighting Islam," as enthusiasts often forgot to add "fundamentalist fanatics." Until September 2001, the worst outrage within America had been the 168 dead in Oklahoma City. Although immediately blamed by senior FBI and CIA officials, as well as by self-styled academic experts on "Islamic" terrorism, that one was inflicted by all-American boys. Heated concerns about "militias" at home followed fast.[39] Before September 11, Americans were thrashing about beneath the unanticipated pains of a different form of danger.

After New York and Washington were struck, President Bush and his secretary of defense each told the nation that no one had imagined the prospect of commercial airliners being used as 120-ton missiles by barbaric suicide squads. Given the vast efforts and the increasing billions of dollars spent in the immediately preceding years to prepare against terror, the critical question might have been "why not?" It was a conventional attack (planes against conspicuously colossal facilities) conducted by a few competently trained men prepared to die. America's total antiterrorism spending for 1991–2001 surpassed any Pentagon annual budget of the late 1940s. Yet additional layers of bureaucracy, and powerful new functionaries had not provided the insights that might have resulted from three solid months of careful thought. "You wouldn't believe how bad it is," remarked Robert Baer, until his resignation in 1997 the CIA's best on-the-ground field officer in the Middle East and a recipient of the Career Intelligence Medal.[40] He was speaking, after the attack, about U.S. intelligence.

A month before, Senator Diane Feinstein, of both the Appropriations Committee and the Select Committee on Intelligence, observed that $13 billion had just been designated for counterterrorism. She added there was little idea of where it was going. Approximately $10 billion had been committed annually since 1996. For several years preceding the attack, the highest U.S. officials had spoken censoriously of the country already being at war. President Clinton had promised "a long, ongoing struggle" and denounced terrorism in his final State of the Union address as one of the greatest dangers to America. His last secretary of state, Madeleine Albright, saw it as a threat even to an expanded NATO.[41] All this was little more than an ill assortment of reaction-formations, throwing money at the issue in the classic Cold War fashion, and entrusting the procedures to the type of people who are pushed aside once matters become serious.

By its nature, counterterrorism keeps strange and dangerous company. It is likely to be staffed by thrill seekers, at least until a national emergency arrives. For the first time, the United States in the late 1990s installed a counterterrorism czar — the National Coordinator for Security, Infrastructure and Counter-Terrorism — to wield secret authority out of Oliver North's old office. Moving from one terror to another, this was the individual who, on the NSC staff, had crafted U.S. policy toward Rwanda. He thereafter morphed into what John le Carré calls an "intellocrat," a figure whose authority rests on allegedly secret knowledge and dark experience, best kept from delicate citizen sensibilities. In the months before September 11, he perceived bin Laden and his men staying awake at night "around the campfire . . . worried stiff about who we're going to get next." Other officials insisted that the CIA and the FBI were clandestinely "picking apart" bin Laden's organization "limb by limb."[42]

Between the mid-1990s and September 2001, the CIA tried to beef up its Counter-Terrorism Center, staffed by hundreds of analysts, linguistically bereft case officers, some truly impressive NSA technologists, and personnel from a constellation of other departments. It was a paper-shuffling unit consumed by internecine warfare until forced to grow up after September 11. Its highly classified monthly publication, *Terrorism Review*, became coveted reading for those in the know. But apparently *Terrorism Review* did not anticipate new uses for 757s and box cutters. For most U.S. experts, weaned for years on academic treatises removed from reality, catastrophic terrorism nearly always meant the use of weapons of mass destruction. Nuclear or biological terrorism received the bulk of attention: aircraft hijackings and aviation terrorism seemed relics of the 1960s and 1970s. Who would think of a "flying bomb" being used as a weapon of catastrophic terror? Once it occurred, predictable remedies were heard: more money for intelligence (which since the late 1990s had already seen treasuries of it), more human intelligence capabilities (which are mostly unrelated to money); less restraint on CIA operations (of which there is little reason to believe they are better than in the decades just past).

On September 12, the day after the attack, it was announced to the federal workforce in Washington that only essential employees need show up for work. Nonessential personnel should stay home. The immense CIA parking lot in Langley, usually filled with thousands of cars as far as the eye can see, was depleted. "The point of the sword," said a senior Agency official, "is incredibly tiny." Less than 1 percent of the 18,000 or so employees, he estimated in the days thereafter, have anything to do with counterterrorism. There are only around 800 field intelligence officers, meaning the people on the ground overseas ferreting out secrets. Of these patriotic men and women, very few have Middle Eastern backgrounds, underscoring the little-noticed public criticism made by a former case officer for the region just weeks before the assault: "America's counterterrorism program in the Middle East and its environs is a myth."[43]

America is a personalist culture, one eager to put faces on formless dangers: Stalin, Khrushchev, Castro, Saddam, and, from the mid-1990s on, Osama bin Laden — a child of privilege like the East bloc–assisted terrorists in Germany and Italy of the 1970s and 1980s, or America's own Weathermen bombers. He had been placed on the FBI's Ten Most Wanted List in 1999 and tagged with a $5 million State Department bounty. For the first time ever, the CIA in 1996 created an overseas station directed at one individual. After the embassy bombings that left 213 dead in Nairobi and 11 in Dar es Salaam, the United States shot off seventy cruise missiles at $1 million each to try to kill him and his key followers. "We took this decision extremely seriously," said President Clinton. But it was the lack of seriousness that was notable, as in the overall effort.

Perhaps several dozen trainees of bin Laden's Al Qaeda were blown away. A simultaneous missile strike was launched against a pharmaceutical plant in Khartoum that might have crafted his chemical-weapon components. No one who knew anything about Sudan or much about chemistry was consulted; the attack was based on incomplete CIA evidence; State Department doubts were ignored; and the drama unfolded at a politically opportune time for the White House. The plant's Saudi owner promptly hired one of the best-connected law firms in Washington and sued the U.S. government. The plaintiff used chemists from Boston University to challenge allegations of weapons making. "If you're going to respond," blurted the director of Middle East Studies at the Army's Special Warfare Center, "you have to be willing to kill a whole lot of people" — precisely the thing *not* to do in these contests.[44] Amid such pre–September 11 fecklessness, the legend of bin Laden grew in Muslim lands.

And not only there. In Colorado, the North American Aerospace Command's headquarters were soon closed to the public tours that had been offered for decades, even during the Cold War's greatest dangers. Terrorism was accomplishing what Soviet SS-18s could not, and the 25-ton metal doors were closed to NORAD's Strangelovian, 4.5-acre granite bunker buried 1,700 feet beneath Cheyenne Mountain. For its part, the National Security Agency constructed new fences and barriers around its metropolis-like headquarters to better protect its 38,000 employees.

When a superpower fires at shadows, the whole world is full of ricochets. But the cruise-missile shootings were only the most dramatic part of the decade's overall ineffectiveness. From the White House, the counterterrorism czar labored to create public-private "partnerships" for every sector of the U.S. economy against one strand of the phenomenon, cyberterrorism. The worst case, officials explained, might include computer-launched attacks from terrorists or "rogue nations" against U.S. electric power, telecommunications, banking, transportation, food distribution, and water systems. Billions more dollars were said to be needed to defend economically critical computer systems, with the administrators of those systems belonging to, say, Pacific Gas & Electric, to be polygraphed regularly. An ROTC-like Cyber Corps was proposed. Housed within the Office of Personnel Management (OPM), it would recruit college students for federal defensive information-technology jobs in exchange for scholarships. There was to be polygraphing too.

Terrorists and rogue nations were grouped with disgruntled employees and hackers. Computer systems in America's electronic marketplace, however, do not lend themselves to the sort of attacks envisioned. Vast data interoperability obstacles exist between industries, companies, and even business units within companies. At least one result of America's serendipitously uncoordinated way of innovation is that no single system or overarching architecture is there to be destroyed. Software and communication industry CEOs paid little time to these interpretations of threat assessments, tending to scoff at the notion of America's best young techies tying themselves to a federal Cyber Corps within OPM.[43] Might this not be thinking somewhat along too familiar lines?

In 2000, the White House staged the largest antiterrorist exercise ever, based on the prospect that three or more attacks would occur all at once. Sound preparation, to be sure, but it became baroque. The Department of Justice hired two contracting firms of former military officers and government officials to manage events in Denver, outside Washington, D.C., and in Portsmouth, New Hampshire. Assuming that national computer networks were already sabotaged, the federal government demonstrated how it would respond to simultaneous radiation, biological, and chemical attack. Several classified millions of dollars were spent. Yet cabinet officers and other senior personnel scheduled to participate found other things to do. As so often during the Cold War, the basics were meanwhile being neglected: in this case, airlines found security measures primarily useful as a way to prevent the exchange of cheap tickets and to circumvent travel agents; little was done at Treasury to "follow the money," given that such steps were not only complex but unsettling to bankers in friendly nations; bureaucratic inertia mixed with turf disputes meant that the FBI, CIA, and Immigration and Naturalization Service (INS) could not coordinate to secure U.S. borders from suspects on an international watch list.

Undoubtedly these and other agencies achieved silent successes. But those were the exceptions. Few of the threat assessments from all the government agencies involved were in accord on what was possible or unlikely.

The following year, even before the September attack, the Office of National Preparedness had to be created within the Federal Emergency Management Agency to oversee all the behind-the-scenes empire building in the name of counterterrorism. Nearly every department had by then established its own counterterrorism budget, including the Department of Agriculture, which uses an island laboratory to study the impact of terrorism on U.S. food supplies. Acronyms abounded: the State Department had created its FEST (Federal Emergency Support Team) and the Department of Health and Human Services weighed in with its MMSTs (Metropolitan Medical Strike Teams). The Department of Energy has long possessed its NEST (Nuclear Emergency Search Teams) with about a thousand personnel. Through the Los Alamos security scandals of 2000 (including ravenous prosecution of Wen Ho Lee in what the laboratory's chief of counterintelligence described as "a career-enhancing opportunity for FBI agents, Justice Department officials, and others"), NEST was bedeviled by infighting with the Defense Department and the FBI over whose clearances would be used.[46]

The FBI manages its own DEST (Domestic Emergency Support Team), with its Washington field office containing a "special weapons of mass destruction" squad, the National Capital Domestic Response Team. The FBI also has set up the Weapons of Mass Destruction Hotline: 202-324-6000. Citizens calling it in the weeks before the attack heard a metallic female voice say, "Your call has been forwarded to an automatic voice messaging system. The mailbox . . . is full. To disconnect, press one . . ."

A lot of this thrashing about permeated outward. The Defense Against Weapons of Mass Destruction Act of 1996 spawned ninety different programs for training local officials. Small towns and big cities alike joined in as they developed SWAT units, with Pentagon training also available. Immense attention was given in the late 1990s to chemical and biological terrorism, creating what was called a "bio-terrorism panic."[47] The TV program *Nightline*, for example, produced a five-part series on "biowar" full of scientific inaccuracies. Money flowed fast, seemingly everywhere. It was important that the Department of Health and Human Services received several hundred million for "bioterrorism preparedness," but then a free-for-all ensued as academia rushed for grants. Johns Hopkins University established its Center for Civilian Biodefense Studies, created a journal, the *Biodefense Quarterly*, and described counter-bioterrorism as requiring "an allocation of money and talent finite neither in amount or time."[48] Dartmouth persuaded the Department of Justice to fund two new laboratories to research ways to fight terrorists of both the cyber and bio variety. Nearly every think tank created a homeland security center. Quoting the counterterrorism chief, defense consultants used full-page newspaper ads to tout their services. When anthrax arrived in October 2001, Americans were primed to be terrified.

"War is the health of the state," but fear is pretty good medicine. Well before September 2001, America had jumped into the most intensive self-protection drive since the investigations of the early Cold War. Suspicion of malicious secret foreign penetration has always been part of American anxiety, going back to the earliest days of the Republic: the Alien and Sedition Acts against what little Jacobinism 1790s America could muster; the Masons, Nazis, Japanese-Americans, and Communists. The fact that the September attack sprang from within — Florida, Massachusetts, New Jersey — ratchets up the fears. As usual, when the drums start beating, such fervor finds itself on a collision course with the Bill of Rights.

After the Oklahoma City bombing, the Antiterrorism and Effective Death Penalty Act followed fast. The Illegal Immigration Reform and Immigrant Responsibility Act also was passed, establishing both the Anti-Terrorism Removal Procedures and the Alien Terrorist Removal Court. This led to the Foreign Intelligence Surveillance ACT (FISA) being amended so as to authorize secret physical searches of homes, something for which the FBI had long lobbied. Well before the September attack, a secret FISA court was granting nearly as many wiretaps as did all other federal courts combined in criminal cases. The Effective Death Penalty Act, moreover, already allowed the INS to arrest, detain, and deport illegal immigrants based on secret evidence — as America's Muslim community quickly discovered well before the towers fell.

Responses were indiscriminate. The number of federal prosecutions based on secret evidence — legal proceedings upheld by courts since the anti-Communist alarms of the early 1950s — had reached an all-time high by the first half of 2001, although a string of them had unraveled before furious judges ready to denounce "government processes initiated and prosecuted in darkness."[49] Back practicing law after serving as CIA director, James Woolsey spent the late 1990s defending six Iraqi refugees who had been airlifted to asylum after the CIA's 1996 debacle. Once they arrived in the United States, along with hundreds of other opponents of Saddam, unparticularized allegations arose that they were somehow tied to terrorism. Classified deportation orders were given to hand them back to Baghdad. The even-tempered Woolsey, denied access to the secret evidence despite retaining the highest clearances, spoke of "blithering incompetence," botched FBI interviews, and "using classified information as a tool of oppression" more appropriate to Iraq than to America."[50] All this did nothing to set priorities straight against real danger.

Even before the attack, discussions of terrorism were straying toward irreversible decisions. From one administration to another, arguments in favor of assassination sound tough and realistic, mostly to the inexperienced. It had never been eliminated "as a last resort option for U.S. policy," as popularly believed, but had been closed off to the CIA because, in the early 1960s, it had become nearly a first-resort option. At one remove, President Ford's 1976 executive order did not stand in the way of Reagan's air strike targeted on Qaddafi, George H. W. Bush's against Saddam during the Gulf War, and Clinton's against bin Laden. Assassination is a method of war, but by no means a winning one. It is totally American to believe that a determined opposition can be beheaded by killing a personifying star figure. The mark of serious organizations — all too common in international terrorism — is their regenerative power. America's enemies are more complicated, as are America's strengths. It is worth recalling that Churchill held back from any assassination attempt on Hitler, as did Wellington on Bonaparte. These were not squeamish men. Their self-restraint sends a message that moderation, even against monsters, can, in most circumstances, be prudently effective. In any event, the CIA by October 2001 was ordered to undertake its most sweepingly lethal operation since 1947.

The CIA spurned the matter in the decades after John Kennedy; there is no reason to believe that its targetable killing abilities have improved since. As to restraints on Agency operations, they have never been as significant as popularly assumed: foreign informants with criminal records or a history of terrorist involvement could always be recruited. Rules put in place in 1995, in the aftermath of the latest Guatemalan outrages, required that there be some purpose to these recruitments and that use of such people be approved by senior intelligence officials. Frequently during the Cold War, there were excellent reasons for the CIA to consort with the dregs of humanity, including Nazis at the start. Screening of agents by a senior review panel in Langley, however, is childish and should be unnecessary. Yet it came about after decades of often-gratuitous intimacy with SAVAK, with Central American psychopaths, and other Cold War defenders of freedom. To argue that this under-mined CIA performance leading up to September 11 is an excuse for the Agency's own failure in long-neglected human intelligence, and for a long-mishandled Directorate of Operations.

During the 1990s, there was a series of CIA blunders in the Indian subcontinent, a part of the world particularly important today. A congressional report then flatly concluded that the CIA lacked sufficient expertise to carry out its duties. One reason for the lack of warning for Indian and then for Pakistani nuclear detona-tions, as an example, was worsening linguistic shortfalls. Inside re-ports on the failure of U.S. intelligence to translate information that could have warned policymakers of the explosions "remain classi-fied," according to the head of the University of Maryland's National Foreign Language Center, "but you can rest assured that those sur-prised people."[51] Larger problems were said to be so pervasive that U.S. intelligence "need[ed] to be scrubbed" from the top down. Whatever the critics concluded, Langley was then, as now, truly American. It enduringly shares the nation's classic assumption — what Congress's investigation of the failure to anticipate India's det-onations criticized as "this 'everybody thinks like us' mindset."[52]

The seventy-eight-day Kosovo air war during 1999 brought worse criticism. The one target the Agency selected proved to be China's embassy in Belgrade, mistaken for the Yugoslav military procurement directorate. Another inspector general's report had to be written, and $4.5 million was paid to Beijing for the destruction and the dead.[53] Several low-level people were fired, one of whom promptly hired the Washington law firm that has built a practice around suing the Agency over wrongful employee terminations based on polygraph exams. It was unjust to blame individuals, said the attorneys, because "the failure was systemic."[54]

The sprawling secrecy system that the Cold War has be-queathed, with so many ways of eluding demands for improvement, helped create the problem: $5.3 billion spent annually to process and protect secrets (not including CIA material); blanket exemption for the FBI to declassify records because of the vastness of its files (6.5 million cubic feet); and millions of man-hours lost each year due to huge delays in background checks. Ultimately, it is the CIA that oversees the highest of all clearances — the SCI category, which takes the most time to obtain and is held by an enormous number of unnecessary people. How many people possess SCI clearances is itself classified, although having this designation was thought essential to the work of Monica Lewinsky.

After September 11, as earlier, Langley frames its shortcomings in terms of money. Nearly ten years after the Cold War, for instance, records of numerous covert operations that occurred under Truman, Eisenhower, and Kennedy had to remain secret. The Agency claimed that it did not have the resources to declassify them — before revealing that those concerning Iran, Indonesia, the Congo, and no doubt a number of other less important countries had been destroyed.[55] Facing congressional anger arising as a result of the events in India and then Kosovo, the CIA director concluded that his organization would "no longer be relevant" unless it received more money. If it were provided, he vowed to restore the Agency to its Cold War strength and "mount increasingly complex and expensive operations."[56] Hundreds of millions of dollars were made available, primarily for the several thousand men and women in the Directorate of Operations — the largest new effort since William Casey presided over the multibillion-dollar expansion of the early 1980s. There was some merit to the funding request, even before 2001's attacks, particularly after having to offer intelligence support for the U.S. military's overseas combat operations during the preceding eight years. But the problem is not just money.

Promises to improve personnel have been heard regularly since the 1950s. One CIA executive director, the third most senior official, testified in the mid-1990s that the Agency's hiring and staffing had been "deteriorating for the past 15 years," during which "there [had] been five major studies of the agency's human resources system with a total of 66 recommendations." Only one, an annual report card, had ever been instituted agency-wide.[57] Today the clandestine service is slated to grow by about 30 percent by 2006. But size is not the critical issue as résumés flooded in after September 11. The problem is a personnel system little changed from the 1980s, or even from the James Schneider and other experiences of the 1990s.

At the CIA's fiftieth anniversary, former president and CIA director George H. W. Bush and another former director, Richard Helms, spoke to a crowd of around four thousand intelligence veterans. They both reflected on the Agency's past difficulties — Bush still angry about Congress's investigations of the mid-1970s, Helms

about the Agency's experience during Vietnam. The entire ceremony was admirably patriotic and warmhearted, except that several
thousand retired officers (from whom the CIA was trying to recruit
a reserve component modeled after the Army's) had not been
invited. No one had been able to find the names and addresses of
people who had served before 1987. The current director sent a letter of apology to a retirees organization. Outsiders would not be told
how many had been overlooked; that number is secret (perhaps to
the Agency, too)

This is the "point of the sword" that the country brings to a new
war. At the start, in September 2001,Washington faced this war as
something disorientingly new, a fanatical enemy barely to be understood by the sedate industrial democracies. Such a reaction is also
entirely reminiscent of the Cold War: guerrilla warfare was once
regarded as a secret art, shadowed by an East Asian mystique; the
Soviet view that nuclear war was winnable was tuned out as pure
noise, unthinkable, surely arising from mistranslations. Terrorism is
an ancient fact of political life no more novel or difficult to comprehend than other forms of war. Its characteristics today have long
precedent: the Assassins of twelfth-century Syria venturing out for
a generation to kill Sunni Moslem and Christian rulers alike; Cava-
liers loyal to the exiled Charles II knocking off Cromwell's diplomatic agents across Europe. Terrorism is one of the permanent
states of mankind, as is cold war.

Religion and terrorism particularly share a long history. What is
new is the greater vulnerability of modern societies (big airplanes,
massive office towers), centralized communications, and the integration of the world that does not stop at learning or trade, but can
weave together European-educated middle-class operatives from
Saudi Arabia with primitive protectors in Afghanistan — to create
cells in Delray Beach and Newark that kill secretaries from Staten
Island, bankers from Connecticut, waiters from Senegal, and stock-
brokers from Brussels.

Just as rust is a slow burning, so terrorism is fine-structure war.
For more than a hundred years, it has possessed a richly imaginative literature at every level of refinement: Henry James's *Princess
Casamassima*; entertainments such as John Buchan's *The Power
House*; and thrillers like Edgar Wallace's *Four Just Men*, in which a
liberal exile from imperial Russia is about to be handed back to the
czarist authorities by George V's obliging ministers. A little band
of stern vindicators of liberty, the "just men," announce that if such

a miscarriage of justice prevails, the responsible official will be assassinated. The Home Secretary is frantically guarded by the strictest powers of Georgian England as he prepares to sign the extradition order. A crowd gathers outside his mansion. When a passerby asks what they're doing, he is told, "They're waiting for a man to be killed." Equally gripping is *The Deed* by Meyer Levin, a novelization of the killing of Lord Moyne (the British Minister Resident in the Middle East) by the Stern Gang in 1944. In such novels, we see the ambiguities of the moral order, the craving for power behind idealism no less than the indifferent ruthlessness of the established state. And we will increasingly live with many more such ambiguities: strange new allies and unfettered procedures are likely to make the Cold War's "fighting fire with fire" look benign.

The first day after the September attack one influential journalist described the fight ahead as World War III.[58] But we know what a third world war would really be — the long-anticipated nuclear exchange in which several hundred million people die in a few hours, with network commentators burning too. Instead, another world*wide* war began, one involving conventional explosives (so far) and painstaking attempts at again making common cause with the shadiest of states and organizations. Terrorism is merely the way war is fought by the weak, by people without government license. The Khobar barracks, the USS *Cole,* the Pentagon are their military targets; New York their Dresden and Tokyo.

Change begets terror. When the world alters, individuals, not nations, fight back. Surprise and otherness are terror's weapons, begetting rage, the sister of fear, which introduces attacks that are anything but constitutional. The enemy is unlikely to be composed of "cowards," which is how the September attackers were first frantically belittled by nearly everyone in Washington. That portrayal is like General Westmoreland insisting that Americans had "more guts" than another determined enemy who relied on mass murder as a means of war. Terrorism, perhaps on the scale of September 2001, will not go away in our lifetime, as did communism. At the worst, it is not altogether difficult to imagine a political culture of terrorist containment. Well-connected interests such as insurance companies might prosper in the long term; the government and military would be free to expand; senior officials could grow more powerful and for a while more eminent; university centers and foundations would flourish amid the new discipline of "terrorism studies"; and exciting technologies would be incubated as Americans went about their business. Then the screw would turn again.

The Cold War was finally won by eschewing such a culture. However, that part of government least publicly accountable has been, in its own way, able to proceed with business as usual right through the Cold War's final years, through the interregnum decade that followed, and into 9/11. In a complex world, we will always be taken by surprise. What occurred during the Cold War, however, and what carries on today, is the absence of an institutional cushion — such as a top intelligence capability — to prevent the country from often stumbling badly. And from laying itself open to assault.

In adding up the price of Cold War victory, the cost of the Central Intelligence Agency is unique. No other single government body has blundered so often in so many ways integral to its designated purpose. Yet another comprehensive review of U.S. intelligence capabilities, ordered by President Bush early in 2001, was already under way when America was attacked. Led by the director of Central Intelligence, and calling upon other establishment experts, it was focusing on ways to end bureaucratic rivalries, to cut waste, and to improve the clandestine service. Even at that time, no attention was paid to prospects for radical change — let alone going as far as Patrick Moynihan, long a member of the Senate's Intelligence Committee, had urged: disband the Agency and give its vital analytical and intelligence gathering functions to the Pentagon (which already handles 85 percent of the intelligence community budget) and the State Department, which could then finally fund a larger, even more accomplished corps of Foreign Service Officers. Since the Agency needs to continue in some form, given that its key function is to steal secrets, it has to be smarter, which does not at all mean bigger.

The value of a hot war is a shakedown in government, the arrival of serious people and procedures. The graver the issue, the faster it passes into the hands of those who have more to do than find their own unchallenged niche. At its best, bureaucracy has great virtues, of dependability, honesty, reasoned inquiry. But when the world starts shaking — as it did after September 11 — something better is required. And there is now opportunity for overhaul at Langley.

✪

The Germanic root of the word *war* means "mixup" or "mess." The way America fought the Cold War, as the CIA exemplifies, reflects this condition. No one should be surprised to find confusion, indeed contradiction, in this most improvised and spontaneous of countries. But when winging it becomes a fifty-year tradition in some of the most sensitive institutions of the nation, a game in which purpose is often forgotten, not a second look but a second approach is required. For the decade after 1991, there was not as adequate a cooling off process as might have occurred had there been a management audit of the CIA, a reconsideration of the U.S. military posture, more skepticism toward the latest overseas entanglements, and a focused confrontation with terror.

As the new century began, "mess" was capped by irony. For instance, Nikita Khrushchev's son, a jovial engineer once involved in the Soviet missile industry, took his oath as a U.S. citizen in 1999, as did Stalin's daughter several years before. Supersecret intelligence satellites from the National Reconnaissance Office were launched from Cape Canaveral in the presence of Russian technicians, because the engine that powers the *Atlas III* is a joint venture involving AMROSS, a Russian space company that is the successor of the one that built most of the engines for Russia's ballistic missiles. Forty years after Francis Gary Powers was downed, another U-2 finally appeared over Russia. Leaving Kiruna, Sweden, it flew over St. Petersburg, then sped in a straight line to Kursk, the site of history's greatest tank battle, in 1943. It made a 180-degree turn and flew directly back. Admirably, the purpose was to collect data for a U.S./Russian/European Community/Japanese study on reduced Arctic ozone levels.

In another reminder of the past, the son of Cambodia's prime minister graduated from West Point. His proud father, previously of the Khmer Rouge, stood by his side. Meanwhile, the "little Stalins" kept hanging on from the Cold War. In one concession to modernity: e-mail can be sent to North Korea's Kim Jong Il, son of the founding tyrant (and only to him). North Korea's website, www.kcna.co.jp, describes him as "the greatest man in the world." It rails against "U.S. Imperialist War Maniacs," the same people who have tried to feed the starving citizens of self-isolated North Korea since a famine in the mid-1990s took the lives of "somewhere" between 270,000 and 2 million people. Aid does not get past the prosperous Marxist-Leninist elite. Castro, for his part, endures as Latin America's only remaining dictator, his regime condemned by Human Rights Watch for its "highly effective machinery of repression."[59]

At the start of the new century, particular reminders surface every so often of the conflict just past. Consider Roswell, New Mexico. After the Cold War, the U.S. Air Force worked assiduously to convince a not insignificant percentage of the public that the silvery wreckage seen in 1947 was from a secret, short-lived effort to monitor the upper atmosphere for potential Soviet atomic tests and that it was not a UFO. A two-and-a-half-inch thick report written in the mid-1990s proved unpersuasive. It was followed by another report, consisting of 231 pages and titled *Case Closed*.[60] The nearly $2 million required to deny that the federal government harbors extraterrestrials is a dot in the budget, but the inherent distrust is telling.

There are many more reminders. "McCarthyism" is a slur so loosely used by left and right that it has practically become meaningless, but artifacts from the events behind it keep popping up. For instance, Anthony Lake, President Clinton's first national security assistant and his ultimately unsuccessful nominee as CIA director, was attacked for suggesting that Alger Hiss might not have been guilty, an opinion quickly recanted. In 2000, the Writers Guild was still correcting credits on more than one hundred movies released from 1951 to 1964, adding the real identities of dozens of screenwriters who had been compelled to practice their craft under pseudonyms. The following year was the centenary of Whittaker Chambers, who had died long before. There was a small ceremony at the White House to honor him.

Also honored that year was a former terrorist. In an egregiously timed story on September 11, 2001, the *New York Times* warmly profiled one Bill Ayers, calling his descriptions of bombing the Pentagon, the U.S. Capitol, and New York police headquarters "daring acts in his youth." Such uncritical acceptance of the 1960s era and "a love of explosives" is unlikely to be seen again anytime soon.

Weirdly, documents emerging from CIA files have created nearly a literary subgenre of how-to manuals for the Agency's own forms of terror (presumably long past). One dating from 1953 was inadvertently declassified five years ago. It reads, "The most efficient accident, in simple assassination, is a fall of 75 feet or more onto a hard surface. Elevator shafts, stairwells, unscreened windows and bridges will serve. . . . The act may be executed by sudden, vigorous [exised] of the ankles, tipping the subject over the edge."[61]

The same vein of bureaucratic cold-bloodedness can be seen in *American Ground Zero: The Secret Nuclear War*, published by the MIT

Press. The book's chilling collection of photographs and interviews of downwind victims documents the feloniously reckless practices surrounding the Nevada Test Site blasts between 1951 and 1963. These were the families considered by some to be part of the "low use population."[62]

In the mid-1990s, a National Cancer Institute study that Congress initiated in 1982 was made public. Its 100,000 pages include explanations of how 160 million U.S. residents between 1953 and 1968 received at least some fallout exposure, causing thousands of thyroid cancers (excess thyroid illness being related to radiation), most of which had not yet been diagnosed, perhaps 10 percent of which were likely to be fatal, and many of which were expected to develop in people who were younger than five at the time of exposure, mainly during 1952, 1953, 1955, and 1957. Controversially, the study asserts that the most affected of America's 3,070 counties are not just those downwind in Nevada and Utah, but areas around Albany, New York, and parts of Massachusetts, Missouri, Tennessee, North and South Dakota, Idaho, and Montana. Since 1990, the Department of Energy has paid more than $260 million to settle claims under that year's Radiation Exposure and Compensation Act.

From late 1943 into the 1950s, about 600,000 Americans worked for government contractors to produce nuclear weapons. Many were sickened and some were killed as a result of the work. The AEC and the Energy Department instructed employers to fight claims of injury from chemicals and radiation, fearing disruption. Moreover, nearly all the affected people were ineligible for workers' compensation because their illnesses developed years or decades after exposure. In 2000, the energy secretary announced a plan to compensate them (or their families) in a five-year payout of $1.8 billion. Into the following year, 2001, some 3,595 people, mostly ailing uranium miners from the 1940s through 1971 (when mining for the nuclear weapons program ended), were receiving only IOUs from the Justice Department, which administers money under the Radiation Exposure and Compensation Act. That program had gone broke. About the same number of people were denied assistance altogether because medical records or company employment logs could not be found.

At least as sad, the Energy Department had to create the Advisory Committee on Human Radiation Experiments to review some four thousand government-sponsored episodes from the end of

World War II to the early 1970s. Records had remained classified, the committee concluded, "out of concern for embarrassments to the Government, potential legal liability, and concern that public misunderstanding would jeopardize Government programs." A final tally showed that about sixteen thousand men, women, and children had been used, mostly without knowing and in numerous experiments having a "dark side," according to Secretary of Energy Hazel O'Leary who eventually opened the files.[63]

These are only a few of the scars. By the time such knowledge about government tests, experiments, and collusion spilled out, it was not difficult for people to hold some pretty lurid suspicions. Several friends and I attended the 1997 movie *Conspiracy Theory* with a neighbor, the economist-as-statesman Herbert Stein. He was a generation older than we and had worked closely with department secretaries and presidents. Dr. Stein found the movie ridiculous. How could anyone conceive of a government so out of control as to contain rival secret agencies — possessing their own SWAT teams and directed by a dispassionate senior official with clear plastic-rim spectacles and a Harvard class ring — that experiment on human beings for reasons of national security? My friends enjoyed the movie and just rolled their eyes.

Americans inflicted a lot on themselves that remains painful. Much worse was meted out by others whenever the Cold War turned hot. In 2000, the Korea Cold War Family Association of the Missing was trying to locate relatives to donate DNA samples for help in identification. Only a few years previously, North Korea had finally allowed the United States to search for evidence of the thousands of men still missing since the Korean War.

As for the war that was supposed to be "not Korea," a 180-person Hawaii-based military task force scours the hills, fields, and jungles of Vietnam to determine the fate of more than a thousand Americans unaccounted for there. When the first serving U.S. defense secretary to visit Vietnam since the war arrived in 2000, he described this search as America's highest priority. Forty-eight cases of men last seen alive in the hands of their captors were still being scrutinized.[64] Personnel from all four U.S. services work as detectives in Vietnam, as well as in Laos and Cambodia, interviewing witnesses, excavating crash sites, draining ponds, and sifting bone fragments from shallow graves. More than 3,000 joint investigations with the countries that once composed French Indochina were conducted in the first post–Cold War decade; 165 sets of remains have been identified, and about 350 others are still waiting to be matched with men lost in long-forgotten ambushes and falling B-52s. The Socialist Republic of Vietnam still searches for some 300,000 of its own missing.

Russia's help has been mixed. Transcripts of communications between Leonid Brezhnev and the North Vietnamese Ministry of Defense concerning prisoners remain unshared. No representatives of the former KGB have ever appeared before the Joint Commission on POW/MIA Affairs, a U.S.-Russian task force established after the Cold War to unearth the range of America's disappeared during those decades. No evidence has been found of U.S. POWs having been transferred to the Soviet Union. "If it had been done," reflected one Russian official once the Soviet Union disappeared, "it would have been done in 'very secret channels' that would not be reflected in the MFA [Ministry of Foreign Affairs] archives."[65] Stranger things had happened.

Also after the Cold War, the story finally became known of the brave South Vietnamese soldiers whom the CIA had infiltrated into the North thirty years earlier. Angry members of Congress promised to compensate each of the surviving "lost commandos," some of whom had spent two decades being taught the error of their ways as only totalitarian regimes know how. The Pentagon was ordered to tender them what they were owed in back pay for their time in captivity — about $2,000 per year (incurred when the dollar was several times more valuable), an aggregate of $20 million — but military bureaucrats stalled on the grounds that Congress's enactment fell short of an actual statute.

There was similar neglect of other brave people long forgotten. Only in 1997 did a lobbying campaign by the Special Forces Association finally squeeze consent from the U.S. government to resettle what were then just 177 surviving Nung in the United States. As for the Hmong, several tens of thousand had quickly perished when Laos went under in 1975. Over the next twenty-two years, they would become the war's last wandering group of refugees. With as many as 100,000 dead from war and reprisal, about 125,000 survivors were finally able to leave Thailand's wretched refugee camps for America, many moving to Minnesota, where, in the late 1950s, CIA money at the state university had been used to create a written language for these tactically useful subsistence farmers.

By 1998, welfare reform meant that food stamps were cut off for the remaining Hmong veterans and their families — many maimed by battle, few with any education, all bereft by exile — to save about one-thirtieth of 1 percent of the annual federal food stamp budget. However, noble assistance came from that old operative, Larry Devlin, who had overseen the secret CIA-directed war in Laos. Among other contributions, he lobbied successfully in 2001 for the Hmong Veterans Naturalization Act, designed to enable forty-five thousand Hmong and Laotian veterans, including widows, to take U.S. citizenship exams with the aid of translators.

Over the years, the United States accepted close to one million of the people who began fleeing Vietnam in 1975. Vietnam is still one of the half dozen places from which flow the greatest number of America's immigrants (Mexico, China, and India being among the others). Mostly from the South, some are still technically refugees. Special programs exist to accept the Amerasian children of servicemen and the survivors of reeducation camps. As a nation, Vietnam is still held back by its Communist regime from becoming an economic dynamo like Taiwan, Malaysia — and South Korea. Persecutions continue. In 2001, more than twenty thousand Montagnards staged the largest antigovernment demonstrations since the country's unification. A military crackdown followed, with more Montagnards fleeing into Cambodia and some thereafter arriving in the United States. Had self-determination ever been among the goals of Ho Chi Minh and his successors, the Vietnamese people would have had free elections long ago.

As for what had been the worst of the killing fields, the United States spent about $1.4 billion between 1980 and 2000 to help Cambodia recover. Congress appropriated several million dollars for the Cambodian Genocide Program, contracted on a rather Cold War pattern by Yale University, to gather evidence for international trials. Only in 1998 did the Khmer Rouge guerrilla movement finally collapse. Most of the leading massacre makers enjoy quiet retirement, although the judicial process is tightening and the prime minister promises trials. A website exists to remind the world of the sixteen thousand men, women, and children who entered Tuol Sleng, the Khmer Rouge's secret police prison, between 1975 and 1979; only seven emerged alive.

The final U.S. combat soldier to leave Vietnam was Max Beilke, an Army master-sergeant who had originally been drafted into the

Korean War from a small farm in Minnesota. Although Marines guarding the U.S. Embassy stayed until South Vietnam fell in April 1975, the Army lists Beilke as the last one out. Working as a civilian for the Army on veterans issues, he was at the Pentagon that September morning when American Airlines flight 77 was rammed into the building. He was among the first killed at the start of the strange new war.

There is tragedy enough from the Cold War years and from times more recent. There is also black humor. With no sense of irony — in light of the histories of South Vietnam, Kurdistan, and other places where the U.S. presence had arrived and departed — the Council on Foreign Relations honored one of its prominent members by creating the Henry A. Kissinger Study Group on Exit Strategies and American Foreign Policy. In 2001, the Library of Congress, where the former secretary's government papers were kept from public view, established its Henry Alfred Kissinger Chair in Foreign Policy and International Relations. That was the year that a quarter-century wrong was partly corrected — once a private group of scholars threatened to sue for access to these public documents.

Looking back at the turn of the century, another eminent man from that troubled era, Paul Nitze, remarked of the Cold War, "We did a goddamn good job." Well, yes and no: yes if the overriding emphasis is that civilization survived more or less intact, that the Soviet Union collapsed peacefully, and that most of the world was liberalized along the way; no if we dwell on the indirection, inexcusable ignorance, political intrusions, personal opportunism, and even crimes underlying this ultimate victory.

The Cold War and the first decade thereafter have brought us to this present point of conflict. We now seem to confront one of those grim epochs . . . in which familiar problems are replaced by authentic, terrible crises: and the worse because they are stoked by the world's trend toward increasingly harsh inequalities. Calvin Coolidge's secretary of war gave his name to the Davis Cup. Forrestal, Marshal, and Lovett soon had to face sterner tasks, think harder thoughts. They had each helped win the greatest war in history, and learned from it. They then thought above all about how the world they confronted was new, to be met with different attitudes and transformed institutions. This is where America and its much wider, better informed array of leaders now stand.

Conclusion

Today, in the Ruhr, whose furnaces fired so much of the twentieth century's heats, stands a 230-acre megamall, Centro, its restaurants anchored until recently by Planet Hollywood. The malling of the Ruhr — cradle of Krupp, target of ten thousand Allied bombings, its surly industrial proletariat the hope of revolutionaries — is essentially complete, and with special fitness, Centro is planted where once stood a Thyssen steel mill. It solicitously maintains a trauma room for overstressed shoppers: "blood and iron" indeed recycled. Perhaps the greatest of victories are those in which the sequel seems to have left all the contestants victorious.

For Japan, the last forgotten World War II prisoners began drifting home from Siberia during the twentieth century's final decade. The fiftieth anniversary of what Americans long celebrated as V-J Day, the grimly sought "Victory in Japan" attained on August 14, 1945, was pervaded by a desire not to hurt Japanese feelings. The commemorations in Hawaii were officially designated EOWP Day, as in "End of the War in the Pacific." In the first week of September 2001, the fiftieth anniversary of the formal peace treaty was similarly diplomatic: a Japanese prime minister, for the first time, acknowledged the ill treatment of prisoners of war. The Pacific war had been a triumph of American arms. By the time of these anniversaries, however, triumph had happily been overshadowed by what it had so largely made possible: the arrival of sovereign trading nations, democratic or working toward democracy, around the great ocean — the real new world of the early millennium. Triumph is vindicated not by what has been destroyed, but by what is made possible.

As for America's foremost wartime allies — Russia, China, Britain, and France — the first two, historically authoritarian, are only now breaking out of their corroded time capsules. Theirs was the heaviest price of world conflict during the Cold War (as during World War II), not the least of which was the risk of near nuclear war with each other during its middle years. Meanwhile, Britain and France were able to contract under American auspices from unprofitable world powers to complacent industrial democracies. As in the early 1980s and 1990s, in fall 2001 Britain is applying its will and resources to a planet-wide defense of the general interest.

The United States, the most heterogeneous of countries, enjoyed the most natural solidarity in a century during which many other nations were splitting wide open. This became ever more apparent during the Cold War's last decade: a conservative president had an African-American general as national security assistant (who would go on to become secretary of state); a dozen years after the fall of Saigon, Vietnamese teenagers in America were climbing quickly to the top of the class, and soon to success in business. The Anglo-Saxon ascendancy so apparent at the Cold War's start had disappeared. Time was moving too fast and demanding too much from everyone for that old social order to prevail. Catalyzed by having to live up to the principles of freedom and equality to which it had so publicly committed itself during the Cold War, the United States ended the century by embodying its own ideas worldwide much more than it applied its power.

Tyranny disintegrated, and with it perished the Soviet Union's dreams of conquering a way out of communism's misfortunes. Yet no one now among us is likely to be alive when the waste products of the Cold War are laid to their final rest: the leftovers of weapons making; the millions of lives wrecked by the Cultural Revolution; whole nations blighted by techno-Leninist arrogance and secret police power; the risky habit in America of odious friends indulged lest they be replaced by worse enemies; the grim "blowbacks" of particular, barely remembered contests with the Soviet Union, as in Afghanistan. Today's newest child almost anywhere in the world will be carrying some of these costs throughout his or her life. Such costs will reach into the late 2000s, and part of the horror is that their origins are found in the early 1900s.

A French poet of the First World War cried that the Gare du Nord (the Paris train station delivering the armies to the Western Front) "had eaten our sons." Looking at the Cold War, we see how much it has eaten of ourselves. America, as well as the world of which it has been the great engine, would be a very different place if it had not had to pump so much of its best efforts into that particular pit for so long.

In the short term, the Cold War accelerated history — international connectedness, racial enlightenment, fascinating technologies. The initial responses to the ruin of 1945 built dikes against the errors of 1919 — collective security, liberalized trade, fruitful generosity to the vanquished (a vanquished convicted of deeds far worse than any the harshly used defeated of 1919 could ever have imagined). New enemies had been identified early, and neither crusade nor militarization followed. Thereafter, certainly by the time Eisenhower described the struggle as "total war," any returns so far won began diminishing fast. What he could not foresee was that bearing this "cross of iron" for decade after decade might tire less the economic body than the very souls of his countrymen.

Despite immense U.S. prosperity, amazing revelations in science, and the burst of communications, Americans have been robbed of part of their future, perhaps the most shining part. They cannot know what they have forgone, but many people sense that things are not as good as they could have been. This shows in polls that reflect a diminished interest in the rest of the world — at least until part of that world came crashing into New York and Washington — and in anxieties about immigrants that should have been left behind in the 1930s.

Had Americans been able to invest their trillions of dollars elsewhere, not only would the country be richer, but its level of confidence, perhaps of generosity to the world's disadvantaged, would be much greater. Splendid cities of the mind and spirit have been lost — ones that might have towered in place of missile silos, command centers, and barracks. The Cold War's most visible memorial, when the defeat of totalitarianism has been forgotten, is likely to remain the myriad lives that would have gone so much further were it not for the chronic drain of those years. Our children will no doubt reap many of the postponed harvests, but they will do so on a planet more heavily armed, more politicized, and much more densely populated than the one in which these problems might otherwise have been faced. It will be more difficult for them to meet the challenges to come.

The Cold War awoke ambitions in all kinds of people who never would have been heard from had they not been pawns on the chessboard. Had Russia left the Afghans in 1979 to cut their own throats in the time-honored fashion, it is unlikely the world would have felt the bite of the Taliban twenty-two years later. Not only has the first war of the twenty-first century involved some of the same characters, but some of the same centers of training, as in Pakistan and northern Afghanistan. War is an abomination against civilization, and one abomination, as was seen after World War II, breeds another.

America is the only society to have reached supremacy as the result of the sustained failure of a world system (World War I–Great Depression–World War II). By the late 1940s, it had arrived at the top in the very moment that it realized that all could be lost. Today it does not know most of its enemies, because America has innumerable enemies it does not know about. September 11, 2001, was an inspiration to all enemies of the human race. Malcontent organizations exist worldwide — certainly including some in middle-class countries, as well as at home. They have yet to exploit the really total technologies of destruction. But mass murder, surprise attack, and hatred borne by envy are inseparable from thousands of years of history.

New challenges mean, among other things, new powers to government. Today such challenges are unlikely to include either a revival of archaic authority or archaic deference. The discovery of 1970s vulnerabilities by twenty-first-century fanatics is not grounds for the revival of 1947 attitudes, pleasant as the return to such futures might be for many lawyers, journalists, academics, businesspeople, and other assorted mandarins. The terrorism that has showed itself terribly is precisely the voice of the past and those who know what is good for us. Jefferson, in his Age of Reason optimism and confidence, fought the Barbary Pirates more effectively, as the pope said, than countries of Old World princes — and resisted an overall increase of state power simultaneously.

Could the Cold War have been fought better? Of course. Yet anyone who knows America might have guessed that such a high-pressure endeavor would be conducted in a typically American fashion — improvised, second-guessed, neglected, and suddenly redynamized toward success at close to the last minute. It might have been a virtue at the outset that this new enterprise, set on avoiding the old mistakes, had to be invented as it was being built. Soon enough, however, improvisation became the excuse for misdirection, when it did not turn into self-deception. Not too long after the start, almost everyone involved — politicians, intellocrats, professors, mandarins of various sorts who frequently enjoyed the self-promotion that comes from maintaining the mystery of high policy — was winging it amid a clamor of faddish policies and "crisis management" styles of governance.

Not that events were ever entirely in the hands of unsubtle, willful people. How much better, George Kennan insinuates, America's foreign policy could have looked if it had been exercised only by wise, dispassionately insightful, less sentimental leaders. This is a dangerous argument that can add further to disappointments. It becomes easy to imply that if the United States did not exactly cause the Cold War, its truculence and hysteria helped maintain it at a ruinous level.

The Cold War was sensibly undertaken in the name of a more secure America — soon of a more secure world, because it would ideally become more like America. Long-term protection had to embrace that of many, but by no means all, of the clients whom it dignified (and deluded itself as to their abilities) by calling them allies. Some far-sighted Americans, strongly influenced by European socialists, knew early on that their country had to buy time. By 1950, every responsible policymaker realized that America's outlandish share of good fortune and its hulking dominance of world commerce should not be allowed to continue. They understood that the prosperity of a liberal society (where the state is an instrument of individual betterment) rises with that of others and that it is reactionary to assume that someone else's success diminishes one's own. U.S. leaders were by and large desperate to see a world in which their country did not possess 40 percent or more of the wealth — not that existing wealth should be redistributed, but that others might create wealth as well. The freedom from envy (of America) was a vital one, to be carried on the back of the freedom from want. This had to be accomplished fast, before resentment again broke the world apart. "Money is like muck," Francis Bacon wrote, "not good except it be spread."

Since 1950, when the United States became a global political-military power, the world economy has grown sixfold. Trade has expanded fourteenfold, driving modernization and ensuring higher incomes, better diets, and longer lives for many of the world's people. By now, resistance to the possibilities of free markets is the near monopoly of ideologues. The growth of democratic capitalism was from the start recognized as something that would work to

America's advantage worldwide. Given the impending technologies, if there had not been a global advance right after World War II, there would have been a global retreat. "By creating a security umbrella over Europe and Asia," said one of the more experienced participants after it was all over, "Americans lowered the business transaction costs in all these regions: North America, Western Europe and Northeast Asia all got richer as a result."[1] Americans followed the principle that wealth would help make other countries not necessarily like their own, but at least citizens of the same world — and in ways that would bring basic improvement. This is not "cold war victor's history"; nearly all the world's people, in Lenin's phrase, ended up voting with their feet.[2] And the few who come in deadly anger seem to be moved by the rage of older orders whose own people are leaving them behind.

Unlike all that went before, the American supremacy that arose during the second half of the twentieth century was not a cumulative imperial darkening of the sun, but the recognition by Europeans, Japanese, and other allies of the plain facts of international life. What passed for British supremacy in the nineteenth century had been toiled for. U.S. political, military, and industrial preeminence arose more haphazardly. It sprang more from productive power, technology breakthroughs, and Hollywood's reflections of the American dream than from any expansionist yearnings in Washington. "The United States is the first nation in history," André Malraux observed, "to become a great power without trying to do so."[3] The optimistic, high-energy democracy had found itself having to settle a problem, not build itself a monument.

Did the United States get anything like maximum benefit from its commitments? No. As the Rothschilds used to say, only fools set out to make the highest returns. How much had it lost? European and Japanese prosperity are fundamental U.S. interests. Endless accommodations — to cartelization within the European Community, to every known mercantilist tactic in Japan, to unequal defense contributions from both — were obviously not a whip-cracking imperial posture, but that of a country prepared to exchange some of its own considerable immediate prosperity to avoid having to extend its power and to be able to skirt the seductive responsibility that comes with it. The goal since 1947 of wiring together the world by general prosperity, however imperfectly pursued, distances the U.S. presence during the Cold War and today from all previous centuries of imperial ambition.

There was no Unified Theory guiding this effort — certainly not containment, which quickly came to mean anything to anyone. Instead, it was essentially a willingness to be guided by three lessons that the United States more or less read into situations and that still shape decisions today: (1) the "Ghost of Versailles Past," which let Americans know that they could never turn their backs on the world again; (2) the "Primrose Path of Smoot-Hawley," the primitive protectionist tariff of 1930 that did much to institutionalize the Great Depression and that thereafter made obvious the advantages of free trade; and (3) the most searing, the "Watchfire of Munich," a dread warning by which the next world war (or something nearly as horrible) was to be prevented.

What the United States found itself undertaking had at the outset neither name nor frame. In retrospect, we may call it the preservation of a liberal world order — a loose term for constitutionalism, resistance to aggression, and cooperation, as much as possible, rather than coercion. Too often, however, decaying colonial realms were shored up until their failures were more catastrophically dramatic than their earlier decline. Too often dictatorships were shamefully indulged. Too often the individuals who lined up against the threat from 1946 to 1991 — including Nobusuke Kishi, Senator Joseph McCarthy, by way of Wernher von Braun and J. Edgar Hoover — were unfortunate companions in a great cause. But the cause was truly greater than any of the figures who crowded to the front of the photograph and of the embarrassments such people added along the way.

Many costly Cold War experiences that these men, and others, injected cannot be explained as tragic necessities. Ventures into atomic testing with "a little bit of the Buchenwald touch," CIA world-order men whose intrigues more often than not started at the incompetent and went down from there, White House claims of "national security" to conceal deceit, and the creation of huge special interests in archaic spending all too easily occurred because most Americans were not preoccupied with the struggle. Had they focused more of their attention on the Cold War itself, let alone winning it, the United States might have become too much like the other side for comfort. Of course, this conclusion is no solace to downwinders, to abandoned Kurds and South Vietnamese, to the Mayans dead at the hands of Guatemalan platoons, to just about every American in the past fifty-plus years — 400-odd million people — each of whose lives has had one or more bits cut out of it by research postponed, investment trammeled, and bureaucracy expanded.

The first justification of any war is that even its horrors are the lesser evil. If the Cold War is construed as having prevented a collapse of the terribly injured remnants of civilization that were still functioning after 1945, we might contemplate the costs of international disorder that otherwise would have been so much to the benefit of the Soviet Union and, before long, China, given the capacity of both to intimidate and subvert. Civilization could not have renewed itself without considerable help from the one unscarred liberal power. Americans paid for it with their taxes and blood. We may gratefully concede to the Russians that the American array of suffering does not compare with what it took to disembowel the Wehrmacht, but "there are no light casualties," as Creighton Abrams said. Shattered men will lie in veterans hospitals for another twenty or thirty years. New ones arrive. The wound bleeds on.

If America lost many opportunities during this era, not all of them stemmed from the Cold War. Sacrifices from thwarting the ambitions of Stalin, Khrushchev, Brezhnev, and Andropov had little to do, for instance, with tolerating mediocre high schools in Massachusetts or emphasizing football over math classes in Texas. During most of those years, the United States was more than rich enough to waste its resources and still to prosper. Now Americans find themselves having to overcome some expensive habits in the freer and undoubtedly more competitive twenty-first-century world of six billion soon-to-be-networked people they helped create. Doing so will not be easy.

So much of the charging about during the Cold War (with its minimum of showdowns and demarches) was like the war America is now experiencing against terrorism. Communism seemed no more likely to wither away than do armed nihilists or drug lords today. In each contest, friends would be bought, and one's allies might often prove repellent. Loss of principle, embezzlement, flipping on unfloppable issues — they were all there. Since shooting wars that too closely involved the superpowers had to be avoided whenever possible, it was appropriate for America to inject the political into all parts of the struggle. But this entailed some strange and expensive brokering. At one end, there were powerful secret officials and too-well-connected journalists and law firms. At the other, there was the reverse of Burckhardt's "emergencymen" — all the clients and despots who were clamoring to Washington for favors so that they would remain "stable" and not themselves become an emergency.

The United States is still whipsawed between the more rewarding activities it can pursue on its own turf and a sense of danger (indeed of responsibility) abroad. Attempts at energetic solutions come naturally to it. More so than that of any other power, U.S. foreign policy remains a function of passions and reactions, as well as of very real dangers. America has always seen itself as an idea, as a dream, more than a place: it is a land where anyone prepared to lift his or her eyes to the horizon can become someone new. To this extent, it is the exception to history.

Americans will keep offering humanitarian relief to the world, just as they will keep absorbing newcomers or fighting international outlaws as did Jefferson. One hundred years ago, after all, Teddy Roosevelt, on his own initiative, rushed supplies to volcano-shattered Martinique. Similarly remarkable was the food aid provided to the unhappy Afghan people while their government harbored the massacre makers of September 11.

The noble readiness to respond to world upheavals is one thing; basing it on a well-thought-out body of principle is another. As during the Cold War, much of the first ten years thereafter showed a recurring belief that goodwill alone could create a policy. The overseas entanglements maximized commitment and clamor going in, ineffectiveness once arrived, and embarrassment when leaving. So much of the Vietnam disaster, for instance, also flowed from ignorant goodwill. Not the least of the drawbacks of the imperial presidency developed by decades of emergency was the need to act, to be decisive. Television provided a convenient way of bypassing the deliberative mechanisms of government. In looking back, we can see that so much of the cost during the Cold War's middle years, 1961 to 1981, was due to America rushing into things — very American, but in un-American contexts.

Other countries' quarrels are real, complicated, exhausting, and often unique, despite most people's eagerness worldwide to try on American popular culture and to concern themselves so largely with making money rather than war. This is still not as obvious as it seems. At the end of the 1990s, one of the longest-serving senior officials in the U.S. administration would ingenuously reflect, "Over time, we have learned and relearned the lesson that other countries shape their own destiny to a far greater extent than we believed."[4] At this stage of the game, such a breathtakingly innocent remark could only have come from a member of the uniquely American mandarinate that has rung up so many avoidable costs since 1946.

The defeat of totalitarianism made it possible for more of the world's people to prosper and to use technology as much as possible to extend their abilities and freedoms. People who have quarrels with secular industrial states now direct them at Russia as well, and, likely soon enough, upon China.

Software, Internet, and other high-tech product advertisements since the Cold War have used familiar images to stress individual choice against a monolith (as did Apple Computer's original "Big Brother" ad during the 1984 Super Bowl). A nationwide campaign for IKON office copiers showed an enormous statue of Lenin being pulled down by ropes to shatter on the bricks below; "Second Place, Cold War" read the caption. "No Empire Lasts Forever," declared the RCN fiber-optic network in its advertisement, which showed a bust of Lenin being hoisted to destruction. "Defenders of the Free World," proclaimed an ad for a free e-mail service. A data exchange company I founded during those years used in its marketing a wall-size, ominous-red poster of Stalin riven from top to bottom over the statement "Systems Which Don't Interface with Others Eventually Fail."

The most useful aftermath of the Cold War is that the world that resulted from it is increasingly one of private causes and individual initiatives. The forces that pulled down totalitarianism came from almost as many points of the compass as can be found on the latest search engine. Despite the unknown dangers ahead, we face a world that stands fair to be made better by people of all sorts, with government in their service and, in the United States, with a government schooled in modesty after its fear-and-pride-driven years on Olympus. This is what Americans bought over these weary decades, and it is worthwhile.

Acknowledgments

Colleagues at Georgetown University offered encouragement throughout, especially Government Department chairs Robert Lieber and Euseblo Mujal-Leon, as well as Michael Ryan at the Business School. Also in Washington, the Center for Strategic and Budgetary Assessments generously assisted by adding a wealth of clarifying detail, as did the late Herbert Stein. Timothy Dickinson, of the *Paris Review*, the *Washington Monthly*, and innumerable consultancies, is among the best of editors, and of friends, for anyone lucky enough to know him.

In so vast a field, the obligations are innumerable. Roger Donald, former editor in chief of Little, Brown and Company, is to be thanked for coming up with the idea for this book. Most of my sources will find themselves acknowledged in the notes, but there are several people who have been particularly generous with their time and wisdom: David G. Bradley, David Braunschvig, Scott Brown, Robert Coulam, Loren Douglass, Donna Farmer, Patricia Fields, Estelle Moeri, Joe Spieler, Marc Wall, David Webster, and my mother. At Harvard University, Professor Paul M. Doty, founder and director emeritus of the Belfer Center for Science and International Affairs, selflessly enabled a generation of young scholars to encounter new fields of study beyond their own areas of special expertise. Initially as a graduate student and then as a colleague, David May applied his expert energies to help with research.

Notes

Chapter 1. 1946: At the Top of the Wave

1. Schlesinger, *Crisis*, p. 74.
2. Holt, "Joint Plan Red," pp. 48–56. Also see Jordan, ed., *Naval Warfare*, pp. 169–170.
3. Bird, *Chairman*, p. 112.
4. Ibid., pp. 19, 661.
5. Ibid., pp. 661, 18. Nor would the country ever agree on something as outlandish as having to "shoulder its imperial responsibilities."
6. Walter Lord, *Day of Infamy* (New York: Holt, 1957), photo page 10.
7. Conversation with Kay Murphy Halle, who was there; June 1987.
8. Correspondence with Ward Elliott, professor of government, Claremont College, May 2001, and Samuel Beer, professor emeritus of government, Harvard University, who was there.
9. Sir Gerald Campbell, *Of True Experience* (London: Hutchinson, 1948), p. 149.
10. Rhodes, *Dark Sun*, p. 192.
11. Schwartz, ed., *Atomic Audit*, p. 58. Brookings presents this sum as $21.6 billion in 1996 dollars.
12. Stalin had thoughtfully offered Berlin much more than it expected from the 1939 treaty of collaboration. The bombers that set London ablaze were serviced with Soviet oil. The first Axis sea raider to decimate British and Australian shipping in the Pacific had been assiduously convoyed through the Northeast Passage by Soviet icebreakers. And German Communists (many of them Jews) who had fled to Moscow during the 1930s were returned to Hitler.
13. Gabriel Peri, Communist deputy, in a smuggled letter from July 1942, as published in the *New York Times*, April 11, 1943, p. 15.
14. Fossedal, *Our Finest Hour*, p. 169.
15. Interview with Carleton Swift, November 1998.
16. Piel, *The Acceleration of History*. The phrase is the book title.
17. Luce, "American Century."
18. *Congressional Record*, September 8, 1949, Hubert H. Humphrey. The much misunderstood "Pax Britannica" was an epoch of peace that happened to occur over the years when Britain was the most pervasive country in the world. British power was significant, especially at sea, but was not shaping

the world system, nor did it uphold the peace. Napoleon III and Bismarck were not swayed by what Britain might decide. Recall the latter's response as to what he would do should the British land troops: "I shall not hesitate to call the police."

19. Council on Foreign Relations, archives, Herbert Morrison speech, March 14, 1948.

Chapter 2: Back to the Future (1946–1950)

1. Smith, *My Three Years*, p. 53.
2. Council on Foreign Relations, archives, Digest of Mtg. with J. F. Dulles, October 30, 1945; Patricia Dawson, *The Threat of Peace: James F. Byrnes and the Council of Foreign Ministers 1945–1946* (Kent: Ohio State University Press, 1979), p. 41; a revisionist description of Bevin as "the dupe of far cleverer minds in the Foreign Office" reflects an utter misreading of the Foreign Office and Cabinet Office records, let alone a failure to interview these "cleverer minds," as in Dorril, *MI6*, p. 37.
3. PRO, CB 131/1 DO (46), October 16, 1946.
4. PRO, Bevin to Warner, FO371/66184 N20/19/38, November 8, 1946.
5. John Updike, *Assorted Prose* (New York: Knopf, 1965), p. 86.
6. *Time*, December 1, 1948.
7. Foot, *Aneurin Bevan*, p. 55.
8. Ku111, *Butter and Guns*, p. 44
9. House Banking Committee, Representative Wolcott, *Times* (London), June 4, 1946; *New York Times*, November 12, 1947.
10. PRO, FO 371/66279, N 222/7/38G, May 28, 1946.
11. Walter Lippmann, Oral History, Columbia University.
12. "Only by utter ignorance could one expect Mao and his comrades to adopt Marshall's mediation," explains Michael M. Sheng, in describing the extent to which China's Communist Party strictly adhered to Stalin's policy advice. Sheng, *Battling Western Imperialism*, p. 194.
13. Universal Military Training: Hearings Before the Senate Armed Services Comm., 80th Congress, 2nd Session, March 17, 1948.
14. By 1947, the number of personnel on active duty had been reduced from 11 million to 2.8 million. N. S. Simonov, *Voyenno-Promyshlennyy Kompleks SSSR v 1920-1950-e Gody* (Military Industrial Complex of the USSR in the 1920s–1950s) (Moscow, Roccpen, 1996), p. 192, citing the USSR Gosplan archives. In 1950–51, the armed forces were remobilized to about 6 million on active duty and remained at that level until 1956–57, followed by reduction back to about the 1947 level by 1961–62.
15. Rhodes, *Dark Sun*, p. 121.
16. Eugene Rabinowitch, "Decision Making in the Scientific Age," in Elbers and Duncan, *Scientific Revolution*, p. 23.
17. Tugwell, *Chronicle of Jeopardy*, p. 60.
18. d'Antonio, "Atomic Guinea Pigs," p. 38. The purpose, it is claimed, was to answer the question "How much radiation can a man take?"
19. Cousins and Finletter, "A Beginning for Sanity."
20. Tugwell, *Chronicle of Jeopardy*, p. 93.
21. Isenberg, *Shield of the Republic*, p. 298.
22. Isaacson and Thomas, *Wise Men*, p. 348.

23. Stein, ed., *Fiscal Revolution*, p. 207.
24. Pogue, *Marshall: Education*, pp. 306–307.
25. PRO, FO 371/67543 UN 173G, December 20, 1946.
26. As extolled by Schlesinger in "The Radical," pp. 3–8, and acclaimed by Thomas Friedman in his column "Now a Word from 'X,'" in the *New York Times*, May 2, 1998.
27. Brinkley, *Dean Acheson*, p. 88; Lambright, *Powering Apollo*, p. 52.
28. Brinkley, *Dean Acheson*, pp. 92, 81.
29. Crossman, "Strange Case X," p. 133.
30. Mayers, *George Kennan*, p. 16, re family records; Halle interview with author about Churchill; Crossman, *Diaries*, p. 352.
31. Isaacson and Thomas, *Wise Men*, p. 579.
32. National Archives, RG 59, PPS, 101st Mtg.
33. Arnold, *First Domino*, p. 46.
34. Mr. X [George Kennan], "Sources of Soviet Conduct," p. 582.
35. Millis with Mansfield, *Arms and the State*, p. 243; PRO, Record of Conversation, FO 371/76301 N j111 11101 10, 1919.
36. Kennan, "Letter on Germany," p. 19.
37. Kennan and Lukas, "From World War to Cold War," pp. 64–65.
38. Bullock, *Ernest Bevin*, p. 840.
39. Kennan and Lukas, "From World War to Cold War," pp. 65, 64.
40. Archives of the former Institute of Marxism-Leninism in East Berlin have disgorged Stalin's outline from June 1945 to first split and then to unite Germany under the German Communist Party, controlled from Moscow. See Raack, "Stalin Plans," pp. 54–55.
41. Leffler, *Preponderance*, pp. 513, 515, 516; also see Meade, "Refighting," p. 4. Given newly available Soviet documents Meade writes matter-of-factly that "the reputation that takes the hardest knock is Josef Stalin's."
42. *Encyclopaedia Britannica*, Vol. 26, 1997, s.v. Roosevelt, Franklin D., p. 937.
43. Leffler echoes Henry Wallace's belief that "toughness would beget toughness" from the Soviets. Leffler, *Preponderance*, p. 139.
44. MacDonald, "Communist Bloc Expansion," p. 185.
45. PRO, FO 371/60996 AN193 160, January 27, 1947.
46. NA, RG 84, London Post Files, "Cards on the Table," 1947.
47. PRO, FO 371/67582A UN2001/1754/78, March 26, 1947; in fact, the United States had already contributed $200 million to support Greece via UN relief efforts, the Export-Import Bank, and a surplus property credit.
48. Gage, *Eleni*, p. 245.
49. Joseph M. Jones, *Fifteen Weeks*, p. 7.
50. NA, RG 218 Leahy Files, August 1947, No. 36, Box 7.
51. PRO, Wilson-Young minute, March 21, 1947, FO 371/67582 AN 2001/1754/78.
52. Marton, *Polk Conspiracy*, p. 93.
53. Clayton cited in Fossdale, *Our Finest Hour*, p. 209; PRO, "Tactics with the United States Administration," FO 371/61003, undated.
54. Not only Merlin engines, but Rolls Royce Derwents and Nerves were transferred in the belief that Moscow was too backward to make much use of such technology, an assumption refuted at the 1947 May Day flypast in Red Square. See PRO May 24, 1947, FO 371/60154 AN 1827/40/45; September

16, 1947, CAB 131/4 DO 47; NA, RG 330 Memorandum for Forrestal, October 10, 1947, CD-6-1-5.

55. Marton, *Polk Conspiracy*, p. 100.

56. PRO, FO 371/67582A UN 2766, Balfour to Jebb, April 19, 1947.

57. NA, RG 218, March 25, 1947, Box 14.

58. Lovett, Oral History, Truman Presidential Library.

59. Ibid.; Harriman, Oral History, Truman Presidential Library: "Bevin did a superb job of getting Molotov out of Paris by careful maneuvering."

60. Kunz, *Butter and Guns*, p. 54.

61. PRO, FO 371/68013B AN/156/6/45, January 21, 1948.

62. Harold Knutson, *Dictionary of American Biography*, Supplement 5, p. 397, column 1.

63. Galbraith, *How to Control*, p. 69. "We can out-invent, out-research, out-develop, out-engineer and out-pace the U.S.S.R.," said LeMay correctly, "and in doing so become more and more prosperous while the Soviets become progressively poorer."

64. *Washington Post*, May 16, 1947.

65. Admiral Richard Conolly, Oral History, Columbia University.

66. *New York Times*, September 25, 1947.

67. Tugwell, *Chronicle of Jeopardy*, p. 13.

68. For a discussion of Alsop, Athens's insatiable appetite, and U.S. ambition, see D. F. Fleming, *The Cold War and Its Origins*, Vol. I (New York: Doubleday, 1969), pp. 299–303.

69. Marton, *Polk Conspiracy*, p. 197.

70. Bird, *Chairman*, p. 296.

71. Bertrand Russell recalls this incident in G. J. Whitrow, *Einstein: The Man and His Achievement* (New York: Dover Publications, 1973), p. 90. These are transcripts of three BBC programs from 1967.

72. *Washington Post*, April 25, 1996, quoting Daniel Goldhagen.

73. NA, Report by Joint Intelligence Committee to the JCS, April 5, 1951, "Denial of German and Austrian Scientists."

74. Interview, April 1998, with Col. Ralph Pate, USA ret., field officer in charge, 1949–51.

75. Arnold Lapiner, "Brain Drain," *American Heritage* (May/June 2000), pp. 36–37.

76. Hunt, *Secret Agenda*, p. 20.

77. NA, Memo, CCS 471.9, Sec 16, November 4, 1948; letter from Javits to SecDef Lovett, April 24, 1952, concerning complaint by Joseph Wilder.

78. Michael Ignatieff, "What Did the CIA Do to His Father?," *New York Times Magazine* (April 1, 2001), pp. 68–70.

79. NA, JCS Files, September 24, 1952, memorandum for the Secretary of Defense.

80. For the scope of Macdonald's opinions of Nazism and other forms of totalitarianism, see Wreszin, *Rebel*.

81. National Security Archive documents cited in the *New York Times* by David Sanger, May 9, 1997, p. 12.

82. "Week in Review," *New York Times*, July 6, 1997, p. 10.

83. Regis, *Biology of Doom*, p. 126.

84. See Patrick Smith's review of Herbert Bix's *Hirohito and the Making of Modern Japan* in *Business Week*, October 16, 2000, p. 28.

85. Peter Maas, "They Should Have Their Day in Court," *Parade,* June 17, 2001, pp. 4–6.
86. National Security Archive, Memorandum from the AEC's Dr. Shields Warren to Dr. Joseph Hamilton, 1950.
87. Sturtevant, "Social Implications."
88. National Security Archive, James Forrestal to President Truman, November 18, 1948, signed and approved by the President (DOE, Doc 0014347-8); letter from Gary Hearne to DDE, April 13, 1953; letter from John C. Bugher, M.D., Director, to Clarence Freund of Minneapolis, July 28, 1953.
89. National Security Archive, Col. O. O. Haywood to Dr. Fidler (DOE, Doc 0000015).
90. National Security Archive, "General Institutional Assurance: Statement of Compliance," signed by James L. Liverman, Associate Director, Oak Ridge, and by William G. Pollard, Executive Director of Oak Ridge Associated Universities, February 28, 1972.
91. Finletter conversation with Timothy Dickinson, New York, November 1973.
92. PRO, FO 371/68018 AN 0849/16/45, March, 2, 1948.
93. Marshall to the Committee on Armed Services, U.S. Senate, "Hearings on Universal Military Training," 80th Congress, 2nd Session March 17, 1948.
94. Reed and Kramish, Trinity," pp. 30–32.
95. *Public Papers,* Truman, Item 52: "Special Message to Congress on the Threat to the Freedom of Europe," March 17, 1948, p. 185; "Final Report as Chief of Staff," Dwight D. Eisenhower, February 7, 1948.
96. Letter to Admiral Forrest Sherman, March 15, 1948, Lippmann Papers, Sterling Library, Yale University.
97. "The Fortune Survey," *Fortune,* June 1948, p. 12.
98. PRO, FO 371/68051 AN 1675/356/45G, April 9, 1948.
99. PRO, FO 371/68014 AN 2076, May 24, 1948.
100. NA, RG 59 840.004-1348, Lovett to Douglas, April 14, 1948.
101. PRO, FO 371/75568 UE/6627/14/53G, October 27, 1949.
102. Friedberg, *In the Shadow,* p. 167.
103. Even during the Korean War, callups never exceeded more than 5 percent of age-eligible men and rarely rose above 1 percent before Selective Service was supplanted in 1973 by the all-volunteer force.
104. Francis Williams, *A Prime Minister Remembers: The War and the Post-War Memoirs of the Rt. Hon. Earl Attlee* (London: Heinemann, 1961), p. 172.
105. Hixson, *George F. Kennan,* p. 79.
106. PRO, FO 371/74183 AN 308/1053/45G, November 5, 1948.
107. Volker Koop, "No Struggle for Berlin?," published by Bouvier Verlag, 1998; Seidman, "Sam Walton."
108. PRO, FO 371/75568 UE/6627/14/53G, October 27, 1949.
109. Kovel, *Red Hunting,* p. 129.
110. Even during Vietnam, Marine Corps officer candidates, such as the author, would be quizzed by equally puzzled NCOs about whether they had ties to it or to any of the by then ancient Communist fronts.
111. *FRUS* 1945–50, "Emergence of the Intelligence Establishment," Document 292, NSC 10/2, June 18, 1948, p. 714.
112. Grose, *Operation Rollback,* pp. 96, 172.
113. Fromkin, "Daring Amateurism," p. 171.

114. Murray Kempton's phrase on Mayor of New York John V. Lindsay, as used during 1966–69.

115. "Morning Edition," National Public Radio, March 16, 2000, transcript, p. 10.

116. Isaacs and Downing, *Cold War,* p. 73.

117. Naval Historical Center, Records of the Strategic Plans Division, February 19, 1948, OP 30, 1948.

118. "A Portrait of American Public Opinion Through the Century," Gallup Poll Releases, Section 8: The Federal Income Tax, p. 7.

119. Tugwell, *Chronicle of Jeopardy,* p. 9.

120. Friedberg, *In the Shadow,* p. 103. Although Friedberg may overemphasize the impact of fiscal restraint in this instance, his book is the definitive study of the effect of liberal philosophy on U.S. national security policy.

121. Valuable work by the Cold War International History Project at the Woodrow Wilson International Center for Scholars has noted the constitution drafting, but not the designation of Seoul, for which see CIA, ORE 15-48.

122. The best supporting arguments for Stalin's early involvement are in Lee, "The Korean War." Dissenting views include those of Alexandre Y. Mansourov as presented at the AEI conference center, "The Outbreak of the Korean War," June 15, 1999.

123. National Security Archive, March 14, 1949, telegram to Molotov, "Khrono logiya," 1949–50, pp. 3, 6; Molotov draft submitted to Stalin and the Politburo, March 11, 1949; Kim telegram to Stalin, May 1, 1949.

124. ORE 3-49, "Consequences of U.S. Troop Withdrawal from Korea in Spring 1949," p. 1.

125. George Sansom's lecture to the Royal Institute of International Affairs, July 1947, RIIA archives.

126. Schaller, *American Occupation,* p. 82.

127. Schaller, *Altered States,* p. 14.

128. McGlothlen, *Controlling the Waves,* pp. 35–38; Kennan as cited in Holt, *Reluctant Superpower,* p. 153; Smith, *Japan,* p. 14, on compromising democracy.

129. PRO, FO 371/76215, Gascoigne to London, February 18, 1949.

130. PRO, FO 371/76215 F 2076/10345/23, February 11, 1949.

131. NA, Daily Summary, Executive Secretariat, U.S. Department of State, June 14, 1949, 2044 to London.

132. *Department of State Bulletin,* May 29, 1949, p. 696.

133. *New York Herald Tribune,* September 6, 1949.

134. Stebbins, *United States,* p. 54.

135. Sheng, *Battling Western Imperialism,* p. 194.

136. McGlothlen, *Controlling the Waves,* p. 140. U.S. business had invested only $100–$200 million in China, while the total value of U.S. trade fluctuated between $100–$125 million a year; Kennan re "empire" in Gardner, *Covenant,* p. 112; Kennan re Japanese control in Ball, *Cold War,* p. 55.

137. What became the Military Defense Assistance Program soon granted $1.314 billion just for 1949–50 to Greece, Turkey, Iran, the Philippines, South Korea, and to countries in Latin America and Western Europe — all this added upon $13.26 billion in outright gifts and grants and another $10.08 billion in reimbursable credits already extended to foreign countries since mid-1945 — 13.4 percent of total U.S. federal spending in those years.

138. Stebbins, *United States,* p. 82.

139. Ibid., p. 104.
140. *FRUS* 1948/1, GFK to Secretary of State, February 24, 1948, p. 509, re lack of knowledge; *FRUS* 1950/2, "Memorandum" by the Counselor of the Department to the Secretary of State, pp. 601, 607.
141. Sorley, *Thunderbolt*, p. 109.
142. Stebbins, *United States*, p. 23.
143. Leffler, *Preponderance*, p. 182; Pogue interview re Marshall and "fire."
144. NA, RG 59 841.248/61449, June 14, 1949; *Times* (London), June 24, 1949.
145. NA, RG 330, CCS 091.3GB, Olney Memorandum for Webb, "The Need for an Assessment of the Full Implications to American Security of the Current British Dollar Crisis," September 1, 1949.
146. NA, RG 59, "American Opinion," No. 9, September 5, 1949.
147. NA, RG 330, CCS 091.3GB, Olney to Webb.
148. As described by Oliver Franks, PRO, FO 371/74252 AN 2902/16313/45, December 2, 1949.
149. PRO, FO 371/76383, Gladwynn Jebb, Record of Conversation, September 20, 1949; NA, Bohlen Papers, Kennan in Position, October 12, 1949.
150. Strauss, *Men and Decisions*, p. 204.
151. NA, RG 59, Policy Planning, December 6, 1949, "Reaction of the American People to U.S. Use of Atomic Bomb in War"; Millis with Mansfield, *Arms and the State*, p. 246.
152. Nitze quoted in *New York Times*, April 23, 1999, p. A8; NA, Kennan in Policy Planning, 171st Mtg., December 16, 1949; for Acheson's opinions of Kennan, see Brinkley, *Dean Acheson*, pp. 79–92.
153. NA, December 6, 1949, "Reaction of the American People," Policy Planning paper.
154. Morgenstern, *Question of National Defense*, p. 125.
155. Reed and Kramish, "Trinity," pp. 32–34.
156. SE-14, "Soviet Capabilities for a Military Attack on the United States Before July 1952," October 23, 1951.
157. Kovel, *Red Hunting*, p. 131; R. C. Lewontin, "The Cold War and the Transformation of the Academy," in Schiffrin, ed., *The Cold War and the University*, pp. 20, 2.
158. Tugwell, *Chronicle of Jeopardy*, p. 168; Stebbins, *United States*, p. 87.
159. Louis Ridenour, "How Effective Are Radioactive Poisons in Warfare?," *Bulletin of the Atomic Scientists* (July 1950), p. 224.
160. Sherry, *In the Shadow*, p. 125.
161. NA, RG 59, Meeting File, Policy Planning, 148 Mtg., October 11, 1949.

Chapter 3: Getting the Habit (1950–1953)

1. When the third Archbishop of Paris in twenty-three years was murdered in 1871, for example, the last words of his chaplain were, "This is like Korea."
2. The common description of America launching itself on a "crusade" is offered, for example, in Evans, *American Century*, p. 396.
3. PRO, FO 371/83108 FJ1023/1G, Franks to Dening, June 4, 1950.
4. Gladwyn Jebb lecture to the Imperial Defence College, RIIA archives, February 24, 1950.
5. *FRUS* 1950, Vol. I, p. 260, "A Report to the President," April 7, 1950, as well as "Comments of the Bureau of the Budget," May 8, 1950, pp. 300–302.

6. Of the U.S. Army's ten divisions, only the 82nd Airborne was combat-ready. All others were at 60–70 percent strength, and training standards were low. U.S. Navy Archives, Ship Force Levels, Memorandum for the CNO, May 31, 1973, "Historic Ship Force Levels," p. 2.

7. Kovel, *Red Hunting*, p. 246; Isaacs and Taylor, *Cold War*, p. 88; Cummings, *Korea's Place*, p. 263.

8. Cold War International History Project, *Bulletin* 10, March 1997, p. 6.

9. Rodman, *More Precious*, p. 50; Katherine Weathersby on Kim taking the initiative, in Cold War International History Project, *Bulletin*, No. 6–7, Winter 1995/96, pp. 120–123; Leffler, *Preponderance*, p. 514, about Stalin's "acquiescence"; Andrew, *For the President's Eyes*, p. 184 re "persuaded."

10. Katherine Weathersby, "Soviet Aims in Korea and the Origins of the Korean War, 1945–1950: New Evidence from Russian Archives," Cold War International History Project, *Working Paper*, no. 8, November 1993.

11. *Sovetskaya Voennaya Entsiklopediya*, Vol. 8, p. 544.

12. National Security Archive, Molotov Telegram to Stalin, March 11, 1949.

13. National Security Archive, Kim telegram to Stalin, May 1, 1949.

14. Gen. Col. Yu. Votintsev, "Neizvestnyye Voiska Ischeznuvshey Sverzhderzhavy," Voennno-Istoricheskaya Zhurnal, No. 8, 1993, p. 57; see Lee, "The Korean War," for conclusive arguments.

15. S. N. Goncharov, John W. Lewis, and Xue Litai, *Uncertain Partners: Stalin, Mao, and the Korean War* (Stanford: Stanford University Press, 1993), p. 213.

16. Patterson, *Grand Expectations*, p. 213.

17. Schaller, *Altered States*, p. 32; Steel, *Walter Lippmann*, pp. 469–476.

18. Kenneth Younger Diary, July 6, 1950, on Aneurin Bevan being ready to back the U.S., with Attlee speaking of "evil."

19. Ridgway, *Soldier*, pp. 5, 6.

20. Philby, *Silent War*, pp. 213, 250.

21. Thomas, *Very Best Men*, p. 65.

22. "S. Korea Killed 2,000 Without Trial, U.S. Data Reveal," *New York Times*, April 21, 2000, p. A6.

23. Patterson, *Grand Expectations*, p. 211.

24. Acheson so described by Anthony Eden's secretary, Evelyn Shuckburgh, in Shuckburgh, *Descent*, p. 57.

25. PRO, FO 371/84087 FK 1022/128/G, July 12, 1950, Dixon minute.

26. NA, State Department Executive Secretariat, Daily Summary, January 3, 1952; the Red Army's strength was not a juggernaut of 175 divisions, since many of those divisions were not fully manned or equipped. But it certainly was one of 90 full-strength divisions.

27. NA, RG 330 Finletter to Johnson, July 7, 1950, CD 092.2 UK; Finletter also warned Truman that only one-tenth of U.S. striking power could operate intercontinentally. The rest of the punch would have to be delivered by B-50s and B-29s, the latter (despite its maximum range of 2,000 miles) being America's nuclear delivery system. It was deemed necessary to imply to Attlee that (as during the Berlin Airlift) the bombers would be "without the nuclear component"; July 9, 1950, Norstad to LeMay, JCS Files; August 9, 1950, Vandenberg to LeMay, JCS Files.

28. *Pravda*, November 27, 1950, signed, very penetrably, "Observer."

29. On "unconditional surrender," see D. Clayton James, *The Years of MacArthur*

(Boston: Houghton Mifflin, 1985), p. 489; on avenging angels, see Oliver Franks, PRO, FO 371/83014 F 1022/24F, August 5, 1950; Attlee's famous visit to Truman in December 1950, however, had less to do with fear of U.S. nuclear first-use, as is often thought, than with U.S. economic policy. His first meetings were with the Treasury Department.

30. Tugwell, *Chronicle of Jeopardy*, p. 224.

31. Andrew Greenwood, "The National Defense Stockpile: A Historical Perspective," *CRS Report for Congress*, December 14, 1994, p. 3.

32. Even before Congress passed the $1.2 billion mutual defense package for 1950–51, Truman asked for an additional $4 billion, with Greece, Turkey, and Iran receiving nearly $200 million.

33. Isenberg, *Shield of the Republic*, p. 223.

34. Brooks, *Seven Fat Years*, p. 209.

35. Paul Weaver, *The Suicidal Corporation* (New York: Simon and Schuster, 1988), pp. 210–212; for a different emphasis, see Friedberg, *In the Shadow*, p. 212, and "Saving the Steel Industry," Kennedy School of Government Case Program, C15-85-625, p. 2.

36. NA, RG 319, Army Ops General File, Section IV-A, December 20, 1950.

37. Acheson to Truman, December 6, 1950, President's Files, Truman Presidential Library.

38. Tor Egil Forland, "Selling Firearms to the Indians: Eisenhower's Export Control Policy, 1953–1954," *Diplomatic History* (Spring 1991), pp. 226–227.

39. PRO, Gen CAB 131/65, Air Chief Marshal Slessor to Attlee, November 23, 1950.

40. Forrest Pogue, General George C. Marshall's biographer, concluded that this was one of Lovett's pivotal contributions at this moment. As discussed with author.

41. Counting U.S. forces in Japan, there were nearly a half million American fighting men in the theater.

42. Ridgway letter to Robert Smith, as cited in *New York Times*, August 12, 1996.

43. Military Situation in the Far East (published as "MacArthur Hearings"), Joint Session of the Senate Committee on Armed Services and Foreign Relations, May 3, 1951, p. 307. Resorting to the ultimate Cold War epithet (fighting the battles, one might say, of the previous cold war), he warned that "to appease or otherwise surrender in Asia, would simultaneously undermine our efforts to halt [Communist] advance in Europe."

44. Donovan, *Tumultuous Years*, p. 176.

45. Ambrose, *Eisenhower*, p. 255; S. J. Ball, *Cold War*, p. 58; NSC 108 "Utilization of Manpower of Other Nations for Military Purposes," April 17, 1951.

46. Pogue, *Marshall: Statesman*, p. 495.

47. *New York Times*, May 14, 1993.

48. PRO, FO 371/100836, Gascoigne to Paul Mason, June 20, 1952; and see Gascoigne to Strang, May 20, 1952.

49. Schaller, *Altered States*, p. 46.

50. U.S. Senate, Committee on Armed Services and Committee on Foreign Relations, 82nd Congress, 1st Session, "Hearings to Conduct an Inquiry into the Military Situation in the Far East and the Facts Surrounding the Relief of General of the Army Douglas MacArthur, Assignments in That Area," 1951, Pt. 1: 312–313.

51. Schaller, *Altered States*, p. 46.

52. Bergsten, "World Economy," p. 98. Between 1950 and 1955, Japan's economy rose 7.3 percent per year, compared to average U.S. growth of 2.4 percent.

53. For the next decade, overall (and increasingly sophisticated) exports rose at least 20 percent a year with 30 percent of them eventually being absorbed by America.

54. Ch. III. Security (Article V: Follow U.N. Principles; Article VI: Allies to Leave Japan).

55. Chang, *Rape of Nanking*, p. 173.

56. Carleton Swift, interview; those particular dollars were the profits of a complicated Agency-bankrolled smuggling operation that used $2.8 million to bring large amounts of tungsten into the United States from Japan, the scarce metal then being sold to the Pentagon. Also see *New York Times*, October 9, 1994.

57. PRO, FO 371/101262 FZ 1193/53G, May 30, 1952.

58. Arnold, *First Domino*, p. 106.

59. NA, RG 218, CJCS 091 England, Bradley File. Omar Bradley to Air Chief Marshal Sir William Elliot, October 20, 1952.

60. PRO, FO 371/101267 FZ 1195/2, February 2, 1952, "Defense of South East Asia in the Context of Global Strategy."

61. NA, RG 330, January 2, 1952, Gen. Bradley to SecDef, "Defense of Southeast Asia," CD 337 Churchill/Truman.

62. NA, RG 59, Policy Planning, June 6, 1950, Paul Nitze, "East and South Asia," and *FRUS*, "Comments of the Bureau of the Budget" (note 5).

63. See Herman, *Joseph McCarthy*, pp. 110–112, in which accusations from McCarthy's list are examined against State Department security breaches.

64. *New York Times*, May 4, 1993.

65. Alger Hiss obituary, *New York Times*, November 16, 1996.

66. Senator Patrick Moynihan, "Secrecy as Government Regulation," Marver H. Bernstein Lecture, March 3, 1997, Georgetown University.

67. Kennan, *Memoirs*, p. 85; Sudoplatov, *Special Tasks*, pp. 84–85.

68. Krock, *Memoirs*, p. 261; *New York Times*, January 19, 1998, Richard Bernstein, "Books of the Times"; Krock admission on Rosenbergs to Roger Donald, editor of his memoirs.

69. Schrecker, *Many Are the Crimes*, pp. 199, 24.

70. Philby, *Silent War*, p. 229.

71. Albright and Kunstel, *Bombshell*, pp. 126–127, argues that the value for Moscow was "priceless," whereas Richard Rhodes, author of *Dark Sun*, argues that the plans that Hall transferred delayed rather than accelerated Soviet programs.

72. Bird, *Color of Truth*, p. 117.

73. Strauss, *Men and Decisions*, p. 259.

74. Testimony of John A. Waters, Director, Division of Security, AEC, Hearings Before Subcommittee on Reorganization, U.S. Senate, on Joint Resolution 21, 84th Congress, 1st Session, 1955.

75. Kovel, *Red Hunting*, p. 142.

76. Schrecker, *Many Are the Crimes*, p. 219.

77. Kovel, *Red Hunting*, p. 129; McCullough, *Truman*, p. 552; Schrecker, *Many Are the Crimes*, p. 209.

78. Kovel, *Red Hunting*, pp. 106, 130; note the CNN series' sixth program, "Reds," broadcast on November 1, 1998; General Lee Butler, USAF (ret.), National Press Club, February 2, 1998.
79. Acheson, *A Democrat Looks*, p. 177. A more expansive Gallup poll in 1954 — asking, "What do you think is the most important problem facing the country today?" — found 17 percent identifying "Communism in U.S." As cited in *New York Times*, August 1, 1999, "The Nation: What's the Problem?," Section 4, p. 4.
80. *Dictionary of American Biography*, Supplement 7, p. 626, column 2.
81. Acheson, *A Democrat Looks*, p. 155.
82. Patricia Bosworth, "The Lives They Lived: Diana Trilling," *New York Times Magazine*, December 29, 1996, p. 18.
83. *New York Times*, October 29, 1999, p. C20.
84. Chambers, *Witness*, p. 725.
85. Michael Dobbs, "Julius Rosenberg Spied, Russian Says," *Washington Post*, March 16, 1997.
86. Author's conversation with D. during the late 1970s.
87. Tony Kahn (host), Tony Kahn Productions, "Blacklisted," National Public Radio/Corporation for Public Broadcasting, 1997.
88. Billingsley, *Hollywood Party*, p. 242; and Dmytryk, *Odd Man Out*, p. 203.
89. "The Century in the Post: The Hollywood 10," *Washington Post*, May 30, 1999, p. F2; Isaacs and Downing, *Cold War*, p. 113.
90. Kazan, *A Life*, p. 449.
91. See Leab, "How Red Was My Valley," pp. 59–88.
92. Leab, " 'The Iron Curtain.' "
93. Daniel J. Robinson and David Kimmel, "The Queer Career of Homosexual Security Vetting in Cold War Canada," *Canadian Historical Review* (September 1994), p. 319.
94. Nasar, *A Beautiful Mind*, pp. 184–189.
95. On Kastler, see Foreman, "Behind Quantum Electronics," p. 174.
96. Schrecker, *Many Are the Crimes*, p. 370.
97. Taylor, *Grand Inquest*, p. 269; total figure undergoing clearance in Ralph S. Brown, "Loyalty-Security Measures," pp. 113, 117; Acheson, *A Democrat Looks*, pp. 154, 166.
98. Catholic University, Department of Archives, Constitution of the American Federation of Labor and Congress of Industrial Organizations, 1955; "Resolution on Expulsion of the URMWA and Withdrawal of Certificate of Affiliation," 11th Constitutional Convention, CIO, Box 2.
99. PRO, FO 371/100836 AS 10345, Gascoigne to Strang, May 20, 1952.
100. Watson, *Lion in the Lobby*, p. 169.
101. Williams, *Thurgood Marshall*, p. 257.
102. Nicholas von Hoffman, "Right About the Left," *Washington Post*, April 14, 1996.
103. Summers, *Official and Confidential*, p. 179.
104. Bosworth, *Anything Your Little Heart Desires*, p. 380.
105. NA, RG 129, Notorious Offender File, Gus Hall, Dr. Joseph Bartone, physical exam, and communications between attorney Richard Gladstein and Warden McDonald, FCI Leavenworth.
106. Ann Marks, interview, January 1999.

107. Swearingen, *FBI Secrets*, p. 34.

108. Summers, *Official and Confidential*, p. 259.

109. Bonavolonta and Duffy, *The Good Guys*, p. 163; Louis Freeh, "Remarks Before the 1996 Meeting of the World Economic Forum," February 4, 1996, www.fbi.gov; Robert Stewart, Chief of the DOJ Organized Crime Strike Force in Newark, noting "the distraction" in "How the Good Guys," p. 18.

110. *FRUS 1952–54*, Vol. VI, Pt. 1, minutes, January 7, 1952, p. 755.

111. Truman/Churchill Talks, January 1952, President's Secretary's Files, Truman Presidential Library.

112. *Washington Post*, June 19, 1952.

113. Isenberg, *Shield of the Republic*, p. 250.

114. See Simon, *Models of My Life*.

115. Foreman, "Behind Quantum Electronics," p. 181.

116. Needle, "Truth Is Our Weapon," pp. 405–408, 416, 418.

117. Herken, *Counsels of War*, p. 59.

118. Treverton, *Covert Action*, p. 42; on paramilitary, Thomas, *Very Best Men*, pp. 37–38.

119. Fineman, *A Special Relationship*, p. 135.

120. Andrew, *President's Eyes*, p. 193.

121. As reported to British diplomat J. W. Russell in Rome by Italy's Foreign Minister after his audience with Stalin. PRO, FO 371/100826 NS 1023/29, J. W. Russell to Paul Mason, October 2, 1952.

122. Hixson, *Kennan*, p. 125, citing Peer de Silva of the CIA. The highly emotional Kennan apparently feared he would break under torture and be forced to make statements damaging to the United States; also see PRO, Gascoigne to Strang, May 20, 1952, FO 371/100836 AS 10345.

123. PRO, FO 371/100826 NS 1023/29, J. W. Russell in Rome to Paul Mason, October 2, 1952.

124. *Forbes*, May 25, 1992, p. 316.

125. Immerman, ed., *Dulles*, p. 263; the slur is in Talbott, *Master of the Game*, p. 61.

126. Despite its economic boom, Washington believed it could only pass the estimated monthly rate of Soviet jet engine production in February 1953.

127. January 9, 1952, Third Formal Session, Truman/Churchill Talks, January 9, 1952, President's Secretary's File, Truman Presidential Library.

128. Gallup poll, "What's the Problem?" (note 79).

129. Friedberg, *In the Shadow*, is a superb antidote to beliefs of Cold War militarization.

130. A sample of this genre's well-received writings include Sherry's *In the Shadow of War*, Engelhardt's *Victory Culture*, Richard Fried's *Nightmare in Red* (New York: Oxford University Press, 1990), plus records of "Fifty Years of Conflict: The National Security State vs. Democracy," Institute of Policy Studies, Washington, DC, March 18, 1998. Kennan's quote is from "The G.O.P. Won the Cold War? Ridiculous," p. A21; as for "the military-industrial complex," see Reynolds, *One World Divisible*, p. 20; "military headquarters" is from Ernest May, "The U.S. Government," p. 218.

131. Wills, *John Wayne's America*, p. 164.

132. Many aspects of German and Japanese society earlier in the twentieth century might be seen as decent. Certainly much of the state apparatus in both

cases was characterized by the high technologies of the day. But neither society can be described as high tech to the extent that the most advanced means
of communication and mobility were widely dispersed.

133. Wills, *John Wayne's America*, p. 24.
134. Sherry, *In the Shadow of War*, p. xi.
135. Higgs, "The Cold War Economy," p. 292. From 1948 to 1989, real government nonmilitary spending increased 4.5 percent annually, with real military
spending growing at 1.9 percent.
136. Kiraly, "Aborted Soviet Military Plans," pp. 273–288. Also see the CIA analyses: ORE 8-50, "Evaluation of Soviet Yugoslav Relations (1950)," May 11,
1950, p. 1, NIE-15, "Probable Soviet Moves to Exploit the Present Situation,"
December 1950; NIE-29, "Probability of an Invasion of Yugoslavia in 1951,"
March 20, 1951, pp. 1, 4.
137. Library of Congress, Task Force Russia Documents, Box 42-17, Shtemenko to
Poskrebyshev, December 2, 1951; also see Douglas MacDonald, "Communist
Bloc Expansion," p. 181.
138. Tugwell, *Chronicle of Jeopardy*, p. 202.

Chapter 4: Nothing So Simple (1953–1956)

1. Moorhead, *Bertrand Russell*, p. 468. Some scholars dispute the claim that
Russell advocated a preemptive attack. See Nicholas Griffen, ed., *The Selected
Letters of Bertrand Russell: The Public Years, 1914–1970* (London: Routledge,
2001), pp. 426–428. Russell's advocacy of a U.S. nuclear strike — on
humanitarian grounds — is corroborated by Lord Lawson. See Letters, *The
Economist*, August 4, 2001, in which he recalls attending the 1948 speech. It
is more likely that Russell favored, between 1946 and 1947, the *threat* of an
attack in order to compel Moscow to accept international controls on nuclear
weapons. Nicholas Griffen and Kenneth Blackwell at the Bertrand Russell
Research Centre have helped me to clarify.
2. *FRUS 1952–54*, Vol. VI, September 18, 1953, Livingston Merchant, p. 669.
3. Engelhardt, *Victory Culture*, p. 75.
4. Fried, *Russians Are Coming*, p. 93.
5. Sloan, *Eisenhower*, p. 81.
6. Alexander, *Holding the Line*, p. 38.
7. NA, State Department, Executive Secretariat, Daily Summary, July 2, 1951.
8. *Public Papers*, Eisenhower, Item 50: "The Chance for Peace," delivered before
the American Society of Newspaper Editors, April 16, 1956, p. 182.
9. Blanche Cook, "First Comes the Lie: C. D. Jackson and Political Warfare," *Radical History Review*, No. 31 (1984), p. 56.
10. *FRUS 1952–54*, Vol. XV, Pt. 2, Korea, December 3, 1953, "Analysis of Possible Courses of Action in Korea," p. 1638.
11. The attacks by the Fifth Air Force's fighter-bombers on dams at Toksan and
then at Chosin were an apparently effective U.S. escalation of the war's intensity, made once armistice negotiations stalled. See Walter G. Hermes, *Truce
Tent and Fighting Front: The United States Army in the Korean War*, Office of the
Chief of Military History, United States Army, Washington, DC, 1966, pp.
460–461.
12. Calvin Sims, *New York Times*, June 25, 2000, p. 6; Defense Department statistics cited in *National Journal*, March 4, 2000, p. 719; also note the *Wall Street*

Journal's national security correspondent stating that between 1988 and 1991, "27,112 Americans died from drug overdoses — more than all the U.S. soldiers killed in the Korean War," in Fialka, *War by Other Means*, p. 140.

13. Sloan, *Eisenhower*, p. 100.

14. Isenberg, *Shield of the Republic*, p. 592.

15. Schwartz, ed., *Atomic Audit*, argues that about one third of the entire military budget from 1945 to 1995 ended up going to nuclear weapons, although the sums cannot help but become arbitrary. Reckoning in R&D costs, delivery systems, communications, and special security, they could add up to roughly $6 trillion, about equivalent to the entire Army or Navy budget since World War II.

16. *FRUS 1952–54*, Vol. II, Memorandum of discussion at the 165th mtg. of the National Security Council, October 7, 1953, pp. 514–534.

17. Gaddis, *Strategies*, p. 166.

18. Ibid. Gaddis shows how the New Look was actually more versatile, linking nuclear deterrence, alliances, psychological warfare, and covert action. See pp. 158–182.

19. Sloan, *Eisenhower*, p. 35.

20. As quoted by Lawrence Korb in Schmertz, *President Reagan*, p. 243.

21. William Pfaff, "Markets Must Be Guided? Tell That to Prospering Sweden," *International Herald Tribune*, October 20, 1997; Isaacs and Downing, *Cold War*, p. 247.

22. Kunz, *Butter and Guns*, p. 2; Isaacs and Downing, *Cold War*, p. 363.

23. Reynolds, *One World Divisible*, p. 511, repeats the common mistake that public spending permitted the creation and widespread adoption of microelectronic innovations, rather than just affected the timing — for better or worse.

24. See arguments by Russet et al. in "Did Americans' Expectations."

25. Engelhardt, *End of Victory Culture*, p. 79.

26. Isenberg, *Shield of the Republic*, p. 729.

27. Tugwell, *Chronicle of Jeopardy*, p. 435.

28. PRO, FO 371/103514 AU 1024/65G, Roberts to Dixon, August 15, 1953.

29. Kunz, *Butter and Guns*, p. 69; and as described by the President in Helsinki during March 1997; the Russian view on the Pact is in L. S. Khalkatsi, "Koreyskaya Voyna i Sovetsko-Amerikansiye Otnosheniya," in L. N. Nezhenskiy, ed., *Sovetskaya Bneshnyaya Politika v Gody Kholodnoy Voiny (1945–1985)* (Moscow, 1995), p. 191.

30. Fairlie, *Kennedy Promise*, p. 173.

31. See Cecil B. Currey, *Edward Lansdale: The Unquiet American* (Washington: Brassey's, 1998) for the scope of Lansdale's involvements. Details are available in the Lansdale Papers, National Security Archive.

32. Philby, *Silent War*, p. 169; Roosevelt quote in the CIA's history of Operation Ajax, "Overthrow of Premier Mossadeq of Iran, November 1952–August 1953," March 1954, CIA Clandestine Service History.

33. Samuel Halpern quoted in Kermit Roosevelt's obituary, *New York Times*, June 11, 2000, p. 37.

34. "A Survey of Foreign Policy Problems," January 27, 1953, in JFD Papers, Vol. III, E. Speeches, Statements, Press Conferences, Box 310.

35. *FRUS 1952–54*, Vol. XIV, Pt. 2, China and Japan, "United States Objectives and Courses of Action with Respect to Japan," NSC, June 29, 1953.

36. Schaller, *Altered States*, p. 65.
37. *FRUS* 1955–57, Japan, NSC Policy Paper 5516, April 9, 1955, p. 19, and Dulles, Department of State, Central Files, 003.9411/83155, Memcom, August 31, 1955, p. 113. The half billion in materiel is reckoned at replacement value.
38. Dulles, "A Survey of Foreign Policy Problems"; Eisenhower's first State of the Union in Fred L. Israel, ed., *The State of the Union Messages of the Presidents, 1790–1966*, vol. III (New York: Chelsea House, 1966), p. 3014.
39. Immerman, *John Foster Dulles*, p. 16.
40. Arnold, *First Domino*, p. 127.
41. *FRUS* 1952–54, Vol. XIII Pt 1 Indochina, quoting General Vandenberg, April 24, 1953, p. 502; Eisenhower at 141st NSC mtg. on April 28, 1953.
42. McKeever, *Adlai Stevenson*, p. 288.
43. British alarm, as well as the extent to which France was echoing British arguments, is shown in PRO, FO 371/101276 FZ1195/2, "Defence of South East Asia in Global Strategy."
44. NA, State Department, Executive Secretariat, Daily Summary, September 22, 1950.
45. See "The United States Government and the Vietnam War," Part I, 1945–61, U.S. Senate Committee on Foreign Relations, 98th Congress, 2nd Session, p. 129.
46. Stennis quote in Arnold, *First Domino*, p. 143.
47. Sorley, *Thunderbolt*, p. 132.
48. *FRUS* 1952–54, Vol. XIII, Pt. 1, Indochina, the Ambassador in the Soviet Union (Bohlen) to the Dept. of State, April 12, 1954, p. 1310.
49. *Public Papers*, Eisenhower, Item 63: "The President's News Conference," March 24, 1954 p. 343.
50. Ibid., News Conference, April 7, 1954, p. 383.
51. *FRUS* 1952–54, Vol. VI, Western Europe and Canada, WSC to DDE, March 24, 1954, p. 1015.
52. Moran, *Churchill*, p. 405.
53. PRO, FO 371/112057/360G, record of Churchill-Radford dinner, Chequers, April 26, 1954.
54. *FRUS* 1952–54, Vol. XIII, Indochina, DDE to WSC, April 4, 1954, p. 1240; "fight for it" on p. 1256; and LBJ April 5, 1954, p. 1224.
55. *FRUS* 1952–54, Vol. XIII, Indochina, April 21, 1954, Saigon to State, p. 1360, and MacArthur to State, April 23, 1954, p. 1371.
56. *FRUS* 1952–54, Vol. XIII, Indochina, 194th NSC mtg., April 29, 1954, p. 1440.
57. Shuckburgh, *Descent to Suez*, diary for May 3, 1954, p. 189.
58. *FRUS* 1952–54, Vol. XIII, Pt. 2, Indochina, "Memorandum of Conversation with the President," May 19, 1954, p. 1584.
59. Arnold, *First Domino*, p. 187.
60. *FRUS* 1952–54, Vol. XIII, Indochina, 202nd NSC mtg., June 17, 1954, p. 1716.
61. *FRUS* 1952–54, Vol. XIII, Indochina, WSC to DDE, June 21, 1954; re "jungle warfare," PRO, FO 371/109100 AU 1013/21.
62. Tugwell, *Chronicle of Jeopardy*, p. 444.
63. NA, Dictabelt transcript, released June 12, 1997, Eisenhower mtg. with Roy Howard, February 24, 1955; Rodman, *More Precious*, p. 71.

64. *FRUS* 1952–54, Vol. XIII, Pt. 2, Indochina, "reluctance" in "Memorandum of Conversation with the President," August 17, 1954, p. 1953; re "aggression" see "The S.E.A. Collective Defense Treaty" in *FRUS* 1954, Vol. XII, Pt. 1, East Asia and the Pacific, pp. 839–848.

65. *FRUS* 1952–54, Vol. VI, Pt. 1, Western Europe and Canada, Mtg. of Dulles and Eden, June 29, 1954, p. 1117.

66. *New York Times*, May 4, 1993.

67. Meers, "British Connection," p. 417.

68. Saunders, *Cultural Cold War,* pp. 139, 141.

69. National Security Archive, Document 1, "CIA and Guatemala Assassination Proposals, 1952–54," CIA History Staff Analysis, Gerald K. Haines, June 1995, pp. 3–6 re "disposal list," p. 3 re "rifles," and p. 6 for "criteria"; Document 2 contains the unsigned, undated manual.

70. Meers, "British Connection," p. 417.

71. Ibid., p. 422.

72. Salisbury, *Without Fear,* pp. 142–143; Tom Weiner, "Role of CIA in Guatemala," *New York Times,* June 6, 1997, p. A25.

73. Roger Donald interview, March 2000.

74. Meers, "British Connection," p. 417.

75. Frederick Hitz quoted in Clifford Krauss, "The Spies Who Never Came in from the Cold War," *New York Times,* March 7, 1999; see *Guatemala: Never Again,* April 24, 1998, report of the Recovery of Historical Memory Project, conducted by the Human Rights Office, Archdiocese of Guatemala.

76. Anderson, *Che Guevara,* p. 163, and pp. 150–159 for Anderson's perspective of the U.S. role.

77. Anthony Eden, *Full Circle: Memoirs of the Rt. Honorable Anthony Eden* (London: Casell, 1960), p. 634.

78. Allen W. Dulles, "The Soviet Challenge," in Elbers and Duncan, *Scientific Revolution,* p. 39.

79. Interview with Walter Pforzheimer, former CIA head of congressional relations, June 1999.

80. Treverton, *Covert Action,* p. 231.

81. *United States–Vietnamese Relations,* 1945–1967 (Study Prepared for the Department of Defense), Vol. 10 (Washington: GPO, 1971), p. 737.

82. CDJ to W. W. Rostow, December 31, 1952, Jackson Papers, Box 75, Eisenhower Presidential Library.

83. Saunders, *The Cultural Cold War,* pp. 225–226.

84. Kovel, *Red Hunting,* p. 180.

85. Lichenstein interview, July 1998.

86. Grose, *Gentleman Spy,* p. 219, for Bruce and Lovett quotes. However, Grose bases his findings on notes taken originally by Arthur Schlesinger Jr. The original report has not been found.

87. John le Carré, *The Secret Pilgrim* (New York: Knopf, 1990), p. 206.

88. Re subsidies, see Tugwell, *Chronicle of Jeopardy,* p. 473.

89. *New York Times*, March 3, 1955.

90. *Time*, January 14, 1952, p. 18.

91. Robert Sevigny interview, December 2000, citing the AEC report to the Joint Committee on Atomic Energy, June 19, 1951.

92. Hacker, "Radiation Safety," p. 52.

93. "Report by the Director of Military Application, Summary of A.E.C. Relationships Between the A.E.C. and the Photographic Industry Regarding Radioactive Contamination from Atomic Weapons Tests, from January Through December, 1951," 1953, via the Institute for Energy and Environmental Research, Takoma Park, MD.

94. "Poisoned Workers and Poisoned Places," *USA Today*, September 7, 2000, pp. A4–5.

95. Hale, Lushbaugh, and Spaulding, *Comparative Study of Experimentally Produced Beta Lesions and Skin Lesions in the Utah Sheep Range*, Los Alamos Scientific Laboratory, November 30, 1953; *Bulloch v. United States*, 133 F. Supp. 885, 1955 US District Court. The case was appealed (Bulloch II, 95 F.R.D. 123, 1982 U.S. District). It was eventually reversed and remanded by the U.S. Supreme Court on November 23, 1983.

96. Schwartz, ed., *Atomic Audit*, p. 421.

97. *New York Times*, April 1, 1954.

98. Nicholas Kristof, "An Atomic Age Eden," *New York Times*, March 5, 1997.

99. A. Costandina Titus, "Selling the Bomb: Public Relations by the Atomic Energy Commission During the 1950s and Early 1960s," *Government Publications Review* 16 (1989), p. 246.

100. *Las Vegas Sun* editorial, February 18, 1955; *Las Vegas Review-Journal*, editorial, February 18, 1955.

101. See the National Academy of Science, Archives, Committees on Biological Effects of Atomic Radiation, Agriculture and Food Supplies, Summary Report, 1956.

102. J. Laurence Kulp, Columbia University, to Division of Biology and Medicine, January 18, 1955, AEC, documents from the Advisory Committee on Human Radiation Testing.

103. Kovel, *Red Hunting*, pp. 105–106; Engelhardt, *Victory Culture*, p. 7.

104. JoAnne Brown, "A Is for Atom," p. 81.

105. Engelhardt, *Victory Culture*, p. 88.

106. Killian, *Sputnik, Scientists, and Eisenhower*, p. 68.

107. Andrew, *President's Eyes*, p. 221.

108. Pedlow and Welzenbach, *CIA and the U-2 Program*, p. 111; LeMay cited in Schwartz, ed., *Atomic Audit*, p. 173.

109. For example, see Gallup poll for 1954, as shown in "What's the Problem?," *New York Times*, August 1, 1999, p. 4.

110. Alsop and Alsop, *Reporter's Trade*, p. 214.

111. Matthew Josephson, "The Big Guns," *The Nation*, January 14, 1956, p. 33.

112. Killian and Hill, "For a Continental Defense," p. 40; Tugwell, *Chronicle of Jeopardy*, p. 411.

113. As cited in Foreman, "Beyond Quantum Electronics," p. 221.

114. *Aviation Week*, April 16, 1956, p. 66; *The Emerging Shield: The Air Force and the Evolution of Continental Air Defense 1945–1960* (USAF Office of the Historian, 1991), p. 210.

115. TIAS 3218, "Establishment in Canada of Warning and Control System Against Air Attack, United States Treaties and Other International Agreements," Vol. 6, Pt. 1 (Washington: GPO, 1955), pp. 763–772.

116. *Science Digest*, July 26, 1956, pp. 25–26.

117. Ibid., pp. 28–29.

118. NA, ODP, "Abstracts from Papers Pertaining to Outdoor Lighting," Report of the Civilian Light Control Session at the Illuminating Engineering Society, September 17, 1954.

119. President's Advisory Committee on a National Highway Program (Washington: GPO, 1955), pp. 5, 158–159.

120. Testimony of General Lucius D. Clay in U.S. Congress, Senate, Committee on Public Works, "A National Highway Program," Hearings Before the Senate Committee on Public Works, 84th Congress, 1st Session (Washington: GPO, 1955), p. 128.

121. Helen Leavitt, *Superhighway-Superhoax* (Garden City, NY: Doubleday, 1970), p. 34.

122. Testimony of Major General Paul F. Yount, "A National Highway Program," p. 158.

123. Ibid., p. 6.

124. Testimony of D. K. Chacey, U.S. Congress, Senate, Committee on Public Works, Defense Highway Needs, 86th Congress, 2nd Session (Washington: GPO, 1960), p. 13.

125. Ibid. "In the days of the guided missile there is more potential in the use of this highway if it is in suburban areas."

126. Bohlen, *Witness to History*, p. 346.

127. Lucius Battle, Oral History, June 23, 1971, Truman Presidential Library.

128. Acheson, *A Democrat Looks*, pp. 86, 99.

129. Brinkley, *Dean Acheson*, p. 80.

130. Ibid., p. 90.

131. Ibid., p. 91.

132. *Washington Post*, November 10, 2000, p. A5.

133. NA, USAF, Escape and Evasion Section of the 6004th Air Intelligence Service Squadron, Report, October 19, 1955.

134. *Washington Post*, May 11, 1997.

135. Peebles, *Shadow Flights*, pp. 49–53.

136. Pedlow and Welzenbach, *The CIA*, pp. 75, 96.

137. Ibid., pp. 110, 112, 124.

138. Walter Lippmann, "The Administration Mind," *Washington Post*, January 20, 1955.

Chapter 5: Settling In for the Long Haul (1956–1961)

1. Bird, *Color of Truth*, citing John Kenneth Galbraith's approving recollection of how his Cambridge colleagues regarded Khrushchev, p. 137.

2. Khrushchev quoted in "Russia's War: Blood in the Snow," television documentary, Part Four.

3. CDJ to William Jackson, May 9, 1956, and CDJ to Luce, May 10, 1956, Box 52, Eisenhower Presidential Library.

4. Saunders, *Cultural Cold War*, pp. 303–304.

5. Coleman, *Decline and Fall*, p. 82.

6. John Foster Dulles, Telephone Memorandum Series, Box 5, Nixon-Dulles Phone Conversation, October 31, 1956, Eisenhower Presidential Library; Pedlow and Welzenbach, *The CIA*, p. 123.

7. As discussed with Laszlo Valki, professor of international law, Eotvos University, Budapest. Author's interview, March 1989.

8. Wolfe, *Man Without a Face*, p. 92; the utter lack of preparation for Hungary's tragedy is apparent in National Security Archive, "U.S. Policy Toward Developments in Poland and Hungary," NSC 5616, October 31, 1956.

9. Working Notes from the Session of the CPSU CC Presidium on November 1, 1956 (regarding Point I of Protocol No. 50), in Mark Kramer, Cold War International History Project, *Bulletin*, Nos. 8–9 (1996/97), pp. 388–410.

10. National Security Archive, see the Working Notes of the CPSU CC Presidium, October 21–November 4, 1956, for arguments among Khrushchev, Molotov, Suslov, Zhukov, Brezhnev, et al.

11. Shuckburgh, *Descent to Suez*, diary entries for March 4, 1951, p. 111, January 24, 1953, p. 75, and December 16, 1951, p. 29.

12. Kunz, *Butter and Guns*, p. 75. Since 1950, the United States had distributed about $30 million worth of military equipment over the Middle East, Israel receiving almost $8 million and Saudi Arabia over $20 million, while Egypt, Syria, Iraq, Lebanon, and Jordan divided the rest. (This was in addition to humanitarian grants of what would be $712 million to the Palestinians from 1950 to 1972.)

13. Churchill, *Anthony Eden*, p. 255.

14. Riley, *Philby*, p. 83, concerning Young and poisoning, Wright, *Spycatcher*, pp. 159, 161, says it was nerve gas.

15. David Rees, *The Age of Containment* (New York: St. Martin's Press, 1967), p. 63.

16. "November 1956 Staff Memoranda," November 5, 1956, Memorandum of a Conference with the President, Box 19, Diary Series, Ann Whitman File, EP, Eisenhower Presidential Library.

17. Ambrose, *Eisenhower*, p. 425; Kunz, *Butter and Guns*, pp. 86–87.

18. Pedlow and Welzenbach, *The CIA*, pp. 116–117, 122–124, emphasis in the original.

19. John Emmet Hughes, *The Ordeal of Power: A Political Memoir of the Eisenhower Years* (New York: Atheneum, 1963), p. 220.

20. *FRUS 1952–54*, Vol. VI, Pt. 1, July 22, 1954, DDE to WSC, pp. 1047–1048; Wong, *Footsteps of Mr. Kurtz*, p. 65.

21. Ayittey, *Africa in Chaos*, p. 7.

22. Isenberg, *Shield of the Republic*, p. 700.

23. Rodman, *More Precious*, p. 66.

24. Piers Brendon, *Ike: His Life and Times* (New York: Harper and Row, 1986), p. 257.

25. Eveland, *Ropes of Sand*, p. 250.

26. Ibid., p. 252.

27. Isenberg, *Shield of the Republic*, p. 714.

28. Gendizer, *Notes from the Minefield*, p. 366.

29. Isenberg, quoting Burke, in *Shield of the Republic*, p. 715.

30. Peebles, *Shadow Flights*, p. 218.

31. Bernstein, *Guns or Butter*, p. 326; *New York Times*, November 24, 1963.

32. As cited in Sloan, *Eisenhower*, p. 53.

33. *Washington Post*, January 26, 1951.

34. Cummings, *Korea's Place*, p. 441.

35. Sherry, *In the Shadow*, p. 147.

36. *New York Times*, March 19, 1998.

37. Duberman, *Paul Robeson*, p. 432; Robeson Archives, Army Intelligence to FBI, May 13, 1947, 100-25857-2891 and FBI New York 100-38128-244.
38. NA, RG 59, 745J.00/3-557, Despatch 242 from Accra, March 3, 1957.
39. NA, Memorandum for the White House from Brig. Gen. Andrew Goodpaster, "Treatment of Minorities in the United States," December 31, 1958, 811.411/12-458 (Goodpaster Report); *The West African Pilot*, September 30, 1958.
40. Ibid., Goodpaster Report.
41. Saunders, *Cultural Cold War*, p. 291.
42. NA, RG 59, 811.411. Despatch 1031, Stockholm to State, April 16, 1956.
43. NA, RG 59, 811.411, The Hague to State, September 24, 1957; February 11, 1958, *al-Gumhuriyah*.
44. NA, RG 59 811.411, Djakarta/USIS to State, October 7, 1957.
45. A&E Network, rebroadcast, June 9, 1997.
46. NA, RG 59, 811.411, The Hague to State, January 30, 1959; RG 59, 811.411, AmConsul Port Elizabeth to State, November 13, 1957; RG 59 811.411, Circular, October 10, 1957. "Talking Points to Overcome Adverse Reaction to Little Rock" were distributed to all East European and African posts.
47. Morris J. MacGregor Jr., *Integration of the Armed Forces, 1940–1965* (Washington: GPO, 1981), p. 579. This report was done for the Army's Center for Military History.
48. Hanson W. Baldwin, "ICBM," *Collier's*, March 16, 1956.
49. Eric Smoodin, "Watching the Skies: Hollywood, the 1950s, and the Soviet Threat," *Journal of American Culture*, Summer 1988, pp. 35–37.
50. Joseph Alsop and Stewart Alsop, "The New Balance of Power," *Encounter*, May 1958, p. 4.
51. Killian, *Sputnik, Scientists, and Eisenhower*, p. 10.
52. Dulles in Ebbers and Duncan, *Scientific Revolution*, p. 74.
53. Letter to the editor from Dr. Leonard Reiffel, who was then working on USAF contracts at Chicago's Armour Research Foundation, *Nature*, May 4, 2000.
54. Dulles in Elbers and Duncan, *Scientific Revolution*, p. 37.
55. Herbert Stein, interview, February 1999.
56. William Broad, "Spy Satellites' Early Role," *New York Times*, September 12, 1995, p. C1.
57. Pedlow and Welzenbach, *The CIA*, p. 144.
58. Ibid., p. 146; Peebles, *Shadow Flights*, re "shot himself," p. 213, and "mobilization," p. 112; R. Cargill Hall in McDonald, ed., *Corona*, p. 41, suggests that these intrusions might have been a reason for new Soviet production of jet fighters and surface-to-air missiles.
59. Lee Auspitz, correspondence with the author, April 2001.
60. Matthew Lyon, discussion with the author, March 2000; Lebow, *Information Highways*, p. 178.
61. Hafner and Lyon, *Wizards*, p. 41; Roberts, "The ARPANET," p. 169.
62. *The Decline of the U.S. Machine-Tool Industry and Prospects for Its Sustainable Recovery* (Santa Monica, CA: Rand Corp, 1994), Vol. 2, p. 106; $273 million was initially committed to develop these tools for working on bombers.
63. Elbers and Duncan, *Scientific Revolution*, p. 255.

64. Burt Solomon, "For High Schools, Small Is Beautiful," *National Journal*, May 29, 1999, p. 1484.

65. *On Further Examination: Report of the Advisory Panel on the Scholastic Aptitude Test Score Decline* (New York: College Entrance Examination Board, 1977). While real spending would double, then triple, for K-12 education, SAT scores plunged well beyond what could be explained by reckoning in the absorption of large and previously neglected minority groups.

66. Bill Clinton, "The President's Radio Address," *Public Papers*, February 8, 1997, p. 133.

67. Louis Menard, "How to Make a Ph.D. Matter," *New York Times Magazine*, September 22, 1996, p. 80. Between 1910 and 1990, federal money for academic research grew by a factor of 25.

68. Isenberg, *Shield of the Republic*, pp. 302, 742.

69. Dr. Otis B. Brown, "Scientific Utility of Naval Environmental Data," published by Medea (Measurements of Earth Data for Environmental Analysis), University of Miami, June 1995; the geophysicist quoted is Gordon MacDonald, University of California at San Diego, in *New York Times*, November 28, 1995.

70. Raymond Siever, "Doing Earth Science Research During the Cold War," in Schiffren, *The Cold War and the University*, p. 162.

71. McDougall, "Sputnik," p. 24.

72. Haines, "C.I.A.'s Role."

73. Crane Brinton et al., *A History of Civilization* (New York: Prentice Hall, 1955), p. 448.

74. Watson and Petre, *Father and Son*, p. 230.

75. Galbraith, *Affluent Society*, p. 86; see Paul Krugman's similarly skeptical treatment of Galbraith in "The Ascent of E-Man," *Fortune*, May 24, 1999.

76. Elbers and Duncan, *Scientific Revolution*, p. 6.

77. C. W. Borklund, *Men of the Pentagon: From Forrestal to McNamara* (New York: Praeger, 1966), p. 186.

78. Personal conversation at the Council on Foreign Relations, 1983.

79. Isenberg, *Shield of the Republic*, p. 68.

80. The temper of the times is shown well in Snead, *The Gaither Committee*.

81. Tobin, "The Eisenhower Economy," p. 324.

82. "Sputnik and the Budget," *Fortune*, November 1957, p. 126.

83. Chalmers Roberts, *Washington Post*, December 20, 1957.

84. Schwartz, ed., *Atomic Audit*, p. 314; "preventive war" being articulated by Robert C. Sprague, as discussed in Perret, *Eisenhower*, pp. 563–564.

85. *The Nation*, August 17, 1957, citing MacArthur's speech to shareholders, p. 62; Ambrose, *Eisenhower*, p. 460.

86. The S&P average annual return was 18.9 percent from 1942 to 1958, with that from 1982 to 1997 being 18.4 percent. Growth was almost identical to that of the post-1982 bull market, and the mild 1957–58 recession was deemed only a check on inflation.

87. *New York Times*, as cited in Elbers and Duncan, *Scientific Revolution*, p. 58; Reeves, *President Kennedy*, p. 540.

88. Lee, *CIA Estimates*, pp. 159, 169.

89. Such a description comes from his assertion that, had he known in 1934 that "millions of people are dying in the Soviet experiment," he would not have

renounced communism because "the chance of a new world being born in great suffering would still have been worth backing." See Conquest, *Reflections*, pp. 10–11.

90. *FRUS 1958–60*, Vol. XVIII, NSC Policy Paper 6008/1, June 11, 1960, pp. 335–349; U.S. direct private investment in Japan by 1960 was still relatively modest at $180 million; author's correspondence with Chalmers Johnson, June 2001.
91. NA, RG 59, 794/6-2958, Memcon, MacArthur, July 29, 1958; 794.00/5-2760, May 27, 1960, "Liberal Democratic Party Secretary General Appeals for Funds"; Schaller, *Altered States*, p. 136.
92. Schwartz, *Atomic Audit*, p. 130.
93. Finletter, *Foreign Policy*, p. 30.
94. Isenberg, *Shield of the Republic*, p. 425; the armed forces were also in a vicious circle of "becoming the biggest vocational training school in the United States," recalls one personnel director in Borklund, *Men of the Pentagon* (note 77), p. 184.
95. Isenberg, *Shield of the Republic*, p. 672.
96. Morgenstern, *Question of National Defense*, p. 209.
97. Isenberg, *Shield of the Republic*, p. 726.
98. Dean Golembeski, "What Sank the *Thresher?*," *Innovation and Technology*, Summer 1997, p. 30.
99. Schwartz, ed., *Atomic Audit*, p. 147.
100. Morgenstern, *Question of National Defense*, p. 111.
101. Ibid., p. 128.
102. Ibid., p. 126.
103. Ibid., p. 120.
104. Ibid., p. 45.
105. Paul Nitze, "Limited Wars or Massive Retaliation," *The Reporter*, September 5, 1957, p. 41; and Nitze, *From Hiroshima to Glasnost*, p. 298.
106. *Statement by the General Advisory Committee of the U.S. Atomic Energy Commission*, May 4, 1959.
107. Gallagher, *American Ground Zero*, pp. xxv, xxiii.
108. National Security Archive, Medical Research Branch, Division of Biology and Medicine, AEC, November 26, 1963, Doc. No. 1026268-71; on mutations, Oak Ridge Intra-Laboratory correspondence, W. S. Snyder to K. Z. Morgan, December 17, 1963, Doc. No. 1026272.
109. National Security Archive, Instructions for the Expenditure of Nuclear Weapons in Accordance with the Presidential Authorization, May 22, 1957, revised 1959.
110. *Technology Review*, October 1996, p. 24; Pedlow and Welzenbach, *The CIA*, p. 135.
111. Kissinger consistently addressed Eisenhower's inadequate defense preparations, arguing that existing trends would "doom our diplomacy to futility" while writing vapidly about "an absence of clear American purpose" and concluding that "vacillating policies will prove disastrous to everybody." See, for example, *New York Times Magazine*, March 8, 1959, pp. 78, 77, and *New York Times*, Letter to the Editor, February 15, 1960, which helped make the case for General Power's $500 million.
112. *Washington Post*, September 18, 1998, p. A3, emphasis in original. The assertion, with underlining for emphasis, is also made in "An Intelligence Success

Story: The U-2 Program: The DCI's Perspective," *Studies in Intelligence* (Winter 1998–1999), published by the CIA, and is repeated by the Brookings Institution in Schwartz, ed., *Atomic Audit*, p. 490. Loath to acknowledge mistakes, the CIA did so only by telephone (July 2001) in response to the author's written request for clarification.

113. Beschloss, *May Day*, p. 334.
114. Central Intelligence Agency, NIE 11-8-1960, August 1, 1960. Note chart 29157 7-60.
115. Roland S. Inlow, "How the Cold War and Intelligence Problems Influenced Corona Operations," in McDonald, ed., *Corona*, pp. 114–129.
116. This strange deployment was due to the already serious Soviet lag in electronics that required aligning the guidance system with the target, a technological shortcoming not known to western intelligence.
117. Interview with Walter Pforzheimer, former CIA head of congressional relations, June 1999.
118. Grose, *Gentleman Spy*, p. 462.
119. *Newsweek*, April 14, 1989.
120. *Public Papers*, Eisenhower, Item 421, "Farewell Radio and Television Address to the American People," January 17, 1961, pp. 1039, 1038.
121. Ambrose, *Eisenhower*, p. 522.
122. Schlesinger, *A Thousand Days*, pp. 197–198; "winning" in Hilsman, *To Move a Nation*, pp. 440, 467.

Chapter 6: The Burden and the Glory (1961–1963)

1. Fairlie, *Kennedy Promise*, p. 106.
2. Ibid., p. 71; Isenberg, *Shield of the Republic*, p. 753.
3. *Public Papers*, Kennedy, Item 1: "Inaugural Address," January 20, 1961, p. 2.
4. Schlesinger, "On Heroic Leadership," pp. 3–11.
5. McNamara, *In Retrospect*, pp. 207, 323.
6. Halberstam, *Best and Brightest*, p. 41.
7. Arthur Schlesinger Jr., *The Imperial Presidency* (Boston: Houghton Mifflin, 1973), p. 169.
8. Schlesinger cited in Kunz, *Butter and Guns*, pp. 126–127; Reeves, *President Kennedy*, p. 261.
9. Norman Podhoretz, "The Kennedy Myths," *Wall Street Journal*, July 29, 1999.
10. Fairlie, *Kennedy Promise*, p. 70.
11. Erwin Glikes, ed., introduction by Arthur Schlesinger Jr., *Of Poetry and Power: Poems Occasioned by the Presidency and by the Death of John F. Kennedy* (New York: Basic Books, 1964), a fatuously sentimentalized anthology by a cross-section of American poets celebrating John Kennedy; JFK, as cited in Fairlie, *Kennedy Promise*, p. 222.
12. Kazin, *Contemporaries*, p. 373.
13. *New York Times*, December 27, 1959.
14. Pointon, "Imagining Nationalism," p. 370.
15. National Arts Legislation, Hearings on S. 165 and S. 1316, Before the Special Subcommittee on the Arts of the Senate Comm. on Labor and Public Welfare, 88th Congress, p. 49, quoting Senator Hubert Humphrey, p. 50.
16. As described in "Great American Monuments," production of the History Channel, 1998.

17. John Emmet Hughes, *America the Vincible* (Garden City, NY: Doubleday, 1959).

18. Malraux, *Felled Oaks*, p. 55.

19. Ward Just, Bundy obituary, *Newsweek*, September 30, 1996.

20. *New York Times* obituary, September 17, 1996, quoting Max Frankel's profile; on "Zionists," see Beschloss, *Taking Charge*, p. 226; Halberstam in Bird, *Color of Truth*, p. 134.

21. Ward Just, *Newsweek* (note 19).

22. White, *Making of the President*, p. 406.

23. McMaster, *Dereliction of Duty*, p. 215; an example of the casualness with which the history of this era is often treated is the belief expressed in a *New York Times Book Review* essay, "Members of the Club," by Mark Dancer (April 4, 1999, p. 7) that it was James Forrestal, the long-deceased first Secretary of Defense, rather than his son, Michael, who worked for Bundy; Michael's claim to then knowing little of the Far East was first made to me in 1975.

24. Like Kahn, Douhet's and Ardant du Picq's doctrines also combined romantic intensity and speculations on the nature of society in the ringing idiom of military science.

25. As quoted in Hilty, *Robert Kennedy*, p. 258.

26. *New York Times*, March 26, 1961.

27. *Public Papers, Kennedy*, Item 475: "Remarks at a Rally in Fort Worth in Front of the Texas Hotel," November 22, 1963, p. 887.

28. The economy was growing more quickly than defense spending, however, thereby permitting the defense component of GDP to keep declining. See Friedberg, *In the Shadow*, p. 140.

29. Shapley, *Promise and Power*, p. 232.

30. Ibid., p. 246.

31. *Public Papers, Kennedy*, Item 234: "Commencement Address at Yale University," June 11, 1962, pp. 470–475.

32. An overview of applying microeconomic principles to policy issues is Zeckhauser and Leebaert, eds., *What Role for Government?* In our Introduction we argue that McNamara-era use of these tools in the Pentagon set back their credibility, and that even twenty years later the quantitative study of defense policy tended to be too weak to include an example in this volume.

33. Interview, March 2001. Coulam is the author of *Illusions of Choice*.

34. William Kaufmann, *The McNamara Strategy* (New York: Harper and Row, 1964), p. 43.

35. Kevin Kelly, "Peters' Provocations," *Wired*, December 1997, p. 210.

36. Michael Forrestal was among those who attributed this statement to McNaughton, specifically recalling how it summed up the perspective within the Office of the Secretary of Defense at that time. As discussed with author.

37. Hersh, *Dark Side*, pp. 252–253, quoting a Kennedy Library oral history interview with LeMoyne Billings, and his own with Hugh Sidey.

38. Fairlie, *Kennedy Promise*, p. 328, re Berlin; *Public Papers, Kennedy*, Item 302: "Radio and Television Report to the American People on the Berlin Crisis," July 25, 1961, p. 536.

39. Bluth, *Soviet Strategic Arms Policy*, p. 69.

40. Bruce Watson, "We Couldn't Run, So We Hoped We Could Hide," *Smithsonian*, April 1994, p. 50.

41. *New York Times*, October 1, 1961.

42. Testimony of Robert S. McNamara, House of Representatives, Subcommittee of the Committee on Government Operations, Civil Defense 1961, 87th Congress, 1st Session, 1961, p. 6.

43. House of Representatives, Hearings Before the Subcommittee of the Committee on Government Operations, 87th Congress, 2nd Session, February 19–27, 1962, p. 283.

44. House of Representatives, Subcommittee of the Committee on Government Operations, "Civil Defense," 87th Congress, 1st Session, 1961, p. 131.

45. *Office of Civil Defense Handbook on Family Shelter Designs* (Washington: GPO, 1962).

46. Updike, *Assorted Prose* (New York: Knopf, 1965), p. 81.

47. Arthur Waskow and Stanley Newman, *America in Hiding* (New York: Ballantine Books, 1962), p. 24.

48. Bruce Watson, "We Couldn't Run, So We Hoped We Could Hide" (note 40). Watson also notes that the Reverend Billy Graham asked Kennedy to deflate the controversy by supporting community shelters.

49. Reeves, *President Kennedy*, p. 229. LeMay has left behind bone-chilling statements about his eagerness to unleash SAC against the Soviet Union. Many were delivered to Rand and DOD civilian analysts. When hearing such thunder from LeMay years later, sitting by his pool in Newport Beach during the summer of 1979 while working at Rand, I suspected that the general relished provoking the academics.

50. McGeorge Bundy, "Possible Nuclear Worlds," pp. 174–175; Bundy offers a more nuanced discussion of McNamara-era nuclear targeting in his *Danger and Survival*, pp. 512–566.

51. Shapley, *Promise and Power*, p. 123.

52. National Security Archive, Document Set, "Checklist of Presidential Actions, L. D. Battle, Executive Secretary, State Department, to McGeorge Bundy, White House, July 28, 1961, pp. 1–4.

53. Herbert Stein made this comparison several times in conversations with the author.

54. Lee, "US-USSR Strategic Arms Control Agreements," p. 416.

55. Dobrynin, *In Confidence*, pp. 151–152.

56. Shapely, *Promise and Power*, pp. 396, 561.

57. William Bundy, *A Tangled Web*, p. 84; Rodman, *More Precious*, pp. 111, 155; the myth has been perpetuated among a wider audience by Isaacs and Downing, *Cold War*, p. 236, and their CNN series *Cold War*.

58. Several of the programs funded were the SS-9 and SS-11 ICBMs, plus the Y Class submarines and SS-N-6 missile. For "on hold," see Bird, *Color of Truth*, p. 249; Russian sources include, among many others, Karpenko, *Otechestvennyye Strategicheskiye Raketnyye Kompleksy*, pp. 197, 207, 215; Ambrose, *Eisenhower*, p. 553.

59. Hersh, *Dark Side*, quoting U.S. ambassador to the Soviet Union, and later presidential assistant, Llewellyn E. Thompson Jr., p. 254; ibid., p. 248, citing Robert Kennedy oral history.

60. Theodore Sorensen, *New York Times*, October 18, 1997; McNamara, *In Retrospect*, p. 341; McNamara et al., *Argument Without End*, p. 151; the latest biography is Thomas, *Robert Kennedy*, pp. 214, 233.

61. Anatoli Grybkov, "Karilskiy Krizis," *Voenno-istorcheskiy*, no. 10, 1992, p. 42.

62. Translation of the Directive by Raymond Garthoff in CWIHP *Bulletin*, no. 11, Winter 1998 (from Volkoganov Papers in the Library of Congress).

63. Col. A. Dokuchaev, "100-Dnevngy Ydarnyy Kruz," *Krasnaya Zvezda*, November 6, 1992, citing General Grybkov as the source; Aleksandr Fursenko and Timothy Naftali, *One Hell of a Gamble* (London: J. Murray, 1997), p. 243, have the same story from an unspecified source.

64. Ibid., Dokuchaev citing Lt. General L. Garbuz, Pliyev's deputy; Freedman, *Kennedy's Wars*, pp. 163–164.

65. Ibid., Dokuchaev. The KGB colonel in charge has been quoted as saying that nuclear weapons were to be used only under "concrete" circumstances specified by Moscow, and that he never received such instructions or codes. Gen. Col. V. I. Esin and Col. Yu. V. Grekov, "Uchastie PVSN v Operatsu: Anadir," *Voennaya Mysl*, no. 5, 1997, p. 70, citing the Central MOD Archives. Grybkov, *VIZh*, No. 12, 1992, p. 35, says the same.

66. See Gribkov and Smith, *Operation ANADYR*, which notes that the September 8, 1962, telegram was "unsent"; in answer to a question by William Lee at the Smithsonian's Woodrow Wilson Center in May 1994, Gribkov also said that Malinovsky never signed that delegation of authority order.

67. Had they remained, these highly vulnerable weapons would have tripled the Soviet missile force of 30 ICBMs already threatening the United States, but only briefly giving a still severely outgunned Moscow a marginal benefit for about a year, by which time approximately 200 new U.S. ICBMs were in place.

68. The U.S. was calculating its overall nuclear advantage as 7:1, whereas the Soviets figured it at 15:1. Another intelligence failure was that the CIA estimated only 12,000–15,000 Soviet troops in Cuba; Bird, *Color of Truth*, p. 16.

69. Dobrynin to Moscow, October 30, 1962, reprinted in Cold War International History Project, *Bulletin* 8–9 (1996–1997).

70. Castro in James Blight, Bruce Allyn, and David Welch, *Cuba on the Brink* (New York: Pantheon, 1993), p. 101.

71. Never of course activated for a nuclear crisis, the warning system was nonetheless used more than 20,000 times just between 1976 and 1996 to broadcast civil emergency messages and severe-weather warnings; on hotline, see Bamford, *Body of Secrets*, p. 193.

72. Michael W. Weinstein, obituary of W. S. Salant, *New York Times*, May 2, 1999, p. 59. The senior official cited is Charles P. Kindleberger.

73. Reeves, *President Kennedy*, p. 328.

74. Interestingly, the aggregate U.S. capital invested overseas at this time was equivalent to 7 percent of that current year's GDP, the same as in 1914 — the point being that the growing U.S. presence overseas was still largely for government purposes.

75. *New York Times*, March 31, 1997; NA, RG 59, 794.00/11961, XR 794.01, November 9, 1961, Memcon, "Control of Communist Subversion in Japan."

76. Paloczi-Horvath, *Facts Rebel*.

77. Lambright, *Powering Apollo*, pp. 93, 94.

78. Pierre Salinger, *John F. Kennedy: Commander in Chief* (New York: Penguin Studio, 1997), p. 97; Lambright, *Powering Apollo*, p. 86.

79. Ambrose, *Eisenhower*, p. 554.

80. Ibid.

81. Beon, *Planet Dora*, pp. xxiii–xxv.

82. Leslie, *Cold War,* p. 27, citing Louis Smullin.
83. Author's conversations with Dan Lynch and Steve Crocker, 1998 and 1999.
84. Review of Space Research: The Report of the Summer Study (NAS-NRC publication 1079, 1962), chapter 16, p. 6.
85. Foreman, "Behind Quantum Electronics," p. 201.
86. Leslie, *Cold War,* p. 9.
87. Beschloss, *Crisis Years,* p. 61; Rodman, *More Precious,* p. 99.
88. Rodman, *More Precious,* p. 116.
89. *Public Papers,* Kennedy, Item 206: "Special Message to the Congress on Urgent National Needs," May 25, 1961, p. 397; "take off" in Rostow, *Stages of Economic Growth,* p. 4.
90. The Peace Corps was proposed in "Remarks of Senator John F. Kennedy, University of Michigan," October 14, 1960. His "Special Message to Congress on the Peace Corps," of March 1, 1961, gives a glimpse of the Cold War value. See *Public Papers,* Kennedy, Item 61.
91. Samuel Berger, May 7, 1997, NBC Evening News, interview with Tom Brokaw.
92. Schlesinger, *A Thousand Days,* p. 554; Jack Raymond, *Power at the Pentagon* (New York: Harper and Row, 1964), p. 112, about courses for Africans.
93. Fairlie, *Kennedy Promise,* p. 135.
94. Knaus, *Orphans of the Cold War,* p. 212.
95. Ibid., p. 157.
96. Ibid., p. 217; "thousands" are postulated by Kai Bird in *Color of Truth,* p. 225.
97. Knaus, ibid., p. 322.
98. Gardner, *Pay Any Price,* p. 32.
99. Engelhardt, *Victory Culture,* p. 163.
100. LeMay, *America Is in Danger,* p. 123.
101. Tim Weiner, "The Spy Agency's Many Mean Ways," *New York Times,* February 9, 1997, p. 7.
102. Russo, *Live by the Sword,* p. 6.
103. The December 1959 CIA memorandum is from the National Security Archive web site, posted March 2001; Patterson, *Contesting Castro,* p. 257.
104. *Public Papers,* Eisenhower, Item 410: "Annual Message to the Congress on the State of the Union," January 12, 1961, p. 925.
105. McNamara in *Alleged Assassination Plots Involving Foreign Leaders* (Washington: GPO, 1975), p. 14; "boy commandoes" cited in Isenberg, *Shield of the Republic,* p. 754.
106. Treverton, *Covert Action,* p. 95; on "disposal," see Freedman, *Kennedy's Wars,* p. 128; "Inspector General's Survey of the Cuban Operation," CIA, February 16, 1962, p. 3 re Hungary; Soviet knowledge of the date is documented in portions of the Taylor Commission report, at the National Security Archive.
107. McGhee, *On the Front Line,* p. 147; on "tears," see Freedman, *Kennedy's Wars,* p. 145.
108. Bird, *Color of Truth,* p. 200.
109. See Hitchens, "Brief Shining Moments"; Dulles's conclusion is contained in the Taylor Commission report; on polygraphing, see Peter Wyden, *Bay of Pigs: The Untold Story* (New York: Simon and Schuster, 1979), p. 49.
110. CIA Director John McCone cited in Russo, *Live by the Sword,* p. 170.
111. "The Inspector General's Survey of the Cuban Operation," Lyman Kirkpatrick, CIA, 1962, National Security Archive.
112. Fairlie, *Kennedy Promise,* p. 193.

113. *Public Papers*, Kennedy, Item 119: "The President's News Conference of April 12, 1961," p. 258.
114. McGhee, *On the Front Line*, pp. 138, 140.
115. Thomas, *Very Best Men*, p. 181.
116. Russo, *Live by the Sword*, p. 19.
117. Harris Wofford, *Of Kennedys and Kings: Making Sense of the Sixties* (New York: Farrar, Strauss & Giroux, 1980), p. 386; Freedman, *Kennedy's Wars*, on "over the top," p. 149.
118. Russo, *Live by the Sword*, pp. 45–46; Allen Dulles, oral history, Kennedy Presidential Library; "The Spy Boss Who Loved Bond," in Sheldon Lane, ed., *For Bond Lovers Only* (New York: Panther Books, 1965), pp. 155–156; Thomas, *Robert Kennedy*, p. 166.
119. Hersh, *Dark Side*, p. 190; Russo, *Live by the Sword*, p. 75, best documents the chain of events surrounding this administration's use of assassination. Freedman, *Kennedy's Wars*, p. 150, makes a strong case about lack of evidence. The likelihood that the President did not know about his brother's inducements of the CIA causes laughter among several former senior officials, such as Thomas Hughes, Hilsman's successor at the State Department's Bureau of Intelligence and Research, as observed at the Woodrow Wilson International Center, February 8, 2001, Freedman book presentation.
120. Schlesinger, *A Thousand Days*, p. 95, and his letter to the editor, *New York Times Book Review*, February 4, 2001.
121. Helms assertion when interviewed for "The CIA: America's Secret Warriors," Discovery Channel, 1997.
122. Russo, *Live by the Sword*, p. 75; Woolsey statement on "Washington Journal," CSPAN, July 19, 2001.
123. Russo, *Live by the Sword*, interview of Sam Halpern, p. 173. About $150 million, more than a half-billion dollars today, was spent on CIA-managed mayhem.
124. Thomas, *Very Best Men*, p. 287; Russo, *Live by the Sword*, p. 46; Freedman, *Kennedy's Wars*, p. 151, discusses Harvey. JFK's disappointment upon meeting him was noted by Hughes and other former officials at Freedman's Woodrow Wilson Center presentation on February 8, 2001.
125. National Security Archive, "Pentagon Proposed Pretexts for Cuban Invasion in 1962, Annex to Appendix: Pretexts to Justify U.S. Military Intervention in Cuba," Memorandum for the Secretary of Defense, March 13, 1962.
126. Wright, *Spycatcher*, p. 160.
127. Hersh, *Dark Side*, p. 380, on raids; McGhee, *On the Front Line*, p. 146; Wofford, *Of Kennedys and Kings* (note 117), p. 426.
128. *New York Times*, July 13, 1998, quoting Luis Posada Carriles.
129. Raymond, *Power at the Pentagon* (note 92), pp. 112–113.
130. National Security Archive, Foreign Police Training file, HQ 62-107929, 1962–1963.
131. Ibid., Hoover to RFK, July 23, 1963.
132. NA, RG 286, May 8, 1963, telegram from DOS, Panama City, IAPA, Farland to AID/W; RG 286, February 21, 1963, telegram from Department of State to Panama USAID and AID/W.
133. "Police Aid and Political Will," The Washington Office on Latin America, 1987, p. 12.
134. Reston, *Deadline*, p. 288. Reston is recalling his meeting with the President at the U.S. Embassy in Vienna, right after the summit.

135. "Security and Assistance in Laos," Rand Corporation, September 1965, Laos Collection, National Security Archive; this staggering sum is also provided in Schlesinger, *A Thousand Days*, p. 325.
136. Isenberg, *Shield of the Republic*, p. 774.
137. May 11, 1961, Task Force Russia Documents, Box 32-1, Library of Congress.
138. Beech, "How the U.S. Fumbled in Laos."
139. *Congressional Record*, August 2, 1961.
140. DCI John McCone, Memorandum for the Record, May 10, 1962. CIA/DCI files, Job No. 80B01285A, Box 2, Folder 2. "Nothing would stop the southward movement of Communism through Indonesia and this would have the effect of cutting the world in half"; re making a stand in Southeast Asia, see Reeves, *President Kennedy*, p. 75.
141. Freedman, *Kennedy's Wars*, p. 360; Shultz, *Secret War Against Hanoi*, p. 316.
142. The 50,000 figure comes from "Vietnam and Laos: The Impasse of War Communism," by Jean-Louis Margolin, in Courtois, *Black Book of Communism*, p. 569; *Public Papers*, Kennedy, Item 205: "Special Message to the Congress on Urgent National Needs," May 25, 1961.
143. Langguth, *Our Vietnam*, writes of Diem's "campaign of torture and terror," p. 99, whereas the "gentle" Ho Chi Minh is described as "never more ruthless than he needed to be," p. 97.
144. *Washington Post*, September 17, 1996.
145. McNamara, *Argument Without End*, p. 61; Bird, *Color of Truth*, p. 327.
146. Schlesinger, "Measure of Diplomacy," p. 146; McNamara, *In Retrospect*, p. 33; that McCarthyism "decimated" the experts is again repeated in Ford, "Revisiting Vietnam," p. 96.
147. *Washington Post*, July 24, 1996, quoting Congressman James Moran concerning State Department appropriations.
148. George Kennan, "A Fresh Look at Our China Policy," *New York Times Magazine*, November 22, 1964, pp. 27, 140. In making a case for his version of the domino theory, Kennan presents China as intending to dominate Asia by expanding its power not only into Indochina but also India, Pakistan, the Philippines, and elsewhere. "We have had no choice but to place ourselves in that path," he writes, while offering bromides such as "we are not the avenging angel of all humanity."
149. McNamara, *In Retrospect*, pp. 108, 55.
150. The best analysis of the subject is William Burr and Jeffrey Richelson, "Whether to 'Strangle the Baby in the Cradle': The United States and the Chinese Nuclear Program, 1960–64," *International Security*, Winter 2000/2001. On "antagonists," p. 67, on Bundy, see pp. 54–56.
151. Ibid., p. 74.
152. Associated Press, "Administrations Considered Bombing Nuclear Sites in China," *New York Times*, January 12, 2001, p. A6. "For a longer term effect it would be necessary to destroy research facilities and personnel," George Rathjens advises in a paper dated December 14, 1964. Given the context, the *Times* describes this as considering "a policy of assassinating Chinese nuclear officials."
153. Jason DeParle, "The Man Inside Clinton's Foreign Policy," *New York Times Magazine*, August 20, 1995.
154. Bernstein, *Guns or Butter*, p. 339, in which "tyranny" is used casually.
155. McNamara, *Argument Without End*, pp. 73, 111, 165.

156. Bird, *Color of Truth*, p. 221.

157. Stanley Karnow, "Spook," *New York Times Magazine*, January 3, 1999, p. 34.

158. Reeves, *President Kennedy*, p. 201.

159. *New York Times*, March 12, 1963.

160. Kennedy, *The Military and the Media*, pp. 98–101.

161. McPherson, *A Political Education*, p. 386.

162. Kenneth O'Donnell and David Power, *Johnny We Hardly Knew Ye: Memories of John Fitzgerald Kennedy* (Boston: Little, Brown, 1972), pp. 13, 16; Michael Beschloss has valuably distilled the costs of war with the political costs to JFK in "The 20th Century with Mike Wallace," History Channel, September 14, 2000.

163. Re "chicken," President Kennedy to aide Theodore Sorensen before the Bay of Pigs, as cited by Russo, *Live by the Sword*, p. 18.

164. Beschloss, *Taking Charge*, p. 14; Dallek, *Flawed Giant*, p. 53.

165. Scripps Howard News Service Poll, *Washington Times*, July 5, 1997.

166. *Public Papers*, Kennedy, Item 475, p. 887.

Chapter 7: The Burden Felt (1964–1969)

1. Dallek, *Flawed Giant*, p. 84, citing political scientist John Roche, president of the Americans for Democratic Action, who came to protest the Vietnam War at the White House and was promptly hired as a presidential assistant.

2. William Burr and Jeffrey Richelson, "Whether to 'Strangle the Baby in the Cradle': The United States and the Chinese Nuclear Program, 1960–64," *International Security*, Winter 2000/2001, p. 79.

3. Beschloss, *Taking Charge*, February 20, 1964, LBJ to McNamara, p. 248.

4. Rusk interview in "Vietnam: The Ten Thousand Day War," segment on airpower. Bonaventure Productions and Informational Television Productions with the Canadian Broadcasting Company, 1980. Peter Arnett, writer/interviewer.

5. Kenneth Adelman, "A Clandestine Clan," *International Security*, Summer 1980, p. 162.

6. Byrne, *Whiz Kids*, p. 406.

7. Conversation with Edwin L. Weisl Jr., Simpson, Thacher & Bartlett partner, and a Johnson assistant attorney general, whose father FDR had ordered to become Johnson's lawyer when LBJ was elected to Congress in 1937.

8. LBJ Library, telephone log, March 21, 1964, released October 11, 1995; McNamara, *Argument Without End*, p. 155; Beschloss, *Taking Charge*, November 30, 1963, LBJ to Cook, pp. 73, 124.

9. Beschloss, *Taking Charge*, February 3, 1964, LBJ to John S. Knight, p. 214, and March 4, 1964, LBJ to McGeorge Bundy, p. 267.

10. Thomas, *Robert Kennedy*, p. 289.

11. Beschloss, *Taking Charge*, May 20, 1994, LBJ and McGeorge Bundy, p. 359.

12. On Taylor's comparison of Korea and Vietnam, see Hersh, *Dark Side*, p. 264; on the advice Korea would never be repeated, see Beschloss, *Taking Charge*, March 4, 1964, LBJ and McGeorge Bundy, p. 267.

13. Dallek, *Flawed Giant*, pp. 147, 255.

14. Beschloss, *Taking Charge*, May 27, 1964, Bundy to LBJ, p. 372.

15. Robert McNamara, Statement to the House Committee on Foreign Affairs, *Congressional Digest*, June–July 1965, p. 181.

16. $533 million, mostly in economic aid, went to Afghanistan from 1956 to 1978 in nominal dollars, with the billions in military assistance then following. Reference to Afghan joking is from William Ogilvie, letter to the editor, *The Economist,* June 13, 1998.

17. Martin, *Overtaken by Events,* p. 667. If U.S. objectives could not even be achieved there, Johnson said to Ambassador Martin, "What can we do in Vietnam?"

18. Alex Shoumatoff, "Mobutu's Final Days," *Vanity Fair,* August 1997, p. 97.

19. Ibid., p. 100.

20. *New York Times,* February 14, 1997, on CIA mercenaries; assistant secretary quote is from Wong, *Footsteps,* p. 204.

21. Kennan quoted in Chomsky, *Year 501,* p. 121.

22. McGhee, *Front Line,* p. 145 on pornography, for which the CIA tried to blame the Soviets; Crosby role in James Strodes, *Allen Dulles: Master of Spies* (Washington: Regnery, 1999), p. 494.

23. National Security Archive, "Story of 'Adhyatmin,'" July 26, 1988, Indonesia, 1965–67, Box 1, on CIA; Chaplen, *Promise and Power,* p. 475.

24. National Security Archive, "Story of 'Adhyatmin,'" including Marshall Green, interview, p. 37.

25. Ibid., p. 71.

26. Edward E. Masters, "The September 30 Affair," October 1965, Counsellor, Political Affairs, U.S. Embassy, Hoover Institution Archives; *Time,* December 17, 1965.

27. Robert F. Kennedy, speech, January 27, 1966, at ADA National Roosevelt Day Dinner, press release, Hoover Institution Archives.

28. *Washington Post,* April 18, 1966.

29. This assertion keeps being repeated in the press and in scholarly papers alike. *Washington Post,* March 7, 1998; Bird, *Color of Truth,* p. 352.

30. Chomsky, *Year 501,* p. 126.

31. J. W. Fulbright, "Foreign Aid? Yes, but with a New Approach," *New York Times Magazine,* March 21, 1965, p. 102.

32. Working Paper series, World Bank, 1997, study by Craig Burnside and David Dollar, as reported by Paul Blustein, *Washington Post,* May 22, 1997; also see the World Bank study on Africa issued on May 31, 2000.

33. Marcus Brauchli, "Speak No Evil," *Wall Street Journal,* July 14, 1998, p. 1; Stephen Rosenfeld, "Banking on Indonesia," *Washington Post,* July 17, 1998, p. A21.

34. IMF bailouts are largely transfer payments from U.S. taxpayers, since the government borrows money in the bond market at a fraction of the rate the recipient would pay, then (through the IMF) loans it to the recipient at a lesser rate, meanwhile forcing up the rates to other (usually more promising) borrowers.

35. *Public Papers,* Johnson, Item 287: "Remarks at the University of Michigan," May 22, 1964, p. 104.

36. Bernstein, *Guns or Butter,* p. 3; Dallek, *Flawed Giant,* p. 421.

37. Bernstein, *Guns or Butter,* pp. 321–323.

38. Shapley, *Promise and Power,* p. 373.

39. Bernstein, *Guns or Butter,* p. 378.

40. Conversation with Michael Forrestal, 1979.

41. Shapley, *Promise and Power*, p. 389.

42. Ibid., pp. 385–387; *Military Support for Youth Development* (Santa Monica, CA: Rand Corp., 1994), table 3.1.

43. Kunz, *Butter and Guns*, p. 158.

44. Amaury de Riencourt, *The American Empire* (New York: Dial Press, 1968), p. 278, citing a U.S. Embassy spokesman in London, and the UPI report of March 3, 1968.

45. In fact, this was only a balance of payments equalization, not a full repayment, since the U.S. had to absorb the domestic costs of production, at least 90 percent of sale price, which could have gone more profitably elsewhere.

46. Schaller, *Altered States*, pp. 189, 186.

47. Ibid., pp. 198, 196.

48. In 1965, no more than 10 percent of U.S. industries experienced significant foreign competition in the U.S. market. Fifteen years later, 70 percent would.

49. McPherson, *A Political Education*, p. 314.

50. "Seaborne Imports into North Vietnam, 1964/65: Shipping into North Vietnam by Flag." Undated NSC document from the Vietnam Archive, Texas Tech.

51. *Washington Post*, April, 21, 1996, citing Jacques Chirac.

52. Jack F. Matlock Jr., "Why Were We in Vietnam," *New York Times Book Review*, August 8, 1999, p. 11.

53. This was a widespread opinion within the French government that flabbergasted General Pierre Gallois, a Gaullist theoretician of nuclear war, with whom I had many conversations in the later 1970s.

54. Ennes, *Assault on the Liberty*, chapter 6; author's interview with Joseph Meadors, USS *Liberty* Veterans Association, April 2001.

55. Dallek, *Flawed Giant*, p. 430; Andrew, *President's Eyes*, p. 334, in which Andrew, one of the world's leading authorities on intelligence history, concludes, "The Israelis had almost certainly decided to destroy the *Liberty*"; the NSA quotes and the war crimes reporting by the Israeli press are in the definitive (unclassified) treatment by Bamford, *Body of Secrets*, pp. 185–239.

56. David Schoenbaum, *The United States and the State of Israel* (New York: Oxford University Press, 1993), p. 158, for Eban quote; I was a student of Eban's at Columbia University in Spring 1975 when he declined to elaborate; for the evidence of a coverup, see Ennes, *Assault*, pp. 200–209.

57. "Mr. McNamara's War," *New York Times*, April 12, 1995, p. 24. This essay was written personally by editorial page editor Howell Raines, according to sources at the *Times*.

58. Douglas Pike, "South Vietnam: Autopsy of a Compound Crisis," in Pipes and Garfinkle, eds., p. 44.

59. Melman, *Permanent War Economy*, p. 264, who writes of "replacing."

60. McPherson, *Political Education*, p. 259.

61. Senate Select Committee on Intelligence, 104th Congress, 2nd Session, Hearings, Vol. 2, "Vietnamese Commandos," Testimony No. 3, June 19, 1996 (Maj. Gen. John Singlaub, USA ret., former Commander MACSOG), p. 15.

62. One U.S. Air Force study concluded that "survival of the tribe was becoming a major concern," as cited in "Many Laotians in the U.S. Find Their Hopes Betrayed," *New York Times*, December 27, 1997, p. 1.

63. Roger Warner, *Shooting at the Moon: The Story of America's Clandestine War in Laos* (South Royalton, VT: Steerforth Press, 1996), p. 125.

64. See Ford, *CIA and the Vietnam Policymakers*, George Carver, the CIA's "expert" on Vietnam, did not appear to speak a word of Vietnamese when later discussing the war with me and several colleagues in 1986.
65. According to diplomat Chester Cooper, traveling with Bundy, in McNamara, *Argument Without End*, p. 205.
66. McMaster, *Dereliction*, p. 215, on the aftermath of Pleiku.
67. Bird, *Color of Truth*, p. 301.
68. Halberstam, *Best and the Brightest*, p. 528.
69. Ambrose, *Eisenhower*, pp. 560, 562.
70. Shultz, *Secret War*, p. 325.
71. Heikal, *Sphinx and the Commissar*, p. 164, who reports Kosygin relaying this to Nasser.
72. See "The Anatomy of Military Failure," chapter 1, in Luttwak, *The Pentagon and the Art of War*, plus my discussions of the subject with Dr. Luttwak during 1997–1998.
73. Bernstein, *Guns or Butter*, citing John P. Roche, p. 350.
74. NA, OJCS, 031 1, Lt. General Oplvcy to Major Gen. Kerwin, February 13, 1968.
75. Sorley, *A Better War*, pp. 14–15, on South Vietnamese reaction; Andrew, *President's Eyes*, p. 341.
76. John Mueller, *War, Presidents and Public Opinion* (New York: Wiley, 1973), pp. 56, 72, 90, 106–107. Seventy percent wanted to continue the bombing, and 53 percent were for intensifying the war.
77. Braestrup, *Big Story*, p. 705.
78. "Vietnam: The Camera at War," A&E network.
79. Richard Bernstein, "Critic's Notebook," *New York Times*, December 1, 1998, p. B2; "A Widow Mourns Her Brutally Executed Husband," *People*, May 1, 2000, p. 91.
80. Handlin, *Distortion of America*, pp. 99–100.
81. McMaster, *Dereliction*, p. 394, quoting Bundy. Nearly twice as many men were drafted in 1951 than in 1966, the year of Vietnam's highest callup from a much larger pool of draft-age men.
82. Johnson, *Modern Times*, p. 637.
83. Dubček, *Hope Dies Last*, p. 212.
84. Jaromir Navratil, ed., *Czechoslovak Government Commission for Analysis of the Events of 1967–70*, published by the Central European University Press and the National Security Archive.
85. Coleman, *Decline and Fall*, pp. 84–85.
86. Mansfield, "Legacy of the Late Sixties," p. 21.
87. Stephen Crocker, interview, June 1999.
88. "Mr. McNamara's War," *New York Times* (note 57).
89. Phil McCombs,"Semper Fi: A Brother's Search," *Washington Post*, July 20, 1998, p. 1.
90. Rosenblatt, *Coming Apart*, p. 216.
91. Isaacs, *Vietnam Shadows*, pp. 38–39, 47. The percentage of twenty-six-year-old veterans was lower in 1973 (40 percent) after seven years of a wartime draft than in 1962 (58 percent) after nearly a decade of peace.
92. Friedberg, *In the Shadow*, p. 189.
93. Higgs, "The Cold War Economy," p. 285; Friedberg, *In the Shadow*, pp. 193, 195.

94. Garfinkle, *Telltale Hearts*, p. 13, who uses the Poe metaphor.
95. Hendrickson, *The Living and the Dead*, p. 315.
96. Kennan, *Democracy and the Student Left*, p. 153.
97. Thomas, *Robert Kennedy*, p. 263.
98. Hilty, *Brother Protector*, p. 227.
99. *New York Times*, May 31, 1995, quoting Jerry Cohen.
100. National Security Archive. From SAC, St. Louis to Director, FBI, January 30, 1970, in Exhibits 19-1, 19-2, 20-1, as released in 1975 intelligence community hearings. She "wouldn't be shucking and jiving with our Black Men in ACTION" if she could "get enough at home," the husband was told; on "pranks," discussion with retired special agent who participated. The FBI undertook many similar racial and sexual harassments during these years.
101. Andrew, *President's Eyes*, p. 355, citing Richard Helms.
102. Wolfe, *Mauve Gloves*, p. 116.
103. "The Osgood File," CBS Radio, January 9, 1996, transcript.
104. Lewin, *Report from Iron Mountain*. Annotated reprint of the original.
105. See "The Sino-Soviet Border" in Tyler, *A Great Wall*, pp. 47–103.
106. For a review of Soviet priorities in a nuclear war, in this case by officers of the Russian Federation's Strategic Rocket Forces, see Volkov, ed., *Mezhkontinental'nye Ballisticheskiye Rakety*.
107. Lee, *CIA Estimates*, p. 157; Yazov quote in Schmertz, ed., *President Reagan*, p. 122.
108. For McNamara quotes, see Adelman, "Clandestine Clan" (note 5), p. 162; the flawed intelligence reports are: SNIE 11-14-61, "The Soviet Strategic Military Posture, 1961–67; NIE 11-8-62, "Soviet Capabilities for Long-Range Attack," which did not forecast any specific new ICBMs; and NIE 11-8-63, "Soviet Capabilities for Surprise Attack," which only foresaw systems designed to strike cities and other "soft" targets. The NIEs backed off in 1968–69 on the matter of the Soviets not going for parity; and in 1975–76 they began acknowledging Soviet war-fighting doctrine. Intelligence officials were shocked by Soviet testing and deployment of the three new, unexpectedly accurate ICBMs with MIRVs.
109. Newhouse, *Cold Dawn*, pp. 20–21.
110. Interviews with participants in this meeting: William Lee, Julian Davidson (Army chief scientist for Nike-X), and Bell Labs vice president Donald Ling.
111. "Notes on Meeting with the President in Austin, Texas, December 6, 1966, with Secretary McNamara and the Joint Chiefs of Staff," December 10, 1966, Walt W. Rostow, Johnson Presidential Library.
112. Kennedy's buildup had raised it 11 percent as of 1962, against 1960. But there followed a three-year decline that brought the real amount below that of 1957. There was then a leap of more than one-third after 1965 through 1968, soon to fall again.
113. William D. Krimer, "Memorandum of Conversation between President Johnson and Premier Kosygin on the Morning 23 June 1967," Johnson Presidential Library.
114. Memorandum for Mr. Kohler from Seymour Weiss, "British Discussions with the Soviets on ABMs," February 27, 1967, FOIA.
115. Dobrynin, *In Confidence*, p. 165; Kosygin made similar arguments at a 1967

press conference in London, which are quoted in Daniel O. Graham, *Confessions of a Cold Warrior* (Fairfax, VA: Preview Press, 1995), p. 192.

116. As cited in Dobrynin, *In Confidence*, p. 166. At the time, the SA-5 was known as the Talinn system after the location of the first site discovered by U.S. intelligence.

117. Shapley, *Promise and Power*, p. 232.

118. See Lee, *CIA Estimates*, p. 142.

119. McNamara publicly accepted the 4:1 ratio in his Statement for Fiscal Years 1968–1972, January 23, 1967, p. 53. It was consistent with a tradeoff band calculated for him by the Stanford and Bell Lab briefers who argued that the ratio was somewhere between 4:1 in favor of the defense and 1:1 in favor of the offense, depending on assumptions. In the briefing, he accepted that argument. In the publication, McNamara said the cost-exchange ratio was between even (1:1 for both offense and defense) and 4:1 in favor of the offense.

120. In 1980, the U.S. strategic arsenal reached 10,768 nuclear warheads and bombs about equally divided between the Navy's SLBMs and the Air Force's ICBMs and bombers. The emphasis on being able to respond to an attack with ICBMs was due to their immediacy and accuracy.

121. The three key elements of the U.S. antiballistic missile system in 1967 (Nike-X) were high-frequency phased array radar; high-acceleration solid-fuel missiles; and IBM 360 class computers. Moscow might have paralleled U.S. progress in radar but lagged far behind both in this type of high-acceleration missile and in microelectronics. It would take the Soviets twenty years to copy the Nike-X system.

122. *Newsweek*, August 25, 1969.

123. In the Nuclear Nonproliferation Treaty, five nations that had already tested nuclear weapons pledged to work toward eliminating them and to help other nations with civilian nuclear energy, provided those other signatories agreed not to develop their own nuclear weapons.

124. *The Pentagon Papers: The Defense Department History of U.S. Decisionmaking on Vietnam* (Boston: Beacon Press, 1971–1972), 5, I.C.6.b., p. 107.

125. *Business Week* so describes Clifford, September 25, 1995.

126. Isaacson and Thomas, *Wise Men*, p. 578; as cited in William Pfaff, *Barbarian Sentiments: How the American Century Ends* (New York: Hill & Wang, 1989), p. 182.

127. As stated by Ball in 1973 to *Harper's* magazine editor Timothy Dickinson and to an eminent journalist who prefers to be unnamed.

128. Lambright, *Powering Apollo*, p. 7.

129. Dalleck, *Flawed Giant*, p. 419.

130. Fareed Zakaria, "Sometimes a Great Nation," *New York Times Book Review*, May 18, 1997, section 7, p. 11.

Chapter 8: Blight on the Battlefield (1969–1975)

1. Kunz, *Butter and Guns*, p. 214.

2. Ibid., p. 258.

3. Author's observation of Nixon's appearance at the Quai d'Orsay, and at his departure from Orly airport in 1969.

4. The impromptu talk with reporters occurred on July 25, 1969, at an officers club. *Public Papers*, Nixon, pp. 544–556. The quote is a description of those

remarks on February 18, 1970, in "First Annual Report to the Congress on United States Foreign Policy for the 1970s."

5. Richard Nixon, "U.S. Foreign Policy for the 1970's: A New Strategy for Peace," Washington, GPO, February 18, 1970. It also included a new approach to budgeting that would try to work back from resources available to the strategies that might then be possible.

6. Earl C. Ravenal, "Large-Scale Foreign Policy Change: The Nixon Doctrine as History and Portent," *Policy Papers in International Affairs*, No. 35, 1989, Institute of International Studies, University of California, Berkeley, pp. 19, 20.

7. Bundy, *A Tangled Web*, p. 508. Although other experts cite a much higher number, one also offers an estimate of just 11,600 by 1975. See Robert S. Litwak, *Détente and the Nixon Doctrine: American Foreign Policy and the Pursuit of Stability, 1969–1976* (New York: Cambridge University Press, 1984), pp. 141, 148. On Israel, Tel Aviv insisted upon military supplies before it would consider U.S.-requested air strikes against Syrian tanks penetrating Jordan during the Palestinian uprising. But Jordanian pilots and artillerymen ended up doing the job themselves.

8. Tyler, *A Great Wall*, pp. 231, 69; Fudan University Professor Ni Shixiong, interviews in 1997.

9. Personal travel in winter 1970/71 around that city.

10. *The NewsHour with Jim Lehrer*, remarks respectively by Haynes Johnson, Michael Beschloss, Doris Kearns Goodwin, June 23, 1998.

11. Christopher Hitchens, "The Case Against Henry Kissinger Part Two," *Harper's*, March 2001, p. 60.

12. Haldeman, *Diaries*, p. 424. One of the most revealing examples of U.S. over-enthusiasm is the July 1971 photo of Kissinger, with a desperately anxious ear-to-ear grin, first shaking hands with the tightly smiling Zhou Enlai.

13. Gromyko as quoted in *Kommunist*, January 1973, p. 39, and cited in Day, *Cold War Capitalism*, p. 262.

14. Episodes of détente are: May 1949–June 1950; from the 19th Party Congress in 1952 to the Missile Crisis ten years later (with regrettable interruptions over Hungary and Berlin); the test-ban summer of 1963 to the invasion of Czechoslovakia 1968; and then the era of SALT and Ostpolitik in the 1970s.

15. The Soviet Union was credited with 1,527 ICBM launchers, 516 SLBM launchers, and 195 heavy bombers and tankers in NIE 11-8-72, "Soviet Forces for Intercontinental Attack," October 26, 1972, p. 2; whereas U.S. forces stood at 1,054 ICBMs, 656 SLBMs, and about 400 B-52s. Comparisons were complicated further by rapid technological advances: the U.S. had a lead in MIRVing its warheads and by 1976 began deploying long-range cruise missiles on its bombers. Moreover, the U.S. had fighter-bombers based in Europe, and two allies with nuclear weapons.

16. Aleksandr Bovin, *Izvestia*, February 6, 1975.

17. For example, the Trident SLBM-carrying submarine, the first new strategic missile program in eight years, made it past the Senate in 1974 with one vote.

18. Gerard C. Smith, *Disarming Diplomat*, pp. 170, 174.

19. Gerard C. Smith, *Doubletalk*, p. 85.

20. Dobrynin, *In Confidence*, p. 210.

21. Savel'yev and Detinov, *The Big Five*, p. 17.
22. Bundy, *Tangled Web*, p. 312.
23. Isaacson, *Kissinger*, p. 431, citing negotiator Raymond Garthoff.
24. Ibid., p. 427.
25. William T. Lee, *ABM Treaty Charade*, pp. 116–117.
26. Soviet ICBMs had originally been designed to destroy all of America's ICBM silos hardened to 300 psi, an objective theoretically achieved by 1976. However, in 1971 U.S. silos began being modified to withstand 2000 psi. Soviet ICBMs could theoretically destroy all of them by 1980, depending on how one interprets Soviet data on airbursts and groundbursts.
27. After the Cold War, Russian sources reported the accuracy and warhead yields. For example: A. V. Karpenko, *Rossiiskoye*, p. 13, and E. B. Volkov, ed., *Mezhkontinental'nye*, pp. 329, 331, 383. All warheads on these Soviet missiles were a minimum of .55 megatons and could go to .75 megatons on the SS-18, in contrast to Minuteman's .17 warheads and .05 on Poseidon. Because of the long time to target, SAC's more numerous bombers were not considered first strike weapons, at least by Americans.
28. Conversation with author, May 1979, Cumberland Park, U.K.
29. Melvin R. Laird, Military Manpower Requirements for Fiscal Year 1972: Hearings Before the House Armed Services Committee, 92nd Congress, 1st Session, March 9, 1971, pp. 1050–1072.
30. Schmertz, *President Reagan*, p. 122, citing Soviet Minister of Defense Yazov on the consequences of Chernobyl is, again, an excellent distillation of this view.
31. See National Security Archive, "Intelligence Community Experiment in Competitive Analysis," December 1976, pp. 9–16 ("Team B" report).
32. Over the past decade, Russian memoirs, official histories, and other sources have together closed critical intelligence gaps on the question of whether the Soviets assembled a national missile defense system from dual purpose "universal anti-aircraft/anti-missile (SAM/ABM) systems" — in violation of the ABM Treaty's Article 1. The majority in the U.S. intelligence community assessed the SA-5 and SA-10 as only for antiaircraft purposes. The conclusion now appears to be wrong. There are two or more independent Russian sources on virtually all major controversial parts of this problem, and they are internally consistent in pointing to a Soviet (and now a Russian) national missile defense capability.
33. Michael Howard, "Nuclear Danger and Nuclear History," *International Security*, Summer 1989, p. 182.
34. *U.S. News and World Report*, October 30, 1972, p. 36.
35. Kissinger, *Years of Renewal*, p. 99.
36. Kissinger, Memorandum for the President, "My Trip to China," March 2, 1973, in Burr, *Kissinger Transcripts*, p. 113.
37. Robert Legvold, "The Nature of Soviet Power," *Foreign Affairs*, October 1977, p. 66, citing Gromyko; "potato" assertion in Memorandum of Conversation, January 24, 1968, of Lt. Gen. John J. Davis, USA, ACDA, with Gen. Maj. V. I. Meshcheryakov, Military Attaché, Washington; "eating grass" said to Leebaert by G. Arbatov, Moscow, March 1981.
38. Day, *Cold War Capitalism*, pp. 275–277. This is a volume of translations from the Soviet press and bureaucracy that documents the shift from respect in the early 1960s to contempt a decade later.

39. Zumwalt, *On Watch*, p. 319; Kissinger rebuttal is included in Isaacson, *Kissinger*, pp. 696–697.
40. As cited in Kovel, *Red Hunting*, p. 41.
41. Shershnev, *Mutual Advantage*, p. 91. Exports of U.S. subsidiaries were approximately $400 million annually in the early 1970s.
42. Kunz, *Butter and Guns*, p. 185.
43. See "The Soviet Natural Gas Pipeline," Harvard Business School Case 9-384-007, 9; "Sunshine and Shadow: The CIA and the Soviet Economy," Kennedy School of Government, C16-91-1096.0, p. 13. In the latter source, an example of a specific deal is cited by one Agency analyst as advising executives "how you can . . . sell Pepsi Cola to the Russians."
44. George Meany, testimony about "Détente," Before the Senate Foreign Relations Committee, 93rd Congress, 2nd Session, October 1, 1974, pp. 380–381.
45. See Thomas G. Patterson and Dennis Merrill, eds., *On Kissinger: Major Problems in American Foreign Relations*, Vol. II (Lexington, MA : D. C. Heath, 1995), p. 60.
46. Andrew and Mitrokhin, *Sword and the Shield*, p. 186.
47. Weiss, "Duping the Soviets."
48. Ibid., p. 71.
49. Andrew and Mitrokhin, *Sword and the Shield*, pp. 215–216, 340; testing could show Moscow how to jam the U.S. device. Interviews with intelligence officials, 1998–99.
50. CIEPSM No. 25, "U.S. Policy on the Export of Computers to the Communist Countries," January 30, 1974, p. 10, emphasis in the original. This was the precursor of National Security Decision Memorandum 247, which followed on March 14, 1974.
51. Ibid.
52. Atomic Industrial Forum, conference on security, Knoxville, Tennessee, October 1976, which author attended.
53. Schaller, *Altered States*, p. 212.
54. Ibid.
55. Herbert Stein interviews with author, 1997–98.
56. Reston, *Lone Star*, p. 409.
57. Herbert Stein interview (note 55).
58. Haldeman, *Diaries*, p. 342.
59. Editorial, *Wall Street Journal*, October 28, 1992.
60. Nakao, "Studies on U.S.-Japan Economic Relations."
61. Interviews with CIA officers at the time.
62. Kunz, *Butter and Guns*, p. 251.
63. Rodman, *More Precious*, p. 82.
64. Ball, *The Past*, pp. 435, 436.
65. Randal, *After Such Knowledge*, p. 156.
66. Ball, *The Past*, pp. 454, 455.
67. Ian Skeet, *OPEC: Twenty-five Years of Prices and Politics* (New York: Cambridge University Press, 1988), p. 61.
68. Frances FitzGerald, *Fire in the Lake: The Vietnamese and the Americans in Vietnam* (Boston: Atlantic–Little, Brown, 1972), p. 442. This aspiration is offered in the book's concluding paragraph.
69. Race, *War Comes to Long An*, p. 253.

70. Ibid., p. 254.
71. Sorley, *Better War*, p. 214.
72. For quote and context, see Mackburn Owens, "Bob Kerry's War: The Fine Line Between Combat and Atrocities," *The Weekly Standard*, May 14, 2001. His perspective is significant because he led a Marine Corps rifle platoon in Vietnam and teaches at the Naval War College.
73. Sorley, *Thunderbolt*, p. 232, citing General Fred Wyand.
74. Small teams of specialists fighting their own version of a "better war" proved able to divert entire divisions of North Vietnam's formidable regulars, plausibly claiming immense kill ratios — although themselves often incurring over 100 percent casualty rates, men getting hit, staying in action, and getting hit again. One Special Forces company, for example, could advise 15,000 Montagnard or South Vietnamese soldiers, as explained in RG 472 Box 3, Senior Officer Debrief, Col. Harold Aaron, CO 5th SFGA, June 12, 1969.
75. On theory, see Schecter, *Palace File*, p. 69.
76. McNamara, *Argument Without End*, p. 253. The strongest argument for the war's unwinnability, even after the successes of the early 1970s, is made by Jeffrey Record, a former pacification advisor, in his *The Wrong War*. Extensive conversations with Dr. Record have shaped my conclusions to the contrary.
77. Ball, *The Past*, p. 417.
78. Bundy, *Tangled Web*, p. 147.
79. Roger Rosenblatt, *Time*, August 19, 1997, p. 26; Henry Kissinger, "The 'Tangled Web': An Exchange," *New York Review of Books*, September 24, 1998, pp. 78–80.
80. Colby, *Lost Victory*, p. 310; Sorley, *Better War*, p. 274.
81. Lewis Sorley, "Courage and Blood: South Vietnam's Repulse of the 1972 Easter Invasion," *Parameters*, Summer 1999, pp. 44–45; Berman, *No Peace*, p. 132.
82. Schecter, *Palace File*, p. 258.
83. Bundy, *Tangled Web*, p. 352. To be sure, there was dissension in Moscow over whether to proceed with the summit. See S. J. Ball, *Cold War*, p. 156.
84. Kissinger, *Years of Renewal*, p. 51; Sorley, *Better War*, p. 282, citing Gallup poll, December 1971.
85. Kissinger, *Years of Renewal*, p. 492.
86. Isaacson, *Kissinger*, p. 486.
87. Schecter, *Palace File*, pp. 1, 189; Berman, *No Peace*, p. 174.
88. Cao Van Vien, *Final Collapse*, pp. 33–34; Andrew, *President's Eyes*, p. 388.
89. Bundy, *Tangled Web*, p. 372; "Ex-POW Identifies Cuban Dignitary as His Chief Tormentor," *Miami Herald*, September 9, 1999, p. A1, based on declassified DOD and USAF documents.
90. Dung, *Our Great Spring Victory*, pp. 17–18.
91. *Public Papers*, Ford, "Special Message to the Congress Requesting Supplemental Assistance for the Republic of Vietnam and Cambodia," January 28, 1975, p. 119.
92. On superiority, see VWP Politburo directive, March 31, 1975, in Ruane, *Vietnam Wars*, p. 146; on "candy," see Pham Van Dong to Politburo, December 18, 1974, ibid.; for force dispositions, see Todd, *Cruel April*, chapter 113.
93. Interview with Nguyen Tien Hung at Howard University, August 2001.
94. Kissinger, *Years of Renewal*, pp. 531–532; Berman, *No Peace*, p. 267. The purpose was to facilitate a coalition government.

95. Arnold Kramish, interview, June 2001.

96. Bamford, *Body of Secrets*, p. 353.

97. Ford, *A Time to Heal*, pp. 253–254.

98. Ron Nessen, *It Sure Looks Different from the Inside* (Chicago: Playboy, 1978), pp. 97–98.

99. Bui Tin, *Following Ho Chi Minh*, pp. 88–93, with the author explaining "we were drunk with victory."

100. Huynh, *South Wind*, on executions; Sorley, *Better War*, p. 383, on 65,000. Ron Frankum, archivist at the Vietnam Archive, Texas Tech, cautions that there is no conclusive figure for the tens of thousands killed. Correspondence with author, June 2001.

101. Rodman, *More Precious*, pp. 185–186.

102. Gaddis, "Tragedy," pp. 11–12.

103. Seth Mydans in *New York Times*, June 28, 1997; Seth Mydans, "Cambodia's 'Year Zero' Haunts a Photographer," *New York Times*, July 6, 2000, p. B2.

104. Isaacson, *Kissinger*, p. 681.

105. Hitchens, "The Case Against," pp. 61–65 (note 11).

106. Stevens, *Vain Hopes*, chapter 14.

107. Shay, *Achilles in Vietnam*, p. 70.

108. James Webb citing 1980 Harris Survey, in *Wall Street Journal*, July 15, 1998.

109. Interview with Dennison Lane (former Deputy Military Attaché in Thailand), October 2000.

110. The suicide figure is from Bernard Siskin and Jerome Staller, *What Are the Chances? Risks, Odds & Likelihood in Everyday Life* (New York: Crown, 1989), p. 164; Daniel Hoffman, ed., *Harvard Guide to Contemporary American Writing* (Cambridge, MA: Harvard University Press, 1979). The quote is from the opening chapter, "Intellectual Background," by Alan Trachtenberg, p. 4.

111. George W. Ball, "Should the U.S. Fight Secret Wars?" p. 37.

112. *New York Times*, April 30, 1975.

113. Haldeman, *Diaries*, p. 376.

114. Ibid., p. 330.

115. Author's observations when, as a graduate student in 1974, he was interviewed for the CIA's Career Trainee program.

116. Yuri Shvets (a former KGB major), "James Jesus Angleton: The Kremlin's Favorite Spook," *Capital Style*, October 1997, p. 62.

117. Castañeda, *Compañero*, p. 370.

118. Bundy, *Tangled Web*, p. 203, on mishandling; Kissinger, *Years of Renewal*, p. 316.

119. National Security Archive, CIA Headquarters to Henry Heckscher, October 16, 1970.

120. Ibid., p. 101; also see *60 Minutes*, CBS News, September 9, 2001, for interviews and documentation concerning Operation Chaos and its aftermath.

121. "Police Aid and Political Will," The Washington Office on Latin America, 1987, p. 7.

122. Dr. Jerome Singer, as cited in *Washington Post*, December 2, 1995.

123. Isaacson, *Kissinger*, p. 201.

124. Kissinger, *White House Years*, p. 730; Memcon, "Chairman Mao's Residence," October 21, 1975, in Burr, *Kissinger Transcripts*, p. 396.

125. James Davis, *Spying on America* (New York: Praeger, 1992), p. 56; Summers, *Official and Confidential*, p. 164.
126. NA, WHCF, Press Releases, Box 41, October 20, 1973.
127. The Phoenix Program is still inaccurately described as targeted against "supposed enemy civilians who worked in the villages of South Vietnam," see Cahn, *Killing Détente*, p. 71. Serious analysis of Phoenix can instead be found in Mark Moyar, *Phoenix and the Birds of Prey: The CIA's Secret Campaign to Destroy the Viet Cong* (Annapolis, MD: Naval Institute Press, 1997).
128. I reached this conclusion several years later during candid conversations with Colby when we were working together on an unrelated article for *International Security*.
129. Interview with Walter Pforzheimer, former CIA head of congressional relations, June 1999.
130. Olmstead, *Challenging the Secret*, pp. 119, 121.
131. Hersh, *Dark Side*, p. 190; David Belin, *Final Disclosure* (New York: Scribner's, 1988), p. 117.
132. Lawrence Meyer, "CIA's Colby Makes Way for Bush," *Washington Post*, January 31, 1976, p. 1.
133. Olmstead, *Challenging the Secret*, pp. 3, 188
134. Executive Order 12333, United States Intelligence Activities, December 4, 1981, pt. 2: Conduct of Intelligence Activities, Section 2.11 (Prohibition on Assassination); also see Stuart Taylor Jr., "Is the Assassination Ban Dead?" *National Journal*, November 21, 1998, p. 2758.
135. Powers, *Not Without Honor*, p. 340.
136. *Washington Post*, April 15, 1997.
137. Stoler, *Allies and Adversaries*, p. 270.

Chapter 9: In the Hollow of the Wave (1975–1981)

1. William Watts and Lloyd A. Free, "A New National Survey: Nationalism, Not Isolationism," *Foreign Policy*, Fall 1976, pp. 5–6.
2. National Security Archive, PD-59 on targeting; PD-13 of May 19, 1977, on weapons transfers.
3. On ass-kissing, see Mann, *About Face*, Woodcock quote, p. 79; Presidential Review Memorandum 31, on technology transfer.
4. Palmer, *25-Year War*, p. 94.
5. Sorley, *Thunderbolt*, p. 350.
6. Burr, *Kissinger Transcripts*, p. 427.
7. Schlesinger aide W. Scott Thompson on the 1975 "tightening up." Interview March 2001.
8. Bundy, *Tangled Web*, p. 505, about Kissinger's paranoia; Thompson interview (note 7) on "defiant talk"; on "assistance," June 2000 interview with Dr. Wolfgang Pordzik, former U.S. representative of the Adenauer Foundation.
9. Thompson interview (note 7).
10. Sciolino and Schmidtt, "Defense Choice Made a Name as an Infighter," *New York Times*, January 8, 2001, p. A13.
11. Nitze, "Assuming," p. 207.
12. Observing the reaction of my colleagues in the library of the Program for Science and International Affairs, Harvard University, to the news of the appointment in the *Boston Globe*, October 20, 1976.

13. "We were outmatched. People like Nitze ate us for lunch," added one of the Team A participants. Quoted in Cahn, *Killing Détente*, p. 158.

14. Cover memo by George Bush for Recipients of National Intelligence Estimate 11-3/8-76; for the critique of the CIA's previous work, see *Intelligence Community Experiment in Competitive Analysis*, "Soviet Strategic Objectives: An Alternative View," "Report of 'Team B,'" December 1976.

15. Even today, a senior CIA analyst from those years asserts, in a book well received by other authorities, that "the principal impetus driving the Soviet armament program was U.S. policy and behavior. . . . Soviet policy was essentially reactive and defensive." See Willard Matthias, *America's Strategic Blunders: Intelligence Analysis and National Security Policy, 1936–1991* (University Park: Pennsylvania State University Press, 2001), p. 318.

16. Kenneth Adelman, ACDA director during the Reagan years, explains how a contractor was hired to scout for other knowledgeable outsiders to critique CIA estimates, but how this initiative was undermined by the covert side of CIA. See Kenneth Adelman, "A Clandestine Clan," *International Security*, Summer 1980, p. 166.

17. Burr, *Kissinger Transcripts*, p. 476; see Zbigniew Brzezinski, "America in a Hostile World," *Foreign Affairs*, Spring 1975, for his opinions at this juncture.

18. Memorandum of Conversation, Brezhnev's Office, The Kremlin, on "US-Soviet Relations; SALT; Other Arms Control," March 25, 1974, in Burr, *Kissinger Transcripts*, p. 242.

19. MIT, Center for International Studies, arms control seminar, May 1977, which the author attended.

20. See William Broad, "Russian Says Soviet Arsenal Was Larger than West Estimated," *New York Times*, September 26, 1993; FBIS-SOV-92-235, December 7, 1992, p. 9; FBIS-SOV-91-226, November 22, 1991, p. 2; FBIS-SOV-92-0090, May 8, 1992, p. 3.

21. "Soviet Capabilities for Strategic Conflict, 1982–1992," 11-3/8-82, p. 7, projected up to 21,000 warheads in the absence of SALT limits.

22. *Soviet Military Power*, Department of Defense, 1981, p. 12. Note the CIA's own retroactive review of its earlier forecasts: CIA, Directorate of Intelligence, "Intelligence Forecasts of Soviet Intercontinental Attack Forces: An Evaluation of the Record," 1989.

23. G. V. Kisun'ko, the chief designer of the original Moscow ABM systems permitted under SALT, states in his autobiography that the SA-5 was a dual-purpose ABM operating with the large phased array radars that provided battle management target tracking data as well as early warning of ballistic missile attack. In 1980 came the SA-10, which had two generations. See Gen. Col. V. M. Smirnov, "30th Anniversary of Missile-Space Defense Troops," FBIS-SOV-97-199, July 18, 1997.

24. Robert Ellsworth, "New Imperatives for the Old Alliance," *International Security*, Spring 1978, p. 138; Statement of Secretary of Defense Harold Brown Before the Senate Foreign Relations Committee, July 9, 1979, "Hearings on the SALT II Treaty," 96th Congress, 1st Session, Part 1, p. 111.

25. The strongest proponent of this view has been Russian expert and former arms negotiator Raymond Garthoff. His arguments are distilled in "Mutual Deterrence, Parity and Strategic Arms Limitation in Soviet Policy," in Leebaert, *Soviet Military Thinking*, and in "Mutual Security and the Future of

Strategic Arms Limitation," in Leebaert, *Soviet Strategy*. His 1,206-page *Détente and Confrontation* is the standard reference for this school.

26. The "Impact Statement" proposal was introduced at Harvard during 1975–1976 by political scientist Ann Cahn, who went on to become a senior official at ACDA in the Carter administration.

27. Powers, *Not Without Honor*, p. 375.

28. Cahn, *Killing Détente*, p. 128.

29. Ford Foundation accounting of grant making in "peace, security, and arms control," for fiscal years 1970–1987. As conveyed to the author on August 13, 1997.

30. Schwartz, ed., *Atomic Audit*, p. 203; Butler at the National Press Club, as quoted in *Washington Post*, December 4, 1996.

31. Gus Weiss, "The Life and Death of COSMOS 954," p. 5.

32. This became abundantly clear to me in working with McGeorge Bundy on his essay "Maintaining Stable Deterrence," which appeared in *International Security*, Winter 1978/1979.

33. Author's conversations with a cross section of FBI agents responsible for counterintelligence and who frequently called upon Harvard and MIT faculty and fellows during the late 1970s

34. Peter Maas, *Underboss: Sammy the Bull Gravano's Story of Life in the Mafia* (New York: HarperCollins, 1997), p. 158; Friedman, *Red Mafiya*, pp. xvii, 23, 33.

35. U.S. Congress, House Subcommittee on Investigations of the Committee on Post Office and Civil Service, 96th Congress, 2nd Session, "Hearings on Federal Personnel Security," pp. 3, 7.

36. Agencies doing the investigating billed the U.S. Treasury differently for identical services. OPM, for example, demanded $1,375 for a background check, whereas DIS asked for only $500, claiming it could handle six times the work with merely twice the staff.

37. U.S. Congress, Senate Permanent Subcommittee on Investigations of the Committee on Government Affairs, 99th Congress, 1st Session, "Federal Government Security Clearance Programs," April 16, 1985, pp. 14, 8. The whole rigmarole was proving to delay the hiring of government workers by an average of 50 days.

38. Ibid., p. 12; James Gordon, "Security Clearance Delays Cost Defense Department $1 Billion a Year," *Aviation Week & Space Technology*, May 13, 1985, pp. 63–68.

39. Rodman, *More Precious*, p. 156; Georgi Arbatov, *The System: An Insider's Life in Soviet Politics* (New York: Times Books, 1991), p. 194.

40. Franklin B. Weinstein, "The United States, Japan and the Security of Korea," *International Security*, Fall 1977, pp. 80, 84.

41. Stockwell, *In Search of Enemies*, p. 180.

42. Ibid., pp. 72, 37.

43. Ibid. This is the title of chapter 9.

44. Kissinger, *Years of Renewal*, pp. 818, 803.

45. Stockwell, *In Search of Enemies*, p. 216.

46. Ibid., p. 221.

47. Interview with Professor Hillary Mukwenha, Dean, Faculty of Commerce, University of Zimbabwe, October 1999.

48. Kissinger et al. and PRC Ambassador Huang Zhen, White House, July 6, 1973, in Burr, *Kissinger Transcripts*, p. 145; ibid., pp. 373, 385, 389, 405.

49. The first five years of the Harvard-based quarterly journal *International Security*, from 1976 to 1981, published only one article concerning the Vietnam War amid dozens on SALT, NATO, proliferation, China, and regional security issues.

50. Handlin, *Distortion of America*, p. 124; Aleksandr Solzhenitsyn, as quoted in Berman, *Solzhenitsyn at Harvard*, pp. 13–14.

51. Handlin, *Distortion of America*, pp. 121–122; *New York Times*, editorial, June 13, 1978; *Washington Post*, editorial, June 13, 1978.

52. Christoph Bertram, "European Security and the German Problem," *International Security*, Winter 1979/80, p. 105.

53. George Urban, "A Conversation with George Kennan," *Encounter*, September 1976, pp. 34–35, 37.

54. Together, the nine members of the European Economic Community roughly equalled the United States in GDP in 1979, at around $2000 billion.

55. Wolf and Leebaert, "Trade Liberalization," pp. 136–139.

56. Snyder, *Warriors of Disinformation*, p. 97, concerning $100 million.

57. Andrew and Mitrokhin, *Sword and the Shield*, p. 298; ie training Italiano, p. 392.

58. Donald McNeil, "The Life of a Terrorist Emerges," *New York Times*, November 15, 2000, p. A6, concerning testimony of Mohamed Abo Talb.

59. Carter, *Keeping Faith*, p. 438.

60. *Public Papers*, Carter, 1977, Vol. 1, "The Energy Problem: Address to the Nation," April 18, 1977, p. 657.

61. Resource Data International, Boulder, Colorado, cites this as the amount spent through 1998.

62. Harvard Center for Risk Analysis. As cited by Lawrence Cranberg, Senior Fellow, American Physical Society, Austin, Texas. Studies repeatedly show that, to generate the amount of electricity, more people will die if coal is used than if nuclear power is the energy source.

63. Hixson, *George F. Kennan*, p. 246; Urban, "Conversation," p. 21, on "stupidities."

64. Melman, *Permanent War Economy*, p. 11.

65. Robert Reich, *The Next American Frontier* (New York: Times Books, 1983), pp. 14, 17. In contrast to progress in Western Europe and Japan, his argument goes, the U.S. is poorly structured politically and economically to adapt to a changing world.

66. Richard Rovere, "Affairs of State," *New Yorker*, August 6, 1979, p. 89; Dobrynin, *In Confidence*, pp. 409–412.

67. CNN's "Cold War Facts and Figures," a two-page compilation that accompanies the *Cold War* TV series, not only ignores inflation but incorrectly reports that the budget increased 20 percent, to $106 billion.

68. AID contractor Flemming Heegaard, who was with Dubbs that final day, convincingly argues how this killing points to Soviet involvement. Interview, March 2001. Also see the *Washington Post*, December 3, 1997, letter to the editor, from former State Department official Eli Flam.

69. See "Concerning the Situation in 'A,'" Odd Arne Westad, Cold War International History Project, *Bulletin*, Winter 1996/97, p. 131; Magnus and Naby, *Afghanistan*, p. 128.

70. Dobbs, *Big Brother*, p. 14; Andrew, *President's Eyes*, p. 448.
71. Hixson, *Kennan*, p. 273.
72. Interview, George Crile, CBS News, January 1996.
73. Gallup Poll, "What do you think is the most important problem facing the country today?" Forty-four percent answered "foreign policy," compared to 40 percent noting "war" in 1950 and "keeping the peace" in 1959, as depicted in the *New York Times*, August 1, 1999, p. WK 4; Whittle Johnston, "Reagan and America's Democratic Mission," in Schmertz, *President Reagan*, p. 22.

Chapter 10: Hard Pounding (1981–1985)

1. Writing in early 1989 about the future of Soviet military thinking, ten of the most conversant students of the problem, covering a broad spectrum of political beliefs and practical experiences, failed to imagine that the empire in some assuredly Communist form would not be around to greet the millennium. See Leebaert, *Soviet Strategy*, which includes chapters by Colin Gray, Raymond Garthoff, Christopher Jones, Mikhail Tsypkin, and others, including this author. Jack Matlock, ambassador in Moscow during 1988–91, is among those who believed it "not true" that the Soviet Union was economically on the point of collapse even as late as 1989. See his interview in Strober and Strober, *Reagan*, p. 573.
2. Henry Kissinger, *Diplomacy* (New York: Simon and Schuster, 1994), p. 772.
3. Fairlie, *Kennedy Promise*, p. 180.
4. Charles Krauthammer, "Reluctant Cold Warriors," *Washington Post*, November 12, 1999, p. A35, citing Anthony Lewis's, Tom Wicker's, and George Ball's reactions respectively.
5. D'Souza, *Ronald Reagan*, p. 230.
6. Author's interviews in Moscow during April 1981.
7. Author's April 1981 conversation with George Kennan in front of Arbatov and other Soviet functionaries.
8. Stanford Center arms control researchers, among many others, insisted that the Krasnoyarsk radar site was merely a satellite-tracking facility. Russians would finally acknowledge the latter in 1989, but not revealing until after the Cold War that orders to violate had come straight from the Politburo. It was the most unambiguous of all violations.
9. Robert Scheer, *With Enough Shovels: Reagan, Bush and Nuclear War* (New York: Random House, 1982), p. 40.
10. Don Oberdorfer in the *Washington Post*, May 20, 1981.
11. Andrew and Mitrokhin, *Sword and the Shield*, p. 213.
12. The "seventeen months" was revealed in interviews by the long-serving senior technical official finally responsible for conducting President Reagan through this exercise; George Keyworth, Reagan's science adviser, quoted in Gregg Herken, "The Earthly Origins of Star Wars," *Bulletin of the Atomic Scientists*, October 1987, p. 23.
13. Minutes of the NSC mtg. of December 16, 1982, "U.S. Relations with the USSR," prepared by Col. Michael Wheeler.
14. By 1983, the Soviets were nearing their goal of being able to kill up to 90 percent of U.S. ICBMs in a preemptive strike. In that year's NIE on Soviet strategic forces, however, the CIA made sharp reductions in its assessment of SS-19

accuracy and of SS-18 warhead yield. The Soviets would thereby appear to have little or no such capability. This revision became the basis for the conventional wisdom that the Soviet ICBM force never achieved, perhaps had not even sought, a counterforce strike capability. This has been disproved. See Lee, "Counterforce Capabilities"; on "arms race," see Shevardnadze in a speech to the Soviet Foreign Ministry, July 1988, as cited in Schmertz, *President Reagan*, p. 33.

15. Author's conversation with Senator Moynihan at the Marver Bernstein lecture, Georgetown University.

16. "Sizing Up the Kremlin," *Washington Post*, February 1, 1981.

17. Arthur Schlesinger delivered the Cyril Foster Lecture at Oxford University in May 1983. Titled "Foreign Policy and the American Character," there was no doubt to several of us in the audience as to which Oval Office occupant was regarded as lacking in character: Reagan was presented as inept for explaining the world struggle as one between "right and wrong." A version was published in *Foreign Affairs*, Fall 1983.

18. George Urban, "Was Stalin Really a 'Great Man'? A Conversation with Averell Harriman," *Encounter*, November 1981.

19. Weinberger, *The Fragment* ████████████ ██ ████

20. Author's interviews with former officials Norman Bailey and with Richard Perle on "economic warfare," 2000–2001.

21. Strobe Talbott, "Playing for the Future," *Time*, April 18, 1983.

22. These views were expressed at a Faculty Club dinner I attended on September 22, 1981, held by the Harvard Strategy and Arms Control Seminar, for Paul Nitze, U.S. Representative for Intermediate Range Nuclear Forces Negotiations, concerning "The Strategic Balance in the 1980s."

23. Kokoshin, *Soviet Strategic Thought*, p. 181.

24. John Newhouse, *War and Peace in the Nuclear Age* (New York: Knopf, 1989), p. 426.

25. The debate at a dinner held by the Harvard Arms Control Seminar (before it expanded its name to include "strategy") on March 21, 1979, had become heated. The guest was George Seignious, director of ACDA.

26. Schultz, *Triumph*, pp. 125–128.

27. NSDD 75, "U.S. Relations with the USSR," January 17, 1983.

28. The pivotal document is NSDD 75, "U.S. Relations with the USSR," January 17, 1983; NSDD 32, "U.S. National Security Strategy," May 20, 1982, p. 6; Memorandum for the President from William P. Clark, NSSD 11-82: Draft NSDD and IG Study, December 16, 1982.

29. Isaacs and Downing, *Cold War*, p. 347.

30. NIE 11-3/8-77, 1977, "Soviet Capabilities for Strategic Nuclear Conflict Through the Late 1980s," p. 48.

31. NSDD 32, "U.S. National Security Strategy," May 20, 1982, p. 5.

32. D. Takhanov, interview with Gen. Col. Yu. Votintsev, "We Defended the USSR Against a Nuclear Strike," *Vecherniy Almaty*, June 1, 2, and 3, 1993, as reported in JPRS-UMA-93-035, September 22, 1993, p. 6.

33. Andrew and Mitrokhin, *Sword and the Shield*, p. 214.

34. Tsarev, "A Diamond Studded Sky," JPRS-UMA-93-039, October 20, 1993, p. 4.

35. Andrew and Mitrokhin, *Sword and the Shield*, p. 214.

36. Votintsev, *VIZh.*, No. 10, 1993, pp. 36–37.
37. Richard Burt, Council on Foreign Relations, mtg. September 1983; *New York Times*, December 9, 1996.
38. Author's interviews with W. Scott Thompson, 1999–2000.
39. Pavel Palazchenko, *My Years with Gorbachev and Shevardnadze: The Memoirs of a Soviet Interpreter* (University Park: Pennsylvania State University Press, 1997), p. 20.
40. Special National Intelligence Estimate (SNIE) 11-10-84/JX, "Implications of Recent Soviet Military Activities," p. 11; Fischer, "A Cold War Conundrum," pp. 12, 18, 20.
41. Andrew and Mitrokhin, *Sword and the Shield*, p. 213.
42. David Pryce-Jones, *The Strange Death*, p. 363; Kalugin in Schweizer, *Victory*, p. xi.
43. Strober and Strober, *Reagan*, p. 152. Matlock's own writings on these years are thorough, although he myopically claims there was no coherent policy toward the Soviet Union when he joined the NSC in 1983, p. 79. His observation is disproved by the formulation of NSDD 75 that January.
44. Leebaert, *Soviet Strategy*, p. 17.
45. Reagan, *An American Life*, p. 262.
46. *New York Times*, April 23, 1998; Yazov quote from Matlock in Schmertz, *President Reagan*, p. 122; interview with William Crowell, Deputy Director, NSA, October 1997.
47. Shultz, *Triumph*, p. 377.
48. Bosch, *Reagan*, p. 280.
49. Schwartz, ed., *Atomic Audit*, p. 82.
50. Bosch, *Reagan*, p. 289.
51. Strober and Strober, *Reagan*, p. 355.
52. Morris, *A Memoir*, p. 662.
53. Dobrynin, *In Confidence*, p. 609.
54. Schwartz, ed., *Atomic Audit*, pp. 298, 297.
55. Lee, *CIA Estimates*, pp. 143–148, 35; the CIA estimate for this period was about 14 percent with no growth in military procurement in 1976–85; even this for accurate estimate may be too low. Recently available Soviet material, as discussed in chapter 11, puts the military's share at 30 percent of official GDP, or 60 percent of the Soviet national budget in the early 1980s.
56. Alibek, *Biohazard*, re dozens of tons of plague and smallpox stockpiled "near Moscow," p. x; re working with U.S. to eradicate smallpox, pp. 110–111; concerning joint eradication efforts, Professor D. A. Henderson of Johns Hopkins called Soviet behavior "unconscionable" on CNN Newsroom with Garrick Utley, interview, May 9, 2000.
57. Lee, *CIA Estimates*, pp. 159–60.
58. Schweizer, *Victory*, p. xiv.
59. Leebaert, *Soviet Strategy*, pp. 16–17.
60. NSDDs 32 and 75. Aleksandr Bessmertnykh elaborates in Schweizer, *Victory*.
61. Norman A. Bailey, "The Strategic Plan That Won the Cold War: NSDD 75" (McLean, VA: The Potomac Foundation, 1998), p. 18.
62. Response to NSSD 11-82, December 6, 1982, Part II, Section A, Subhead c.
63. Bailey, "Strategic Plan," p. 18.
64. Schweizer, pp. 109–110.

65. The alliance controversy is examined in Kennedy School Case, "The Reagan Administration and the Soviet Pipeline Embargo."

66. NSC mtg., December 16, 1982 (note 13); Reagan's intense involvement with these parts of the policy-making process is also unanimously reported by the senior NSC staff during 1981–84, including scholars such as Pipes, CUNY's Norman Bailey, Guy Weiss, and the University of Virginia's Carey Lord.

67. NSDD 48, July 23, 1982.

68. Interview, Richard Perle, May 2001.

69. U.S. Department of Commerce, "Quantification of Western Exports of High-Technology Products to Communist Countries Through 1983" (Washington: GPO, 1985), p. 28.

70. Weiss, "Farewell," plus extensive discussions with Weiss during 1998–2000.

71. See Gen. Yakolev, C-in-C Russian Federation Strategic Rocket Forces (chief editor), *Raketnyy Shchit Oteckestva* (m.TsIPK RVSN, 1999), pp. 184–185.

72. NSDD 75 (note 27).

73. Fialka, *War by Other Means*, pp. 120, 10.

74. Ibid., p. 75.

75. *Public Papers*, Reagan, "Address to the Nation on Defense and National Security," March 23, 1983, pp. 442–443.

76. Broad, *Teller's War*, p. 99.

77. Schweizer, *Victory*, p. 136.

78. Daniel O. Graham, *Confessions of a Cold Warrior* (Fairfax, VA: Preview Press, 1995), p. 144.

79. Author's discussions at the time with Lord St. Brides (Maurice James), previously high commissioner to both India and Pakistan.

80. See William T. Lee, "High-Tech Adventurism," in Stephen J. Cimbala, ed., *Mysteries of the Cold War* (Aldershot, UK: Ashgate Publishing, 1999), pp. 137–139. Also see the trip report by Robert Molloy, director of Martin Marietta's Directed Energy Systems Division, in "SpaceTrans: The Newsletter of the Space Transportation Association," March/April 1994.

81. William T. Lee offers new evidence in "Counterforce Capabilities."

82. Ball, "The War for Star Wars," p. 38.

83. "Maginot . . . in space" cited in Reynolds, *One World*, p. 489; "decline" is Mao's statement at the Tenth Party Congress, as cited in Ball, *Cold War*, p. 199; Ross, "China Learns to Compromise," pp. 766, 769.

84. Graham, *Confessions* (note 78), p. 153; Strober and Strober, *Reagan*, interviewing Gennadi Gerasimov, chief of the Soviet Foreign Ministry Information Department, and spokesman for Secretary General Gorbachev, pp. 357–358.

85. Broad, *Teller's War*, p. 283; Schmertz, *Reagan*, p. 138.

86. "When 'Star Wars' came on the scene," said one political activist, the Reverend William Sloane Coffin, "*pfft* went Nuclear Freeze." He is quoted in Graham, *Confessions* (note 78), p. 190.

87. Strober and Strober, *Reagan*, p. 248.

88. Shultz, *Triumph*, pp. 250, 492.

89. Broad, *Teller's War*, pp. 138, 210.

90. Ibid., pp. 252, 253.

91. Strober and Strober, *Reagan*, p. 244.

92. Graham, *Confessions* (note 78), p. 155; I heard Garwin address the concept while we were both affiliated with Harvard's CSIA during the later 1970s,

and we together discussed his views on deterrence while working on his essay "Launch Under Attack to Redress Minuteman Vulnerability?" *International Security*, in 1979.

93. FitzGerald, *Way Out in the Blue*, pp. 86–87, 95, 115–116, 330, 407–408, 442, 474–475. Among the Russian sources useful for examining the preemptive capabilities behind Moscow's strategic doctrines of the time are Volkov, ed., *Mezhkontinental'nye*; Karpenko, *Otechestvennyye*; and Podvig, *Strategicheskoye*.

94. Interview with Angelo Codevilla, Hoover Institution, SDI analyst and former Wallop defense aide, October 1999.

95. Rodman, *More Precious*, p. 310, citing Vyacheslav Dashichev, a prominent analyst at the Institute for the Study of the Economics of the World Socialist System. "This proved that our foreign policy was not cost-effective," added Dashichev.

96. Lawrence Korb, an assistant secretary of defense under Reagan, in Schmertz, *President Reagan*, p. 247.

Chapter 11: Shaking Loose (1985–1989)

1. D'Souza, *Reagan*, p. 193.
2. Jeffrey E. Garten, "The Gradual Revolution," *New York Times Book Review*, February 8, 1998, p. 7.
3. Hixson, *Kennan*, pp. 275–276.
4. Mark Kramer, "Colonel Kuklinski and the Polish Crisis," Cold War International History Project *Bulletin*, Winter 1998, pp. 48–49, and "Soviet Preparations," pp. 102–103; Dobbs, *Big Brother*, pp. 73, 463.
5. NSDD 75, January 17, 1983.
6. NSDD 45, July 15, 1982.
7. Snyder, *Warriors of Disinformation*, p. 166.
8. D'Souza, *Reagan*, p. 231.
9. Strober and Strober, *Reagan*, p. 207.
10. Ibid., interview with John Vessey, p. 214.
11. Ibid., p. 289.
12. Ibid., interview with Robert McFarlane, p. 262.
13. Powell, *American Journey*, p. 292.
14. Rodman, *More Precious*, p. 371.
15. Ibid., p. 454.
16. Kennedy School Case, "Politics of a Covert Action."
17. Milt Bearden recounts this order in the *Washington Post*, December 12, 1998.
18. Author's interviews with Michael Pillsbury, December 2000, April 2001.
19. NSDD 166, U.S. Policy Programs and Strategy in Afghanistan, March 27, 1985 (classified); Rodman, *More Precious*, p. 338.
20. Kennedy School Case, "Politics of a Covert Action," p. 34; Pillsbury interviews (note 18).
21. Bearden is quoted in "One Man and a Global Web of Violence," *New York Times*, January 14, 2001, p. A16; the observer who predicted trouble was Lord St. Brides, the former high commissioner to Pakistan and to India, in discussions with the author; Mary Anne Weaver, "Letter from Pakistan," *New Yorker*, June 12, 1995, p. 44.
22. Leogrande, *Our Own Backyard*, p. 23.

23. Bosch, *Reagan*, p. 277; the best evidence for Castro's shipments is in Timothy C. Brown, *Real Contra War*. He is a Stanford University researcher who served in the late 1980s as the senior U.S. State Department liaison to the Contras.

24. Rodman, *More Precious*, p. 47.

25. Author's USIA-sponsored meetings with academics and government officials in Britain, France, and West Germany during 1984 and 1985.

26. Timothy C. Brown, *Real Contra War*, pp. 3–11, 204–206.

27. Charles Krauthammer, "Reluctant Cold Warriors," *Washington Post*, November 12, 1999, p. A35.

28. Strober and Strober, *Reagan*, interview with George Shultz, p. 153.

29. Edwin Meese, *With Reagan* (Washington: Regnery, 1992), pp. 238–240; Rodman, *More Precious*, pp. 430–431; conversations with former NSC staffer Paula Dobriansky, October 1997.

30. Rod McDaniel to author, July 1984.

31. Strober and Strober, *Reagan*, interview with Admiral William Crowe, p. 512.

32. Leebaert, "U.S. Policies in the Third World," p. 63.

33. Richard Haass, Assistant Secretary of State for Policy Planning in 2001, spoke of those ties as minimal on "Washington Journal," CSPAN, June 1, 2001; on intelligence partner, see Bamford, *Body of Secrets*, pp. 544–545.

34. Clarridge, *A Spy for All Seasons*, p. 16.

35. Gerecht (writing as Shirley), "Can't Anybody?," p. 48.

36. McCullough, "Coping with Iran-Contra," p. 87.

37. Powell, *American Journey*, p. 340.

38. Strock, *Reagan on Leadership*, p. 98; the conclusion of Reagan's biographer that the President's last years in office were encumbered by recovery from both the 1981 shooting and the 1987 prostatectomy were quickly refuted by Drs. John Hutton and Benjamin Aaron, the two personal physicians Edmund Morris had used as sources. *Washington Post*, October 30, 1999, p. A23.

39. Rodman, *More Precious*, p. 430.

40. Peter Rodman in Schmertz, *President Reagan*, p. 33.

41. Rodman, *More Precious*, p. 284.

42. Report by the American Committee on U.S.-Soviet Relations cited in "Superpower Proxies in Third World Deplored," *New York Times*, May 6, 1988.

43. See the "Dark Alliance" series in the *San Jose Mercury News* of August 1996, subsequently published as a highly misleading book by the same author, Gary Webb, *Dark Alliance: The CIA, the Contras and the Crack Cocaine Explosion* (New York: Seven Stories Press, 1998).

44. CIA statement to the court at his trial, although he claimed his retainers added up to $10 million.

45. National Security Archive, the 450-page Inspector General's report concerning Contra drug links was released October 1998. Frederick P. Hitz is quoted in the *Washington Post*, November 3, 1998.

46. This 211-page Inspector General's report was released to the Human Rights Commissioner of Honduras, October 1998; Donald H. Winters is quoted by Tim Golden in "Honduran Army's Abuses Were Known to the CIA," *New York Times*, October 24, 1998.

47. The aftermath of Archbishop Romero's 1980 assassination is but one example, as explained by former ambassador Robert E. White in "Call Off the Spies," *Washington Post*, February 7, 1996, p. A19.

48. Tim Golden, "Forgiven Enemy: From Suspect in Murders to a New Life in America," *New York Times*, November 22, 1996, p. 18.

49. Xuncax v. Gramajo, Nos. CIV. A. 9111564-DPW, CIV.A. 91-11612-DPW 1995 WL 54818 (D. Mass., April 12, 1995).

50. Strober and Strober, *Reagan*, p. 169, Adolfo Calero interview.

51. Clarridge, *A Spy*, p. 208.

52. Andew and Mitrokhin, *Sword and the Shield*, p. 343.

53. According to Charles A. Peters, who edited the President's Daily Brief, and served in that role for fourteen years. See *Washington Post*, April 23, 1999.

54. Firth and Noren, *Soviet Defense Spending*, pp. 66, 169.

55. Ibid., pp. 53, 63–64, 151, 221; William T. Lee, *The Estimation of Soviet Defense Expenditures, 1955–75* (New York: Praeger, 1976), p. 66, and Lee, *CIA Estimates*, pp. 42–50, 123–132.

56. Letter from Professor Genrikh Trofimenko, Russian Academy of Sciences, to William T. Lee, November 18, 1995; also see *Segodnya* (Today), June 18, 1993, in which a GRU colonel cites the analyses of Birman and Lee.

57. James H. Noren, "The Economic Impact of Soviet Military Spending, CIA, ERIR 75-3, April 1975, pp. 5–11.

58. James H. Noren, "The Controversy over Western Measures of Soviet Defense Expenditures," *Post-Soviet Affairs*, no. 3, July–September 1995, p. 266; Firth and Noren (note 54), pp. 180, 182; CIA, "The Soviet Release of Defense Spending Data to the United Nations: Less Than Meets the Eye," May 1991, p. 6.

59. Lee, *CIA Estimates*, pp. 34–41; the CIA also sought outsider opinion during the 1980s by contracting with Rand economist Charles Wolf Jr., MIT defense analyst Stephen Meyer, and several others to referee the Agency's economic analyses.

60. Ibid., figures 2.3 and 2.4, p. 51.

61. Laurie Kurtzweg, "Measures of Soviet Gross National Product in 1982 Prices," prepared for the Joint Economic Committee (Washington, DC, 1990), table A-9, pp. 80–81. Although the Soviets themselves admitted that household consumption had ceased to grow in 1982–83, and even then probably postdated the fact by at least five years, the CIA discerned a 3 percent annual advance during the 1970s, dropping to a sedate pace of still over 2 percent from 1980 to 1987. The Agency calculated the growth of Soviet GDP at about 2.4 percent annually in 1970–80, dropping to 2 percent over the 1980s. This would have seen the Soviet economy increase 150 percent over its 1981 size by around year 2005.

62. Shultz, *Triumph*, p. 507. George Shultz, himself an economist, has been the most outspoken secretary of state about CIA shortcomings.

63. Author's interviews with intelligence community analysts during 2000 and 2001.

64. At the Princeton conference, Charles Wolf Jr., a former dean of the Rand Corporation's Graduate School, graded the CIA's Soviet economic analyses like this: "Scholarly approach — 'B.' Results — 'C.' Answers provided to policymakers — 'A,' splendidly right even if for the wrong reasons."

65. The quote is that of Richard Kerr, deputy director in 1989–92, in the *New York Times*, March 17, 2001, p. A17.

66. Taubman et al., *Nikita Khrushchev*, p. 318.

67. Melvin Goodman, "Ending the CIA's Cold War Legacy," *Foreign Policy*, Winter 1996/97, pp. 130–132, and Spring 1997, pp. 179–180.

68. MacEachin, "CIA Assessments," pp. 58, 59; "Domestic Stresses on the Soviet System," NIE 11-18-85, November 1985, p. 3; also see Kennedy School Case, "The Soviet Economy in a Global Perspective."

69. "The Soviet Economy in a Global Perspective" (note 68), p. 22; author's conversations with Trofimenko in 1981 and 1983. In May 1991, CIA analysts foresaw a 10–15 percent decline in Soviet GDP but still did not recognize the extent of its collapse since 1988. See CIA, Directorate of Intelligence, "Soviet Economic Futures: The Outlook for 1991," May 1991, pp. iii–iv.

70. Hough cited in the *Washington Post*, November 7, 1999, p. B4; Stansfield Turner, "Intelligence for a New World Order," *Foreign Affairs*, Fall 1991, p. 162, plus author's interview with Turner, July 1998.

71. Paul Samuelson and William Nordhaus, *Economics*, 12th edition (New York: McGraw Hill, 1985), pp. 775, 776; Mark Skousen, *Economics on Trial: Lies, Myths, and Realities* (Homewood, IL: Business One Irwin, 1991), p. 208.

72. Wolf, *Man Without a Face*, p. 316.

73. Jay Taylor, "A Leaner, Keener CIA," *Washington Post*, December 22, 1996, p. C7.

74. See Gerecht (writing as Shirley), *Know Thine Enemy*.

75. Wise, *Nightmover*, p. 200.

76. Ibid., p. 316.

77. Gerecht (writing as Shirley), "Can't Anybody?," p. 50. He confirms from experience that "some good agents, and many mediocre or worthless ones, died for the case officers' mistakes."

78. Ibid., p. 58.

79. *Interview*, July 1986, William Casey interview conducted by Ira Ginsburg, pp. 42–44.

80. Casey invoked this vision of truly mechanical security around the time that Margaret Thatcher experimented with lie-detector vetting within the British intelligence services, grudgingly accepting six polygraph machines and their staffs from a missionary CIA. In a 1984–85 pilot program, polygraph tests of 200 members of British counterintelligence (MI5) brought a preposterous 37 percent failure rate under interrogation. See the *Sunday Telegraph*, October 5, 1986, p. 40.

81. Author's interviews during 2000–2001 with neuroscientists at the Krasnow Institute for Advanced Study, under contract with the CIA.

82. Norman Pattis, "Worried About Your Masculinity? The Polygraph Lies," *Hartford Courant*, June 8, 1986, p. C4.

83. Charles Hall, "Official at State Failed CIA, FBI Polygraphs," *Washington Post*, September 24, 1996, p. B1. Rick Osborn is the spokesman quoted.

84. Peter Finn, "Hiker Finds Man's Body in U.S. Park: Foreign Service Officer Was Missing 2 Months," *Washington Post*, October 28, 1996, p. B1. I also interviewed Schneider family attorneys in 1997.

85. Author's interviews. Employee polygraphing has intensified. Today about 90 percent of those tested are called for a second test in attempts to resolve "discrepancies."

86. Clarridge, *A Spy*, pp. 303, 305.

87. Wolf, *Man Without a Face*, p. 315; "seedy" extended to the commonplace wearing of gold chain necklaces, after office hours, among DO personnel in the Northern Virginia suburbs. As observed by author.

88. CIA director Tenet threatened to resign in 1998 when an Israeli prime minister pressured the White House to release traitor Jonathan Pollard.

89. Discussion with former Special Agent Ted Frauman, September 2000.

90. Marie Brenner, "A Traitor's Life: Why Edward Pitts Betrayed His Country," *Washington Post Magazine*, September 21, 1997, p. 19.

91. *New York Times*, April 20, 1997, quoting John F. Lewis Jr.

92. Elisabeth Frater, "Polarized Over Polygraphs," *National Journal*, September 9, 2000, quoting Donald M. Kerr, director of the FBI's lab division.

93. "Military decade" became a common description among academic critics of the time; one of the many unoriginal uses of the latter term is Barbara Ehrenreich, *The Worst Years of Our Lives: Irreverent Notes from the Decade of Greed* (New York: HarperCollins, 1991).

94. Arthur Schlesinger Jr., "Anticommunism's Two Faces," *Foreign Affairs*, January/February 1996, p. 156; Bosch, *Reagan*, interviewing Lewis, p. 339.

95. Samuelson, *Good Life*, p. 159; Keith Bradsher, "Partnership in the Deficit: Parties Share Blame Over Three Decades," *New York Times*, December 3, 1995, p. 1. Merely two government programs were cut during the Reagan years, general revenue sharing and urban development action grants.

96. David Calleo, *The Bankrupting of America: How the Federal Budget Is Impoverishing the Nation* (New York: Morrow, 1992), p. 21, on taxes; talk of "racing to bankruptcy" can be found in David Stockman, *Triumph of Politics: Why the Reagan Revolution Failed* (New York: Harper and Row, 1986), p. 395.

97. Samuelson, *Good Life*, p. 161, cites 20.2 percent of GDP.

98. Laura D'Andrea Tyson, "Who's Bashing Whom? Trade Conflict in High-Technology Industries" (Washington: Institute for International Economics, 1992), pp. 25, 39.

99. *New York Times*' David Sanger to author in Tokyo, October 1991.

100. For another view of Japanese software development, see Leebaert, *Future of Software*, pp. 19–20, 215–225; the prominent "cold fusion" policy advocate was management consultant and future Clinton adviser Ira Magaziner, who lobbied for the University of Utah, from where the "breakthrough" had emerged.

101. Paul Volcker and Toyoo Gyohten, *Changing Fortune: The World's Money and the Threat to American Leadership* (New York: Times Books, 1992), p. xiv.

102. Reynolds, *One World*, p. 646.

103. Pete Peterson, "The Morning After," *The Atlantic*, October 1987, pp. 44, 49, 55.

104. Kenichi Ohmae, "After the Crash: Patching Up a World of Trouble: A Japanese View," *Washington Post*, November 1, 1987, p. C1.

105. David Halberstam, *The Next Century* (New York: Morrow, 1991), pp. 15–16. The term is also used in John K. White, *Still Seeing Red: How the Cold War Shapes the New American Politics* (Boulder, CO: Westview Press, 1997), p. 205. Senator Paul Tsongas and others additionally adopted this wisdom at the time. Today, in correspondence with the author, Johnson explains that Japan "has not adjusted to the changed circumstances of the post–Cold War world."

106. Higgs, "Cold War Economy," p. 291. Between 1948 and 1989, an average of 7.5 percent of GDP was expended annually on defense, according to Budget of the U.S. Government (Washington: GPO, 1997), table 6.1.
107. Strober and Strober, *Reagan,* interview with Oliver Wright, p. 242.
108. D'Souza, *Reagan,* p. 228.

Chapter 12: Unintended Consequences (1989–)

1. Former *Washington Post* editorialist Charles Paul Freund wrote "Might and Fog: Reich Makes Might-Have-Been," in the *City Paper,* June 10, 1988, pp. 12–16; the descriptions of "fatigue" and "impatience" come from the real event with the Soviets, as presented by Talbott in *Master of the Game,* p. 390.
2. For example, see Robert Thruston, *Life and Terror in Stalin's Russia* (New Haven, CT: Yale University Press, 1996).
3. Courtois, *Black Book of Communism,* details between 85 and 100 million dead, with determinations of class being comparable to those of race under Nazism as each ideology killed to create a "pure" society.
4. Strobe Talbott, "Rethinking the Red Menace," *Time,* January 1, 1990.
5. Testimony of George F. Kennan, "The Future of Europe," in Hearings on the Soviet Bloc and Europe's Future Before the Subcommittee on European Affairs of the Committee on Foreign Relations, January 17, 1990, 101st Congress, 2nd Session, Vol. 6, p. 77.
6. Matlock, *Autopsy,* pp. 590–591.
7. Ligachev, *Inside Gorbachev's Kremlin,* p. 363.
8. Isaacson, *Kissinger,* pp. 727–728.
9. See, for instance, Mark Helprin, "A Marshall Plan for Russia," *Wall Street Journal,* September 9, 1998.
10. Schmertz, ed., *President Reagan,* p. 141.
11. Missy Ryan, "Arrested Development," *National Journal,* June 10, 2000, p. 1822.
12. Paul Sarobin, "What Went Wrong," *National Journal,* p. 3454.
13. Odom, *Collapse of the Soviet Military,* p. 277. Dr. Odom's opinions are significant not only as a Sovietologist and retired Air Force general, but as a former NSA director.
14. Isaacs and Downing, *Cold War,* p. 377.
15. *New York Times,* December 8, 1998, p. A12; Judith Miller, "U.S. Aid Is Diverted to Germ Warfare," *New York Times,* January 26, 2000. U.S. taxpayers also met a first installment of at least $8 million in the late 1990s to upgrade security at Vector, Russia's germ bank for all strains of smallpox, to be followed by around $20 million annually on joint research. Also see Judith Miller, "Flying Blind in a Dangerous World," *New York Times,* Week in Review, February 6, 2000, p. 5.
16. Hundreds of thousands of tons of uranium ore were also processed, although releasing far less radiation into the environment than the Soviet weapons complex. U.S. plants generated billions of gallons of wastewater and 105 million gallons of highly radioactive and hazardous chemical wastes.
17. *Estimating the Cold War Mortgage: The 1995 Baseline Environmental Management Report,* U.S. Department of Energy, Office of Environmental Management, March 1995.
18. *Washington Post,* August 11, 2000.

19. Kenneth Timmerman, "Missile Defense Deployed in Russia," *Insight*, April 30, 2001, p. 33. This journalist's interview was with the most senior DIA official responsible for the issue. The "nor did he know anyone" assertion was not included in the article.

20. William Safire, "Friendly Dissuasion," *New York Times*, May 3, 2001; just one of the terms reads, "A Missile Shield: Grand Vision or Maginot Line," *New York Times*, May 3, 2001, editorials/letters.

21. Adam Coymer, "Russia Tries to Pierce Missile Shield with Charm," *New York Times*, August 4, 2001, p. A3.

22. Former DOJ counterintelligence official John Martin sees in the FBI's lack of expertise about China "disaster waiting to happen." As he explained on NPR News, Barbara Bradley interview, May 19, 2000; also see *The NewsHour with Jim Lehrer*, June 9, 1999, interview with former FBI agent Paul Moore on the Bureau needing new methods to confront Chinese espionage; FBI/Lee quote in *Time*, January 17, 2000, p. 24.

23. Also reminiscent of Vietnam, a small scientific industry arose around the issue of chronic illness among veterans — $115 million going to 121 research projects, millions more to create medical registries.

24. Cockburn and Cockburn, *Out of the Ashes*, p. 54.

25. Reuel Marc Gerecht, "Liberate Iraq," *Weekly Standard*, May 14, 2001, p. 25; Cockburn and Cockburn, *Out of the Ashes*, pp. 174, 197, 229, 230.

26. Richard L. Kuglar, "Costs of NATO Enlargement: Moderate and Affordable," Strategic Forum, National Defense University, October 1997.

27. George F. Kennan, "A Fateful Error," *New York Times*, February 5, 1997, op/ed; Thomas Friedman, "Now a Word from 'X,'" *New York Times*, May 2, 1998; Friedman, *Red Mafiya*, p. xix for Yeltsin quote; Nicholas Lemann, "The Provocateur," *New Yorker*, November 13, 2000, p. 100.

28. Chris Hedges, "Leaders in Bosnia Are Said to Steal Up to $1 Billion," *New York Times*, August 17, 1999, p. A1.

29. Samantha Power, "Bystanders to Genocide: Why the United States Let the Rwanda Tragedy Happen," *Atlantic Monthly*, September 2001, pp. 103–104.

30. Tim Weiner quoting the NSC's Morton Halperin, *New York Times*, March 26, 1998.

31. Samantha Power, "Bystanders to Genocide: Why the United States Let the Rwanda Tragedy Happen," *Atlantic Monthly*, September 2001, p. 107.

32. White House correspondent John F. Harris on polls, *Washington Post*, December 31, 2000, p. A1; *Time*, September 2, 1996, p. 24, on Morris.

33. For fiftieth-anniversary conclusions about compartmentalization and inward focus, see those of the congressionally chartered defense panel on this subject, as reported in *New York Times*, December 2, 1997; criticism of Pentagon purchasing has best been made by Inspector General Eleanor Hill, testimony to the Acquisition Subcommittee, Senate Armed Services Committee, March 18, 1998; a succinct analysis of failure to adapt to electronic systems is Edward Luttwak's essay, "Situational Awareness," in *New York Times Book Review*, January 21, 2001, p. 21; the Clinton failure is from Bradley Graham, *Washington Post*, May 11, 1997, p. A7.

34. See the testimony of Charles A. Bowsher, General Accounting Office, Before the Senate Armed Services Subcommittee on Readiness, May 16, 1996. Other bureaucracies, of course, such as HHS and the Healthcare Financing Administration, are in an at least equal mess.

35. *Defense Week*, special edition, May 6, 1996, quoting John Nelson.
36. Eric Bloch in "Commentary: Throwing Money at Science Just Creates a Monster," *Business Week*, June 19, 1995; GAO report, January 1997, as cited by Daniel Greenberg in *Washington Post*, May 21, 1997; author's observation in working with NRL's biology laboratory.
37. For example, Vice President Gore acclaimed one high-tech firm in Massachusetts (backed by a campaign aide) as "a shining example of American ingenuity," immediately before it went bankrupt, sopping up millions of dollars in U.S. Energy Department subsidies. See Gore's description of Molten Metals Technology, Inc., in *Washington Post*, December 4, 1997.
38. Dana Priest in *Washington Post*, July 12, p. A23; author's interview with Michael Ratner, Director, Center for Constitutional Rights, May 2001.
39. Stephen Jones, *Others Unknown: The Oklahoma Bombing Case and Conspiracy* (New York: Public Affairs, 1998), pp. 105–107.
40. Seymour Hersh, "What Went Wrong: The C.I.A. and the Failure of American Intelligence," *New Yorker*, October 8, 2001, p.36.
41. White House press transcript, August 21, 1998, on "struggle"; State of the Union 2000 is on www.whitehouse.gov; Albright is quoted in Jane Perlez, "Expanding Alliance. The Overview," *New York Times*, March 13, 1999, p. A1; testimony of George Tenet, "Counterterrorism," before the Committee on Appropriations, U.S. Senate, 105th Congress, 1st Session, May 13, 1997, p. 41; Senator Diane Feinstein on CNN *Late Edition*, July 1, 2001.
42. Gerecht, "Counterterrorism Myths," p. 38.
43. Ibid. On remarks of senior CIA official, confidential to author.
44. Col. Norvell De Atkine, USA, ret., as quoted in the *Wall Street Journal*, September 4, 1998.
45. See interview with this author in William Greider, "The White House Goes After Cyberterrorists," *Rolling Stone*, August 19, 1999, p. 51; *Washington Post*, April 2, 2000, p. A20.
46. Robert Vrooman interviewed on *The NewsHour with Jim Lehrer*, September 13, 2000.
47. Donald Henderson, M.D., "Dangerous Fictions About Bioterrorism," *Washington Post*, November 8, 1999. The person interviewed needs to be unnamed.
48. Daniel Greenberg, "The Bioterrorism Panic," *Washington Post*, March 16, 1999; for the example of profitable opportunism at Johns Hopkins University, see www.hopkinsbiodefense.org.
49. Federal District Judge William H. Walls is quoted in the case of Hany Kiareldeen, *New York Times*, October 21, 1999.
50. *Washington Post*, June 26, 1998, p. A3; also see R. James Woolsey, "Iraqi Dissidents Railroaded — by U.S.," *Wall Street Journal*, June 10, 1998, op/ed.
51. Dr. Richard Brecht is quoted by Diana Schemo, "Use of English as World Tongue Is Booming," *New York Times*, April 16, 2001, p. A1.
52. Tim Weiner citing report of Adm. David E. Jeremiah, USN, ret., *New York Times*, June 3, 1998.
53. Beijing's representatives made the mistake of having moved their embassy. The CIA, in turn, had relied on an intercepted envelope to find the address of the Yugoslav Army's procurement directorate, believing that street addresses in Belgrade were numbered as uniformly as those in, say, McLean, Virginia. It also relied on satellite imagery, which nonetheless clearly showed that the tar-

get looked nothing like a Yugoslav government building. The correct address was easily available on the procurement directorate's web site.

54. *New York Times*, April 9, 2000.

55. In a comment that applies equally well to the Agency's overall behavior as to its aborted archives, Woolsey speaks of "a terrible breach of faith with the American people." Author's conversation with Woolsey.

56. George Tenet speech of May 5, 1998, CIA press office; and the argument of former case officer Brian P. Fairchild in "Terrorism and Intelligence Operations," Hearings Before the Joint Economic Committee, 105th Congress, 2nd Session, May 20, 1998, pp. 15–18, 79–98.

57. Testimony of Nora Slatkin, Executive Director of the CIA on "Human Resources and Diversity," Hearings on H431-1 Before the Permanent House Select Committee on Intelligence, 104th Congress, 2nd Session, September 20, 1996, pp. 18–24.

58. Thomas Friedman, "World War III," *New York Times*, September 12, 2001, column.

59. *Cuba's Repressive Machinery: Human Rights Forty Years After the Revolution*, Human Rights Watch, Washington, D.C., 1999, p. 1.

60. *The Roswell Report: Fact or Fiction in the New Mexico Desert* (Washington: GPO, 1994).

61. As cited in Michael Ignatieff, "What Did the CIA Do to His Father?" *New York Times Magazine*, April 1, 2001, p. 60.

62. Gallagher, *American Ground Zero*, p. xxv.

63. Concerned that a proliferation of grievances would precipitate an open-ended run on the U.S. Treasury, the Committee recommended that less than three dozen remaining victims be compensated, that only a few hundred should receive a formal apology, and that the government not notify those people who were unaware of their experience. The U.S. government paid $4.8 million for having injected 12 people with plutonium or uranium.

64. Only in 1995 would Washington acknowledge publicly that the MIAs were nearly entirely KIAs — killed in action with bodies not recovered, and with at least 567 cases in which the Pentagon finally noted that "no actions by any government will result in the recovery of remains."

65. Volkoganov, Task Force Russia Documents, Report, March 17, 1993, p. 4, annex to the 18th report; V. Svivdov, Task Force Russia Bi-Weekly Report, September 25, 1992, 6th Report. Library of Congress.

Conclusion

1. William Odom, "NATO's Expansion: Why the Critics Are Wrong," *National Interest*, Spring 1995, p. 44.

2. Reynolds, *One World*, p. 3. "Victor's history" became the simplistic post–Cold War put-down for viewpoints generally favorable to the U.S. achievement, and skeptical of Soviet legitimacy.

3. Makin and Ornstein, *Debt and Taxes*, p. 101.

4. David Sanger, "So Much for Grand Theories," *New York Times*, March 7, 1999, Week in Review, p. 3.

Bibliography

Archives
U.S. National Archives (NA)
RG 59 General Records of the Department of State
RG 84 London Post Files
RG 129 Notorious Offenders
RG 218 Records of the JCS
RG 316 Army-Ops General
RG 319 Records of the Army Staff
RG 330 Office of the Secretary of Defense
RG 335 Indochina
Department of State, Executive Secretariat, Daily Summary
Department of State, Division of Public Studies, Schuyler Foster Files

Public Record Office, United Kingdom (PRO)
FO Foreign Office Papers
CAB Cabinet Minutes and Papers
DEF Ministry of Defence
PREM Prime Minister's Office

Catholic University, Department of Archives, CIO papers
Charles Bohlen Papers, NA
Collections and oral histories from the Truman, Eisenhower, Kennedy, Johnson,
    and Reagan Presidential Libraries
Columbia University, Oral History Collection
    Admiral Richard Conolly
    Walter Lippmann
Council on Foreign Relations Archives
Ford Foundation Archives
John Foster Dulles Papers, Princeton
Kenneth Younger Papers, Diary, University of Leicester
Library of Congress, Task Force Russia Documents
National Academy of Science, Committee on Biological Effects of Atomic Radiation
National Security Archive, Washington, DC

Naval Historical Center, Washington, DC, Records of the Strategic Plans Division
New-York Historical Society (Robert Lovett, Daily Log Sheet, Diary)
Paul Robeson Archives
Royal Institute of International Relations Archives
Vietnam Archive, Texas Tech University
Yale University
    Walter Lippmann Papers
    Sherman Kent Papers

Selected Books and Articles

Acheson, Dean. *A Democrat Looks at His Party.* New York: Harper & Brothers, 1955.

———. *Present at the Creation: My Years at the State Department.* New York: Norton, 1969.

Albright, Joseph, and Marcia Kunstel. *Bombshell: The Secret Story of America's Unknown Atomic Spy Conspiracy.* New York: Times Books, 1997.

Alexander, Charles C. *Holding the Line: The Eisenhower Era, 1952–1961.* Bloomington, IN: University of Indiana Press, 1975.

Alibek, Ken. *Biohazard: The Chilling True Story of the Largest Covert Biological Weapons Program in the World.* New York: Random House, 1999.

Alsop, Joseph, and Stewart Alsop. *The Reporter's Trade.* New York: Reynal & Co., 1958.

Ambrose, Stephen. *Eisenhower: Soldier and President.* New York: Touchstone, 1990.

Anderson, Jon Lee. *Che Guevara: A Revolutionary Life.* New York: Grove Press, 1997.

Andrew, Christopher. *For the President's Eyes Only: Secret Intelligence and the American Presidency from Washington to Bush.* New York: HarperCollins, 1995.

Andrew, Christopher, and Vasili Mitrokhin. *The Sword and the Shield: The Secret History of the KGB.* New York: Basic Books, 1999.

Arbatov, Georgi. *The System: An Insider's Life in Soviet Politics.* New York: Times Books, 1991.

Arnold, James R. *The First Domino: Eisenhower, the Military, and America's Intervention in Vietnam.* New York: Morrow, 1991.

Avittey, George B. N. *Africa in Chaos.* New York: St. Martin's Press, 1998.

Ball, George W. *The Past Has Another Pattern: Memoirs.* New York: Norton, 1992.

———. "Should the U.S. Fight Secret Wars?" *Harper's* (September 1984).

———. "The War for Star Wars." *New York Review of Books* (April 11, 1985).

Ball, S. J. *The Cold War: An International History.* New York: Arnold, 1998.

Bamford, James. *Body of Secrets: Anatomy of the Ultra-Secret National Security Agency, from the Cold War Through the Dawn of a New Century.* New York: Doubleday, 2001.

Beech, Keyes. "How the U.S. Fumbled in Laos." *Saturday Evening Post* (April 22, 1961).

Beon, Yves. *Planet Dora: A Memoir of the Holocaust and the Birth of the Space Age.* Boulder, CO: Westview, 1997.

Bergsten, Fred. "The World Economy After the Cold War." *Foreign Affairs* (Summer 1990).

Berman, Larry. *No Peace, No Honor: Nixon, Kissinger, and Betrayal in Vietnam.* New York: Simon and Schuster, 2001.

Berman, Ronald, ed. *Solzhenitsyn at Harvard.* Washington: Ethics and Public Policy Center, 1980.

Bernstein, Irving. *Guns or Butter: The Presidency of Lyndon Johnson.* New York: Oxford University Press, 1996.

Bertram, Christoph. "European Security and the German Problem." *International Security* (Winter 1979/80).

Beschloss, Michael R. *The Crisis Years: Kennedy and Khrushchev, 1960–1963.* New York: HarperCollins, 1991.

———. *May Day.* New York: Harper & Row, 1986.

Beschloss, Michael, ed. *Taking Charge: The Johnson White House Tapes, 1963–1964.* New York: Simon and Schuster, 1997.

Billingsley, Kenneth. *Hollywood Party: How Communism Seduced the American Film Industry in the 1930s and 1940s.* Rocklin, CA: Prima Publishing 1998.

Bird, Kai. *The Chairman: John J. McCloy, The Making of the American Establishment.* New York: Simon and Schuster, 1992.

———. *The Color of Truth: McGeorge Bundy and William Bundy, Brothers in Arms.* New York, Simon and Schuster, 1998.

Bluth, Christopher. *Soviet Strategic Arms Policy Before SALT.* New York: Cambridge University Press, 1992.

Bohlen, Charles E. *Witness to History, 1919–1969.* New York: Norton, 1973.

Donavolonta, Jules, and Brian Duffy. *The Good Guys: How We Turned the FBI 'Round.* New York: Simon and Schuster, 1996.

Bosch, Adriana, foreword by David McCullough. *Reagan: An American Story.* New York: TV Books, 1998, for *The American Experience*, WGBH Education Foundation.

Bosworth, Patricia. *Anything Your Little Heart Desires: An American Family Story.* New York: Simon and Schuster, 1997.

Braestrup, Peter. *Big Story: How the American Press and Television Reported and Interpreted the Crisis of Tet 1968 in Vietnam and Washington,* vol. 1. Boulder, CO: Westview Press, 1977.

Brinkley, Douglas. *Dean Acheson, The Cold War Years, 1953–1971.* New Haven, CT: Yale University Press, 1992.

Broad, William J. *Teller's War: The Top Secret Story Behind the Star War's Deception.* New York: Simon and Schuster, 1992.

Brooks, John. *The Seven Fat Years: Chronicles of Wall Street.* New York: Harper, 1958.

Brown, JoAnne. "A is for Atom, B is for Bomb: Civil Defense in American Public Education, 1948–1963." *Journal of American History,* no. 69 (1988).

Brown, Ralph S. Jr. "Loyalty-Security Measures and Employment Opportunities." *Bulletin of the Atomic Scientists* (April 1955).

Brown, Timothy C. *The Real Contra War: Highlander Peasant Resistance in Nicaragua.* Norman: University of Oklahoma Press, 2001.

Brzezinski, Zbigniew. *Power and Principle: Memoirs of the National Security Advisor, 1977–1981.* New York: Farrar, Straus and Giroux, 1983.

Bullock, Alan. *Ernest Bevin: Foreign Secretary.* Oxford: Oxford University Press, 1983.

Bundy, McGeorge. *Danger and Survival: Choices About the Bomb in the First Fifty Years.* New York: Random House, 1988.

———. "Maintaining Stable Deterrence." *International Security* (Winter 1978/1979).

———. "Possible Nuclear Worlds." *International Security* (Winter 1980).

Bundy, William. *A Tangled Web: The Making of Foreign Policy in the Nixon Presidency.* New York: Hill and Wang, 1998.

Burr, William, ed. *The Kissinger Transcripts: The Top Secret Talks with Beijing and Moscow.* New York: W. W. Norton, 1999.

Byrne, John A. *The Whiz Kids: The Founding Fathers of American Business — and the Legacy They Left Us.* New York: Doubleday, 1993.

Cahn, Anne. *Killing Détente: The Right Attacks the CIA.* University Park: Pennsylvania State University Press, 1998.

Carter, Jimmy. *Keeping Faith: Memoirs of a President.* New York: Bantam Books, 1992.

Castenada, Jorge G. *Compañero: The Life and Death of Che Guevara.* New York: Knopf, 1997.

Chang, Iris. *Rape of Nanking: The Forgotten Holocaust of World War II.* New York: Basic Books, 1997.

Chomsky, Noam. *Year 501: The Conquest Continues.* Boston: South End Press, 1993.

Churchill, Randolph. *The Rise and Fall of Sir Anthony Eden.* London: MacGibbon and Kee, 1960.

Clarridge, Duane R. *A Spy for All Seasons: My Life in the CIA.* New York: Scribner's, 1997.

Cockburn, Christopher, and Patrick Cockburn. *Out of the Ashes: The Resurrection of Saddam Hussein.* New York: HarperPerennial, 2000.

Colby, William. "Intelligence Secrecy and Security in a Free Society." *International Security* (Fall 1976).

——. *Lost Victory: A Firsthand Account of America's Sixteen-Year Involvement in Vietnam.* New York: Contemporary Books, 1989.

Coleman, Fred. *The Decline and Fall of the Soviet Empire: Forty Years That Shook the World, from Stalin to Yeltsin.* New York: St. Martin's Press, 1996.

Conquest, Robert. *Reflections on a Ravaged Century.* New York: W. W. Norton, 1999.

Coulam, Robert. *Illusions of Choice: The F-111 and the Problem of Weapons Acquisition Reform.* Princeton, NJ: Princeton University Press, 1978.

Courtois, Stephane, et al. *The Black Book of Communism.* Cambridge, MA: Harvard University Press, 1999.

Cousins, Norman, and Thomas Finletter. "A Beginning for Sanity." *Saturday Review* (June 15, 1946).

Crossman, Richard. *The Diaries of a Cabinet Minister,* vol. III. New York: Holt, Rinehart, 1977.

——. "The Strange Case of Mr. X." *The Charm of Politics.* London: Hamish Hamilton, 1958.

Cummings, Bruce. *Korea's Place in the Sun: A Modern History.* New York: Norton, 1997.

d'Antonio, Michael. "Atomic Guinea Pigs." *New York Times Magazine* (August 31, 1997).

D'Souza, Dinesh. *Ronald Reagan: How an Ordinary Man Became an Extraordinary Leader.* New York: Free Press, 1997.

Dalleck. Robert. *Flawed Giant: Lyndon Johnson and His Times.* New York: Oxford University Press, 1998.

Day, Richard B. *Cold War Capitalism: The View from Moscow, 1945–1975.* Armonk, NY: M. E. Sharpe, 1995.

Dmytryk, Edward. *Odd Man Out: A Memoir of the Hollywood Ten.* Carbondale: Southern Illinois University Press, 1996.

Dobbs, Michael. *Down With Big Brother: The Fall of the Soviet Empire.* New York: Knopf, 1996.

Dobrynin, Anatoly. *In Confidence.* New York: Times Books, 1995.

Donovan, Robert J. *Tumultuous Years: The Presidency of Harry S. Truman, 1949–1953.* New York: Norton, 1982.

Dorril, Stephen. *MI6: Inside the Covert World of Her Majesty's Secret Intelligence Service.* New York: Free Press, 2000.

Dubček, Alexander. *Hope Dies Last: The Autobiography of Alexander Dubček.* New York: Kodansha, 1993.

Duberman, Martin. *Paul Robeson.* New York: Knopf, 1988.

Dung, Van Tian. *Our Great Spring Victory.* London: Monthly Review Press, 1977.

Elbers, Gerald, and Paul Duncan, eds. *Scientific Revolution: Challenge and Promise.* Washington: Public Affairs Press, 1959.

Elegant, Robert. "How to Lose a War: Reflections of a Foreign Correspondent." *Encounter* (August 1981).

Englehardt, Tom. *The End of Victory Culture: Cold War America and the Disillusioning of a Generation.* New York: Basic Books, 1995.

Ennes, James M. Jr. *Assault on the Liberty: The True Story of the Israeli Attack on the American Intelligence Ship.* New York: Random House, 1979.

Evans, Harold. *The American Century.* New York: Knopf, 1990.

Eveland, Wilbur Crane. *Ropes of Sand.* New York: Norton, 1980.

Fairlie, Henry. *The Kennedy Promise: The Politics of Expectation.* Garden City, NY: Doubleday, 1973.

Ferrell, Robert, ed. *The Eisenhower Diaries.* New York: Norton, 1981.

Fialka John. *War by Other Means: Economic Espionage in America.* New York: Norton, 1997.

Fineman, Daniel. *A Special Relationship: The United States and Military Government in Thailand, 1947–1958.* Honolulu: University of Hawaii Press, 1997.

Finletter, Thomas K. *Foreign Policy: The Next Phase.* New York: Council on Foreign Relations, 1958.

Firth, Noel E., and James H. Noren. *Soviet Defense Spending.* College Station: Texas A&M University Press, 1998.

FitzGerald, Frances. *Way Out There in the Blue: Reagan, Star Wars, and the End of the Cold War.* New York: Simon and Schuster, 2000.

Foot, Michael. *Aneurin Bevan,* vol. II. New York: Atheneum, 1974.

Ford, Gerald. *A Time to Heal.* New York: Harper and Row, 1979.

Ford, Harold P. "Revisiting Vietnam." *Studies in Intelligence* (1996).

Foreman, Paul. "Behind Quantum Electronics: National Security as the Basis for Physical Research in the United States, 1940–1960." *Historical Studies in the Physical and Biological Sciences* (18), part 1.

Fossdale, Gregory. *Our Finest Hour: Will Clayton, the Marshall Plan and the Triumph of Democracy.* Stanford, CA: Hoover Institution Press, 1993.

Freedman, Lawrence. *Kennedy's Wars: Berlin, Cuba, Laos and Vietnam.* New York: Oxford University Press, 2000.

Fridrich, Otto. "How to Be a War Correspondent." *Yale Review* (Spring 1959).

Fried, Richard M. *The Russians Are Coming! Pageantry and Patriotism in Cold-War America.* New York: Oxford University Press, 1998.

Friedberg, Aaron L. *In the Shadow of the Garrison State: America's Anti-Statism and Its Cold War Grand Strategy.* Princeton, NJ: Princeton University Press, 2000.

Friedman, Robert I. *Red Mafiya: How the Russian Mob Has Invaded America.* Boston: Little, Brown, 2000.

Fromkin, David. "Daring Amateurism." *Foreign Affairs* (January/February 1996).

————. *In the Time of the Americans: FDR, Truman, Eisenhower, Marshall, Mac-Arthur — The Generation That Changed America's Role in the World.* New York: Knopf, 1995.

————. *Kosovo Crossing: American Ideals Meet Reality on the Balkan Battlefields.* New York: Free Press, 1999.

Gaddis, John Lewis. *Strategies of Containment: A Critical Appraisal of Postwar American National Security Policy.* New York: Oxford University Press, 1982.

————. "The Tragedy of Cold War History." *Diplomatic History* (Winter 1993).

————. *We Now Know: Rethinking Cold War History.* New York: Oxford University Press, 1997.

Gage, Nicholas. *Eleni.* New York: Random House, 1983.

Galbraith, John Kenneth. *The Affluent Society.* Boston: Houghton Mifflin, 1957.

————. *How to Control the Military.* Garden City, NY: Doubleday, 1969.

Gallagher, Carole. *American Ground Zero: The Secret Nuclear War.* Cambridge, MA: MIT Press, 1993.

Gardner, Lloyd. *A Covenant with Power: America and World Order from Wilson to Reagan.* New York: Oxford University Press, 1984.

Gardner, Lloyd C. *Pay Any Price: Lyndon Johnson and the Wars of Vietnam.* Chicago: Ivan R. Dee, 1995.

Garfinkle, Adam. *Telltale Hearts.* New York: St. Martin's Press, 1995.

Garthoff, Raymond. *Conflict and Confrontation: American-Soviet Relations from Nixon to Reagan.* Washington: Brookings Institution, 1994.

Gendizer, Irene. *Notes from the Minefield: The United States Intervention in Lebanon and the Middle East, 1945–1958.* New York: Columbia University Press, 1997.

Gerecht, Marc Reuel (writing as Edward G. Shirley). "Can't Anybody Here Play This Game?" *Atlantic Monthly* (February 1998).

————. *Know Thine Enemy: A Spy's Journey into Revolutionary Iran.* New York: Farrar, Straus and Giroux, 1997.

Gerecht, Marc Reuel. "The Counterterrorism Myths." *The Atlantic* (July/August 2000).

Glikes, Erwin, ed. *Of Poetry and Power: Poems Occasioned by the Presidency and by the Death of John F. Kennedy,* introduction by Arthur Schlesinger. New York: Basic Books, 1964.

Goldhagen, Daniel. *Hitler's Willing Executioners: Ordinary Germans and the Holocaust.* New York: Knopf, 1996.

Goodman, Melvin. "Ending the CIA's Cold War Legacy." *Foreign Policy* (Winter 1996/1997).

Greider, William. "The White House Goes After Cyberterrorists." *Rolling Stone* (August 19, 1999).

Gribkov, Anatoli, and William Y. Smith. *Operation ANADYR: U.S. and Soviet Generals Recount the Cuban Missile Crisis.* Chicago: edition q, 1997.

Grose, Peter. *Gentleman Spy: The Life of Allen Dulles.* Boston: Houghton Mifflin, 1994.

————. *Operation Rollback: America's Secret War Behind the Iron Curtain.* Boston: Houghton Mifflin, 2000.

Hacker, Barton. "Radiation Safety, the AEC, and Nuclear Weapons Testing." *The Public Historian,* no. 1 (1992).

Hafner, Katie, and Matthew Lyon. *Where Wizards Stay Up Late.* New York: Simon and Schuster, 1996.

Haines, Gerald K. "C.I.A.'s Role in the Study of U.F.O.s, 1947–1990." *Studies of Intelligence* (1997).

Halberstam, David. *The Best and the Brightest.* New York: Random House, 1972.

Haldeman, H. R. *The Haldeman Diaries: Inside the Nixon White House.* New York: G. P. Putnam, 1994.

Hamilton-Merrit, Jane. *Tragic Mountains: The Hmong, the Americans, and the Secret Wars for Laos, 1942–1992.* Bloomington: Indiana University Press, 1993.

Handlin, Oscar. *The Distortion of America.* New Brunswick, NJ: Transaction Books, 1981.

Heikal, Mohammed. *The Sphinx and the Commissar: The Rise and Fall of Soviet Influence in the Middle East.* New York: Harper and Row, 1978.

Hendrickson, Paul. *The Living and the Dead: Robert McNamara and Five Lives of a Lost War.* New York: Knopf, 1996.

Herken, Gregg. *Counsels of War.* New York: Knopf, 1985.

———. "The Earthly Origins of Star Wars." *Bulletin of the Atomic Scientists* (October 1987).

Herman, Arthur. *Joseph McCarthy: Reexamining the Life and Legacy of America's Most Hated Senator.* New York: Free Press, 2000.

Hersh, Seymour M. *The Dark Side of Camelot.* Boston: Little, Brown, 1997.

Higgs, Robert. "The Cold War Economy: Opportunity Costs, Ideology, and the Politics of Crisis." *Explorations in Economic History* 31 (1994).

Hilsman, Roger. *To Move a Nation: The Politics of Foreign Policy in the Administration of John F. Kennedy.* New York: Doubleday, 1967.

Hilty, James W. *Robert Kennedy: Brother Protector.* Philadelphia: Temple University Press, 1997.

Hitchens, Christopher. "Brief Shining Moments." *London Review of Books* (February 19, 1998).

——— *The Trial of Henry Kissinger.* London: Verso, 2001.

Hixson, Walter L. *George F. Kennan: Cold War Iconoclast.* New York: Columbia University Press, 1989.

Holt, Richard. *The Reluctant Superpower: A History of America's Global Economic Reach.* New York: Kodansha, 1995.

Holt, Thaddeus. "Joint Plan Red." *Quarterly Journal of Military History* (Autumn 1988).

Hunt, Linda. *Secret Agenda: The United States Government, Nazi Scientists and Project Paper Clip, 1945–1990.* New York: St. Martin's Press, 1993.

Huynh, Jade Ngoc Quang. *South Wind Changing.* St. Paul, MN: Graywolf Press, 1994.

Immerman, Richard H., ed. *John Foster Dulles and the Diplomacy of the Cold War.* Princeton, NJ: Princeton University Press, 1990.

Isaacs, Arnold R. *Vietnam Shadows: The War, Its Ghosts, and Its Legacy.* Baltimore: Johns Hopkins University Press, 1997.

Isaacs, Jeremy, and Tony Downing. *Cold War: The Book of the Ground-Breaking TV Series.* London: Bantam Press, 1998.

Isaacson, Walter. *Kissinger: A Biography.* New York: Simon and Schuster, 1992.

Isaacson, Walter, and Evan Thomas. *The Wise Men: Six Friends and the World They Made.* New York: Simon and Schuster, 1986.

Isenberg, Michael. *Shield of the Republic: The United States Navy in an Era of Cold War and Violent Peace, 1945–1962.* New York: St. Martin's Press, 1993.

Ishihara, Shintaro. *The Japan That Can Say No: Why Japan Will Be First Among Equals.* New York: Simon and Schuster, 1989.

Johnson, Loch K. *Secret Agencies: U.S. Intelligence in a Hostile World.* New Haven, CT: Yale University Press, 1996.

Johnson, Paul. *Modern Times: The World from the Twenties to the Nineties.* New York: HarperCollins, 1991.

Jones, Joseph M. *The Fifteen Weeks.* New York: Viking Press, 1955.

Jones, Stephen. *Others Unknown: The Oklahoma Bombing Case and Conspiracy.* New York: Public Affairs, 1998.

Jordan, Gerald, ed. *Naval Warfare in the Twentieth Century.* London: Croom Helm, 1977.

Kazan, Elia. *A Life.* New York: Knopf, 1988.

Kazin, Alfred. *Contemporaries from the 19th Century to the Present.* New York: Horizon Press, 1982.

Kennan, George F. *Democracy and the Student Left.* Boston: Little, Brown, 1968.

———. "The G.O.P. Won the Cold War? Ridiculous." *New York Times* (October 28, 1992).

———. "A Letter on Germany." *New York Review of Books* (December 3, 1998).

———. *Memoirs 1925–1950.* Boston: Little, Brown, 1967.

———. *The Nuclear Delusion: Soviet American Relations in the Atomic Age.* New York: Pantheon, 1982.

———. *Realities of American Foreign Policy.* Princeton, NJ: Princeton University Press, 1954.

Kennan, George ["Mr. X."]. "The Sources of Soviet Conduct." *Foreign Affairs* (July 1947).

Kennan, George F., and George Urban. "A Conversation with George F. Kennan." *Encounter* (September 1976).

Kennan, George F., and John Lukas. "From World War to Cold War." *American Heritage* (December 1995).

Kennedy, Paul. *The Rise and Fall of the Great Powers: Economic Change and Military Conflict from 1500 to 2000.* New York: Random House, 1987.

Kennedy, William V. *The Military and the Media.* Westport, CT: Praeger, 1993.

Killian, James R. *Sputnik, Scientists, and Eisenhower: A Memoir of the First Special Assistant to the President for Science and Technology.* Cambridge, MA: MIT Press, 1977.

Killian, James R., and A. G. Hill. "For a Continental Defense." *Atlantic Monthly* (November 1953).

Kiraly, Bela K. "The Aborted Soviet Military Plans Against Tito's Yugoslavia." *War and Society in East Central Europe,* vol. X, Wayne S. Vucinich, ed. New York: Columbia University Press, 1982.

Kissinger, Henry. *Diplomacy.* New York: Simon and Schuster, 1994.

———. *White House Years.* Boston: Little, Brown, 1979.

———. *Years of Renewal.* New York: Simon and Schuster, 1999.

Klitgaard, Robert. *Tropical Gangsters.* New York: Basic Books, 1990.

Knaus, John Kenneth. *Orphans of the Cold War: America and the Tibetan Struggle for Survival.* New York: Public Affairs, 1999.

Kokoshin, Andrei. *Soviet Strategic Thought, 1917–91.* Cambridge, MA: MIT Press, 1998.

Kovel, Joel. *Red Hunting in the Promised Land: Anticommunism and the Making of America.* New York: Basic Books, 1994.

Krock, Arthur. *Memoirs.* New York: Funk and Wagnalls, 1968.

Kunz, Diane B. *Butter and Guns: America's Cold War Economic Diplomacy.* New York: Free Press, 1997.

Lambright, W. Henry. *Powering Apollo: James E. Webb of NASA.* Baltimore: Johns Hopkins University Press, 1995.

Langguth, A. J. *Our Vietnam War, 1954–1975.* New York: Simon and Schuster, 2000.

Leab, Daniel J. "How Red Was My Valley: Hollywood, the Cold War Film, and 'I Married a Communist.'" *Journal of Contemporary History* (1984).

———. "'The Iron Curtain': Hollywood's First Cold War Movie." *Historical Journal of Film, Radio and Television* 8, no. 2 (1988).

Lebow, Irwin. *Information Highways and Byways.* New York: IEEE Press, 1995.

Lee, William T. *The ABM Treaty Charade: A Study in Elite Illusion and Delusion.* Washington: Council for Social and Economic Studies, 1997.

———. *CIA Estimates of Former Soviet Union Military Expenditures: Errors and Waste.* Washington: American Enterprise Institute, 1995.

———. "Counterforce Capabilities of Soviet ICBMs During the Cold War." *Journal of Cold War Studies* (Spring 2002).

———. "US–USSR Strategic Arms Control Agreements: Expectations and Reality." *Comparative Strategy* (October–December 1993).

Leebaert, Derek. "Innovation and Private Initiatives as Frontiers Fall." *Washington Quarterly* (Spring 1992).

———. "U.S. Policies in the Third World: Objectives, Instruments, and Constraints." *Superpower Competition and Crisis Prevention in the Third World,* Allison, Roy, ed. New York: Cambridge University Press, 1990.

Leebaert, Derek, ed. *The Future of the Electronic Marketplace.* Cambridge, MA: MIT Press, 1998, 1999.

———. *The Future of Software.* Cambridge, MA: MIT Press, 1995.

———. *Soviet Military Thinking.* Boston: Allen and Unwin, 1982.

———. *Soviet Strategy and New Military Thinking,* Foreword by Sir Michael Palliser. New York: Cambridge University Press, 1992.

———. *Technology 2001: The Future of Computing and Telecommunications.* Cambridge, MA: MIT Press, 1991.

Leffler, Melvyn P. *A Preponderance of Power.* Stanford, CA: Stanford University Press, 1992.

LeMay, Curtis. *America Is in Danger.* New York: Funk and Wagnalls, 1968.

Leogrande, William. *Our Own Backyard: The United States in Central America, 1977–1992.* Chapel Hill: University of North Carolina Press, 1998.

Leslie, Stuart W. *The Cold War and American Science: The Military-Industrial-Academic Complex at MIT and Stanford.* New York: Columbia University Press, 1993.

Lewin, Leonard C. *Report from Iron Mountain on the Possibility and Desirability of Peace.* New York: Free Press, 1996.

Ligachev, Y. *Inside Gorbachev's Kremlin.* Boulder, CO: Westview Press, 1996.

Luce, Henry R. "The American Century." *Life* (February 17, 1941).

Luttwak, Edward. *The Pentagon and the Art of War.* New York, Simon and Schuster, 1984.

Lynn, Kenneth S. *Charlie Chaplin and His Times.* New York: Simon and Schuster, 1997.

Maass, Peter. *Underboss: Sammy the Bull Gravano's Story of Life in the Mafia.* New York: HarperCollins, 1997.

MacDonald, Douglas J. "Communist Bloc Expansion in the Early Cold War." *International Security* (Winter 1995/1996).

MacEachin, Douglas J. "CIA Assessments of the Soviet Union: The Record Versus the Charges." *Studies in Intelligence*, no. 1 (1997).

Magnus, Ralph, and Eden Naby. *Afghanistan: Mullah, Marx, and Mujahid.* Boulder, CO: Westview Press, 1998.

Makin, John, and Norman Ornstein. *Debt and Taxes.* New York: Times Books, 1994.

Malraux, André. *Falled Oaks: Conversations with DeGaulle.* London: Hamish Hamilton, 1972.

Mandelbaum, Michael. *The Dawn of Peace in Europe.* New York: Twentieth Century Fund, 1996.

———. *The Nuclear Question: The United States and Nuclear Weapons, 1946–1976.* New York: Cambridge University Press, 1979.

Mann, James. *About Face: A History of America's Curious Relationship with China, from Nixon to Clinton.* New York: Knopf, 1999.

Mansfield, Harvey. "The Legacy of the Late Sixties." *Reassessing the Sixties: Debating the Political and Cultural Legacy,* Stephen Macedo, ed. New York: Norton, 1997.

Martin, John Bartlow. *Overtaken by Events: The Dominican Crisis from the Fall of Trujillo to the Civil War.* Garden City, NY: Doubleday, 1966.

Marton, Kati. *The Polk Conspiracy: Murder and Cover-up In the Case of CBS News Correspondent George Polk.* New York: Farrar, Straus and Giroux, 1990.

Matlock, Jack. *Autopsy on an Empire.* New York: Random House, 1995.

May, Ernest. "The U.S. Government: A Legacy of the Cold War." *The End of the Cold War: Its Meaning and Implications,* Michael J. Hogan, ed. New York: Cambridge University Press, 1992.

McCullough, David. *Truman.* New York: Simon and Schuster, 1992.

McCullough, James. "Coping with Iran-Contra: Personal Reflections on Bill Casey's Last Month at CIA." *Studies in Intelligence* (1996).

McDonald, Robert, ed. *Corona: Between the Sun and the Earth.* Bethesda, MD: American Society for Photogrammetry and Remote Sensing, 1997.

McDougall, Walter A. "Sputnik, the Space Race, and the Cold War." *Bulletin of the Atomic Scientists* (May 1985).

McGhee, George. *On the Front Line in the Cold War.* Westport, CT: Praeger, 1997.

McGlothlen, Donald. *Controlling the Waves: Dean Acheson and U.S. Foreign Policy in Asia.* New York: Norton, 1993.

McKeever, Porter. *Adlai Stevenson: His Life and Legacy.* New York: William Morrow, 1989.

McMaster, H. R. *Dereliction of Duty: Lyndon Johnson, Robert McNamara, the Joint Chiefs of Staff, and the Lies That Led to Vietnam.* New York: HarperCollins, 1997.

McNamara, Robert. *In Retrospect.* New York: Random House, 1995.

McNamara, Robert, et al. *Argument Without End: In Search of Answers to the Vietnam Tragedy.* New York: Public Affairs, 1999.

McPherson, Harry. *A Political Education: A Washington Memoir.* Boston: Houghton Mifflin, 1988.

Meade, Walter Russell. "Refighting Yesterday's Battles." *Washington Post Book World* (July 6, 1997).

Meers, Sharon. "The British Connection: How the United States Covered Its Tracks in the 1954 Coup in Guatemala." *Diplomatic History* (Summer 1992).

Melman, Seymour. *The Permanent War Economy: American Capitalism in Decline.* New York: Simon and Schuster, 1974.

Millis, Walter, with Harvey Mansfield. *Arms and the State: Civil-Military Elements in National Policy.* New York: Twentieth Century Fund, 1958.

Moorehead, Caroline. *Bertrand Russell.* New York: Viking, 1992.

Moran, Lord Charles McMoran Wilson. *Churchill: The Struggle for Survival, 1940–1965.* Boston: Houghton Mifflin, 1966.

Morgenstern, Oskar. *The Question of National Defense.* New York: Random House, 1959.

Morris, Edmund. *Dutch: A Memoir of Ronald Reagan.* New York: Random House, 1999.

Moyar, Mark. *Phoenix and the Birds of Prey: The CIA's Secret Campaign to Destroy the Viet Cong.* Annapolis, MD: Naval Institute Press, 1997.

Nasar, Sylvia. *A Beautiful Mind.* New York: Simon and Schuster, 1998.

Needle, Alan. "Truth Is Our Weapon." *Diplomatic History* (Summer 1993).

Neustadt, Richard, and Ernest May. *Thinking in Time: The Uses of History for Decision Makers.* New York: Free Press, 1986.

Newhouse, John. *Cold Dawn: The Story of SALT.* New York: Holt, Rinehart, 1973.

Nitze, Paul H. *From Hiroshima to Glasnost: At the Center of Decision   A Memoir.* New York: Grove Weidenfeld, 1989.

———. "Assuming Strategic Stability in an Era of Détente." *Foreign Affairs* (January 1976).

Odom, William. *The Collapse of the Soviet Military.* New Haven, CT: Yale University Press, 1998.

Olmstead, Kathryn S. *Challenging the Secret Government: The Post-Watergate Investigations of the CIA and FBI.* Chapel Hill: University of North Carolina Press, 1996.

Palmer, Bruce Jr. *The 25-Year War: America's Military Role in Vietnam.* Lexington: University Press of Kentucky, 1984.

Paloczi-Horvath, George. *The Facts Rebel.* Cambridge: Cambridge University Press, 1963.

Patterson, James T. *Grand Expectation: The United States, 1945–1974.* New York: Oxford University Press, 1996.

Patterson, Thomas G. *Contesting Castro: The United States and the Triumph of the Cuban Revolution.* New York: Oxford University Press, 1994.

Peebles, Curtis. *Shadow Flights: America's Secret Air War Against the Soviet Union.* Novato, CA: Presidio Press, 2000.

Perret, Geoffrey. *Eisenhower.* New York: Random House, 1999.

Philby, Kim. *My Silent War.* New York: Grove Press, 1968.

Piel, Gerald. *The Acceleration of History.* New York: Knopf, 1972.

Pillar, Paul R. *Terrorism and U.S. Foreign Policy.* Washington: Brookings Institution, 2001.

Pipes, Daniel, and Adam Garfinkle, eds. *Friendly Tyrants: An American Dilemma.* New York: St. Martin's Press, 1991.

Pogue, Forrest C. *George C. Marshall: Education of a General.* New York: Viking, 1963.

———. *George C. Marshall: Statesman, 1945–1959.* New York: Viking, 1987.

Pointon, Marcia. "Imaging Nationalism in the Cold War: The Foundation of the American Portrait Gallery." *Journal of American Studies* (December 1992).

Powell, Colin. *My American Journey.* New York: Random House, 1995.

Powers, Richard Gid. *Not Without Honor: The History of American Anticommunism.* New York: Free Press, 1995.

Pryce-Jones, David. *The Strange Death of the Soviet Empire.* New York: Henry Holt, 1995.

Raack, R. C. "Stalin Plans His Post-War Germany." *Journal of Contemporary History* 28, no. 1 (1993).

Race, Jeffrey. *War Comes to Long An: Revolutionary Conflict in a Vietnamese Province.* Berkeley: University of California Press, 1972.

Randal, Jonathan C. *After Such Knowledge, What Forgiveness? My Encounters with Kurdistan.* New York: Farrar, Straus and Giroux, 1997.

Reagan, Ronald. *An American Life.* New York: Simon and Schuster, 1990.

Record, Jeffrey. *The Wrong War: Why We Lost in Vietnam.* Annapolis, MD: Naval Institute Press, 1998.

Reed, Thomas, and Arnold Kramish. "Trinity at Dubna." *Physics Today* (1996).

Reeves, Richard. *President Kennedy: Profile of Power.* New York: Simon and Schuster, 1993.

Regis, Edward. *The Biology of Doom: The History of America's Secret Germ Warfare Project.* New York: Henry Holt, 1999.

Reiss, Mitchell. *Without the Bomb: The Politics of Nuclear Proliferation.* New York: Columbia University Press, 1988.

Reston, James. *Deadline: A Memoir.* New York: Random House, 1991.

Reston, James Jr. *Lone Star: The Life of John Connally.* New York: Harper and Row, 1989.

Reynolds, David. *One World Divisible: A Global History Since 1945.* New York: Norton, 2000.

Rhodes, Richard. *Dark Sun: The Making of the Hydrogen Bomb.* New York: Simon and Schuster, 1995.

Ridgway, Matthew. *Soldier: The Memoirs of Matthew B. Ridgway.* New York: Harper Brothers, 1956.

Riley, Morris. *Philby: The Hidden Years.* London: Janus Publishing, 1998.

Roberts, Larry. "The ARPANET and Computer Networks." *A History of Personal Workstations,* Adele Goldberg, ed. New York: ACM Press, 1988.

Rodman, Peter. *More Precious than Peace: The Cold War and the Struggle for the Third World.* New York: Scribner's, 1994.

Rosenblatt, Roger. *Coming Apart.* Boston: Little, Brown, 1997.

Ross, Robert. "China Learns to Compromise: Change in US-China Relations, 1982–1984." *China Quarterly* 128 (1991).

Rostow, Walt Whitman. *The Stages of Economic Growth: A Non-Communist Manifesto.* New York: Cambridge University Press, 1960.

Ruane, Kevin. *The Vietnam Wars.* New York: Manchester University Press, 2000.

Rusk, Dean. *As I Saw It.* New York: Norton, 1990.

Russet, Bruce, et al. "Did Americans' Expectations of Nuclear War Reduce Their Savings?" *International Studies Quarterly* (1994).

Russo, Gus. *Live by the Sword.* Baltimore: Bancroft Press, 1998.

Salisbury, Harrison. *Without Fear or Favor.* New York: Times Books, 1980.

Samuelson, Robert J. *The Good Life and Its Discontents: The American Dream in the Age of Entitlement.* New York: Basic Books, 1995.

Saunders, Frances Stonor. *The Cultural Cold War: The CIA and the World of Arts and Letters.* New York: New Press, 1999.

Sayel'yev, A. G., and N. N. Detinov. *The Big Five: Arms Control Decision Making in the Soviet Union.* New York: Praeger, 1995.

Schaller, Michael. *Altered States: The United States and Japan Since the Occupation.* New York: Oxford University Press, 1997.

———. *The American Occupation of Japan: The Origins of the Cold War in Asia.* New York: Oxford University Press, 1985.

Schecter, Jerrold, and Tien Hung Nguyen. *The Palace File.* New York: Harper and Row, 1986.

Schoor, Robert. *With Enough Shovels: Reagan, Bush and Nuclear War.* New York: Random House, 1982.

Schiffren, Andre, ed. *The Cold War and the University: Toward an Intellectual History.* New York: New Press, 1997.

Schlesinger, Arthur Jr. *The Crisis of the Old Order.* Boston: Houghton Mifflin, 1957.

———. "Foreign Policy and the American Character." *Foreign Affairs* (Fall 1983).

———. "The Measure of Diplomacy." *Foreign Affairs* (July/August 1994).

———. "On Heroic Leadership and the Dilemma of Strong Men and Weak Peoples." *Encounter* (December 1960).

———. "The Radical." *New York Review of Books* (February 11, 1993).

———. *A Thousand Days: John F. Kennedy in the White House.* Boston: Houghton Mifflin, 1965.

Schmertz, Eric, ed. *President Reagan and the World.* Westport, CT: Greenwood Press, 1997.

Schoenbaum, David. *The United States and the State of Israel.* New York: Oxford University Press, 1993.

Schrecker, Ellen. *Many Are the Crimes: McCarthyism in America.* Boston: Little, Brown, 1997.

Schwartz, Stephen, ed. *Atomic Audit: The Costs and Consequences of U.S. Nuclear Weapons Since 1940.* Washington: Brookings Institution, 1998.

Schweizer, Peter. *Victory: The Reagan Administration's Secret Strategy That Hastened the Collapse of the Soviet Union.* New York: Atlantic Monthly Press, 1994.

Seideman, Tony. "What Sam Walton Learned from the Berlin Airlift." *Audacity* (Spring 1996).

Shapley, Deborah. *Promise and Power: The Life and Times of Robert McNamara.* Boston: Little, Brown, 1993.

Shay, Jonathan. *Achilles in Vietnam.* New York: Atheneum, 1994.

Sheng, Michael M. *Battling Western Imperialism: Mao, Stalin, and the United States.* Princeton, NJ: Princeton University Press, 1997.

Sherry, Michael S. *In the Shadow of War: The United States Since the 1930's.* New Haven, CT: Yale University Press, 1995.

Shershnev, E. S. *On the Principle of Mutual Advantage: Soviet-American Economic Relations.* Moscow: Progress, 1978.

Shuckburgh, Evelyn. *Descent to Suez: Diaries, 1951–56.* New York: Norton, 1987.

Shultz, George. *Triumph and Turmoil: My Years as Secretary of State.* New York: Scribner's, 1993.

Shultz, Richard Jr. *The Secret War Against Hanoi.* New York: HarperCollins, 1999.

Simon, Herbert A. *Models of My Life.* New York: Basic Books, 1991.

Sloan, John W. *Eisenhower and the Management of Prosperity.* Lawrence: University of Kansas Press, 1991.

Smith, Gerard C. *Disarming Diplomat: The Memoirs of Gerard C. Smith, Arms Control Negotiator.* New York: Madison Books, 1996.

———. *Doubletalk: The Story of SALT I.* New York: Doubleday, 1980.

Smith, Patrick. *Japan: A Reinterpretation.* New York: Pantheon, 1997.

Smith, Walter Bedell. *My Three Years in Moscow.* New York: Lippincott, 1950.

Snead, David L. *The Gaither Committee, Eisenhower, and the Cold War.* Columbus: Ohio State University Press, 1999.

Snepp, Frank. *Decent Interval: An Insider's Account of Saigon's Indecent End.* New York: Random House, 1977.

Snyder, Alvin A. *Warriors of Disinformation: American Propaganda, Soviet Lies, and the Winning of the Cold War.* New York: Arcade, 1995.

Sorley, Lewis. *A Better War: The Unexamined Victories and Final Tragedy of America's Last Years in Vietnam.* New York: Harcourt Brace, 1999.

———. *Thunderbolt: General Creighton Abrams and the Army of His Times.* New York: Simon and Schuster, 1992.

Stebbins, Richard P., and Staff for the Council on Foreign Relations. *The United States in World Affairs.* New York: Harper and Brothers, 1950.

Steel, Ronald. *Temptations of a Superpower: America's Foreign Policy After the Cold War.* Cambridge, MA: Harvard University Press, 1995.

———. *Walter Lippmann and the American Century.* Boston: Atlantic–Little, Brown, 1981.

Stein, Herbert. *The Fiscal Revolution in America: Policy in Pursuit of Reality,* rev. ed. Washington: AEI Press, 1996.

Stevens, Robert Warren. *Vain Hopes, Grim Realities.* New York: New Viewpoints, 1976.

Stewart, Robert. "How the Good Guys Caught Up to the Wise Guys." *New Jersey Law Journal* (October 1994).

Stockwell, John. *In Search of Enemies: A CIA Story.* New York: Norton, 1978.

Stoler, Mark A. *Allies and Adversaries: The Joint Chiefs of Staff, the Grand Alliance, and U.S. Strategy in World War II.* Chapel Hill: University of North Carolina Press, 2000.

Strauss, Lewis L. *Men and Decisions.* London: Macmillan, 1963.

Strober, Deborah Hart, and Gerald S. Strober. *Reagan: The Man and His Presidency.* Boston: Houghton Mifflin, 1998.

Strock, James M. *Reagan on Leadership.* Rocklin, CA: Prima Publishing, 1998.

Sturtevant, A. H. "Social Implications of the Genetics of Man." *Science* (September 10, 1954).

Sudoplatov, Anatoli, with Jerrold and Leona Schecter. *Special Tasks: The Memoirs of an Unwanted Witness.* Boston: Little, Brown, 1995.

Summers, Anthony. *Official and Confidential: The Secret Life of J. Edgar Hoover.* New York: Putnam, 1993.

Swearingen, Wesley. *FBI Secrets: An Agent's Exposé.* Boston: South End Press, 1995.

Talbott, Strobe. *The Master of the Game: Paul Nitze and the Nuclear Peace.* New York: Knopf, 1988.

Tanenhaus, Sam. *Whittaker Chambers: A Biography.* New York: Random House, 1997.

Taubman, William, Sergei Khrushchev, and Abbot Gleason, eds. *Nikita Khrushchev.* New Haven, CT: Yale University Press, 2000.

Taylor, Telford. *Grand Inquest: The Story of Congressional Investigations.* New York: Simon and Schuster, 1955.

Thomas, Evan. *Robert Kennedy: His Life.* New York: Simon and Schuster, 2000.

———. *The Very Best Men. Four Who Dared: The Early Years of the CIA.* New York: Simon and Schuster, 1995.

Tin, Bui. *Following Ho Chi Minh, The Memoirs of a North Vietnamese Colonel.* London: Hurst and Co., 1995.

Tobin, James. "The Eisenhower Economy and National Security: Two Views." *Yale Law Review* (March 1958).

Todd, Oliver. *Cruel April: The Fall of Saigon.* New York: Norton, 1990.

Treverton, Gregory. *Covert Action.* New York: Basic Books, 1987.

Tugwell, Rexford G. *A Chronicle of Jeopardy, 1945–55.* Chicago: University of Chicago Press, 1955.

Tyler, Patrick. *A Great Wall: Six Presidents and China.* New York: Public Affairs, 1999.

Walzer, Michael. "Political Action: The Problem of Dirty Hands." *War and Moral Responsibility,* Marshall Cohen et al., eds. Princeton, NJ: Princeton University Press, 1981.

Watson, Denton. *Lion in the Lobby: Clarence Mitchell, Jr.'s Struggle for the Passage of Civil Rights Laws.* New York: Morrow, 1990.

Watson, Thomas J., and Peter Petre. *Father and Son & Co.: My Life at IBM and Beyond.* New York: Bantam, 1990.

Watts, William, and Lloyd A. Free. "A New National Survey: Nationalism, Not Isolationism." *Foreign Policy* (Fall 1976).

Weiss, Gus. "Dupping the Soviets: The Farewell Dossier." *Studies in Intelligence* 39, no. 5 (1996).

White, Theodore. *The Making of the President, 1960.* New York: Atheneum, 1961.

Williams, Juan. *Thurgood Marshall: American Revolutionary.* New York: Random House, 1998.

Wills, Garry. *John Wayne's America.* New York: Touchstone, 1997.

Wise, David. *Nightmover: How Aldrich Ames Sold the CIA to the KGB.* New York: HarperCollins, 1995.

Wolf, Charles Jr., and Derek Leebaert. "Trade Liberalization as a Path to Weapons Standardization in NATO." *International Security* (Winter 1977/78).

Wolf, Markus. *Man Without a Face: The Autobiography of Communism's Greatest Spymaster.* New York: Public Affairs, 1997.

Wolfe, Tom. *Mauve Gloves & Madmen, Clutter & Vine.* New York: Farrar, Straus and Giroux, 1976.

Wong, Michela. *In the Footsteps of Mr. Kurtz.* New York: HarperCollins, 2001.

Wreszin, Michael. *A Rebel in Defense of Tradition: The Politics of Dwight MacDonald.* New York: Basic Books, 1995.

Wright, Peter. *Spycatcher: The Candid Autobiography of a Senior Intelligence Officer.* New York: Viking, 1987.

Zakaria, Fareed. "Sometimes a Great Nation." *New York Times Book Review* (May 18, 1997).

Zeckhauser, Richard, and Derek Leebaert, eds. *What Role for Government? Lessons from Policy Research.* Durham, NC: Duke University Press, 1983.

Zumwalt, Elmo R. *On Watch: A Memoir.* New York: Times Books, 1976.

Personal Interviews and Correspondence

Edward Atkeson
Lee Auspitz
Norman Bailey
Stephen Crocker
Angelo Codevilla
Robert Coulam
George Crile
William Crowell
Timothy Dickinson
Paula Dobriansky
Roger Donald
Ward Elliott and Samuel Beer
Richard B. Foster
Victor Galinsky
Fleming Heegaard
Arnold Kramish
Dennison Lane
William Lee
Charles Lichenstein
Edward Luttwak
Ann Marks
Joe Meadors
Hilary Mukwenha

Halle Murphy Kay
William Niskanen
Macburn Owens
Ralph Pate
Richard Perle
Walter Pforzheimer
Michael Pillsbury
Forrest Pogue
Wolfgang Pordzick
Michael Ratner
Jeffrey Record
Roger Robinson
Robert Sevigny
Ni Shixiong
Robert Sorely
Herbert Stein
Carleton Swift
Scott Thompson
Hung Tien Nguyen
Stansfield Turner
Gus Weiss
Edwin Wiesel Jr.
James Woolsey

Monographs, Case Studies, and Reports

At Cold War's End: U.S. Intelligence on the Soviet Union and Eastern Europe, 1989–1991. Center for the Study of Intelligence, CIA, 1999.

Bailey, Norman, "The Strategic Plan That Won the Cold War: NSDD 75." McLean, VA: The Potomac Foundation, 1998.

Benson, Robert Louis, and Michael Warner, eds. *Venona: Soviet Espionage and the American Response 1939–1957.* Washington: National Security Agency/Central Intelligence Agency, 1996.

CIA Analysis of the Soviet Union, 1947–1991. Center for the Study of Intelligence, CIA, 2001.

Cuba's Repressive Machinery: Human Rights Forty Years After the Revolution. Human Rights Watch, Washington, DC, 1999.

The Emerging Shield: The Air Force and the Evolution of Continental Air Defense, 1945–1960. USAF Office of the Historian, 1991.

Estimating the Cold War Mortgage: The 1995 Baseline Environmental Management Report. U.S. Department of Energy, Office of Environmental Management, March 1995.

Fischer, Benjamin B. *A Cold War Conundrum.* Center for the Study of Intelligence, CIA, 1997.

———. *The 1983 War Scare in US-Soviet Relations.* Center for the Study of Intelligence, CIA, 1996.

Ford, Harold P. *CIA and the Vietnam Policymakers: Three Episodes, 1962–1968.* Center for the Study of Intelligence, CIA, 1998.

Kuhns, Woodrow. *Assessing the Soviet Threat: The Early Cold War Years.* Center for the Study of Intelligence, CIA, 1997.

Lee, William T., "The Korean War Was Stalin's Show." Occasional Paper 99-1, Center for National Security Law, University of Virginia, 1999.

MacEachin, Douglas J. *U.S. Intelligence and the Polish Crisis, 1980–81.* Center for the Study of Intelligence, CIA, 2001.

Nakao, Mitsuyuki. "Studies on US-Japan Economic Relations in the Post Cold War Era." *Bulletin of the Faculty of Commerce,* Nagoya University, September 1990.

Pedlow, Gregory W., and Donald E. Welzenbach. *The CIA and the U-2 Program, 1954–1974.* Center for the Study of Intelligence, CIA, 1998.

Police Aid and Political Will. Washington: The Washington Office on Latin America, 1987.

"Politics of Covert Action: The U.S., the Mujahiddeen, and the Stinger Missiles," Kennedy School of Government Case C15-99-15446.0, 1999.

President's Advisory Committee on a National Highway Program. *A Ten Year National Highway Program.* Washington: GPO, 1955.

Ravenal, Earl C. "Large-Scale Foreign Policy Change: The Nixon Doctrine as History and Portent." *Policy Papers in International Affairs,* no. 35, Institute of International Studies, University of California, Berkeley 1980.

"The Reagan Administration and the Soviet Pipeline Embargo." Kennedy School of Government Case C16-91-1016.0

Report by the Director of Military Application, Summary of A.E.C. Relationships between the A.E.C. and the Photographic Industry Regarding Radioactive Contamination from Atomic Weapons Tests, from January Through December, 1951," via the Institute for Energy and Environmental Research, Takoma Park, MD.

The Roswell Report: Fact or Fiction in the New Mexico Desert. Washington: GPO, 1994.

"Saving the Steel Industry." Kennedy School of Government Case C15-85-625.

Security and Assistance in Laos. Rand Corporation, September 1965 National Security Archives Laos Collection.

"The Soviet Natural Gas Pipeline." Harvard Business School Case 9-384-007, 9.

"Soviet Strategic Objectives: An Alternative View," "Report of 'Team B.'" *Intelligence Community Experiment in Competitive Analysis* (December 1976).

"Sunshine and Shadow: The CIA and the Soviet Economy." Kennedy School of Government Case C16-91-1096.0.

"The Two Paths of Richard Helms." Kennedy School of Government Case C14-83-525, 1983.

Vien, Gen. Cao Van. *The Final Collapse.* Indochina Monographs, Washington, DC, U.S. Army Center of Military History, 1983.

Weiss, Gus. "The Life and Death of COSMOS 954," published in the CIA's classified version of *Studies in Intelligence,* 1978. Declassified under the Freedom of Information Act.

Selected Russian Sources on Soviet Strategic Missile Programs

Fedosev, E. A. *Gosudarstvenniy Nauchno-issledovatel'skiy Instituti Aviatsionykh System, 1946–1996.* Moscow, 1996.

Karpenko, A. V., ed. *Otechestvennyye Strategicheskiye Raketnyye Kompleksy.* St. Petersburg: Nevskiy Bastion, 1999.

———. *Protivoraketnaya i Protivokosmicheskaya Oborona.* St. Petersburg: Nevskiy Bastion, 1998.

———. *Rossiiskoye Raketnoye Oruzhnye, 1943–1993.* St. Petersburg: PIKA, 1993.

Kisun'ko, G. V. *Sekretnaya Zona.* Moscow: Sovremennik, 1996.

Kolesnikiov, S. G. *Strategicheskoye Raketno-Yadernoye Oruzhiye.* Moscow: Arsenal Press, 1996.

Magritskiy, A. G. *Zinitnaya Ravetnaya Sistema S-300.* St. Petersburg: Nevskiy Bastion, 1997.

Minayev, A. V., ed. *Sovetskaya Voyennaya Mosch' Ot Stalina do Gorbacheva.* Moscow: Voyenniy Parad, 1999.

Pervov, M. *Zenitnoye Raketnoye Oruzhiye Protivovozdyshnoy Oborony Strany.* Moscow: ZAO PFG, 2001.

Podvig, P. L., ed. *Strategicheskoye Ydernoye Vooruzeniye Rossii.* Moscow: Izdat, 1998.

Volkov, E. B., ed. *Mezhkontinental'nye Ballisticheskiye Rakety, SSSR (R.F.) and SshA.* Moscow: Strategic Rocket Forces, 1996.

Yakolev, Gen. Col. V. *Raketn'yy Shchit Otechestva.* Moscow: RVSN, 1999.

Index